D0142107

ADVANCED COBOL

ADVANCED COBOL

Second Edition

A. S. Philippakis
Leonard J. Kazmier
Arizona State University

McGraw-Hill Book Company
New York   St. Louis   San Francisco   Auckland
Bogotá   Hamburg   Johannesburg   London
Madrid   Mexico   Milan   Montreal   New Delhi   Panama
Paris   São Paulo   Singapore   Sydney   Tokyo   Toronto

ADVANCED COBOL

Copyright © 1987 by McGraw-Hill, Inc. All rights reserved.
Printed in the United States of America. Except as permitted under the United
States Copyright Act of 1976, no part of this publication may be reproduced or
distributed in any form or by any means, or stored in a data base or retrieval
system, without the prior written permission of the publisher.

1 2 3 4 5 6 7 8 9 0   D O C D O C   8 9 4 3 2 10 9 8 7

ISBN 0-07-049813-X

This book was set in Optima by Americomp.
The editor was Gerald A. Gleason;
the cover was designed by Infield and D'Aftolfo Associates;
the production supervisor was Leroy A. Young.
Project supervision was done by
Editing, Design & Production, Inc.
R. R. Donnelley & Sons Company was printer and binder.

Library of Congress Cataloging-in-Publication Data

Philippakis, Andreas S.
  Advanced COBOL.

  Includes index.
  1. COBOL (Computer program language)   I. Kazmier,
Leonard J.   II. Title.
QA76.73.C25P48   1987   005.13′3   86-15177
ISBN 0-07-049813-X

ABOUT THE AUTHORS

Andy Philippakis is Professor of Information Systems and a Director of Computer Resources at Arizona State University. Professor Philippakis did his undergraduate work at Gannon College in Erie, Pennsylvania, and received master's and Ph.D. degrees from the University of Wisconsin at Madison. Coauthor of several McGraw-Hill books on computer programming, Professor Philippakis has published many journal articles, has taught introductory and advanced courses, and has served as consultant to many business organizations.

Leonard Kazmier is Professor of Decision and Information Systems at Arizona State University. He completed the bachelor's and master's degrees at Wayne State University, Detroit, and earned the Ph.D. at The Ohio State University. Professor Kazmier has authored or coauthored books in management concepts, statistical analysis, and computer applications, all published by McGraw-Hill. He is a charter member of the Decision Sciences Institute and is also a member of the Academy of Management and the American Statistical Association. He has taught at Wayne State University, the University of Notre Dame, and Arizona State University.

To our wives
Patricia and Lorraine

CONTENTS

PREFACE

This second edition of ADVANCED COBOL has been designed as an updated improvement of the successful first edition. Like the first edition, the book presents material on the implementation of COBOL that is beyond the introductory level.

The book has been developed in response to the increased role of COBOL in college and university curricula. In most college-level programs, COBOL is included in a two- and often three-semester sequence of courses. Yet, there is a very limited choice of text materials to support the second or third course.

The new edition represents a total restructuring of the book to reflect recent advances in programming concepts and practices and to incorporate the extensive enhancements to the language included in the new standard adopted by the American National Standards Institute (ANSI) in 1985.

The contents of the book are grouped into five parts, each covering a cohesive group of topics. The first part consists of two chapters on program structure, and includes coverage of diagrammatic representations of programs as well as an advanced treatment of structured programming. The core of the language features are covered in the second part of the book, which offers an intermediate-level coverage of the common features of the language.

File processing, the "heart" of COBOL applications in business and government, is covered by the four chapters that constitute the third part of the book. The reader will find that these important topics are covered in a rigorous and comprehensive manner. The fourth part of the book contains a set of special topics, including subprograms and nested programs, the report writer feature, interactive programming, and data structures. Devoting a complete chapter to each of these advanced topics is a unique and powerful feature of this book. Mastery of such topics can serve to differentiate between intermediate-level and advanced-level students. Courses that are at the intermediate level may choose to omit or overview some of the topics in this part of the book. Courses that are at the advanced level should cover these topics in detail.

The book concludes with the fifth part, on program design concepts and methods. Of the two chapters, one covers program cohesion and design while the final chapter describes methods of program testing.

Given the diversity of topics and extent of coverage, this book includes more material than it is feasible to cover in a typical one-semester college course. However, students who have already had work in COBOL programming, which is the intended prerequisite for this book, can cover selected topics deemed most suitable by the instructor. Furthermore, the order of coverage need not be the same as the order of presentation in the book. For example, courses that emphasize file processing may wish to cover Chapters 8 through 11 early in the semester.

Special features of the book include extensive use of self-study review items, numerous exercises, and ample use of illustrations.

The authors express their appreciation to Christina Mediate of the McGraw-Hill Book Company for her very capable supervision of this project. We also extend thanks to the following for their comments and recommendations: Albert Croker, New York University; David F. Harris, Bentley College; Charles Litecky, University of Missouri, Columbia; and Marilyn Meyers.

A. S. Philippakis
Leonard J. Kazmier

ACKNOWLEDGMENT

The following acknowledgment is reprinted from *American National Standard Programming Language COBOL, X3.23-1974* published by the American National Standards Institute, Inc.

Any organization interested in reproducing the COBOL standard and specifications in whole or in part, using ideas from this document as the basis for an instruction manual or for any other purpose, is free to do so. However, all such organizations are requested to reproduce the following acknowledgment paragraphs in their entirety as part of the preface to any such publication (any organization using a short passage from this document, such as in a book review, is requested to mention 'COBOL' in acknowledgment of the source, but need not quote the acknowledgment):

COBOL is an industry language and is not the property of any company or group of companies, or of any organization or group of organizations.

No warranty, expressed or implied, is made by any contributor or by the CODASYL Programming Language Committee as to the accuracy and functioning of the programming system and language. Moreover, no responsibility is assumed by any contributor, or by the committee, in connection therewith.

The authors and copyright holders of the copyrighted material used herein

FLOW-MATIC (trademark of Sperry Rand Corporation), Programming for the UNIVAC I and II, Data Automation Systems copyrighted 1958, 1959, by Sperry Rand Coporation; IBM Commerical Translator Form No. F28-8013, copyrighted 1959 by IBM; FACT, DSI 27A5260-2760, copyrighted 1960 by Minneapolis-Honeywell

have specifially authorized the use of this material in whole or in part, in the COBOL specifications. Such authorization extends to the reproduction and use of COBOL specifications in programming manuals or similar publications.

ADVANCED COBOL

1 Program structure

1

REPRESENTING PROGRAM STRUCTURE BY DIAGRAMS

INTRODUCTION
PARTITIONING
HIERARCHIES AND NETWORKS
STRUCTURE CHARTS
ALTERNATIVE FORMS OF STRUCTURE CHARTS
EXERCISES

INTRODUCTION

Program structure consists of the identification of the individual functions that constitute a program and the specification of their relationships. The use of program structure with respect to a programming project is analogous to the use of an architectural plan in constructing a building. In contrast, the term *structured programming* refers to the use of certain principles and methods for developing a good program code. The purpose of the code is to execute each of the component functions that comprise the overall program structure.

Effective completion of a programming project requires both the creation of a well-designed architectural plan (program structure) and a well-executed construction process (structured programming). Therefore, the first two chapters of this book are devoted to the topics of program structure and structured programming, respectively. The broader consideration of effective program design is covered in the last two chapters of the book.

PARTITIONING

A fundamental concept of program design is that of *partitioning*, which refers to the process of subdividing a programming task into smaller parts or functions.

Partitioning is a pervasive phenomenon in human activities. One common form of partitioning in organizations is the division of labor, or functional specialization. For example, an automobile manufacturing plant includes departmental units which may be further subdivided according to specific functions. A Painting Department, for instance, could include such separate functions as cleaning, spraying, baking, inspecting, and the like. Similarly, an Information Services Department could include such separate functions as programming, systems analysis, data entry, and input/output control. The common occurrence of partitioning in a variety of situations is reflective of the physical and mental limits of human beings. A given person can only do so much and attend to so much at a given time. Therefore, we find it not only beneficial, but also necessary, to partition large and complex tasks into smaller and more specialized tasks.

A computer programming task generally is complex enough to make partitioning desirable. From the standpoint of the individual programmer, the partitioning of the overall task allows the programmer to concentrate on particular program functions. From the standpoint of the organization, partitioning makes it possible to complete complex programming tasks in a shorter time by having a team of programmers working simultaneously on different specific tasks that constitute the overall program.

In the context of computer programming, a widely used term associated with partitioning is *modularity*. A program module is a well-defined program segment. Modular programming has been recognized as a desirable practice for many years. In practice, all programs include some degree of modularity by necessity: no programmer can write a monolithic program that is not partitioned into some kinds of parts, or modules. Thus, it is not just presence of modularity that is important. Rather, we need to develop an understanding of how to design programs whose modules are so constructed as to lead to good programs.

To be useful, a module should not only be a program segment, but a *well-defined* program segment. More specifically, a module should be a named program segment that carries out a specific program function. In the context of COBOL programming, a module eventually is represented in one of five forms in the program:

1   As a single paragraph

2   As a series of two or more consecutive paragraphs which are the object of a PERFORM PA THRU PZ, where PA and PZ stand for the first and last paragraphs in a consecutive series of paragraphs

3   As a single section

4   As a subprogram

5   In ANS 1985 COBOL, a *contained* program in a *nested* program (as described in Chapter 12, Subprograms and Nested Programs)

Review

1   The process of subdividing a large programming task into smaller, more specific tasks is called _____.

partitioning

2   In terms of human endeavors, partitioning is a [long-standing/recently developed] concept.

long-standing

3   "A named program segment that carries out a specific program function" is a definition of a program _____.

module

4   Of the five forms by which a program module can be represented physically in a COBOL program, the simplest form is a single _____.

paragraph

HIERARCHIES AND NETWORKS

As described in the preceding section, partitioning is the process by which a programming task can be subdivided into smaller parts. But there must be an integrating force in order to attain coordinated results with respect to the parts. This force is provided by *structure,* which refers to the identification of system components and their interrelationships. The two basic forms of structure are *hierarchies* and *networks.*

Hierarchies are often referred to as *tree structures.* A hierarchy, or tree, is a structure in which there is a single module at the top, (the *root* module) with one or more *subordinate* modules. The singular root module is *superordinate,* or *superior,* to its subordinate modules, and these subordinate modules may themselves have additional subordinate modules to which they are superior. Any given module can be subordinate to only one superior, but may itself be superior to one or more subordinate modules. Figure 1-1 portrays a typical hierarchical structure. As can be observed, the single root module A is at the top (level 0) of the structure. This module has two subordinate modules, B and C, which comprise level 1 in the hierarchy, and which have further subordinates. The designation of superiors and subordinates constitutes the specification of the relationships. Two basic characteristics of a strict hierarchy structure is that there is a single superior module for the entire hierarchy and that there is only one superior module for each subordinate module.

As contrasted to a hierarchy structure, in a *network structure* there is no single module that is superior to all others, and relationships among modules are unrestricted. In other words, two modules may relate to each other in both directions, so that we cannot say that one is superior to the other. Figure 1-2 includes two examples of networks. In the first network module A is superior to all three of the other modules B, C, and D, as indicated by the direction of the arrows. But notice that B is also subordinate to C, and C is also subordinate to D, which violates the rule for hierarchies that a subordinate should have only one superior. The second diagram in Figure

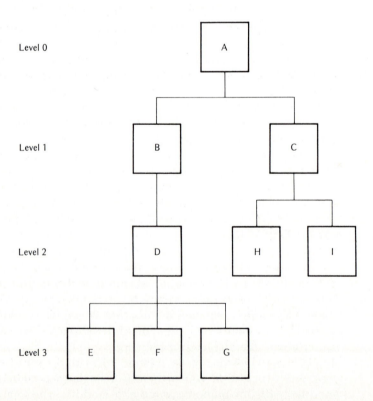

FIGURE 1-1   REPRESENTATION OF A HIERARCHY (TREE) STRUCTURE.

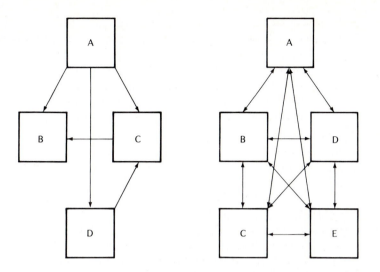

FIGURE 1–2   REPRESENTATIONS OF NETWORK STRUCTURES.

1-2 illustrates a network in which every possible relationship is used: all modules are interconnected and all arrows point in both directions.

Although the number of modules in a system is indicative of program complexity, the greatest source of complexity is the number of intermodule relationships. Such relationships tend to undo the benefits derived from partitioning by making functional distinctions between program modules less clear. Therefore hierarchies, rather than networks, are the preferred form of program structure.

Let us now relate the general concepts of program structure to the specific context of COBOL programming. Figure 1-3 depicts the typical representation of a hierarchy in both structure chart and program outline form. The letters A through I in the figure stand for paragraph names in a COBOL program. PERFORM is the imperative programming statement that specifies execution of the referenced paragraph and subsequent return to the statement immediately following the PERFORM. Each horizontal line in the program outline in Figure 1-3 represents one or more programming statements, the detail of which is not relevant for our present discussion.

Reviewing Figure 1-3, we can observe that a line connecting two modules in the structure chart is represented in the program as a PERFORM statement. For instance, the conecting line between modules A and B is represented in the program by "PERFORM B," which is a statement within module A. Thus, a tree structure can be implemented in COBOL by use of appropriate PERFORM statements. Notice that the PERFORM statement is directed toward a subordinate module, and never toward either a superior or a peer module. Thus in order to conform to the requirements of a hierarchy, one could not have the statement PERFORM C within module G, nor the statement PERFORM F within module E.

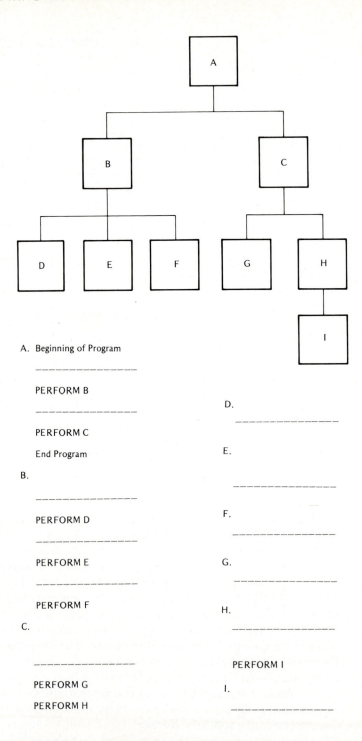

A. Beginning of Program

—————————————

PERFORM B

—————————————

PERFORM C

End Program

B.

—————————————

PERFORM D

—————————————

PERFORM E

—————————————

PERFORM F

C.

—————————————

PERFORM G

PERFORM H

D.

—————————————

E.

—————————————

F.

—————————————

G.

—————————————

H.

—————————————

PERFORM I

I.

—————————————

FIGURE 1-3   REPRESENTATION OF HIERARCHY IN STRUCTURE DIAGRAM AND IN COBOL PROGRAM OUTLINE.

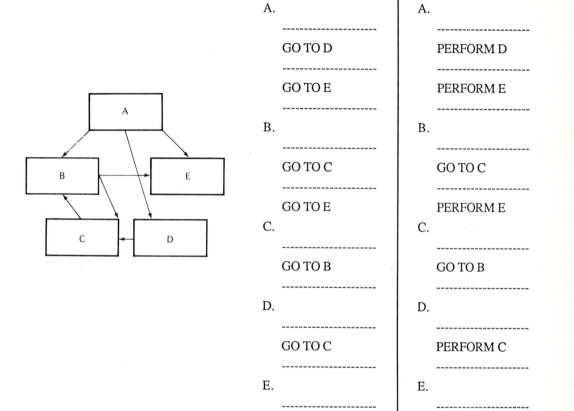

	USING GO TO	USING PERFORM
A.		
	----------------------	----------------------
	GO TO D	PERFORM D
	----------------------	----------------------
	GO TO E	PERFORM E
	----------------------	----------------------
B.		
	----------------------	----------------------
	GO TO C	GO TO C
	----------------------	----------------------
	GO TO E	PERFORM E
C.		
	----------------------	----------------------
	GO TO B	GO TO B
	----------------------	----------------------
D.		
	----------------------	----------------------
	GO TO C	PERFORM C
	----------------------	----------------------
E.		
	----------------------	----------------------
	----------------------	----------------------

FIGURE 1-4   REPRESENTATION OF NETWORK IN STRUCTURE DIAGRAM AND IN COBOL PROGRAM OUTLINE.

Figure 1-4 depicts a network chart and associated program outlines. Notice that a network structure is represented in COBOL by the use of GO TO or PERFORM statements. The rules governing the use of the PERFORM statement do not allow this command to be used when two modules reference each other. In the case of any such mutual references the GO TO statement must be used. Thus in Figure 1-4 the references between B and C and then between C and B are implemented by the use of GO TO statements in both versions of the program outline.

Notice the dashed line connecting module A to module B in the network chart in Figure 1-4. The use of a dashed line indicates that the control structure is a result of physical position. Module B is physically located after module A, and thus will be executed only when the execution of module A is completed. Thus, module B is effectively a subordinate of module A by implicit reference, based on its physical position.

The highly abstract form of the program outlines in Figure 1-4 may leave the reader wondering how there could be two GO TO statements in module A and how there could be additional statements (represented by dashed lines) following a GO TO statement. In such cases, the GO TO statements are assumed to be embedded in conditional statements that allow one GO TO *or* another GO TO to be executed. Similarly, the code could specify that either a GO TO *or* the succeeding statements be executed.

As we have observed, network structures are undesirable because they undermine some of the benefits of partitioning and result in program structures that are complex, difficult to understand, and difficult to modify. Yet network structures probably characterize the majority of the older programs in the libraries of most computer installations. Because of their wide use in early programs, it is worthwhile to extend our coverage of network structures by means of two examples.

Consider a program task to copy the contents of one file onto another, as for instance listing the contents of a disk file on a printer. A typical network-oriented implementation is represented by the following:

A.

　Open Files
　Print Report Heading.
B.
　Read Input-File Record
　　If End-of-File GO TO C
　Move the Input Record to the Output Record
　Write the Output Record
　GO TO B.
C.
　Close Files and do other End-of-Program Tasks.

Figure 1-5(a) presents a network chart that corresponds to this program. Notice that in the pseudocode program outline above, module A is superordinate to B by virtue of the physical sequence of A and B. Then notice that, by means of the statement, GO TO B, B serves as its own superior and subordinate, thereby constituting a nonhierarchical structure. Figure 1-5(b) clarifies this point by adding a new module, B-1. The program outline could also be modified in paragraph B to reflect this change in the structure chart, as follows:

B.
　Read Input-File Record
　　If End-of-File GO TO C.
B-1.
　Move Input Record to the Output Record
　Write the Output Record
　GO TO B.

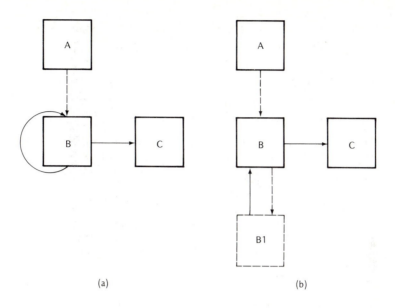

(a)   (b)

FIGURE 1–5   STRUCTURE REPRESENTATION OF SAMPLE PROGRAM.

The simplicity of the above programming example may well lead us to question why the network structure is considered undesirable. Therefore, let us consider a somewhat more complex programming task as further practice in understanding networks and in recognizing some of the difficulties that they introduce.

Figure 1-6 is a flowchart for updating a sequential master file based on transaction records. Master records for which there are no corresponding transaction records are simply copied, while the other master records are updated based on the *one* transaction in each case. Figure 1-7 is a program outline for the updating task, while Figure 1-8 is a corresponding network structure chart. This example is typical of the way that such a task could have been programmed in earlier years, and such structures are likely to be encountered by programmers who are called upon to modify existing programs.

Notice the large number of intermodule connections in Figure 1-8. The function of a program with such a network structure is difficult to determine without careful study. One way is to resort to running test data through the flowchart or the program a few times and observing the result. Further, any attempt to revise a module in a network structure includes a high risk of error. For example, suppose we wish to change this sample program so that a validity check of the transaction is performed when the transaction is read. The structure chart in Figure 1-8 is of no help in making this change, and neither would the complete program listing be of much help. The reading of transactions is a function interspersed throughout the logic of the program. Similarly, if we wish to revise the Update Master module we need to recognize that the Write Master and Read Master modules are its

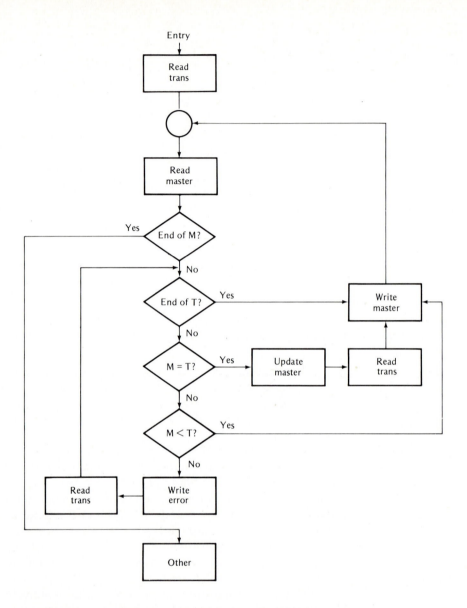

FIGURE 1-6   FLOWCHART FOR THE SEQUENTIAL FILE UPDATING TASK.

subordinates, even though they are not clearly designated as such in the structure chart.

We conclude this section by restating the point that the hierarchy structure is the preferred structure, and the one that leads to the development of good programs. Network structures lead to inherent difficulties in both writing and revising programs, and therefore should be avoided whenever possible.

```
READ-TRANS.
   Read Transaction File.
READ-MASTER.
   Read Master File
        At End of Master File GO TO OTHER.
PROCESS-DATA.
   If End of Transaction File
        GO TO WRITE-MASTER
   ELSE
        IF M = T
          GO TO UPDATE-MASTER
        ELSE
          IF M < T
             GO TO WRITE-MASTER
          ELSE
             GO TO WRITE-ERROR.
UPDATE-MASTER.
   Update Master
   Read Transaction
WRITE-MASTER.
   Write Master Record
   GO TO READ-MASTER.
WRITE-ERROR.
   Write error message
   Read Transaction
   GO TO PROCESS-DATA.
OTHER.
   (etc.)
```

FIGURE 1–7   PROGRAM OUTLINE FOR THE SEQUENTIAL FILE UPDATING TASK.

Review

1   The two basic forms of program structure are _____ structure and _____ structure.

hierarchy; network

2   A hierarchy, or tree, structure always has only one root module at the [top/base] of the structure.

top

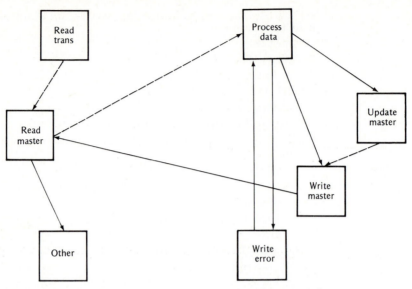

Dashed lines represent relationships due to physical positions of modules in the program.

FIGURE 1–8   NETWORK STRUCTURE CHART FOR THE SEQUENTIAL FILE UP-DATING TASK.

3   In a hierarchy, any given module can be subordinate to [only one/several superior(s) and any given module can be superior to [only one/several] subordinate(s).

only one; several

4   As contrasted to a hierarchy structure, in a network structure the relationships among modules are [more/less] restricted.

less

5   When a hierarchy structure is depicted in program outline form, each line connecting two modules in the structure chart is represented in the program as the imperative programming statement _____.

PERFORM

6   A network structure is represented in COBOL by the use of _____ and PERFORM statements.

GO TO

7   The use of a dashed line in a network chart indicates module control as a result of _____.

physical position

8   The type of structure whose use leads to programs that are complex, difficult to understand, and difficult to modify is the _____ structure.

network

9   The type of structure that leads to the development of good programs, and is therefore preferred, is the _____ structure.

hierarchy

STRUCTURE CHARTS

As already introduced in this chapter, a structure chart is a graphic representation that portrays program modules as rectangular boxes and shows their interrelationships by means of connecting lines. Because the network structure is so undesirable, program structure charts should always follow the hierarchical approach. The mutual vertical positioning of two modules serves to differentiate superordinate (top) and subordinate (bottom) modules. Because peer modules are independent of one another, no horizontal connecting lines are needed for modules at the same level.

Figure 1-9 presents the two most common forms of structure charts. Figure 1-9(a) illustrates the convention in which all superior-subordinate relationships are portrayed by rectangular lines, while Figure 1-9(b) illustrates a less restrictive form in which connecting lines are not drawn at right angles. Either form is acceptable, but within a given organization it is desirable to follow consistently either one convention or the other.

In addition to describing the hierarchical relationships, a structure chart can also be enhanced to include:

Loops (repetitive invocation of subordinate modules)

Decision points (conditional invocation of subordinate modules)

Data (input to and output from modules)

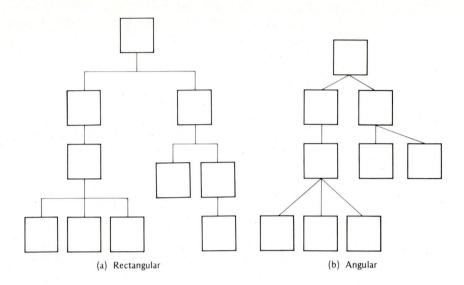

(a) Rectangular   (b) Angular

FIGURE 1–9   RECTANGULAR AND ANGULAR STRUCTURE CHARTS.

Figure 1-10 is a structure chart that includes these additional features. Module A passes X as input data to module B, which returns output data Y to module A. Then, modules C and D are executed repetitively, as indicated by the curved arrows below B; the inner loop involves module C while the outer loop involves both C and D. Finally, module F invokes modules G and H conditionally, as indicated by the diamond symbol at F.

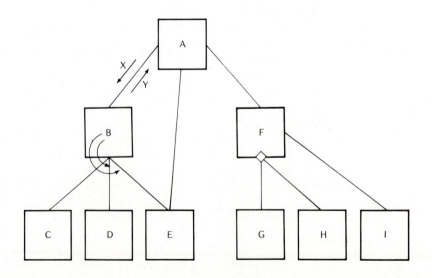

FIGURE 1–10   STRUCTURE CHART SHOWING DATA, LOOPS, AND DECISION POINT.

Notice that module E in Figure 1-10 is subordinate to both modules A and B. Often, there will be such modules that have multiple superiors because they represent common functions in the program. When a module is subordinate to many superior modules it would be confusing to draw many crossing connecting lines. Therefore, in such cases the module representation is repeated and a corner of the block is shaded to alert the reader of the chart to the repetition. For example, in Figure 1-11 module Q is repeated many times. A common reason for such repetition is invocation of a standard error-message module.

It should be observed that the case of a module being subordinate to more than one module is a violation of the general hierarchical rule that a module should be subordinate to only one superior. However, application of the rule is bypassed for the sake of practicality in circumstances such as here described. The strict hierarchy concept could be observed by giving the four module Q representations in Figure 1-11 different names and having each such module contain identical code. However, such an approach would be counterproductive because of the redundant code. When the hierarchical rule is bent to allow for multiple superiors, such instances should be clearly documented. If a future program change requires modifica-

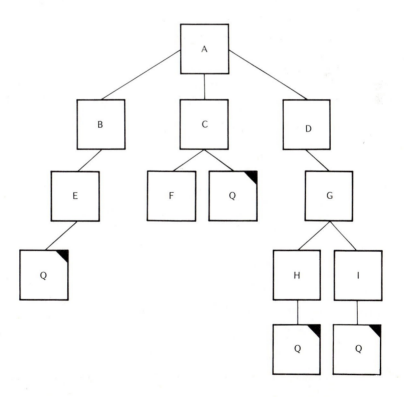

FIGURE 1-11   STRUCTURE CHART ILLUSTRATING A COMMON FUNCTION (Q).

tion of a repeated module, it would have to be ascertained whether or not the change is appropriate for all uses of the subordinate module. If not, a new module may then have to be created.

Depicting the data flow into and out of modules is often useful as an aid for understanding the data processing task. When the modules represent subprograms, then the list of arguments in the CALL statement is the natural data to depict. When the modules represent sections or paragraphs of the same program the data involved can still be identified, even though the program code does not identify the data as part of the PERFORM verb that invokes module execution.

It may be useful at this point to contrast a structure chart with a flowchart. A structure chart is based on hierarchical program structure, whereas a flowchart is based on sequential procedure. In order to design a good program, first a good structure chart should be developed. After the structure chart has been completed, a flowchart may then be developed as an additional aid for coding the program logic into program procedures.

The concept of hierarchy is implemented in COBOL by use of the PERFORM and CALL verbs. A module A that PERFORMS or CALLs module B is the superordinate of B. Therefore, when a program is well-structured it tends to consist of top-level modules that act as superiors which PERFORM or CALL lower-level modules to execute most of the "work."

Review

1   Program structure charts should always follow the [hierarchical/network] approach.

hierarchical

2   In addition to describing hierarchical relationships, a structure chart can also identify input of data into and output of data from particular

_____ .

modules

3   A structure chart can also identify conditional invocation of subordinate modules, as represented by decision _____, and repetitive invocation of subordinate modules, as represented by program

_____ .

points; loops

4   From the standpoint of the strict hierarchy concept, a module [may sometimes/should never] be subordinate to more than one superior module.

should never

5   When the hierarchical rule is bent to allow for multiple superiors, a corner of the [superior/subordinate] block is shaded to alert the reader of the structure chart.

subordinate

6   A structure chart is based on [hierarchical/sequential] program structure, whereas a flowchart is based on [hierarchical/sequential] procedure.

hierarchical; sequential

7   The concept of hierarchy is implemented in COBOL by use of the verbs _____ and _____ in superordinate modules.

PERFORM; CALL

ALTERNATIVE FORMS OF STRUCTURE CHARTS

The preceding section presented some basic conventions for representing program structure in the form of structure charts. However, there is no one universal format for drawing such charts; rather, there are several somewhat competing alternative formats. Each alternative encompasses a design methodology that provides a standard set of conventions for representing program structure, data structure, and program code. In a given organization, it makes good sense to use one of the alternative formats consistently, so that efficient and clear communication among the programming professionals in that organization is achieved. In a general context, such as in this book, it is impractical to attempt the simultaneous use of different diagramming conventions. For this reason, a simplified set of formats is used in the text examples, leaving the choice of a specific convention to the preference of the reader.

Of the many available diagrammatic conventions for representing program structure, we present a brief overview of two of them: HIPO charts and Warnier–Orr charts.

Hierarchical Input-Process-Output (HIPO) is the set of diagramming conventions developed by IBM that focuses on the inputs, processes, and outputs of programs. Figure 1-12 includes a sample HIPO chart. Figure 1-12(a) is a Visual Table of Contents (VTOC) diagram that essentially is a hierarchical structure chart very similar to the type used throughout this book. At the lower right corner of each block in the VTOC diagram, a number is included as a reference to an associated HIPO chart. The HIPO chart included in Figure 1-12(b) is for block 1.0, which is the root module representing the entire program. As illustrated in Figure 1-12(b), a HIPO chart consists of three portions, labeled INPUT, PROCESS, and OUTPUT, respectively. As part of the HIPO methodology, a similar chart would be prepared for *each* of the 12 blocks included in the VTOC structure chart in Figure 1-12(b). Thus, HIPO charts provide documented detail for the input, the process, and the output for each module or function in the program, and therefore can be used as the basis for writing the program code.

Warnier–Orr charts are named after Jean-Dominique Warnier and Ken Orr, who were the principal developers of this approach to representing program structure. Figure 1-13 presents a Warnier–Orr chart corresponding to the structure chart in Figure 1-12(a). The notable characteristic of such charts is that they use horizontally arranged brackets rather than vertically placed blocks to represent the hierarchical structure of a program. Warnier–Orr charts focus on the hierarchical relationships of the functions to be

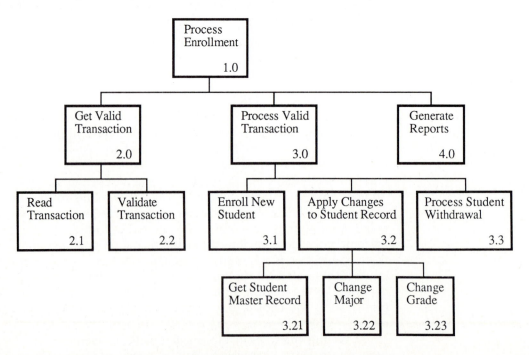

FIGURE 1-12   A HIERARCHICAL STRUCTURE CHART AND ONE ASSOCIATED HIPO CHART. (a) Hierarchical Structure Chart.

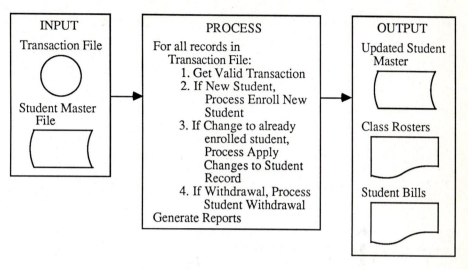

FIGURE 1-12 (Continued)   (b) An Associated HIPO Chart.

performed, and, as is the case for HIPO charts, they can be used as the basis for writing the program code. Warnier–Orr charts are generally more compact than corresponding HIPO charts because they incorporate the functions of both the VTOC and HIPO charts into one diagram. However, combination of the two types of functions into one chart results in a somewhat more complex diagram.

Review

1   The type of chart developed by IBM that focuses on the inputs, processes, and outputs of programs is the _____ chart.

HIPO

2   Reflecting the focus of such a chart, the term *HIPO* stands for _____.

HIERARCHICAL INPUT-PROCESS-OUTPUT

3   The type of chart that utilizes horizontally arranged brackets rather than vertically placed blocks to represent the hierarchical structure of a program is the _____ chart.

WARNIER-ORR

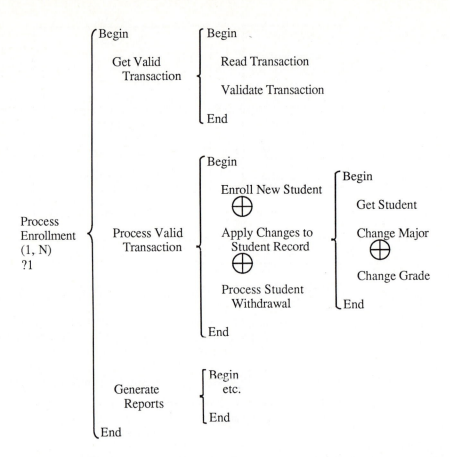

FIGURE 1–13   SAMPLE WARNIER-ORR CHART. (1,N) means that this process is repeated N times and ?1 is an indication that there is a footnote and it is labeled 1. Warnier-Orr diagrams use footnotes to explain control logic; for this example, footnote 1 might state that the N repetitions are terminated when the end-of-file condition is true. ⊕ is a symbol to indicate the exclusive *or*; for example, either Enroll New Student *or* Apply Changes to Student Record will be executed.

4   Of the two approaches to diagrammatic representation that were described, the one that requires that two types of associated charts be prepared is the _____ chart.

HIPO

5   Of the two approaches to diagrammatic representation, the one that incorporates all information in one rather than two types of charts, with greater complexity generally resulting in the one chart, is the _____ chart.

WARNIER-ORR

Exercises

1.1   Distinguish between the concepts *structured programming* and *program structure and design.*

1.2   Is a modular program a well-partitioned program? Is a well-partitioned program a modular program?

1.3   What are the five forms of representing program modules in COBOL?

1.4   Distinguish between the concepts of *hierarchy* and *network* in reference to program structure.

1.5   Why are hierarchies preferred as program structures over networks?

1.6   Draw structure diagrams representing each of the following two program outlines:

a PROCEDURE DIVISION.
   A.
     PERFORM B
     PERFORM C
   B.
     PERFORM I
   C.
     PERFORM L
     PERFORM M

b PROCEDURE DIVISION.
   A.
     PERFORM B
     GO TO C
   B.
     GO TO D
   C.
     GO TO B
     GO TO A
   D.
     GO TO B

1.7   Draw a Warnier–Orr diagram for the first program outline (labeled "a") in Exercise 1.6, above.

1.8   Take a program which you have written previously and draw a structure chart that represents that program. Was it a hierarchy- or network-oriented structure?

1.9   Apply the HIPO approach to a program that you have previously written.

1.10   Apply the Warnier–Orr diagramming method to represent the structure of a program that you have previously written.

2

STRUCTURED PROGRAMMING

INTRODUCTION

For the first quarter-century of programming practice, most programs were characterized by "spaghetti bowl logic." Programmers had no clear concepts or guidelines on which to rely for writing good programs in a systematic way. Programs differed in their structure as the intuition and experience level of individual programmers differed. Then, starting with the late 1960s and culminating in the mid-1970s, there was developed a set of concepts and methods that could be used to write good programs that have common structural elements. *Structured programming* is the label that was given to this development.

Today, structured programming is almost universally accepted as the preferred method for writing programs. People differ on minor issues, but basically everyone agrees that programs developed under the structured programming approach are less error-prone and can be understood and modified more easily when they are reviewed subsequent to their initial development.

In this chapter we describe concepts related to structured programming and we conclude with methods for converting unstructured programs to structured form.

BASIC PROGRAM STRUCTURES

Briefly stated, structured programming is based on the use of the five standard constructs presented in Figure 2-1. For a program to be considered structured, one should be able to portray the program by the use of any combination of these standard structures.

A fundamental property of the basic structures is that each has one entry and one exit. Based on that property, we may represent a structure either in detail or in summary form. A given block structure may represent a series of interrelated blocks with the same entry and exit point. Figure 2-2 illustrates the point. The rectangular borders in Figure 2-2(a) illustrate how we can use different levels of abstraction depending on our needs. In part (b), one block has been substituted for the entire diagram in part (a). This is the highest level of abstraction. Then in part (c) we represent the entire part (a) structure as a simple selection. Finally, part (d) presents more detail by demonstrating the nested selection structure of part (a).

The one-entry, one-exit property can be used as a powerful tool both when developing a new program and when trying to review or comprehend an existing one. We can deal with minute details of code or we can focus on higher levels of abstraction, as needed.

Review

1   Structured programming is based on the use of [any one/any combination] of the standard structures presented in Figure 2-1.

                                                          any combination

2   A fundamental property of all five basic structures is the existence of [only one/several] entry point(s) and [only one/several] exit point(s).

                                                          only one; only one

COBOL IMPLEMENTATION OF BASIC STRUCTURES

The COBOL language now provides for convenient implementation of all five basic program structures. In some cases, the 1974 standard was incapable of straightforward implementation, but the 1985 standard has removed

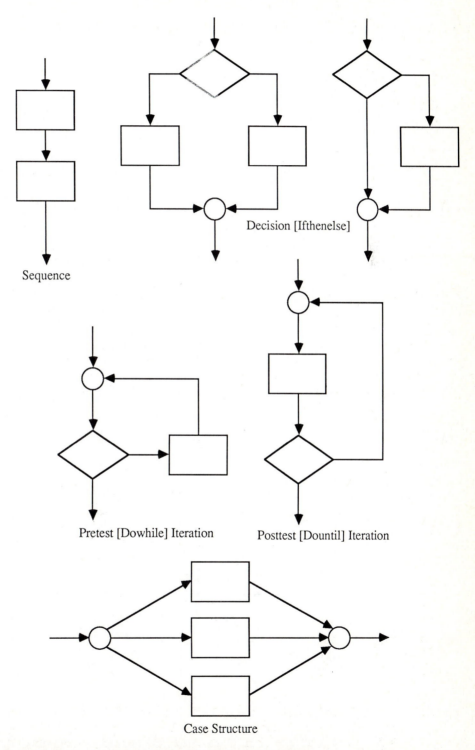

Sequence

Decision [Ifthenelse]

Pretest [Dowhile] Iteration

Posttest [Dountil] Iteration

Case Structure

FIGURE 2-1   STANDARD PROGRAM STRUCTURES.

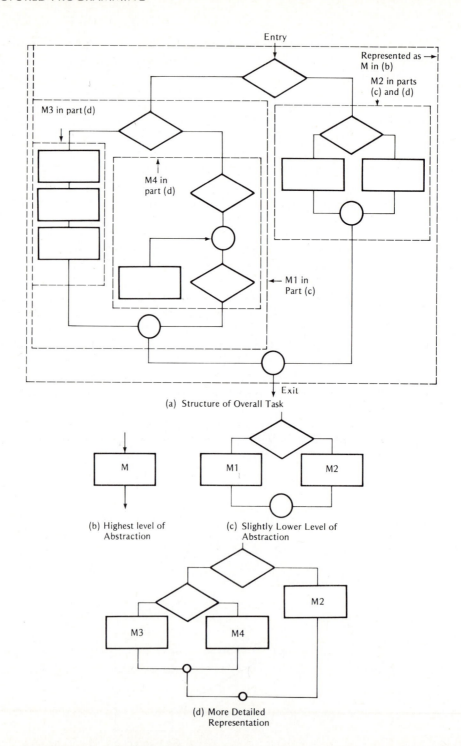

(a) Structure of Overall Task

(b) Highest level of
    Abstraction

(c) Slightly Lower Level of
    Abstraction

(d) More Detailed
    Representation

**FIGURE 2-2   ILLUSTRATION OF LEVELS OF ABSTRACTION BASED ON THE
ONE-ENTRY ONE-EXIT PROPERTY.**

such deficiencies. A series of examples are presented in this section to demonstrate how COBOL language statements can be used to implement each of the basic structures.

Figure 2-3 presents the implementation of the *sequence structure* in COBOL. This is the most basic form of structure, and represents the successive execution of statements or modules in a program. As exemplified by the set of statements for the second module in that figure, a conditional statement that is properly marked by an END-IF scope terminator may be viewed as one step (block) in the sequence.

The implementation of the *decision structure* (also called the *selection* or *ifthenelse structure*) is illustrated in Figure 2-4. There are two forms of the decision structure. The first form is used when one specific action is taken given that the condition is true, and another specific action is taken given that the condition is false. In the second form, one of the "legs" is null, and no action is taken in that case. Either the "true" or the "false" case may be null.

As presented in Figure 2-5, there are two *iteration structures:* the *pretest* (or *dowhile*) and the *posttest* (or *dountil*). In the pretest iteration, a test is performed before any execution of a module, whereas in the posttest iteration, the module is executed once, and then may be executed more times according to the result of the test which follows. There was no direct way of implementing the posttest iteration structure in the 1974 version of COBOL, but this deficiency has been removed in the 1985 standard with the addition of the PERFORM WITH TEST AFTER option.

Finally, alternative implementations of the *case structure* are presented in Figure 2-6. The case structure is convenient when we have need for

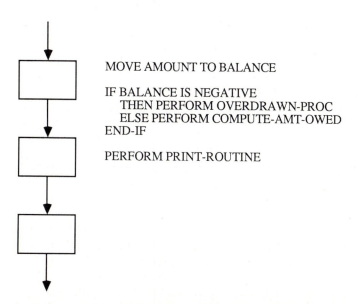

FIGURE 2–3   **COBOL IMPLEMENTATION OF SEQUENCE STRUCTURE.**

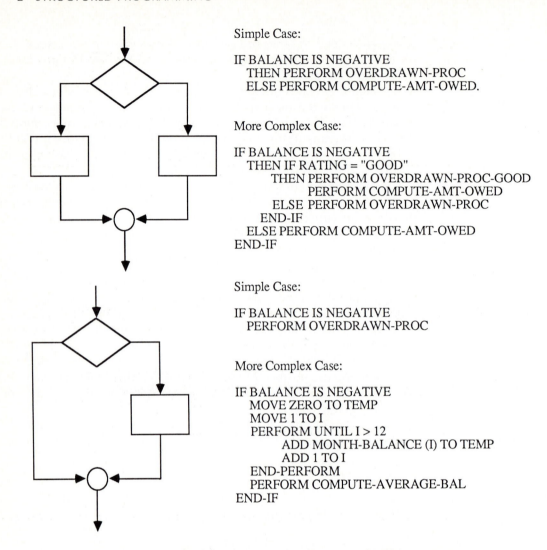

Simple Case:

IF BALANCE IS NEGATIVE
    THEN PERFORM OVERDRAWN-PROC
    ELSE PERFORM COMPUTE-AMT-OWED.

More Complex Case:

IF BALANCE IS NEGATIVE
    THEN IF RATING = "GOOD"
        THEN PERFORM OVERDRAWN-PROC-GOOD
             PERFORM COMPUTE-AMT-OWED
        ELSE PERFORM OVERDRAWN-PROC
    END-IF
    ELSE PERFORM COMPUTE-AMT-OWED
END-IF

Simple Case:

IF BALANCE IS NEGATIVE
    PERFORM OVERDRAWN-PROC

More Complex Case:

IF BALANCE IS NEGATIVE
    MOVE ZERO TO TEMP
    MOVE 1 TO I
    PERFORM UNTIL I > 12
        ADD MONTH-BALANCE (I) TO TEMP
        ADD 1 TO I
    END-PERFORM
    PERFORM COMPUTE-AVERAGE-BAL
END-IF

FIGURE 2–4   COBOL IMPLEMENTATION OF DECISION STRUCTURES.

the selection of a module from among more than two alternative modules, as for example the processing of many types of transactions in a file update program. As illustrated in the first implementation in Figure 2-6, in the 1985 standard the EVALUATE statement provides for a direct way of implementing the case structure. As illustrated by the other three implementations in Figure 2-6, however, use of the 1974 standard requires the use of a more complex programming logic. In general, the nested IF illustrated in Figure 2-6(b) is the preferred approach when the number of alternatives is small— say, no greater than six. When the number of alternatives is large, the COBOL code in Figure 2-6(d) is preferred because it avoids the use of a deeply nested IF structure. The implementation in Figure 2-6(c), using GO TO . . . DEPENDING ON, is suitable only if we have a numeric code that assumes consecutive numeric values ranging as 1, 2, . . . *n*. For instance, if the

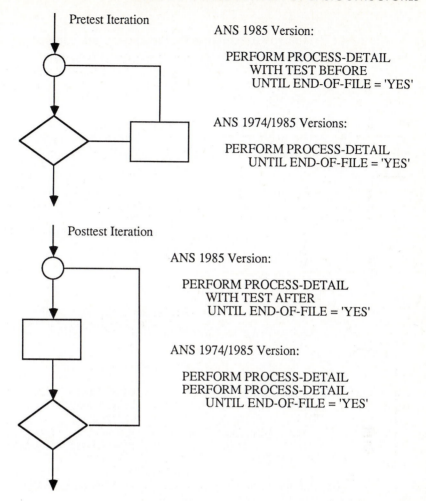

Pretest Iteration

ANS 1985 Version:

PERFORM PROCESS-DETAIL
WITH TEST BEFORE
UNTIL END-OF-FILE = 'YES'

ANS 1974/1985 Versions:

PERFORM PROCESS-DETAIL
UNTIL END-OF-FILE = 'YES'

Posttest Iteration

ANS 1985 Version:

PERFORM PROCESS-DETAIL
WITH TEST AFTER
UNTIL END-OF-FILE = 'YES'

ANS 1974/1985 Version:

PERFORM PROCESS-DETAIL
PERFORM PROCESS-DETAIL
UNTIL END-OF-FILE = 'YES'

FIGURE 2-5   COBOL IMPLEMENTATION OF ITERATION STRUCTURES.

numeric code represents the last school grade completed from the first grade through the fourth year of college and we process each of the 16 possibilities separately, then the implementation in Figure 2-6(c) would be convenient. Otherwise, the generally preferred choices using the 1974 standard are those illustrated in Figure 2-6(b) and Figure 2-6(d), with the choice being based on the depth of nesting that is involved.

Review

1   The program structure that simply indicates that processing is to continue with the next statement or module is the _____ structure.

sequence

2   The type of structure that involves a selection of one of two alternative actions, or of one action versus no action, is the _____ structure.

decision (or selection, or ifthenelse)

3   The two forms of program structure that represent a repeating process, or program loop, are the _____ structures.

iteration

4   The form of the iteration structure in which a test is done before the execution of a program module is the _____ iteration.

pretest (or dowhile)

5   The form of the iteration structure in which the program module is

```
EVALUATE TRUE
    WHEN    FRESHMAN        PERFORM     FROSH-PAR
    WHEN    SOPHOMORE       PERFORM     SOPH-PAR
    WHEN    JUNIOR          PERFORM     JUNIOR-PAR
    WHEN    SENIOR          PERFORM     SENIOR-PAR
    WHEN    OTHER           PERFORM     ERROR-PAR
END-EVALUATE
```

(a) Case Implementation using the EVALUATE Statement (ANS 1985)

```
IF FRESHMAN
    PERFORM FROSH-PAR
ELSE
    IF SOPHOMORE
        PERFORM SOPH-PAR
    ELSE
        IF JUNIOR
            PERFORM JUNIOR-PAR
        ELSE
            IF SENIOR
                PERFORM SENIOR-PAR
            ELSE
                PERFORM ERROR-PAR.
```

(b) Case Implementation using Nested IF Statements

FIGURE 2-6   ALTERNATIVE COBOL IMPLEMENTATIONS OF CASE STRUC-TURE.

```
02   YEAR-OF-STUDIES PIC 9.
     88     FRESHMAN       VALUE 1.
     88     SOPHOMORE      VALUE 2.
     88     JUNIOR         VALUE 3.
     88     SENIOR         VALUE 4.
```
(Notice that values start with 1 and
are consecutive—a requirement for
correct use of the GO TO . . .
DEPENDING ON statement.)

```
ENTRY-PAR.
     GO TO FROSH-PAR
           SOPH-PAR
           JUNIOR-PAR
           SENIOR-PAR
     DEPENDING ON YEAR-OF-STUDIES.
     GO TO ERROR-PAR.

FROSH-PAR.
     ---------------------------
     ---------------------------
     GO TO EXIT-PAR.

SOPH-PAR.
     ---------------------------
     ---------------------------
     GO TO EXIT-PAR.

JUNIOR-PAR.
     ---------------------------
     ---------------------------
     GO TO EXIT-PAR.

SENIOR-PAR.
     ---------------------------
     ---------------------------
     GO TO EXIT-PAR.

ERROR-PAR.
     ---------------------------
     ---------------------------
     GO TO EXIT-PAR.
```
*(In case EXIT-PAR is not physically
contiguous.)*

EXIT-PAR.   *(This is the converging point for all cases, so that the one-
                   entry one-exit structure is preserved and GO TO's are in
                   control.)*

(c) Case Implementation using GO TO . . . DEPENDING ON. . . .

**FIGURE 2–6   ALTERNATIVE COBOL IMPLEMENTATIONS OF CASE STRUC-
TURE.   (Continued)**

```
IF    FRESHMAN
      PERFORM FROSH-PAR
      GO TO EXIT-PAR.

IF    SOPHOMORE
      PERFORM SOPH-PAR
      GO TO EXIT-PAR.

IF    JUNIOR
      PERFORM JUNIOR-PAR
      GO TO EXIT-PAR.

IF    SENIOR
      PERFORM SENIOR-PAR
      GO TO EXIT-PAR.

      PERFORM ERROR-PAR
      GO TO EXIT-PAR.        (in case EXIT-PAR is not physically
                             contiguous.)
```

EXIT-PAR.   *(This is the converging point for all cases, so that the one-entry one-exit structure is preserved and GO TO's are in control.)*

(d) Case Implementation using Simple Conditionals and GO TO

FIGURE 2–6   ALTERNATIVE COBOL IMPLEMENTATIONS OF CASE STRUC-TURE.   (Continued)

executed once, and then may be executed more times according to the result of a test, is the _____ iteration.

posttest (or dountil)

6   The type of program structure in which selection of program modules is made from more than two alternatives is the _____ structure.

case

7   In the 1985 standard, the case structure can be implemented directly by use of the COBOL verb _____.

EVALUATE

8   When the number of alternative modules is small, the preferred COBOL code to implement the case structure in the 1974 standard is to use [GO TO . . . DEPENDING/nested IF] statements.

nested IF

FORMATTING RULES FOR PROGRAMS

Form and substance are highly interrelated. A number of the benefits associated with structured programming derive from use of certain form. Proper substance must be there as a prerequisite to good programming, but proper substance cast in obscure form is hardly worthwhile. In this section we provide some basic guidelines for writing structured programs in readable form. These guidelines are not exhaustive nor are they imperative, but they represent collectively the consensus of good formatting rules practiced in the field.

1   *In the source program use physical spacing to enhance visibility and to denote logical groupings.*

- Use asterisks in column 7 of the COBOL coding form to separate major items. For instance, precede each new 01 item in the WORK-ING-STORAGE with an asterisk. Similarly, in the PROCEDURE DIVISION, separate logical groups by a comment line. If there is a series of MOVE statements and then a WRITE, put a blank comment line before the WRITE to block together the MOVEs that perform a common function.

- Use the stroke (/) in column 7 to start a new page. For instance, always begin the DATA DIVISION on a new page and the PROCEDURE DIVISION on a new page. Then within each of these divisions, start a new page when a major logical unit begins. If you have, for example, three 01 heading descriptions and they require about 20 lines of codes, it is much better to start a new page and to precede the program code with a comment such as:

THE FOLLOWING THREE ITEMS DESCRIBE THE PAGE HEADERS OF THE SALES REPORT.

Then the reader can quickly grasp the common element in the items on the page, and can choose either to give attention to the page or to bypass it.

- In the PROCEDURE DIVISION it is a good practice to list a PROGRAM SUMMARY type of module on the first page and, if there is enough space, all of its immediate subordinates as well. If there is not enough space for all the immediate subordinates, then start a new page for each first level module, and, similarly, place all its immediate subordinates on one page.

2   *Use vertical alignment of similar items to convey similarity of function.*

- Align all PICTURE and VALUE clauses on the same column when possible, especially with respect to each 01-level item. For example:

```
01  A.
    02 B   PIC   9(6).
    02 C   PIC   X(2)       VALUE 'ABC'.
    02 D   PIC   99V9.
    02 E   PIC   99V9.
    02 F   PIC   X(3)       VALUE 'XYZ'.
    02 G   PIC   X(29)      VALUE
               'LONG LITERAL ON SEPARATE LINE'.
```

- Align similar verbs and their operands in the PROCEDURE DIVISION. For instance:

```
OPEN   INPUT     FILE-A
                 FILE-B
         OUTPUT  FILE-C
MOVE AMOUNT         TO ED-AMOUNT
MOVE RATE           TO FACTOR
MOVE PREVIOUS-BAL   TO TEST-VALUE.
```

- Indent subordinate clauses under the main clause.
  In the DATA DIVISION, for instance, 88 items should be indented as follows:

```
02  TRANS-CODE  PIC  X.
    88   CHANGE-RATE  VALUE '1'.
    88   CHANGE-BAL   VALUE '2'.
    88   ERROR-CODE   VALUE LOW-VALUES THRU ZERO
                            '3' THRU HIGH-VALUES.
```

In the PROCEDURE DIVISION we can use indentation as follows:

```
READ   SOURCE-FILE RECORD
         AT END ...

WRITE   DISK-FILE RECORD
          INVALID KEY ...

PERFORM PROCESS-RATE-CHANGE
        UNTIL AMOUNT-OWED > MAX-LIMIT
            OR ERROR-CODE
```

```
MOVE LAST-NAME OF TRANSACTION-FILE-REC
    TO LAST-NAME OF REPORT-REC

CALL 'SUB' USING NO-OF-TRANS
              POLICY-NO
              PREMIUM RATE.
```

These illustrations should serve to suggest the various possibilities. There is no reason why one should commit to memory any detailed rules of indentation. Instead, one should develop a general practice and a state of mind to indent to advantage. Within a given organization there may be "standard" indentation rules developed, but petty adherence to any strict set of rules may defeat the main purpose of indentation, which is to facilitate writing readable programs.

3   *Use group labels to convey common functions.*
- In the DATA DIVISION, it is desirable to group similar items under the same group item. For instance, if there are four totals accumulated in a report-generating program, it is preferable to write them under one group name:

```
01   REPORT-TOTALS.
     02   PRODUCT TOTAL
     02   SALESPERSON-TOTAL
     02   DEPARTMENT-TOTAL
     02   GRAND-TOTAL
```

- In the PROCEDURE DIVISION, group labels can be written in many ways. As one approach, a comment line preceding a group of statements may in effect be a group label that explains the common function:

```
*
*Test IF GROSS-PAY falls within reasonable limits
*
     IF SALARIED-EMPL
         IF GROSS-PAY-THIS WEEK > MIN-SAL-LEVEL
             AND GROSS PAY-THIS-WEEK < MAX-SAL-LEVEL
             PERFORM COMPUTE-NET
         ELSE
             PERFORM UNREASONABLE-SALARY
     ELSE ...
```

Another way of creating a group label is, of course, by the paragraph name. It should be chosen to convey the function of the paragraph.

- Whenever a series of paragraphs constitutes a logical unit, then the SECTION name should be used to give a name to the function of the whole group. Remember, though, that the end of a section is signaled when another section begins. Thus if there is one section, there must be at least one additional section unless the single section is in the last physical position in the program. In general, instead of using PERFORM A THRU B it is better to give a section name to the paragraphs A through B and then say "PERFORM section-name" instead.

4   *Use similar names for similar items.*
- In most programs we encounter fields such as Name or Employee-Number that are present in an input file record, an output file record, and a report record. All three records contain similar items, and we should use a naming convention that facilitates recognition of this similarity. One way to approach the nomenclature is to use qualification:

MOVE NAME OF EMPL-SOURCE-FILE
    TO NAME OF PAY-REG-REPORT
MOVE ADDRESS OF EMPL-SOURCE REC
    TO ADDRESS OF EMPL-NEW-MAST-REC.

But qualification requires more extensive writing, and therefore programmers avoid qualification in their hurry to complete the program. Actually, the keyboarding effort associated with a programming task is a very small portion of the total programming effort. Therefore, qualification should be considered a good approach to naming similar items and achieving good program documentation.

- Another way of naming similar items is to use a mnemonic prefix or suffix to differentiate the items. For example:

NAME-OMR [OMR understood to mean Old Master Record]
NAME-RR   [RR = Report Record]
NAME-WS   [WS = Working Storage]

Review

1   The purpose of this section has been to present the consensus of rules relating to the _____ of structured COBOL programs.

format

2   Many of the rules are concerned with spacing and indentation, with the objective particularly being to make the programs easier to [read/write].

read

3   The use of group labels in the program and the use of similar data-names for similar items particularly [minimize writing time/enhance readability] for the program.

enhance readability

4   The rules presented in this section [should be followed strictly/are general guidelines] for establishing the format for a COBOL program.

are general guidelines

PROGRAM LAYOUT

Program layout refers to the physical arrangement of procedures (para-graphs/sections) in the PROCEDURE DIVISION of the program. Our main objective is to arrange procedures in ways that make the program readable and understandable.

Figure 2-7 presents the structure chart for a sample program. The two-dimensional feature of the structure chart provides a high level of visi-bility and affords easy grasp of intermodule relationships. However, pro-grams can only be written in a one-dimensional mode, line after line, and we wish to develop a linear representation that preserves as much of the two-dimensional structure as possible. In general, no single representation will achieve the same level of visibility as the structure chart. Rather, we can choose one of two basic layouts, each of which is better suited to a different objective.

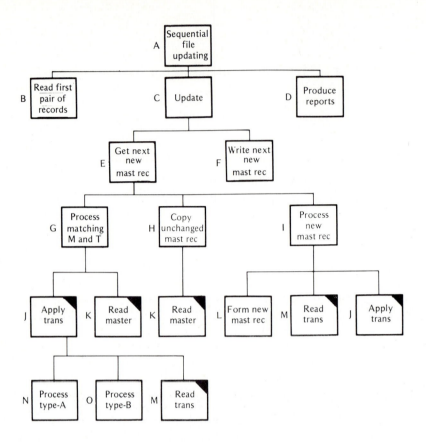

FIGURE 2-7   SAMPLE STRUCTURE CHART.

One layout is oriented to facilitate comprehension of the depth structure of the structure chart, and can be called the *vertical layout.* Figure 2-8(a) illustrates the vertical layout. The letters inside the blocks represent the corresponding modules in Figure 2-7. Referring to Figures 2-7 and 2-8(a), the rationale is that each vertical path is completed before another path begins, and that program modules are *not* repeated. Beginning from the top of Figure 2-8(a), the listed modules A and B represent the first vertical path. Because B has no subordinates, the path terminates at B. The next vertical path is represented by the series of modules A, C, E, G, J, and N. Notice that the A module is not repeated, but the rest of the modules are new and therefore are listed. The next vertical path comprises the modules A, C, E, G, J, N, and O. All these modules have already been listed except O, and so only the O module is listed next. The process of listing modules continues until all modules are included. The vertical layout is well-suited for occasions when we need to traverse a complete path of processing. For instance, if we are interested in reviewing all successive subordinates of a given module, the vertical layout would be convenient.

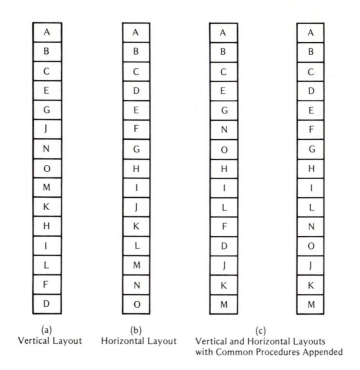

| (a)
Vertical Layout | (b)
Horizontal Layout | (c)
Vertical and Horizontal Layouts
with Common Procedures Appended |

FIGURE 2-8   VERTICAL AND HORIZONTAL LAYOUTS FOR STRUCTURE CHART OF FIGURE 2-7.

The horizontal layout is illustrated in Figure 2-8(b). Notice that it represents the program by hierarchical level. This layout is convenient when we are interested in reviewing all the *immediate* subordinates of a module such as E. The immediate subordinates of E, identified as G, H, and I in Figure 2-7, can be easily located in Figure 2-8(b).

It may be noted that both representations suffer from inadequate treatment of common modules, the ones identified in the structure chart by the shaded corners. For instance, if M is listed after O in the vertical layout, then it is not present after L; the reader would have to "hunt" for M when he encountered it in I. Figure 2-8(c) illustrates the convention of appending common modules (in this case J, K, and M) at the end of the program. When following this convention, if a procedure is not present in the stream of code, it is sought at the "end" of the program listing.

It is clear from the above discussion that no single layout is perfectly suited for program representation. For this reason, the prevalent practice is to use a numeric prefix that corresponds to the physical order of modules. By this approach, the prefix number serves to indicate physical position in the program. Figure 2-9 illustrates the use of a 3-digit prefix. If we encountered a PERFORM 090-READ-TRANS within module I (120–PROCESS-NEW-MAST-REC), we would scan the paragraph names, seeking the paragraph that

PROCEDURE DIVISION

010-SEQ-FILE-UPDATE
020-READ-FIRST-PAIR
030-UPDATE
040-GET-NEXT-NEW-MAST-REC
050-PROCESS-MATCHING-M-T
060-APPLY-TRANS
070-PROCESS-TYPE-A
080-PROCESS-TYPE-B
090-READ-TRANS
100-READ-MASTER
110-COPY-UNCHANGED-MAST-REC
120-PROCESS-NEW-MAST-REC
130-FORM-NEW-MAST-REC
140-WRITE-NEXT-NEW-MAST-REC
150-PRODUCE-REPORTS

(a)

Order is: A,B,C,E,G,J,N,O,M,K,H,I,
          L,F,D

PROCEDURE DIVISION

010-SEQ-FILE-UPDATE
020-READ-FIRST-PAIR
030-UPDATE
040-PRODUCE-REPORTS
050-GET-NEXT-NEW-MAST-REC
060-WRITE-NEXT-NEW-MAST-REC
070-PROCESS-MATCHING-M-T
080-COPY-UNCHANGED-MAST-REC
090-PROCESS-NEW-MAST-REC
100-APPLY-TRANS
110-READ-MASTER
120-FORM-NEW-MAST-REC
130-READ-TRANS
140-PROCESS-TYPE-A
150-PROCESS-TYPE-B

(b)

Order is: A,B,C,D,E,F,G,H,I,J,K,L,
          M,N,O

FIGURE 2-9   VERTICAL AND HORIZONTAL LAYOUTS OF MODULES, WITH PREFIX NUMBERS. (a) Modules arranged and prefixed by vertical hierarchical level. (b) Modules arranged and prefixed by horizontal hierarchical level.

begins with 090. Incidentally, since there are fewer than 99 modules in this program, a 2-digit prefix would suffice.

Yet another approach to layout is to use a prefix designed to convey the hierarchical relationship of modules. This approach is illustrated in Figure 2-10, in which the codes inside the blocks represent the corresponding prefix. Notice that the first-level main module is labeled 0. Then the first-level modules are labeled alphabetically and the subordinates of each module are labeled so as to reflect the hierarchical level as well as the serial order of the modules. For example, the prefix C124 in Figure 2-10 designates that the module is under C, is under the first descendent of C, is under the second descendent of that first descendent, and, finally, is the fourth descendent of the latter module. At first blush such a coding scheme appears to give us the two-dimensional property that we have been seeking. However, unless the program is small, deciphering the coded prefix is rather distracting and has been known to defeat the very purpose for which it was designed.

In summary, the best layout method is use of a prefix denoting the serial order of modules, as illustrated in Figure 2-9, and to sort the modules in the order of their prefix.

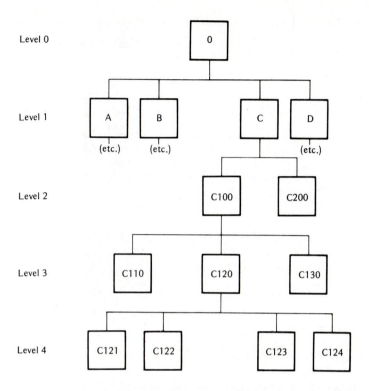

FIGURE 2-10   HIERARCHICAL ENCODING OF PREFIX NUMBERS.

Review

1   Program layout refers specifically to the physical arrangement of paragraphs/sections in the _____ DIVISION of a COBOL program.

PROCEDURE

2   The basic difficulty associated with achieving a clear physical arrangement of the procedures to be executed is that whereas a structure chart is _____-dimensional, the program statements are in a _____-dimensional format.

two; one

3   The two general approaches to program layout are _____ layout and _____ layout.

vertical; horizontal

4   The type of layout that represents the program by hierarchical level is _____ layout, while the type well-suited to traverse a complete path of processing is _____ layout.

horizontal; vertical

5   Because no single layout is perfectly suited for program representation, the prevalent practice is to use a numeric [prefix/suffix] to indicate physical position in the program.

prefix

6   Another approach, which can lead to too much time being devoted to deciphering the coded prefix, is to use the prefix to convey the specific _____ relationship of the modules.

hierarchical

CONVERTING UNSTRUCTURED PROGRAMS TO STRUCTURED FORM

As mentioned in the Introduction to this chapter, programs written during the first quarter-century of programming practice do not conform to the recent techniques of structured programming. Still, these programs are in use and may continue to be used for a long time to come. Thus, it is a common occurrence for a programmer to be asked to modify an existing program. If the required modification is extensive enough, it may be worth redesigning and rewriting the program "from scratch." In the more typical case, an organization cannot afford to rewrite whole programs, and we have to work with "local" modifications to the program. In such instances it may be helpful to revise the appropriate part of the program into structured form. Again, form and substance are not equivalent. If the program was poorly designed in the first place, the benefit of converting the form without converting the substance is questionable. Still, it is often useful to convert an old program into structured form so that modifications can then be incorporated with minimal risk of error. In this section we describe some conversion approaches that may be useful for unstructured programs.

Use of Duplicate Code to Achieve Structured Form

It is often possible to achieve proper structured form by duplicating the same instructions in several places in the program. First, consider a case such as portrayed in Figure 2-11(a). While the form is in fact structured, ANS 1974

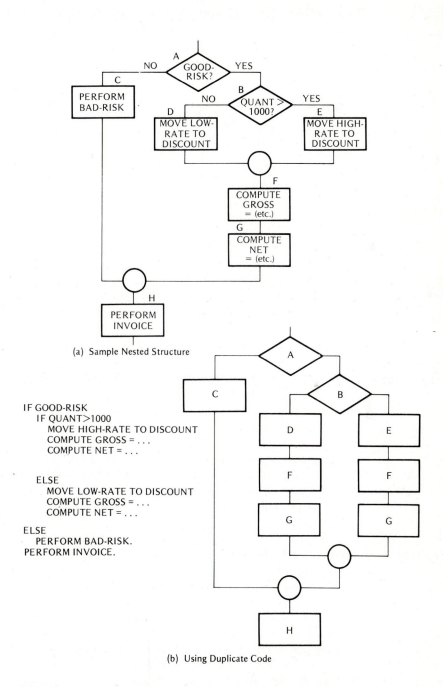

(a) Sample Nested Structure

```
IF GOOD-RISK
   IF QUANT>1000
      MOVE HIGH-RATE TO DISCOUNT
      COMPUTE GROSS = . . .
      COMPUTE NET = . . .

   ELSE
      MOVE LOW-RATE TO DISCOUNT
      COMPUTE GROSS = . . .
      COMPUTE NET = . . .

ELSE
   PERFORM BAD-RISK.
PERFORM INVOICE.
```

(b) Using Duplicate Code

**FIGURE 2-11   DUPLICATION OF CODE TO IMPLEMENT A NESTED STRUC-
TURE IN THE ABSENCE OF THE END-IF SCOPE TERMINATOR.**

COBOL cannot represent the form directly without the duplication of code, as illustrated in Figure 2-11(b). However, in the 1985 standard, the availability of the END-IF makes it possible to code the structured form directly, without the use of duplicate code, as follows:

```
IF GOOD RISK
   THEN IF QUANT > 1000
           THEN MOVE HIGH-RATE TO DISCOUNT
           ELSE MOVE LOW-RATE TO DISCOUNT
        END-IF
   ELSE PERFORM BAD-RISK
END-IF
PERFORM INVOICE.
```

Lacking the END-IF capability for programs written before the 1985 standard was available, duplicate code was the most straightforward approach.

Now let us apply duplication of code in a more complex and more realistic example. Consider the program outline in Figure 2-12(a) and its associated flow diagram in Figure 2-12(b). Using the concept of duplication of code, we revise the program structure as presented in Figure 2-13. Notice that we have achieved the one-entry, one-exit property at all levels, and we can now make our program modifications much more easily than before. For instance, if we wanted to make a change to the program under condition C4 when the path was from C to C3 to D to C4, we could make the change and leave the rest of the program unaffected.

Duplication of coding appears to be against "efficiency" in program coding. Yet writing a few additional instructions may be a small investment with a high payoff. Further, the duplication is often only conceptual, as illustrated in Figure 2-13(b), where the use of PERFORMs has reduced the actual duplicate code.

Use of a Binary Switch to Control Loop Execution

Unstructured programs often contain intermeshed multiple loops that are difficult to unravel without rewriting the entire program segment involved. To convert an unstructured loop into structured form we employ the approach illustrated in Figure 2-14. The method relies on setting a switch (S) to an initial value, S=1 in the example, and forming a pretest loop structure based on using this switch as the selection variable.

Now let us illustrate application of this method in a rather difficult but common case of overlapping loops. In Figure 2-15 we have a program segment that is diagrammed in part (b). Notice that there are two overlapping loops, and to make matters worse the selection step of the first loop is the first step of the second loop.

Figure 2-16 represents a conversion of Figure 2-15 into structured

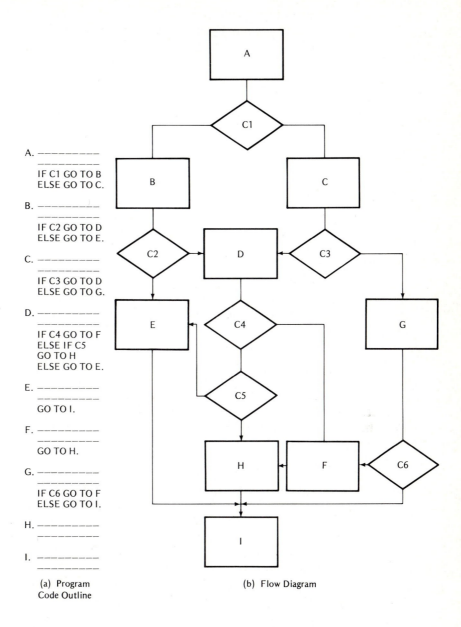

A. ----------

   IF C1 GO TO B
   ELSE GO TO C.

B. ----------

   IF C2 GO TO D
   ELSE GO TO E.

C. ----------

   IF C3 GO TO D
   ELSE GO TO G.

D. ----------

   IF C4 GO TO F
   ELSE IF C5
   GO TO H
   ELSE GO TO E.

E. ----------

   GO TO I.

F. ----------

   GO TO H.

G. ----------

   IF C6 GO TO F
   ELSE GO TO I.

H. ----------

I. ----------

(a) Program
Code Outline

(b) Flow Diagram

FIGURE 2-12   SAMPLE UNSTRUCTURED PROGRAM.

form using two binary switches, S1 and S2, to control execution of the two loops. Notice the inset in the upper right corner, which employs the concept of levels of abstraction to highlight the structured form of the converted figure.

An alternative solution is given in Figure 2-17. In this case we first employ duplication of coding to set off the first loop by itself, at the top

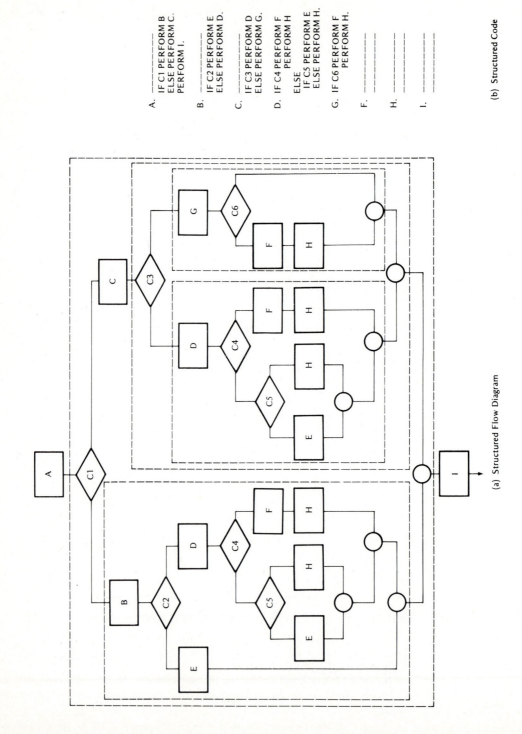

A.   IF C1 PERFORM B
     ELSE PERFORM C.
     PERFORM I.

B.   IF C2 PERFORM E
     ELSE PERFORM D.

C.   IF C3 PERFORM D
     ELSE PERFORM G.

D.   IF C4 PERFORM F
     PERFORM H

     ELSE
     IF C5 PERFORM E
     ELSE PERFORM H.

G.   IF C6 PERFORM F
     PERFORM H.

F.   _____

H.   _____

I.   _____

(b) Structured Code

(a) Structured Flow Diagram

FIGURE 2-13   STRUCTURED VERSION OF THE PROGRAM IN FIGURE 2-12.

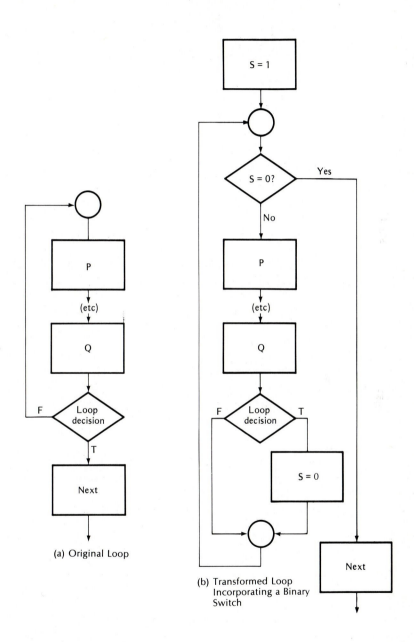

FIGURE 2-14   USING A BINARY SWITCH TO CONTROL LOOP EXECUTION IN STRUCTURED FORM.

A.
```
WRITE PRINT-REC
MOVE AMOUNT TO SUBTOTAL.
```

B.
```
MOVE TEMP-SUM TO PREV-TEMP-SUM.
```

C.
```
IF PROD-CLASS-1
    GO TO B
ELSE
    MOVE DISC-CODE TO SAVE-CODE
    WRITE PRINT-REC FROM MESSAGE-3.
IF CUST-CLASS-B
    GO TO C
ELSE
    WRITE PRINT-REC FROM MESSAGE-5.
```

(a) Sample Unstructured Code Involving Loops

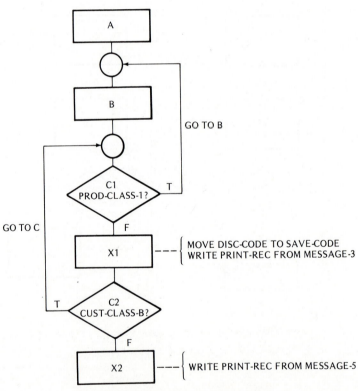

(b) Flow Diagram for Unstructured Code

**FIGURE 2–15   SAMPLE UNSTRUCTURED PROGRAM INVOLVING OVERLAP-
PING LOOPS.**

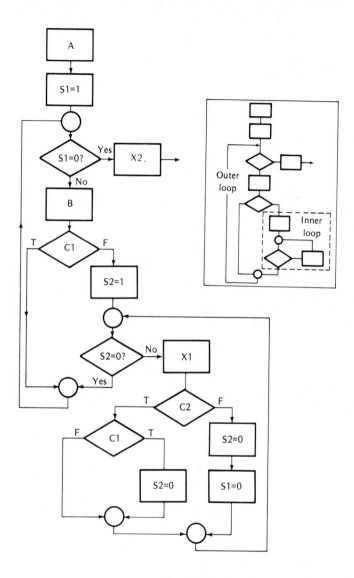

FIGURE 2-16   USING TWO BINARY SWITCHES TO CONVERT THE PROGRAM IN FIGURE 2-15 TO STRUCTURED FORM.

of the flow diagram. Then, we use two switches in the lower half to control iterative execution of the two loops after we have exited from the first loop.

The two alternatives in Figures 2-16 and 2-17 serve to demonstrate that the conversion to structured form is not a fixed procedure, but can be done in different ways.

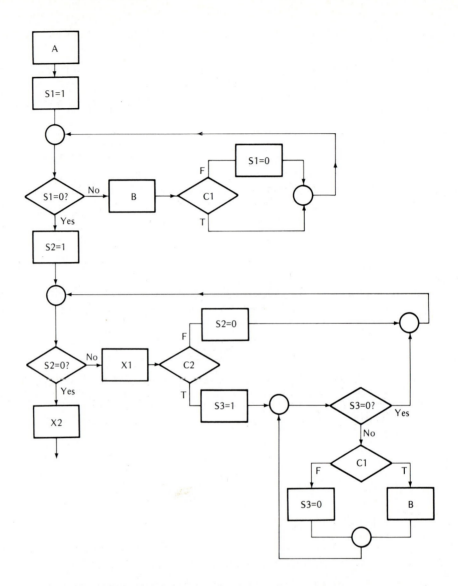

**FIGURE 2-17   USING DUPLICATION OF CODING AND BINARY SWITCHES
TO CONVERT THE PROGRAM IN FIGURE 2-15 TO STRUCTURED FORM.**

Review

1   The need to convert unstructured programs to structured form typically is associated with [the objective that all programs be structured/the need to modify an existing older program].

> the need to modify an existing older program

2   Duplication of modules in a structure chart done to achieve structured form [does/does not] thereby result in the program code also being duplicated the same number of times.

> does not

3   In the 1985 standard, duplication of code in order to achieve a structured form is avoided by the use of the command _____.

> END-IF

4   The principal methods used to convert overlapping program loops into structured form involve the introduction of binary _____ in the program.

> switches

Exercises

2.1   Describe and illustrate diagrammatically the five basic program structure forms discussed in this chapter.

2.2   A program is to be developed to represent the basic logic and function of a vending machine that accepts nickels, dimes, and quarters; dispenses a 30-cent candybar; and provides the correct change, if any. Coins other than nickels, dimes, and quarters are either rejected or do not fit. We assume that we want to develop a program that reads data records, with each data record representing one coin. The program reads the data, processes it, and either "delivers" a product and the change or reads another record representing another coin. The last record in the input contains a special code that indicates the end of data. After processing such a record, the program stops. Develop a flowchart of the program logic, using the basic program structures discussed in this chapter.

2.3   For the following structure chart illustrate the vertical and the horizontal approaches to program layout:

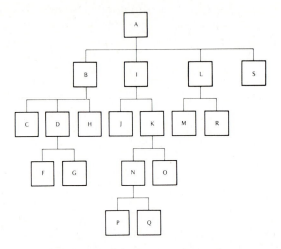

2.4   Assume the use of the vertical layout with respect to the structure chart in the preceding exercise. Now assign a numeric prefix to indicate the physical position of each module in the program.

2.5   Consider the following structured program segment:

```
PAR-A.
    IF COND-A GO TO PAR-C.
    PERFORM PAR-M.
PAR-B.
    IF COND-B GO TO PAR-X.
PAR-C.
    PERFORM PAR-N
    GO TO PAR-B.
PAR-M.
    ⋮
PAR-N.
    ⋮
PAR-X.
    ⋮
```

a Draw the corresponding logic in flowchart form.
b Apply use of duplicate code to achieve structured form. Show the structured form both by means of flowcharting and by means of program statements.
c Apply use of binary switches to achieve structured form. Show the structured form both by means of flowcharting and by means of program statements.

2.6   Revise the following chart to structured form using both flowcharting and program statements. Enhance the program logic so that when either file ends we exit from this procedure.

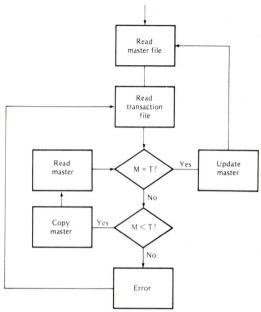

2.7   Consider the program excerpt below, which is not in proper structured form.

    a   Draw a flowchart to highlight the essential control logic of the program.

    b   Revise the flowchart constructed in part **a**, above, so that it is in structured form by using binary switch(es) and/or duplicate code.

    c   Demonstrate application of the concept of *levels of abstraction* in your structured flowchart in part **b**, above.

    d   Rewrite the program excerpt below in proper structured form.

```
PAR-1.
    MOVE AMOUNT TO BALANCE
    IF BALANCE IS NEGATIVE GO TO PAR-4.
    PERFORM READ-INVENTORY
    IF END-INV GO TO PAR-3
    ELSE MOVE PART-LOC TO WHSE-CODE
        MULTIPLY QUANT BY PRICE GIVING TOTAL
        MOVE INV-LIMIT TO LIMIT-FIELD.
PAR-2.
    PERFORM CHECK-INVENTORY
    IF TOTAL > MAX-QUANT GO TO PAR-1
    ELSE PERFORM PROCESS-SHIPPING-PREP.
    IF FULL-LOAD PERFORM TRUCK-LOAD
```

```
      ELSE PERFORM COMBINE-SHIPMENT.
      IF SHIPPING ERROR GO TO PAR-2.
PAR-3.
      MOVE CUST-ADDRESS TO REPORT-ADDRESS
      PERFORM PRINT-LABEL.
PAR-4
      (etc.)
```

II   Selected program language features

3

ENVIRONMENT DIVISION

INTRODUCTION

Use of the ENVIRONMENT DIVISION is optional under the new standard but is required under the 1974 standard. When it is used, the statements in this division define aspects of the program that are dependent upon the specific computer that is to be used in executing the program.

The ENVIRONMENT DIVISION can include two sections: the CONFIGURATION SECTION and the INPUT-OUTPUT SECTION. The coverage of this chapter is concerned only with the CONFIGURATION SECTION. The INPUT/OUTPUT SECTION is used only in conjunction with file processing, and therefore is described in Chapters 8 through 11, which are devoted to this topic.

Figure 3-1 presents the general format for the CONFIGURATION SECTION. The remainder of this chapter is devoted to explaining the options that are available in this section of the ENVIRONMENT DIVISION.

ENVIRONMENT DIVISION.
CONFIGURATION SECTION.
SOURCE-COMPUTER. [Computer-name   [WITH DEBUGGING MODE].]
OBJECT-COMPUTER.   [Computer-name
                    [PROGRAM COLLATING SEQUENCE IS alphabet-name].]
SPECIAL-NAMES.
  [[Implementor-name-1

$\left\{\begin{array}{l}\text{IS mnemonic-name-1}\\ \quad\text{[\underline{ON} STATUS IS condition-name-1 [\underline{OFF} STATUS IS Condition-name-2]]}\\ \text{IS mnemonic-name-2}\\ \quad\text{[\underline{OFF} STATUS IS condition-name-1 [\underline{ON} STATUS IS condition-name-2]]}\\ \underline{\text{ON}}\text{ STATUS IS condition-name-1 [\underline{OFF} STATUS IS condition-name-2]]}\\ \underline{\text{OFF}}\text{ STATUS IS condition-name-2 [\underline{ON} STATUS IS condition-name-1]]}\end{array}\right\}$ . . .

[ALPHABET alphabet-name-1 IS]

$\left\{\begin{array}{l}\underline{\text{STANDARD-1}}\\ \underline{\text{STANDARD-2}}\\ \underline{\text{NATIVE}}\\ \text{implementor-name-2}\\ \left\{\text{literal-1}\quad \left[\left\{\begin{array}{l}\underline{\text{THROUGH}}\\ \underline{\text{THRU}}\end{array}\right\}\text{ literal-2 . . .}\right]\right.\\ \qquad\qquad\qquad \underline{\text{ALSO}}\quad\text{literal-3 . . .}\end{array}\right\}$ . . .

$\left[\underline{\text{SYMBOLIC}}\text{ CHARACTERS}\quad \left\{\left\{\text{symbolic-character-1}\right\}\text{ . . . }\left\{\begin{array}{l}\text{IS}\\ \text{ARE}\end{array}\right\}\{\text{integer-1}\}\text{ . . .}\right\}\right.$ . . .

  [IN alphabet-name-2] } . . .

$\left[\underline{\text{CLASS}}\text{ class-name IS}\quad \left\{\text{literal-4}\quad\left[\left\{\begin{array}{l}\underline{\text{THROUGH}}\\ \underline{\text{THRU}}\end{array}\right\}\text{ literal-5}\right]\right\}\text{ . . .}\right]$ . . .

[CURRENCY SIGN IS   literal-6]
[DECIMAL-POINT IS COMMA].]

FIGURE 3-1   GENERAL FORMAT FOR THE CONFIGURATION SECTION OF THE ENVIRONMENT DIVISION.

THE SOURCE-COMPUTER PARAGRAPH

The SOURCE-COMPUTER *paragraph* is an optional paragraph used to identify the computer on which the COBOL source program is to be compiled. If this paragraph is omitted, the default is the computer on which the source program in fact is compiled. Because of the default, it might seem that this paragraph would never be needed. But note that use of the following optional clause requires the existence of this paragraph.

The WITH DEBUGGING MODE clause provides a switch mechanism for activating/deactivating debugging lines in a source program during its compilation. A debugging line is identified by a *D* character in column 7 of the COBOL coding form, as explained in Chapter 16, Program Cohesion. In a source program that includes such lines, the WITH DEBUGGING MODE clause specifies that such lines should be compiled along with the rest of the program. Omission of this clause results in the debugging lines (if any) being treated as if they were comment lines in the process of compilation.

In the typical situation, if a program includes debugging lines, then the WITH DEBUGGING MODE option is used until program testing is completed. At that point the clause is removed and the program is compiled again, thereby deactivating the effect of the debugging lines without physically erasing them or having to change them to comment lines (which could be done by changing the *D* in column 7 to a *).

Review

1   As indicated by the paragraph name, the purpose of the SOURCE-COMPUTER paragraph is to identify the name of the _____ on which the COBOL source program is to be compiled.

computer

2   If the SOURCE-COMPUTER paragraph is omitted, then the source computer is identified as being the one on which the COBOL source program is _____.

compiled

3   The optional clause that provides a switch mechanism for activating/deactivating debugging lines in a source program during its compilation is the _____ clause.

WITH DEBUGGING MODE

THE OBJECT-COMPUTER PARAGRAPH

The OBJECT-COMPUTER *paragraph* is an optional paragraph used to identify the name of the computer on which the compiled program is to be executed and to identify the collating sequence to be used during program execution. As explained in the next section of this chapter, on the SPECIAL-NAMES PARAGRAPH, the alphabet-name in the COLLATING SEQUENCE clause can be defined in several ways. For example, suppose that *alphabet-name* has been defined as ASCII-CODE. Then we could have the following:

```
OBJECT-COMPUTER.   ABC-480
                PROGRAM COLLATING SEQUENCE IS ASCII-CODE.
SPECIAL-NAMES.
    ALPHABET ASCII-CODE IS STANDARD-1.
```

In the example above, we have specified that alphanumeric comparisons and any SORT or MERGE operations are to be based on STANDARD-1, which is explained in the following section, on the SPECIAL-NAMES paragraph. The above specifications could be used in conjunction with systems, such as some IBM systems, in which the native collating sequence is *not* the one defined by STANDARD-1. Omission of the optional PROGRAM COLLATING SEQUENCE clause defaults to the use of the native collating sequence for that computer system.

In a related matter, use of the CODE-SET clause (see Chapter 8, Sequential Files) and the COLLATING SEQUENCE clause in the SORT and MERGE statements (see Chapter 9, Sorting and Merging) are ways of overriding the PROGRAM COLLATING SEQUENCE defined in the OBJECT-COMPUTER paragraph in selected areas within the program.

Because the topic of collating sequence is of considerable importance, it is explained in greater detail in the following paragraphs.

Every computer system has a *native* set of characters, or alphabet. The term *alphabet* here has a broader meaning than usually implied, and includes all the characters in use, such as the letters of the alphabet, special symbols, and the numeric digits. Of course, uppercase characters are distinct from lowercase characters and both types are included in the alphabet.

A standard alphabet is the ASCII, represented in Figure 3-2. This is an 8-bit character code. Another alphabet, shown in Figure 3-3, is the EBCDIC code used by large IBM and IBM-compatible systems. Other computer alphabets are also available.

For each alphabet there is a *collating sequence* which assigns an ordinal value to each character. For instance, in the ASCII code "null" is the smallest character, with a collating sequence of zero, and the tilde (~) is the largest character, with a value of 126. Note that the bit configurations for the collating sequence 1–31 and above 126 are undefined. The collating sequence in a computer is used in alphanumeric comparisons. For instance, in the ASCII system a field whose content is 9A is smaller than a field whose content is aA, whereas in EBCDIC 9A is larger than aA.

COBOL provides for some control over the alphabet and the collating sequence by use of the PROGRAM COLLATING SEQUENCE option, and can therefore facilitate some compatibility of data files created with different computers and different alphabets and collating sequences.

Review

1   The paragraph in the CONFIGURATION SECTION of the ENVIRONMENT DIVISION that identifies the computer on which the compiled program is to be executed is the _____ paragraph.

OBJECT COMPUTER

COLLATING SEQUENCE	BIT CONFIGURATION	SYMBOL	MEANING
0	00000000		Null
32	00100000	SP	Space
33	00100001	|	Logical OR
34	00100010	"	Quotation mark
35	00100011	#	Number sign
36	00100100	$	Dollar sign
37	00100101	%	Percent
38	00100110	&	Ampersand
39	00100111	'	Apostrophe, prime
40	00101000	(	Opening parenthesis
41	00101001	)	Closing parenthesis
42	00101010	*	Asterisk
43	00101011	+	Plus
44	00101100	,	Comma
45	00101101	−	Hyphen, minus
46	00101110	.	Period, decimal point
47	00101111	/	Slant
48	00110000	0	
49	00110001	1	
50	00110010	2	
51	00110011	3	
52	00110100	4	
53	00110101	5	
54	00110110	6	
55	00110111	7	
56	00111000	8	
57	00111001	9	
58	00111010	:	Colon
59	00111011	;	Semi-colon
60	00111100	<	Less than
61	00111101	=	Equals
62	00111110	>	Greater than
63	00111111	?	Question mark
64	01000000	@	Commercial At
65	01000001	A	
66	01000010	B	
67	01000011	C	
68	01000100	D	
69	01000101	E	
70	01000110	F	
71	01000111	G	
72	01001000	H	
73	01001001	I	
74	01001010	J	
75	01001011	K	
76	01001100	L	

FIGURE 3-2   ASCII ALPHABET AND CODING SEQUENCE.

COLLATING SEQUENCE	BIT CONFIGURATION	SYMBOL	MEANING
77	01001101	M	
78	01001110	N	
79	01001111	O	
80	01010000	P	
81	01010001	Q	
82	01010010	R	
83	01010011	S	
84	01010100	T	
85	01010101	U	
86	01010110	V	
87	01010111	W	
88	01011000	X	
89	01011001	Y	
90	01011010	Z	
91	01011011	[	Opening bracket
92	01011100	\	Reverse slant
93	01011101	]	Closing bracket
94	01011110	^	Circumflex, Logical NOT
95	01011111	___	Underscore
96	01100000	`	Grave Accent
97	01100001	a	
98	01100010	b	
99	01100011	c	
100	01100100	d	
101	01100101	e	
102	01100110	f	
103	01100111	g	
104	01101000	h	
105	01101001	i	
106	01101010	j	
107	01101011	k	
108	01101100	l	
109	01101101	m	
110	01101110	n	
111	01101111	o	
112	01110000	p	
113	01110001	q	
114	01110010	r	
115	01110011	s	
116	01110100	t	
117	01110101	u	
118	01110110	v	
119	01110111	w	
120	01111000	x	
121	01111001	y	
122	01111010	z	

FIGURE 3–2   ASCII ALPHABET AND CODING SEQUENCE.
(Continued)

COLLATING SEQUENCE	BIT CONFIGURATION	SYMBOL	MEANING
123	01111011	{	Opening Brace
124	01111100	|	Vertical Line
125	01111101	}	Closing Brace
126	01111110	~	Tilde

FIGURE 3-2   **ASCII ALPHABET AND CODING SEQUENCE.**
(Continued)

COLLATING SEQUENCE	BIT CONFIGURATION	SYMBOL	MEANING
0	00000000		
.			
.			
74	01001010	¢	Cent sign
75	01001011	.	Period, decimal point
76	01001100	<	Less than sign
77	01001101	(	Left parenthesis
78	01001110	+	Plus sign
79	01001111	|	Vertical bar, Logical OR
80	01010000	&	Ampersand
.			
.			
90	01011010	!	Exclamation point
91	01011011	$	Dollar sign
92	01011100	*	Asterisk
93	01011101	)	Right parenthesis
94	01011110	;	Semi-colon
95	01011111	^	Logical not
96	01100000	−	Minus, hyphen
97	01100001	/	Slash
.			
.			
107	01101011	,	Comma
108	01101100	%	Percent sign
109	01101101	__	Underscore
110	01101110	>	Greater than sign
111	01101111	?	Question mark
.	.		
.			
122	01111010	:	Colon
123	01111011	#	Number sign
124	01111100	@	At sign
125	01111101	'	Apostrophe, prime
126	01111110	=	Equals sign

FIGURE 3-3   **EBCDIC ALPHABET AND CODING SEQUENCE.**

COLLATING SEQUENCE	BIT CONFIGURATION	SYMBOL	MEANING
127	01111111	''	Quotation marks
.			
.			
129	10000001	a	
130	10000010	b	
131	10000011	c	
132	10000100	d	
133	10000101	e	
134	10000110	f	
135	10000111	g	
136	10001000	h	
137	10001001	i	
.			
.			
145	10010001	j	
146	10010010	k	
147	10010011	l	
148	10010100	m	
149	10010101	n	
150	10010110	o	
151	10010111	p	
152	10011000	q	
153	10011001	r	
.			
.			
162	10100010	s	
163	10100011	t	
164	10100100	u	
165	10100101	v	
166	10100110	w	
167	10100111	x	
168	10101000	y	
169	10101001	z	
.			
.			
193	11000001	A	
194	11000010	B	
195	11000011	C	
196	11000100	D	
197	11000101	E	
198	11000110	F	
199	11000111	G	
200	11001000	H	
201	11001001	I	
.			
.			
209	11010001	J	

FIGURE 3-3   EBCDIC ALPHABET AND CODING SEQUENCE.
(Continued)

COLLATING SEQUENCE	BIT CONFIGURATION	SYMBOL	MEANING
210	11010010	K	
211	11010011	L	
212	11010100	M	
213	11010101	N	
214	11010110	O	
215	11010111	P	
216	11011000	Q	
217	11011001	R	
.			
.			
226	11100010	S	
227	11100011	T	
228	11100100	U	
229	11100101	V	
230	11100110	W	
231	11100111	X	
232	11101000	Y	
233	11101001	Z	
.			
.			
240	11110000	0	
241	11110001	1	
242	11110010	2	
243	11110011	3	
244	11110100	4	
245	11110101	5	
246	11110110	6	
247	11110111	7	
248	11111000	8	
249	11111001	9	

FIGURE 3-3   EBCDIC ALPHABET AND CODING SEQUENCE. (Continued)

2   The optional clause in the OBJECT COMPUTER paragraph that identifies the collating sequence to be used during program execution is the PROGRAM _____ clause.

COLLATING SEQUENCE

3   The native set of characters associated with a computer system, which includes the alphabetic characters, special symbols, and numeric digits, is referred to as the _____ of the system.

alphabet

4   Associated with every alphabet is a system by which an ordinal value is assigned to each character, which is called the _____ sequence.

collating

THE SPECIAL-NAMES PARAGRAPH

As can be seen in Figure 3-1, the SPECIAL-NAMES paragraph provides for a host of definitions for special features to be used in a program. The available features are described in the following subsections.

Defining Implementor Switches and Devices

In general, an *implementor* is the supplier of the operating system and the COBOL processor. Specifically, implementors may define switches and devices which can be accessed by a COBOL program. The SPECIAL-NAMES paragraph then can be used to associate specific implementor switches and devices with the general structure of the language in a particular program. The following numbered examples under the SPECIAL-NAMES paragraph heading serve to illustrate the concepts that are involved.

```
SPECIAL-NAMES.
1  UPSI-O   ON STATUS IS END-OF-MONTH
             OFF STATUS IS NOT-END-OF-MONTH
2  C01 IS TOP-OF-PAGE
   C06 IS MIDDLE-OF-PAGE
   C12 IS BOTTOM-OF-PAGE
3  CONSOLE IS OPERATOR-WORKSTATION
   SYSOUT IS DISPLAY-FILE
```

The first example defines an external switch by the implementor-name UPSI-O. It is to be referenced by the condition-names END-OF-MONTH and NOT-END-OF-MONTH as corresponding to an ON and OFF status, respectively. The switch is set by an action external to the COBOL program, usually through the operating system. The definition in Example 1 could be applied in the following program segment:

```
IF END-OF-MONTH
  THEN PERFORM CLOSE-THE-BOOKS
  ELSE PERFORM DAILY-PROCESSING
END-IF
```

In essence, the above program segment says "If the external switch called UPSI-O is ON at the time of execution, do one thing; if it is OFF, do another thing." The program can then "sense" the operating environment at the time of program execution and take the appropriate action.

Example 2 in the numbered list above illustrates three similar applications. C01, C06, and C12 are implementor-names that are given mnemonic names. The mnemonic names then can be used in a program as follows:

WRITE REPORT-REC AFTER ADVANCING MIDDLE-OF-PAGE

For the above program segment, *MIDDLE-OF-PAGE* was previously defined as a mnemonic-name standing for C06, which is also an implementor-name. The result, presumably, would be to advance the vertical carriage of the printer to a prespecified channel.

Finally, Example 3, above, illustrates two more mnemonic names that can be used in ACCEPT and DISPLAY statements, as in the following two examples:

ACCEPT BEGINNING-CHECK-N0 FROM OPERATOR-WORKSTATION

DISPLAY 'CONTENT OF SALES-TOTAL = TOTAL = ' UPON DISPLAY-FILE

In the program illustrations above, OPERATOR-WORKSTATION and DISPLAY-FILE are mnemonic-names for what are implementor-defined as CONSOLE and SYSOUT, respectively.

In general, use of mnemonic-names allows the programmer to use meaningful names in place of implementor-names that may not be meaningful, such as the use of the mnemonic-name DISPLAY-FILE in place of SYSOUT in Example 3.

Defining Alphabets

The ALPHABET clause allows the user to name one of the three choices shown in Figure 3-1. STANDARD-1 refers to the American National Standard Code X3.4-1977 for Information Interchange. STANDARD-2 refers to the International Standard 646 Code for Information Processing Interchange. Finally, NATIVE refers to the code that is native to that computer, such as the EBCDIC code used in most IBM mainframe systems. Such codes specify the collating sequence of characters.

We now give some additional examples to illustrate use of these language facilities. Suppose we want to define a collating sequence that starts with space as the smallest character, followed by the 10 digits, followed by the remaining native sequence. We could write:

OBJECT-COMPUTER.   ABC-480
                        PROGRAM COLLATING SEQUENCE IS NEW-CODE.
SPECIAL-NAMES.
  ALPHABET NEW-CODE IS ' ', '0', '1', '2', '3', '4', '5', '6', '7', '8', '9'.

Now in the alphabet named NEW-CODE the figurative constant LOW-VALUE will be the space, since it is listed as the first character in the NEW-CODE alphabet. The characters not explicitly defined remain in their native order and immediately follow the explicitly defined characters.

If we wanted to define the % sign as the largest character (HIGH-VALUE) and if we assume an IBM system whose native code is EBCDIC, we could write:

NEW-CODE IS 0 THROUGH 107, 109 THRU 249, '%'.

When we use numeric literals such as 0, 107, 109, and 249, above, they stand for the characters in the native collating sequence. In other words, we consulted Figure 3-3, and observed that % is 108 in the EBCDIC sequence. In the above example we write 0 THRU 107 to leave the first part of the native sequence intact, and 109 THRU 249 to continue with the remaining native sequence except for character 108 (the % sign), which we wrote last and thereby made it the highest character. We used 249 as the last reference before the % because it is the highest value in EBCDIC code.

We may also specify equality of characters. For example, if we write:

ALPHABET CODE-XYZ IS ' ' ALSO '0', 'A' THRU 'X', 'Y' ALSO 'Z'

the space and the zero, and the Y and the Z, would be equal to one another, respectively. Use of ALSO equates characters in the collating sequence. If CODE-XYZ is used, a non-numeric field containing zeros would be compared as being equal to another field containing spaces.

As another option, the sequence may be reversed by writing, for example:

ALPHABET REVERSE-CODE IS 'Z' THRU 'A', '9' THRU '0'.

Now the Z is the smallest letter followed by Y, and so on, while 9 is the smallest digit for purposes of comparison (but not for purposes of arithmetic). In the MERGE and SORT verbs there is a COLLATING . . . option. If we were performing a sort on the S-FILE and we wrote SORT . . . COLLATING SEQUENCE IS REVERSE-CODE (as defined above), the sort would operate in descending order for alphabetic and numeric characters.

Overall, the COLLATING SEQUENCE option is particularly helpful in handling data created under a different alphabet or using a program whose logic is directly dependent on a certain collating sequence that is different from the native sequence. In such cases we can define a new alphabet to simulate the required collating sequence.

Defining Symbolic Characters

The SYMBOLIC CHARACTER clause allows the programmer to give a (mnemonic) name to a character which may not be in the principle set of characters. For example, consider the following:

```
SPECIAL-NAMES.
   ALPHABET ASCII IS STANDARD-1
   SYMBOLIC CHARACTER BEEP IS 7 IN ASCII.
```

The SYMBOLIC CHARACTER specification uses the alphabet-name ASCII, as defined by ALPHABET ASCII IS STANDARD-1. If the character value 7 in the collating sequence of STANDARD-1 causes the terminal bell to ring, then the following program statements would cause the bell to ring:

```
01   DISPLAY-FIELD PIC X.
      .
      .
      .
     MOVE BEEP TO DISPLAY-FIELD.
     DISPLAY DISPLAY-FIELD . . .
```

Defining a Data Class

The CLASS clause in the SPECIAL-NAMES paragraph can be used to define a set of characters and to assign a class-name to them. The program can then refer to this class-name to test whether it is true or false that a data item consists exclusively of the characters identified in the definition of the class-name. Consider the following example:

```
SPECIAL-NAMES.
   CLASS SPOKEN-NUMERIC
      IS '0' THRU '9'
         'o', 'O'. [these are the lowercase and uppercase letter 'o']
```

In the above example SPOKEN-NUMERIC is defined as the 10 numeric digits and the letter "o", to allow for the use of "o" as an alternate to zero, such as in "the course number is three-o-two" (perhaps as heard and interpreted by a speech-recognition data-input device). In the PROCEDURE DIVISION we could now write:

IF STREET-NUMBER IS SPOKEN-NUMERIC . . .

The condition is true if STREET-NUMBER contains only the characters in the defined set SPOKEN-NUMERIC.

It should be noted that class-names are different from condition-names. Condition-names can be used to define a "class" of characters, but such names limit the order of the characters, the number of occurrences of individual characters, and the data-names to which they apply. This can be seen by contrasting the following condition-name with the class-name in the preceding example:

02 STREET-NUMBER PIC X.
    88 SPOKEN-NUMERIC VALUES '0' THRU '9', 'o', 'O'.

SPOKEN-NUMERIC is true in the above example when STREET-NUMBER contains a "0" or a "1", or a "2", and so forth. Furthermore, SPOKEN-NUM-BER applies to STREET-NUMBER only.

The CURRENCY and DECIMAL-POINT Clauses

COBOL includes provisions for international usage with respect to monetary currencies and numeric values. Changing the dollar sign and using a comma in lieu of a decimal point can be accommodated by the use of two special clauses, as explained below.

By use of the following format specification in the SPECIAL-NAMES paragraph, one can thereafter use a sign other than $ in PICTURE clauses that are included in the program.

CURRENCY SIGN IS literal

For example, suppose that 'F' is the appropriate currency sign. We could write CURRENCY SIGN IS 'F', and then in PICTURE clauses we would use 'F' in place of $. The currency sign *cannot* be chosen from the following:

a.   The digits 0 through 9;

b.   The alphabetic characters consisting of the uppercase letters A, B, C, D, P, R, S, V, X, Z; the lowercase letters a through z; or the space;

c.   The special characters * + − , . : ( ) " = /.

In many countries outside of the United States, the functions of the decimal point and comma are reversed. Thus, the values 1,35 and 2.534,99 would be equivalent to the U.S. 1.35 and 2,534.99, respectively. The format of the clause in the SPECIAL-NAMES paragraph to accommodate the difference in these conventions is:

DECIMAL-POINT IS COMMA

Once this clause has been used, the function of the comma and period are interchanged in the character string of the PICTURE clause and in numeric literals. Thus, suppose we use the following specification in the ENVIRON-MENT DIVISION:

```
SPECIAL-NAMES.
    CURRENCY SIGN IS 'F'
    DECIMAL-POINT IS COMMA.
```

Given the above specification, the following PICTURE definition is valid in the DATA DIVISION:

```
02   AMOUNT-1   PIC FFFF.FF9,99.
```

The floating currency sign in the PICTURE definition above is the character 'F' and the roles of the decimal point and comma have been reversed. Also, note that given the CURRENCY and DECIMAL-POINT specifications above, a PICTURE definition cannot include the floating $ sign nor the "usual" use of the comma and decimal point in a PICTURE definition.

Review

1   The paragraph in the CONFIGURATION SECTION that provides for a variety of definitions for special features to be used in a COBOL program is the _____ paragraph.

SPECIAL-NAMES

2   The specification of mnemonic-names in the SPECIAL-NAMES paragraph allows the programmer to use meaningful names in place of _____-names that may not be meaningful.

implementor

3   The clause that is used to specify the collating sequence of characters during program processing is the _____ clause.

ALPHABET

4   The clause that is used to give a name to a character which may not be in the printable set of characters, such as may be useful in causing a bell to ring, is the _____ clause.

SYMBOLIC CHARACTER

5   The clause in the SPECIAL-NAMES paragraph that can be used to define a set of characters and to assign a class-name to them is the _____ clause.

CLASS

6   Changing the dollar sign to a sign associated with another currency can be achieved by use of the _____ clause.

CURRENCY

7   The clause in the SPECIAL-NAMES paragraph that makes it possible to interchange the meaning of the comma and decimal point in PICTURE clauses for monetary amounts that are defined in the DATA DIVISION is the _____ clause.

DECIMAL-POINT

Exercises

3.1   Describe the principal uses of the SOURCE-COMPUTER paragraph in the CONFIGURATION SECTION of the ENVIRONMENT DIVISION.

3.2   Describe the principal uses of the OBJECT-COMPUTER paragraph.

3.3   Give some reasons why a programmer may want to specify an alphabet that is different from the code that is native to a given system.

3.4   Distinguish class-names as specified in the SPECIAL-NAMES paragraph of the CONFIGURATION SECTION of the ENVIRONMENT DIVISION from condition-names as defined in the DATA DIVISION.

4

DATA DIVISION

INTRODUCTION

This chapter presents a number of topics relating to the DATA DIVISION that go beyond the elementary level. The topics are grouped according to two main functions: data reference and data definition.

DATA REFERENCE

The following topics and features relating to the DATA DIVISION are all concerned with data reference.

Level Numbers and Data-Names

The use of level numbers and data-names provides the basis by which data can be referenced in the PROCEDURE DIVISION. Consider the following generalized example:

```
01   A.
     02   B-0.
          03   B-1
          03   B-2
     02   C-0.
          03   C-1.
               04   C-1-1
               04   C-1-2
          03   C-2.
```

By the use of level numbers and data-names, the above description provides reference information such as the following:

- The data-name A refers to the entire group of data (record). Any instruction that references A also references all of its subordinates by implication.

- In addition to A, there are three other group items: B-0, C-0, and C-1.

- There are five elementary data items: B-1, B-2, C-1-1, C-1-2, and C-2.

By the above level numbers and data-names, either particular groups of items or particular elementary items can be referenced in the PROCEDURE DIVISION as needed.

In addition to level numbers and data-names, there are four other means of controlling the ways in which data can be referenced: by use of the REDEFINES clause, by the definition of multiple data records in the FILE SECTION, by use of the RENAMES clause, and by use of reference modification. These topics are discussed after the following subsection on the optional use of FILLER.

Review

1 When a group item (record) is referenced in the PROCEDURE DIVISION, the elementary items included in that group thereby [also are/are not] referenced.

also are

2 It [is/is not] possible to reference an elementary item without referencing the group (if any) to which it belongs.

is

The Optional Use of FILLER

The recognition that there are fields in a program that will not be referenced explicitly has led to the option of omitting the generic data-name FILLER in the 1985 standard. Thus we are now able to specify "nameless" fields, as follows:

```
01  REPORT FOOTING.
    02                               PIC  X(5)      VALUE  'TOTAL'.
    02                               PIC  X(14)     VALUE  SPACES.
    02  REPORT-TOTAL-UNITS           PIC  ZZZ9.
    02                               PIC  X(8)      VALUE  SPACES.
    02  REPORT-TOTAL-NET-SALES  PIC  ZZZ9.99.
```

For entries that contain no data-names, such as the ones in the above program segment, the record description is treated exactly as if FILLER had been specified.

Review

1   In the 1985 standard, use of FILLER [is/is not] required for entries that do not require data-names for later reference.

is not

2   The data descriptions that include no data-names [are/are not] treated the same way as those specifying FILLER.

are

The REDEFINES Clause

The REDEFINES clause can be used to allow the same storage location to be referenced by different data-names or to allow a regrouping or different description of the data in a particular storage location. The general format associated with the use of this option is:

```
level-number   data-name-1 REDEFINES data-name-2
```

The following example illustrates the use of this option:

```
01  SAMPLE.
    02  RECEIVABLE.
        03  CUSTOMER-NUMBER        PICTURE 9(8).
        03  CUSTOMER-NAME          PICTURE X(11).
        03  AMOUNT                 PICTURE 9(4)V99.
    02  PAYABLE REDEFINES RECEIVABLE.
        03  VENDOR-NUMBER          PICTURE 9(6).
        03  VENDOR-NAME            PICTURE X(12).
        03  VENDOR-OWED-AMOUNT     PICTURE 9(5)V99.
```

In this example, use of the REDEFINES option allows the data-names RECEIVABLE and PAYABLE to refer to the same 25 positions in internal storage.

The format of these two data items in internal storage can be portrayed as follows:

RECEIVABLE

CUSTOMER-NUMBER	CUSTOMER-NAME	AMOUNT

PAYABLE

VENDOR-NUMBER	VENDOR-NAME	VENDOR-OWED AMOUNT

In this example, notice that the format of the data items was also changed by the use of the REDEFINES option, but that the overall size of the item was not changed.

It should be made clear that the redefinition applies to the storage area involved and not to the data that may be stored in that area at any point in time. The programmer is responsible for providing the necessary program logic so that correct reference is made to the actual data stored. In the previous example, if we write ADD VENDOR-OWED-AMOUNT TO..., the result will be to add the contents of the last 7 storage positions, whatever these contents might be.

There are certain conditions under which the REDEFINES clause cannot be used. Two such conditions are:

1   The REDEFINES clause cannot be used at the 01 level in the FILE SECTION. The use of multiple data records in the FD entry has the same effect as use of the REDEFINES option, in that it permits use of the same storage location for different records.

2   The REDEFINES clause cannot be used when the levels of data-name-1 and data-name-2 are different. Further, the level number must not be at the 66 or 88 level.

Review

1   The same storage location can be used in conjunction with two different data-names by use of the _____ clause.

REDEFINES

2   When the REDEFINES option is used, the format of the data item [can/cannot] be changed as well.

can

3   Generally, the REDEFINES clause can be used when the two data items have the same level number. The exceptions are when the special-purpose 66- or 88-level numbers are used and when the level

number is at 01 in the _____ SECTION, in which case the REDE-
FINES clause cannot be used.

FILE

Multiple Data Records in the FILE SECTION

The REDEFINES clause cannot be used at the 01 level in the description of
record-names in the FILE SECTION. Instead, the following option is available
in the file description to indicate the existence of more than one type of data
record in the file:

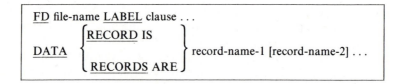

FD file-name LABEL clause . . .

DATA $\begin{Bmatrix} \text{RECORD IS} \\ \text{RECORDS ARE} \end{Bmatrix}$ record-name-1 [record-name-2] . . .

Consider an example. Suppose that a bank's customers may make
three kinds of transactions: deposits, withdrawals, and change of address. A
record containing information about a deposit or withdrawal has a different
format than one pertaining to a change of address. We assume that all
records identify the account by a 5-digit number in the first 5 columns and
the type of transaction by a transaction code in column 6. Then, if it is a deposit or withdrawal record, the amount is recorded in columns 7–12, while if
it is a change of address the new address is recorded in columns 7–50. We
can write the following data entries:

```
FD TRANSACTION-FILE
   LABEL RECORDS OMITTED
   DATA RECORDS ARE FINANCIAL-REC
                    ADDRESS-REC.
01 FINANCIAL-REC.
    02  ACCOUNT       PIC 9(5).
    02  TRANS-CODE    PIC 9.
    02  AMOUNT        PIC 9(4)V99.
    02  FILLER        PIC X(38).
01 ADDRESS-REC.
    02  ACCOUNT       PIC 9(5).
    02  TRANS-CODE    PIC 9.
    02  NEW-ADDRESS   PIC X(44).
```

In this example, the FD entry has specified two types of data records, named
FINANCIAL-REC and ADDRESS-REC. It is important to emphasize that,

physically, a record in this file will consist of 50 characters of data (the sum of all PIC clauses in either record description). Use of two record descriptions simply allows us to reference that data by different names and in different ways.

Both record names reference the entire 50 columns of data. Thus, MOVE FINANCIAL-REC or MOVE ADDRESS-REC do exactly the same thing: they MOVE these 50 columns of data. Similarly, ACCOUNT of FINANCIAL-REC and ACCOUNT of ADDRESS-REC refer to the same first 5 columns of data, as do the TRANS-CODE names. However, AMOUNT refers to the data in columns 7–12 and, according to the PIC clause, it is assumed that the data are numeric. It should be recalled that a PICTURE clause simply specifies the storage allocation to data, and not the actual contents. The actual contents come about through input or MOVE type operations. Thus, if we were dealing with a change-of-address transaction and columns 7–12 contained the first 6 characters of the new address, a statement such as ADD 1 TO AMOUNT would produce unpredictable results, since we are performing arithmetic with nonnumeric data. More appropriately, we first would test to see what type of record we actually had before referencing the data in question. For this purpose, assume that we use a code of 1 for a deposit, 2 for withdrawal, and 3 for change of address. We could write:

```
IF TRANS-CODE OF FINANCIAL-REC = 1
   PERFORM PROCESS-DEPOSIT.
```

This statement checks to see if column 6 contains the value 1. Notice that, if we had used IF TRANS-CODE OF ADDRESS-REC = 1, it would be exactly the same thing, since both refer to column 6. To further clarify this point, we could have used this data description for ADDRESS-REC:

```
01  ADDRESS-REC.
    02  FILLER          PIC X(6).
    02  NEW-ADDRESS     PIC X(44).
```

ACCOUNT and TRANS-CODE need no qualification now, since they are unique names in FINANCIAL-REC. Use of TRANS-CODE still refers to column 6 of the data. Beginning students often equate the generic data-name FILLER with blank spaces. This should be a good point to discard any such misconception. In this example, the FILLER in ADDRESS-REC refers to the first 6 columns, which we know will contain data—the account number and the transaction code.

In general, a file may consist of more than one type of data record. As a rule, there should be a field that designates the type of record involved. In our example we used TRANS-CODE as a field that was in a fixed location no matter what the record type. Then we tested the value of that field to ascertain the type of record. In general, this identifying field should be common to all record types so that, no matter what the data are in other fields, this field can be tested.

Review

1   When there is more than one type of data record in a file, the file description in the FILE SECTION of the DATA DIVISION should identify [only one/more than one] file-name.

only one

2   When there is more than one type of data record in a file, the file description should identify [only one/more than one] record-name.

more than one

3   A coded entry in a specified field serves to differentiate the different input records when there is more than one data record. Particularly when the records are of variable length, the differentiating field should be located in the [left/right] part of the record field.

left

4   In the case of multiple-type record files, at any given time the internal storage can contain [only one/more than one] type of record.

only one

The RENAMES Clause

The RENAMES clause provides the programmer with the capability of regrouping elementary data items. In a sense, it resembles the REDEFINES clause, except that it can form a new grouping of data items that combines several items. Use of the RENAMES clause always is signaled by the special 66-level number. The general format is:

```
66   data-name-1 RENAMES data-name-2 [THRU data-name-3]
```

Consider the following example, which includes use of the RENAMES clause.

```
01  TAX-RECORD.
    02  SOC-SEC-NUMBER            PICTURE X(9).
    02  NAME.
        03  FIRST-NAME            PICTURE X(10).
        03  MIDDLE-INITIAL        PICTURE XX.
        03  LAST-NAME             PICTURE X(15).
    02  TOTALS-YEAR-TO-DATE.
        03  GROSS-PAY             PICTURE 9(8)V99.
        03  NET-PAY               PICTURE 9(8)V99.
        03  FED-TAX               PICTURE 9(6)V99.
        03  STATE-TAX             PICTURE 9(4)V99.
    66  LAST-GROSS RENAMES LAST-NAME THRU NET-PAY.
```

Schematically, the regrouping of data fields by use of the RENAMES clause in the last statement can be portrayed as follows:

NAME				TOTALS-YEAR-TO-DATE			
SOC-SEC-NUMBER	FIRST-NAME	MIDDLE-INITIAL	LAST-NAME	GROSS-PAY	NET-PAY	FED-TAX	STATE-TAX
			LAST-GROSS				

In the example, LAST-GROSS is a storage field that consists of the LAST-NAME, GROSS-PAY, and NET-PAY fields. In this way, we can make reference to those three fields as one group, which would not be possible without use of the RENAMES clause.

As an example of another application of the RENAMES clause, suppose that an interactive program asks the user: "DO YOU WANT TO ADD, VIEW, OR DELETE A RECORD?" We may have defined the field in which the user response is entered as follows:

```
01  RESPONSE.
    02  CHARS-1-TO-3      PIC XXX.
    02  CHAR-4           PIC X.
    02  CHARS-5-TO-6     PIX XX.
    66  ADD-RESPONSE     RENAMES CHARS-1-TO-3.
    66  VIEW-RESPONSE    RENAMES CHARS-1-TO-3 THRU CHAR-4.
    66  DELETE-RESPONSE  RENAMES CHARS-1-TO-3 THRU CHARS-5-TO-6.
```

We recognize that the response may be in the first 3, the first 4, or all 6 characters of RESPONSE, according to whether the viewer responded with "ADD," "VIEW," or "DELETE." In the PROCEDURE DIVISION we could check to see which response was given by statements such as:

IF ADD-RESPONSE = 'ADD' ...
IF VIEW-RESPONSE = 'VIEW' ...

Such a structure is particularly useful in subprograms when passing values of literals as arguments. This point will be elaborated upon in Chapter 12, Subprograms and Nested Programs.

Review

1   Elementary data items that are part of different storage fields can be regrouped and formed into a new field by use of the _____ clause.

RENAMES

2   The DATA DIVISION statement in which the RENAMES clause is used is always assigned the level number _____ (number).

66

Reference Modification

It is possible to reference a portion of a data field without using REDEFINES or group items in the data description. The general format for such reference is:

> data-name 1 (leftmost-character-position: [length])

Note the colon (:) character in the above format. This is a new addition to the COBOL character set, introduced in the 1985 standard.
    Suppose that we have a field A, containing a 9-digit social security number, and we want to access the last four digits of that number and store them in a field called B. The fields are defined as:

```
01  A   PIC 9(9).
01  B   PIC 9(4).
```

We can use the reference modification feature and write:

MOVE A (6:4) TO B.

The '6' inside the parenthesis specifies the starting byte for the MOVE. The colon is the required separator, and the '4' specifies the number of bytes being referenced.

In the general format above note that the "length" item is optional. Its absence implies a reference to the remainder of the field. Thus, MOVE A (6:) TO B, means to move to B the data stored in A beginning with the sixth byte up to and including the end of the field.

In essence, the reference modification concept is an indirect definition of a field. As such, it reduces the effort that is required to write DATA DIVISION entries. On the other hand it allows the programmer to define fields "on the fly," so to speak, and thereby runs counter to the documentation spirit of COBOL. Still, let us consider an example that illustrates the time-saving effect of using the reference modification feature. Assume the following field definitions:

```
01   REPORT-LINE.
     02   FILLER                    PIC X(10)   VALUE SPACES.
     02   SALESMAN-NAME-OUT         PIC X(15).
     02   FILLER                    PIC X(5)   VALUE SPACES.
     02   PRODUCT-NUMBER-OUT        PIC 999.
     02   FILLER                    PIC X(11)   VALUE SPACES.
     02   SALES-AMOUNT-OUT          PIC Z,ZZ9.99.
     02   FILLER                    PIC X(8)   VALUE SPACES.
     02   TOTAL-SALES-OUT           PIC $$$,$$9.99.
```

The above field definitions are sufficient for a report containing a salesman heading, product heading, and detail lines. For purposes of footings, however, we need not create separate data definitions. Instead, we can make use of reference modification. For a salesman footing condition, for example, we could write the following:

```
MOVE SPACES TO REPORT-LINE
MOVE '**TOTAL FOR SALESMAN ' TO REPORT-LINE (13:24)
MOVE PREVIOUS-SALESMAN-NAME TO REPORT-LINE (37:15)
MOVE SALESMAN-TOTAL-SALES TO TOTAL-SALES-OUT.
```

The two middle MOVE statements above, which contain the reference modification feature, eliminate the need to define a new group item.

The above example illustrates some of the positive aspects of reference modification. It can be seen that use of reference modification to simplify the code needed to position header-type data into a working storage field does not complicate program logic and does not degrade the clarity of the program. As such, it is a useful application of reference modification.

Review

1   The COBOL feature by which a portion of a data field can be referenced in a PROCEDURE DIVISION statement is the _____ _____ feature.

reference modification

2   Suppose we wish to MOVE the 4th through 8th bytes of a 10-byte data field A to field B. The appropriate command is _____.

MOVE A (4:5) TO B

3   Suppose we wish to MOVE the 9th and 10th bytes of a 10-byte data field A to field C. The two alternative forms of the command that can be used are MOVE A _____ TO C or MOVE A _____ TO C.

(9:2); (9:)

DATA DEFINITION

The following topics and features relating to the DATA DIVISION are all concerned with data definition.

Class and Category Distinctions by Level

There are three main concepts associated with defining data in a COBOL program: the level, class, and category of a data item.

In terms of *level*, a data item can be either an *elementary* or a *group* (nonelementary) data item. An elementary data item is one that is not further subdivided. A group item describes a combination of two or more elementary items.

In terms of *class*, a data item can be *alphabetic, numeric,* or *alphanumeric*. If the item is at the elementary level, then its class is determined by its data content at a given point in time. Alphabetic data consist of the letters of the alphabet and the space (blank). Numeric data consist of the ten numeric digits 0–9 with or without an operational sign. Alphanumeric data include special symbols as well as the letters of the alphabet and numeric digits. If an item is at the group, or nonelementary, level, then its class automatically is considered to be alphanumeric. This is so regardless of the class of its constituent elementary items. For example, consider the following data description:

```
02  A.
    03  B  PIC 99  VALUE 10.
    03  C  PIC 99  VALUE 25.
```

The class of the A group item is alphanumeric even though the classes of B and C are numeric in each case.

The topic of utilizing a class test in the PROCEDURE DIVISION is discussed in Chapter 6, in the section "Conditional Statements and Expressions." With respect to such a class test, the class of an item can be NUMERIC, ALPHABETIC, ALPHABETIC-LOWER, ALPHABETIC-UPPER, AND "class-name," where the latter refers to user-defined classes of data in the ENVIRONMENT DIVISION, as explained in Chapter 3. Thus, in a class test, more detailed forms of class can be specified than the basic three classes. Nevertheless, in the context of data transfer (MOVE, and so forth) the relevant class definitions are the alphabetic, numeric, and alphanumeric. For this reason, these are considered to be the three main classes.

The third concept associated with data definition is the *category* of data. There are five categories of data, as presented in Figure 4-1, which also relates these categories to the levels and classes of data. The category of data is defined by use of a PICTURE clause. Notice in Figure 4-1 that for alphabetic and numeric items the class and category are synonymous. Every elementary item belongs to one of the three classes and one of the five categories. However, as we noted previously, the class of a group item is treated as being alphanumeric regardless of the class of its subordinate elementary items.

The category of a receiving data item is critical in determining the alignment of data in a MOVE statement. For numeric and numeric-edited receiving items, the actual or implied position of the decimal point serves to align the data that are received. For alphabetic, alphanumeric, and alphanumeric-edited receiving items, data are aligned at the leftmost character position (unless the JUSTIFIED clause has been used) and truncation or padding by spaces takes place at the right.

LEVEL OF ITEM	CLASS	CATEGORY
Elementary	Alphabetic	Alphabetic
	Numeric	Numeric
	Alphanumeric	Numeric edited Alphanumeric edited Alphanumeric
Group (Nonelementary)	Alphanumeric	Alphabetic Numeric Numeric edited Alphanumeric edited

FIGURE 4-1   LEVEL, CLASS, AND CATEGORY RELATIONSHIPS.

Having discussed the definitional concepts of level, class, and category of data items, in the following subsections we will describe a number of specialized clauses used in defining data in the DATA DIVISION.

Review

1   In terms of *level*, a data item can be described as being either at the _____ or _____ level.

elementary; group

2   The three principal *classes* of data are the _____, _____, and _____.

alphabetic; numeric; alphanumeric

3   In addition to the alphabetic letters and numeric digits, alphanumeric data items can also include special _____.

symbols

4   The class of a group item is always considered to be _____.

alphanumeric

5   There are five *categories* of data items. The particular category for a given data item is defined by use of a _____ clause.

PICTURE

6   In conjunction with a MOVE statement, alignment of receiving items is done with respect to the decimal point for the _____ and _____ categories of items.

numeric; numeric-edited

7   In conjunction with a MOVE statement, alignment of receiving items is at the leftmost character for the _____, _____, and _____ categories of items.

alphabetic; alphanumeric; alphanumeric-edited

The PICTURE Clause

The PICTURE clause is the principal means of defining data items and their data categories. Figure 4-2 presents the types of characters available for use in PICTURE clauses, while Figure 4-3 summarizes the role of PICTURE characters in defining the categories of data.

The SIGN Clause

The S character specifies that the field is signed. The SIGN clause specifies the position and the mode of representation of the operational sign when it is necessary to describe these properties explicitly. The general format for the SIGN clause is:

TYPE OF CHARACTER	SYMBOL	USE
Field definition characters	9	Numeric field
	A	Alphabetic field
	X	Alphanumeric field
Numeric field special character	V	Assumed decimal point
	P	Decimal scaling
	S	Operational (arithmetic) sign included
Editing characters	$	Dollar sign
	Z	Zero suppression
	*	Check protection
	.	Decimal point
	,	Comma
	+	Plus sign
	−	Minus sign
	DB	Debit
	CR	Credit
	B	Blank insertion
	0	Zero insertion
	/	Stroke insertion

FIGURE 4–2   TYPES OF CHARACTERS AVAILABLE FOR USE IN PICTURE CLAUSES

Numeric items	The PICTURE may contain suitable combinations of the following characters: 9 V P and S.
Alphabetic items	The PICTURE clause contains only the A character.
Alphanumeric items	The PICTURE clause consists of A 9 and X characters. It cannot contain all A or all 9 characters, but it may contain a mixture of A and 9 characters.
Numeric edited items	The PICTURE clause can contain suitable combinations of the following characters: B P V Z 0 9 , . + – CR DB $ and /.
Alphanumeric edited items	The PICTURE clause can contain combinations of the following characters: A X 9 B 0 and /.

FIGURE 4–3   THE FIVE CATEGORIES OF DATA

If we write:

```
02  AMOUNT-A  PICTURE  S999  SIGN  IS  LEADING.
02  AMOUNT-B  PICTURE  S999  SIGN  IS  TRAILING.
```

we are specifying that these two signed fields contain the operational sign in the first and in the last digit position, respectively. Thus, if they both contained the numeric value −243 and the character K happened to represent −2 while L happened to represent −3, the contents of these fields would be shown as follows:

AMOUNT-A		
K	4	3

AMOUNT-B		
2	4	L

The convention is to store the sign in the rightmost digit position; therefore, the absence of the SIGN clause defaults to that case. The choice of LEADING rather than TRAILING is difficult to justify, but the option is available.

When the SEPARATE CHARACTER option is used, then the operational sign *is* actually represented as a separate leading or trailing character and requires a separate storage position. Consider these examples:

```
02  AMOUNT-A  PIC S999 SIGN IS LEADING SEPARATE CHARACTER.
02  AMOUNT-B  PIC S999 SIGN IS TRAILING SEPARATE CHARACTER.
```

MOVE   15   TO   AMOUNT-A
MOVE   −156   TO   AMOUNT-B

After these MOVE instructions are executed the contents of these two fields will be:

AMOUNT-A			
+	0	1	5

AMOUNT-B			
1	5	6	−

Notice that each field consists of four positions. In AMOUNT-A the + sign is inserted as the first character. A field containing S always contains a sign, whether positive or negative. The leading zero, of course, was inserted by the MOVE so that all the characters in the field are numeric digits. In the case of AMOUNT-B the sign is negative and it is trailing.

Fields containing the SIGN clause must include the S character and are considered numeric. The system treats the sign as part of the field in MOVE and arithmetic operations. A MOVE from an S99 field to S99 SIGN IS . . . SEPARATE will be suitably converted by the system to change the sign representation. Similarly, reversing the sending and receiving fields in the above example will also produce conversion to the appropriate sign representation.

When the SIGN . . . SEPARATE clause is used, then source data may be entered via a terminal with a sign. However, care must be taken to put the sign in the correct place and to use numeric values only, as always. For the field

AMOUNT-A   PIC   S9999   SIGN   LEADING   SEPARATE

the following data would be correct: +0010, +1234, −1000, −0001, +0000. Notice that a sign must always be present, even to represent a (positive) zero.

Review

1   When it is necessary to describe the position of the operational sign for a field explicitly, the _____ clause is included with the data description.

SIGN

2   Fields containing the sign clause [must/need not] include the S character and [must/need not] be described by 9 PICTURE characters.

must; must

3   The operational sign is represented as a separate character and requires a separate storage position when the _____ option is used in the SIGN clause.

SEPARATE CHARACTER

The BLANK WHEN ZERO Clause

Use of the BLANK WHEN ZERO clause achieves the same result as Z PICTURE, but it is more general. Consider the statement 02 AMOUNT PIC ZZ9.99 BLANK WHEN ZERO. If AMOUNT contains a zero value, the field will be blanked (six blanks); otherwise, the PICTURE string will provide the editing.

Review

1   In the event that an entire data field contains a zero value, the field can be output as all blanks by use of the _____ clause.

BLANK WHEN ZERO

Data Representation

We digress now from the COBOL-language orientation of these topics to establish a common foundation for understanding the two special definitional clauses, USAGE and SYNCHRONIZED, that are described after the following subsections on character data and numeric data.

Computers utilize the binary characters (bits) of zero and one to represent data because the physical basis of electromagnetic circuitry is binary. However, there is a great variety of ways that these binary bits are used to represent data in computer systems.

Table 4-1 lists the most common ways of representing data. As indicated in the table, we need to make a distinction between character data, which are used to represent nonquantitative data, and numeric data, which are used to represent quantitative measures. Only a brief explanation of the categories included in Table 4-1 is presented in this section of the chapter. More detailed coverage can be found in introductory texts on computer science and data processing.

TABLE 4-1   DATA REPRESENTATION

DATA REPRESENTATION	
CHARACTER DATA	NUMERIC DATA
6-bit BCD	*Binary* quarterword, halfword, fullword, doubleword
8-bit ASCII	*Scientific Notation* single-precision double-precision
8-bit EBCDIC Other vendor-based codes	*Hexadecimal* *Packed Decimal* *Zoned Decimal* *Character Representation* BCD, ASCII, EBCDIC, other

Character Data

A character may be an alphabetic letter, a numeric digit (but not amenable to arithmetic operations), or any special symbol. Characters are represented by grouping a number of bits together and associating a specific bit pattern with a specific character. Following is a description of each category of character data listed in Table 4-1.

BCD.   The 6-bit binary-coded decimal code uses 6 binary bits per character. For instance the letter A is represented as 110001 while the digit 9 is represented as 001001. This coding method is not as widely used today as it was earlier. However, it is currently used with some 36-bit word-oriented computers, such as the 1100 series of UNIVAC, because a 36-bit word can hold an even number of six BCD-type 6-bit characters. The 6-bit BCD can provide $2^6 = 64$ unique bit patterns, so it cannot be used to represent both lower and upper-case alphabetic characters as well as other required characters.

ASCII.   The American Standard Code for Information Interchange, or ASCII (pronounced "as-kee") uses 8 bits per character and can therefore be used to represent $2^8 = 256$ unique bit patterns. Since there are fewer than 100 characters available in all Western languages, the majority of bit patterns are unused. As the name implies, this is a *standard code* that can be used to transmit data to all systems that accept this standard.

As examples, the representations for the characters A,), and 9 are 01000001, 00101001, and 00111001, respectively. Figure 3-2 in the preceding chapter includes the complete ASCII code.

EBCDIC.   The Extended Binary Coded Decimal Interchange Code, or EBCDIC (pronounced "ib-se-dic"), is also an 8-bit code developed and favored by IBM. As examples, the character representations for A,), and 9 are 11000001, 01011101, and 11111001, respectively. The complete EBCDIC code is included in Figure 3-3 in the preceding chapter.

Numeric Data

A number is a collection of digits representing a quantity. Numbers may be signed as positive or negative and may represent integer values or decimal values. Following is a description of each category of numeric data listed in Table 4-1, at the beginning of this section on data representation.

Binary.   Numeric data in binary representation consist of zeros and ones having position-values represented as powers of the (binary) base 2. As an illustration, Figure 4-4 presents a 12-bit binary field. The leftmost bit is used for the sign, 0 = positive, 1 = negative. Then, the remaining 11 bits can be used to represent any number ranging from 0 to $2^{11} - 1$. In the illustration, the positive decimal quantity +1,234 is represented as 010011010010. The number can be converted to its decimal equivalent by multiplying each digit by its position value and forming the sum, as illustrated in the figure.

Positions to the right of the "decimal" point have position values of ½, ¼, ⅛, and so forth, and therefore fractional quantities may also be represented. However, note that for a specified number of binary positions to the right of the decimal point some decimal values cannot be represented exactly. For instance, with 2 binary positions to the right of the decimal point we could not represent ⅕, but we could come "close" to it by using 6 positions and writing 0.001101, which is equivalent to ⅛ + 1/16 + 1/64 = 13/64. In administrative uses of the computer "close" to a value is usually not good enough, and we may choose not to use binary representation for fractional values or to use it only after making appropriate adjustments. For instance, for dollar and cents values we could convert to integer form by multiplying by 100, do the arithmetic in binary form, and then adjust the final result by dividing by 100 in decimal representation.

The number of bits used in a binary field is dependent on the machine used and the size of the values. For large IBM systems, binary fields are

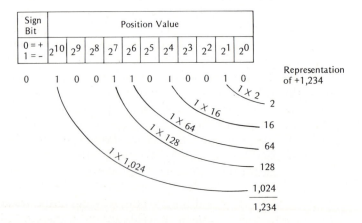

FIGURE 4-4   REPRESENTATION OF +1234 AS A 12-BIT SIGNED BINARY NUMBER.

HEXADECIMAL DIGIT	BIT CONFIGURATION	HEXADECIMAL DIGIT	BIT CONFIGURATION
0	0000	8	1000
1	0001	9	1001
2	0010	A	1010
3	0011	B	1011
4	0100	C	1100
5	0101	D	1101
6	0110	E	1110
7	0111	F	1111

FIGURE 4–5   HEXADECIMAL DIGIT BIT CONFIGURATIONS.

either 16 bits (= 2 bytes, or 1 halfword), 32 bits (= 4 bytes, or 1 fullword), or 64 bits (= 8 bytes, or 2 fullwords). For 36-bit word machines, such as some UNIVAC and Honeywell systems, binary fields may be 12 bits (quarterword), 18 bits (halfword), 36 bits (fullword), or 72 bits (doubleword).

Scientific Notation.   Numbers may be represented by a sign bit, a value (mantissa) of fixed length and an exponent as a power of 10. Thus +12,345,600 and +12,345,666 could both be represented as +1.23456E7, thereby losing the precision of the last two digit positions. This notation is useful in scientific applications but is hardly ever needed in administrative uses, in which precision is as important as the magnitude of quantities.

Hexadecimal.   This representation is widely used by large IBM systems and it is even externally shown on such printed outputs as "core dumps," which display the contents of memory. Because of its wide use by IBM, we consider it worthwhile to elaborate to some extent. Figure 4-5 presents the 16 hexadecimal digits and their binary bit configurations. A hexadecimal digit can have a value from 0 to 15 and can be represented by a group of 4 bits, since 4 bits provide 2^4 = 16 unique bit patterns. Since IBM-type systems use the 8-bit byte as an addressable unit of storage, 2 hexadecimal digits can be stored in 1 byte. Similarly, since a halfword is 2 bytes, a word is 4 bytes, and a doubleword is 8 bytes, there can be 4, 8, and 16 hexadecimal digits stored, respectively, in such units of central storage.

   As an illustration, suppose that we have a 2-byte field containing the binary equivalent of the decimal value +1,234. As shown in Figure 4-4 and adding 4 leading zeroes to have 2 full bytes, the binary value would be 0000010011010010. In hexadecimal form the content could be represented as 04D2, which can be ascertained by referring to Figure 4-5 and substituting the hexadecimal equivalent for each group of 4 binary bits.

   It may be useful to transform 04D2 from hexadecimal to decimal form. Recall that the first digit, 0, represents the sign and has no numeric value. The 4D2 part can be converted keeping in mind that the position values in the hexadecimal system are, from left to right, . . . 16^2, 16^1, 16^0. Thus we have:

$$2 \times 16^0 = 2 \times 1 = 2$$
$$D \times 16^1 = 13 \times 16 = 208$$
$$4 \times 16^2 = 4 \times 256 = \underline{1{,}024}$$
$$1{,}234$$

Packed Decimal.   This representation is widely used for numeric computational data by COBOL programmers in IBM systems. A packed-decimal field consists of an integer number of bytes and stores 2 digits per byte, except that the last half of the last byte is used to store the sign. For example, +1,234 would be stored on 3 bytes even though 2½ bytes would appear to be enough. The hexadecimal representation is 01234C, where the first zero represents 4 leading binary zeroes to make it an even 3-byte field, and the C is the hexadecimal representation of the + sign. The number −1,234 is represented in hexadecimal form as 01234D, where D is the negative sign in the rightmost half-byte.

Zoned Decimal.   This IBM representation uses a whole byte per decimal digit, but the sign of the field is stored in the last byte along with the last digit. In each byte the first half is the "zone-bits" that are essentially unused, while the decimal digit is stored in the second half of the byte. Then, in the last byte the first 4 bits represent the sign while the last 4 bits represent the last digit.

As an illustration, +1,234 would require 4 bytes, 1 for each decimal digit. The hexadecimal representation is F1F2F3C4, where F is represented by the zone bits 1111, as can be observed in Figure 4-5. The C represents the positive sign in the upper half of the last byte. As another example, −1,234 has the hexadecimal representation F1F2F3D4, where now D is the negative sign.

Character Representation.   Numeric data can be represented as characters. In the 8-bit ASCII code, the decimal 19 is represented as 0011000000111001, where the first 8 bits represent 1 and the last 8 bits represent 9. Notice that if we treated this code as a single 16-bit binary number, it would instead represent 12,345!

Computer systems convert numeric character data into an appropriate computational form before performing arithmetic operations, and then reconvert the data for storage in character form.

The foregoing overview on data representation will now be applied to COBOL-related issues in the following sections of this chapter.

Review

1   Of the two basic forms of representation, the one that is used to represent nonquantitative data is _____ data.

character

2   Of the two basic forms of data representation, the one that is used to represent quantitative measures is _____ data.

> numeric

3   The 6-bit BCD, 8-bit ASCII, and 8-bit EBCDIC are all ways of representing _____ data.

> character

4   Binary, scientific notation, hexadecimal, packed decimal, and zoned decimal are all ways of representing _____ data.

> numeric

5   Numeric data can also be represented as characters, and such representation [is/is not] directly amenable to arithmetic operations.

> is not (conversion to a
> computational form is done)

The USAGE Clause

In COBOL, data in character mode are described as being in DISPLAY mode, while data in numeric mode are described as being in COMPUTATIONAL mode. DISPLAY is the default condition: All data items are assumed to be in DISPLAY mode unless they are declared to be COMPUTATIONAL. The declaration is done in the DATA DIVISION with the USAGE clause. Figure 4-6 presents the general format of this clause. In terms of the character description in the PICTURE clause, numeric data in the DISPLAY mode can be designated PIC 9 or PIC X (numeric or alphanumeric); however, data in the COMPUTATIONAL mode can only be PIC 9. Of course, whether data are designated PIC 9 or PIC X, it is understood that any fields involved in arithmetic computations will include only numeric data, and not any letters,

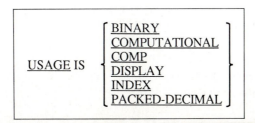

FIGURE 4–6   GENERAL FORMAT OF THE USAGE CLAUSE.

spaces, decimal points, or other special symbols. Consider the following examples:

```
02   AMOUNT-1                        PIC 99.
02   AMOUNT-2                        PIC 99  USAGE DISPLAY.
02   AMOUNT-3                        PIC XX USAGE DISPLAY.
02   AMOUNT-4                        PIC 99  USAGE COMPUTATIONAL.
02   AMOUNT-5                        PIC 99  USAGE COMP.
02   AMOUNT-6  USAGE COMP  PIC 99  VALUE ZERO.
```

The first example omits the USAGE clause, and the item will be in DISPLAY mode by default. The second example makes the declaration explicit. The third example describes the data item as being alphanumeric and in the character mode. The fourth and fifth examples illustrate the COMPUTATIONAL declaration in full and abbreviated form, respectively. The last example illustrates the point that the order of USAGE, PIC, and VALUE is immaterial.

The USAGE of a numeric item determines its size in terms of bits, but the size also depends on the coding scheme used. For instance, if we declare USAGE DISPLAY and use a 6-bit code for each 9 in the PICTURE clause, there are 6 bits in central storage for each 9 in the PICTURE. On the other hand if we use an 8-bit code, then there are 8 bits for each 9 in the PICTURE. If a choice is available as to what bit code to use, then it is communicated either by job control statements or by invoking the appropriate compiler version.

For numeric DISPLAY items the sign is represented in combination with the last digit in ways similar to the description under the zoned-decimal heading in the preceding section of this chapter. When data are entered on a terminal, we must be careful to cause the correct bit representation by entering an alphabetic character for the last digit.

As explained earlier in this chapter, the SIGN clause can be used in conjunction with the USAGE clause, and it affects the way that DISPLAY numeric data are treated. For illustration, we follow the IBM conventions. Suppose that we have PIC S9999 USAGE DISPLAY SIGN IS LEADING and we have the value −1,234. In hexadecimal form (consult Figure 4-5 again) the representation is D1F2F3F4, where D is the *leading* negative sign in this case. It may be instructive to pause for a moment to further "decode" the hexadecimal form. D1 translates to 11010001, which is the EBCDIC representation of the uppercase letter J, while F2, F3, and F4 are the EBCDIC representations of 2, 3, and 4 respectively. Thus, for the item in this example J234 is the equivalent of −1,234. Had the number been +1,234, we would have A234, since a +1 is a C1 in hexadecimal, or A in EBCDIC.

As a further example, suppose that we have PIC S9999 USAGE IS DISPLAY SIGN IS TRAILING SEPARATE and we consider the value −1,234. Now we need to represent the sign as a separate, trailing character. In hexadecimal form it is F1F2F3F460, where 60 is the hexadecimal negative sign which is also the EBCDIC (01100000) negative sign. To represent +1,234, the hexadecimal form would be F1F2F3F44E, where 4E is the positive sign (01001110).

It is clear from the preceding examples that the COBOL programmer has to have knowledge of the specific coding system that the compiler is using in order to be able to decode core dump type of outputs, or to be able to enter data correctly in DISPLAY usage fields with signed data. Such machine dependence is contrary to the spirit of standardized COBOL, but it is at times necessary to accept the realities of the imperfect world of "standard" languages.

The COMPUTATIONAL option of the USAGE clause specifies that the data are in the form in which the respective machine does its computations. Typically, the form is binary and the size of the field in terms of bits is determined by the compiler. For instance, for some IBM compilers the following rule is used:

DIGITS IN PICTURE CLAUSE	STORAGE OCCUPIED
1-4	2 bytes
5-9	4 bytes
10-18	8 bytes

Care must be taken in handling group fields or records containing USAGE COMP fields. For instance, if we have

```
01  A.
    02  B  PIC  X(6).
    02  C  PIC  9(6) USAGE COMP.
```

and we write MOVE A TO..., we should realize that we are moving 10 bytes, since C now requires just 4 bytes as presented in the preceding rule. Without the USAGE COMP we would, of course, be moving 12 bytes!

In addition to the COMP option most compilers will implement additional variants, such as COMP-1, COMP-2, COMP-3, etc. In the case of some compilers, for instance, COMP-1 (or COMPUTATIONAL-1) and COMP-2 mean respectively single- and double-precision floating-point scientific notation representation (both of which are rarely used in COBOL programs). Further, COMP-3 for IBM 1974 standard COBOL is the packed-decimal representation which was described in the preceding section, while DISPLAY is the zone-decimal representation.

These options, which include some standard (COMP) and some non-standard (COMP-1, COMP-2, COMP-3) options provide the programmers with a dubious tool for improving computational efficiency. The case is often made that USAGE COMP in one form or another increases speed of execution because data need not be converted from character mode to computational mode and back. We feel that in terms of today's economics of machine instructions per dollar we should have good reasons before we consider machine efficiency in executing arithmetic operations. Most COBOL programs do relatively so little arithmetic that it is not worth the trouble to write machine-dependent programs. Particularly, we should not include COMP fields in file descriptions that may need to be portable to other systems.

In a related context, it should be noted that moving zeros to a group item whose elementary items contain USAGE COMPUTATIONAL clauses may result in nonzero data. Consider this group item:

```
01   GROUP-ITEM.
     02   AMOUNT-1   PIC 99V99 USAGE COMPUTATIONAL.
     02   AMOUNT-2   PIC 9999V99 USAGE COMPUTATIONAL.
```

A statement such as MOVE ZERO TO GROUP-ITEM will move "character" zeros into GROUP-ITEM. A zero in character mode is different from a zero in binary numeric mode. Therefore, if we subsequently write ADD TOTAL TO AMOUNT-1, erroneous results will be obtained from the arithmetic operation, since AMOUNT-1 does not contain a numeric-mode zero value. To avoid such problems, we should move zeros to each individual numeric field which has been defined as USAGE COMPUTATIONAL. Thus MOVE ZERO TO AMOUNT-1, AMOUNT-2 would be the appropriate instruction for setting these two fields equal to zero. Of course, in the absence of the USAGE COMPUTATIONAL clauses, MOVE ZERO TO GROUP-ITEM would have resulted in proper zeros in the elementary fields. The fact that the numeric data is in the character mode would be clear because of the (default) DISPLAY mode being designated, in this case. Another alternative would have been to have declared the GROUP-ITEM USAGE COMPUTATIONAL, in which case a MOVE ZEROS to GROUP-ITEM would have resulted in numeric zero being stored in the subordinate fields.

Figure 4-6 also includes the BINARY, INDEX, and PACKED-DECIMAL representations as options in the USAGE clause. The BINARY option specifies that data will be represented in base 2 notation; however, the precise implementation is dependent on the specific implementor. Thus, you would have to consult the language manual of the computer to determine the exact form of binary representation. For example, in a 32-bit machine, binary integers may utilize the leading bit as a sign bit (such as 0 = negative and 1 = positive) and the remaining bits may be used for the actual binary values. The number of binary bits that are available must be sufficient to accommodate the maximum range of values specified by the associated decimal PIC-

TURE character string. Consider the following example:

02   AMOUNT   PIC S9(3)   USAGE   BINARY.

The maximum decimal value is +999, which requires 10 binary bits plus the sign bit (since $2^{10} = 1023$). Whether a particular compiler uses 11 bits or some other, larger, number with respect to the above example cannot be known except by reference to the appropriate manual.

The INDEX option of the USAGE clause is described in Chapter 7, Table Handling. Briefly, an index value is a value that corresponds to an occurrence number in a table. The specific form of an INDEX item depends on the implementor, so, again, you would need to consult a local source for details.

When the USAGE IS PACKED-DECIMAL options is used, the data are stored in the packed-decimal form described in the preceding subsection of this chapter, "Data Representation." Many computers are designed for efficient execution of computations with respect to data in the packed-decimal form. Therefore, for such computers it is advantageous to use such a definition for computational fields.

Review

1   In COBOL, the two modes in which numeric data can be represented are DISPLAY and COMPUTATIONAL. The appropriate form of the data can be indicated by use of the _____ clause in the DATA DIVISION.

USAGE

2   When the USAGE clause is not used, the field is automatically defined as being [DISPLAY/COMPUTATIONAL] in form.

DISPLAY

3   For numeric DISPLAY items the sign is represented in combination with the [first/last] digit of the item.

last

4   For numeric DISPLAY items the sign can be represented in combination with the first digit of the item by use of the _____ clause.

SIGN

5   The option of the USAGE clause that specifies that the data are in the form in which the computer does its calculations is the _____ option.

COMPUTATIONAL

6   In addition to the COMP option, most compilers will implement nonstandard options designated by such an option name as _____.

COMP-1 (*or* COMP-2 *etc.*)

7   In general, the use of the COMP options improves [machine/programmer] efficiency but as a trade-off against [machine/programmer] time.

machine; programmer

8   If zeros are moved into a group item that includes elementary items that are designated COMP, such zeros will be in the [character/numeric] mode.

character
(Unless the USAGE COMP applies to the group item.)

9   If the BINARY option is used in the USAGE clause, the number of binary bits available must be sufficient to accommodate the maximum range of values specified by the associated decimal _____ character string.

PICTURE

10   The option of the USAGE clause that corresponds to an occurrence number in a table is the _____ option.

INDEX

11   In addition to BINARY, COMPUTATIONAL, DISPLAY, and INDEX USAGE, the 1985 standard defines the _____ USAGE option.

PACKED-DECIMAL

The SYNCHRONIZED Clause

The SYNCHRONIZED clause can be used to improve arithmetic execution speed. It is a machine-dependent instruction, and for that reason unless the need for it is imperative its use should be avoided. In order to use the instruction effectively, the programmer has to study the rules that apply to the specific computer system. Even then, it is an error-prone instruction due to the complexity of the rules and the indirect ways by which the instruction works.

By DATA DIVISION descriptions the programmer can specify data items to be stored adjacent to one another in storage. However, execution of arithmetic operations is affected by the extent to which computational items have been "properly" aligned for a given computer system. In other words, there are some naturally good boundaries for computational data, and the SYNCHRONIZED clause provides a means for controlling the alignment to desired advantage. In the course of doing so, however, we typically introduce _slack bytes,_ or unused storage interspersed among the useful data. Future oversight of such slack bytes is a main reason for recommending avoidance of the SYNCHRONIZED clause.

Let us consider an example:

```
01  A.
    02  B  PIC  X(5).
    02  C  PIC  X(2).
    02  D  PIC  S9(8) USAGE COMP SYNCHRONIZED.
```

For an IBM system, synchronization would mean the addition of 1 slack byte between items C and D in storage, so that the synchronized item is aligned to start on a fullword boundary (multiple of 4). To be more specific, if the COMP SYNC field has a PICTURE in the range S9 to S9(4), alignment takes place on a halfword. On the other hand, if the item is in the range S9(5) to S9(18), alignment is on a fullword. Rules such as these are machine-dependent, and the reader should be aware that these rules are different for each system.

The programmer should be aware of the availability of the clause. If a program is encountered in which extensive arithmetic computation takes place, the technical manual for the computer system should be consulted for its evaluation of the SYNCHRONIZED clause as a tool for improving program execution.

Review

1   The option that can be used in elementary field descriptions in the DATA DIVISION to improve efficiency of arithmetic execution by the assignment of aligned storage boundaries is the _____ clause.

SYNCHRONIZED

2   Use of the SYNCHRONIZED clause typically introduces some unused storage, or so-called _____ bytes, interspersed among the useful data.

slack

3   A problem associated with the SYNCHRONIZED option is that its use may make the program incompatible for different [input data/computers].

computers

The JUSTIFIED RIGHT Clause

The JUSTIFIED RIGHT clause is used with elementary alphabetic or alphanumeric items only, and its effect is to override the convention of left-justifying nonnumeric data. Suppose we have the record description 02 TITLE PIC X(10). If we write MOVE 'JONES' TO TITLE, the effect in TITLE will be [J][O][N][E][S][ ][ ][ ][ ][ ], with the name left-justified. However, if in the DATA DIVISION we had written 02 TITLE PICTURE X(10) JUSTIFIED RIGHT, execution of the above MOVE instruction would result in [ ][ ][ ][ ][ ][J][O][N][E][S] in TITLE.

As indicated by the above example, the JUSTIFIED RIGHT clause is always used in conjunction with the PICTURE clause for elementary items. However, it cannot be used with level-66 or level-88 items, which are concerned with use of the RENAMES and condition-names, respectively. In addition to arranging right justification, the JUSTIFIED RIGHT clause also affects truncation. Without the JUSTIFIED RIGHT clause, truncation takes place from the right for alphabetic and alphanumeric data. When the JUSTIFIED RIGHT clause is used, truncation takes place from the left, as is the case for numeric data.

Review

1   Elementary alphabetic or alphanumeric items can be positioned in the rightmost portion of the field by the use of the _____ clause in the DATA DIVISION.

JUSTIFIED RIGHT

2   For alphabetic and alphanumeric data, truncation normally occurs from the [left/right]. However, when the JUSTIFIED RIGHT clause is used, truncation occurs from the [left/right].

right; left

Exercises

4.1   "The PICTURE clause can be used only with elementary items." True or false? Indicate the reason for your answer.

4.2   Indicate the size of each of the following fields:

PICTURE	SIZE
99V99	
9(3).9	
S999V9	
ZZ,ZZZ	
+(3).99	
$***,**9.99	
VPP99	
ZZZ000	

4.3   Suppose it has become necessary to change an existing COBOL program. The original version of the relevant DATA DIVISION entries is as follows:

```
02  FIELD-A
    03  FIELD-B
    03  FIELD-C
    03  FIELD-D
02  FIELD-E
```

In the revised version it is required that the fields be restructured so that (a) reference can be made to all the fields as one unit; (b) reference can be made to fields B and C as a unit; and (c) reference can be made to fields D and E as a unit. Show how this can be done.

4.4   Write DATA DIVISION entries for the WORKING-STORAGE record named SALES-DATA whose description is given in the following table. Data are moved from the items whose PICTURE description is shown.

SOURCE ITEM PICTURE	RECEIVING ITEM-NAME	PRINT POSITIONS	EDITING REQUIRED
99999	SALE-NUMBER	1–5	Suppress all leading zeros
		6–7	Blank
(X)25	NAME	8–32	None
		33–34	Blank
S9999V99	DOLLARS	35–?	Insert comma, decimal point. Dollar sign immediately to the left of leftmost nonzero digit. Show negative sign if negative.
		2 positions	Blank
S9(3)V9(4)	PROFIT	?–?	Show decimal point. Suppress leading zeros. Show negative sign to left of leftmost nonzero digit.

4.5   Suppose it is claimed that the following is equivalent to the example at the end of The RENAMES Clause section in this chapter. Explain how this equivalent form can be used instead of the original one. Which form is better? Why?

```
01  RESPONSE.
    02 ADD-RESPONSE PIC XXX.
    02 CHAR-4        PIC X.
    66 VIEW-RESPONSE RENAMES ADD-RESPONSE THRU CHAR-4.
```

4.6   Assume that in all cases the following two instructions apply:

```
MOVE A TO B
MOVE B TO C
```

where C has been defined as:

01   C   PIC   X(11).

Show the resulting contents in C, assuming each cell stands for one character position.

CONTENT OF A	PICTURE OF B	RESULTING CONTENT IN C										
10.125	9999V99											
10000.00	Z,ZZZ.ZZ											
900.15	$$,$$Z.99											
0.08	$$,$ZZ.ZZ											
50.50	$***.99DB											
−25.25	+,+++.99											
25.25	$$$$.99−											
WELCOME	XXXBXXX											

4.7   Assume the following DATA DIVISION entries:

```
01   A.
     02   X.
          03   Y.
     02   W.
          03   Y.
01   B.
     02   X.
          03   Y.
     02   W.
          03   Y.
```

Write PROCEDURE DIVISION statement(s) to move the last elementary item in A to the first elementary item in B.

4.8   A file contains name and address data for college students and their parents or guardians. The file is arranged so that for each student there are two records. The first record contains the name and address of the student, and the second record contains the name and address of parent or guardian. The record formats are as follows:

STUDENT RECORD		PARENT RECORD	
FIELD	**COLUMNS**	**FIELD**	**COLUMNS**
Student number	1–9	Student number	1–9
Student name	10–30	Parent name	10–30
Street	31–60	Street	31–60
City	61–79	City	61–79
Record code = 1	80	Record code = 2	80

a Write ENVIRONMENT and DATA DIVISION file and record entries to describe this file.

b Write PROCEDURE DIVISION statements to read two consecutive records, testing to ascertain that they are student and parent records, respectively. When the first record is read, if it is a student record, it is stored in REC-WORK-AREA. If the first record is not a student record or if the second record is not a parent record for the same student, the program branches to a paragraph called ERROR-ROUTINE. If the records are correct, the program branches to a paragraph called PROCESS.

4.9 In the following diagram there is a record called BIGFIELD. The numbers running from 1 to 13 indicate respective character positions. Thus, the record consists of 13 character positions. We want to be able to reference the following positions while also preserving the current structure of the record. Indicate how to accomplish this objective.

BIGFIELD

GROUP-A					GROUP-B				
AA		AB		AC		BA	BB		BC
1	2	3	4	5	6	7	8	9	10	11	12	13

a Reference 1, 2, 3, 4 by one name
b Reference 5, 6, 7 by one name
c Reference 8, 9, 10 by one name
d Reference 11, 12, 13 by one name
e Reference 1, 2, 3, 4, 5, 6, 7 by one name
f Reference 8, 9, 10, 11, 12, 13 by one name
g Reference 3, 4, 5, 6, 7, 8, 9, 10 by one name

4.10 Incorporate the reference modification feature in a program that you have previously written. Evaluate its impact on program documentation.

4.11 Consider the following program segments:

```
01  LAST-NAME PIC X (15).
    PERFORM VARYING I FROM 13 BY −1
        UNTIL I < 1
        OR LAST-NAME (I:3) = 'VEZ'
    END-PERFORM.
```

    a. Describe the function of the program segment above.

    b. What would be an alternative way of doing the same task without the use of reference modification?

    c. Is reference modification a useful feature for such an application?

4.12   How many classes of data are there in COBOL? Name and briefly explain each class of data and its use.

4.13   Discuss the relationship between *classes* and *categories* of data.

4.14   Given that all data in a computer are represented by binary (0,1) bits, in what way are character data different from numeric data?

4.15   How many unique characters can be represented by a 4-bit code? a 6-bit code? a 7-bit code? Generalize to an *n*-bit code.

4.16   If numeric data is in binary form, how is the sign represented?

4.17   What would be the minimum number of bits required to store a field whose PIC is S999? Explain.

4.18   In the discussion in this chapter it was mentioned that some COBOL systems allocate 2 bytes to COMP fields whose PICTURE clauses include 1 to 4 digits. Suppose that for such a system we have:

```
01  A.
    02  B  PIC  X(3).
    02  C  PIC  S9(3) COMP.
    02  D  PIC  9(5).
    02  E  PIC  S9(2) COMP.
```

What is the size of A in terms of bytes? Explain.

4.19   Explain how the SIGN clause can be used with USAGE DISPLAY numeric items.

4.20   Suppose that we have a 36-bit word-oriented computer system and that its COBOL compiler allocates a full word to each SYNC item. Further, assume that we use the ASCII code and have the following DATA DIVISION items:

```
01  X.
    02  A  PIC  XX.
    02  B  PIC  99.
    02  C  PIC  XXX.
```

a. Draw a storage layout for the above X record, using the diagram below. Be sure to designate the exact starting and ending storage bits for each item.

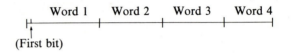

(First bit)

b. Now suppose that everything was the same except that we have 02 B PIC 99 SYNC. Redraw the storage layout and explain the effect of SYNC.

4.21   Are the SYNCHRONIZED and JUSTIFIED clauses related? Explain.

5

PROCEDURE DIVISION STATEMENTS

INTRODUCTION

In this chapter we describe a number of PROCEDURE DIVISION features that tend to receive minimal attention in introductory texts but that have broad applicability in COBOL programs. Other, more specifically oriented PROCEDURE DIVISION statements are included in the remaining chapters of this book as they relate to particular applications.

ARITHMETIC VERBS

Appendix C includes the standard formats for the five arithmetic verbs: ADD, SUBTRACT, MULTIPLY, DIVIDE, and COMPUTE. As can be seen by reviewing these specifications, a variety of statement formats can be written. Before presenting examples of using these verbs, we first describe four specialized clauses that can be used with arithmetic statements: the ROUNDED, [NOT] ON SIZE ERROR, and REMAINDER clauses, and the END-verb scope terminators.

ROUNDED Clause

A frequent need exists for rounding numeric values. For example, even though prices or rates of interest may be quoted to three or four decimal places, any billing must be rounded to two decimal places, since the smallest monetary unit is the cent. COBOL provides automatic rounding by use of the ROUNDED clause, which can be used with all arithmetic verbs.

Execution of the statement ADD A TO B ROUNDED will result in a rounded number in B. If B was specified as containing two decimal places in the DATA DIVISION description, rounding is accomplished by adding 0.005 to the result of the addition and truncating the third place. Therefore, when the remainder which is to be dropped begins with a 5 or higher value, the number is rounded up; otherwise it is rounded down. If B was specified to contain one place to the right of the decimal point, 0.05 is added to the result of the addition, and the second place is truncated.

If values are to be summed, it is an error to round the values before summing. Rather, the sum should be determined with all available digit positions and then the sum should be rounded. Rounding each individual value can lead to a considerable accumulation of rounding error.

[NOT] ON SIZE ERROR Clause

The case may arise in which an arithmetic result is larger than anticipated, in terms of the number of digit positions available. For example, a person earning $10.00 per hour should have a weekly gross pay well under $999.99. But suppose that by some mistake in the program, or more likely in the input, the computed weekly pay figure is over $1,000.00. Rather than allow truncation of this figure to occur, such "overflows" can be detected by use of the ON SIZE ERROR clause. For example, assume GROSS has PICTURE 999V99. We can write:

```
MULTIPLY RATE BY HOURS GIVING GROSS
   ON SIZE ERROR
   MOVE 'GROSS PAY EXCEEDS $999.99' TO MESSAGE.
```

The ON SIZE ERROR clause is simply a conditional statement that says: If the size of a value does not fit in the field, do whatever is indicated in the statement that follows in that sentence. The statement that follows must be imperative; that is, it cannot be conditional. When ON SIZE ERROR is used and the condition is fulfilled, the arithmetic operand intended to receive the result is not altered from its previous value. In other words, it is as if the arithmetic operations had not happened.

In addition to "large" results, the ON SIZE ERROR condition is also fulfilled by a zero division. As you may recall from algebra, division by zero is an undefined operation yielding an "infinitely" large quotient.

The 1985 standard COBOL provides an "else" alternative path with respect to the ON SIZE ERROR conditional, namely, the NOT ON SIZE ERROR. The program segment included in Figure 5-1 illustrates use of this option, while the flowchart in this figure portrays the chronological sequence of steps that occurs by execution of the sample ADD statement. Review both the program segment and the flowchart at this time.

Using the 1974 version of COBOL, which does not have the [NOT] ON SIZE ERROR option, you can code the programming task presented in Figure 5-1 as follows:

```
MOVE 'NO' TO SIZE-ERROR-TEST
ADD X Y GIVING W
   ON SIZE ERROR MOVE 'YES' TO SIZE-ERROR-TEST.
IF SIZE-ERROR-TEST = 'YES'
   MOVE ZERO TO Z
ELSE
   MOVE W TO Z.
MOVE Z TO A.
```

REMAINDER Clause

The REMAINDER clause can be used in conjunction with a DIVIDE instruction. The REMAINDER option can only be used with the DIVIDE GIVING format and must follow the ROUNDED clause if ROUNDED is also present. Use of the REMAINDER clause is illustrated in the examples that follow.

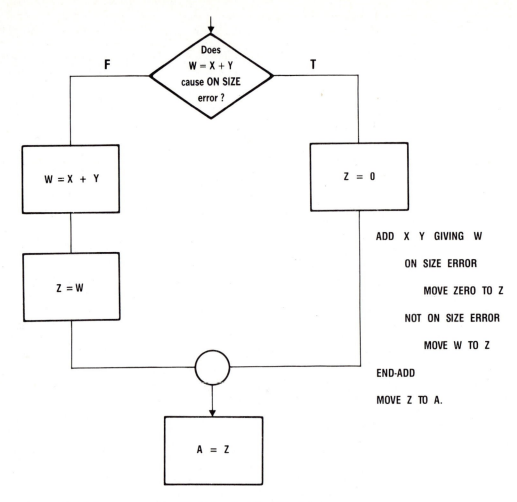

FIGURE 5-1   ON SIZE ERROR ILLUSTRATION.

Examples of Using Arithmetic Verbs

Figure 5-2 presents a set of examples involving the use of arithmetic verbs. Review these examples and note the effects of the various forms of instructions on the data fields. In addition, the following paragraphs direct your attention to some particular results.

Example 4 illustrates the effect of the ROUNDED clause. The result of 132.456 has been rounded to 132.46 because Y has two decimal positions.

Example 5 shows the effect of the ON SIZE ERROR clause. Since Y has three positions to the left of the decimal point, the result 1030.25 is too large. Incidentally, if the ON SIZE had not been used, the result in Y would have been stored as 030.25, due to truncation of the first significant digit.

Example 7 illustrates that a negative result is stored as an absolute value (without sign) if the numeric field does not include the S PICTURE character.

Example 8 illustrates the application of the rule of arithmetic that

		W	X	Y	Z
	PICTURE:	S999V99	999V99	999V99	999
	INITIAL VALUE:	010∧0̄0̄	090∧00	030∧00	040
1	ADD X TO Y			120∧00	
2	ADD X, Y TO Z				160
3	ADD 5 Y GIVING W	035∧00			
4	ADD X, 12,456 TO Y ROUNDED			132∧46	
5	ADD 1000.25 TO Y ROUNDED ON SIZE ERROR MOVE ZERO TO Z				000
6	SUBTRACT Y FROM X		060∧00		
7	SUBTRACT X FROM Y			060∧00	
8	SUBTRACT X Y FROM W	130∧0̄0̄			
9	SUBTRACT W FROM X GIVING Y			100∧00	
10	SUBTRACT 1260.256 FROM Y ROUNDED ON SIZE ERROR MOVE ZERO TO Z				000
11	MOVE 10 TO X MULTIPLY X BY Y		010∧00	300∧00	
12	MULTIPLY X BY Y			700∧00	
13	MULTIPLY X BY Y ON SIZE ERROR MOVE ZERO TO Z				000
14	MULTIPLY Y BY 0.2453 GIVING X ROUNDED		007∧36		
15	DIVIDE X INTO Y			000∧33	
16	DIVIDE Z INTO 100 GIVING Y			002∧50	
17	DIVIDE 12.2 INTO X Y ROUNDED		007∧37	002∧46	
18	DIVIDE 12.2 INTO Y GIVING Z REMAINDER X		005∧60		002
19	DIVIDE Z BY 12.2 GIVING Y ROUNDED REMAINDER X		000∧10	003∧28	
20	COMPUTE Y ROUNDED = Z/12.2			003∧28	

FIGURE 5-2   EXAMPLES OF THE USE OF ARITHMETIC VERBS.

subtracting from a negative value is equivalent to adding the number to be subtracted to that negative value.

Example 12 illustrates that truncation will occur if the number is larger than the defined field.

Example 17 shows the effects of the absence of ROUNDED in the result in X and the presence of ROUNDED in the result in Y. Incidentally, it is permissible to write DIVIDE 12.2 INTO X ROUNDED Y ROUNDED.

Example 18 illustrates the storage of the integer result in Z (since the PICTURE of Z is integer) and storage of the remainder in X. The remainder is determined as follows. Because the *integer* quotient is $30.00 \div 12.2 = 2$, the remainder is $30.00 - (2 \times 12.2) = 5.6$.

Example 19 shows that the value is stored in the REMAINDER field *before* the rounding takes place. Thus, the unrounded quotient is 3.278, which if stored in Y would have been stored unrounded as 3.27. The remainder is, then, $40 - (3.27 \times 12.2) = 0.106$, which is stored (right-truncated) in X as 0.10.

The END-Verb Scope Terminator

All five arithmetic verbs include an END-verb scope terminator that can be used to terminate the range of the [NOT] ON SIZE ERROR conditionals. In Figure 5-1, for example, the END-ADD terminates the scope of the NOT ON SIZE ERROR clause, whereas MOVE Z TO A is executed unconditionally. In contrast, we could write:

```
ADD X Y GIVING W
   ON SIZE ERROR
      MOVE ZERO TO Z
MOVE Z TO A.
```

Absence of the END-ADD scope terminator results in the last statement above, MOVE Z TO A, being executed conditionally based on the ON SIZE ERROR condition, since no period follows the statement MOVE ZERO TO Z. This is so despite the deceiving alignment of the statements in the above program segment.

In general, the END-ADD, END-SUBTRACT, END-MULTIPLY, END-DIVIDE, and END-COMPUTE are useful in defining the range of the [NOT] ON SIZE ERROR conditions when these conditionals are included with the arithmetic verbs.

Review

1   If the result of an arithmetic operation is 45.4545, rounding to three decimal places will result in the value _____ being placed in a storage location, whereas rounding to two places will result in the value _____ being placed in the storage location.

45.455; 45.45

2   If the ROUNDED option is not used, 45.4545 reported to three places would result in the value _____, whereas the value reported to two places would be _____.

45.454; 45.45

3   When the number of digits of an arithmetic result is greater than the number defined in the DATA DIVISION specifications, the likely reason is an error in the data input. Such an overflow can be signaled by use of the _____ clause.

ON SIZE ERROR

4   The alternative option to the ON SIZE ERROR in the 1985 standard is the _____ option.

NOT ON SIZE ERROR

5   The scope terminators for arithmetic verbs that can be used to define the range of [NOT] ON SIZE ERROR conditions used with arithmetic verbs are the _____-ADD, _____-SUBTRACT, _____-MULTIPLY, _____-DIVIDE, and _____-COMPUTE.

END; END; END; END; END

6   The remainder associated with the arithmetic process of division can be output by using the _____ clause with DIVIDE GIVING.

REMAINDER

7   Complete the following table by entering the numeric result of each arithmetic operation:

			W	X	Y	Z
		PICTURE:	99V9	99	99V9	S999.9
		INITIAL VALUE:	15∧0	10	12∧8	100∧0

1 ADD W, Y TO X

2 ADD W, Y GIVING X ROUNDED

3 SUBTRACT W FROM Y

4 SUBTRACT W FROM Y GIVING Z

5 MULTIPLY W BY Y

6 MULTIPLY X BY Y GIVING Z
         ROUNDED

7 DIVIDE W INTO W
       DIVIDE W INTO Z GIVING Y
           ON SIZE ERROR
               MOVE ZERO TO X
           NOT ON SIZE ERROR
               MOVE 1 TO X.

8 DIVIDE X INTO Y ROUNDED
         REMAINDER Z

1	X = 37
2	X = 28
3	Y = 02∧2
4	Z = 002∧$\bar{2}$
5	Y = 92∧0
6	Z = 128∧8
7	W = 1∧0, Y = 12∧8, X = 0
8	Y = 1∧3; Z = 008∧8
	[computed as 12.8 − (1.2 × 10)]

ARITHMETIC PRECISION

Numeric data in COBOL may contain up to 18 digits. In administrative uses of the computer rarely is there a need for very large or very small numbers, and thus 18 digits is more than adequate. For example, dollar values, even for the federal government, do not exceed 13 digits (trillions), inventories rarely exceed counts in hundreds of thousands, customers or clients do not exceed 100 million, and interest rates are seldom quoted to more than three to five decimal places.

Given the capacity of 18 digits, it would seem that arithmetic precision should not be an issue. Yet it is a matter that must be noted by the programmer for three main reasons. First, there is a tendency to ignore the issue of precision on the part of programmers, and fields are often defined with inadequate size. As a result, a MOVE instruction may result in truncation of integer digits, resulting in incorrect values, or truncation of decimal digits, resulting in arithmetic results that are less precise than desired. Of course, compilers often diagnose the possibility of truncation and, as we saw in a preceding section, the ON SIZE ERROR clause can be used to detect such problems.

The second reason for considering precision is the fact that some quantities cannot be represented exactly in any finite number of digits. For instance, an asset depreciated on a straight-line basis over 3 years would require an annual depreciation of ⅓ the original asset value, which is not a finite decimal number. Thus, after 3 years of depreciation the book value would not be exactly zero.

In such a case, a recommended procedure is illustrated in the following examples. Suppose we have:

```
01   ASSET-VAL    PIC   9(8)V99.
01   DEPREC       PIC   9(8)V99.
01   BOOK-VAL     PIC   9(8)V99.
```

Then we could write:

```
MOVE   ASSET-VAL   TO   BOOK-VAL
COMPUTE   DEPREC   ROUNDED   =   BOOK-VAL   /   3.00
COMPUTE   BOOK-VAL   =   BOOK-VAL   −   DEPREC
```

for the first 2 years' computation. For the third and final year we could write:

```
MOVE BOOK-VAL   TO   DEPREC
MOVE ZERO TO BOOK-VAL
```

thus forcing the third-year depreciation to be equal to the remaining book value. Alternately, we could have written a more general expression:

```
COMPUTE DEPREC = ASSET-VAL − 2.00 * DEPREC,
```

where 2 is the number of years of depreciation taken up to this time.

The third and primary reason for being concerned about arithmetic precision is the matter of *intermediate results.* Statements like:

```
ADD A B C GIVING D
COMPUTE E = A + B * (C / D)
```

require intermediate results. Arithmetic operations are carried out one at a time, meaning that for the first example A and B are added giving an intermediate result to which C is then added before storing the result in D.

Review

1   The maximum number of numeric digits that may be contained in a numeric field in COBOL is _____ (number).

18

2   One reason for concern about precision is that MOVEment of data from a larger to a smaller field may result in arithmetic results that are less precise than desired or in _____ of integer digits.

truncation

3   The second reason for the concern about truncation is that some quantities, such as ⅙, [can/cannot] be represented exactly in any finite number of digits.

cannot

4   The third reason for being concerned about precision is the matter of [preliminary/intermediate/final] results in arithmetic operations.

intermediate

Treatment of intermediate results is specific to each compiler used, and the appropriate manual must be consulted in each case. We illustrate here the procedures used by large-scale IBM systems, such as the IBM 370 and 303X systems. In these systems, intermediate results can be carried to 30 digits. The symbol system used in each of the arithmetic operations described below is:

$i Vd$ means a field with i integer and d decimal digits.
The two operands involved in any arithmetic operation are designated $i_1 Vd_1$ and $i_2 Vd_2$.

Addition

The intermediate result from two given operands has precision $i Vd$, where i is determined by the result that would be obtained by transforming the PICTURE for each operand to its maximum decimal value. For instance, if A and B are being added and their PICTUREs are 9V9 and 99V99, respectively, we can imagine that the addition (9.9 + 99.99) is performed, which yields three integer places. This rule taken from IBM COBOL manuals for large-scale systems can be translated to mean that the intermediate result is 1 + the larger of i_1 or i_2 in the two operands involved.

If one of the operands involved is a constant, then the integer precision of the intermediate result is determined by adding the constant itself. For instance, if:

A   PIC   9V9
B   PIC   99V99

and we write

ADD   A   10.25   B   GIVING . . .

the intermediate result of (A + 10.25) is determined to need integer precision of 2, since (9.9 + 10.25) cannot give a result of more than two integer places. Contrast this to the above example of adding two data-names with respective PICTURE strings of 9V9 and 99V99.

The *decimal* precision d in the intermediate result i Vd is the larger of d_1 or d_2 in the two operands involved. Thus for two operands with PIC 99V9 and PIC 9V99 the intermediate result would have the precision represented by 999V99.

The above rules govern the precision of a pair of operands. When a series of operands is involved, the precision of the maximum intermediate result applies to the final result. For instance if we have:

A   PIC 9V9
B   PIC 99V99
C   PIC 9V999
D   PIC 9999V99
ADD A   B   C   GIVING   D

the following process takes place. The intermediate result of A + B is determined to have precision 999V99. Then the sum represented by that intermediate result plus C is determined to have precision of 9(4)V999 (the intermediate result of A + B is treated as if it were an individual operand in the addition to C). Since D includes only two decimal places, truncation will take place from the right. Had D been erroneously defined with PIC 9(3)V99, the compiler might not diagnose the fact that there could be an inadequate number of integer places. The program may be tested and used extensively and, by chance A, B, and C may have small enough values that no errors occur. Then, some day A, B, and C may finally contain large enough values to cause truncation. The result will be either an undetected error or a "surprise" as to how this "thoroughly tested and extensively used program" could fail!

Subtraction

The integer and decimal precision for the intermediate result iVd in the case of subtraction is the same as for addition. Thus, the precision for integer precision is 1 + the larger of i_1 or i_2 while the decimal precision is the larger of d_1 or d_2 in the two operands involved.

On the face of it, it might appear that the precision for the integer is simply the larger of i_1 or i_2. For example, if A has the PICTURE 9V9 and B has the PICTURE 99V99, then it would seem that the maximum result associated with subtracting A from B is 2 integer places (99.99 − 0.0). However, note that because numeric data can be signed, one of the operands may be negative, and therefore the process of subtraction by the rules of algebra will lead to *addition* of the two operands in such a case. Thus, if B in the example above is negative, the subtraction (−99.99 − 9.9) yields three integer positions. For the same reason, if one of the operands in the subtraction is a constant, the integer position of the intermediate result is determined by *adding* the absolute value of the constant. Thus, if A has the PICTURE S9V9, the instruction SUBTRACT 5.0 FROM A requires integer precision of 2. Again, note that the value of A could be the negative −9.9, and in this case the subtraction (−9.9 − 5.0) in fact results in addition of the two values and integer precision of 2.

Multiplication

When two operands i_1Vd_1 and i_2Vd_2 are multiplied together, the intermediate result iVd is determined as follows: $i = (i_1 + i_2)$ and $d = d_1 + d_2)$. Thus, if A and B have PICTUREs of 9V9 and 99V99, respectively, the intermediate result is determined to have precision of 999V999.

Recalling that throughout this discussion we have been illustrating IBM practices, we should state that the above result for the integer precision is obtained by multiplying the corresponding PIC equivalents 9.9 and 99.99. By this procedure, if one of the operands is a constant, then the value of the constant is used in determining i and d. Thus in the expression A * 10.1, where A has PIC 9V9, the intermediate result precision is 99V99, since 10.1 * 9.9 yields a result in two integer places and two decimal places.

Division

Division is the most common source of arithmetic computational errors and it requires the greatest amount of attention in determining precision.

When two operands i_1Vd_1 and i_2Vd_2 are involved in division, the precision of iVd of the intermediate result is obtained as follows. The integer part, i, is determined by dividing i_1 by the minimum nonzero value that the division can have. Thus, for A/B, where A has PIC 9V9 and B has PIC 9V99, it is assumed that 9.9 is divided by 0.01, which in turn implies that three integer positions are needed for the intermediate result. In essence, this procedure translates to $i = i_1 + d_2$.

The required number of decimal positions, d, in division is determined by the greater of d_1, or the decimal precision of the final result field. It may seem pointless to carry more decimal positions than required in the final result field. But recall that in general the intermediate result may be one of a sequence of calculations, and therefore full precision should be maintained until any final rounding, or truncation. Thus, if we have:

```
A   PIC 9V99
B   PIC 99V99
C   PIC 999V999
COMPUTE C = A/B
```

then $i = 3$ and $d = 3$ for a 999V999 equivalent. However, if C had PIC 999V9, the intermediate result precision would be $d = 2$, since d_1 would be the greater value in this case.

If the divisor is a constant, then the constant is used in determining the intermediate precision for i and d. Thus if A is described by PICTURE 99V9 and the final result field B also is described by 99V9, and B = A/10.0, then the intermediate result precision is 9V99. In this example $i = 1$ and $d = 2$ because these are the number of positions resulting from the division (99.9/10.0). Note that the value $d = 2$ exceeds the decimal positions in the final result field B, and therefore $d = 2$ prevails for the intermediate result precision.

Consider now the following example:

```
A   PIC 99
B   PIC 9
C   PIC 999
MOVE 2 TO A
MOVE 8 TO B
MOVE 100 TO C
COMPUTE C = C * (A/B).
```

The expression in parentheses is the one evaluated first and the precision of the intermediate result will be $i = 2$ and $d = 0$. Then, because 2 divided by 8 gives a value less than 1, the intermediate result is zero, and multiplication by zero results in a value of zero for C, instead of 25! Had we defined A as PIC 99V99, the intermediate result would have had sufficient decimal precision $d = 2$ to carry the intermediate result of 2/8 = 0.25.

Again, the above example emphasizes the importance of being careful when coding division operations in a program.

Exponentiation

The exponent is assumed to be either an integer (whole number) or, if a fraction, it should have only a value of 0.5, signifying the square root. If the exponent is a literal, whether integer or 0.5, then the required i value for the intermediate result is equal to multiplying the i_2 (of the base) by the literal. If the product is a fraction, which will occur if a base with an odd-numbered i_1 is raised to the 0.5 power, then it is rounded up to the next whole number. For example, if the base is A PIC 999V9, then A ** 2 has $i = 3 \times 2 = 6$ integer digits required for the intermediate result. For the same data-name, A ** 0.5 has $i = 3 \times 0.5 = 1.5 = 2$ (rounded) for the required integer digits.

If the exponent is a data-name, then the required i value for the intermediate result is equal to raising the base to the numeric equivalent of the PICTURE. For instance, if the two operands are A PIC 9V9 and B PIC 9, then for A ** B the system would compute i as if we were multiplying (9.9) * (9.9) * $\cdots$ * (9.9) nine times, giving 9, which is i_1 times the maximum numeric equivalent of the PICTURE of the exponent. Note that the implication of this rule is that the exponent in COBOL can never have a picture greater than PIC 9 if the base is at least $i_1 = 1$. For example, if the two operands are A PIC 9V9 and B PIC 99, then the required number of integer digits for the intermediate result is $i = 1 \times 99 = 99$, which is well in excess of the 30 digits available!

For the decimal part of the intermediate result precision, if the exponent is a data name or 0.5, then $d =$ either d_1 (of the base) or the d of the final result field, whichever is larger. If the exponent is an integer literal, then $d = d_1$ times the literal. For example, for the expression A ** B, if A has PIC 9V9 and B has PIC 9, then either $d = 1$ or the d of the final result, as for instance $d = 3$ in COMPUTE C = A ** B where C has PIC 9(9)V9(3). As another example, if A has PIC 9V9 and we write A ** 4, the intermediate result will have $d = 4$, which is d_1 times the literal exponent value (1×4). This is consistent with the general rule of assuming the operation to be (9.9) * (9.9) * (9.9) * (9.9), which would generate four decimal places.

In general, compilers provide reasonable rules for intermediate result precision, but it is the responsibility of the programmer to provide the correct size and form of data fields. Most of the common errors can be avoided by providing for larger fields both on the integer and decimal side. Arithmetic operations constitute such a small part of the machine resources consumed by a typical COBOL program that it should not really matter whether we define a WORKING-STORAGE item to be PIC 9(4)V99 vs. PIC 9(6)V9(6). In the same vein, when constants (numeric literals) are used, it is preferable to include decimal places. Thus use 2.00 . . . instead of 2, especially in operations involving division, unless the application specifically requires integer arithmetic.

Further, it is often useful to consider the order of execution of arithmetic operations and its impact on arithmetic precision. If we have 100 * (2/8), the result will be zero, whereas 100 * 2/8 or (10 * 2)/8 will yield the correct result of 25. In other words, where both multiplication and division are involved, do the multiplication first. However, caution should be exercised that the multiplication does not lead to excessively large intermediate results, which can easily occur if several successive multiplications and/or exponentiations are involved prior to division. For instance, in the case of the expression

(1200 * 65879 * 50.00 ** 8)/(150.00 ** 5)

it would be better to write it as

((50.00 ** 8)/(150.00 ** 5)) * 1200 * 65879

to avoid a size error.

Review

1   Given the two fields described by A PIC 99V999 and B PIC 999V9, the intermediate result of ADD A B has the integer and decimal precision $i\,Vd = $ _____.

9999V999

2   Given the two fields described by A PIC 99V999 and B PIC 999V9, the intermediate result of SUBTRACT A FROM B has the integer and decimal precision $i\,Vd = $ _____.

9999V999

3   Given the field described by A PIC 99V999, the intermediate result of ADD A 1.0 has the precision $i\,Vd = $ _____.

999V999

4   Given the field described by A PIC 99V999, the intermediate result of SUBTRACT 1.0 FROM A has the precision $i\,Vd = $ _____.

999V999

5   When a series of operands, rather than simply a pair of operands, is involved, the precision of the [minimum/maximum] intermediate result applies to the final result.

maximum

6   Given the two fields described by A PIC 99V999 and B PIC 999V9, the intermediate result of A * B has the precision $i\,Vd$ = _____.

9(5)V9(4)

7   Given the field described by A PIC 99V999, the intermediate result of A * 5.0 has the precision $i\,Vd$ = _____.

999V999

8   Given the two fields described by A PIC 99V999 and B PIC 999V9, if the intermediate result of A/B is to be stored in the final result field C PIC 99V99, the precision of the intermediate result is $i\,Vd$ = _____.

999V999

9   Given the field A PIC 99V999 and the final result field B PIC 99V99, the precision of the intermediate result of the division A/25.0 is $i\,Vd$ = _____.

9V999

10   Given the field A PIC 9V99 and the final result field C PIC 9(10)V9(8), the precision of the intermediate result required for A ** 3 is $i\,Vd$ = _____.

9(4)V9(6)

11   Given the field A PIC 9V99 and the final result field C PIC 9(10)V9(8), the precision of the intermediate result required for A ** 0.5 is $i\,Vd$ = _____.

9V9(8)

12   Given the fields A PIC 9V99 and B PIC 9, and the final result field C PIC 9(109V)(8), the precision of the intermediate result required for A ** B is $i\,Vd$ = _____.

9(9)V9(8)

DATA TRANSFER

In this section of the chapter we consider a number of statements that can be used to transfer data in storage during program execution.

Data can be transferred into a receiving field in a variety of ways. The most common method is by use of the MOVE verb, whose function it is to transfer either a direct copy or an edited copy of the contents of a sending field to a receiving field. Sometimes the function of a MOVE statement is expressed through syntax *other* than the MOVE verb, as in the following cases:

The effect of using the GIVING option with arithmetic verbs is the same as if a MOVE statement had been used.

The COMPUTE verb itself includes an implied MOVE statement to store the results in a specified field.

The READ . . . INTO and the WRITE . . . FROM options include implied MOVE statements.

The VALUE clause in the DATA DIVISION is an implied MOVE statement (albeit it is as if it were executed only once, at the start of program execution).

The MOVE Statement

The effects of a MOVE statement depend on the sizes and PICTURE specifications of the sending and receiving fields. Further, the category of the sending and receiving fields is a factor in determining whether a MOVE statement is valid or invalid. Figure 5-3 summarizes the legal and illegal MOVE commands according to the data categories of the sending and receiving fields.

A critical factor in determining the effect of a MOVE statement is the

CATEGORY OF SENDING DATA DATA ITEM	CATEGORY OF RECEIVING DATA ITEM		
	ALPHABETIC	ALPHANUMERIC; ALPHANUMERIC EDITED	NUMERIC INTEGER; NUMERIC NONINTEGER; NUMERIC EDITED
Alphabetic	YES	YES	NO
Alphanumeric	YES	YES	NO
Alphanumeric edited	YES	YES	NO
Numeric integer	NO	YES	YES
Numeric noninteger	NO	NO	YES
Numeric edited	NO	YES	YES

FIGURE 5-3   LEGAL AND ILLEGAL MOVE COMMANDS.

level of the items involved in the operation. Sending fields at the group (nonelementary) level are always considered to be in the alphanumeric class even if the subordinate items are all numeric. The significance of the above rule is illustrated in the MOVE statement examples that follow and relate to the following program segment:

```
02  A.
    03  B                         PIC 99V9.
02  C.
    03  D  OCCURS 2 TIMES  PIC 9V9.
02  E                             PIC 9(4).
```

MOVE 1.1 TO B
MOVE A TO E

As a result, E will contain 0011. The sending item, A, is alphanumeric by virtue of being at the group level. Therefore the sending item is treated as if it were an unsigned numeric integer.

MOVE 1 TO D (1)
MOVE 2 TO D (2)
MOVE C TO E

As a result, E will contain 1020. The sending item, C, is considered as being alphanumeric and the numeric value that it contains is treated as an unsigned numeric integer.

The effect of a MOVE statement is also influenced by the presence of the SYNCHRONIZED or USAGE COMPUTATIONAL options, which are described in the respective subsections of Chapter 4, on the DATA DIVISION.

Review

1   When a MOVE statement is executed, a sending field that is at the group level is always considered to be in the _____ class in terms of category of data, regardless of the type of content in the subordinate fields.

alphanumeric

2   When data are transferred by use of the MOVE instruction, one might say more correctly that the data have been _____, rather than "moved."

duplicated

3   When numeric data are moved from a sending field to a receiving field, alignment takes place with respect to the _____.

decimal point

4   When nonnumeric data are moved from a sending field to a receiving field, alignment takes place at the [left/right] margin.

left

The MOVE CORRESPONDING

The concept of qualification allows the programmer to use the same subordinate data-name in more than one place in the program, thus allowing nonunique data-names. The CORRESPONDING option, available for use with MOVE and with the arithmetic verbs, simplifies the program in cases in which the same operation is to be performed on one or several pairs of elementary, nonunique data-names. Let us take an example. Suppose we have the following two records:

```
01  PAY-RECORD.
    02  GROSS        PIC 9999V99.
    02  NET          PIC 9999V99.
    02  TAXES        PIC 999V99.
01  EDITED-RECORD.
    02  GROSS        PIC ZZZ9.99.
    02  TAXES        PIC ZZ9.99.
    02  NET          PIC ZZZ9.99.
```

If we want to move PAY-RECORD to EDITED-RECORD, we *cannot* do it in one statement. Writing MOVE PAY-RECORD to EDITED-RECORD would be incorrect, because the order of the fields NET and TAXES is not the same in the two records and the receiving elementary items involve editing. Of course, the move could be accomplished by a separate MOVE statement for each of the three fields; however, the same result can be accomplished more easily by use of the CORRESPONDING option:

MOVE CORRESPONDING PAY-RECORD TO EDITED-RECORD.

The general format associated with the use of the CORRESPONDING option is:

$$
\text{\underline{MOVE}} \quad \left\{ \begin{array}{l} \text{CORRESPONDING} \\ \text{CORR} \end{array} \right\} \quad \text{identifier-1 \underline{TO} identifier-2}
$$

CORR is the abbreviated form of the option. Unlike the situation in the previous example, the two data-names may contain only some items that correspond, as in the following example:

```
01  INSPECTION.
     03   TOTAL-QUANTITY ...
     03   REJECTED ...
     03   ACCEPTED ...
     03   QUALITY-RATIO ...

01  QUALITY-REPORT.
     02   TOTAL-QUANTITY ...
     02   QUALITY-RATIO ...
```

Executing the statement MOVE CORR INSPECTION TO QUALITY-REPORT will result in the two items or fields, TOTAL-QUANTITY and QUALITY-RATIO, being moved.

In order for the CORRESPONDING option to be used, there must be pairs of items having the same name in two group items, and at least one of the items in each pair must be elementary. Another rule to remember is that any items that are subordinate to identifier-1 and identifier-2 and have RE-NAMES, REDEFINES, or OCCURS clauses are ignored in the move. Therefore, we cannot use the MOVE CORRESPONDING option to move a table of values, for example. However, the identifier-1 and identifier-2 items themselves may have REDEFINES or OCCURS clauses or may be subordinate to data items with such clauses.

The CORRESPONDING option also is available with ADD and SUB-TRACT, as can be observed in the format specifications in Appendix C. In general, the option should be avoided or used sparingly with respect to both MOVE and the arithmetic verbs. Use of the CORRESPONDING option may result in errors when programs are modified subsequently, and therefore most programming managers tend to limit or even forbid use of this option.

Review

1   The abbreviated form of the CORRESPONDING option is
_____. Use of this option in conjunction with the MOVE in-

struction results in transfer of only the _____ items contained in two records.

CORR; common
(or corresponding)

2   When the MOVE CORRESPONDING option is used, an item will be moved if at least one of the items in each pair is at the _____ level and only if the receiving group item has an item with the same [storage capacity/name].

elementary; name

3   The MOVE CORRESPONDING option can be used to move elementary items [including/but not including] tables of values at the elementary level.

but not including

De-Editing

Figure 5-3, presented previously, identifies legal and illegal MOVE commands in COBOL. As indicated in the figure, it is permissible to move a numeric edited field to a numeric unedited field. This option thus allows for *de-editing* of data. As an example of de-editing, consider the following program statements:

```
02   COMP-AMOUNT   PIC   9(5)V99.
02   EDIT-AMOUNT    PIC   $$,$$9.99.
```

```
MOVE 1234.56 TO EDIT-AMOUNT
MOVE EDIT-AMOUNT TO COMP-AMOUNT.
```

When the statements above have been executed, EDIT-AMOUNT will contain $1,234.56 while COMP-AMOUNT will correctly contain 0123456. The last statement, MOVE EDIT-AMOUNT TO COMP-AMOUNT strips the data of such editing characters as the dollar sign, comma, and decimal point, and moves the numeric edited data to the numeric unedited field. Such a move is not valid in the 1974 version of COBOL.

The SET Verb for Condition-Names

The language provides for a convenient way to move data into fields for which condition-names have been defined. The 88-level condition-name feature of COBOL is very meaningful for conducting tests as to whether a condition is true. But in the 1974 version of COBOL there was something lacking with respect to moving values that correspond to defined condition-names. Consider the following example:

```
01   TOTAL-CREDIT-HOURS   PIC 999.
01   STUDENT-CLASS-CODE   PIC X.
     88   FRESHMAN            VALUE '1'.
     88   SOPHOMORE           VALUE '2'.
     88   JUNIOR              VALUE '3'.
     88   SENIOR              VALUE '4'.

     IF TOTAL-CREDIT-HOURS < 33
       MOVE '1' TO STUDENT-CLASS-CODE
     ELSE IF TOTAL-CREDIT-HOURS < 65
         MOVE '2' TO STUDENT-CLASS-CODE
       ELSE IF TOTAL-CREDIT-HOURS < 97
           MOVE '3' TO STUDENT-CLASS-CODE
         ELSE MOVE '4' TO STUDENT-CLASS-CODE.
```

In the program segment above, statements like MOVE '1' TO STUDENT-CLASS-CODE do not take advantage of the 88 FRESHMAN condition-name specification. In contrast, consider the following program segment:

```
IF TOTAL-CREDITS < 33
  SET FRESHMAN TO TRUE
ELSE IF TOTAL-CREDITS < 65
    SET SOPHOMORE TO TRUE
  ELSE IF TOTAL-CREDITS < 97
      SET JUNIOR TO TRUE
    ELSE SET SENIOR TO TRUE.
```

In the program segment above the SET verb has been used to take advantage of the convenient condition-names provided by the 88-level items. The format of the SET verb used for this purpose is:

```
SET { condition-name-1} ... TO TRUE
```

In the above format, the SET verb directs that the value specified in the VALUE clause is to be moved to the identified field. If a range of values is specified, then the first value is moved, as in the following example:

```
01  STUDENT-CLASS-CODE PIC X.
    88  UNDERCLASSMAN   VALUES ARE '1' THRU '2'.
    88  UPPERCLASSMAN   VALUES ARE '3' THRU '4'.
```

Use of SET UNDERCLASSMAN TO TRUE in the above example is equivalent to saying MOVE '1' TO STUDENT-CLASS-CODE.

If multiple condition-names are specified in the same SET statement, the effect is the same as using multiple SET statements. This is illustrated in the following example:

```
01  CREDIT-RATING       PIC XX.
    88  DOUBLE-A        VALUE 'AA'.
    88  GOOD            VALUES ARE 'BA' THRU 'BB'.
01  ACCOUNT-CLASS       PIC X.
    88  INSTITUTIONAL   VALUE 'I'.
    88  PERSONAL        VALUE 'P'.
```

```
        SET DOUBLE-A PERSONAL TO TRUE.
```

The SET statement immediately above is equivalent to:

```
SET DOUBLE-A TO TRUE
SET PERSONAL TO TRUE.
```

The latter style is the recommended approach because the style makes it clear that two separate condition-names are set to true. Of course, in either form it would not be logical to use two condition-names from the *same* field, such as:

```
SET DOUBLE-A TO TRUE
SET GOOD     TO TRUE.
```

The INITIALIZE Verb

The addition of the INITIALIZE statement provides a structured method of documenting the initial value of fields. The most common use of this verb is for setting numeric fields to zero and nonnumeric fields to spaces.

Figure 5-4 presents the general format for the INITIALIZE verb while Figure 5-5 includes several examples of using the verb. When used without the REPLACING option, spaces are moved to alphabetic, alphanumeric, and alphanumeric-edited data items while zeros are moved to numeric and numeric-edited items. When identifier-1 is a group item, as in the first INITIALIZE A example, it is as if we wrote a series of elementary MOVE statements to move either spaces or zeros, depending on the data category of the receiving field.

When the REPLACING option is used, only the items that match the specified category are initialized. Thus, the third example in Figure 5-5 illustrates that only D is affected by the INITIALIZE statement.

Notice the inclusion of the reserved words ALPHANUMERIC-EDITED and NUMERIC-EDITED in the format statement in Figure 5-4. Overall, the INITIALIZE verb serves as a convenient alternative to the use of the VALUE clause in the DATA DIVISION or the associated use of a MOVE statement in the PROCEDURE DIVISION.

Review

1   De-editing is accomplished by the ability to move a numeric edited field to a numeric field that is not _____.

edited

2   The COBOL verb that provides a convenient way to move data into fields for which condition-names have been defined is the _____ verb.

SET

3   The COBOL verb that provides a structured method of documenting the initial value of a constant is the _____ verb.

initialize

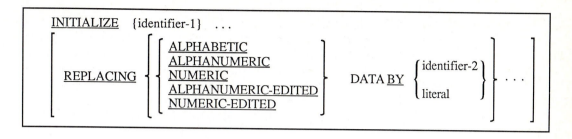

FIGURE 5–4   FORMAT AND SAMPLE USES OF THE INITIALIZE VERB.

DATA DIVISION· SPECIFICATIONS

```
01  A.
    02  B  PIC  A(2).
    02  C  PIC  X(2).
    02  D  PIC  9V9.
    02  E  PIC  X/X.
    02  F  PIC  $9.99.
    02  G  PIC  X(2).
01  M  PIC   9V9    VALUE 1.2.
01  N  PIC   XX     VALUE '12'.
```

INITIALIZE Statement Examples	Equivalent MOVE Statements
INITIALIZE B	MOVE SPACES TO B
INITIALIZE A	MOVE SPACES TO B, C, E, G MOVE ZERO TO D, F
INITIALIZE A REPLACING NUMERIC BY ZERO	MOVE ZERO TO D

INITIALIZE A
   REPLACING
      ALPHABETIC   DATA BY 'NO'
      ALPHANUMERIC   DATA BY N
      NUMERIC   DATA BY M
      NUMERIC-EDITED   DATA BY 9.1
      ALPHANUMERIC-EDITED DATA BY N
	MOVE 'NO' TO B
	MOVE N TO C, G
	MOVE M TO D
	MOVE 9.1 TO F
	MOVE N TO E

FIGURE 5–5   EXAMPLES OF USING THE INITIALIZE VERB.

CHARACTER PROCESSING

COBOL statements use entire fields as operands. The fields may be elementary or group items; but, in either case, the bytes that constitute a field are referenced as a group. Yet there are instances when we need to process individual characters within fields, and COBOL provides three verbs that can be used for such character processing: STRING, UNSTRING, and INSPECT. These three verbs are very effective in performing the functions for which they were designed. However, they are specialized verbs that are limited to their respective functions.

Before describing each of these three character-processing verbs, it is appropriate to point out that the most flexible form of character processing can be achieved by means of defining a field as individual bytes through an appropriate OCCURS clause and using a PERFORM . . . VARYING iteration. Such a generalized approach can always be a substitute for use of the specialized STRING, UNSTRING, and INSPECT verbs but requires longer and more complex coding.

Consider the following example in which we contrast use of the OCCURS clause and the PERFORM . . . VARYING iteration with the alternative use of the STRING verb. First, suppose that we have two fields, as follows:

```
02   FIRST-NAME    PIC X(10).
02   LAST-NAME     PIC X(12).
```

We wish to move the contents of the above two fields to the following field in such a way that the first name follows the last name and the two names are separated by a comma and *one* space.

```
02   FULL-NAME   PIC X(24)
```

For example, FULL-NAME might contain either of the following names:

```
JONES, ED
HERNANDEZ, CHRISTOPHER
```

We could write the following program code to do this task:

```
02   CHAR-FIELD.
     03   CHAR OCCURS 12 TIMES              PIC X.
02   FULL-NAME                             PIC X (24).
02   FL-NAME-CHAR REDEFINES FULL-NAME.
     03   FL-CHAR OCCURS 24 TIMES          PIC X.
```

```
MOVE SPACES TO FULL-NAME
MOVE LAST-NAME TO CHAR-FIELD
MOVE 1 TO K
PERFORM MOVE-CHAR VARYING I FROM 1 BY 1
                    UNTIL I > 12
                            OR CHAR (I) = SPACE.
MOVE ',' TO FL-CHAR (I)
ADD 1 TO I
MOVE SPACE TO FL-CHAR (I)
ADD 1 I GIVING K
MOVE FIRST-NAME TO CHAR-FIELD
PERFORM MOVE-CHAR VARYING I FROM 1 BY 1
                    UNTIL I > 12
                            OR CHAR (I) = SPACE.
MOVE-CHAR.
    MOVE CHAR (I) TO FL-CHAR (K)
    ADD 1 TO K.
```

In the program code above we define a temporary CHAR-FIELD into which we MOVE the FIRST-NAME and then the LAST-NAME. Each byte in CHAR-FIELD is moved to FULL-NAME until the end of the sending field is reached or a space is encountered. The REDEFINES clause is used with respect to the receiving field in order to control the positioning of each byte, including the comma and the space separating the last name from the first name.

Now, contrast the approach above with the following alternative approach using the STRING verb:

```
MOVE SPACES TO FULL-NAME
STRING LAST-NAME DELIMITED BY SPACE
    ',  ' DELIMITED BY SIZE
    FIRST-NAME DELIMITED BY SPACE
  INTO FULL-NAME.
```

With the use of the STRING there is no need to use REDEFINES, no need to use an extra field such as CHAR-FIELD, and no need to write a procedure consisting of 10 statements, including the two PERFORM . . . VARYING statements. Clearly, STRING is a powerful and useful verb, as are the UNSTRING and INSPECT verbs to be described in the following subsections of this chapter. When a programming task is suited to the respective function of each of these verbs, it is done easily, with no explicit procedural logic required.

Review

1 Of the two approaches to character processing illustrated in this section, the more complex procedure involves use of the _____ clause in a data definition along with a PERFORM . . . _____ iteration in the PROCEDURE DIVISION.

OCCURS; VARYING

2 The specialized verb for character processing whose use was briefly illustrated in this section is the _____ verb.

STRING

The STRING and UNSTRING Statements

The STRING and UNSTRING verbs are designed to facilitate transfer of data from several sources into one destination and from one source to many destinations, respectively. In effect, use of these verbs allows one statement to be used in lieu of multiple uses of the MOVE verb and, possibly, in lieu of some DATA DIVISION entries.

We begin with two examples that illustrate uses of the STRING verb.

Suppose that EDIT-SOC-SEC contains a social security number, including hyphens after the third and fifth digits, as for instance '123-45-6789'. We wish to move the social security number to SOC-SEC while also removing the hyphens. The following data description entries are given:

```
01  SOC-SEC        PIC X(9).
01  EDIT-SOC-SEC.
    02  PART-1      PIC 999.
    02  FILLER      PIC X VALUE  '-'.
    02  PART-2      PIC 99.
    02  FILLER      PIC X  VALUE  '-'.
    02  PART-3      PIC 9999.
```

We now use the STRING statement:

```
STRING  PART-1 DELIMITED BY SIZE
        PART-2 DELIMITED BY SIZE
        PART-3 DELIMITED BY SIZE
  INTO  SOC-SEC.
```

The STRING here specifies moving the three fields, PART-1, PART-2, and PART-3, and positioning them adjacent to each other. The transfer of data can be thought of as taking place character by character. Thus, the data in PART-1 would be transferred into the first three positions of SOC-SEC, the data in PART-2 would be transferred into the next two positions of SOC-SEC, and so on. The DELIMITED BY SIZE clause specifies that the transfer of data from the associated field will stop at (be delimited by) the point when as many characters have been transferred as the size of the source field. The next example illustrates the availability of other alternatives.

Assume that we want to print a report that lists a company name in columns 5–20, a city name starting with column 26, 1 blank space, and then the ZIP code. The source of data is VENDOR-RECORD:

```
01   VENDOR-RECORD.
        02    COMPANY-NAME   PIC X(15).
        02    STREET         PIC X(40).
        02    CITY-STATE     PIC X(20).
        02    ZIP            PIC 9(5).
```

The data in CITY-STATE are recorded so that the city-name is followed by a comma, a space, and then the state code, e.g., LOS ANGELES, CA.

The output record is described as:

```
01   OUTPUT-REC   PIC X(132).
```

We use the STRING verb as follows:

```
MOVE SPACES TO OUTPUT-REC
MOVE 5 TO STARTING-PLACE.
STRING COMPANY-NAME DELIMITED BY SIZE
    '      '            DELIMITED BY SIZE
    CITY-STATE          DELIMITED BY','
    SPACE, ZIP          DELIMITED BY SIZE
    INTO OUTPUT-REC
    WITH POINTER STARTING-PLACE.
```

The first MOVE statement clears the output record of any previous contents. The second MOVE sets STARTING-PLACE to a value of 5 so that the beginning of data transfer into OUTPUT-REC will begin in column 5 (WITH POINTER STARTING-PLACE). Of course, STARTING-PLACE is an arbitrary name chosen by the programmer; but it must be an integer field for obvious reasons.

The STRING statement specifies that, in effect, five fields will be transferred: COMPANY-NAME, the 5-byte nonnumeric literal '   ', CITY-STATE,

$$\underline{\text{STRING}} \quad \left\{\begin{Bmatrix} \text{identifier-1} \\ \text{literal-1} \end{Bmatrix} \cdots \underline{\text{DELIMITED}} \text{ BY} \begin{Bmatrix} \text{identifier-2} \\ \text{literal-2} \\ \underline{\text{SIZE}} \end{Bmatrix}\right\} \cdots$$

$$\underline{\text{INTO}} \text{ identifier-3}$$
[WITH $\underline{\text{POINTER}}$ identifier-4]
[ON $\underline{\text{OVERFLOW}}$ imperative-statement-1]
[$\underline{\text{NOT}}$ ON $\underline{\text{OVERFLOW}}$ imperative-statement-2]
[END-STRING]

FIGURE 5-6   GENERAL FORMAT FOR THE STRING VERB.

the figurative constant SPACE, and ZIP. Thus, starting with column 5 of OUTPUT-REC, the entire (DELIMITED BY SIZE) COMPANY-NAME is transferred and it is followed by the 5-blank nonnumeric constant. The next data item to be transferred comes from CITY-STATE; this data item is transferred character by character until a comma is encountered (DELIMITED BY ','). One blank follows (SPACE) and then the ZIP code. It should be pointed out that use of figurative constants, such as SPACE, ZEROS, or the like, always means one occurrence of the implied character. Thus, we would obtain one blank even if we had used SPACES instead of SPACE.

The general format for the STRING verb is presented in Figure 5-6.

Our two examples have illustrated all but the OVERFLOW option. If the data specified to be transferred are greater than the size of the receiving item (identifier-3) during execution of a STRING statement, then the imperative statement of the OVERFLOW clause is executed. If the optional OVERFLOW is not used and the overflow condition arises, then the STRING operation is discontinued and the next program statement is executed. During execution, identifier-4, if used, is incremented by 1 as each character is transferred. It is the value of this identifier that is checked in determining an overflow condition. If identifier-4 is not used, an implied counter is used to fulfill the same function.

The UNSTRING verb, as its name implies, acts in the reverse direction of the STRING verb. We present two examples to illustrate use of this verb.

Suppose that data are recorded in free form (without predefined fields) as follows:

TED S BROWN,4,15,3.52
TINA LORI CHRISTIANSON,1,12,2.50

As we can see, name fields are separated by 1 or more blank spaces; then commas separate the remaining three fields. We would like to move these data fields to a fixed-format record, as shown on the following page:

```
01   STUDENT-RECORD.
     02   FIRST-NAME        PIC X(15).
     02   MIDDLE-NAME       PIC X(15).
     02   LAST-NAME         PIC X(20).
     02   CLASSIFICATION    PIC 9.
     02   CREDIT-LOAD       PIC 99.
     02   GPA               PIC XXXX.
```

Assuming that the source data are in

```
01   FREE-FORM-RECORD   PIC X(57).
```

we can write:

```
UNSTRING   FREE-FORM-RECORD
           DELIMITED BY ALL SPACES OR ';'
    INTO   FIRST-NAME
           MIDDLE-NAME
           LAST-NAME
           CLASSIFICATION
           CREDIT-LOAD
           GPA.
```

The DELIMITED clause specifies that fields in the source record are separated by 1 or more blank spaces (ALL SPACES), or single commas (OR ','). In essence, the source record is scanned character by character from left to right. When a blank or a comma appears, it is assumed that a new field begins. The delimiters in this case are blanks or commas, and they are not included in the data transfer, although the UNSTRING statement does include an option allowing the transfer of delimiters themselves.

Consider now a second example that expands on UNSTRING and illustrates combined use of STRING and UNSTRING.

Data records contain numbers in columns 1–6, followed by a name and a header separated from each other by a dollar sign. As in the previous example, a delimiter such as a dollar sign can be used to allow recording of data without adherence to predefined field positions. When data length is highly variable, such free-form data can save a lot of space. Two sample records are as follows:

```
349687INTERNATIONAL TOOLS, INC.$BALANCE SHEET$
135002ACME CORP.$INCOME STATEMENT$
```

We are interested in printing the company name, centered at column 40 on the top of a new page, followed by the name of the report on the third line, also centered at column 40. Solution of the problem involves separating the two fields, determining their size; and, on the basis of their size, centering the data with respect to column 40. We also assume that we wish to ascertain that there are indeed two fields available in the relevant part of the source record. First, we define some data fields:

```
01   FREE-FORM-RECORD   PIC X(47).
01   FIRST-LINE         PIC X(26).
01   SECOND-LINE        PIC X(26).
01   LENGTH-1           PIC 99.
01   LENGTH-2           PIC 99.
01   STARTING-POINT     PIC 99.
01   NO-OF-FIELDS       PIC 9.
01   OUTPUT-RECORD      PIC X(132).
```

Figure 5-7 presents a program segment written to accomplish the desired task. The NO-OF-FIELDS item is used to count the number of fields transferred. Notice its use in the TALLYING clause in the UNSTRING statement. The value 7 is moved to STARTING-POINT because the first 6 columns of FREE-FORM-RECORD contain a number that we wish to ignore. Notice the clause WITH POINTER STARTING-POINT. Using the $ as a delimiter, we transfer data from the source record into two fields, FIRST-LINE and SECOND-LINE. In the process, we obtain a count of the characters moved into each receiving field in LENGTH-1 and LENGTH-2, respectively. The COUNT option provides this length count. Finally, use of the OVERFLOW specifies execution of PERFORM ERROR-ROUTINE-1 if the data being transferred exceed the size of the receiving field. This could happen in our example if the delimiting dollar sign was missing, or if one field was longer than 26 characters—the size specified for FIRST-LINE and SECOND-LINE.

After the UNSTRING statement, we check to see that we indeed had two fields transferred; if not, we PERFORM ERROR-ROUTINE-2.

The PRINT-HEADERS paragraph computes the starting point of each line to the left of column 40. We divide the length of the field involved by 2 and we subtract this amount from 40. We then use the STRING verb to move the data, using LENGTH-1 as the pointer. Actually, it is the availability of the POINTER option in the STRING verb that makes it capable of achieving what the MOVE verb could not accomplish in this case. After the transfer of the data, we print the record and repeat the process for the next line of printed output. The general format for the UNSTRING verb is present in Figure 5-8.

We have illustrated all the options except the DELIMITER IN clause. When used, the clause specifies the identifier to be used to receive the delimiter(s). This option is used if we wish to move the delimiters themselves.

```
    MOVE ZERO TO NO-OF-FIELDS
    MOVE 7 TO STARTING-POINT
    UNSTRING FREE-FORM-RECORD DELIMITED BY '$'
      INTO FIRST-LINE
          COUNT IN LENGTH-1
        SECOND-LINE
          COUNT IN LENGTH-2
      WITH POINTER STARTING-POINT
      TALLYING IN NO-OF-FIELDS
      ON OVERFLOW
        PERFORM ERROR-ROUTINE-1.
    IF NO-OF-FIELDS NOT = 2
      PERFORM ERROR-ROUTINE-2
    ELSE
      PERFORM PRINT-HEADERS.
      .
      .
      .

PRINT-HEADERS.
    COMPUTE LENGTH-1 = 40 − (LENGTH-1 / 2)
    COMPUTE LENGTH-2 = 40 − (LENGTH-2 / 2)
    MOVE SPACES TO OUTPUT-RECORD
    STRING FIRST-LINE DELIMITED BY SIZE
      INTO OUTPUT-RECORD
      WITH POINTER LENGTH-1
    WRITE OUTPUT-RECORD AFTER ADVANCING PAGE
    MOVE SPACES TO OUTPUT RECORD
    STRING SECOND-LINE DELIMITED BY SIZE
      INTO OUTPUT-RECORD
      WITH POINTER LENGTH-2
    WRITE OUTPUT-RECORD AFTER ADVANCING 2 LINES.
```

FIGURE 5–7   EXAMPLE PROGRAM INVOLVING THE USE OF UNSTRING AND STRING.

Review

1   The verb that is used to transfer data from several sources to one destination is the _____ verb.

STRING

UNSTRING identifier-1

$$\left[\underline{\text{DELIMITED}} \text{ BY } [\underline{\text{ALL}}] \quad \begin{Bmatrix} \text{identifier-2} \\ \text{literal-1} \end{Bmatrix} \quad \left[\underline{\text{OR}} \, [\underline{\text{ALL}}] \quad \begin{Bmatrix} \text{identifier-3} \\ \text{literal-2} \end{Bmatrix} \right] \ \cdots \right]$$

INTO {identifier-4   [DELIMITER IN identifier-5]   [COUNT IN identifier-6]}   ...
[WITH POINTER identifier-7]
[TALLYING IN identifier-8]
[ON OVERFLOW imperative-statement-1]
[NOT ON OVERFLOW imperative-statement-2]
[END-UNSTRING]

FIGURE 5–8   GENERAL FORMAT FOR THE UNSTRING VERB.

2   The verb that is used to transfer data from one source to many destinations is the _____ verb.

UNSTRING

3   When the DELIMITED BY SIZE clause is used in conjunction with the STRING verb, transfer of data from the sending field stops when the number of characters which have been transferred equals the size of the [sending/receiving] field.

sending

4   If an OVERFLOW clause is not used in conjunction with a STRING verb and an overflow condition occurs, then [the STRING operation/program execution] is terminated.

the STRING operation

5   Used in conjunction with the UNSTRING verb, the DELIMITED BY clause specifies the basis used to signal the beginning of a new record in the [sending/receiving] field.

sending

6   The clause that is used if delimiters themselves, such as commas or spaces, are to be transferred to receiving fields during the UNSTRING operation is called the _____ clause.

DELIMITER IN

The INSPECT Statement

At times we need to access and manipulate individual characters in a field. One very common use is to edit input data, such as replacing leading blanks by zeros. COBOL provides the INSPECT verb to accomplish such character manipulations. This verb replaces the EXAMINE verb, which served a similar but more limited purpose in pre-1974 versions of the language.

The INSPECT verb is powerful but a bit complicated. Three formats are available, and these are presented in the format specifications in Appendix C. Discussion of the complete set of options would exceed the intended scope of this text. We present some examples to illustrate the basic options.

EXAMPLE 1: Suppose we wanted to replace all *leading* blanks by leading zeros in a field called TEST. We would write:

INSPECT TEST REPLACING LEADING ' ' BY '0'.

EXAMPLE 2: Suppose we wanted to replace *all* blanks by zeros in a field called TEST. We would write:

INSPECT TEST REPLACING ALL ' ' BY '0'.

EXAMPLE 3: If we wanted to replace the first zero by a +, we would write:

INSPECT TEST REPLACING FIRST '0' BY '+'.

EXAMPLE 4: Suppose we wanted to ask the question: How many dollar signs are in TEST? We would write:

INSPECT TEST TALLYING COUNT-A FOR ALL '$'.

After this instruction is executed, the numeric field COUNT-A will contain a value equal to the number of $ in TEST. (COUNT-A would have been defined in the DATA DIVISION.)

EXAMPLE 5: Suppose we wanted to ask the question: How many zero characters are there to the left of the decimal point and how many zeros are there to the right of the decimal point: We would write:

INSPECT TEST TALLYING COUNT-A FOR ALL '0' BEFORE INITIAL '.'
                       COUNT-B FOR ALL '0' AFTER '.'.

This instruction would result in COUNT-A containing the number of zeros before the decimal point and COUNT-B containing the number of zeros after the decimal point.

EXAMPLE 6: We want to count the number of dollar signs in TEST and replace all dollar signs after the first one by asterisks. We write:

```
INSPECT TEST TALLYING COUNT-A FOR ALL '$'
    REPLACING ALL '$' BY '*' AFTER INITIAL '$'.
```

EXAMPLE 7: We want to ask the question: Assuming that TEST contains a name left-justified, how long is the name? (Unused positions are blank.) We write:

```
INSPECT TEST TALLYING COUNT-A FOR CHARACTERS BEFORE INITIAL
'  '.
```

EXAMPLE 8: An untrained data-entry operator did not depress the numeric key; all numbers have been mistyped. For example, instead of a zero there is a/; instead of a 1 there is a U. To correct the data, we write:

```
INSPECT TEST REPLACING ALL '/' BY '0'
                         'U' BY '1'
                         'I' BY '2'
                          ⋮
                         '.' BY '9'.
```

EXAMPLE 9: An integer field ABC of six positions may have leading blanks and a sign. We want to move the correct numeric value represented in ABC to S-ABC whose PIC is S9(6). We could write:

```
MOVE ZERO TO PLUS-SIGN, MINUS-SIGN
INSPECT ABC
    TALLYING
        PLUS-SIGN FOR ALL '+'
        MINUS-SIGN FOR ALL '−'
    REPLACING
        LEADING SPACES BY ZERO
        FIRST '+' BY ZERO
        FIRST '−' BY ZERO.
```

```
IF ABC IS NOT NUMERIC
    PERFORM INCORRECT-DATA
ELSE
    MOVE ABC TO S-ABC
    IF MINUS-SIGN NOT = ZERO
    MULTIPLY −1 BY S-ABC.
```

We initialize two counters, PLUS-SIGN and MINUS-SIGN, to zero and we use them for TALLYING the occurrence of + and −, respectively. Notice, however, that we are REPLACING . . . FIRST. In the unlikely event that more than one sign is present, the statement IF ABC IS NOT NUMERIC would sense the presence of the unconverted extra sign(s). If the field is unsigned or positive, MOVE ABC to S=ABC is sufficient. If the field is negative, however, then MINUS-SIGN would have a nonzero value and we multiply S-ABC by −1 to attain the proper sign.

EXAMPLE 10: Suppose that we want to convert all uppercase letters to lowercase. We can write:

```
INSPECT TEST REPLACING 'A' BY 'a'
                       'B' BY 'b'
                        •
                        •
                        •
                       'Z' BY 'z'.
```

Alternately, we can use the CONVERTING option to achieve the same result more easily:

```
INSPECT TEST CONVERTING 'ABCDEFGHIJKLMNOPQRSTUVWXYZ'
                     TO 'abcdefghijklmnopqrstuvwxyz'.
```

Review

1   Individual characters in a field can be accessed and possibly changed by use of the _____ verb.

INSPECT

2 Use of the TALLYING option in conjunction with the INSPECT verb makes it possible to _____ designated characters.

count

3 Use of the REPLACING option in conjunction with the INSPECT verb makes it possible to _____ designated characters.

change

4 The option that can be used with the INSPECT verb to change any of the designated group of characters to a corresponding character in another designated group is the _____ option.

CONVERTING

Exercises

5.1 Test the arithmetic precision characteristics of your compiler by incorporating the following computational expressions in a program:

```
ADD A B C GIVING D
SUBTRACT A B C FROM D
COMPUTE D = A * B
COMPUTE D = A / B
COMPUTE D = A * B / C
COMPUTE D = A * (B / C)
COMPUTE D = A ** B / C
COMPUTE D = 100 * (2 / 8)
COMPUTE D = 100 * (2.00 / 8.00)
```

Experiment with different PICTUREs and values for A, B, and C. After each arithmetic statement, print the value of D to observe the result of the arithmetic operations.

5.2 Consider the following record:

```
01  A.
    02  B  PIC X(10).
    02  C  PIC $$$9.99−.
```

```
02   D   PIC X(2).
02   E   PIC Z9.
02   F   PIC X(5).
02   G   PIC 99.
```

Use the INITIALIZE verb to set E and G to zero value and to set the rest of the record to spaces.

5.3   We want to print the following format:

VENDOR-NO. 1234   P.O. NO. A350

Assume that VENDOR-NO and P-O-NO contain the relevant data. Use the STRING verb to position the data in PRINT-REC for printing. Leave blanks where needed and choose how many to leave.

5.4   A free-form NAME-REC contains first name, middle name, and last name separated by either a # or a comma. When no middle name is available there are two successive delimiters to indicate so. If the name is for a woman the # is used, while comma is used for men. Write instructions to store the data in W-FIRST, W-MIDDLE, and W-LAST for women and M-FIRST, M-MIDDLE, and M-LAST for men.

5.5   A field ABC consists of 10 positions and contains numeric integer data with commas. For instance, it might contain data such as the following: 12,345,678. The commas are assumed to be placed correctly. Write instructions to store the numeric value in ABC into NUM without the commas.

6

PROGRAM FLOW CONTROL STATEMENTS

INTRODUCTION

This chapter describes a number of PROCEDURE DIVISION features that give the programmer control over the flow of program execution. The chapter consists of two main sections. The first section, Conditional Statements and Expressions, is devoted to conditional statements and conditional expressions. The second section of the chapter, Program Flow Control, describes the PERFORM, CONTINUE, and EVALUATE statements. The PERFORM and especially the EVALUATE have conditional statement features included in them; however, they are described separately from the conditional statements because their main effects are not the conditions per se, but rather, control of the program flow based on possible conditional determination.

CONDITIONAL STATEMENTS AND EXPRESSIONS

Conditional expressions are either true or false at execution time, and the flow of program execution is controlled accordingly. A conditional expression identifies the conditions that are to be tested. The conditions may be simple or complex. A simple condition is one specific condition such as relation conditions, class conditions, condition-name conditions, sign conditions, and switch-status conditions; and these are explained in the following subsections of this chapter. A complex condition includes multiple simple or multiple complex conditions by use of one or more of the logical operators AND, OR, or NOT, as explained in the later subsection, Complex Conditions.

Conditional expressions are incorporated in conditional statements formed by the use of IF, EVALUATE, PERFORM, and SEARCH. Since the IF statement is the predominant form of conditional statement, we begin our coverage of conditional statements by considering this type of statement in the following subsection.

Review

1   In terms of level of complexity, a conditional expression can be described as being either _____ or _____.

simple; complex

2   In addition to the use of the IF statement, conditional expressions can be incorporated into statements by use of the verbs _____, _____, or _____.

PERFORM; EVALUATE; SEARCH

The IF Statement and Nested Conditions

Figure 6-1 presents the general format for the IF statement. In this format, condition-1 is either a simple or complex conditional expression. Statement-

IF condition-1 THEN $\left\{\begin{array}{l} \{\text{statement-1}\} \quad \ldots \\ \underline{\text{NEXT SENTENCE}} \end{array}\right\}$ $\left\{\begin{array}{l} \underline{\text{ELSE}} \{\text{statement-2}\} \ldots [\underline{\text{END-IF}}] \\ \underline{\text{ELSE NEXT SENTENCE}} \\ \underline{\text{END-IF}} \end{array}\right\}$

FIGURE 6–1   GENERAL FORMAT FOR THE IF STATEMENT.

1 and statement-2 represent either an imperative or a conditional statement optionally preceded by an imperative statement. The ELSE NEXT SENTENCE phrase may be omitted if it immediately precedes the terminal period of the sentence. The END-IF is a scope terminator for the IF statement. If the END-IF is specified, then the ELSE NEXT SENTENCE must not be specified.

When statement-1 and/or statement-2 in the IF statement format are conditional statements, then a nested conditional exists. Figure 6-2 presents a nested conditional in both flowchart and program form and demonstrates the effect on the program code of either not using or using the END-IF scope terminator. In the absence of END-IF, either some program code has to be duplicated, as in Figure 6-2, or a separate paragraph has to be created and referenced by a PERFORM statement in lieu of the explicit duplication of code.

Nested conditions can be quite extensive. Figures 6-3a and 6-3b illustrate an extensively nested condition in both flowchart and program-code form. The brackets inserted on the right side of Figure 6-3b serve to identify the sequence of program code associated with each condition that is tested. Use of the END-IF scope terminator helps to block and identify related units of code in Figure 6-3b. Still, as the levels of nesting are increased, it becomes difficult to follow the logic of the program. Figure 6-4 illustrates a deeply nested structure that would be very difficult to comprehend without a pictorial aid such as a flowchart. But rather than finding aids to cope with such complexity, our objective should be to reduce the complexity and thereby make the program logic more understandable and easier to code. One effective way of reducing program complexity is to decompose a complex structure into simpler but interrelated modules. Figure 6-5 illustrates one possible decomposition of the nested structure in Figure 6-4. Each of the M . . . modules can be referenced by a PERFORM statement. The result is that the amount of program code is reduced, while the dependency in program execution is preserved.

A nested structure can also be used to implement a *case* form of program structure. Figure 6-6 illustrates a case structure implemented as a nested conditional. Prior to the introduction of the EVALUATE statement in the 1985 standard, the case structure typically was implemented in this way. However, use of the EVALUATE statement, described in a subsection later in this chapter, is now a much preferred way of implementing the case structure.

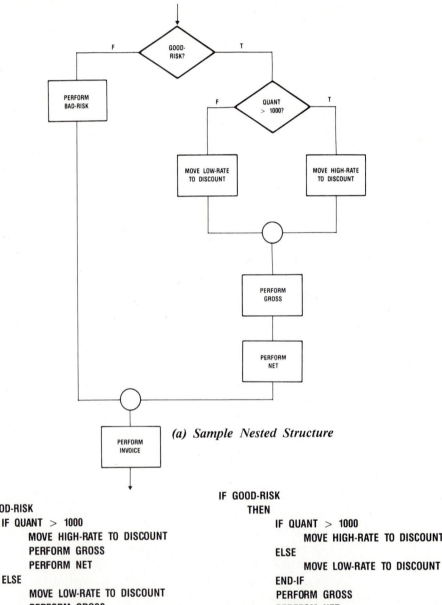

(a) Sample Nested Structure

```
IF GOOD-RISK                                    IF GOOD-RISK
    IF QUANT > 1000                                THEN
        MOVE HIGH-RATE TO DISCOUNT                     IF QUANT > 1000
        PERFORM GROSS                                      MOVE HIGH-RATE TO DISCOUNT
        PERFORM NET                                    ELSE
    ELSE                                                   MOVE LOW-RATE TO DISCOUNT
        MOVE LOW-RATE TO DISCOUNT                      END-IF
        PERFORM GROSS                                  PERFORM GROSS
        PERFORM NET                                    PERFROM NET
ELSE                                               ELSE
        PERFORM BAD-RISK.                              PERFORM BAD-RISK
PERFORM INVOICE.                                END-IF
                                                PERFORM INVOICE.

(b) Without use of END-IF                       (c) With use of END-IF
```

FIGURE 6–2   ILLUSTRATION OF NESTED IF WITH AND WITHOUT END-IF.

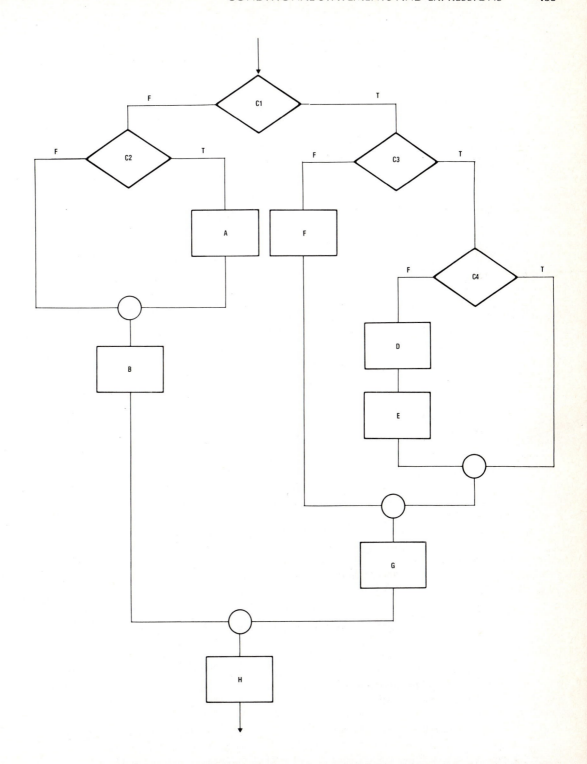

FIGURE 6-3   ILLUSTRATION OF DEEPLY NESTED PROGRAM STRUCTURE.

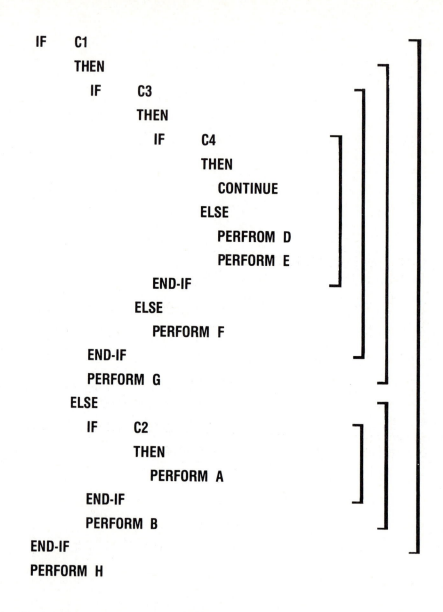

```
IF    C1
      THEN
            IF      C3
                  THEN
                        IF      C4
                              THEN
                                    CONTINUE
                              ELSE
                                    PERFROM D
                                    PERFORM E
                        END-IF
                  ELSE
                        PERFORM F
            END-IF
            PERFORM G
      ELSE
            IF      C2
                  THEN
                        PERFORM A
            END-IF
            PERFORM B
      END-IF
      PERFORM H
```

(b) Coded Representation of Program Logic Using END-IF.

FIGURE 6–3   ILLUSTRATION OF DEEPLY NESTED PROGRAM STRUCTURE.
(Continued)

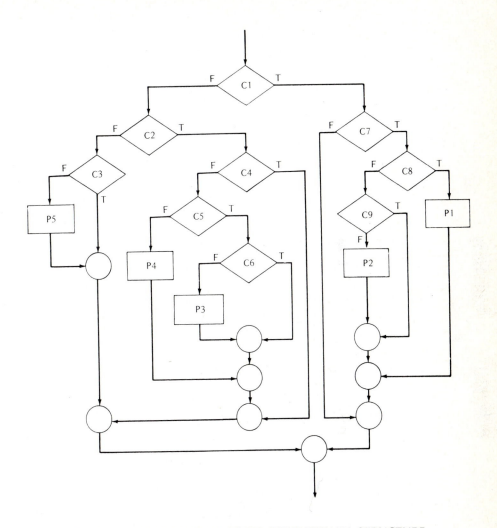

FIGURE 6-4   SAMPLE DEEPLY NESTED CONDITIONAL STRUCTURE.

Review

1   A nested conditional is said to exist when statement-1 and/or statement-2 in the IF statement format are themselves _____ statements.

conditional

2   Related units of code that are associated with an IF statement can be blocked and readily identified with the statement by use of the _____ scope terminator.

END-IF

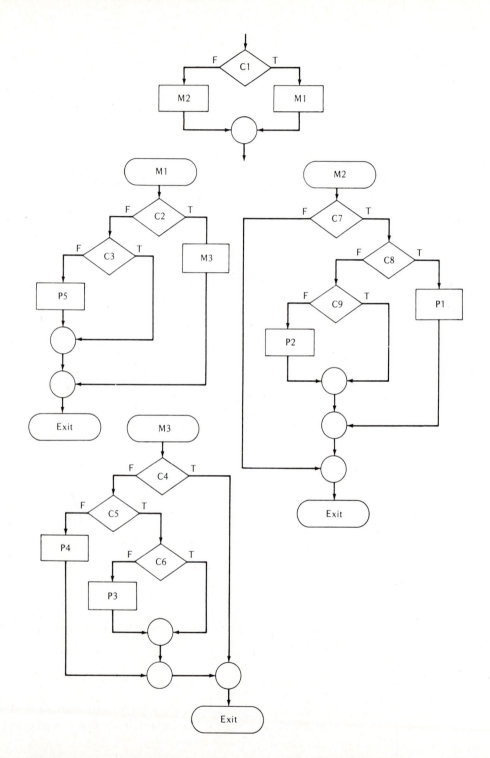

FIGURE 6-5   **DECOMPOSITION OF A DEEPLY NESTED CONDITIONAL STRUCTURE.**

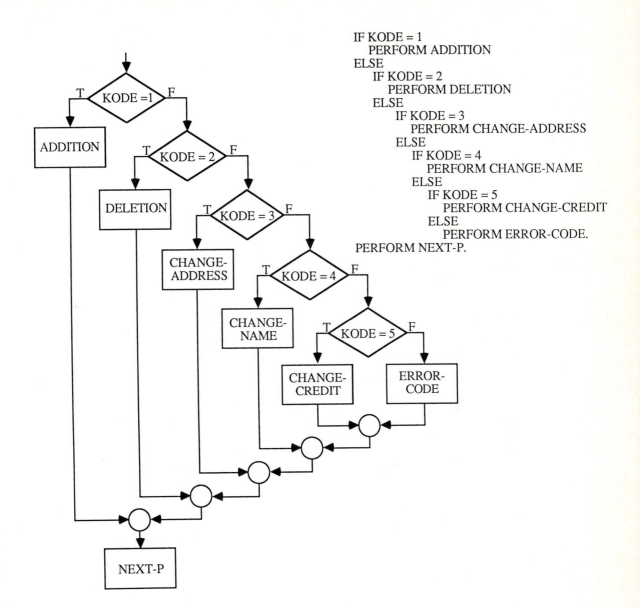

```
IF KODE = 1
   PERFORM ADDITION
ELSE
   IF KODE = 2
      PERFORM DELETION
   ELSE
      IF KODE = 3
         PERFORM CHANGE-ADDRESS
      ELSE
         IF KODE = 4
            PERFORM CHANGE-NAME
         ELSE
            IF KODE = 5
               PERFORM CHANGE-CREDIT
            ELSE
               PERFORM ERROR-CODE.
PERFORM NEXT-P.
```

FIGURE 6-6   SAMPLE NESTED CONDITIONAL STRUCTURE THAT INCLUDES FIVE LEVELS.

3   One way of eliminating deeply nested structures, and thereby reducing program complexity, is to decompose a complex structure into simpler but interrelated _____.

modules

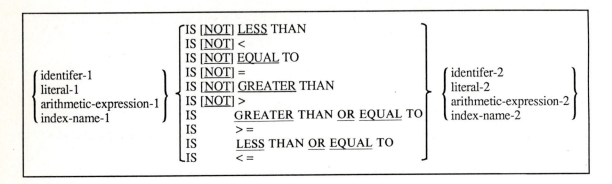

FIGURE 6–7 GENERAL FORMAT FOR RELATION CONDITIONS.

Relation Conditions

Relation conditions are concerned with comparisons between two items. The type of comparison is indicated by the relational operator, which may be in the form of words or symbols. The general format for relation conditions is presented in Figure 6-7. When identifier-1 and identifier-2 are the operands and are both numeric, then the comparison is based on the arithmetic value of their contents. If the identifiers are nonnumeric, then the comparison is based on the collating sequence in effect.

The topic of alphabets and collating sequences was included in Chapter 3. Described there is the means by which a programmer can choose among STANDARD-1, STANDARD-2, NATIVE (explicitly or by default), an implementor-defined choice, or a "custom-made" alphabet defined in the program. Thus, it is possible that in one program A1 is smaller than a1, while in another program the reverse is true. Normally, there is no reason to "tinker" with the standard collating sequence. But we point out the possibility of doing this in case of special circumstances, such as a program that is to be run on different computers with different default collating sequences.

Review

1   Relation conditions are concerned with comparisons between two items. The words or symbols that serve to indicate the type of comparison to be made are called relational _____.

operators

2   When the operands in a relation condition are both numeric, then the comparison is based on the _____ values of their contents.

arithmetic

3 When the operands in a relation condition are nonnumeric, then the comparison is based on the _____ in effect.

collating sequence

4 Relational operators can be in the form of either words or symbols. In the following spaces, enter the symbols that are equivalent to the listed relational operators:

LESS THAN _____   <
EQUAL TO _____   =
GREATER THAN _____   >
LESS THAN OR EQUAL TO _____   <=
GREATER THAN OR EQUAL TO _____   >=

5 Of the following three relation conditions, the one that is invalid as a COBOL expression is the one identified by the letter [a/b/c].

a   IF GROSS-PAY IS GREATER THAN 99 . . .
b   IF 100 < ORDER-AMT . . .
c   IF 500 > 400 . . .

c

Class Conditions

The use of a class condition test makes it possible to determine whether or not an identifier belongs to one of the five classes included in the format for the class condition, as identified in Figure 6-8.

A data field is numeric if it contains only the digits 0-9, with or without an operational sign. Alphabetic items, on the other hand, consist of the letters A-Z and/or blanks. It is not valid to perform a NUMERIC class test on an alphabetic field or an ALPHABETIC class test on a numeric field. Thus, suppose we have the DATA DIVISION specifications on the following page:

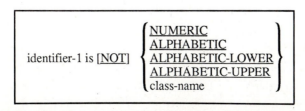

identifier-1 is [NOT] { NUMERIC / ALPHABETIC / ALPHABETIC-LOWER / ALPHABETIC-UPPER / class-name }

FIGURE 6-8   GENERAL FORMAT FOR THE CLASS CONDITION.

AMOUNT   PICTURE 9(4)V99.
NAME   PICTURE A(l5).

It would be improper to write:

IF AMOUNT IS ALPHABETIC . . .   or IF NAME IS NUMERIC . . .

Instead, the AMOUNT field just given can be tested to determine if the content is in fact NUMERIC or if it is NOT NUMERIC. Similarly, the NAME field can be tested only to determine if the content is ALPHABETIC or NOT AL-PHABETIC. A common case of a numeric field not containing numeric data involves reading a field from a record that contains one or more blanks. Specifying the PICTURE with 9s does not guarantee that the field will contain numeric digits. Table 6-1 summarizes the valid uses of the class condition test for different kinds of fields. Note that any of the condition tests may be used with an alphanumeric field.

In general, the class condition test is useful as a check to determine if particular data classes contain the type of data as defined in the DATA DI-VISION: numeric, alphabetic, or alphanumeric. The tests for NUMERIC and ALPHABETIC are straightforward, such as:

IF AMOUNT IS NUMERIC . . .
IF NAME IS NOT ALPHABETIC . . .

In effect, the first statement directly tests the appropriateness of the content in the numeric field called AMOUNT, whereas the second statement tests for inappropriateness of the content in the alphabetic field called NAME. Since an alphanumeric field can have both alphabetic and numeric content, the alphanumeric content can be ascertained indirectly by determining that the content is not entirely numeric and that it is not entirely alphabetic, as follows:

IF   FIELD-A IS NOT NUMERIC
     IF   FIELD-A IS NOT ALPHABETIC
             PERFORM ALPHA-NUM-PAR . . .

TABLE 6-1 VALID USES OF THE CLASS CONDITION TEST FOR DIFFERENT KINDS OF FIELDS

FIELD CLASS	VALID TEST
Numeric	NUMERIC, NOT NUMERIC
Alphabetic	ALPHABETIC, NOT ALPHABETIC
Alphanumeric	NUMERIC, NOT NUMERIC, ALPHABETIC, NOT ALPHABETIC

The class condition test cannot be used with numeric items whose USAGE has been declared COMPUTATIONAL. Thus the usage must be explicitly or implicitly DISPLAY. The COMPUTATIONAL and DISPLAY clauses are discussed in Chapter 4, in the subsection, The USAGE Clause.

The ALPHABETIC-LOWER and ALPHABETIC-UPPER provide a way of testing the content of a nonnumeric field for the presence of lowercase and uppercase alphabetic characters, respectively. Although data fields may contain lowercase letters, however, COBOL programs themselves must be written in uppercase except for the nonnumeric literals. For example, the following statements are valid:

02   NAME-FIELD   PIC X(8)   VALUE 'John Doe.'

MOVE 'incompatible codes' TO ERR-MESSAGE.

The fifth class condition in the general format in Figure 6-8, *class-name*, can be used for a user-defined class. Such a class can be defined in the SPECIAL-NAMES paragraph of the ENVIRONMENT DIVISION, as explained in Chapter 3. The user defines a set of characters, assigns them a class-name, and then can refer to that class-name to test whether it is true or false that a data item consists exclusively of the characters identified in the definition of the class-name. Here is an example:

SPECIAL-NAMES.

   .

   .

   .

   CLASS SPOKEN-NUMERIC
         IS '0' THRU '9'
            'o,' 'O'.   [these are the lowercase and uppercase letter 'o']

In the above example, SPOKEN-NUMERIC is defined as the 10 numeric digits and the letter "o", to allow for the use of "o" as an alternate to zero, such as in "the course number is three-o-two" (perhaps as heard and interpreted by a speech-recognition data-input device). In the PROCEDURE DIVISION we could now write:

IF STREET-NUMBER IS SPOKEN-NUMERIC . . .

The condition is true if STREET-NUMBER contains only the characters in the defined set SPOKEN-NUMERIC.

Review

1   The purpose of a class condition test is to determine if the actual content of a storage field is _____, _____, or _____.

> numeric, alphabetic,
> alphanumeric

2   Suppose that a field named VENDOR has been defined as an alphabetic field in the DATA DIVISION. If we wish to check for the possibility that numeric data have been entered into this field, we could do so by the statement IF VENDOR IS _____.

> NOT ALPHABETIC

3   Suppose that a field named ADDRESS has been defined as an alphanumeric field in the DATA DIVISION. If we wish to ascertain that the content of the field is in fact alphanumeric, we can do so by the statement _____.

> IF ADDRESS IS NOT NUMERIC
> IF ADDRESS IS NOT
> ALPHABETIC

4   The content of a nonnumeric field can be tested for the presence of lowercase and uppercase alphabetic characters by the respective keywords _____ and _____.

> ALPHABETIC-LOWER; ALPHABETIC-UPPER

Condition-Name Conditions

Condition-names are defined in the DATA DIVISION by means of the special 88-level number, as explained in Chapter 4. Although the use of condition-name conditions is quite straightforward, we point out one common practice that leads to possible errors. Numeric values often are used as labels rather than as quantitative measures. Examples are account numbers and transaction codes. Such numeric values should be defined as being alphanumeric, and the associated condition-names should account for all possibilities. Consider the following example of condition-names:

```
02   TRANS-CODE   PIC 9.
     88   ADD RECORD          VALUE 1.
```

```
88   DELETE-RECORD      VALUE 2.
88   CHANGE-RECORD      VALUE 3.
88   ERROR-TRANS-CODE   VALUES ARE ZERO, 4 THRU 9.
```

At first glance, it may appear that the 88-level condition-names defined above constitute an exhaustive set. Now consider the following revision of the definitions:

```
02   TRANS-CODE                              PIC 9.
02   C-TRANS-CODE REDEFINES   TRANS-CODE  PIC X.
     88   ADD-RECORD          VALUE '1'.
     88   DELETE-RECORD       VALUE '2'.
     88   CHANGE-RECORD       VALUE '3'.
     88   ERROR-TRANS-CODE    VALUES ARE
                              LOW-VALUES THRU ZERO,
                              '4' THRU HIGH-VALUES.
```

The REDEFINES in the definition above is used on the assumption that somewhere in the program the transaction code is treated as a numeric value. If this were not the case, then TRANS-CODE could be defined with PICTURE X in the first place. Note that the last 88-level condition-name above includes the entire remaining set of characters, not just the numeric digits. For example, if the transaction code has been mistakenly keyed-in as a space or other nonnumeric value, the error would be detected by the all-inclusive LOW-VALUES THRU ZERO, '4' THRU HIGH-VALUES. Such an error would not be detected by the preceding set of condition-names.

Review

1   Numeric values, such as account numbers, that are used as labels rather than as quantitative values should be defined as being [alphabetic / numeric / alphanumeric].

alphanumeric

2   If a numeric value is used as a label and is defined as being alphanumeric, then the associated condition-names should account for all _____ as well as numeric possibilities.

nonnumeric

Sign Conditions

The sign condition determines whether or not the algebraic value of an identifier or arithmetic expression is greater than, less than, or equal to zero. The general format for the sign condition is:

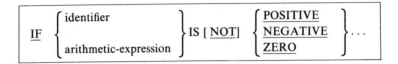

The subject of the condition must be a numeric field or arithmetic expression. If the value contained in the field is greater than zero, it is POSITIVE; if the value is equal to zero, it is ZERO; and if it is less than zero, it is NEGATIVE.

Review

1   The sign condition can be used to test for three specific types of conditions in regard to the content held in a particular field: whether it is positive, _____, or _____.

negative; zero

2   The subject of the sign condition must be a _____ field, or a _____.

numeric;
numeric expression

Switch-Status Conditions

The implementor of a compiler may define certain "switches" and give them associated names. Then such switches can be set as being "on" or "off" at program execution time by the operating system, and the executing program can include a test to determine the status of the switch.

The implementor-name and the ON and OFF values associated with each switch are specified in the SPECIAL-NAMES paragraph of the ENVIRONMENT DIVISION, as explained in Chapter 3, in the section, The SPECIAL-NAMES Paragraph. The following example taken from that section serves to illustrate such a specification:

SPECIAL-NAMES.
UPSI-O   ON STATUS IS END-OF-MONTH
                OFF STATUS IS NOT-END-OF-MONTH.

The example above defines an external switch by the implementor-name UPSI-O. It is to be referenced by the condition-names END-OF-MONTH and NOT-END-OF-MONTH as corresponding to the ON and OFF status, respectively. The switch is set by an action external to the COBOL program, usually through the operating system. The definition could be applied in the following PROCEDURE DIVISION segment:


```
IF END-OF-MONTH
   THEN PERFORM CLOSE-THE-BOOKS
   ELSE PERFORM DAILY-PROCESSING
END-IF
```


In essence, the above program segment says: If the external switch called UPSI-O is ON at the time of program execution, do one thing; if it is OFF, do another thing. The program can then "sense" the operating environment at the time of program execution and take the appropriate action.

Review

1   As indicated by its name, the purpose of a switch-status conditional is to determine if a switch is in an _____ or _____ condition.

ON; OFF

2   The implementor-names and the ON and OFF values associated with each such switch are specified in the _____ paragraph of the ENVIRONMENT DIVISION.

SPECIAL-NAMES

Complex Conditions

A complex condition is formed by combining simple and/or complex conditions with the logical connectors AND, OR, or NOT. OR means either *or* both, while AND means both. Thus, consider the following statement:

IF BALANCE IS NEGATIVE AND DAYS-OVERDUE > 10
   PERFORM PAR-A.

The instruction indicates that the program should execute PAR-A when both the balance is negative and the number of overdue days exceeds 10.
   On the other hand, consider the following statement:

IF INPUT-DATA IS NOT NUMERIC OR NAME-IS-MISSING
   MOVE 'CANT PROCESS, INCORRECT DATA' TO MESSAGE.

The program will move the indicated message to MESSAGE if either the input data are not numeric (perhaps because of a keying error) or the condition-name condition defined as NAME-IS-MISSING in the DATA DIVISION holds.
   Parentheses can be used to clarify the meaning of a complex condition. For example, we can write:

IF (AGE IS GREATER THAN 28) OR ((EXPERIENCE = 4)
   AND (EDUCATION IS GREATER THAN HS)) . . .

This condition holds either if age is greater than 28 or if both experience = 4 and education is greater than high school (HS). As another example, consider the following:

IF (KODE = 2) OR (KODE = 3) AND (BALANCE-CODE = 1)
   MOVE SPACES TO ERROR-MESSAGE
   PERFORM OLD-ITEM-2.

In this example, the condition is true if KODE is equal to 2 or 3 and BALANCE-CODE is equal to 1.
   In the absence of parentheses, the order of precedence is NOT, AND, and OR. Thus,

IF A > B OR NOT C = 10 AND D < K

is equivalent to:

IF A > B OR ((NOT C = 10) AND D < K)

With reference to the examples above, it is obvious that omission of parentheses may result in unnecessary greater effort to understand a complex conditional expression.

A complex condition can also be abbreviated by omitting the subject of the relation condition or by omitting both the subject and the relational operator in any relational condition except the first. The format for the abbreviated combined relation condition is:

relation-condition $\left\{\begin{Bmatrix} \underline{\text{AND}} \\ \underline{\text{OR}} \end{Bmatrix} \text{[NOT] [relational operator] object} \right\} \dots$

Presented below are some relational examples in both expanded and abbreviated form:

Expanded
(A NOT = B) OR (A NOT = C)

Abbreviated
A NOT = B OR C

Expanded
((A > B) and (A NOT < C)) OR (A NOT < D)

Abbreviated
A > B AND NOT < C OR D

Expanded
(NOT (A = B)) OR (A = C)

Abbreviated
NOT A = B OR C

Expanded
NOT ((((A NOT > B) AND (A NOT > C)) AND (NOT (A NOT > D))))

Abbreviated
NOT (A NOT > B AND C AND NOT D)

Brevity of expression may or may not be desirable, depending on the conditional expression. For instance, in the last example above, the multiple parentheses in the expanded version are more confusing than they are helpful, and the abbreviated version is easier to understand. In the immediately preceding example, however, the expanded version is less likely to be misinterpreted than is the abbreviated version.

Review

1   In contrast to the use of simple conditionals, a combination of tests can be included in one statement by the use of _____ conditionals.

complex

2   The use of a complex conditional requires the use of one of the logical operators: _____, _____, or _____.

OR; NOT; AND

3   When the logical operator OR is used in a complex conditional test, the presence of [either / both / either or both] of the conditional states constitutes a true condition.

either or both

4   When the logical operator AND is used in a complex conditional test, the presence of [either / both / either or both] of the conditional states constitutes a true condition.

both

5   Generally, the abbreviated form of a complex conditional requires [more / fewer] parentheses and is [easier / more difficult] to interpret in terms of meaning.

fewer; easier

Verb-Related Conditions

There are several verbs in COBOL that contain "built-in" conditionals. These are summarized in Table 6-2, along with the verb or verbs with which each of these conditionals is associated. The designers of COBOL chose to use

TABLE 6-2 SPECIALIZED CONDITIONALS RELATED TO COBOL VERBS

CONDITIONAL	RELATED VERB
[NOT] AT END	READ
[NOT] AT { END-OF-PAGE / EOP }	WRITE
[NOT] INVALID KEY	DELETE, READ, REWRITE, START, WRITE
[NOT] ON EXCEPTION	CALL
[NOT] ON OVERFLOW	STRING, UNSTRING
[NOT] ON SIZE ERROR	ADD, COMPUTE, DIVIDE, MULTIPLY, SUBTRACT

such specialized conditionals to serve as special purpose "if" statements, in contrast with the general purpose IF.

Review

1   [NOT] ON OVERFLOW and [NOT] ON SIZE ERROR are examples of _____-related conditionals.

verb

2   In its effect, a verb-related conditional serves as a special "_____" statement.

if

PROGRAM FLOW CONTROL

The following subsections describe four types of statements that can be used to control the flow of program logic: PERFORM, EVALUATE, CONTINUE, AND EXIT. Other flow-controlling statements, such as STOP RUN, EXIT PROGRAM, and GO TO, are described elsewhere in this book. In brief, the STOP RUN terminates program execution, while the EXIT PROGRAM terminates subprogram execution. The GO TO transfers control to the specified procedure-name, which can be a paragraph or a section. Finally, there are two implicit control-directing clauses embedded in the SORT and MERGE statement: INPUT PROCEDURE and OUTPUT PROCEDURE. In terms of their effect, these are alternate forms of the out-of-line PERFORM statement.

The PERFORM Statement

Figure 6-9 presents two formats for the PERFORM statement, one associated with use of the UNTIL option and one associated with use of the TIMES option. In each case there is an out-of-line and an in-line alternative. Whereas out-of-line PERFORM statements reference separate procedure-names, there is no such reference in the in-line PERFORM statements. Instead, it is as if we said, "PERFORM the statements that follow."

As a simple illustration of using the in-line PERFORM, consider the following program segment:

```
PERFORM
    MOVE   NAME-IN TO NAME-OUT
    MOVE   ACCOUNT-NO TO ACCOUNT-NO-OUT
    ADD    AMOUNT-IN TO TOTAL
    WRITE REPORT-LINE
END-PERFORM
```

Notice the absence of a procedure-name after the word PERFORM in the above program code.

As another illustration, consider the following code:

```
IF N > ZERO
    THEN MOVE ZERO TO SUM-OF-DIGITS
        MOVE 1 TO YEAR-COUNTER
        PERFORM UNTIL YEAR-COUNTER > N
            ADD YEAR-COUNTER TO SUM-OF-DIGITS
            ADD 1 TO YEAR-COUNTER
        END-PERFORM
        PERFORM DEPRECIATION
    ELSE
        MOVE 'INVALID N' TO ERR-MESSAGE
END-IF.
```

In the illustration above, the END-PERFORM delimits the scope of the first PERFORM so that DEPRECIATION is executed after the in-line iterative procedure has been completed. The same procedure could be coded as follows using the TIMES option:

```
IF N > ZERO
    THEN
        MOVE ZERO TO SUM-OF-DIGITS
        MOVE 1 TO YEAR-COUNTER
```

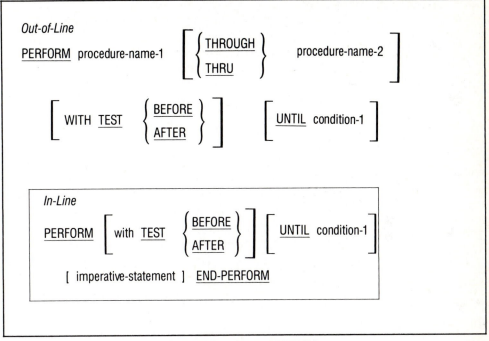

(a) UNTIL Option PERFORM

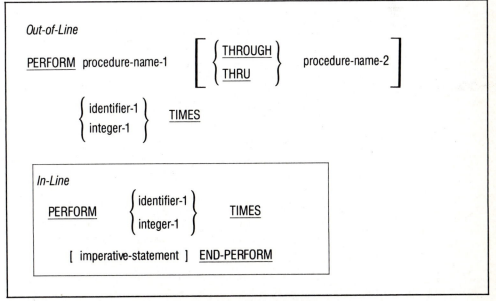

(b) TIMES Option PERFORM

FIGURE 6–9   IN-LINE AND OUT-OF-LINE PERFORM FORMATS.

```
        PERFORM N TIMES
            ADD YEAR-COUNTER TO SUM-OF-DIGITS
            ADD 1 TO YEAR-COUNTER
        END-PERFORM
        PERFORM DEPRECIATION
      ELSE
        MOVE 'INVALID N' TO ERR-MESSAGE
END-IF.
```

The TEST option allows for greater control over the repeated execution of a procedure. If we want to do a procedure and then determine if it should be done again, we use the WITH TEST AFTER option. If we want to determine if a procedure should be done beforehand, then we can either use the TEST BEFORE option or omit the TEST option altogether. Figure 6–10 presents a flowchart and an example of each of the two TEST options available in the PERFORM . . . UNTIL statement.

Review

1   Of the two formats of the PERFORM statement, one is associated with use of the _____ option and one is associated with use of the _____ option.

UNTIL; TIMES

2   The type of PERFORM statement that references separate procedure-names, in lieu of the statements that follow, is the _____ PERFORM statement.

out-of-line

3   The type of PERFORM statement that signifies that the statements that follow should be executed is the _____ PERFORM statement.

in-line

The EVALUATE Statement

The new EVALUATE statement provides a powerful and convenient way of implementing the "case" structure in structured programming. Use of the EVALUATE statement eliminates the need to use complicated nested IF statements and allows the programmer to express conditional logic in a

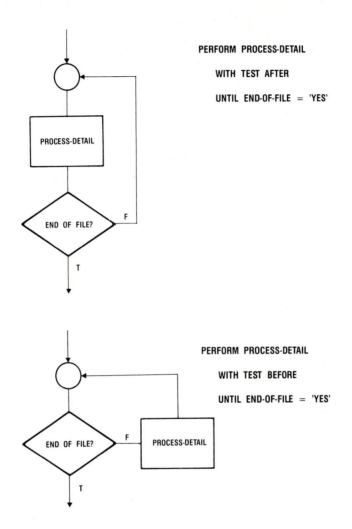

PERFORM PROCESS-DETAIL

WITH TEST AFTER

UNTIL END-OF-FILE = 'YES'

PERFORM PROCESS-DETAIL

WITH TEST BEFORE

UNTIL END-OF-FILE = 'YES'

FIGURE 6–10   PERFORM . . . UNTIL WITH USE OF TEST OPTION.

well-documented manner. The general format of the statement is presented in Figure 6-11.

As the general format indicates, there are many options available in using the EVALUATE statement, hence its power and flexibility. Let us begin by considering the following simple example:

```
EVALUATE TRANSACTION-CODE
    WHEN 1        PERFORM P-A
    WHEN 2        PERFORM P-B
    WHEN 3        PERFORM P-C
    WHEN OTHER PERFORM P-D.
```

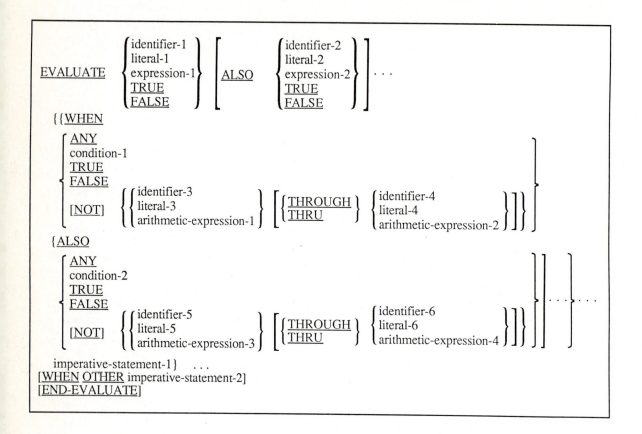

FIGURE 6–11   FORMAT OF THE EVALUATE STATEMENT.

The above statement says to "evaluate" TRANSACTION-CODE and if it is equal to 1 to PERFORM P-A, if it is equal to 2 to PERFORM P-B, and so on. If TRANSACTION-CODE is not 1, 2, or 3, then it is to PERFORM P-D. TRANS-ACTION-CODE is the evaluation *subject,* and as we shall explain below, multiple evaluation subjects may be included in an EVALUATE statement. The literals 1, 2, and 3 and the keyword OTHER that follow each WHEN in the above example are the evaluation *objects.* Again, as explained below, there may be a single object or multiple objects associated with each WHEN.

Execution of an EVALUATE statement involves evaluating each subject with respect to each corresponding object for each of the WHEN statements. Evaluation means substituting each subject and each object with one of the following:

TRUE or FALSE   (a) if these very keywords are written as a subject or object
                     (b) if the subject/object is a condition

A value (numeric or alphanumeric)	(a) if the subject/object is a literal or an identifier
	(b) if the subject/object is an arithmetic expression
A range of values (numeric or alphanumeric)	if the object is written with the THROUGH or THRU option

The evaluation subject(s) and the corresponding object(s) are compared for each WHEN statement. If they match, then the imperative statement that follows the WHEN is executed. If no such statement immediately follows the WHEN, then the next encountered imperative statement associated with a subsequent WHEN is the one executed, as will be illustrated later in this section in Figure 6-16.

We now illustrate the uses of the EVALUATE command by a series of sample applications.

Figure 6-12 presents a sample case structure that is implemented in Figure 6-13 by use of an EVALUATE statement. Figure 6-14 represents the EVALUATE statement in flowchart form in order to focus on the chronological order of execution of the commands. Finally, Figure 6-15 presents an

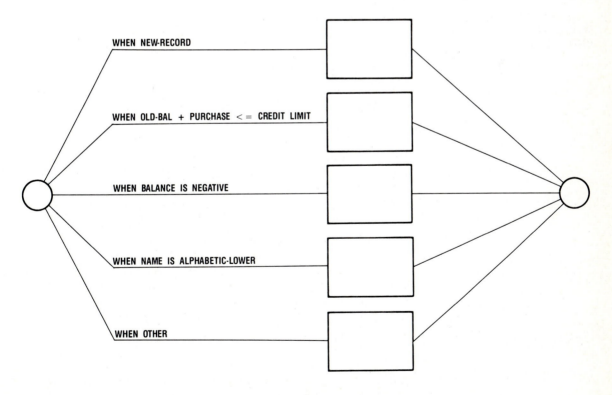

FIGURE 6-12   SAMPLE CASE STRUCTURE.

EVALUATE TRUE	The evaluation subject is "true".
WHEN NEW-RECORD	NEW-RECORD is a condition-name and is the first evaluation object. If the condition NEW-RECORD is true then P-1 is executed and A is MOVED to B and program control continues with execution of P-6.
PERFORM P-1	
MOVE A TO B	
WHEN OLD-BAL + PURCHASE $<=$ CREDIT-LIMIT	The second evaluation object is a relational condition. If it is true, then P-2 is executed and program control continues with execution of P-6.
PERFORM P-2	
WHEN BALANCE IS NEGATIVE	
PERFORM P-3	
IF X $>$ Y	
THEN	The third evaluation object is a sign condition. If it is true, P-3 is executed, followed by the conditional statement and then program control continues with execution of P-6.
MOVE P TO Q	
ELSE	
MOVE R TO Q	
END-IF	
WHEN NAME IS ALPHABETIC-LOWER	The fourth evaluation object is a class condition. If it is true then P-4 is executed and program control continues with P-6.
PERFORM P-4	
WHEN OTHER	If none of the above four evaluation objects were TRUE, then P-5 is executed and program control continues with P-6.
PERFORM P-5	
END-EVALUATE	
PERFORM P-6	

FIGURE 6-13　SAMPLE EVALUATE STATEMENT.

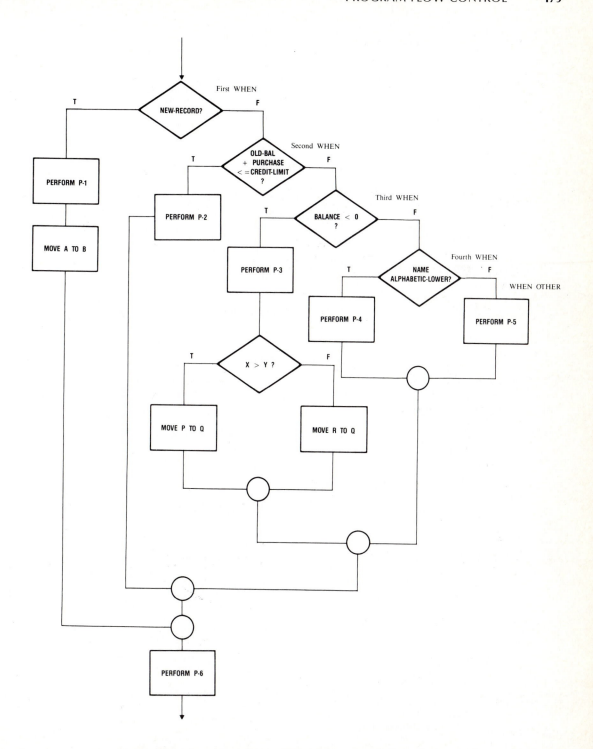

FIGURE 6–14   FLOWCHART REPRESENTATION OF SAMPLE EVALUATE STATEMENT.

```
IF NEW-RECORD
    THEN
        PERFORM P-1
        MOVE A TO B
    ELSE
        IF OLD-BAL + PURCHASE < = CREDIT-LIMIT
            THEN
                PERFORM P-2
            ELSE
                IF BALANCE IS NEGATIVE
                    THEN
                        PERFORM P-3
                        IF X > Y
                            THEN
                                MOVE P TO Q
                            ELSE
                                MOVE R TO Q
                        END-IF
                    ELSE
                        IF NAME IS ALPHABETIC-LOWER
                            THEN
                                PERFORM P-4
                            ELSE
                                PERFORM P-5
                        END-IF
                END-IF
        END-IF
END-IF
PERFORM P-6.
```

FIGURE 6–15   NESTED IF ALTERNATIVE TO SAMPLE EVALUATE STATEMENT.

equivalent nested IF coding of the same logic, so that this approach can be contrasted with the EVALUATE code in Figure 6-13.

Figure 6-16 illustrates use of the EVALUATE statement with multiple subjects and objects. There are three evaluation subjects: TRUE, TRUE, and FALSE; therefore, each WHEN (except a WHEN OTHER) must have three evaluation objects, although some may include the null ANY, which satisfies any comparison. Notice that the third and fourth WHEN "share" the PER-FORM P-C imperative statement. If either of these two WHEN statements is satisfied, P-C is executed.

Figure 6-17 illustrates the incorporation of the EVALUATE verb in a conditional statement and omission of the optional WHEN OTHER clause.

As the final example of using the EVALUATE statement, Figure 6-18 presents a decision table that shows two fields, YEAR-CODE and LETTER-GRADE. There are four actions specified depending on the joint values of the two fields. For instance, when YEAR-CODE has a value of 4, then the procedure called PROC-3 is executed regardless of the value of LETTER-GRADE. Figure 6-18 also includes an EVALUATE statement to implement the decision table. For example, the first WHEN clause is interpreted as follows:

If the value of YEAR-CODE is 1 thru 2 and the value of LETTER-GRADE is A thru C, then PERFORM PROC-1.

The ANY option in the third WHEN in Figure 6-18 specifies that any value of LETTER-GRADE fulfills the evaluation criterion for this WHEN conditional. Finally, the WHEN OTHER refers to both the YEAR-CODE and LETTER-CODE; it is equivalent to saying:

Any other combination of values of YEAR-CODE and LETTER-GRADE other than the ones specified in the previous WHEN statements.

EVALUATE	TRUE	ALSO	TRUE	ALSO	FALSE
WHEN	ACCOUNTANT PERFORM P-A	ALSO	EXPERIENCED	ALSO	WILLING-TO-TRAVEL
WHEN	ACCOUNTANT PERFORM P-B	ALSO	INEXPERIENCED	ALSO	WANTS-TO-STAY-PUT
WHEN	COMPUTER-SCIENTIST	ALSO	ANY	ALSO	UNDERPAID
WHEN	SYSTEMS-ANALYST PERFORM P-C	ALSO	EXPERIENCED	ALSO	ANY
WHEN	EXPERIENCED PERFORM P-D	ALSO	ANY	ALSO	ANY

FIGURE 6–16   ADDITIONAL SAMPLE EVALUATE ILLUSTRATION.

```
IF  A = B
    THEN
        EVALUATE    TRUE            ALSO  BALANCE  ALSO  BALANCE + (PRICE * QUANTITY) < CREDIT-LIMIT
            WHEN    EXCELLENT              ALSO              ANY              ALSO              ANY
                    PERFORM  P-1
            WHEN    AVERAGE           ALSO  LOW-BAL  THRU  MEDIUM-BAL         ALSO              ANY
                    PERFORM  P-2
            WHEN    MARGINAL          ALSO  LOW-BAL  THRU  HIGH-BAL           ALSO              TRUE
                    PERFORM  P-3
            WHEN    DAYS-SINCE-LAST-PMT < LATE-LIMIT  ALSO  ANY              ALSO              TRUE
                    PERFORM  P-4
        END-EVALUATE
    ELSE
        PERFORM  P-A
END-IF
```

FIGURE 6–17   SAMPLE EVALUATE AS PART OF A CONDITIONAL STATEMENT.

Review

1   A powerful and convenient way of implementing the "case" structure is provided by the _____ statement.

EVALUATE

2   For each of the WHEN statements, execution of an EVALUATE verb involves evaluating each _____ with respect to its corresponding _____.

subject; object

The CONTINUE statement

The CONTINUE verb is used to indicate that no executable statement is present. It may be used anywhere that a conditional statement or an imperative statement may be used. Its most likely use is in the null branch of a conditional statement. The example on the bottom of the following page includes two instances of such use:

CONDITION		ACTION
YEAR-CODE	**LETTER-GRADE**	
1 or 2	A, B, or C	execute PROC-1
3	A or B	execute PROC-2
4	any	execute PROC-3
any other	any	execute PROC-4

```
EVALUATE        YEAR-CODE       ALSO      LETTER-GRADE

    WHEN 1 THRU 2               ALSO      'A' THRU 'C' PERFORM PROC-1

    WHEN 3                      ALSO      'A' THRU 'B' PERFORM PROC-2

    WHEN 4                      ALSO      ANY          PERFORM PROC-3

    WHEN OTHER PERFORM PROC-4

END-EVALUATE
```

FIGURE 6–18   SAMPLE USE OF THE EVALUATE VERB.

```
IF C1
   THEN
      IF C2
         THEN
            PERFORM P-1
         ELSE
            CONTINUE
      END-IF
   ELSE
      IF C3
         THEN
            CONTINUE
         ELSE
            PERFORM P-2
      END IF
END-IF.
```

As the example shows, use of the CONTINUE option allows the programmer to preserve the symmetry of the If-Then-Else structure. As an alternative, we could have used the NEXT SENTENCE instead of the CONTINUE.

Another convenient use of CONTINUE is to form "do-nothing" paragraphs marking the end of a section or the last paragraph in a PERFORM procedure-1 THRU procedure-n series of paragraphs.

Review

1   The verb that can be used to indicate that no executable statement is present is the _____ verb.

CONTINUE

The EXIT Statement

In terms of its lack of effect, the EXIT statement is similar to the newer (1985) CONTINUE statement, but it is designed for use as the only statement in a paragraph. Similar to the CONTINUE, the EXIT is a "no op" (no operation) statement; it has no operational effect because of its presence. But unlike the CONTINUE, the EXIT statement provides documentation as to the end of a multiparagraph procedure, such as a section of the program.

Consider the following example:

```
      PERFORM ABCD
         .
         .
         .
ABCD SECTION.
P1.
      PERFORM XYZ
      PERFORM PDQ
         .
         .
         .
      GO TO ABCD-END.
XYZ.    . . .
      .
      .
      .
PDQ.    . . .
```

.

.

.

ABCD-END.
    EXIT.
VWZ SECTION.

In the above example we PERFORM a section named ABCD. As always, the section begins with its name and the section-header keyword SECTION and ends when another section begins. When the section is the last section of the program, it ends at the physical end of the program. In the sample program outline above, P1 contains the summary logic of the ABCD section. When P1 is completed, the section is completed. Yet there is no COBOL statement that in effect says, "Exit this section now." The only way to exit the section is to reach its *physical* end. For this purpose, the GO TO ABCD-END statement was included to reference the null paragraph that was created to contain the EXIT verb. After the ABCD-END paragraph is executed, program control returns immediately after the PERFORM ABCD statement.

    It would appear that the EXIT verb is suspect of mismatching name and function. It would make a lot of sense if EXIT did what is implied by its name and, in fact, provide an exit. But its effect is to do nothing. As in the example, its use is recommended only for its documentation value. But it is very important to understand that any other statement could have been included in the ABCD-END paragraph with the same program-flow effect. For instance, suppose a field named TEMP with PIC X had been defined and we wrote:

ABCD-END.
    MOVE SPACE TO TEMP.

Assuming that MOVE SPACE TO TEMP serves no purpose in the logic of the task, the program flow would be exactly the same as in the example using the EXIT verb.

    Avoiding use of the EXIT verb is not easy. In the program outline above you could suggest placing paragraphs XYZ and PDQ outside of the ABCD section so that the end of P1 would be the end of ABCD. However, if the logic of P1 is such that under certain conditions execution of the section should be terminated, then we may be forced to use a deeply nested or extensively partitioned structure in the attempt to avoid use of EXIT.

    As a final comment, the use of EXIT as illustrated in the example almost always requires use of the GO TO. Such use is harmless from the standpoint of complicating the program logic, however, because it is contained within a one-entry one-exit procedure, which is the ABCD SECTION in the example.

Review

1   The verb that can provide documentation as to the end of a multiparagraph procedure but that has no operational effect is the _____ verb.

EXIT

2   Unlike the similar CONTINUE verb, the EXIT verb can be used [only once / many times] in a given paragraph.

only once

SAMPLE PROGRAM: USING CONDITIONALS TO CHECK INPUT DATA

The well-known GIGO (Garbage In, Garbage Out) acronym summarizes effectively the importance of accurate input data. Before data can be processed, they must be checked for correctness and completeness. Errors creep into source data for a variety of reasons, but are due mainly to human error. A good data processing system accepts reasonable error rates in input data as a fact of life and screens the data through so-called edit programs. Such programs use conditional expressions that check input data to determine that they are complete and that they are valid or at least reasonable. Errors that are detected are listed for manual correction and resubmission.

Figure 6-19 presents a simplified program that checks employee records that contain payroll data. Sample input and output are shown in Figure 6-20. As the program illustrates, it is a good practice to list the record that contains the error and to check for all possibilities. If there is one error, the chances are that there may be several errors, and we should identify all of them the first time through. An error message is printed for each error that is detected. It is worth noting that the PAY-RATE field is checked for reasonableness by comparing it to maximum and minimum values, but such a test is meaningful only if the PAY-CODE is correct (either salaried or hourly).

Review

1   A good data processing system is based on the assumption that there will be [no / some] errors in input data.

some

```
 IDENTIFICATION DIVISION.
 PROGRAM-ID.  DATAEDIT.
*
 ENVIRONMENT DIVISION.
*
 CONFIGURATION SECTION.
 SOURCE-COMPUTER.  ABC-480.
 OBJECT-COMPUTER.  ABC-480.
*
 INPUT-OUTPUT SECTION.
*
 FILE-CONTROL.
*
     SELECT EMPLOYEE-FILE ASSIGN TO  File Device.
     SELECT PRINT-FILE    ASSIGN TO  Printer.
*
 DATA DIVISION.
*
 FILE SECTION.
*
 FD   EMPLOYEE-FILE       LABEL RECORDS ARE OMITTED
                          RECORD CONTAINS 27 CHARACTERS
                          DATA RECORD IS EMPLOYEE-RECORD.
 01   EMPLOYEE-RECORD.
      02 EMPL-NAME             PIC X(15).
      02 EMPL-NO               PIC 9(4).
      02 PAY-CODE              PIC X.
         88   SALARIED         VALUE 'S'.
         88   HOURLY           VALUE 'H'.
         88   VALID-PAY-CODE   VALUE 'H', 'S'.
         88   ERROR-PAY-CODE   VALUES ARE LOW-VALUES THRU 'G'
                                      'I' THRU 'R'
                                      'T' THRU HIGH-VALUES.
      02 PAY-RATE              PIC 9(4)V99.
      02                       PIC X.
*
 FD   PRINT-FILE          LABEL RECORDS ARE OMITTED
                          RECORD CONTAINS 80
                          DATA RECORD IS PRINT-RECORD.
*
 01   PRINT-RECORD        PIC X(80).
*
 WORKING-STORAGE SECTION.
*
 01   END-OF-FILE-INDICATOR  PIC XXX VALUE 'NO '.
      88 END-OF-FILE          VALUE 'YES'.
*
 01   RECORD-PRINT-SWITCH           PIC 9.
      88 RECORD-HAS-BEEN-PRINTED        VALUE 1.
      88 RECORD-HAS-NOT-BEEN-PRINTED VALUE ZERO.
```

FIGURE 6-19   LISTING OF THE PROGRAM TO CHECK INPUT DATA.

```
01    PAY-LIMITS.
      02 MINIMUM-SALARY        PIC 9(4)V99 VALUE   600.00.
      02 MAXIMUM-SALARY        PIC 9(4)V99 VALUE 6800.00.
      02 MINIMUM-WAGE          PIC 9(4)V99 VALUE     3.50.
      02 MAXIMUM-WAGE          PIC 9(4)V99 VALUE    18.99.
*
01    ERROR-MESSAGE-RECORD.
      02 FILLER                PIC X(20) VALUE SPACES.
      02 ERROR-MESSAGE         PIC X(50).
*
01    INPUT-RECORD-OUT.
      02 FILLER                PIC X(5) VALUE SPACES.
      02 INPUT-RECORD          PIC X(27).
*
01    HEADING-1.
      02 FILLER                  PIC X(30) VALUE SPACES.
      02 FILLER PIC X(24) VALUE 'INPUT DATA ERROR LISTING'.
*
01    HEADING-2.
      02 FILLER                PIC X(27) VALUE SPACES.
      02 FILLER                PIC X(36) VALUE
       '(RECORD PRECEDES ITS ERROR MESSAGES)'.

PROCEDURE DIVISION.
*
PROGRAM-SUMMARY.
*
    OPEN INPUT    EMPLOYEE-FILE
         OUTPUT   PRINT-FILE
*
    WRITE PRINT-RECORD FROM HEADING-1 AFTER PAGE
    WRITE PRINT-RECORD FROM HEADING-2 AFTER 1
*
    PERFORM WITH TEST AFTER
            UNTIL END-OF-FILE
*
       READ EMPLOYEE-FILE RECORD
            AT END
                 SET END-OF-FILE TO TRUE
            NOT AT END
                 SET RECORD-HAS-NOT-BEEN-PRINTED TO TRUE
                 PERFORM ERROR-CHECKING
       END-READ
*
    END-PERFORM
*
    CLOSE EMPLOYEE-FILE,   PRINT-FILE
*
    STOP RUN.
```

FIGURE 6-19   LISTING OF THE PROGRAM TO CHECK INPUT DATA.
(Continued)

```
   ERROR-CHECKING.
*
     IF EMPL-NAME = SPACES
        MOVE 'EMPLOYEE NAME IS MISSING' TO ERROR-MESSAGE
        PERFORM ERROR-PRINT.
*
     IF EMPL-NO NOT NUMERIC
        MOVE 'EMPLOYEE NUMBER CONTAINS NON-NUMERIC CHARACTERS'
            TO ERROR-MESSAGE
        PERFORM ERROR-PRINT.
*
     IF (NOT SALARIED) AND (NOT HOURLY)
        MOVE 'PAY CODE IS NEITHER S NOR H' TO ERROR-MESSAGE
        PERFORM ERROR-PRINT.
*
     IF PAY-RATE NOT NUMERIC
        MOVE 'PAY RATE CONTAINS NON-NUMERIC CHARACTERS'
            TO ERROR-MESSAGE
        PERFORM ERROR-PRINT.
*
     IF VALID-PAY-CODE
        THEN
          IF SALARIED AND (PAY-RATE < MINIMUM-SALARY)
                      OR  (PAY-RATE > MAXIMUM-SALARY)
            THEN
              MOVE 'UNREASONABLE PAY RATE FOR SALARIED EMPLOYEE'
                  TO ERROR-MESSAGE
            PERFORM ERROR-PRINT
          ELSE
            IF HOURLY AND (PAY-RATE < MINIMUM-WAGE)
                      OR  (PAY-RATE > MAXIMUM-WAGE)
              THEN
              MOVE 'UNREASONABLE PAY RATE FOR HOURLY EMPLOYEE'
                  TO ERROR-MESSAGE
                PERFORM ERROR-PRINT
            END-IF
          END-IF
     END-IF.
*
   ERROR-PRINT.
*
     IF RECORD-HAS-BEEN-PRINTED
        NEXT SENTENCE
     ELSE
        SET RECORD-HAS-BEEN-PRINTED TO TRUE
        MOVE EMPLOYEE-RECORD TO INPUT-RECORD
        WRITE PRINT-RECORD FROM INPUT-RECORD-OUT AFTER 2.
*
     WRITE PRINT-RECORD FROM ERROR-MESSAGE-RECORD AFTER 1.
```

FIGURE 6-19   LISTING OF THE PROGRAM TO CHECK INPUT DATA.
(Continued)

```
INPUT

BROWN,R.K.        12345156035
DAVIS,M.O.         5246H250603
GARCIA,L.A.       3345H000676
HARRISON,P.N      21005000700
MARTIN,A.C.       5123512000
MARTINEZ,P.M.     44335800000
PETERSON,R.A.     6161H0001256



OUTPUT

                      INPUT DATA ERROR LISTING
                (RECORD PRECEDES ITS ERROR MESSAGES)


BROWN,R.K.        12345156035
                  PAY CODE IS NEITHER S NOR H

DAVIS,M.O.         5246H250603
                  EMPLOYEE NUMBER CONTAINS NON-NUMERIC CHARACTERS
                  PAY CODE IS NEITHER S NOR H
                  PAY RATE CONTAINS NON-NUMERIC CHARACTERS

HARRISON,P.N      21005000700
                  PAY CODE IS NEITHER S NOR H

MARTIN,A.C.       5123512000
                  PAY CODE IS NEITHER S NOR H
                  PAY RATE CONTAINS NON-NUMERIC CHARACTERS

MARTINEZ,P.M.     44335800000
                  PAY CODE IS NEITHER S NOR H

PETERSON,R.A.     6161H0001256
                  UNREASONABLE PAY RATE FOR HOURLY EMPLOYEE
```

FIGURE 6-20   SAMPLE INPUT AND OUTPUT FOR THE PROGRAM TO CHECK INPUT DATA.

2   The purpose of a typical edit program is to test for the [accuracy / reasonableness] of input data.

reasonableness

3   For each apparent error detected by use of an edit program, it is good practice to [list only the item in error / list the entire record that contains an error].

list the entire record that contains
an error

Exercises

6.1   Write PROCEDURE DIVISION statements to implement the logic included in the following (unstructured) flowchart:

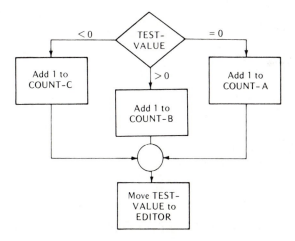

6.2   An input field has been defined as:

03   IN-FIELD   PICTURE X(10).

Two other fields in WORKING-STORAGE have been defined as:

01   AMOUNT   PICTURE 9(10).
01   NAME   PICTURE A(10).

We wish to test the content of IN-FIELD and, if it contains a number, to store it in AMOUNT; if it contains a name, to store it in NAME; and if a mixture of characters, to execute a paragraph called ERRORS.

a   Write PROCEDURE DIVISION statements to accomplish this task.

b   Suppose that, if the IN-FIELD contains a number, it is actually in dollars and cents. What would you do to make the number available in dollars and cents instead of as an integer? (*Hint:* Be careful!)

6.3   Using the 88-level number indicator in the DATA DIVISION and suitable condition-name clauses, the following obvious identifiers have been defined.

MALE
FEMALE
SINGLE-M
MARRIED-M
DIVORCED-M
WIDOWED-M
SINGLE-F
MARRIED-F
DIVORCED-F
WIDOWED-F

Assume we want to tabulate the number of individuals falling in the last eight classes, as, for example, the number of single males (SINGLE-M). We thus want to test the field containing the identifying code and ADD 1 TO the corresponding counter. Assume the following fields are to be used as counters: SM, MM, DM, WM, SF, MF, DF, WF (where SM stands for single males etc.).

a   Draw a flowchart corresponding to your program logic.

b   Write *one* nested conditional expression to accomplish the required testing and tabulating.

6.4   Consider the following DATA DIVISION entries relating to a personnel record:

```
02   EDUCATION                              PICTURE 99.
      88   H-S GRAD              VALUE 12.
      88   COLLEGE-GRAD          VALUE 16.
      88   MASTERS-GRAD          VALUE 17.
      88   DOCTORATE-GRAD        VALUE 20.
02   YEARS-OF-EXPERIENCE                    PICTURE 99.
```

```
02  SEX                                           PICTURE 9.
    88  MALE                      VALUE 1.
    88  FEMALE                    VALUE 2.
02  GEOGRAPHIC-PREFERENCE                         PICTURE 9.
    88  EAST                      VALUE 1.
    88  MIDWEST                   VALUE 2.
    88  WEST                      VALUE 3.
    88  SOUTH                     VALUE 4.
    88  WILLING-TO-TRAVEL         VALUE 5.
```

Suppose that we want to find individuals who fulfill one of these three requirements:

a   Five years of experience, male, high school graduate, willing to travel

b   Male, one year of experience, master's degree, preferring the West or South

c   Three years of experience, female, doctorate, preferring the East

Write *one* compound conditional sentence by which we can check whether a record in question fulfills the first, second, or third of these requirements. If one of these requirements is met, we WRITE PRINT-LINE FROM NAME. If the requirement is not met, we execute PAR-A.

6.5   Consider the following table of conditions:

QUANTITY	PRICE	RATING	DISCOUNT
>100	>10	<2	0.05
>100	>10	≥2	0.10
>100	≤10	<2	0.15
>100	≤10	≥2	0.20
≤100	$\begin{cases} < \\ =10 \\ > \end{cases}$	$\begin{cases} < \\ =2 \\ > \end{cases}$	0.25

a   Write instructions—using nested IF—to MOVE to DISCOUNT the value shown depending on the conditions.

b   Using the EVALUATE statement, write instructions to MOVE to DISCOUNT the value shown depending on the conditions.

c   Draw a structured flowchart corresponding to the data in the table.

6.6   Draw in flowchart from the following, where C1 stands for condition 1 and F1 stands for function (statement) 1.

```
IF   C1 AND (C2 OR C3)
       F1
       F2
ELSE
       IF C3 OR (C6 AND C7)
          F3
       ELSE
          NEXT SENTENCE
```

6.7   Write PROCEDURE DIVISION statements corresponding to the flowchart in Figure 6-21. Assume that each function block is a paragraph to be PERFORMed; for example, your first statement would be PERFORM CLEAR-ACCUMULATORS.

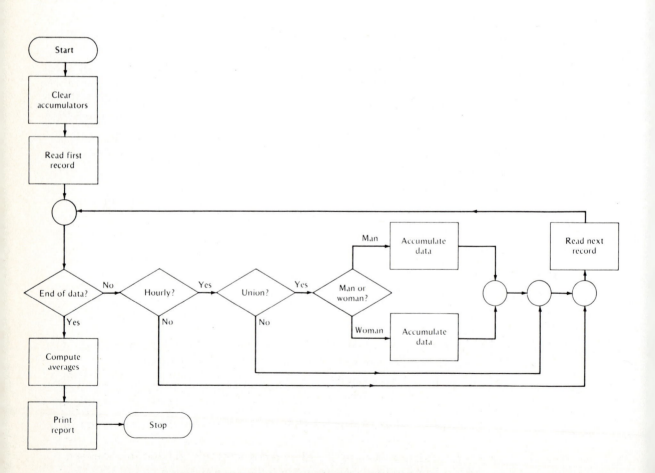

FIGURE 6–21   FLOWCHART FOR EXERCISE 6.7.

7

TABLE HANDLING

TABLE DEFINITIONS IN COBOL

A table, like a file, is a collection of logically related entries. Examples are tax rates for different municipalities in a metropolitan area, commission rates for different product classes, and income tax rates for different levels of income and numbers of dependents. Such data are normally short enough to be placed in central storage and thus constitute a table. Table handling is fundamental to data processing. COBOL recognizes this fact and includes specialized instructions for table definition and manipulation.

A table is simply a set of values stored in consecutive storage locations and assigned one data-name. Reference to specific entries in the table is made by the use of one name along with a subscript that identifies the location of the particular entry. Entries in a one-dimensional table are numbered sequentially 1, 2, 3, . . . , on to the last. Thus, in an example of the average household income for the 50 states, imagine that we have a table of 50 entries. If the entries are arranged alphabetically and we wish to reference the average income for Arizona, the subscript will have a value of 3. Similarly, the subscripts for Washington and Wyoming will be 49 and 50, respectively. Use of the OCCURS clause in conjunction with the PICTURE clause enables the programmer to set up tables so that reference can be made to entire tables or individual values in tables by means of subscripts. A DATA DIVISION entry involving an OCCURS clause includes the following: the data-name assigned to the table, the number of dimensions (up to seven), the number of entries in each dimension, and the field characteristics of the entries.

A one-dimensional table may be defined as it is identified in the example below, for a table to contain the average household income for each of the 50 states:

```
01   STATE-INCOME-TABLE.
     02   AVERAGE-INCOME OCCURS 50 TIMES       PICTURE 9(6)V99.
```

The OCCURS 50 TIMES clause sets up a table in storage that has the following conceptual structure:

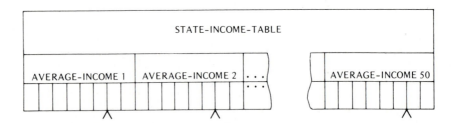

Execution of the PROCEDURE DIVISION statement MOVE STATE-INCOME-TABLE . . . will result in the entire table of 50 fields being moved. In order to move (or otherwise process) a single field of entry in the table, the subscript is included in parentheses and separated from the name by a space, as follows: MOVE AVERAGE-INCOME (12) TO. . . . This statement, of course, refers to the twelfth table entry. The subscript may be a variable instead of a constant, but it always must be an integer (whole number).

The OCCURS clause need not be used alone in a record; other reference entries may be included as well. For example, the record might have been structured as in the format shown in the following material:

01 STATE-INCOME-TABLE.
    02   AVERAGE-INCOME OCCURS 50 TIMES   PICTURE 9(6)V99.
    02   NATIONAL-AVERAGE   PICTURE 9(6)V99.

Notice, however, that STATE-INCOME-TABLE now refers to more than the table of 50 entries. If we want to make specific reference to the table of 50 entries, we will have to write something like this:

01 STATE-INCOME-TABLE.
    02   AV-TABLE.
        03   AVERAGE-INCOME OCCURS 50 TIMES   PICTURE 9(6)V99.
    02   NATIONAL-AVERAGE   PICTURE 9(6)V99.

As a further illustration of a one-dimensional table, assume that we want to include the names of the states along with their corresponding average income figures:

01 STATE-INCOME-TABLE.
    02   NAME-INCOME OCCURS 50 TIMES.
        03   NAME   PICTURE X(12).
        03   INCOME   PICTURE 9(6)V99.

The OCCURS 50 TIMES clause sets up a table in storage that has the following structure:

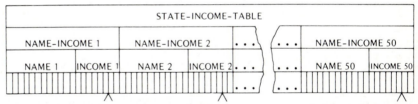

If we write NAME (1), we are referring to a storage field of 12 positions, whereas INCOME (1) refers to an 8-position field. If we write NAME-INCOME (1), we are referring to a storage field of 20 positions. Finally, STATE-INCOME-TABLE refers to the entire table of 100 fields.

Two-dimensional tables require two subscripts to locate an individual entry or field. For an example of a two-dimensional table, assume that a particular state has three state universities and we desire to set up a table that will contain the enrollment figures for each university according to class standing: freshman, sophomore, junior, senior, and graduate. Conceptually, the following type of table is required:

	ENROLLMENT BY UNIVERSITY		
YEAR	1	2	3
FR SO JR SR GR			

In order to set up the required storage locations, the following DATA DIVISION entries can be written:

```
01   ENROLLMENT-TABLE.
      02   UNIV-ENROL   OCCURS 3 TIMES.
            03   YEAR-ENROL   OCCURS 5 TIMES.
                  04   ENROLLMENT   PIC 9(5).
```

Compilation of these DATA DIVISION statements results in the following conceptual storage layout:

ENROLLMENT-TABLE					
UNIVERSITY 1					UNIVERSITY 2 . . .
YEAR 1	YEAR 2	YEAR 3	YEAR 4	YEAR 5	. . .
					. . .

Thus, for each of the three universities there are five fields, corresponding to the five class-standing classifications. Notice that the level number of YEAR-ENROL is lower (03) than that of UNIV-ENROL (02). If the level number of YEAR-ENROL were the same as that of UNIV-ENROL, then the table would not be two-dimensional. To illustrate the use of the table, consider the following examples.

UNIV-ENROL (3) refers to all five fields associated with the third university.

ENROLLMENT (2, 4) refers to the senior (4) enrollment in the second (2) university. ENROLLMENT always must be used with double subscripts. The first subscript refers to the superior hierarchical level (in this case, UNIV-ENROL, and the second subscript refers to the specific entry in the YEAR-ENROL table.

ENROLLMENT (5, 2) is incorrect, since only three values have been defined for UNIV-ENROL. However, ENROLLMENT (2, 5) is correct and identifies the graduate student enrollment in the second university.

YEAR-ENROL and ENROLLMENT can be used interchangeably, since YEAR-ENROL is a group item consisting of only the one subordinate, ENROLLMENT. As a general rule, we recommend using each OCCURS clause with a name that signifies the nature of the dimension involved, which in this example is enrollment by year. The name of each elementary item should signify the nature of the data in the table, while the subscript names identify the dimensions involved. For example, ENROLLMENT (UNIV, YEAR) makes it clear that we are referencing ENROLLMENT data for a given UNIVersity for a given YEAR. Similarly, UNIV-ENROL (UNIV) conveys the meaning that we are referencing a (group) item pertaining to enrollment data for a given UNIVersity.

Subscripts are enclosed in parentheses, and there must be as many subscripts as there are dimensions corresponding to the subscripted item. Subscripts must be integer literals or integer variables. In the 1985 standard it is also permissible to perform arithmetic operations within the subscript references, as in the following examples:

MOVE A (I) TO A (I + 1)
ADD AMOUNT TO B (I, J + 1)
IF C (I, J − K) = C (I + 1, J − K)

In the examples above, notice that the plus or minus symbol can be used to increase or decrease the value of a given subscript.

Notice that, even though we have defined a two-dimensional table (YEAR-ENROL), we also have defined a one-dimensional table (UNIV-ENROL) and one field (ENROLLMENT-TABLE). This again exemplifies the power of COBOL to reference with great flexibility data at different hierarchical levels.

It is worthwhile to consider the process by which the compiler transforms the two-subscript reference scheme into the one-dimensional reference scheme utilized in central storage. Let r and c represent the maximum number of entries in a two-dimensional table of the following definition:

02   A   OCCURS r TIMES
     03   B   OCCURS c TIMES . . .
          04   T PIC X(1).

A two-subscript reference such as B(I, J) can be transformed into a one-dimensional reference by the formula B (I, J) = [(I − 1) × c] + J, which computes the displacement from the beginning of the table. Thus, if r = 4 and c = 5, T(3, 4) = [(3 − 1) × 5] + 4 = 14, meaning that T(3, 4) is the fourteenth element in the table. We can see this by thinking of the table as consisting of four groups of five values each. Since T(3, 4) refers to the fourth value in the third group, and each of the first two groups has five values each, we are referring to the fourteenth value (5 + 5 + 4).

If the PICTURE of T in the above example had been X(6), then a reference such as T(3, 4) refers to the field that starts at byte 79 from the beginning of the table. Since each of the 5 fields at the B level consists of 6 bytes, it follows that each of the A fields is 5 × 6 = 30 bytes long. Therefore, the first two occurrences of A take up 2 × 5 × 6 = 60 bytes, and the first three occurrences of B take up 3 × 6 = 18 bytes, leaving us with the conclusion that T(3, 4) is a 6-byte field that starts at the 60 + 18 + 1 = 79th byte of the table storage. In general terms, the beginning byte of T(I, J) is computed as:

$$[(I - 1) \times c \times p] + [(J - 1) \times p] + 1$$

where p = the field size of the elementary item, as defined by the PICTURE clause; c is the number in the OCCURS c TIMES; and I and J are the subscript references.

The compilation process stores the beginning address of a table and the c and p values; then during execution of the program, a double-subscript reference is transformed into a storage address by a formula such as the one given above.

The foregoing discussion has two important implications. First, we can observe what happens when we use improper subscripts. If we used OCCURS clauses that defined a 3 × 4 table and then used subscripts (4, 3), we would be referencing a place in storage that was past the table content. In such a case we might get unpredictable results, depending on what happened to be stored at that address and what operation we were executing. Because COBOL compilers (unlike BASIC compilers, for instance) generally do not check for out-of-bounds subscript references, it is particularly important that such errors be avoided. When debugging a table-handling program, it is a good idea to display the subscript value(s) first and then the subscripted reference. For instance, suppose a program abends (*abnormally ends*) on the following statement:

COMPUTE TOTAL = PRICE (I) * QUANT (I)

We could trace the subscript values as follows:

DISPLAY I
DISPLAY PRICE (I)   QUANT (I)
COMPUTE TOTAL = PRICE (I) * QUANT (I).

The inadvertent use of illegal subscript values often is subtle and not immediately obvious, as in the following illustration:

02   A OCCURS 20 TIMES   PIC 9

PERFORM XYZ VARYING I BY 1
                UNTIL A (I) = ZERO
                OR I > 20
XYZ.
   CONTINUE.

If there is no zero value in any of the 20 occurrences of A, when I = 21 the A (I) = ZERO test makes reference to an illegal address. To avoid the error, the test should have been written in the order:

. . . UNTIL I > 20 OR A (I) = ZERO.

A second implication of the concept that subscripts are transformed into storage addresses is the fact that the decoding of subscripts requires computations. Of course, the number of computations that is required increases substantially with each additional table dimension. While the computations may not be highly time consuming, it is still advisable in programs involving extensive computations to use several tables with a small number of dimensions, for example, rather than one table with a large number of dimensions.

In the 1974 standard, tables of up to only three dimensions were allowed. In contrast, in the 1985 standard, up to seven dimensions are allowed. As an example of defining a table with more than three dimensions, the following statements define a table with four dimensions:

01   FOUR-LEVEL-TABLE-EXAMPLE.
     02   STATE-DATA OCCURS 50 TIMES.
        03   YEAR-DATA OCCURS 10 TIMES.
           04   MAJOR-DATA OCCURS 100 TIMES.
              05   GRADE-DATA OCCURS 5 TIMES.
                 06   STUD-GRADE PICTURE X.

The following rules serve to summarize the requirements associated with the use of subscripted tables:

1   The OCCURS clause cannot apply to the 01 level. In other words, there cannot be a table of "records." However, this is a language rule and in no way prevents us from assigning a "record" to the 02 level and defining an 01 level name above it, as shown in the following example:

```
01   STATE-INCOME-TABLE.
     02   AVERAGE-INCOME OCCURS 50 TIMES   PICTURE 9(6)V99.
```

2   The OCCURS clause cannot be used with level-77 items.

3   Subscripted tables may have up to seven dimensions.

4   The PICTURE clause applies to the elementary items only. Notice, for instance, the example of the four-dimensional table that was given previously.

5   Only one PICTURE description can be given for all like entries in a table, but there may be several entries that are not alike. The latter is exemplified by the example given earlier and reproduced here:

```
01   STATE-INCOME-TABLE.
     02   NAME-INCOME OCCURS 50 TIMES.
          03   NAME      PICTURE X(12).
          03   INCOME   PICTURE 9(6)V99.
```

The same PICTURE clause applies to all 50 NAME fields above. Thus, OCCURS is used for homogeneous sets of data.

6   The subscripts may be integer constants, or they may be integer variables. Their values must be positive. They must not be zero or negative.

7   The subscript or subscripts are enclosed in one set of parentheses and are separated from the table-name by a space. Multiple subscripts are separated from each other by *commas* and *spaces*. Examples are:

```
A-TABLE (1)
A-TABLE (IDEN)
B-TABLE (3, COUNT)
C-TABLE (GRADE, 3, YEAR)
SEX-ENROL (UNIVERSITY, YEAR, SEX-CODE)
```

Review

1   The programmer can set up tables by using the _____ clause in the DATA DIVISION.

OCCURS

2   The OCCURS clause indicates the number of _____ in the table.

entries

3   Suppose a STATE-POPULATION-TABLE is to include the population figures for all 50 states in alphabetical order. Complete the description below by writing the appropriate OCCURS clause. Assume that the PICTURE for POPULATION is 9(8):

```
01  STATE-POPULATION TABLE.
    02  STATE-DATA _____
        03  POPULATION _____
```

OCCURS 50 TIMES

PICTURE 9(8).

4   Suppose that both the state names and the population figures are read in and we wish to set up a STATE-POPULATION-TABLE such that the 50 state names are located first in the table, followed by the 50 population figures. Complete the following description, assuming that the PICTURE for NAME is X(12).

```
01  STATE-POPULATION-TABLE.
    02  NAME _____
    02  STATE-DATA _____
        03  POPULATION _____
```

OCCURS 50 TIMES
PICTURE X(12).

OCCURS 50 TIMES

PICTURE 9(8).

5   The PICTURE clause is used only at the [highest / lowest] hierarchical level of a table.

lowest

6   The integer subscripts used in conjunction with subscripted variables [may/may not] be constants and [may/may not] be variables.

may; may

7   A subscript used in conjunction with subscripted variables [may/may not] be zero and [may / may not] have a negative value.

may not; may not

8   In contrast to the 1974 standard, in which tables of up to only three dimensions were all allowed, the 1985 standard allows tables of up to _____ _____ dimensions.

seven

AN EXAMPLE OF A TABLE OF CONSTANT VALUES

It often is desirable to build tables that contain specified constant values. One way to accomplish this objective is to define the table by using the OCCURS clause in the DATA DIVISION and then, through suitable PROCEDURE DIVISION instructions, to read in the desired values. There is yet another way of initializing a table with constant values; as the following example illustrates, the joint use of the OCCURS and REDEFINES clauses accomplishes this task.

Suppose that we want to have a table that contains the names of the 12 months of the year, so that we can reference these names by use of the table name and a subscript. For instance, we may want to reference the fifth month or the twelfth month, and so on. Using numeric values to reference the months is desirable, because arithmetic can be performed with numeric values. For instance, if we are on the sixth month and we want to reference the next month, we can simply add 1 to 6 and then make reference to the resulting month. The following example illustrates the common way of accomplishing this task:

```
01   MONTH-TABLE.
       02   FILLER      PICTURE X(9)   VALUE 'JANUARY   '.
       02   FILLER      PICTURE X(9)   VALUE 'FEBRUARY '.
       02   FILLER      PICTURE X(9)   VALUE 'MARCH     '.
       02   FILLER      PICTURE X(9)   VALUE 'APRIL     '.
       02   FILLER      PICTURE X(9)   VALUE 'MAY       '.
       02   FILLER      PICTURE X(9)   VALUE 'JUNE      '.
       02   FILLER      PICTURE X(9)   VALUE 'JULY      '.
       02   FILLER      PICTURE X(9)   VALUE 'AUGUST    '.
       02   FILLER      PICTURE X(9)   VALUE 'SEPTEMBER'.
       02   FILLER      PICTURE X(9)   VALUE 'OCTOBER   '.
       02   FILLER      PICTURE X(9)   VALUE 'NOVEMBER '.
       02   FILLER      PICTURE X(9)   VALUE 'DECEMBER '.
01   MONTHS REDEFINES MONTH-TABLE.
       02   MONTH       PICTURE X(9) OCCURS 12 TIMES.
```

Notice that the record MONTH-TABLE consists of 12 fields. The VALUE clause is used to assign the constant (nonnumeric literal) values. The record called MONTHS is a table consisting of 12 entries. Each entry is referenced by the use of MONTH and a subscript. Thus, executing the instruction MOVE MONTH (3) TO PRINTAREA WRITE PRINTAREA results in the word MARCH being printed.

The procedure may seem unnecessarily roundabout. Let us justify the rationale. The VALUE clause cannot be used with the OCCURS clause because the VALUE clause references *one* value and the OCCURS clause refers to several values. Thus, we use the REDEFINES clause with the OCCURS clause, after we have described each individual field. Of course, all entries in MONTH-TABLE must be of equal field size for the procedure to accomplish the correct result.

USE OF THE VALUE CLAUSE

Unlike the 1974 version of COBOL, the 1985 version permits the use of the combination of the OCCURS and VALUE clauses in order to enter the same constant into all positions in a table. For example, we can write:

```
01   SAMPLE-TABLE.
       02   TABLE-CELL   OCCURS 100 TIMES
                         PIC 9(5)V99 VALUE ZERO.
```

When the above program segment is compiled, each of the 100 fields in the table is set equal to zero.

Review

1 Use of the VALUE clause in conjunction with the OCCURS clause results in [variable values / a constant] being entered in all positions in a table.

a constant

THE OCCURS ... DEPENDING ON OPTION

Sometimes the number of entries in a table varies. The number of entries may be given by the value of a data-name. In such cases we may want to use the DEPENDING ON option of the OCCURS clause. We illustrate the use of variable records with the OCCURS and DEPENDING ON clauses.

A bank has a file containing transactions of checking account customers. Some customers have a greater number of transactions than others; that is, they write more checks or make more deposits. It seems natural that records should be variable. Let us assume the following record layout:

FIELD	NUMBER OF POSITIONS
Customer number	6
Number of transactions	3
Transaction code	1
Date	5
Amount	7
Transaction code	1
Date	5
Amount	7
(etc. for up to 100 transactions)	

This is a case where a record may contain from 0 to 100 transactions. Notice that the minimum number of character positions is 9: 6 for the customer number and 3 for the number of transactions. The maximum size is 9 + (100 transactions × 13 characters per transaction) = 1,309. We then can have the following file description, assuming blocks of three records each:

```
FD  TRANS-FILE   LABEL RECORD STANDARD
                 BLOCK CONTAINS 3 RECORDS
                 RECORD CONTAINS 9 TO 1309 CHARACTERS
                 DATA RECORD IS CHECKING-ACCOUNT-RECORD.
01  CHECKING-ACCOUNT-RECORD.
    02  CUSTOMER-NUMBER              PICTURE 9(6).
    02  NUMBER-OF-TRANSACTIONS       PICTURE 999.
    02  TRANSACTION OCCURS 0 TO 100 TIMES
                 DEPENDING ON NUMBER-OF-TRANSACTIONS.
        03  TRANSACTION-CODE         PICTURE 9.
        03  TRANSACTION-DATE         PICTURE 9(5).
        03  TRANSACTION-AMOUNT       PICTURE 9(5)V99.
```

It should be pointed out that NUMBER-OF-TRANSACTIONS does not auto-matically contain the number of transactions. It is the responsibility of the program logic to store the proper data in the data-name of the DEPENDING ON clause.

The general form of the DEPENDING ON option is

> . . . <u>OCCURS</u> integer-1 <u>TO</u> integer-2 TIMES <u>DEPENDING</u> ON data-name.

The programmer must take care that the DEPENDING ON field is up-dated before a reference is made to a subscripted entry in a record such as the above. For example, if NUMBER-OF-TRANSACTIONS has a value of 20 and we write MOVE ZERO TO TRANSACTION-AMOUNT (I) where I has a value greater than 20, the results will be erroneous. Since NUMBER-OF-TRANSACTIONS is 20, the operating system generally allocates only enough space to the record to store 20 occurrences. To avoid such errors, something like the following should be written:

MOVE I TO NUMBER-OF-TRANSACTIONS
MOVE ZERO TO TRANSACTION-AMOUNT (I).

In other words, we must first update the DEPENDING ON field to a higher value and then make a subscripted reference that is not greater than the value of that field.

As another illustration, suppose that NUMBER-OF-TRANSACTIONS is equal to 20 and we write:

MOVE CHECKING-ACCOUNT-RECORD TO WORKING-STORAGE-RECORD.

The effective move is for $9 + (13 \times 20) = 269$ bytes. In other words, at execu-tion time the system checks the value of the DEPENDING ON field to deter-mine the effective size of the record at that time.

Review

1   The OCCURS . . . DEPENDING ON option can be used when the num-ber of entries to be included in a table is [predetermined / variable].

variable

2   When the DEPENDING ON option is used, the word OCCURS in the program statement always is followed by a specified [value / range of

values], and the phrase DEPENDING ON always is followed by a [data-name / specified value].

range of values; data-name

THE PERFORM VERB AND TABLE HANDLING

Table handling operations often involve iterative references to subscripted entries, and the PERFORM . . . VARYING statement is particularly well suited for such operations. Figure 7–1 presents the general format for this statement.

As an example of using the PERFORM . . . VARYING statement, consider the following:

```
PERFORM READER
    VARYING TERRITORY FROM 1 BY 1
        UNTIL TERRITORY > 5
    AFTER QUARTER FROM 1 BY 1
        UNTIL QUARTER > 4.
    .
    .
    .

READER.
    READ SALES-FILE
        AT END MOVE 'YES' TO END-OF-FILE-SWITCH.
    IF NOT END-OF-FILE
        MOVE SALES-VALUE
            TO QUARTER-SALES (TERRITORY, QUARTER).
```

FIGURE 7–1   **FORMAT OF THE PERFORM . . . VARYING STATEMENT.**

Notice that TERRITORY is varied *after* varying QUARTER. Thus, the sequence of values contained in these two fields is:

TERRITORY	QUARTER
1	1
1	2
1	3
1	4
2	1
2	2
2	3
2	4
.	.
.	.
.	.
5	1
5	2
5	3
5	4

The paragraph called READER will be executed 20 times, as QUARTER and TERRITORY are varied through their specified ranges. Each time the READER paragraph is executed, the pair of values of the subscripts is unique, so that we store each input value in a new QUARTER-SALES cell of the table.

Now consider the following four-dimensional table that was also included in the preceding section of this chapter:

```
01   FOUR-LEVEL-TABLE-EXAMPLE.
     02   STATE-DATA OCCURS 50 TIMES.
          03   YEAR-DATA OCCURS 10 TIMES.
               04   MAJOR-DATA OCCURS 100 TIMES.
                    05   GRADE-DATA OCCURS 5 TIMES.
                         06   STUD-GRADE   PICTURE X.
```

As another example, suppose that we are interested in tabulating five categories of grades (A, B, C, D, F) into the following one-dimensional table:

```
01   GRADE-SUMMARY-TABLE.
     02   SUMMARY-GRADE OCCURS 5 TIMES   PIC 9(5).
```

The following program code will achieve the above objective:

```
MOVE ZEROS TO GRADE-SUMMARY-TABLE
PERFORM TABULATE-GRADES
```

```
VARYING STATE FROM 1 BY 1
            UNTIL STATE > 50
AFTER YEAR FROM 1 BY 1
            UNTIL YEAR > 10
AFTER MAJOR FROM 1 BY 1
            UNTIL MAJOR > 100
AFTER GRADE FROM 1 BY 1
            UNTIL GRADE > 5.
TABULATE-GRADES.
    EVALUATE STUD-GRADE (STATE, YEAR, MAJOR, GRADE)
    WHEN 'A' ADD 1 TO SUMMARY-GRADE (1)
    WHEN 'B' ADD 1 TO SUMMARY-GRADE (2)
    WHEN 'C' ADD 1 TO SUMMARY-GRADE (3)
    WHEN 'D' ADD 1 TO SUMMARY-GRADE (4)
    WHEN 'F' ADD 1 TO SUMMARY-GRADE (5).
```

In the general format in Figure 7-1, when procedure-name-1 is speci-fied in the 1985 standard, then the imperative-statement-1 and the END-PERFORM are omitted. Conversely, when procedure-name-1 is omitted, then imperative-statement-1 must be present and the AFTER phrase must not be used. As an example of a case in which procedure-name-1 is omitted, we could have:

```
PERFORM VARYING I FROM 1 BY 1
        UNTIL I > 10
    ADD SALES (I) TO TOTAL-SALES
    IF SALES (I) > 0
        ADD 1 TO NON-ZERO-COUNT
    ELSE
        ADD 1 TO ZERO-COUNT
    END-IF
END-PERFORM.
```

In the program segment above, we form the sum of the first 10 values in SALES and we count the number of SALES values as nonzero and as zero, re-spectively. In this example "imperative-statement-1" consists of the ADD and the IF statements, illustrating the fact that "imperative-statement-1" can consist of multiple statements and can include conditional statements as long as they are delimited by an explicit scope terminator (in our example, the END-IF).

Figures 7-2 and 7-3 are flowcharts that illustrate the effects of using WITH TEST BEFORE and WITH TEST AFTER, respectively. As can be ob-served, with TEST BEFORE, the specified statements may not be executed even once if the conditions are true. On the other hand, the TEST AFTER

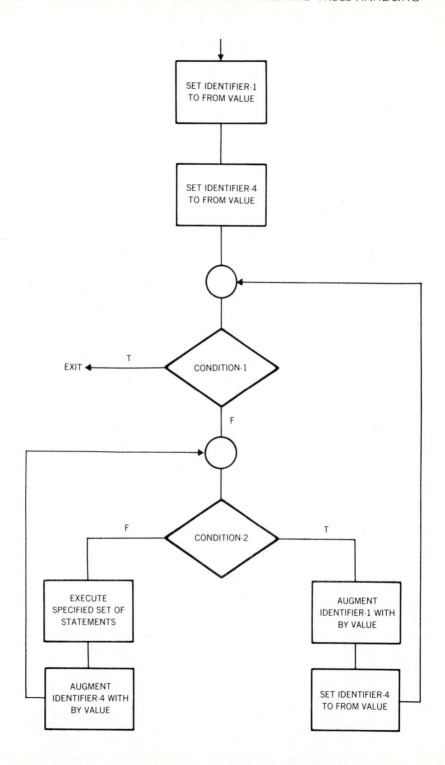

FIGURE 7-2   THE PERFORM . . . VARYING OPTION WITH TEST BEFORE.

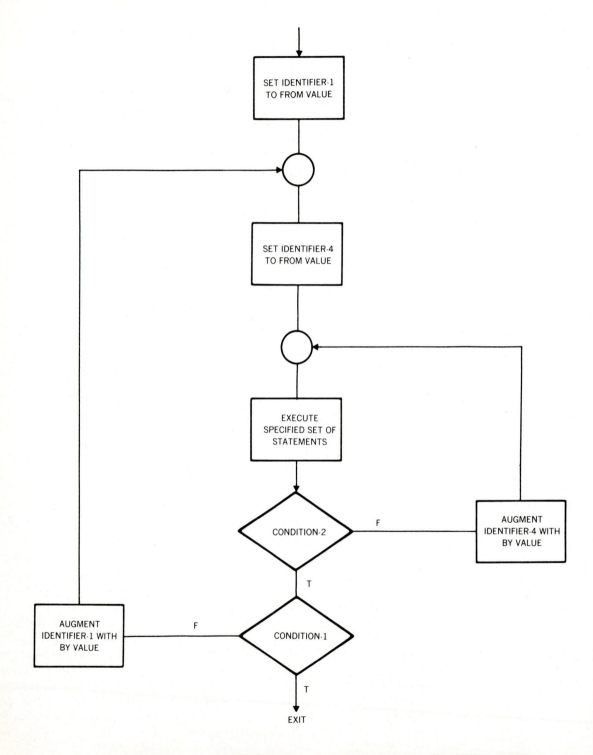

FIGURE 7–3   THE PERFORM . . . VARYING OPTION WITH TEST AFTER.

Use of TEST BEFORE   Use of TEST AFTER

PERFORM LISTING   PERFORM LISTING
   WITH TEST BEFORE   WITH TEST AFTER
   VARYING I FROM 1 BY 1   VARYING I FROM 1 BY 1
    UNTIL I > 2   UNTIL I > 2
   AFTER J FROM 1 BY 1   AFTER J FROM 1 BY 1
    UNTIL J > 3.   UNTIL J > 3.

LISTING.   LISTING.

  DISPLAY I J.   DISPLAY I J.

Resulting Output   Resulting Output

I	J
1	1
1	2
1	3
2	1
2	2
2	3

I	J
1	1
1	2
1	3
1	4
2	1
2	2
2	3
2	4
3	1
3	2
3	3
3	4

FIGURE 7–4   ILLUSTRATION OF TEST BEFORE AND TEST AFTER OPTIONS.

option executes the specified statements at least once before testing whether or not execution should be repeated. Omission of both the BEFORE and AFTER options is understood to imply the BEFORE option.

Figure 7-4 illustrates the effect of the BEFORE and AFTER options by means of an example. In the TEST AFTER case, the conditions are tested after each execution of the iteration; therefore, the number of iterations is different from the TEST BEFORE case.

As a final point regarding the PERFORM ... VARYING statement, if procedure-name-1 is omitted with respect to the general format presented in Figure 7-1, thus constituting an in-line PERFORM, then the AFTER phrase following the VARYING must not be used. In order to use the AFTER phrase with the VARYING option, either procedure-1 must be specified, thereby utilizing an out-of-line PERFORM, or nested multiple PERFORM statements can be used to achieve the same effect. An example of using nested multiple PERFORM statements follows on page 214.

```
PERFORM VARYING I FROM 1 BY 1
          UNTIL I > 12
    PERFORM VARYING I FROM 1 BY 1
              UNTIL J > 31
        ADD SALES (I, J) TO TOTAL-SALES
    END-PERFORM
END-PERFORM.
```

The equivalent out-of-line formulation is:

```
PERFORM ADD-SALES
        VARYING I FROM 1 BY 1 UNTIL I > 12
        AFTER J FROM 1 BY 1 UNTIL J > 31.
ADD-SALES.
    ADD SALES (I, J) TO TOTAL-SALES.
```

Review

1   The option of the PERFORM that is particularly useful for iterative references to subscripted entries is the PERFORM ... _____ option.

VARYING

2   Each identifier may represent a subscript. For a two-dimensional table, for example, _____ (number) subscripts are involved.

2

3   If there are two categories in the first dimension of a table, three in the second, and two in the third, addition of all values in the table involves the summation of _____ (number) values.

$2 \times 3 \times 2 = 12$

4   The option of the PERFORM by which specified statements are executed at least once before testing whether or not execution should be repeated is the [WITH TEST BEFORE / WITH TEST AFTER] option.

WITH TEST AFTER

5   If neither the BEFORE nor AFTER option is specified in conjunction with a test contained in a PERFORM statement, the default is the [BEFORE / AFTER] option.

BEFORE

6   If procedure-name-1 is omitted in a PERFORM ... VARYING statement, thus constituting an in-line PERFORM, then the AFTER phrase following the VARYING [must / cannot] be used.

cannot

SAMPLE TABLE HANDLING PROGRAM

This section of the chapter illustrates application of table handling features in the context of a complete program. The program involves a three-dimensional table and brings out the fact that print formats for complicated tables require programming efforts both in the DATA DIVISION and in the PROCEDURE DIVISION.

The task involves an input file with the following data:

COLUMN	FIELD
1	Store identification (M = Metro, F = Fiesta)
2	Day of the week (1 = Sunday, 2 = Monday, etc.)
3–4	Month (1 = January, 2 = February, etc.)
5–7	Amount of sales (no decimal values)

Because the inclusion of error-checking logic would detract from the table handling focus of this sample program, it is assumed that the data have already been checked by another program and that there are no data errors. The data are input and tabulated into a three-dimensional table and, after appropriate computations, are output in the form illustrated in Figure 7-5.

The sample program is presented in Figure 7-6. The program consists of three sections. The first section, 100-INPUT-DATA, inputs and tabulates the source data. Next, the 200-ACCUMULATE-DATA section forms totals and computes percentages by store and quarter. Notice that out-of-line PERFORM statements are used in this section because there is need to use the VARYING and AFTER clauses. (Recall from the preceding section of this chapter that the AFTER clause cannot be used in an in-line PERFORM involving the VARYING option. Also, the AFTER refers to the AFTER clause following the VARYING and is not to be confused with the TEST AFTER clause.) We could have used nested multiple PERFORM statements instead of the out-of-line PERFORM structure, but the program code would be less clear in its meaning.

The last section of the program, 300-PRINT-DATA, produces the printed report in the form presented in Figure 7-5. Notice that this section and the previous section of the program each contain a GO TO statement. In each case the GO TO transfers control to the end of the section that contains the GO TO, thereby preserving the one-entry/one-exit property of structured programming. The approach that is used allows all paragraphs comprising the logical function of a section to be included in that section while allowing use of out-of-line PERFORM statements when there is good reason to use them, which is the case in this example.

TABLE SEARCHING

One of the most common procedures involving tables is *table searching*. A table is searched to locate an entry that matches a search criterion. Examples would be searching a table of student exam data to find a student with a perfect score, or searching a table of employee data to find the name of employee number 1234.

Two common table searching methods are the *linear search* and the *binary search*. Linear search can be applied to any table, whereas binary search requires that the table data be in sorted order. Figure 7-7 presents the logic of linear search for a sorted table.

Assume that T is the name of the table and therefore T(I) is a subscripted reference to the Ith entry of the table. The subscript I is initialized to a value of 1. We compare X, the key of the record we are seeking, to T(I), the key of the Ith record in the table. If X is less than T(I), this indicates that the point at which the record being sought would have been stored has been passed, and therefore the record is not contained in the table. For instance, if

American Sales Corporation
Annual Sales by Quarter and Day of the Week

DAY	JAN–MAR		APR–JUN		JUL–SEP		OCT–DEC		DAILY TOTAL			% OF YR. TOTAL	
	METRO	FIESTA	METRO	FIESTA	METRO	FIESTA	METRO	FIESTA	METRO	FIESTA	TOTAL	METRO	FIESTA
SUNDAY	50	30	20	0	30	10	40	20	140	60	200	5%	2%
MONDAY													
.													
.													
.													
SATURDAY													
TOTAL	120	80							1000	2000	3000		
% OF QUARTER TOTAL	60%	40%							33%	66%	100%		

FIGURE 7–5   FORM OF OUTPUT FOR THE THREE-DIMENSIONAL TABLE.

```
      IDENTIFICATION DIVISION.
      PROGRAM-ID. STORE-SALES.
*
      ENVIRONMENT DIVISION.
      CONFIGURATION SECTION.
      SOURCE-COMPUTER.   ABC-480.
      OBJECT-COMPUTER.   ABC-480.
*
      INPUT-OUTPUT SECTION.
      FILE-CONTROL.
          SELECT SOURCE-FILE ASSIGN TO Input File
          SELECT REPORT-FILE ASSIGN TO Printer.
*
      DATA DIVISION.
*
      FILE SECTION.
*
      FD   SOURCE-FILE    LABEL RECORDS STANDARD
                          RECORD CONTAINS 7 CHARACTERS
                          DATA RECORD IS SOURCE-RECORD.
      01   SOURCE-RECORD.
           02   STORE-NAME-IN      PIC X.
           02   DAY-NO-IN          PIC 9.
           02   MONTH-NO-IN        PIC 99.
           02   AMOUNT             PIC 9(3).
*
      FD   REPORT-FILE     LABEL RECORDS OMITTED.
*
      01   REPORT-REC              PIC X(102).
*
      WORKING-STORAGE SECTION.
*
      01   END-OF-DATA-TEST        PIC X(3) VALUE 'NO '.
           88   END-OF-FILE   VALUE 'YES'.
*
      01   SUBSCRIPTS.
           02   QUARTER-NO         PIC 9.
           02   DAY-NO             PIC 9.
           02   STORE-NO           PIC 9.
*
      01   DAY-NAMES-1.
           02   FILLER             PIC X(9) VALUE 'SUNDAY    '.
           02   FILLER             PIC X(9) VALUE 'MONDAY    '.
           02   FILLER             PIC X(9) VALUE 'TUESDAY   '.
           02   FILLER             PIC X(9) VALUE 'WEDNESDAY'.
           02   FILLER             PIC X(9) VALUE 'THURSDAY '.
           02   FILLER             PIC X(9) VALUE 'FRIDAY    '.
           02   FILLER             PIC X(9) VALUE 'SATURDAY '.
*
      01   DAY-NAMES-2 REDEFINES DAY-NAMES-1.
           02   DAY-NAME OCCURS 7 TIMES PIC X(9).
NEWA GE
      01   SALES-DATA-TABLES.
*
```

FIGURE 7-6   PROGRAM TO OUTPUT THE THREE-DIMENSIONAL TABLE.

```
        02   SALES-TABLE.
             03   QUARTERLY-DATA OCCURS 4 TIMES.
                  04   DAILY-DATA OCCURS 7 TIMES.
                       05   STORE-DATA OCCURS 2 TIMES.
                            06 STORE-SALES PIC 9(4).
  *
        02   DAY-TOTAL-DATA        OCCURS 7 TIMES.
             03   STORE-DAY-TOTAL  OCCURS 2 TIMES PIC 9(4).
        02   DAY-GRAND-TOTAL       OCCURS 7 TIMES PIC 9(4).
        02   YEAR-PERCENTS         OCCURS 7 TIMES.
             04 STORE-PERCENT      OCCURS 2 TIMES PIC 999.
  *
        02   STORE-QUART-TOTALS    OCCURS 5 TIMES.
             03   STORE-QUART-TOT  OCCURS 2 TIMES PIC 9(4)V99.
        02   SALES-GRAND-TOTAL                   PIC 9(4)V99.
        02   STORE-QUART-PERCNTS   OCCURS 5 TIMES.
             03   STORE-QUART-PRCNT OCCURS 2 TIMES PIC 999.
  *
   01  REPORT-HEADINGS.
  *
        02   HEADING-1.
             03   FILLER PIC X(37) VALUE SPACES.
             03   FILLER PIC X(26) VALUE
                     'AMERICAN SALES CORPORATION'.
  *
        02   HEADING-2.
             03 FILLER PIC X(29) VALUE SPACES.
             03 FILLER PIC X(43) VALUE
                     'ANNUAL SALES BY QUARTER AND DAY OF THE WEEK'.
  *
        02   HEADING-3.
             03   FILLER PIC X(9) VALUE SPACES.
             03   FILLER PIC X(78) VALUE ALL '*'.
             03   HD-3-L PIC X(14) VALUE ALL '*'.
  *
        02   HEADING-4.
             03   FILLER PIC X(9) VALUE SPACE.
             03   FILLER PIC X(14) VALUE '*   JAN - MAR   '.
             03   FILLER PIC X(14) VALUE '*   APR - JUN   '.
             03   FILLER PIC X(14) VALUE '*   JUL - SEP   '.
             03   FILLER PIC X(14) VALUE '*   OCT - DEC   '.
             03   FILLER PIC X(21) VALUE '*    DAILY TOTAL    '.
             03   FILLER PIC X(15) VALUE '* % OF YR-TOT *'.
  *
        02   HEADING-5.
             03   FILLER PIC X(9) VALUE SPACES.
             03   FILLER PIC X(70) VALUE ALL '* METRO*FIESTA'.
             03   FILLER PIC X(22) VALUE '* TOTAL* METRO*FIESTA*'.
```

FIGURE 7-6   PROGRAM TO OUTPUT THE THREE-DIMENSIONAL TABLE. (Continued)

```
        02   HEADING-6.
            03   HD-6-NAME PIC X(9) VALUE SPACES.
            03   FILLER PIC X(79) VALUE ALL '*        *           '.
            03   HD-6-L PIC X(13) VALUE '        *        *'.
*
   01   OUTPUT-LINE.
        02   DAY-NAME-OUT    PIC X(9).
        02   OUT-1 PIC X(70) VALUE ALL '*        '.
        02   OUT-2 REDEFINES OUT-1.
            03   QUART-DATA-OUT   OCCURS 5 TIMES.
                04 STORE-DATA-OUT OCCURS 2 TIMES.
                    05   FILLER PIC X.
                    05   SALES-OUT   PIC Z,ZZZ.
                    05   FILLER PIC X.
        02   FILLER    PIC X VALUE '*'.
        02   DAY-TOT-OUT   PIC ZZ,ZZZ.
        02   FILLER   PIC XX VALUE '* '.
        02   YR-PCNT-OUT-1 PIC X(14) VALUE ALL '   % * '.
        02   YR-PRCNT-OUT-DATA REDEFINES YR-PCNT-OUT-1.
            03   STORE-YR-PRCNT-OUT-DATA   OCCURS 2 TIMES.
            04   STORE-YR-PRCNT-OUT   PIC ZZ9.
            04   FILLER              PIC X(4).
*
   01   QUART-TOT-OUT-DATA.
        02   TOT-NAME-OUT    PIC X(9).
        02   Q-TOT-OUT-1 PIC X(78) VALUE ALL '*        '.
        02   Q-TOT-OUT-2 REDEFINES Q-TOT-OUT-1.
            03   QUART-TOT-OUT   OCCURS 5 TIMES.
                04   STORE-TOT-OUT OCCURS 2 TIMES.
                    05 FILLER PIC X.
                    05 TOT-OUT PIC Z,ZZZ.
                    05 FILLER PIC X.
            03   FILLER PIC X.
            03   GRAND-TOT-OUT   PIC Z,ZZZ.
*
   01   QUART-PRCNT-OUT-REC.
        02   QUART-NAME-OUT PIC X(9).
        02   Q-PCNT-OUT-1 PIC X(70) VALUE ALL '*    % '.
        02   QUART-PRCNT-OUT-DATA REDEFINES Q-PCNT-OUT-1.
            03 QUART-PRCNT-OUT OCCURS 5 TIMES.
                04   STORE-PRCNT-OUT OCCURS 2 TIMES.
                    05 FILLER PIC XX.
                    05 PRCNT-OUT   PIC ZZ9.
                    05 FILLER PIC XX.
        02   FILLER              PIC XXX VALUE '*  '.
        02   COL-100-PRCNT-OUT   PIC ZZZ.
        02   FILLER              PIC XX VALUE '%*'.
*
   PROCEDURE DIVISION.
*
   010-PROGRAM-SUMMARY.
        PERFORM 100-INPUT-DATA
        PERFORM 200-ACCUMULATE-DATA
        PERFORM 300-PRINT-DATA
        STOP RUN.
```

FIGURE 7-6   PROGRAM TO OUTPUT THE THREE-DIMENSIONAL TABLE.
(Continued)

```
 100-INPUT-DATA SECTION.
*
 110-INPUT-SECTION-START.
     OPEN INPUT  SOURCE-FILE
*
     MOVE ZEROS TO SALES-DATA-TABLES.
*
     PERFORM WITH TEST AFTER
             UNTIL END-OF-FILE
        READ SOURCE-FILE
             AT END SET END-OF-FILE TO TRUE
*            NOT AT END PERFORM 120-LOAD-DATA
        END-READ
     END-PERFORM
*
     CLOSE SOURCE-FILE
     GO TO 130-INPUT-SECTION-END.
*
 120-LOAD-DATA.
*
     IF STORE-NAME-IN = 'M'
        MOVE 1 TO STORE-NO
     ELSE
        MOVE 2 TO STORE-NO.
*
     EVALUATE MONTH-NO-IN
        WHEN 1 THRU 3
          MOVE 1 TO QUARTER-NO
        WHEN 4 THRU 6
           MOVE 2 TO QUARTER-NO
        WHEN 7 THRU 9
           MOVE 3 TO QUARTER-NO
        WHEN OTHER
           MOVE 4 TO QUARTER-NO
     END-EVALUATE
*
     MOVE DAY-NO-IN TO DAY-NO
     ADD AMOUNT TO STORE-SALES (QUARTER-NO, DAY-NO, STORE-NO)
*
 130-INPUT-SECTION-END.
     EXIT.
/
 200-ACCUMULATE-DATA SECTION.
*
 210-ACCUMULATE-SECTION-START.
     PERFORM 220-SUM-DATA
                VARYING QUARTER-NO FROM 1 BY 1
                     UNTIL QUARTER-NO > 4
                AFTER DAY-NO FROM 1 BY 1
                    UNTIL DAY-NO > 7
                AFTER STORE-NO FROM 1 BY 1
                    UNTIL STORE-NO > 2
```

FIGURE 7-6   PROGRAM TO OUTPUT THE THREE-DIMENSIONAL TABLE. (Continued)

```
            PERFORM 230-COMPUTE-STORE-PERCENTS
                       VARYING DAY-NO FROM 1 BY 1
                             UNTIL DAY-NO > 7
                       AFTER STORE-NO FROM 1 BY 1
                             UNTIL STORE-NO > 2
*
            PERFORM 240-COMPUTE-QUART-PERCENTS
                       VARYING QUARTER-NO FROM 1 BY 1
                             UNTIL QUARTER-NO > 5
                       AFTER STORE-NO FROM 1 BY 1
                             UNTIL STORE-NO > 2
            GO TO 250-ACCUMULATE-SECTION-END.
*
 220-SUM-DATA.
       ADD STORE-SALES (QUARTER-NO, DAY-NO, STORE-NO)
           TO STORE-DAY-TOTAL (DAY-NO, STORE-NO)
               DAY-GRAND-TOTAL (DAY-NO)
               STORE-QUART-TOT (QUARTER-NO, STORE-NO)
               STORE-QUART-TOT (5, STORE-NO)
               SALES-GRAND-TOTAL.
*
 230-COMPUTE-STORE-PERCENTS.
       COMPUTE STORE-PERCENT (DAY-NO, STORE-NO) ROUNDED =
         100.0 * ( STORE-DAY-TOTAL (DAY-NO, STORE-NO)
                 / SALES-GRAND-TOTAL).
*
 240-COMPUTE-QUART-PERCENTS.
       COMPUTE STORE-QUART-PRCNT (QUARTER-NO, STORE-NO) ROUNDED =
           100.0 * (STORE-QUART-TOT (QUARTER-NO, STORE-NO)
               / (STORE-QUART-TOT (QUARTER-NO, 1)
               +   STORE-QUART-TOT (QUARTER-NO, 2))).
*
 250-ACCUMULATE-SECTION-END.
       EXIT.
/
 300-PRINT-DATA SECTION.
*
 310-PRINT-SECTION-START.
       OPEN OUTPUT REPORT-FILE
       WRITE REPORT-REC FROM HEADING-1 AFTER PAGE
       WRITE REPORT-REC FROM HEADING-2 AFTER 1
       WRITE REPORT-REC FROM HEADING-3 AFTER 1
       WRITE REPORT-REC FROM HEADING-4 AFTER 1
       WRITE REPORT-REC FROM HEADING-6 AFTER 1
       WRITE REPORT-REC FROM HEADING-5 AFTER 1
       WRITE REPORT-REC FROM HEADING-6 AFTER 1
       WRITE REPORT-REC FROM HEADING-3 AFTER 1
*
       PERFORM 320-MOVE-PRINT-DAILY-DATA
                   VARYING DAY-NO FROM 1 BY 1 UNTIL DAY-NO > 7
```

FIGURE 7-6   PROGRAM TO OUTPUT THE THREE-DIMENSIONAL TABLE.
(Continued)

```
            MOVE ' TOTAL' TO TOT-NAME-OUT
            PERFORM 350-MOVE-QUART-TOTALS
                    VARYING QUARTER-NO FROM 1 BY 1
                            UNTIL QUARTER-NO > 5
                    AFTER STORE-NO FROM 1 BY 1
                            UNTIL STORE-NO > 2
            MOVE SALES-GRAND-TOTAL TO GRAND-TOT-OUT
            MOVE SPACES TO HD-6-L
            MOVE SPACES TO HD-3-L
            WRITE REPORT-REC FROM HEADING-6 AFTER 1
            WRITE REPORT-REC FROM QUART-TOT-OUT-DATA AFTER 1
            WRITE REPORT-REC FROM HEADING-6 AFTER 1
            WRITE REPORT-REC FROM HEADING-3 AFTER 1
            MOVE ' % OF' TO HD-6-NAME
            WRITE REPORT-REC FROM HEADING-6 AFTER 1
            MOVE 'QUART-TOT' TO QUART-NAME-OUT
*
            PERFORM 360-MOVE-QUART-PRCNTS
                    VARYING QUARTER-NO FROM 1 BY 1
                            UNTIL QUARTER-NO > 5
                    AFTER STORE-NO FROM 1 BY 1 UNTIL STORE-NO > 2
*
            MOVE 100.0 TO COL-100-PRCNT-OUT
            WRITE REPORT-REC FROM QUART-PRCNT-OUT-REC AFTER 1
            MOVE SPACES TO HD-6-NAME
            WRITE REPORT-REC FROM HEADING-6 AFTER 1
            WRITE REPORT-REC FROM HEADING-3 AFTER 1.
*
            CLOSE REPORT-FILE
            GO TO 370-PRINT-SECTION-END.
*
        320-MOVE-PRINT-DAILY-DATA.
            MOVE DAY-NAME (DAY-NO) TO DAY-NAME-OUT
            PERFORM 330-MOVE-QUART-DATA
                    VARYING QUARTER-NO FROM 1 BY 1
                            UNTIL QUARTER-NO > 4
                    AFTER STORE-NO FROM 1 BY 1
                            UNTIL STORE-NO > 2.
*
            PERFORM 340-MOVE-STORE-TOT-PCNT VARYING STORE-NO FROM 1 BY 1
                    UNTIL STORE-NO > 2
            MOVE DAY-GRAND-TOTAL (DAY-NO) TO DAY-TOT-OUT.
            WRITE REPORT-REC FROM HEADING-6 AFTER 1
            WRITE REPORT-REC FROM OUTPUT-LINE AFTER 1
            WRITE REPORT-REC FROM HEADING-6 AFTER 1
            WRITE REPORT-REC FROM HEADING-3 AFTER 1.
*
        330-MOVE-QUART-DATA.
            MOVE STORE-SALES (QUARTER-NO, DAY-NO, STORE-NO)
                TO SALES-OUT (QUARTER-NO, STORE-NO).
```

FIGURE 7-6   PROGRAM TO OUTPUT THE THREE-DIMENSIONAL TABLE.
(Continued)

```
340-MOVE-STORE-TOT-PCNT.
    MOVE STORE-DAY-TOTAL (DAY-NO, STORE-NO)
        TO SALES-OUT (5, STORE-NO)
    MOVE STORE-PERCENT (DAY-NO, STORE-NO)
        TO STORE-YR-PRCNT-OUT (STORE-NO).
*
350-MOVE-QUART-TOTALS.
    MOVE STORE-QUART-TOT (QUARTER-NO, STORE-NO)
        TO TOT-OUT (QUARTER-NO, STORE-NO).
*
360-MOVE-QUART-PRCNTS.
    MOVE STORE-QUART-PRCNT (QUARTER-NO, STORE-NO)
        TO PRCNT-OUT (QUARTER-NO, STORE-NO).
*
370-PRINT-SECTION-END.
    EXIT.
```

FIGURE 7-6   PROGRAM TO OUTPUT THE THREE-DIMENSIONAL TABLE. (Continued)

we are seeking employee number 123 and the current (Ith) record being compared has a value of 152, there is no point to continuing the search. All records subsequent to 152 will have key numbers larger than 152. On the other hand, as long as X is greater than T(I) we continue to increment the value of I, but with the provision that I should not exceed N, which is the number of records in the table. We repeat the process until either the record is found or it can be established that the record is not in the table. Should the table be unsorted we would modify Figure 7-7 by deleting the "X < T(I)?" block, as well as the two blocks following the "Yes" branch of that block.

The linear search method is generally the simplest procedure to use. It is particularly well suited for unsorted tables, since the method does not require that the table be in any particular order. In practice, many tables are unsorted. If the membership of a table is dynamic, that is, changing often, it may be very costly in terms of overall efficiency to sort the table every time an entry is added or deleted from the table. Furthermore, it may be that other uses of the data require an order that is based on a different key from the one under consideration. The task of sorting the table in one order and then resorting back to the original order may not be worth the effort. For example, suppose we are processing daily credit purchases which have been sorted by customer number. For credit-screening purposes we may want to identify the customers who made purchases of $10,000 or more. If we have a block of 20 customers as a table in central storage, it is much simpler to employ a linear search rather than to sort the records by amount of purchase and then back to customer number. Of course, for an unsorted table the search should continue until all entries have been checked, since the record which is sought can be in any location in the table.

The method of binary search is also referred to as dichotomous

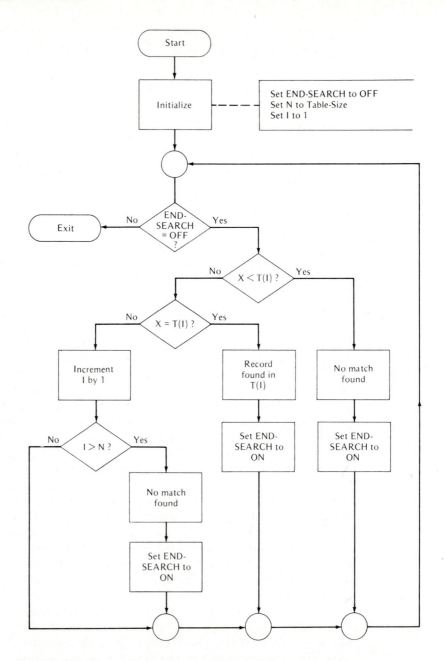

FIGURE 7-7   FLOWCHART FOR THE LINEAR SEARCH OF A SORTED (SEQUENTIALLY ORGANIZED) TABLE.

search. It has the feature that each comparison eliminates from further consideration half the entries that could contain the record being sought. The method requires that the table be sorted. We begin by checking the record at the midpoint of the table. If that record is not the one being sought, it can be determined whether that record is smaller or larger than the one being sought, thereby eliminating half the records from further consideration. For example, if the midpoint record is larger than the one being sought, the record being sought must be in the first half of the table, if it is included in the table at all. Conversely, if the midpoint record is smaller than the record being sought, the first half of the table can be eliminated from further consideration. After half the table is eliminated from consideration, we proceed to the midpoint of the remaining half and again compare the record with the record being sought. The procedure is repeated until the record being sought is found or until it can be concluded that the record is not included in the table. The flowchart in Figure 7-8 presents the logic associated with the binary search method.

Referring to Figure 7-8 we begin by setting two data-names, LO and HI, equal to zero and to the table size plus 1, respectively. The midpoint of the table, MID, is determined by adding LO to HI, dividing by 2, and rounding any fraction upward. Thus, if LO = 0 and HI = 9 for a table with eight entries, MID = (0 + 9)/2 = 4.5, which is rounded to 5. MID is then used as the subscript of T, and the value of the record sought, X, is compared with the MIDth record in the table. If X is less than T(MID), the record being sought could only be located below the MID position, and therefore we set HI = MID. Similar reasoning leads to setting LO = MID when X is greater than or equal to T(MID). Then the difference between HI and LO is checked. If it is less than 2, and since any fractional value would have been rounded upward, this indicates that the last record was the last possible location at which the record being sought might have been located, and that the record being sought is not in the table. For example, for a table with eight entries the first MID = 5, as above. Suppose X > T(MID). Then LO = MID = 5 and HI − LO = 9 − 5 = 4, which is *not* less than 2. The value of MID in the next iteration is (5 + 9)/2 = 7. Again, suppose X > T(MID). Then LO = 7 and HI − LO = 9 − 7 = 2. The next MID = (7 + 9)/2 = 8. If X is unequal to T(MID), the HI − LO comparison will yield one of these two results: If X < T(MID), then HI − LO = 8 − 8 = 0. If X > T(MID), then HI − LO = 9 − 8 = 1. In either case the expression HI − LO will be less than 2 and the search will be terminated with no match found.

Figure 7-9 illustrates the procedure by which the name "Myrtle" would be found in an alphabetically ordered list by means of the binary search method. Notice that a match occurred on the third item considered. If we had been looking for "Mark," one more time through the loop would have been required, for a total of four look-ups. With a table size of 11, four look-ups is in fact the maximum number that can be required, as explained below.

Figure 7-10 presents the sample code for implementing the binary search logic of Figure 7-7. Binary search is an efficient method. Its relative

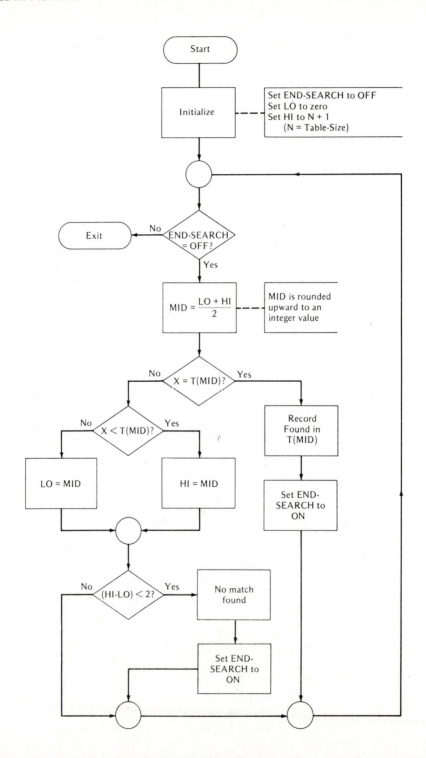

FIGURE 7-8   FLOWCHART FOR THE BINARY SEARCH OF A SORTED TABLE.

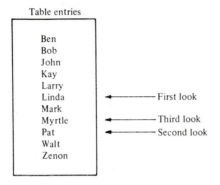

Table entries

Ben	
Bob	
John	
Kay	
Larry	
Linda	◄——— First look
Mark	
Myrtle	◄——— Third look
Pat	◄——— Second look
Walt	
Zenon	

FIGURE 7–9   ILLUSTRATION OF A BINARY SEARCH WITH AN ALPHABETI-CAL LIST, WHERE THE RECORD SOUGHT = MYRTLE.

efficiency becomes more pronounced as the table size is increased. This is so because the maximum number of comparisons required by this method increases only linearly when the table size increases exponentially. Table 7-1 presents the mathematical relationship which is involved. Thus, for example, whereas a table with 15 entries requires a maximum of four comparisons, a table with 255 entries requires a maximum of just eight comparisons.

For the reason described above, the binary search method also becomes increasingly more efficient than the linear search method as table size is increased. The general comparison is presented in Table 7-2. The table sizes listed in the first column of Table 7-2 increase exponentially. Note that the maximum number of comparisons for the linear search method also increases exponentially, whereas the maximum number of comparisons for the binary search method increases approximately on a linear basis. The

TABLE 7-1   MAXIMUM NUMBER OF COMPARI-SONS REQUIRED BY THE BINARY SEARCH METHOD FOR TABLES OF VARIOUS SIZES

TABLE SIZE		MAXIMUM NUMBER OF COMPARISONS
RANGE	AS A POWER OF 2	
1	2^0	1
2	2^1	2
3-4	2^2	3
5-7	less than 2^3	3
8-15	less than 2^4	4
16-31	less than 2^5	5
32-63	less than 2^6	6
64-127	less than 2^7	7
128-255	less than 2^8	8
256-511	less than 2^9	9

```
*
*    We are looking for value X in table T.
*    N is the table size.
*    WHERE-FOUND will contain the subscript value of where X was found in T, or it
         will contain a zero to signify that X was not found in T.
*    END-SEARCH and NOT-END-SEARCH are logical flags to control the iterative
         procedure.
*


BINARY-SEARCH.
     MOVE ZERO TO LO
     COMPUTE HI = N + 1
     SET NOT-END-SEARCH TO TRUE
     PERFORM UNTIL END-SEARCH
          COMPUTE MID = (LO + HI) / 2
          IF X = T (MID)
             THEN MOVE MID TO WHERE-FOUND
                  SET END-SEARCH TO TRUE
             ELSE
                  IF X < T (MID)
                    THEN MOVE MID TO HI
                    ELSE MOVE MID TO LO
                  END-IF
                  IF (HI − LO) < 2
                    THEN MOVE ZERO TO WHERE-FOUND
                         SET END-SEARCH TO TRUE
                    ELSE CONTINUE
                  END-IF
          END-IF
     END-PERFORM.
```

FIGURE 7–10   SAMPLE BINARY SEARCH PROCEDURE.

"average" figures reported in Table 7-2 are based on the assumption that the records being sought are randomly and uniformly distributed in the tables. That is, they have not been ordered according to frequency of use. As can be seen in the table, the binary search method outperforms the linear search method by a wide margin, especially when the table size is relatively large. Remember, though, that the binary method specifically requires that the table be sorted, whereas linear search can be used with either a sorted or unsorted table. The time required to sort a table may then have to be balanced against the search time by the binary method. If the membership of a table is stable and the table is used frequently, binary search is likely to be the better choice. Otherwise, linear search may be preferred.

TABLE 7-2   LINEAR AND BINARY SEARCH COMPARED

TABLE SIZE	NUMBER OF COMPARISONS			
	LINEAR		BINARY	
	MAXIMUM	AVERAGE	MAXIMUM	AVERAGE
5	5	3	3	2
10	10	5	4	3
50	50	25	6	5
100	100	50	7	6
1,000	1,000	500	10	9
10,000	10,000	5,000	14	13
100,000	100,000	50,000	17	16

Review

1   The two methods of table searching described in this section are _____ search and _____ search.

linear; binary

2   The method of table searching that generally is the simplest to use is _____ search.

linear

3   The method of table searching that requires that the table data be in sorted order is _____ search.

binary

4   The table search procedure by which each comparison eliminates from consideration half the entries that could contain the record being sought is called _____.

binary search

5   Suppose that a sorted table contains 30 entries. By the logic of the binary search method the initial value of LO is set equal to _____ and the initial value of HI is set equal to _____.

0; 31

6   For Question 5, the value of MID in the first loop through the program would be _____ (value).

16

COBOL LANGUAGE OPTIONS IN TABLE SEARCHING

Because of the frequency with which table searching is used in computer programs, the COBOL language includes a specialized set of instructions to facilitate programming.

The OCCURS Clause

First, let us consider the format associated with the OCCURS clause:

```
OCCURS integer TIMES
    [ { ASCENDING  } KEY IS data-name-1 [data-name-2] ... ]
    { DESCENDING }
    [ INDEXED BY index-name-1 [index-name-2] ...]
```

Some examples may help illustrate the available forms of the OCCURS option. Let us consider this one first:

```
02  SAMPLE OCCURS 100 TIMES
    ASCENDING KEY IS YEAR MONTH.
    03  OTHER-DATA          PICTURE X(20).
    03  MONTH               PICTURE 99.
    03  YEAR                PICTURE 99.
    03  REST-OF-IT          PICTURE X(40).
```

In this example there are two keys, YEAR and MONTH. Keys are listed in decreasing order of significance. Thus, the months are sorted in ascending sequence within the years, which are also in ascending sequence. As the example illustrates, the order in which the keys appear in the KEY clause is *not* related to their physical order in the record.

Here is a second example:

```
02  SAMPLE PICTURE 9(8) OCCURS 100 TIMES
    INDEXED BY N.
```

In this case we specify an index called N, presumably for the purpose of later using this index in a SEARCH statement.

The USAGE IS INDEX Clause

Consider now the USAGE IS INDEX clause. We can specify the USAGE of a data item is INDEX, so that the item can be used in conjunction with SET, SEARCH, or PERFORM statements.

As an example of implementing the USAGE clause, consider the following program segment:

```
01  SAMPLE.
    02  FIRST-PART     PICTURE X(10).
    02  K USAGE IS INDEX.
```

The item called K is an INDEX item; therefore, no PICTURE clause is given. All index items are handled according to the rules associated with particular computer systems. Normally, index items are in binary form.

When a table is declared to be INDEXED BY an index item, the index item is expressed in terms of displacement values from the beginning of the table. Following are the corresponding subscript and index item values for a table defined as T OCCURS 4 TIMES PICTURE X(3):

Subscript Value	Index Item Value
1	0
2	3
3	6
4	9

The index item value indicates the position at which the item begins with respect to the beginning of the table; thus, for the above example with PICTURE X(3), the index value is 6 for a subscript of 3, because the third item in the table begins at the sixth byte from the beginning of the table.

Indexing makes for more efficient table operations. On the other hand, it is not reasonable to require a programmer to think explicitly of the value of index items. For this reason, the programmer can think of index items as if they were subscripts. However, when a subscript value is moved to an index, or vice versa, then the special verb SET is used to make it clear that it is not a MOVE operation, but rather it is a transformation and move. Suppose S is a subscript and I is an index; then if S contains 3, SET I TO S will result in I being set to a value of 6. Conversely, if I = 6, SET S TO I will result in S being set to 3. In a similar way, SET I UP BY 1 increases I not by 1 but by the unit displacement value determined by the PICTURE clause. If, as in the example above, the PICTURE clause defines a size of 3, then UP BY 1 or DOWN BY 1 changes the index item by 3.

Generally, use of index items is required only in SEARCH operations. However, use of index items is encouraged in all table handling operations because indexes are processed more efficiently than subscripts. An index can be stored in a register during a table operation, whereas a subscript is stored in main memory and has to be brought to a register each time the subscript is used. Also, in serial operations an index is increased by a fixed displacement value. In contrast, a subscript has to be decoded each time by means of multiplication, which is more time consuming than addition (or subtraction).

The SEARCH Verb

Consider now the SEARCH verb, which is the cornerstone of a search instruction. Two principal formats are available, as presented in Figure 7-11. In Format 1, identifier-1 is an item whose description in the DATA DIVISION contains an OCCURS and an INDEXED BY clause. When the VARYING option is used, index-name-2 or identifier-2 is varied in the same way as the index specified in the relevant INDEXED BY clause. Identifier-2 must be specified as USAGE IS INDEX, or it must be an elementary integer item. The AT END clause is optional. If it is omitted, program control will pass to the next sentence when the table has been searched and no match has been found. If AT END is included and imperative-statement-1 does not terminate with GO TO, a branch to the next sentence will be made (in effect bypassing the WHEN clauses). WHEN introduces another form of conditional expression.

Format 2 is used with sorted tables, that is, tables for which the OCCURS clause contains a KEY in addition to the INDEXED BY option. The search may be a binary search, or any other method included in a particular compiler; however, as far as the programmer is concerned, only the instructions included in Format 2 are required.

Notice that in Format 2 only one WHEN option is available, but multiple AND conditions are allowed. Thus, all the conditions must be true in order for the search to be satisfied. In contrast, whenever multiple WHEN statements are used in Format 1, any one of these conditions being true constitutes a sufficient reason for search termination.

Also notice that the conditions tested in the WHEN clauses of Format 1 and Format 2 are different. In Format 1, condition-1 is any condition. For example, we could search a table to find an entry whose squared value plus 100 is greater than some constant. The point is that in a linear search, we can

FORMAT 1

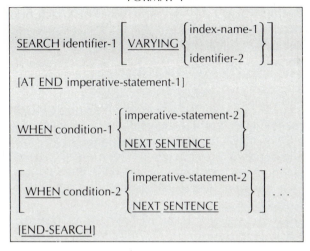

FORMAT 2

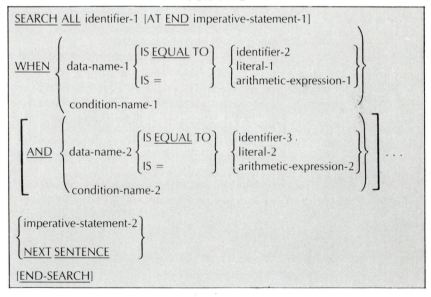

FIGURE 7-11   SEARCH VERB FORMATS.

test for *any* condition, not just the direct content of the table. On the other hand, in the binary search as specified by Format 2, the condition tests for *equality* of data-name-1 to a specified comparand, or for the truth of a condition-name, which is another form of testing for equality. Since a binary search "jumps around" the table based on the values of the sort keys, it follows that the value of the sort key must be tested at each step of the search. Put another way, in a binary search it would not make any sense to test a WHEN condition that did not involve the sort key(s) (indicated in Format 2 as data-name-1, data-name-2, etc.).

The SET Verb

Basically, the SET verb is a variation of MOVE and provides a way of handling index items. Two formats are available, as presented in Figure 7-12.

In Format 1, if we use index-name-1, we can set it equal to index-name-3, identifier-3, or integer-1. If identifier-3 is used, it must be defined as an elementary integer item; if integer-1 is used, it must be a positive integer. If we set identifier-1 and it has not been defined by a USAGE IS INDEX clause, it can be set only to index-name-3.

If we write SET A TO B, we basically are moving the value of B to A. In this way, we can transfer data to an index item or an identifier, for use either in a SEARCH or after a SEARCH. For instance, we may have two tables, one INDEXED BY A and the other INDEXED BY B. After performing a search and finding a match on the first table, we may want to reference the corresponding entry in the second table. We then SET B TO A so that B can be used as a subscript or index in the second table.

In Format 2 in Figure 7-12, we can increase or decrease the value of index-name-1 either by a positive integer (integer-1) or by the value of identifier-1, which must be a field that has not been defined as USAGE IS INDEX. The effect of UP BY is to increase the value of index-name-1, while the effect of DOWN BY is to change index-name-1 by the indicated decrement, as explained in the USAGE IS INDEX subsection earlier in this chapter.

We now illustrate application of these language features using some examples.

Suppose that employee data are contained in a sorted table sequenced by employee NAME:

FORMAT 1

$$\underline{SET} \left\{ \begin{array}{l} \text{index-name-1 [index-name-2]} \dots \\ \text{identifier-1 [identifier-2]} \dots \end{array} \right\} \underline{TO} \left\{ \begin{array}{l} \text{index-name-3} \\ \text{identifier-3} \\ \text{integer-1} \end{array} \right\}$$

FORMAT 2

$$\underline{SET} \text{ index-name-1 [index-name-2]} \dots \left\{ \begin{array}{l} \underline{UP} \ \underline{BY} \\ \underline{DOWN} \ \underline{BY} \end{array} \right\} \left\{ \begin{array}{l} \text{identifier-1} \\ \text{integer-1} \end{array} \right\}$$

FIGURE 7-12   SET VERB FORMATS.

```
01   DATA-TABLE.
     02   NAME-NUMBER OCCURS 400 TIMES
          ASCENDING KEY IS NAME
          INDEXED BY WHICH-ONE.
          03   NAME        PICTURE X(16).
          03   EMPL-NO   PICTURE 9999.
```

EMPL-NAME is a field that contains a name for which we want to determine the associated employee number (EMPL-NO). In order to accomplish this task, we can execute the following statements:

```
SEARCH ALL NAME-NUMBER
    AT END PERFORM CANT-FIND
    WHEN NAME (WHICH-ONE) = EMPL-NAME
        MOVE EMPL-NO (WHICH-ONE) TO EDIT-NUMBER.
```

The instruction SEARCH ALL NAME-NUMBER is an application of the second format of the SEARCH verb. Since the table was defined with ASCENDING KEY IS NAME, the SEARCH ALL will result in a binary search on the NAME field. When a match is found, program execution is transferred to the instruction MOVE EMPL-NO (WHICH-ONE) TO EDIT-NUMBER following the WHEN. Notice that WHICH-ONE has the reference value of the record for which the match occurred; thus, it is used as a subscript, or index, to reference the correspondig EMPL-NO.

Next consider an example of a sorted table with two sort keys:

```
01   TABLE.
     02   SALES-DATA OCCURS 100 TIMES
          ASCENDING KEY IS YEAR
          ASCENDING KEY IS MONTH
          INDEXED BY N.
          03   SALES-AMOUNT   PIC 9(4)V99.
          03   YEAR             PIC 99.
          03   MONTH            PIC 99.
              .
              .
              .

SEARCH ALL SALES-DATA
    AT END SET NOT-FOUND TO TRUE
    WHEN YEAR (N) = YEAR-IN
        AND MONTH (N) = MONTH-IN
        COMPUTE YEAR-SUB = YEAR-IN − BASE YEAR
        ADD SALES-AMOUNT TO SALES-TOTAL (YEAR-SUB, MONTH-IN).
```

In the example above, we test both YEAR (N) and MONTH (N) because the table is sorted on both of these fields.

As another example, suppose the following table definitions were written:

```
01   DATA TABLE.
      02   NAME OCCURS 400 TIMES             PICTURE X(16)
               INDEXED BY NAME-INDEX.
      02   EMPL-NO OCCURS 400 TIMES          PICTURE 9999
               INDEXED BY NO-INDEX.
```

In effect, two tables are defined, one called NAME and the other called EMPL-NO. The NAME table is indexed by NAME-INDEX, while the EMPL-NO table is indexed by NO-INDEX.

In relation to these table descriptions, the following statements then can be written:

```
SET NAME-INDEX TO 1.
SET NO-INDEX TO 1.
SEARCH NAME VARYING NO-INDEX
    AT END PERFORM NO-MATCH
    WHEN EMPL-NAME = NAME (NAME-INDEX)
        MOVE EMPL-NO (NO-INDEX) TO EDIT-FIELD.
```

The SEARCH statement contains the VARYING option, which in effect indicates that NO-INDEX is to be varied in the same way as the index of the table being searched (in this case NAME-INDEX). Thus, for example, when NAME-INDEX refers to the 10th entry, NO-INDEX also refers to the 10th entry. As a result, the EMPL-NO (NO-INDEX) in the MOVE statement corresponds to the NAME for which a match was found. If a match occurred in the 34th position of the NAME table, for example, NAME-INDEX and NO-INDEX both would have a value corresponding to their respective displacement values for the 34th occurrence. Since NAME has PICTURE X(16), NAME-INDEX would have a displacement value of $(34 - 1) \times 16 = 528$, while NO-INDEX would have a value of $(34 - 1) \times 4 = 132$. Thus, the employee number that is accessed corresponds to the name of the employee for which a match was found. Since the ALL option was not used with the SEARCH verb, the search procedure involves accessing every entry in the table in sequence until a match is found or the entire table is searched. In effect, then, we perform a linear search.

It should be noted that the VARYING item is incremented from its initial value. In the above example we initialized it with SET NO-INDEX TO 1. If NO-INDEX was not so initialized but happened to contain the value 5 from previous operations, it then would be incremented to values that correspond to entries 6, 7, 8, . . . as NAME-INDEX was incremented to values that correspond to entries 1, 2, 3, ...

As a general example of program code that can be applied to the latter situation, the program segment below is concerned with a table of last names for which we are interested in finding the average length of the names:

```
    02   NAME-TABLE OCCURS 100 TIMES INDEXED BY I.
        03   NAME-LETTERS OCCURS 20 TIMES INDEXED BY N.
            04   LETTER        PIC X.


01   K USAGE INDEX.
01   TOTAL-LETTER-COUNT   PIC 9(5).
01   AVG-NAME-LENGTH      PIC 9(2)V9.
    .
    .
    .

SET K TO 1
PERFORM VARYING I FROM 1 BY 1
        UNTIL I > 100
    SET N TO 1
    SEARCH NAME-LETTERS VARYING K
        WHEN LETTER (I, N) = SPACE
            NEXT SENTENCE
    END-SEARCH
    SET K DOWN BY 1
END-PERFORM
SET TOTAL-LETTER COUNT TO K
DIVIDE TOTAL-LETTER-COUNT BY 100 GIVING AVG-NAME-LENGTH.
```

In the above program segment, K is a USAGE INDEX item that is not associated with a specific table. It is used as an accumulator of all of the name lengths because its value is not reSET in the program code. Thus, if the first name encountered is 5 characters long, K would be equal to 5. If the second name encountered is 6 characters long, then K would become 11; during the second execution of the SEARCH, K is incremented in the order 6, 7, . . . , while N is incremented in the order 1, 2, ... Incidentally, N would be incremented by 1 in the above example because the PIC clause of LETTER was X. If the PIC had been X(4), for instance, N would be incremented by 4 each time. But in the latter case, K would still be incremented by 1 because K is not associated with a table. If the VARYING item (K, in this case) were associated with a table, then it would be varied by the amount that is appropriate for its respective table.

Review

1   The COBOL language option used to indicate the total number of table entries and to identify the key or keys associated with the records is the _____ clause.

                                                                          OCCURS

2   The COBOL option used to identify a particular data item as being an index is the _____ clause.

                                                                          USAGE

3   The COBOL verb that identifies the table to be searched and also includes options to indicate what should be done when a match is found as well as when it is not found is _____.

                                                                          SEARCH

4   The COBOL verb that is a variation of the MOVE verb and provides the basis for designating the value to be assigned to an INDEX is _____.

                                                                          SET

SAMPLE PROGRAM WITH INDEXING AND SEARCHING

An input file consists of records containing a student name and the numeric score for each of eight parts of a standardized test. Our objective is to store the data in a table and then to illustrate use of SEARCH to identify those students who either scored 100.0 on any part of the test or scored less than 50.0 on any part of the test.

The program is presented in Figure 7-13. Notice that S is designated in the WORKING-STORAGE in INDEXED BY S, and then it is used in the PERFORM . . . VARYING of the PROGRAM-SUMMARY paragraph. Then observe that, after the PERFORM statement, we write SET S DOWN BY 1. After so adjusting S, it represents the number of student records that were read in. We then save the value of S in M (SET M TO S) to be used to control the printing task. Notice that M is a WORKING-STORAGE USAGE INDEX item.

After the table has been stored, we search it in the CHECK-SCORES-AND-PRINT paragraph. Notice that we did not include the AT END option

```
 IDENTIFICATION DIVISION.
 PROGRAM-ID. GRADES.
*
 ENVIRONMENT DIVISION.
*      CONFIGURATION SECTION.
 SOURCE-COMPUTER.  ABC-480.
 OBJECT-COMPUTER.  ABC-480.
*
 INPUT-OUTPUT SECTION.
 FILE-CONTROL.
     SELECT EXAM-FILE   ASSIGN TO Input File
     SELECT REPORT-FILE ASSIGN TO Printer.
*
 DATA DIVISION.
*
 FILE SECTION.
*
 FD   EXAM-FILE       LABEL RECORDS OMITTED
                      DATA RECORD IS EXAM-REC.
 01   EXAM-REC.
      02  STUDENT-NAME                 PIC X(10).
      02  EXAM-SCORES.
          03 SCORES-IN  OCCURS 8 TIMES  PIC 9(3)V9.
*
 FD   REPORT-FILE     LABEL RECORDS OMITTED
                      DATA RECORD IS REPORT-REC.
 01   REPORT-REC                       PIC X(75).
*
 WORKING-STORAGE SECTION.
*
 01   END-OF-FILE-SWITCH        PIC XXX VALUE 'NO '.
      88  END-OF-FILE           VALUE 'YES'.
*
 01   M    USAGE INDEX.
*
 01   EXAM-TABLE.
*
      02   STUDENT-DATA    OCCURS 50 TIMES
                          INDEXED BY  S.
*
           03   STUDENT-NAME       PIC X(10).
*
           03   EXAM-SCORES.
*
                04   SCORE   OCCURS 8 TIMES PIC 9(3)V9
                          INDEXED BY Q.
*
 01   HEADING-1.
      02  FILLER                PIC X(40) VALUE SPACES.
      02  FILLER                PIC X(9)  VALUE 'EXAM PART'.
```

FIGURE 7-13   LISTING FOR PROGRAM WITH INDEXING AND SEARCHING.

```
01    HEADING-2.
      02    FILLER                PIC X(3)  VALUE SPACES.
      02    FILLER                PIC X(12) VALUE 'STUDENT NAME'.
      02    FILLER                PIC X(6) VALUE SPACES.
      02    FILLER                PIC X(50) VALUE
            '1      2      3      4      5      6      7      8'.
*
01    REPORT-LINE.
      02    FILLER                PIC X(2)  VALUE SPACES.
      02    STUDENT-NAME          PIC X(10).
      02    FILLER                PIC X(2)  VALUE SPACES.
*
      02    SCORES-OUT     OCCURS 8 TIMES   PIC ZZZ99.9.
                          INDEXED BY R.
*
/
 PROCEDURE DIVISION.
*
 PROGRAM-SUMMARY.
      OPEN   INPUT   EXAM-FILE
             OUTPUT  REPORT-FILE.
*
      PERFORM READ-EXAM-REC
*
      PERFORM STORE-RECORD
            VARYING   S  FROM  1  BY  1
                      UNTIL  S > 50
                      OR END-OF-FILE.
*
      SET   S  DOWN  BY  1.
      SET   M  TO  S.
*
      WRITE REPORT-REC FROM HEADING-1 AFTER PAGE
      WRITE REPORT-REC FROM HEADING-2 AFTER 2.
*
      PERFORM CHECK-SCORES-AND-PRINT
            VARYING   S  FROM  1  BY  1
                      UNTIL  S > M.
*
      CLOSE EXAM-FILE  REPORT-FILE
*
      STOP RUN.
*
 READ-EXAM-REC.
      READ EXAM-FILE RECORD
            AT END SET END-OF-FILE TO TRUE.
```

**FIGURE 7-13   LISTING FOR PROGRAM WITH INDEXING AND SEARCHING.
(Continued)**

```
*
 STORE-RECORD.
     MOVE STUDENT-NAME OF EXAM-REC
          TO STUDENT-NAME OF EXAM-TABLE (S)
*
     MOVE EXAM-SCORES OF EXAM-REC
          TO EXAM-SCORES OF EXAM-TABLE (S).
     PERFORM READ-EXAM-REC.
*
 CHECK-SCORES-AND-PRINT.
     SET Q TO 1
     SEARCH SCORE
          WHEN   SCORE (S, Q) = 100.0
                 PERFORM PRINT-SCORES
*
          WHEN   SCORE (S, Q) < 50.0
                 PERFORM PRINT-SCORES.
*
 PRINT-SCORES.
     PERFORM MOVE-SCORES
          VARYING  Q  FROM  1  BY  1
                 UNTIL  Q > 8.
*
     MOVE STUDENT-NAME OF EXAM-TABLE (S)
          TO SUDENT-NAME OF REPORT-LINE
     WRITE REPORT-REC FROM REPORT-LINE AFTER 2 LINES.
*
 MOVE-SCORES.
     SET R TO Q
     MOVE SCORE (S, Q) TO SCORE-OUT (R).
```

FIGURE 7-13   LISTING FOR PROGRAM WITH INDEXING AND SEARCHING. (Continued)

in this use of Format 1 of the SEARCH, since it was not needed. If neither a score of 100 nor a score of less than 50 is found for a given student, we simply want to continue with the next student without doing anything AT END.

When either one of the two search conditions is true, we PERFORM PRINT-SCORES and the search for that student record terminates. Then, because of the PERFORM CHECK-SCORES-AND-PRINT in the PROGRAM-SUMMARY, we repeat the search for the next student.

The MOVE-SCORES paragraph illustrates again the use of SET. Since SCORE-OUT was indexed by R, we SET R TO Q so that in the MOVE statement we reference the corresponding scores.

Figure 7-14 illustrates sample input and output for the program. The data provide a somewhat contrived set of cases to illustrate the options. Exercise 7-14 at the end of the chapter asks the student to modify the example in order to incorporate other features of searching.

SAMPLE INPUT

STUDENT-1	09051000082306000900089909770777
STUDENT-2	02000732066605920812085503000600
STUDENT-3	09000820100008320777075306890920
STUDENT-4	07450789082306950765074806780802
STUDENT-5	04500720073010000235024506250213

SAMPLE OUTPUT

| | EXAM PART | | | | | | | |
STUDENT NAME	1	2	3	4	5	6	7	8
STUDENT-1	90.5	100.0	82.3	60.0	90.0	89.9	87.7	77.7
STUDENT-2	20.0	73.2	66.6	59.2	81.2	85.5	30.0	60.0
STUDENT-3	90.0	82.0	100.0	83.2	77.7	75.3	68.9	92.0
STUDENT-4	74.5	78.9	82.3	69.5	76.5	74.8	67.8	80.2
STUDENT-5	45.0	72.0	73.0	100.0	23.5	24.5	62.5	21.3

FIGURE 7-14   SAMPLE INPUT AND OUTPUT FOR THE PROGRAM WITH INDEXING AND SEARCHING.

Exercises

7.1   Consider the following table definition:

```
01  TABLE.
      02   A OCCURS i TIMES.
          03   B OCCURS j TIMES.
              04   C OCCURS k TIMES.
                  05   D OCCURS l TIMES.
                      06   T   PIC p. (where p = field length)
```

For a reference such as T (I, J, K, L), develop a formula to compute the displacement value from the start of the table to determine the first byte of the T (I, J, K, L) field.

As a test case, check to determine that your formula agrees with the following: If i = 50, J = 10, k = 100, l = 5, and p = 1, then T (3, 2, 20, 4) begins at byte 10599, counting the first byte in the table as 1.

7.2   Write DATA DIVISION entries to set up a table that is to contain annual dollar sales for the years 1980–1990. No value will exceed $100,000,000.00.

7.3   Write DATA DIVISION entries to set up a table to contain dollar and unit sales for the years 1980–1990. We want to be able to reference the dollar sales or the unit sales individually for each year, as well as to reference as a group the dollar sales and unit sales pertaining to a given year. The general format of the table is as follows:

YEAR	DOLLAR SALES	UNIT SALES
1980		
1981		
.	.	.
.	.	.
.	. .	.
1990		

7.4   Use DATA DIVISION entries to form a table containing the names of the days of the week so that the names are referenced by a subscript; thus, Monday would have a subscript 1 and Sunday would have a subscript 7.

7.5   Assume that TAX-TABLE contains 30 values (V999). Write the PROCEDURE and DATA DIVISION statements required to print the contents of the table in the following formats:

a   Print the 30 values in one column of 30 lines.
b   Print the 30 values at the rate of 7 per line for as many lines as are needed.

7.6   For the following table, write the necessary program instructions to find the smallest value and to place it in SMALLEST. Disregard the possibility of ties.

    02   TABLE OCCURS 50 TIMES   PICTURE X(12).

7.7   In the following two-dimensional table, we want to form the sum of each row and the sum of each column, as well as the grand total. The results of the summations are to be saved so that they can be printed later in the program. Write relevant DATA and PROCEDURE DIVISION entries.

    01   SALES-DATA-TABLE.
        02   SALES-TERRITORY OCCURS 5 TIMES.
            03   QUARTER-SALES OCCURS 4 TIMES
                        PICTURE 9(6)V99.

7.8   A header is to be centered with respect to column 40 of a printed page. The size of the header is variable, but it is always 20 or fewer characters long. The header is stored in a field called HEADER and we wish to move it and print it from the output record called OUT-PUT-RECORD. Apply the STRING verb as well as table-oriented instructions to accomplish this task.

7.9 A marketing survey conducted by a company involved administering a questionnaire of 25 questions. The responses to each question have been coded by a 1-digit code, ranging from 0 to 9. We want to accumulate a table of the responses to each of the 25 questions, as shown in the following diagram. Write DATA DIVISION entries to form such a table. It should be possible to make reference to each individual cell in the table, as well as each row (question).

Question	Response Code									
	0	1	2	3	4	5	6	7	8	9
1										
2										
.										
.										
24										
25										

7.10 Suppose that source records contain a quarter value in column 1, a region value in column 2, and a sales amount in columns 3–5. Write a complete COBOL program to read such a file and produce a report that presents total sales by quarter and region, as illustrated in the following table:

QUARTER	REGION			
	EAST	SOUTH	MIDWEST	WEST
1				
2				
3				
4				

7.11 Write a complete COBOL program that utilizes table-handling concepts to produce graphic printer output in the form of a bar chart. The output format is illustrated in Figure 7-15. For each common stock, a bar is to be printed whose length corresponds to the percent yield of the stock.

The yield is computed as the percent ratio of the dividend per share to the price per share. It is assumed that no yield can ex-

PERCENT YIELD

```
              0    5   10   15   20   25   30   35   40   45   50
STOCK NAME    I....I....I....I....I....I....I....I....I....I....I
              I
FORD MOTOR CO.        IXXXXXXXX
              I
GENERAL MOTORS CORP.  IXXXXXXXXXX
              I
CONTROL DATA CORP.    IXX
              I
IBM CORP.             IXXXXX
              I
SPERRY RAND CORP.     IXXX
              I
HONEYWELL CORP.       IXXXX
              I
DIGITAL EQUIPMENT CO. IXXXX
              I
EXAMPLE ERROR-1       IINVALID INPUT DATA
              I
EXAMPLE ERROR-2       IINVALID INPUT DATA
              I
JACK-POT CORP.        IYIELD HIGHER THAN 50%
```

FIGURE 7–15   SAMPLE GRAPHIC OUTPUT FOR THE STOCK-YIELD PROGRAM.

ceed 50 percent, but if the computed yield does exeed this percentage, the error message YIELD HIGHER THAN 50% should be printed.

The input consists of records containing the stock name as X(20), the stock price as 9(3)V99, and the dividend as 9(2)V99.

7.12   Data records contain sales data as follows:

COLUMN	DATA
1–5	Amount (whole dollar)
6	Region code: 1 = West, 2 = Midwest 3 = South, 4 = East
7–8	Month code (numeric)

We want to be able to read the data and produce the sales analysis report presented in Figure 7-16. Input records that contain error region codes, error month codes, or nonnumeric amounts should be excluded from the tabulation and are to be printed with a suitable error message. Write a program to produce such a report.

ACME Corporation
Sales Analysis Report

MONTH	WEST	MIDWEST	SOUTH	EAST	MONTHLY TOTAL	PERCENT OF YEAR TOTAL
JANUARY						
FEBRUARY						
MARCH						
APRIL						
MAY						
JUNE						
JULY						
AUGUST						
SEPTEMBER						
OCTOBER						
NOVEMBER						
DECEMBER						
TOTAL						
PERCENT OF TOTAL						

FIGURE 7-16   FORM OF REQUIRED SALES ANALYSIS REPORT.

7.13   The function of a program is to output a sales forecast based on the following input:

NEXT-MONTH: A numeric value that designates the first month to be included in the forecast

HOW-MANY-MONTHS: A 2-digit number that designates the number of months to be included in the forecast

BASE: A dollar value used as the base for the forecast formula

COEFFICIENT: A numeric coefficient used in the forecast formula

The forecasting formula used is:

$$F_i = B + cN$$

The forecast for month i (F_i) is equal to the base B plus a coefficient c times the number of months N from the starting point. If the first month is 2 (February), then the forecast for April will be:

$$F_{April} = B + c\,(2)$$

Thus, $N = 2$ in this case, since April is two months after February, which is the starting month.

If the following input were used, the resulting output would be as shown below.

INPUT:

NEXT-MONTH	05	
HOW-MANY-MONTHS		09
BASE	00100000^00	
COEFFICIENT	0000025000	

OUTPUT:

	PROJECTED SALES
MAY	100250.00
JUNE	100500.00
JULY	100750.00
AUGUST	101000.00
SEPTEMBER	101250.00
OCTOBER	101500.00
NOVEMBER	101750.00
DECEMBER	102000.00
JANUARY	102250.00

7.14   Modify the sample searching program in the last section of the chapter as follows. Assume that the student names are sorted in ascending sequence. After the table is created, read records, each of which contains a student name. Search the table and print the test score data for that student. If the name of the student cannot be found, print a suitable error message.

7.15   Write a COBOL program segment to perform a search in a sorted table called TABLE, searching for an entry that matches THIS-RECORD. If a match is found, the program performs the paragraph MATCHED; otherwise, it performs the paragraph NO-MATCH. Use I to hold the position of the matching table entry, if there is a match. Assume the following data descriptions:

```
01   THIS RECORD      PICTURE X(12).
01   I                PICTURE 999.
```

```
01   TABLE.
     02   CELL            PICTURE X(12) OCCURS 100 TIMES
                          INDEXED BY N.
```

7.16   Consider the following definitions:

```
01   TABLE-OF-NAMES.
     02   NAMES OCCURS 100 TIMES
               INDEXED BY I.
          03   NAME-LETTERS OCCURS 20 TIMES
                    INDEXED BY C V.
               04   LETTER   PIC X.
01   VOWEL-FLAG            PIC XXX.
     88   VOWEL-FOUND VALUE 'YES'.
     88   VOWEL-NOT-FOUND VALUE 'NO'.
01   CONSONANT-FLAG   PIC XXX.
     88   CONSONANT-FOUND VALUE 'YES'.
     88   CONSONANT-NOT-FOUND VALUE 'NO'.
```

Write instructions to find the first vowel after the first consonant for a given name, say the 10th one. If there is a first vowel after the first consonant, then V should contain the location of that vowel and C should contain the location of the first consonant within the name. Use VOWEL-FLAG and CONSONANT-FLAG as defined above. (*Note:* When a table is indexed by two index items, as in INDEXED BY C V, if VARYING is used and specifies C or V, then the index specified is the one used in the search. If VARYING is omitted, then the first item, in this case C, is the one used in the search.)

7.17   How does COBOL differentiate between searching sorted and unsorted tables?

7.18   What is the difference between an index and a subscript in COBOL?

7.19   Review the meaning of the following search-related COBOL features, explaining the use of each feature:

a   OCCURS accompanied by the ASCENDING (DESCENDING) KEY options
b   INDEXED BY
c   USAGE IS INDEX
d   SEARCH and its several optional forms
e   SET TO and SET UP BY or SET DOWN BY

7.20   It is desired to write a program to read in numeric data and to output a bar chart depicting the frequency as percent values. Input consists of records of three types: The first record contains a free-form report header. The second record contains three parameter values:

1   *The number of classes in the bar chart:* This indicates the number of classes in the bar chart.

2   *The limiting value of the first class:* All values equal to or less than this limiting value will be grouped in the first class.

3   *The class size:* This parameter defines the range of values that constitute a class, or group.

These three values are sufficient to define the bar chart. For instance, in the sample output of Figure 7-17 the number of classes was 5 (assume the maximum number of classes is 25). The limiting value of the lowest class was 1,000 while the class size is 2,000. Also notice that all values above 7,000 in the example are grouped in the highest class.

Write a program that reads in the header and the three parameter values discussed above and the data and prints a bar chart such as shown in Figure 7-17.

The input data should have a PICTURE of S9(7) with 8 values per record. The program should check for nonnumeric data and print out those records that contain such data. However, spaces are not considered errors; they simply indicate the end of data. For instance, if we had 19 data values, there would be 8 values in the first record, 8 values in the second, and 3 values in the third record followed by blanks. Your program should scan each record and sense the end of data when blanks are encountered. Figure 7-18 shows sample error message output for some records which happened to contain nonnumeric data.

Finally, your program should be capable of printing a statistical summary such as illustrated in Figure 7-19, showing the number of correct data values, the mean of these values, the minimum, and

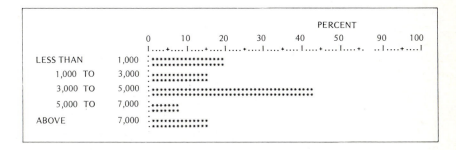

FIGURE 7-17   SAMPLE BAR CHART.

the maximum. The mean is the arithmetic average of the sum of all correct data values divided by the number of correct data values. Use the sample data in Figure 7-20 to check your program. It should give the output shown in Figures 7-17, 7-18, and 7-19.

```
SAMPLE BAR CHART
INCORRECT DATA IN THIS CARD
ERROR      0007000      0008000      0002500      0001000      0002000      0007000      0004500
INCORRECT DATA IN THIS CARD
0004500      0003000      A003000      0004400
```

FIGURE 7-18   SAMPLE OUTPUT ERROR MESSAGES.

```
SUMMARY STATISTICS

NO. OF VALUES   =    26

MEAN            =         3,611

MINIMUM         =           400

MAXIMUM         =         8,000
```

FIGURE 7-19   SAMPLE OUTPUT STATISTICS.

```
SAMPLE BAR CHART
0500010000002000
0000500      0000400      0003000      0004000      0002000      0001500      0006000      0008000
0000500      0000600      0004000      0003000      0003000      0006000      0004000      0003500
ERROR        0007000      0008000      0002500      0001000      0002000      0007000      0001500
0004500      0003000      A003000      0004400
```

FIGURE 7-20   SAMPLE INPUT DATA.

III   File Processing

8

SEQUENTIAL FILES

FILE ORGANIZATION

The concept of file organization refers to the manner in which data records are arranged on a file storage medium. There are three principal methods of file organization in COBOL: sequential, indexed, and relative.

In a sequential file, the records are written in a serial order and are accessed (read) in the same order as written. The serial order need not be in any particular sequence, such as according to account number. Files assigned to the printer and magnetic tape drive always are organized as sequential files. On the other hand, files stored on magnetic disk and other direct access storage devices may be sequential, indexed, or relative files.

Although the language does not require it, sequential files on tape or disk most commonly are sorted so that the records are in some logical sequential order. For instance, if we have a customer file, we might choose to sort the records on the basis of customer number. Then, if customer numbers are unique, each successive record read from the file should have a higher customer number than the one before. This practice of sorting the records is convenient when processing "batch" jobs, such as payroll. In such jobs, we sort the "transaction" data, such as time cards, in the same order as the employee payroll file. Then we need to go through that file only once, rather than go back and forth looking for employee records in random order.

Indexed file organization means that an index has been created so that records can be located directly without accessing them in sequence. We describe this file organization method in Chapter 10, "Indexed Files."

Relative file organization means that the file is stored in such a way that each record has an identifier by which it can be accessed directly. This method is covered in Chapter 11, "Relative File Processing."

Review

1   The manner in which data records are arranged on a file storage medium is referred to as file _____.

organization

2   The type of file for which the records are written in a serial order and for which the records must be accessed in the same order as written is the _____ file organization.

sequential

3   The type of file for which the records have been read and stored in a

serial order, but for which access can be direct, is the _____ file organization.

indexed

4   The type of file for which records are both stored and accessed directly according to the value of an identifier is the _____ file organization.

relative

FILE LABELS

Files stored on magnetic tape or disk involve the use of *label* records in addition to the data records in the file. These label records precede and follow the data records in the file and are used to achieve proper identification and control over file use and disposition.

Label records are processed by special routines in the operating system of each computer installation. These routines create and process labels according to the standardized conventions of that installation. In general, the installation will adopt a standard label record layout specifying the fields comprising a label record and the rules for processing data in these fields. These conventions vary substantially in terms of detail, but they are quite similar to one another in concept. Thus, the discussion that follows describes typical treatment of labels, rather than any universal practice.

A reel of tape or a disk unit (pack) is often referred to as a *volume*. A volume may contain one or more complete files, or it may contain a portion of a file. At the beginning of the volume there is a *volume label* record that contains information about the contents of the volume. Then, a *header label* precedes the data records of the file while a *trailer label* marks the end of the file.

Figure 8–1 presents the file layout for the case of a multifile volume and a multivolume file. In part (a) there are two files stored in the same volume. In such a case both files are identified by the same volume reference, but each file is uniquely identified by an identification field in its header and trailer labels. If the volume is a reel of tape, users of both files need to know the common volume identification, and they would specify it in job control statements submitted at job execution time. Further, one must know the relative position of a given file on a tape, and again, that information is specified by job control statements. For example, if we wanted to process file XYZ, which is the third file on tape volume 12345, we would submit job control statements to specify the volume number and the position (3) of the file. The file is then identified by reference to a cataloged file name supplied in job control statements. In addition, the COBOL program itself may con-

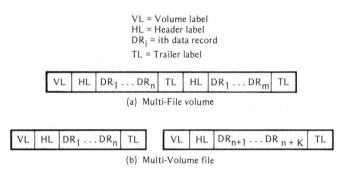

FIGURE 8-1   **GENERAL FILE LAYOUT.**

tain some further identification information in the corresponding FD entry of the DATA DIVISION.

When the storage medium is disk, the volume label typically contains a reference to a "table of contents" for the volume which serves as the location directory for the files in the volume. This locational directory enables the disk device to take a direct path to the beginning of the file, where the header label is read and processed. Magnetic tape, on the other hand, lacks the direct access feature, and the preceding tape footage has to be taken up before getting to a file other than the first file.

In part (b) of Figure 8-1 there is an illustration of a file residing in two volumes. In such a case the trailer label of the first volume and the volume label of the second volume typically contain appropriate information to identify the continuation and to ensure proper processing. For instance, we would want to know that the file is not finished when we have reached the end of the first volume, and that another volume should be accessed next for the continuation of the file.

At this point it is appropriate to consider some physical characteristics of magnetic tape files. We may wonder, for example, about the location of the trailer label in a multivolume file. Obviously, it cannot be located at the very physical end of the tape because of threading requirements. The beginning and the end of usable tape is marked by a reflective adhesive marker. Thus a leader is provided for threading at the beginning and at the end of the tape. When we create a file that exceeds one volume, the system senses the *end-of-reel marker* and proceeds to write a trailer label at the end of the block being written. Therefore, enough tape must be left after the marker so that both the unfinished block and the trailer label can be written without running out of tape.

As far as label processing is concerned, we can differentiate the processing on the basis of whether a file is opened for *output* or *input*.

When a file is used in the output mode, the three main actions are *open*, *write*, and *close*. The following general operations take place with respect to label processing:

When the file is opened for output the beginning label is checked for the field that contains the expiration date of the previously written file. If the expiration date has not yet been reached, then label processing results in some appropriate diagnostic message and prevention of the output function. Thus, a file is protected from inadvertent overwriting. If the expiration date indicates that the previous file can be overwritten, then the beginning label of the new file is written.

Write operations proceed normally until the physical end of the file is reached. If the file is on magnetic tape and it is to be continued on another reel, a trailer label is written indicating that this is the end of the reel and not the end of the file. Then the operator is notified to make the next reel available by replacing the present reel with a "fresh" reel on the same tape drive or by providing for continuation on another drive. A beginning volume label and a header label is then written before the next record block is written on the new reel. Thus, three label records are written between the last data record on the first reel and the first data record on the new reel.

If the file is stored on magnetic disk and it is to continue on another disk, the actions parallel those of tape. However, in the case of a disk file, the physical end of the file may be reached without it being the end of the volume. For example, we may have allocated cylinders 21 to 80 to the file, but because of planning error the file requires more than 60 cylinders. In such a case the operating system will issue a diagnostic message to the operator and the job will be abnormally terminated (although some operating systems may allow the machine operator to expand file size immediately).

When a close-file command is carried out, the resulting operation is the writing of a trailer label at the end of the file. As records are written into the file their number typically is accumulated by the label-processing routine, and this "block count" is written as a field in the trailer label. When the file is used as input on future occasions, the counting is repeated, and the new count is compared to the count in the trailer label to ascertain that all the records in the file have been read by the time the trailer label is processed.

When a file is used in the input mode, the three main actions are *open, read,* and *close.* The following general operations take place with respect to label processing:

When the file is opened for input the beginning labels are read to ascertain that the file identification provided in the job control statements agrees with the information in the label record.

The read operation proceeds normally until the trailer label is reached. If the label signifies the end of the file, then the operating system communicates this information to the program (recall READ . . . AT END . . .) and aborts the program if a further attempt is made to read from the file. If the file is a multivolume file, the end-of-volume label will signify such a condition and will result in reading and processing the volume and file header labels on the next volume. Of course, the label-processing routine will check to ascertain that the correct sequence of volumes is presented.

When an input file is closed the trailer label is processed to verify that all records have been read. If the file is on tape, the reel is normally rewound as a result of closing the file. In some instances it is desirable to read a file in reverse order, in which case an "open reverse" command may be issued after a suitable "close with no rewind" command. The trailer label then acts as a header label. Such a role reversal is possible because the header and trailer labels contain almost identical information. However, a block count is not present in the header label, since there is no knowledge of the block count when this label is written.

In general, label processing involves a number of specialized functions having to do with proper identification of data files and ensuring the data integrity in such files. As stated earlier, it is a function governed by localized operating conventions and procedures, and the programmer has to obtain specific instructions from the particular installation.

Review

1 The records in magnetic tape or disk files that are used to achieve proper identification and control over file use are the _____ records.

label

2 A *volume* typically includes [only one / several] reel(s) of tape or disk unit(s).

only one

3 The record that contains information about the contents of the volume is the _____ label.

volume

4   Following the volume label, the record that precedes the data records of a file is the _____ label.

header

5   It [is / is not] possible for more than one file to be stored in the same volume, and it [is / is not] possible for a file to be stored in more than one volume.

is; is

6   In the case of a multifile volume, the two or more files are identified by the same volume reference but are uniquely identified by an information field in their respective _____ labels.

header

7   In the case of a multivolume file, the _____ label of the first volume and the _____ label of the second volume typically contain information to identify the continuation.

trailer; header

8   The physical end of a reel of magnetic tape is signaled by the _____ marker.

end-of-reel

9   When the end-of-reel marker is sensed during data output, the block of data being written is completed and a(n) _____ label is written.

trailer

10   For a file used in the output mode, the three main actions are _____, _____, and _____.

open; write; close

11   For a file used in the input mode, the main three main actions are
_____, _____, and _____.

open; read; close

12   The specific procedures associated with label processing [have generally been standardized / are governed by localized conventions].

are governed by localized
conventions

RECORD BLOCKING

Data records handled in a program are called *logical records,* as distinguished from the *physical records* written on a file device such as tape or
disk. A physical record is defined as a group of bytes written or read in one
I/O (input-output) operation. The physical and logical records are related to
each other in many possible ways:

They may be identical.

A physical record may consist of several complete logical records.

A physical record may consist of a portion of one logical record or
may consist of a mixture of several complete and partial logical
records.

The term *block* often is used as being synonymous with *physical
record,* while the term *blocking factor* denotes the number of logical records
per block. When the blocking factor is 1, the physical and logical records are
equivalent, and we often refer to them as *unblocked* records. When the
blocking factor is greater than 1, then a block contains several logical
records, and we refer to them as *blocked* records. Finally, if the blocking
factor is less than 1, we have *spanned* records, in which case a logical record
is written in two or more physical records. If the logical record is not an integer multiple of the block, then there may be one or two partial logical
records in a block. For example if logical records are 1,200 bytes long and
physical records are 500 bytes long, the third block will contain the last 200
bytes of the first logical record and the first 300 bytes of the second logical
record.

Logical records may be fixed-length or variable-length. For example,
an employee record that contains the names of dependents would be a can-
didate for variable-length format, since some employees may have no dependents while other may have a large number of dependents. If we used
fixed-length records in such a case, all records would have the length re-

quired for the record with the maximum number of dependents, thus wasting a lot of file storage.

Whether fixed or variable in length, records may be blocked or spanned. When records vary in length, blocks normally would also vary in length, unless they contain "padding" or the records are spanned across blocks. For instance, suppose block length is fixed at 1,000 bytes and we have records of 300, 450, and 280 bytes. The first block could contain the first two records and 250 bytes of padding (special characters recognized as not being data). However, if records were spanned, then the first block would contain the first two records plus the first 250 bytes of the third record. The second block would contain the last 30 bytes of the third record plus data from the following records.

Instead of using either padding or spanned records, however, the preferred alternative is to use variable-length blocks. In such cases there are block-length and record-length fields. For simplicity, assume a maximum block length of 100 and records of length 25, 50, 30, 20, and 40. Figure 8–2 illustrates the block data format. The first field contains the block length which includes the (assumed) 2 bytes needed for this field. Then each record is preceded by a 2-byte record-length field. Thus, in the first block, 81 is derived from the 75, (25 + 50), data bytes required for the first two records plus the total of 6 bytes required for the block-length and the two record-length fields.

In summary, records may be fixed or variable in length and they may be blocked or unblocked. Records may also be spanned across blocks. Of these options, the most widely used is the fixed-blocked, since it is best suited to the most common needs in data processing and it entails the least complexity.

Record blocking is done to compact data in file storage media and to improve processing time. Blocking results in data compaction because of the fact that a "dead space" *interblock gap* is necessary between physical blocks. With typical-length records of a few hundred bytes, unblocked records can result in having as much as 80 to 90 percent of the file device consisting of interblock gaps. Besides compaction, blocking improves processing time because the number of physical read and write operations is reduced by the blocking factor. I/O operations are very slow compared to central processing, and blocking helps reduce the incidence of a program being "I/O-bound," that is, waiting for the reading or writing of data before processing can continue. To further improve I/O operations most operating systems use *double-buffering*.

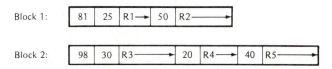

FIGURE 8–2   ILLUSTRATIONS OF BLOCKED, VARIABLE-LENGTH RECORD FORMAT.

A *buffer* is a storage space. Data read from a file medium is always stored in an I/O buffer; similarly data is always sent to the file device from an I/O buffer. This I/O buffer must be at least equal to the block size, so that a complete block is read from or written into a file. Double-buffering refers to the nearly universal practice of allocating twice the buffer size needed to store a block of data from a given file. If the file is an input file, *anticipatory double-buffering* is practiced. When an OPEN command is encountered, the system proceeds to read the first block and store it in the first buffer and then continues reading the second block into the second buffer. When the program has processed all the records from the first buffer, processing continues with the records in the second buffer while the first buffer is being refilled with the third block of data. In a similar fashion, when a block has been completed in one buffer for an output file, formation of the second block begins in the second buffer while the first buffer is being emptied. Thus, double-buffering cuts down on the waiting period between read-write operations. Of course, one can see that the advantage of double-buffering is enhanced as the blocking factor is increased.

With respect to storage, block length is a crucial variable in determining the total physical file size. For instance, magnetic tapes come in 2,400-foot reels and commonly in densities of 556, 800, 1,600, and 6,250 bytes per inch. The following formula can be used for IBM system files to compute tape length needed to store a file:

$$\text{Length} = (\text{number of records}) \frac{\left(\dfrac{\text{block size}}{\text{density}}\right) + k}{12 \text{ (records per block)}}$$

where k is the interblock gap (0.6 inch for 1,600 density and 0.3 inch for 6,250 density).

Consider a file of 100,000 customer records each containing 500 bytes. If we choose four records per block and we assume 6,250 bytes per inch tape density, the length of magnetic tape required is:

$$\text{Length} = (100,000) \frac{\left(\dfrac{6,000}{6,250}\right) + 0.3}{12(4)} = 1291.66 \text{ feet}$$

However, if the blocking factor is increased to 12 records per block, then the length required is:

$$\text{Length} = (100,000) \frac{\left(\dfrac{6,000}{6,250}\right) + 0.3}{12(12)} = 875 \text{ feet}$$

Thus, it can be seen that block size has a significant impact on the total physical file size for magnetic tape. This consideration is in fact even more important for disk files, and tables or formulas are available for estimating the amount of disk space required as a function of block size.

Review

1   The type of record that is defined as a group of bytes written or read in one I/O operation is the _____ record.

physical

2   In contrast to physical records, the data records handled in a program are called _____ records.

logical

3   The term "block" is another name for a [logical / physical] record.

physical

4   The blocking factor represents the number of _____ per block.

logical records

5   When the records are described as being "unblocked," then by definition the blocking factor has the value _____.

1

6   The term "spanned records" indicates that the blocking factor is [less than / greater than] 1.

less than

7   Suppose each logical record is 1,000 bytes long and each block is 500 bytes long. In such a case the blocking factor has the value _____.

8   The logical records in a program may be fixed-length or variable-length. If fixed-length blocks are used with variable-length records, then each block can be restricted to an integer number of records by filling in the unused portion of the block with _____.

padding

9   When variable-length blocks are used with variable-length records, then each block contains not only the data but also separate fields for _____ length and _____ length.

block; record (Note: There may
be more than one record, and
therefore more than one
record-length field.)

10   In terms of actual practice, records are most often [fixed / variable] in length and [blocked / unblocked].

fixed; blocked

11   A principal advantage of record blocking is that it results in data compaction and a reduction in the physical read and write operations, thereby also reducing processing _____.

time

12   In addition to using blocking, the practice associated with defining the buffer size that further reduces the time devoted to I/O operations is called _____.

double-buffering

13   Given a particular number of records all of the same length and given that blocking is used, the larger the block size, the [smaller / larger] is the total physical file size for either magnetic or disk files.

smaller

COBOL INSTRUCTIONS FOR SEQUENTIAL FILES

We will now describe a number of COBOL instructions and features pertaining to sequential files. We will consider the features and instructions that are relevant particularly with respect to disk and magnetic tape files.

ENVIRONMENT DIVISION Features

For sequential files, the SELECT and ASSIGN statements in the FILE-CONTROL paragraph of the INPUT-OUTPUT SECTION have the format presented in Figure 8–3. The instruction for each file must begin with the key word SELECT. OPTIONAL should be used only with input files, and its inclusion signifies that a file may or may not be present. For example, two

```
FILE-CONTROL

    SELECT   [ OPTIONAL ]   file-name

        ASSIGN TO        { implementor-name-1 }  ...
                         { literal-1           }

        [ RESERVE integer-1  [ AREA  ] ]
                             [ AREAS ]
    [[ ORGANIZATION IS ]  SEQUENTIAL.]


    [ PADDING CHARACTER IS  { data-name-1 } ]
                            { literal-2   }

    [ RECORD DELIMITER IS  { STANDARD-1          } ]
                           { implementor-name-2  }


    [ ACCESS MODE IS SEQUENTIAL ]

    [ FILE STATUS IS data-name-2 ]
```

FIGURE 8-3   FILE-CONTROL FORMAT FOR SEQUENTIAL FILES.

types of input files may be included in a given program: one for current transactions and the other for corrected previous-error transactions. The second file can be declared OPTIONAL if we anticipate occasions of no previous-error transactions. (Of course, the program logic is responsible for handling the presence or absence of an optional file.) In the 1985 standard, OPTIONAL files in the FILE-CONTROL paragraph must be OPENed in the INPUT, I-O, or EXTEND modes.

In the ASSIGN statement, the implementor-name refers to the storage device designation. The designation may vary from complicated forms, such as ASSIGN TO SYS005-UT-3410-S-MAST, to simpler forms such as ASSIGN TO MASS-STORAGE A. Obviously, you must consult your computer manual for local file designations. In the 1985 version of COBOL, a file can be ASSIGNed to literal-1, which may be a file-name. For example, for a disk file on the "B:" drive of a personal computer, we could have:

SELECT STUDENT-FILE ASSIGN TO "B:STUDENT.DAT".

If a file consists of more than one tape reel or disk unit, then the assignment is made to two or more implementor-names, such as SELECT PAYROLL-FILE ASSIGN TO TAPE-UNIT-MR02, TAPE-UNIT-MR03.

The ORGANIZATION clause is optional; but when it is omitted, the file is assumed to be SEQUENTIAL. The ACCESS MODE also is assumed to be SEQUENTIAL when not stated. We will further describe the use of these two clauses in Chapters 10 and 11, where we will consider the options associated with indexed and relative files.

The PADDING CHARACTER choice allows the programmer to specify the character to be used to fill the remainder of a partially filled block. Both data-name-1 and literal-1 must be one character long. When a PADDING option is not specified, then the padding character is the default character used by that particular operating system.

The RECORD DELIMITER allows the programmer to identify the method of determining the length of a variable-length record. If STANDARD-1 is used, then the file must be on magnetic tape and the method used is that specified in American National Standard X3.27-1978 and International Standard 1001 1979, both entitled "Magnetic Tape Labels and File Structure for Information Interchange." If "RECORD DELIMITER IS implementor-name-2" is specified, then the method is determined by the implementor and corresponds to the implementor-name. If the RECORD clause is omitted and the file contains variable-length records, then the method used for determining the length is the default method specified by the implementor. The method often used is to prefix a record-length field at the beginning of a record.

We will discuss the FILE STATUS clause later in this chapter in the section entitled I/O Exception Processing.

The I-O-CONTROL paragraph of the INPUT-OUTPUT SECTION of

the ENVIRONMENT DIVISION can be used to express some aspects particular to tape and disk files:

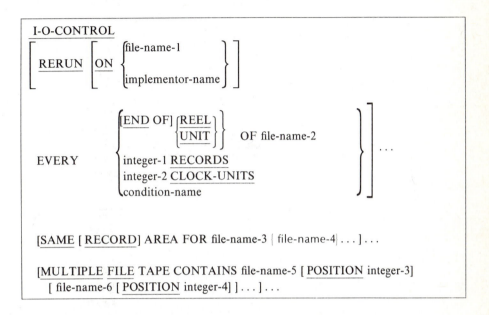

The RERUN clause can be used to instruct the computer to store the program status, as it is in internal storage, onto a device— commonly a magnetic tape. Such a periodic recording of the program status permits restart of the program from the "middle" should an interruption become necessary. Such "checkpoints" are particularly useful in long program runs. For example, suppose a file update program has been running for 1 hour and there is a physical imperfection in the transactions tape, so that the last few transactions cannot be processed. Rather than correct the situation and rerun the entire program from its beginning, we could interrupt and restart it from the point where the last program status was recorded. The EVERY integer RECORDS clause specifies how often we record the program status. For example, we may have:

RERUN ON tape-unit-1 EVERY 1000 RECORDS OF TRANSACTION-FILE.

In this case, at most we would have to reprocess 1,000 TRANSACTION-FILE records should a program interruption occur. Additional options are available with the RERUN clause, which are self-explanatory for the most part.

Although the RERUN clause can be very useful, it has been declared "obsolete" in the 1985 standard because it was deemed to be properly a function of the operating system rather than of COBOL. Still, many old programs may include use of this clause, and therefore we have described it in this section.

The SAME RECORD AREA clause allows two or more files to share the same internal storage area (buffer). This option would be used if the internal storage available were insufficient and two files were not in use at the same time. As an example we have:

SAME RECORD AREA FOR MONTHLY-FILE, QUARTERLY-FILE.

The MULTIPLE FILE clause can be used when more than one file is recorded on the same tape reel. The POSITION integer specifies the relative position of the file—in effect, whether the file is in the first position, the second, the third, etc. For example:

MULTIPLE FILE TAPE CONTAINS WEEKLY-FILE POSITION 2
MONTHLY-FILE POSITION 4

could mean that WEEKLY-FILE is the second file in the reel and MONTHLY-FILE is the fourth file in the reel.

The 1985 version of COBOL modified the I-O-CONTROL paragraph of the ENVIRONMENT DIVISION by making the MULTIPLE FILE TAPE CONTAINS clause obsolete. As such, the clause can continue to be used, but it is understood that it will be deleted in a future revision of the language. The clause has been infrequently used, in any case.

Review

1   In the FILE-CONTROL SECTION of the ENVIRONMENT DIVISION the instruction for each file must start with the key word [SELECT / RESERVE], followed by the file-name.

SELECT

2   The ASSIGN TO implementor-name clause identifies the _____ to be used with each file.

storage device

3   When use of the optional ORGANIZATION clause is omitted, the file is assumed to be a(n) _____ file.

sequential

4   When the ACCESS MODE clause is omitted, file access is assumed to be _____.

                                                                          sequential

5   The clause in the FILE-CONTROL paragraph of the ENVIRONMENT DIVISION that allows the programmer to specify the character to be used to fill the remainder of a partially filled block is the _____ _____ clause.

                                                              PADDING CHARACTER

6   The clause that allows the programmer to identify the method of determining the length of a variable-length record is the _____ _____ clause.

                                                                RECORD DELIMITER

7   In the I-O-CONTROL paragraph of the INPUT-OUTPUT SECTION, the RERUN clause is declared "obsolete" in the [1974 / 1985] COBOL standard.

                                                                                1985

8   The SAME RECORD AREA clause generally is used in the INPUT-OUTPUT SECTION in order to conserve the amount of internal _____ that is used.

                                                                            storage

9   The MULTIPLE FILE clause, declared obsolete in the 1985 standard, is used in the INPUT-OUTPUT SECTION when more than one file is recorded on the same tape reel. The POSITION integer specifies the relative position of the _____ on the reel.

                                                                                file

DATA DIVISION Features

Figure 8-4 presents the general format for a file description entry, with some options being particularly meaningful for sequential files. FD marks the beginning of a file description entry and is followed immediately by the name

```
FD  file-name
    [IS EXTERNAL]
    [IS GLOBAL]
    [BLOCK CONTAINS  [integer-1 TO]  integer-2  {RECORDS   }]
                                                {CHARACTERS}

    [                 {CONTAINS integer-3 CHARACTERS                              }]
    [RECORD           {IS VARYING IN SIZE [[FROM integer-4] [TO integer-5] CHARACTERS]}]
    [                 {     [DEPENDING ON data-name-1]                          }]
    [                 {CONTAINS integer-6 TO integer-7 CHARACTERS                 }]

    [LABEL  {RECORD IS   }  {STANDARD}]
           {RECORDS ARE }  {OMITTED }

    [VALUE OF  {implementor-name-1 IS  {data-name-2}} ... ]
                                       {literal-1  }

    [DATA  {RECORD IS   }  {data-name-3} ... ]
           {RECORDS ARE }

    [LINAGE IS  {data-name-4}  LINES  [WITH FOOTING AT  {data-name-5}]
                {integer-8  }                            {integer-9  }

        [LINES AT TOP  {data-name-6}]  [LINES AT BOTTOM  {data-name-7 }]]
                       {integer-10 }                      {integer-11 }
    [CODE-SET IS alphabet-name-1].
```

FIGURE 8–4   FORMAT FOR A FILE DESCRIPTION ENTRY.

of the file. The name of the file already has been declared in the ENVIRON-MENT DIVISION, where it was assigned to a hardware device.

The EXTERNAL and GLOBAL options are included in the format in Figure 8–4 for completeness but will not be considered until Chapter 12, "Subprograms and Nested Programs."

If records are grouped together, the BLOCK CONTAINS clause is used. If each record constitutes one block, the clause may be omitted or the equivalent BLOCK CONTAINS 1 RECORD can be used. When a block contains several records, then the clause must be used. Typically, this clause is used with the RECORDS option indicated above. In such a case it references the number of records per block. For example, if we have:

FD   PAYROLL-FILE BLOCK CONTAINS 10 RECORDS

each block will contain 10 records. However, if the records are of variable size, BLOCK CONTAINS 10 RECORDS will be interpreted to mean the maximum block size. Thus, if the records varied between 10 and 100 characters (this would be so identified in the record description), BLOCK CONTAINS 10 RECORDS would mean that blocks can be as short as 10 × 10 = 100 characters in length or as long as 10 × 100 = 1,000 characters in length. (Actually, the number of characters will be slightly different, depending on the *control fields* used by different compilers in recording variable-length blocks.)

If the option

FD   PAYROLL-FILE BLOCK CONTAINS 5 TO 12 RECORDS

were used, it would imply that the number of records per block might be a number between 5 and 12, again giving variable block size.

The option BLOCK CONTAINS integer CHARACTERS is used when the block contains padding—the last part of the block may consist of unusable characters. This could be the case when it is desired that block size be fixed, but, because of variable record length, it is not possible to fill the entire block without splitting records across blocks.

RECORD CONTAINS [integer-1 TO] integer-2 CHARACTERS can be used for documentary purposes only. The record description will provide all such information to the compiler since, we recall, the record description specifies all the fields and their length.

Variable-length records are specified in two ways. One way was explained in Chapter 7 in connection with the OCCURS . . . DEPENDING ON clause. We repeat the example presented there for ease of reference:

```
FD   TAPE-FILE   LABEL RECORD STANDARD
                 BLOCK CONTAINS 3 RECORDS
                 RECORD CONTAINS 9 TO 1309 CHARACTERS
                 DATA RECORD IS CHECKING-ACCOUNT-RECORD.
01   CHECKING-ACCOUNT- RECORD.
     02   CUSTOMER-NUMBER                PICTURE 9(6).
     02   NUMBER-OF-TRANSACTIONS         PICTURE 999.
     02   TRANSACTION OCCURS 0 TO 100 TIMES
                    DEPENDING ON NUMBER-OF-TRANSACTIONS.
          03   TRANSACTION-CODE          PICTURE 9.
          03   TRANSACTION-DATE          PICTURE 9(5).
          03   TRANSACTION-AMOUNT        PICTURE 9(5)V99.
```

This is a case in which a record may contain from 0 to 100 transactions. Notice that the minimum number of character positions is 9: 6 for the customer number and 3 for the number of transactions. The maximum size is $9 + (100 \text{ transactions} \times 13 \text{ characters per transaction}) = 1,309$.

Note that NUMBER-OF-TRANSACTIONS does not automatically contain the number of transactions. It is the responsibility of the program logic to store the proper data in the data-name of the DEPENDING ON clause and to do so prior to a subscripted reference that uses a subscript value as high as the value of NUMBER-OF-TRANSACTIONS. For example, if NUMBER-OF-TRANSACTIONS contains 10 and we want to add a new transaction (the 11th one), we should do something like the following:

```
ADD 1 TO NUMBER-OF-TRANSACTIONS
MOVE T-DATE-IN TO TRANSACTION-DATE (NUMBER-OF-TRANSACTIONS)
(etc.)
```

The second method of using variable-length records utilizes the IS VARYING IN SIZE clause included in the general format for file description presented in Figure 8–4. The following program segment will serve to illustrate such use of this clause:

```
FD   CUSTOMER-FILE
     BLOCK CONTAINS 1000 CHARACTERS
     RECORD IS VARYING IN SIZE
        FROM 20 TO 100 CHARACTERS
        DEPENDING ON CUST-REC-SIZE
     LABEL RECORDS ARE OMITTED
     DATA RECORD IS CUSTOMER-REC.
 01  CUSTOMER-REC
     02   CUSTOMER-NAME      PIC X(20).
     02   CUSTOMER-ADDRESS   PIC X(80).
        .
        .
        .
WORKING-STORAGE SECTION.
        .
        .
        .
     01   CUST-REC-SIZE      PIC 999.
```

In the above example, each customer record consists of a 20-byte fixed-length field containing the customer name. A second field in the record, CUSTOMER-ADDRESS, is assumed to be variable in terms of content. A customer whose address is not available would be so designated by placing a 20 in CUST-REC-SIZE, the field identified in the DEPENDING clause. Similarly, for a customer whose address is 65 bytes long, CUST-REC-SIZE would be set to 85. Then, when outputting of data takes place in CUSTOMER-FILE by use of the WRITE verb, the system strings as many whole records as will fit into each of the 1,000 character blocks. When there is insufficient space for one more whole record in the block, then that block is written onto the file, including end-of-block padding.

When a READ or RETURN is executed successfully, the DEPENDING ON field contains the record size of the record that was just read. Similarly, if the READ . . . INTO option is used, the receiving field will also be sent as many bytes as the value in the DEPENDING ON field. With respect to the data description above, assume that we write READ CUSTOMER-FILE INTO WORK-REC and that the specific record that was just read is 60 bytes long. After execution of the READ statement, CUST-REC-SIZE will contain the value 60, while WORK-REC will contain the appropriate content based on execution of a MOVE statement that sent 60 bytes. If WORK-REC were defined as PIC X(80), for example, the last 20 bytes would be filled with blanks, in accordance with the rules of MOVE associated with sending a shorter field to a longer one. Finally, a statement such as MOVE CUSTOMER-REC would result in 60 bytes being sent, if executed after the above READ example. But suppose we wrote the following succession of commands instead:

READ CUSTOMER-FILE
SUBTRACT 5 FROM CUST-REC-SIZE
MOVE CUSTOMER-REC . . .
WRITE CUSTOMER-REC

For the above program segment, the MOVE and the WRITE statements would handle a $60 - 5 = 55$ byte record. Thus, the programmer can control the effective length of a record defined by the VARYING clause in Figure 8-4 by manipulating the content of the DEPENDING ON field. Of course, care must be taken to avoid incorrect or illogical manipulation. For example, MOVE 120 TO CUST-REC-SIZE would be incorrect. Similarly, ADD 5 TO CUST-REC-SIZE in the above example in which a 60-byte record was read would be illogical, since there are no additional bytes available.

If data-name-1 in the RECORD clause in Figure 8-4 is not specified, then the length of the variable-length record is determined by the record description. If the record description itself contains a variable portion (as indicated by an OCCURS . . . DEPENDING ON clause), then the length of the record is the sum of the fixed plus the variable portion of the record. If no variable portion exists, then the record length is determined by the number of positions defined in the data description, including any implicit FILLER ("slack bytes") associated with the possible use of the SYNCHRONIZED option.

The LABEL RECORDS clause is optional. The OMITTED option indicates that the file has no beginning or ending label. If the STANDARD option is used, it is understood to be the standard labels for the particular computer installation. The natural question may be: Granted that they are "standard" for an installation, how do we communicate what the label should be in the context of the COBOL program? Recall that the label record contains data that identify the file, and obviously each file is identified uniquely. There are two basic ways of specifying the contents of a label. By the first and most common approach, this information is communicated through job control statements submitted external to the COBOL program. Thus, this information is not communicated in the COBOL language as such. Another way of communicating the contents of a label record is by use of the VALUE OF clause, which, however was designated as obsolete in the 1985 standard. As an example of the latter approach for specifying the content of a label, we could have:

```
FD   PAYROLL-FILE BLOCK CONTAINS 10 RECORDS
     LABEL RECORDS ARE STANDARD
     VALUE OF IDENTIFICATION IS 'A2359'
     RETENTION-PERIOD IS 090
     DATA RECORD IS PAY-REC.
```

In the example above, the words IDENTIFICATION and RETENTION-PERIOD are meaningful in a particular installation, and they indicate that the STANDARD label contains a field, called IDENTIFICATION, whose content should be A2359. When the file is opened, the field is checked to ascertain that the A2359 data are there—in other words, that the correct file is available. The RETENTION-PERIOD implies that this file cannot be written on until 90 days have elapsed. Of course, other similar fields are used in the VALUE clause option for a more complete description of a file label.

The LINAGE clause in Figure 8-4 applies to printer-assigned files and is used to control page size. We will further discuss the use of this clause in Chapter 13, "Report Generation."

Finally, the CODE-SET option in Figure 8-4 is used to specify the character code convention used to represent data on a file. As described in Chapter 3 on the ENVIRONMENT DIVISION, the alphabet-name associated with CODE-SET would have been defined in the SPECIAL-NAMES paragraph. The rarely used CODE-SET option allows us to read or write data onto a file using a different alphabet from the standard one, presumably for the purpose of communicating data to another computer.

Review

1   The beginning of a new file description in the FILE SECTION of the DATA DIVISION is signaled by the letters _____, followed immediately by the name of the file.

FD

2   If records are grouped together, then the clause that is included in the file description is the _____ clause.

BLOCK CONTAINS

3   Use of the OCCURS . . . DEPENDING ON clause is one way by which [fixed / variable]-length records can be specified.

variable

4   Use of the IS VARYING IN SIZE clause is a second method by which _____-length records can be specified.

variable

5   When the STANDARD option is used with the LABEL RECORDS clause, this indicates that there [is / is not] a beginning label and there [is /is not] an ending label.

is; is

6   The option in the file description entry that allows us to read or write data onto a file by using a different alphabet from the standard one for the computer system being used is the _____-SET option.

CODE

The OPEN and CLOSE Verbs

The OPEN verb initiates processing of a file and performs appropriate label processing. If the file is to be used as output, when the file is opened the existing label is checked to ascertain that the previous file can be "scratched." If so, the header label is written on the file. Similarly, if the file is opened for input, its label is read and checked for proper identification.

If an error condition arises as a result of such label processing, it either is reported by the operating system, which normally terminates the program, or it is handled by the program itself, as explained in a subsequent section of this chapter, I/O Exception Processing.

The OPEN verb has the following format:

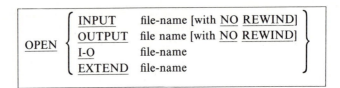

The I-O option can be used only for mass storage files. It allows the program to both input and output on the file. It is used if we want to change a record that we have just read. With tape files, however, we cannot rewrite a record that we have just read in.

The EXTEND option positions the file after its last record. It can be used to add new records at the end of the file and is really a special case of the OUTPUT mode option.

Correct use of input-output verbs depends on the option, or mode, used in the OPEN statement. Table 8-1 summarizes this relationship, with an X designating each permissible combination. For instance, if the INPUT mode option is used, then the READ verb can be used, but the WRITE or RE-WRITE verbs cannot be used.

The CLOSE verb has the following expanded format:

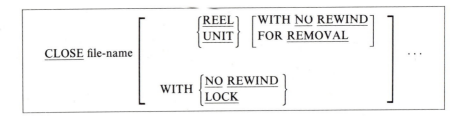

Prior to closing, a file must have been opened. "CLOSE file-name" results in end-of-file procedures. If label records have not been omitted, a trailer label is written and the tape is rewound automatically. If the option CLOSE file-name REEL is used, this results in closing that reel but not the file as such. Thus, the file itself still will be in an open status. The only circumstance in which the REEL option is used is the case of multireel files, where the processing of a particular reel for a file may have been completed but other reels for the file still might remain to be processed. If we are using disk files, then the term UNIT is used instead of REEL. When the indicated LOCK option is used instead, the file is locked once the tape is rewound and can be reopened only by restarting the program. The LOCK option thereby serves as protection against accidentally opening and misusing a file whose data have already been processed. The FOR REMOVAL option is used to allow the operator to intervene, remove the reel (at least logically), and replace it with another reel. The specific procedure that should take place in conjunction with using the FOR REMOVAL option is not defined by COBOL; rather, it is determined by the user.

**TABLE 8-1   PERMISSIBLE COMBINATIONS OF
OPEN-MODE OPTIONS AND INPUT-OUTPUT VERBS**

	OPEN MODE			
STATEMENT	INPUT	OUTPUT	I/O	EXTEND
READ	x		x	
WRITE		x		x
REWRITE			x	

Review

1   Processing of a file is initiated by the use of the _____ verb.

OPEN

2   If the READ verb is to be used subsequent to a file being opened, then the INPUT mode option should be included in the OPEN statement. Similarly, if the WRITE verb is to be used, then the _____ mode option should be included in the OPEN statement.

OUTPUT (OR EXTEND)

3   End-of-file procedures are invoked by use of the _____ verb.

CLOSE

4   The option in the closing routine that serves to protect the file from use (and misuse) is the [NO REWIND / LOCK] option.

LOCK

The READ, WRITE, and REWRITE Verbs

The format for the READ verb for sequential files is:

> READ FILE-name-1 [NEXT] [INTO identifier-1]
>
> [AT END imperative-statement-1]
>
> [NOT AT END imperative-statement-2]
>
> [END-READ]

However, if a file was designated as OPTIONAL in the SELECT statement and the file is not present, the AT END condition occurs when the first READ is executed. As Table 8-1 indicates, a READ is valid when a file has been opened as INPUT or I-O.

The relevant WRITE format is:

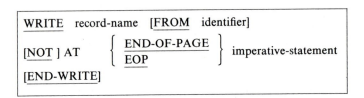

As Table 8-1 indicates, the file must be opened as either OUTPUT or EXTEND if the WRITE verb is to be used.

If a BLOCK CONTAINS clause was used in the file description, the system will automatically control the operations needed to form an appropriate block prior to a physical write of the block itself. The programmer need not be concerned about the blocking operation.

For printer-oriented files for which the LINAGE clause has been described, the NOT AT END-OF-PAGE and NOT AT EOP options may be used, as described in Chapter 13, "Report Generation."

The REWRITE statement is a specialized instruction for mass storage files. Its format is:

> REWRITE record-name [FROM identifier]

In order to update a sequential file on disk we may use "OPEN-I-O file-name." Then, after issuing a READ command that accesses the record to be updated, we use the REWRITE verb to replace the updated record in the same file instead of WRITE on a different file. With magnetic tape files, we must read a record from one file and MOVE and write the updated record on a new file.

It should be noted that REWRITE can be used only to update an existing file. If we are creating a new file, we use the WRITE verb.

Review

1   If the READ verb is to be used, the file must be opened in the
_____ or _____ mode.

INPUT; I-O

2   If the WRITE verb is to be used, the file must be opened in the
_____ or _____ mode.

OUTPUT; EXTEND

3   The verb that is used to update an existing file is the _____ verb.
To use this verb, the file must be opened in the _____ mode.

REWRITE; I-O

SAMPLE PROGRAM TO CREATE A SEQUENTIAL FILE

Figure 8-5 illustrates the process of creating a sequential file on magnetic
tape or disk. The source records are assumed to be in CUST-SOURCE-FILE.
Each record is read in and checked for sequence on a field called CUST-NO
in columns 1-6. If a record is not in ascending sequence, it is listed on the
printer for visual review and correction.

I/O EXCEPTION PROCESSING

We are familiar with the AT END clause associated with the READ statement.
Its purpose is to provide for specific processing when a particular exception
occurs during input, namely, when an end-of-file condition occurs. Other
I/O verbs, such as OPEN, WRITE, and CLOSE, do not have clauses paralleling the AT END feature of READ. Yet it is important for the programmer to
be able to test for exceptions and treat them under control of program logic.
For example, if we are opening a file and for some reason the command is
not successfully completed, we should be able to recognize the exceptional
condition and be able to continue with appropriate processing.
        COBOL provides for I/O exception processing in two ways. First, a
FILE STATUS may be declared with each file that can be tested for the presence of exceptions during I/O operations. Second, DECLARATIVES may be
used to provide for implicit processing of exceptions. We now describe each
of these approaches in turn.

```
       IDENTIFICATION DIVISION.
       PROGRAM-ID. CREATE-FILE.
     *
       ENVIRONMENT DIVISION.
     *
       CONFIGURATION SECTION.
       SOURCE-COMPUTER.   ABC-480.
       OBJECT-COMPUTER.   ABC-480.
     *
       INPUT-OUTPUT SECTION.
       FILE-CONTROL.
           SELECT CUST-MAST-FILE ASSIGN TO MASTOUT.
     *
           SELECT CUST-SOURCE-FILE   ASSIGN TO READER
                   FILE STATUS IS CUST-FILE-STATUS.
     *
           SELECT ERROR-FILE  ASSIGN TO PRINTER.
     *
       DATA DIVISION.
     *
       FILE SECTION.
     *
       FD   CUST-MAST-FILE
            LABEL RECORDS ARE STANDARD
            BLOCK CONTAINS 5 RECORDS
            DATA RECORD IS CUST-MAST-REC.
       01   CUST-MAST-REC              PIC X(75).
     *
       FD   CUST-SOURCE-FILE
            LABEL RECORDS OMITTED
            DATA RECORD IS CUST-SOURCE-REC.
       01   CUST-SOURCE-REC.
            02   CUST-NO              PIC 9(5).
            02   CUST-NAME            PIC X(20).
            02   CUST-ADDRESS         PIC X(50).
            02   FILLER               PIC X(5).
     *
       FD   ERROR-FILE
            LABEL RECORDS ARE OMITTED
            DATA RECORD IS ERROR-REC.
       01   ERROR-REC                 PIC X(132).
     *
       WORKING-STORAGE SECTION.
     *
       01   END-OF-FILE-INDICATOR     PIC XXX VALUE 'NO'.
            88 END-OF-FILE.           VALUE 'YES'.
     *
       01   CUST-FILE-STATUS          PIC XX.
     *
       01   PREVIOUS-CUST-NO          PIC 9(5) VALUE ZERO.
```

FIGURE 8-5   SAMPLE PROGRAM TO CREATE A SEQUENTIAL FILE.

```
01   SEQ-ERROR-MESSAGE.
     02   FILLER               PIC X VALUE SPACE.
     02   FILLER               PIC X(13) VALUE 'ERROR RECORD:'.
     02   RECORD-OUT           PIC X(75).
*
 01  I-O-ERROR-MESSAGE.
     02 FILLER                 PIC X(25) VALUE
                               'CUST-MASTER I/O EXCEPTION'.
     02 FILLER                 PIC X(16) VALUE
                          '   FILE STATUS = '.
     02 ERR-MESS-FILE-STATUS   PIC XX.
*
 01  JOB-TERMINATOR     PIC XXX VALUE 'NO'.
     88 END-OF-JOB      VALUE 'YES'.
/
 PROCEDURE DIVISION.
*
 100-PROGRAM-SUMMARY.
     OPEN INPUT CUST-SOURCE-FILE
          OUTPUT ERROR-FILE.
*
     OPEN OUTPUT CUST-MAST-FILE.
*
     IF CUST-FILE-STATUS = '00'
        PERFORM 200-CREATE-MASTER
     ELSE
        PERFORM 500-I-O-EXCEPTION.
*
     CLOSE CUST-SOURCE-FILE
           ERROR-FILE
           CUST-MAST-FILE.
*
     STOP RUN.
*
 200-CREATE-MASTER.
     PERFORM 300-READ-MASTER.
*
     PERFORM 400-CHECK-WRITE-READ UNTIL END-OF-FILE
                 OR END-OF-JOB.
*
 300-READ-MASTER.
     READ CUST-SOURCE-FILE RECORD.
     IF CUST-FILE-STATUS = '10'
        MOVE 'YES' TO END-OF-FILE-INDICATOR
     ELSE
        IF CUST-FILE-STATUS NOT = '00'
           PERFORM 500-I-O-EXCEPTION.
```

**FIGURE 8-5   SAMPLE PROGRAM TO CREATE A SEQUENTIAL FILE.
(Continued)**

```
400-CHECK-WRITE-READ.
    IF CUST-NO NOT > PREVIOUS-CUST-NO
        MOVE CUST-SOURCE-REC TO RECORD-OUT
        WRITE ERROR-REC FROM SEQ-ERROR-MESSAGE AFTER 2
    ELSE
        WRITE CUST-MAST-REC FROM CUST-SOURCE-REC
        MOVE CUST-NO TO PREVIOUS-CUST-NO.
*
    PERFORM 300-READ-MASTER.
*
 500-I-O-EXCEPTION.
    MOVE CUST-FILE-STATUS TO ERR-MESS-FILE-STATUS
    WRITE ERROR-REC FROM I-O-ERROR-MESSAGE AFTER 1
    MOVE 'YES' TO JOB-TERMINATOR.
```

**FIGURE 8-5   SAMPLE PROGRAM TO CREATE A SEQUENTIAL FILE.
(Continued)**

The FILE STATUS Feature

The programmer may declare a special FILE STATUS field for any file in the program. Then, at the completion of an I/O command this field contains code values that signify whether or not the I/O operation was successful. Consider this example:

```
SELECT CUSTOMER-FILE ASSIGN TO Device
        FILE STATUS IS I-O-STATUS.
    .
    .
WORKING-STORAGE SECTION.
    .
    .
01  I-O-STATUS  PIC XX.
```

In the SELECT statement above, notice that a field called I-O-STATUS is declared to be the FILE STATUS for this file. Then in WORKING-STORAGE, the file status is defined as consisting of 2 bytes. Figure 8-6 presents status codes and their meanings.

The FILE STATUS can be tested within the program to ascertain the outcome of an I/O operation. For example, we may have:

```
OPEN INPUT CUSTOMER-FILE.
IF I-O-STATUS = '00'
    PERFORM PROCESS-CUST
ELSE
    IF I-O-STATUS = '05'
```

STATUS CODE	EXPLANATION
00	Successful execution.
04	A record whose length is inconsistent with the record description for the file that has been read.
05	A file has been OPENed which is not present.
07	The file device is not magnetic tape, yet a CLOSE or OPEN involved a corresponding NO REWIND, REEL, FOR REMOVAL phrase.
10	End-of-file condition.
15	Attempt to read an optional file which is not present.
16	A READ statement was executed while the AT END condition is true (attempt to read past the end of the file).
30	A permanent error exists; no further information is available.
34	An attempt to write beyond the boundaries of the file.
35	Attempt to OPEN as INPUT, I-O, or EXTEND a non-optional file.
37	Attempt to OPEN a file that should be on mass storage but is not.
38	Attempt to OPEN a file that has been CLOSED with LOCK.
39	Error during OPEN execution, due to inconsistency between the file description and the actual file.
41	Attempt to OPEN a file that is already opened.
42	Attempt to CLOSE a file that is not open.
43	A successful READ did not precede execution of the current REWRITE command.
44	A boundary violation due to attempt to WRITE or REWRITE a record of improper length.

FIGURE 8-6   SEQUENTIAL FILE STATUS CODES AND THEIR MEANINGS.

STATUS CODE	EXPLANATION
46	Attempt to READ the next nonexistent record.
47	Attempt to READ from a file not open INPUT or I-O mode.
48	Attempt to WRITE on a file not open in OUTPUT or EXTEND mode.
49	Attempt to REWRITE on a file not open in I-O mode.
9X	An error condition defined by the particular system in use.

**FIGURE 8-6   SEQUENTIAL FILE STATUS CODES AND THEIR MEANINGS.
(Continued)**

```
            MOVE 'ERROR DURING OPEN' TO MESSAGE
      .
      .
      .
      ELSE
          IF I-O-STATUS = '10'
              MOVE 'END-OF-FILE' TO MESSAGE
          .
          .
```

For the above program segment, recall that I-O-STATUS was the name given to the FILE STATUS field for the CUSTOMER-FILE. After the OPEN statement, I-O-STATUS is tested for the possible conditions. Thus, the FILE STATUS feature can be used to detect exceptions during I/O operations. The data-name following FILE STATUS must be a 2-character field and may be qualified by a file-name if the same data-name was used for more than one file.

In practice, the operating systems in use almost always detect an I/O error, give a diagnostic message, and abend the job. If automatic abending is undesirable, the FILE STATUS feature allows the program to assume control over the exception situation and recover, or at least execute some procedure, before termination.

Use of DECLARATIVES

At the start of a PROCEDURE DIVISION the programmer may include a set of DECLARATIVES, as outlined in Figure 8–7. Notice that we begin immediately after the PROCEDURE DIVISION heading and signify the end by END DECLARATIVES. Within this portion of the program there may be one or more sections. The procedures within each section are *conditionally* executed on encountering an exception in conjunction with one of the five

```
PROCEDURE DIVISION.

DECLARATIVES.

section-name SECTION.

     USE AFTER { EXCEPTION }  PROCEDURE ON   ⎧ INPUT  ⎫
               { ERROR     }                 ⎪ OUTPUT ⎪
                                             ⎨ I-O    ⎬
                                             ⎪ EXTEND ⎪
                                             ⎩ file-name ⎭

paragraph-1.
     .
     .
     .
paragraph-n.

section-name SECTION.

     USE AFTER. . . .

paragraph-1.
     .
     .
     .
paragraph-m.
     .
     .
     .
END DECLARATIVES.

PROGRAM-SUMMARY.  (First nondeclarative paragraph)
     .
     .
     .
     (etc.)
```

FIGURE 8-7   OUTLINE OF DECLARATIVES USE WITHIN A COBOL PROGRAM.

available choices: INPUT, OUTPUT, I-O, EXTEND, and file-name. The USE AFTER EXCEPTION is really a conditional statement. It can be paraphrased to say: "If an exception is encountered during INPUT [for instance], execute the instructions in this section." Incidentally, the words ERROR and EXCEPTION are synonyms.

Consider an example:

```
PROCEDURE DIVISION.
DECLARATIVES.
CUST-FILE-EXCEPTION SECTION.
    USE AFTER EXCEPTION PROCEDURE ON CUSTOMER-FILE.
WRITE-EXCEPTIONS.
    IF FILE-STATUS-1 = '34'
      MOVE 'FILE-BOUNDARY VIOLATION' TO ERR-MESSAGE
      WRITE ERROR-RECORD
    ELSE
```

```
         MOVE 'UNSPECIFIED ERROR CONDITION' TO ERR-MESSAGE
         WRITE ERROR-RECORD.
 PRODUCT-FILE SECTION.
     USE AFTER EXCEPTION PROCEDURE ON PROD-FILE.
 OPEN-EXC.
     IF FILE-CODE-1 = '90'
         MOVE 'FILE CANNOT BE OPENED' TO ERR-MESSAGE
         WRITE ERROR-RECORD
     ELSE
         IF FILE-CODE-2 = '05'
             MOVE 'LABEL ERROR DURING OPEN' TO ERR-MESSAGE
             WRITE ERROR-RECORD
         ELSE
             MOVE 'UNSPECIFIED ERROR DURING OPEN' TO ERR-MESSAGE
             WRITE ERROR-RECORD.
```

In the above example, the action resulting from detection of a specific exception is to MOVE and WRITE some message. Obviously, this is only one illustration, and any processing could be done. For instance we might proceed to the printing of reports accumulated thus far or to providing additional information about the status of the program at the time that the exception occurred.

The first section in the example would work as follows. Every time that WRITE is executed for CUSTOMER-FILE, the system places the corresponding values in the FILE STATUS fields. If nonsuccessful completion is indicated, the program executes the WRITE-EXCEPTIONS paragraph as if it were under a PERFORM verb, and finally returns to the statement after the original WRITE (in the non-DECLARATIVES part of the program).

In the last paragraph (OPEN-EXC) of the example, we illustrate the possibility that an implementor has chosen a code of 90 to signify an OPEN exception and a code of 05 to signify a label error. Again this is a hypothetical meaning, not a standardized convention.

The use of DECLARATIVES need not involve use of the FILE STATUS feature. For instance, we could specify a procedure within the DECLARATIVES portion of the program which makes no reference to the file status key. Had we written USE AFTER EXCEPTION PROCEDURE ON I-O, we would know that execution of the associated procedure has to do with I/O (or, alternatively, OUTPUT, EXTEND, or file-name) and we could execute statements without testing the FILE STATUS values.

Overall, through the FILE STATUS feature and/or the DECLARATIVES portion of the PROCEDURE DIVISION we can intervene after I/O operations to treat exceptions. The AT END with READ and the INVALID KEY with WRITE (see Chapters 10 and 11) already provide for exception processing. With the options described in this section we extend these capabilities to all I/O verbs and also have the choice of implementing AT END (and INVALID

KEY) in an alternate way. For example, we can write a READ without AT END and use the FILE STATUS or the DECLARATIVES approach to process the AT END exception.

Review

1 Both the FILE STATUS feature and DECLARATIVES can be used in conjunction with the processing of _____ for I/O verbs.

exceptions

2 When a FILE STATUS field is declared for a file in the program, at the completion of the I/O command this field contains a code value to signify the _____ of the I/O operation.

success

3 In order to ascertain the outcome of an I/O operation, the FILE STATUS [can / cannot] be tested within the program.

can

4 When the FILE STATUS is tested within the program, it is usually in the context of being used as the basis for a(n) [imperative / conditional] statement.

conditional

5 When DECLARATIVES are used, they are entered in the program immediately after the _____ heading.

PROCEDURE DIVISION

6 The procedures included within each section of the DECLARATIVES portion of the program are executed [conditionally / unconditionally] upon encountering a(n) _____.

conditionally; exception

7   Overall, the FILE STATUS feature and/or DECLARATIVES can be used to detect and treat exceptions in conjunction with _____ operations.

I/O (or input-output)

MASTER FILE MAINTENANCE

Files on magnetic tape or disk are maintained or updated to reflect changes that take place. We speak of *master* and *transaction* files as being involved in the updating process.

A *master* file contains reference data that reflect the cumulative status as of a point in time. For example, a payroll master file would contain data on each employee, such as name, address, pay rate, year-to-date earnings, and so forth.

A *transaction* file contains records that either reflect events or indicate changes to the master file. For example, a transaction record at a bank might be a deposit made or a check written. Other examples of transactions would be the addition of a new customer to the master file, deletion of a former customer's name, or a change of the customer's address.

Updating involves processing the transaction file against the master file. The process of updating varies a little, depending on whether we use magnetic tape or disk for storing the master file.

File maintenance is a primary activity in the batch-processing of sequential files. Although it is true that reports are the important result of data processing, it is necessary to maintain the master files in order to produce the reports. Once the file is in the right state (updated and suitably ordered), report production is simply a matter of extracting the desired information. File maintenance and report production are frequently consolidated in the same run, but this need not be the case.

Since it is the transactions that affect the state of the master file, which in turn reflects the state of the activity system, it is imperative that the transactions be screened for possible errors prior to being used to update the master file. In this respect, it is useful to distinguish between data verification and data validation.

Verification is concerned with establishing that original data (usually manually produced) has been correctly transcribed into machine processable form. Verification is typically accomplished by duplicating the transcription effort, using suitable equipment. Since verification which is achieved by duplicating the transcription effort is relatively costly, we should examine whether the value of such verification justifies the cost. For example, verification of hours worked is desirable in a payroll situation but may be questionable when data is to be used in summary form or for statistical analyses in which a small margin of error would not affect the usefulness of the report.

In addition to duplicating the data transcription, the accuracy of certain types of input can be verified by the use of self-checking numbers. A self-checking number is one which has a precalculated check digit appended to the basic number in order to detect input or transmission errors. Normally, the check digit is used in conjunction with such identification codes as employee numbers, customer numbers, and part numbers. A self-checking number which includes the check digit will of course contain 1 more digit than the basic number. For example, a 6-digit customer number would become a 7-digit number.

Although several techniques exist for calculating the check digit, the so-called modulus 10 method is most commonly used. The procedure is described and illustrated below.

1   The units (rightmost) position and every alternate position thereafter in the basic code number are multiplied by 2.

2   The individual digits in the product and the individual digits in the basic code number which were not multiplied by 2 are summed.

3   The sum is subtracted from the next higher number ending in zero.

4   The difference is the check digit, which is to be appended to the basic code number in order to form the self-checking number. Example:

Basic code number:	345798
Units and every alternate position:	4 7 8
Multiply by 2:	×2
Product:	956
Digits not multiplied by 2:	359
Sum of individual digits:	$9 + 5 + 6 + 3 + 5 + 9 = 37$
Next-higher number ending in zero:	40
Subtract sum of individual digits:	−37
Check digit:	3
Self-checking number:	3457983

When self-checking numbers are used, an error can be detected by the fact that the check digit is not appropriate for the basic number to which it is appended. It is possible that an incorrect basic number will have the same check digit as the original (correct) number. However, this can occur only if there is more than one transcription error in the basic number, and it is therefore a rare occurrence.

As contrasted to verification, which is concerned with correct individual transcription, *validation* is concerned with the completeness and internal consistency of the set of data. The use of *control totals* is a very common approach to validation, and a *batch total* is one such control total. For example, a bank teller may produce a tape of the amounts deposited for batches of 50 deposits. These batch totals are identified with their corresponding batches and become part of the input for subsequent computer processing. The computer program duplicates the batch total accumulation process and compares these computer-generated totals with the totals determined manually. If they are not equal, an error has been made. In this example the most likely source of error is the transcription process from the manual deposit slip to the magnetically encoded document. Once an error has been detected, we need only search the particular batch in order to pinpoint the error entry or entries. As it can be seen, there is some advantage to keeping batch sizes small. If a batch contains 1,000 entries instead of the 50 described above, we might have to examine as many as 1,000 entries to locate the error.

A second type of control total is called a *hash total*. When a payroll file is formed, the hash total could be the sum of the social security numbers of all employees. In subsequent processing of this file the total could be formed again and compared with the previous total. If the two totals are not the same, this may indicate that one or more records were missed. The word "hash" indicates that the total has no meaning of its own and is used only for comparison purposes.

A third type of control total is often referred to as *crossfooting*. For example, the following relationship may apply to each item in an inventory file:

Opening balance + receipts − issues = on hand

Utilizing this known relationship, it must then be true that the totals for each of the four fields above for all items processed must also conform to the above formula.

As contrasted to the use of control totals, another form of validation relies on the use of *range checks*. This approach is based on the fact that classes of transactions must occur within certain numerical limits. For example, a transaction showing the amount charged for a pair of shoes in a discount department store should not exceed $99. Similarly, the Internal Revenue Service can check to determine if deductions exceed a certain percent of income. In a particular form of the range check, we may check as to whether the amount sold is blank—thus performing a check to determine if the amount was left out. Such a determination is referred to as a *completeness check*.

A third form of validation is referred to as a *consistency check*. Such checks are directed toward determining if the input data is consistent with known constraints of reality. For example, hourly rates of pay may always be expressed in dollars and cents rather than whole numbers, and the quantity of a particular item may always be in terms of pounds rather than some other unit of measurement.

The term *data editing* is often used in the context of data validation procedures, even though detection of errors as such may not be involved. Data editing is concerned mainly with accomplishing desired changes in the form of data. For example, blanks might be changed to leading zeros in a numeric field, and a date in the form of XX-XX-XX might be changed to the form XXXXXX, thereby eliminating the hyphens.

When an error is detected through the process of data validation, some corrective action must be taken. Ideally, the computer program should provide the corrective action which is necessary, and occasionally this is possible. But in most cases there is no way to correct the error based on the input data alone. Therefore, the fact that a certain type of error has been detected is reported either on magnetic tape for subsequent printer listing, directly on the printer, or directly on the operator's console, for eventual manual correction. Figure 8–8 is a flowchart for a master file update run that includes data verification and validation. In this typical case, manual documents contain the original data, which are keyed and verified, then transferred to magnetic tape, validated, sorted, and finally processed to update the master file. Depending on the extent of data validation, such procedures may be a subpart of the total update job or they may require a separate computer run. More often than not, validation procedures are a separate run, followed by a sort run, which is in turn followed by the main update run. Thus, computer programs concerned with updating master files are not simple programs but rather are concerned with a series of complex tasks.

Review

1   The procedures which are directed toward ascertaining that original data has been correctly transcribed are concerned with the general process called data _____.

verification

2   Data verification is typically accomplished by duplicating the transcription process. However, as an alternate to this approach, certain types of numeric input, such as part numbers, can be verified as to accuracy by the use of _____ numbers.

self-checking

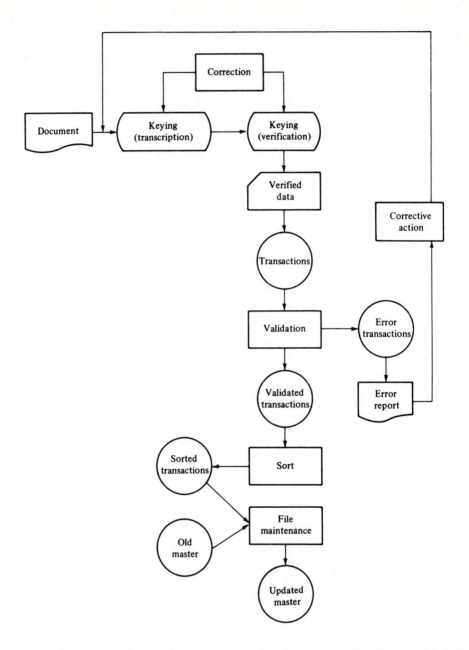

FIGURE 8-8   MASTER FILE UPDATE RUN WITH DATA VERIFICATION AND VALIDATION.

3 As contrasted to verification, data _____ is concerned with the completeness and internal consistency of a set of data, rather than the accuracy of individual transcriptions taken singly.

validation

4 Data validation is generally accomplished by making use of various types of _____ totals.

control

5 When the totals for groups of 100 sales transactions are included with the individual transaction values as the computer input, the type of control total being used for the purpose of validation is the _____ total.

batch

6 When the sum of all the customer numbers for accounts which have had a sales transaction is used for data validation purposes, the control total would be described as being a _____ total. On the other hand, the type of control total that is based on known numerical relationships among such totals as the total amount of payments and total account balances is referred to as _____.

hash; crossfooting

7 As contrasted to the use of control totals, the method of validation based on the fact that certain transactions can occur only within prescribed numerical limits involves the use of _____ checks. A third form of validation is based on the fact that transactions must conform to certain constraints of reality, such as being expressed in certain types of units, and this type of validation is therefore called a _____ check.

range; consistency

8 The procedure which is sometimes associated with validation procedures and which is concerned with changing the form of the input data, such as replacing $ signs with zeros and eliminating commas included in numeric input, is called _____.

data editing

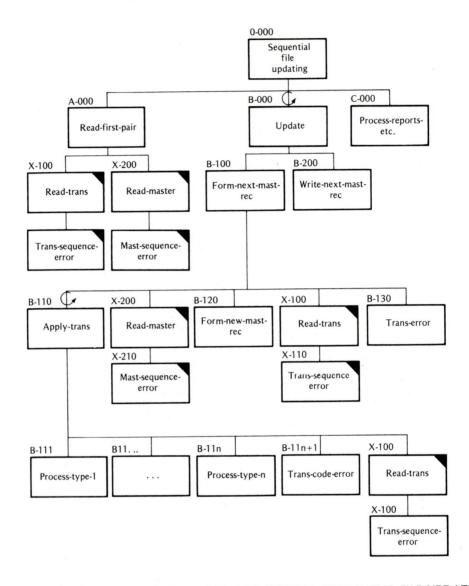

FIGURE 8–9   STRUCTURE CHART FOR GENERAL SEQUENTIAL FILE UPDATE PROGRAM LOGIC.

A GENERAL PROGRAMMING MODEL FOR UPDATING SEQUENTIAL FILES

Because the updating of sequential files is such a common occurrence, we present a general programming model that can be used as the basis for writing the specific logic for most such programs. Figure 8–9 presents a structure chart for this general program model, while Figure 8–10 presents a program statement outline. The logic is designed to handle the following main types of processing:

There can be one or many types of transactions.

There can be one or many transactions pertaining to a given master file record.

New records may be added to the master file by submitting a suitable transaction record. Such records may be added in the front, in the "middle," or at the end of the master file.

A new master file record may also be updated by one or more transaction records. The only requirement is that the sort procedure must ensure that the "add new" transactions precede the "update"-type transactions.

The meanings of some important data-names are described below:

T-END: A condition-name signifying the end of the transaction file. The condition is true when T-I-D is equal to HIGH-VALUES.

M-END: A condition-name signifying the end of the old master file. The condition is true when M-I-D is equal to HIGH-VALUES.

TERMINAL-ERROR: A condition-name signifying the occurrence of a type of error that should result in program termination.

M-I-D: The record key or identifier of a master file record, such as customer number, employee name, etc.

T-I-D: The record key or identifier of a transaction file record.

PREV-M-I-D: A working-storage field containing the M-I-D of the previously read master file record. It is used to ascertain that the master records are in ascending sequence.

PREV-T-I-D: A working-storage field containing the T-I-D of the previously read transaction file record. It is used to ascertain that the transaction records are in proper sequence.

WORK-NEW-MAST-REC: A working-storage field which is used to build a new master file record or update an existing master file record. When a record is ready to be written into the new master file, it is moved from WORK-NEW-MAST-REC to NEW-MAST-REC.

PREV-NEW-REC-I-D: A working-storage field containing the T-I-D of an "add new" transaction. When such a transaction is read in, its T-I-D is stored in PREV-NEW-REC-I-D. Then, the T-I-D of subsequent transactions is compared against the saved value. When T-I-D is not equal to PREV-NEW-REC-I-D, then the new master record is ready to be written onto the updated master file. In this way it is possible to add a new master record and update it by a series of transactions that immediately follow the "add new" transaction.

```
PROCEDURE DIVISION.
0-000-PROGRAM-SUMMARY.
    OPEN INPUT OLD-MAST-FILE, TRANS-FILE
        OUTPUT NEW-MAST-FILE, REPORT-FILE, ERROR-MESS-FILE.
    MOVE 'NO' TO END-OF-TRANS-SWITCH
                END-OF-MAST-SWITCH
                TERMINAL-ERROR-SWITCH.
    PERFORM A-000-READ-FIRST-PAIR.
    PERFORM B-000-UPDATE UNTIL (T-END AND M-END)
                                OR TERMINAL-ERROR.
    CLOSE OLD-MAST-FILE NEW-MAST-FILE
        TRANS-FILE REPORT-FILE ERROR-MESS-FILE.
    PERFORM C-000-PROCESS-REPORTS-ETC.
    STOP RUN.
A-000-READ-FIRST-PAIR.
    MOVE LOW-VALUES TO PREV-T-I-D
        PERFORM X-100-READ-TRANS
        MOVE LOW-VALUES TO PREV-M-I-D
        PERFORM X-200-READ-MASTER.
B-000-UPDATE.
    PERFORM B-100-FORM-NEXT-MAST-REC
    PERFORM B-200-WRITE-NEXT-MAST-REC.
B-100-FORM-NEXT-MAST-REC.
    EVALUATE TRUE
        WHEN M-I-D = T-I-D
                MOVE OLD-MAST-REC TO WORK-NEW-MAST-REC
                PERFORM B-110-APPLY-TRANS UNTIL M-I-D NOT = T-I-D
                                                OR T-END
                                                OR TERMINAL-ERROR

                PERFORM X-200-READ-MASTER
        WHEN M-I-D < T-I-D
                MOVE OLD-MAST-REC TO WORK-NEW-MAST-REC
                PERFORM X-200-READ-MASTER
        WHEN M-I-D > T-I-D AND ADD-NEW
                PERFORM B-120-FORM-NEW-MAST-REC
                MOVE T-I-D TO PREV-NEW-REC-I-D
                PERFORM X-100 READ-TRANS
                PERFORM B-110-APPLY-TRANS UNTIL PREV-NEW-REC-I-D
                                                NOT = T-I-D
                                                OR T-END
                                                OR TERMINAL-ERROR

        WHEN OTHER
                PERFORM B-130-TRANS-ERROR
                PERFORM X-100-READ-TRANS
    END-EVALUATE.
```

FIGURE 8-10   PROGRAM OUTLINE FOR GENERAL SEQUENTIAL FILE UP-DATE PROGRAM LOGIC.

```
B-110-APPLY-TRANS.
    EVALUATE TRUE
        WHEN TRANS-TYPE-1
            PERFORM B-111-PROCESS-TYPE-1
        WHEN TRANS-TYPE-2
            PERFORM B-112-PROCESS-TYPE-2
        WHEN TRANS-TYPE-3
            PERFORM B-113-PROCESS-TYPE-3
            .
            .
        WHEN OTHER
            PERFORM B-114-TRANS-CODE-ERROR
    END-EVALUATE
    PERFORM X-100-READ-TRANS.
B-111-PROCESS-TYPE-1.
    Process transaction type 1
B-112-PROCESS-TYPE-2.
    Process transaction type 2
B-113-PROCESS-TYPE-3.
    Process transaction type 3
    .
    .
B-114-TRANS-CODE-ERROR.
    Process a transaction whose code does not match any of the
    defined transaction types.
B-120-FORM-NEW-MAST-REC.
    Transfer data from the source record to WORK-NEW-MAST-REC and
    do the necessary processing.
B-130-TRANS-ERROR.
    Issue appropriate error message to indicate that this is a
    record with a new identifier (T-I-D is less than M-I-D), yet
    it does not contain an "add-new" type transaction code.
B-200-WRITE-NEXT-MAST-REC.
    Do any processing needed before writing the updated record.
    Then, if not a deleted record,
    MOVE WORK-NEW-MAST-REC TO NEW-MAST-REC
    WRITE NEW-MAST-REC.
C-000-PROCESS-REPORTS-ETC.
    Do any post-update processing such as printing of reports, etc.
X-100-READ-TRANS.
    READ TRANS-FILE RECORD
        AT END MOVE HIGH-VALUES TO T-I-D.
    IF NOT T-END
        IF T-I-D < PREV-T-I-D
            PERFORM X-110-TRANS-SEQUENCE-ERROR
            MOVE 'YES' TO TERMINAL-ERROR-SWITCH
        ELSE
            MOVE T-I-D TO PREV-T-I-D.
```

**FIGURE 8-10   PROGRAM OUTLINE FOR GENERAL SEQUENTIAL FILE UP-
DATE PROGRAM LOGIC.   (Continued)**

X-110-TRANS-SEQUENCE-ERROR.
    Issue suitable error message indicating that the transaction
    file is not properly sorted, etc.
X-200-READ-MASTER.
    READ OLD-MAST-FILE-RECORD
      AT END MOVE HIGH-VALUES TO M-I-D.
    IF NOT M-END
      IF M-I-D NOT > PREV-M-I-D
        PERFORM X-210-MAST-SEQUENCE-ERROR
        MOVE 'YES' TO TERMINAL-ERROR-SWITCH
      ELSE
        MOVE M-I-D TO PREV-M-I-D.
X-210-MAST-SEQUENCE-ERROR.
    Issue suitable error message indicating that the master file
    is not properly sorted, etc.

FIGURE 8-10   **PROGRAM OUTLINE FOR GENERAL SEQUENTIAL FILE UP-DATE PROGRAM LOGIC.**   **(Continued)**

Reviewing the program outline in Figure 8–10, we see that paragraphs which are subordinate to more than one module are prefixed with an X and are positioned at the end of the program. Otherwise, the program layout is of the vertical type.

The program outline is substantially self-documenting even though it is context-free. It can be adopted to any specific situation with minimum logic modification.

Review

1   This section includes a general model that can be followed for writing program statements to update a _____ file.

                            sequential

2   In the general procedure for updating sequential files that is presented in this section there can be [only one / many] types of transactions and [only one / many] transactions pertaining to a given master file record.

                            many; many

3   When a new master record is to be updated, the sort procedure must

ensure that "update"-type transactions [precede / follow] the "add new" transactions.

follow

SEQUENTIAL UPDATE SAMPLE PROGRAM

Task Description

We wish to write a program to update a simplified payroll master file. The master is sequenced on employee number, and records have the following layout:

Employee number	PIC 9(5)
Employee name	PIC X(20)
Pay rate	PIC 9(2)V99
Withholding rate	PIC V99
Year-to-date gross pay	PIC 9(5)V99
Year-to-date net pay	PIC 9(5)V99

The transaction records are of two types. The first type contains changes to the master file and has the following layout:

Employee number	PIC 9(5)
Employee name	PCI X(20)
Transaction code	PIC X
1 = Create new record	
2 = Delete record	
3 = Change pay rate	
Pay rate	PIC 9(2)V99
Withholding rate	PIC V99

The second type of transaction record is daily time cards that have the following layout:

Employee number	PIC 9(5)
Employee name	PIC X(20)
Transaction code	PIC 9
4 = Time card	
Hours worked	PIC 9(2)V99

In addition to the updated master file, the program should produce a printed report as follows:

EMPLOYEE NO.	EMPLOYEE NAME	THIS WEEK GROSS	NET	YEAR-TO-DATE GROSS	NET
.	.	.	.	.	.
.	.	.	.	.	.
.	.	.	.	.	.
TOTAL PAYROLL		xxx	xxx	xxx	xxx

For each employee, a week's gross pay is computed by multiplying pay rate times the hours worked for the whole week (remember that time cards are daily records). If the hours worked exceed 40, time-and-a-half is paid for the hours over 40; however, no employee should work more than 10 hours in a given day nor more than 48 hours in a given week. Either condition is an error, and the employee would not be paid; instead, an error message would be printed.

Net pay is computed by multiplying gross pay by the withholding rate and subtracting this amount from the gross pay. The year-to-date gross and net given in the report include the addition of the latest week's gross and net pay to the previously accumulated amounts.

Structure Chart

Figure 8–11 presents a structure chart developed for the payroll task described above. It should be noticed that the B-200-WRITE-NEXT-MAST-REC module has now been expanded to consist of three subordinate modules, since the writing function is not simple because of the required payroll computations. Such an example demonstrates the relative ease with which the general updating model in Figure 8–9 can be adapted to varying situational needs.

Another point worth mentioning is the development of two "error handling" modules, B-114-TRANS-CODE-ERROR and B-130-TRANS-ERROR, and their placement under different superior modules. In the course of being ready to apply a transaction, it may be discovered that the transaction code is not a valid one. In such a case B-110-APPLY-TRANS invokes the execution of B-114-TRANS-CODE-ERROR.

Another type of transaction error may also occur which needs to be handled by a higher-level module than B-110-APPLY-TRANS. Specifically, one of the types of transactions allowed is the addition of new records to the master file, and this is handled by B-120-FORM-NEW-MAST-REC. It is logically necessary that a new record that is to be added must be lower in sequence than the last-read master record. Further, our task description allows transactions (time cards, etc.) to be applied to a new record. There then may

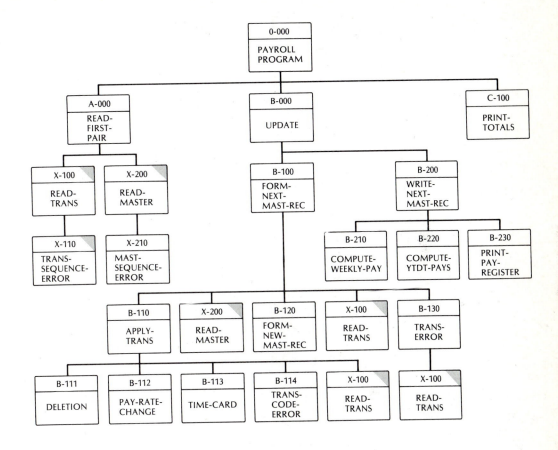

FIGURE 8-11   STRUCTURE CHART FOR PAYROLL PROGRAM.

be a number of transaction records pertaining to the same employee, and the employee may be a new individual being added to the file. However, it is assumed that in such a case the *first* of these transactions is the add-new transaction; if it is not, then we have an error condition arising from the presence of transactions pertaining to a nonexisting master record. This type of error condition is handled by B-130-TRANS-ERROR under control of B-100-FORM-NEXT-MAST-REC.

Sample Program

Figure 8–12 presents a sample program written for the payroll programming tasks. A few comments follow.

Module B-111-DELETION consists of only one line. One can question the need for creating one-line paragraphs. However, deleting a record is a distinct, cohesive function, and it has clear logical identity. Further, in most

```
 IDENTIFICATION DIVISION.
 PROGRAM-ID. PAYROLL.
*
 ENVIRONMENT DIVISION.
 CONFIGURATION SECTION.
 SOURCE-COMPUTER. ABC-480.
 OBJECT-COMPUTER. ABC-480.
*
 INPUT-OUTPUT SECTION.
 FILE-CONTROL.
     SELECT OLD-PAY-MASTER   ASSIGN TO OLDMASTR.
     SELECT NEW-PAY-MASTER   ASSIGN TO NEWMASTR.
     SELECT TRANS-FILE       ASSIGN TO TRANS.
     SELECT ERR-MESS-FILE    ASSIGN TO ERRORRPT.
     SELECT REPORT-FILE      ASSIGN TO TRANSRPT.
*
 DATA DIVISION.
*
 FILE SECTION.

 FD  OLD-PAY-MASTER  LABEL RECORDS OMITTED
              BLOCK CONTAINS 10 RECORDS
              DATA RECORD IS OLD-PAY-MASTER-REC.
 01  OLD-PAY-MASTER-REC.
     02  OLD-PAY-MASTER-DATA.
         04 OLD-EMPLOYEE-NO         PIC X(5).
         04 OLD-EMPLOYEE-NAME       PIC X(20).
         04 OLD-PAY-RATE            PIC 99V99.
         04 OLD-WITHHOLDING-RATE    PIC V99.
         04 OLD-YTDT-GROSS          PIC 9(5)V99.
         04 OLD-YTDT-NET            PIC 9(5)V99.
*
 FD  NEW-PAY-MASTER  LABEL RECORDS STANDARD
              BLOCK CONTAINS 10 RECORDS
              DATA RECORD IS NEW-PAY-MASTER-REC.
 01  NEW-PAY-MASTER-REC            PIC X(80).
*
 FD  TRANS-FILE LABEL RECORDS OMITTED
              DATA RECORD IS TRANS-REC.
 01  TRANS-REC.
     02  TRANS-REC-DATA.
         04 TRANS-EMPLOYEE-NO       PIC X(5).
         04 TRANS-EMPLOYEE-NAME     PIC X(20).
         04 TRANS-CODE              PIC X.
            88 ADDITION             VALUE '1'.
            88 DELETION             VALUE '2'.
            88 PAY-RATE-CHANGE      VALUE '3'.
            88 TIME-CARD            VALUE '4'.
            88 ERROR-CODE           VALUE LOW-VALUE THRU '0'
                                          '5' THRU HIGH-VALUE.
         04 TRANS-PAY-RATE          PIC 99V99.
         04 TRANS-HOURS-WORKED REDEFINES TRANS-PAY-RATE PIC 99V99.
         04 TRANS-WITHHOLDING-RATE PIC V99.
```

FIGURE 8-12   LISTING OF PAYROLL PROGRAM.

```
FD   REPORT-FILE LABEL RECORDS OMITTED
                DATA RECORD IS REPORT-REC.
*
01   REPORT-REC                      PIC X(132).
*
FD   ERR-MESS-FILE
     LABEL RECORDS ARE OMITTED
     DATA RECORD IS ERROR-REC.
01   ERROR-REC                       PIC X(132).
*
WORKING-STORAGE SECTION.
*
01   WORK-NEW-MAST-REC.
     02 NEW-EMPLOYEE-NO              PIC X(5).
     02 NEW-EMPLOYEE-NAME            PIC X(20).
     02 NEW-PAY-RATE                 PIC 99V99.
     02 NEW-WITHHOLDING-RATE         PIC V99.
     02 NEW-YTDT-GROSS               PIC 9(5)V99.
     02 NEW-YTDT-NET                 PIC 9(5)V99.
     02 FILLER                       PIC X(35).
*
01   END-OF-TRANS-SWITCH PIC XXX VALUE 'NO'.
     88 TRANS-ENDED VALUE 'YES'.
*
01   END-OF-MASTER-SWITCH            PIC XXX      VALUE 'NO'.
     88 MASTER-ENDED                              VALUE 'YES'.
*
01   TERMINAL-ERROR-SWITCH           PIC XXX      VALUE 'NO'.
     88 TERMINAL-ERROR                            VALUE 'YES'.
*
01   WRITE-FLAG                      PIC XXX      VALUE 'YES'.
     88 WRITE-REC                                 VALUE 'YES'.
     88 NOT-WRITE-REC                             VALUE 'NO '.
*
01   ACCUMULATORS.
     02 WEEKLY-HOURS                 PIC 99V99    VALUE ZEROS.
     02 TEMP-GROSS                   PIC 9(6)V99  VALUE ZEROS.
     02 TEMP-NET                     PIC 9(6)V99  VALUE ZEROS.
     02 TOT-GROSS                    PIC 9(7)V99  VALUE ZEROS.
     02 TOT-NET                      PIC 9(7)V99  VALUE ZEROS.
     02 TOT-GROSS-YTDT               PIC 9(7)V99  VALUE ZEROS.
     02 TOT-NET-YTDT                 PIC 9(7)V99  VALUE ZEROS.
*
01   HEADER-1.
     02      PIC X(39)   VALUE SPACES.
     02      PIC X(9)    VALUE 'THIS WEEK'.
     02      PIC X(13)   VALUE SPACES.
     02      PIC X(12)   VALUE 'YEAR TO DATE'.
```

FIGURE 8-12   LISTING OF PAYROLL PROGRAM.   (Continued)

```
01   HEADER-2.
     02    PIC X        VALUE SPACE.
     02    PIC X(28)    VALUE 'EMPLOYEE NO.   EMPLOYEE NAME'.
     02    PIC X(8)     VALUE SPACES.
     02    PIC X(5)     VALUE 'GROSS'.
     02    PIC X(6)     VALUE SPACES.
     02    PIC X(3)     VALUE 'NET'.
     02    PIC X(7)     VALUE SPACES.
     02    PIC X(5)     VALUE 'GROSS'.
     02    PIC X(7)     VALUE SPACES.
     02    PIC X(3)     VALUE 'NET'.
*
01   HEADER-3.
     02    PIC X(18)    VALUE SPACES.
     02    PIC X(24)    VALUE 'TRANSACTION ERROR REPORT'.
     02    PIC X(90)    VALUE SPACES.
*
01   REPORT-LINE.
     02 FILLER                  PIC X(4) VALUE SPACE.
     02 EMPLOYEE-NO             PIC 9(5).
     02 FILLER                  PIC X(5) VALUE SPACE.
     02 EMPLOYEE-NAME           PIC X(20).
     02 WEEK-GROSS              PIC Z(4),Z(3).99.
     02 WEEK-NET                PIC ZZZZ,ZZZ.99.
     02 YTDT-GROSS              PIC ZZZZ,ZZZ.99.
     02 YTDT-NET                PIC ZZZZ,ZZZ.99.
*
01   PREV-TRANS-ID             PIC  X(5).
*
01   PREV-MASTER-ID            PIC X(5).
/
PROCEDURE DIVISION.
*
0-000-PROGRAM-SUMMARY.
    OPEN INPUT   OLD-PAY-MASTER
                 TRANS-FILE
         OUTPUT  NEW-PAY-MASTER
                 REPORT-FILE
                 ERR-MESS-FILE
    WRITE REPORT-REC FROM HEADER-1
    WRITE REPORT-REC FROM HEADER-2 AFTER ADVANCING 2 LINES
    WRITE ERROR-REC FROM HEADER-3 BEFORE 3 LINES
    PERFORM A-000-READ-FIRST-PAIR
    PERFORM B-000-UPDATE UNTIL (TRANS-ENDED AND MASTER-ENDED)
                         OR TERMINAL-ERROR
    PERFORM C-000-PRINT-TOTALS
    CLOSE OLD-PAY-MASTER
          TRANS-FILE
          NEW-PAY-MASTER
          REPORT-FILE
          ERR-MESS-FILE
    STOP RUN.
```

FIGURE 8-12   LISTING OF PAYROLL PROGRAM.   **(Continued)**

```
 A-000-READ-FIRST-PAIR.
     MOVE LOW-VALUES TO PREV-TRANS-ID,
                         PREV-MASTER-ID.
     PERFORM X-100-READ-TRANS.
     PERFORM X-200-READ-MASTER.
*
 B-000-UPDATE.
     PERFORM B-100-FORM-NEXT-MAST-REC.
     PERFORM B-200-WRITE-NEXT-MAST-REC.
*
 B-100-FORM-NEXT-MAST-REC.
*
     EVALUATE TRUE
*
        WHEN OLD-EMPLOYEE-NO = TRANS-EMPLOYEE-NO
           MOVE OLD-PAY-MASTER-REC TO WORK-NEW-MAST-REC
           PERFORM B-110-APPLY-TRANS
              UNTIL (OLD-EMPLOYEE-NO NOT EQUAL TRANS-EMPLOYEE-NO)
                 OR TRANS-ENDED
                 OR TERMINAL-ERROR
           PERFORM X-200-READ-MASTER
*
        WHEN  OLD-EMPLOYEE-NO  < TRANS-EMPLOYEE-NO
           MOVE OLD-PAY-MASTER-REC TO WORK-NEW-MAST-REC
           PERFORM X-200-READ-MASTER
*
        WHEN  ADDITION
           PERFORM B-120-FORM-NEW-MAST-REC
           PERFORM X-100-READ-TRANS
           PERFORM B-110-APPLY-TRANS
               UNTIL (NEW-EMPLOYEE-NO NOT EQUAL TRANS-EMPLOYEE-NO)
                  OR TRANS-ENDED
                  OR TERMINAL-ERROR
*
        WHEN  OTHER
           MOVE TRANS-EMPLOYEE-NO TO NEW-EMPLOYEE-NO
           PERFORM B-130-TRANS-ERROR WITH TEST AFTER
               UNTIL (NEW-EMPLOYEE-NO NOT = TRANS-EMPLOYEE-NO)
                  OR TRANS-ENDED
                  OR TERMINAL-ERROR
           SET NOT-WRITE-REC TO TRUE
     END-EVALUATE.
*
 B-110-APPLY-TRANS.
*
     EVALUATE TRUE
*
        WHEN DELETION
           PERFORM B-111-DELETION
*
        WHEN PAY-RATE-CHANGE
           PERFORM B-112-PAY-RATE-CHANGE
```

FIGURE 8-12   LISTING OF PAYROLL PROGRAM.   (Continued)

```
            WHEN TIME-CARD
                PERFORM B-113-TIME-CARD
    *
            WHEN OTHER
                PERFORM B-114-TRANS-CODE-ERROR
                                      *
        END-EVALUATE
    *
        PERFORM X-100-READ-TRANS.
    *
     B-111-DELETION.
        SET NOT-WRITE-REC TO TRUE.
    *
     B-112-PAY-RATE-CHANGE.
        MOVE TRANS-PAY-RATE TO NEW-PAY-RATE.
    *
     B-113-TIME-CARD.
        IF TRANS-HOURS-WORKED GREATER THAN 10
            MOVE SPACES TO ERROR-REC
            STRING
                    TRANS-REC-DATA,
                    '  TRANSACTION HOURS > 10 HOURS'
                        DELIMITED BY SIZE
                INTO ERROR-REC
            WRITE ERROR-REC
        ELSE
            ADD TRANS-HOURS-WORKED TO WEEKLY-HOURS.
    *
     B-114-TRANS-CODE-ERROR.
        MOVE SPACES TO ERROR-REC.
        STRING
                TRANS-REC,
                '  INVALID TRANSACTION CODE'
                    DELIMITED BY SIZE
            INTO ERROR-REC.
        WRITE ERROR-REC.
    *
     B-120-FORM-NEW-MAST-REC.
        MOVE SPACES TO WORK-NEW-MAST-REC.
        MOVE TRANS-EMPLOYEE-NO TO NEW-EMPLOYEE-NO.
        MOVE TRANS-EMPLOYEE-NAME TO NEW-EMPLOYEE-NAME.
        MOVE TRANS-PAY-RATE TO NEW-PAY-RATE.
        MOVE TRANS-WITHHOLDING-RATE TO NEW-WITHHOLDING-RATE.
        MOVE ZERO TO NEW-YTDT-GROSS,
                        NEW-YTDT-NET.
     B-130-TRANS-ERROR.
        MOVE SPACES TO ERROR-REC.
        STRING
                TRANS-REC-DATA
                '  TRANSACTION SEQUENCE ERROR'
                    DELIMITED BY SIZE
            INTO ERROR-REC
        WRITE ERROR-REC.
        PERFORM X-100-READ-TRANS.
```

FIGURE 8-12   LISTING OF PAYROLL PROGRAM.   **(Continued)**

```
B-200-WRITE-NEXT-MAST-REC.
    IF WRITE-REC
        IF WEEKLY-HOURS GREATER THAN 48
            MOVE SPACES TO ERROR-REC
            STRING
                    WORK-NEW-MAST-REC,
                    ' WEEKLY HOURS > 48 HOURS'
                        DELIMITED BY SIZE
                INTO ERROR-REC
            WRITE ERROR-REC
            WRITE ERROR-REC FROM WORK-NEW-MAST-REC
        ELSE
            PERFORM B-210-COMPUTE-WEEKLY-PAY
            PERFORM B-220-COMPUTE-YTDT-PAYS
            PERFORM B-230-PRINT-PAY-REGISTER
            WRITE NEW-PAY-MASTER-REC FROM WORK-NEW-MAST-REC
    END-IF
*
    MOVE ZERO TO WEEKLY-HOURS TEMP-GROSS TEMP-NET
    SET WRITE-REC TO TRUE.
*
 B-210-COMPUTE-WEEKLY-PAY.
*
    IF WEEKLY-HOURS GREATER THAN 40
        THEN
            COMPUTE TEMP-GROSS = 40.0 * NEW-PAY-RATE
                    + (WEEKLY-HOURS - 40.0) * 1.5 * NEW-PAY-RATE
        ELSE
            COMPUTE TEMP-GROSS = WEEKLY-HOURS * NEW-PAY-RATE
    END-IF
    COMPUTE TEMP-NET = TEMP-GROSS -
            (TEMP-GROSS * NEW-WITHHOLDING-RATE).
*
 B-220-COMPUTE-YTDT-PAYS.
*
    ADD TEMP-GROSS TO TOT-GROSS
    ADD TEMP-NET TO TOT-NET
    ADD TEMP-GROSS, NEW-YTDT-GROSS TO TOT-GROSS-YTDT
    ADD TEMP-NET, NEW-YTDT-NET TO TOT-NET-YTDT
    ADD TEMP-GROSS TO NEW-YTDT-GROSS
    ADD TEMP-NET TO NEW-YTDT-NET
*
 B-230-PRINT-PAY-REGISTER.
*
    MOVE NEW-EMPLOYEE-NO TO EMPLOYEE-NO
    MOVE NEW-EMPLOYEE-NAME TO EMPLOYEE-NAME
    MOVE TEMP-GROSS TO WEEK-GROSS
    MOVE NEW-YTDT-GROSS TO YTDT-GROSS
    MOVE NEW-YTDT-NET TO YTDT-NET
    MOVE TEMP-NET TO WEEK-NET
    WRITE REPORT-REC FROM REPORT-LINE AFTER 2
```

FIGURE 8-12   LISTING OF PAYROLL PROGRAM.   **(Continued)**

```
        C-000-PRINT-TOTALS.
            MOVE SPACES TO REPORT-LINE.
            MOVE 'T O T A L' TO EMPLOYEE-NAME.
            MOVE TOT-GROSS TO WEEK-GROSS.
            MOVE TOT-NET TO WEEK-NET.
            MOVE TOT-GROSS-YTDT TO YTDT-GROSS.
            MOVE TOT-NET-YTDT TO YTDT-NET.
            WRITE REPORT-REC FROM REPORT-LINE.
   *
        X-100-READ-TRANS.
            READ TRANS-FILE
               AT END
                   MOVE HIGH-VALUES TO TRANS-EMPLOYEE-NO
                   SET TRANS-ENDED TO TRUE
               NOT AT END
                   CONTINUE
                   IF TRANS-EMPLOYEE-NO LESS THAN PREV-TRANS-ID
                       PERFORM X-110-TRANS-SEQUENCE-ERROR
                       SET TERMINAL-ERROR TO TRUE
                   ELSE
                       MOVE TRANS-EMPLOYEE-NO TO PREV-TRANS-ID
                   END-IF
            END-READ.
   *
        X-110-TRANS-SEQUENCE-ERROR.
            MOVE SPACES TO ERROR-REC
            STRING
                  TRANS-REC-DATA,
                  '   TRANSACTION RECORD OUT OF SEQUENCE'
                  DELIMITED BY SIZE
               INTO ERROR-REC
            WRITE ERROR-REC.
        X-200-READ-MASTER.
            READ OLD-PAY-MASTER
               AT END
                   SET MASTER-ENDED TO TRUE
                   MOVE HIGH-VALUES TO OLD-EMPLOYEE-NO
               NOT AT END
                   CONTINUE
                   IF OLD-EMPLOYEE-NO NOT GREATER THAN PREV-MASTER-ID
                       PERFORM X-210-MAST-SEQUENCE-ERROR
                       MOVE 'YES' TO TERMINAL-ERROR-SWITCH
                   ELSE
                       MOVE OLD-EMPLOYEE-NO TO PREV-MASTER-ID
                   END-IF
            END-READ.
        X-210-MAST-SEQUENCE-ERROR.
            MOVE SPACES TO ERROR-REC.
            STRING
                  OLD-PAY-MASTER-REC,
                  '   OLD MASTER RECORD OUT OF SEQUENCE'
                  DELIMITED BY SIZE
               INTO ERROR-REC.
            WRITE ERROR-REC.
```

FIGURE 8-12   LISTING OF PAYROLL PROGRAM.   (Continued)

cases deleting a record involves a whole procedure, rather than simply omitting the record from the updated file as was done in the abbreviated example. In *principle* a separate paragraph is better, especially if the program is modified in the future with respect to the way that deleted records are processed. However, in a specific case like this it would be futile to try to argue either for or against a separate module for the deletion function.

In this sample program the input data is not extensively validated. If we needed to add such a feature, we could easily modify the structure by adding a validation function subordinate to the input module (X-100-READ-TRANS).

Both input files are sequence-checked, and if a record is found to be out of sequence, the program terminates by use of the TERMINAL-ERROR-SWITCH. Such a termination may or may not be appropriate in a given case. However, because the whole logic of sequential file updating is based on the assumption of correctly sequenced files, it is important to always do sequence checking in such programs.

As a final point we consider how the program handles the error condition of there being one or more transactions for a nonexistent master record. As was stated earlier in the comments regarding the structure chart, the assumption is made that the data are sequenced so that an add-new transaction record must precede any other transactions (if any) pertaining to that new record. In the B-100-FORM-NEXT-MAST-REC the following statements implement an appropriate procedure:

```
... WHEN ADDITION
     PERFORM B-120-FORM-NEW-MAST-REC
     PERFORM X-100-READ-TRANS
     PERFORM B-110-APPLY-TRANS UNTIL
        (NEW-EMPLOYEE-NO NOT EQUAL TRANS-EMPLOYEE-NO)
        OR TRANS-ENDED
        OR TERMINAL-ERROR
   WHEN OTHER
     MOVE TRANS-EMPLOYEE-NO TO NEW-EMPLOYEE NO
   PERFORM B-130-TRANS-ERROR WITH TEST AFTER UNTIL
     (NEW-EMPLOYEE-NO NOT = TRANS-EMPLOYEE NO)
     OR TRANS-ENDED
     OR TERMINAL-ERROR
   SET NOT-WRITE-REC TO TRUE
```

Notice that B-130-TRANS-ERROR is executed (possibly) many times, so that if the condition of ADDITION is not signified by the *first* transaction, all transactions having the same employee number are bypassed. For the purpose, the program states

...PERFORM B-130-TRANS-ERROR WITH TEST AFTER UNTIL...

to form a do-until type of iterative program structure.

TRANSACTION RECORDS AND FILE MAINTENANCE

There are two basic types of transactions in master file updating: transactions that change the values of fields in the master records and transactions that result in whole records being added to or deleted from the file. For instance, in the updating of an inventory file the following types of transactions would result in changes in the values of the fields in the master records:

Receipt transactions, indicating a shipment of items received from the vendor

Issue transactions, indicating items taken out of inventory for the purpose of sale to customers or for release to the production floor

Adjustment transactions, indicating corrections of errors, reconciliation of discrepancies between recorded data and physical inventory count, and the like

On-order transactions, indicating items ordered but not yet received

Committed-item transactions, indicating quantities encumbered or reserved for specified future issue

The program used in a file update process will examine the input transaction records, determine the transaction codes, and apply the appropriate adjustments to the records in the master file. For example, for a receipt record corresponding amounts would be added to the "on hand" and "available" fields of the master record for the item in question. Regardless of the specific processing required for such transactions, the final result is that the master record is updated and written onto the new master file.

The second type of transaction results in the addition or deletion of master records. For example, in a payroll-processing run we will typically have occasion to add new employees to the master file or to delete some employee records from the file. To add a record to the master file we simply encode the transaction record to indicate the addition of a record and we include it in the appropriate sequence in the transactions file. Normally, "add-type" transactions are longer than other types. In the payroll example, most of the usual transactions will involve only one transaction record containing such input as employee number and hours worked. However, the formation of a master record will probably require several records for such information as full name and address, social security number, rate of pay, tax exemptions, and insurance and other deductions.

Once an add-on type transaction is read, we may simply insert it in the updated file, or we may process any transactions which follow and which pertain to the new record. For example, it could be that we have a new employee and that he or she in fact worked during the pay period of concern. In addition to adding the record to the master file we must also read the input regarding the amount of time worked and compute gross pay, taxes, and so on. Note that the inclusion of add-type transactions complicates the processing logic to some extent. In practice, it is not unusual to have one processing run in which the master file is updated with respect to additions and deletions and to have a separate processing run which updates the file with respect to data modifications. This becomes desirable if the number of added or deleted records is large, as it might be for a magazine subscriber list or in a company that has substantial employee turnover.

Deletions from the file are also handled by submitting an encoded transaction record. At first it might seem a simple matter to delete a record from the file: simply do not write the old record in the updated master file. Practical considerations dictate that a series of steps be followed in the case of deletions, however. For one thing, we will want to print full information regarding the deleted records so that the fact of deletion can be communicated to and reviewed by those who have managerial responsibility over the deleted items. Further, the deletion procedure itself has to take into consideration the continued need to work with the records in certain aspects. For example, in a payroll situation we may owe the employee some back pay and make appropriate adjustments for his or her deductions. We may still want to maintain the record (perhaps on a separate file) for such reasons as end-of-year tax reports and for reasons of recall in case the layoff proves to be temporary in nature.

In addition to transactions which change data on the records and those which alter the composition of the records in a file, there is a third type of transaction which logically could fall into the second category but which is usually considered to be a separate type of transaction. It often happens that we need to change the order of records in the master file. One simple example would be the need to change the order of listing in an alphabetical file for women who are married and thus change their last names. If Mary Zacher marries and becomes Mary Brown, her record must be repositioned in the file. Another example would be that situation in which the employee identification number includes a department number and some employees are transferred between departments. With such examples in mind, let us consider two common ways for processing such changes.

One approach is to introduce two transactions in the same run. One involves the addition of a new record, and the other involves the deletion of an old one. In the example of the woman who changed her name from Zacher to Brown, we would provide an add-type transaction for Brown and a delete transaction for Zacher. If the volume of such changes is low, this is probably a satisfactory approach. However, if the volume of such transac-

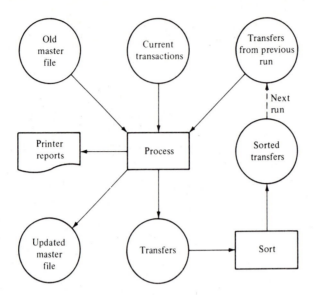

FIGURE 8-13   FILE UPDATING INVOLVING TRANSFER RECORDS.

tions is high, this approach has the disadvantage that it requires whole new master entries, which may involve considerable work. For instance, in a university each student may have a record approximately 2,000 characters in length, containing his or her name, parents' names, local address, home address, transcript data, and so forth. The prospect of manually recreating a new master record is undesirable, and even the prospect of automatic creation of the data may require reading and searching an entire file consisting of several reels of tape.

An alternative approach by which the order of records in a master file can be changed is to alter the record to be relocated, for example, by changing the last name and then writing this altered record on a special "transfer" file and eliminating the record from the currently updated master. This transfer file is then sorted, and in the next run it is merged with the old master file onto the updated master. The process chart in Figure 8–13 presents the logic of the file processing in this case. By this approach we would read and merge the old master file and the transfers-from-previous-run file as the current transactions are being processed. As the process is portrayed in Figure 8–13, five files are required for each update run: one each for the input from the old master file, current transactions file, and transfers from previous run, and one each for output to the updated master file and (new) transfers.

The disadvantage associated with the method portrayed in Figure 8–13 is that the master file is split into two parts. If we wanted to generate a report based on the master file at any other time than during the update procedure, there would be some problems. Figure 8–14 portrays an alternate method that requires an extra merging operation, but that concludes with a complete, updated, and sorted master file.

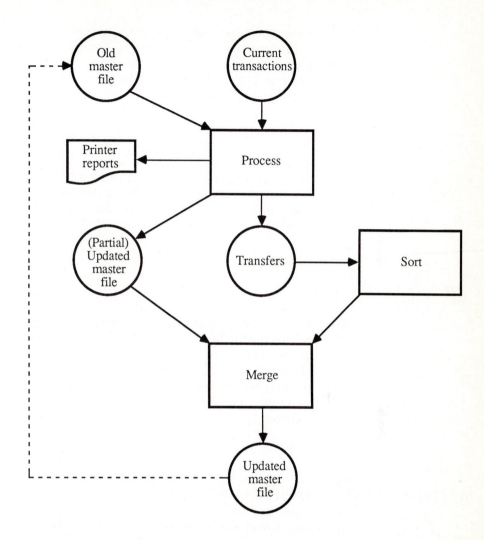

FIGURE 8-14   ALTERNATE METHOD OF FILE UPDATING WITH TRANSFER RECORDS.

Review

1   Of the two basic types of transactions in master file updating, one is concerned with transactions which change the values of _____ contained in master records, while the second is concerned with transactions which result in addition or deletion of whole _____ as such.

fields; master records

2   Suppose an inventory file is updated and there have been no changes in the items held in inventory (although particular inventory levels have changed). Such an updating run would be entirely concerned with changing [values of fields in master records / the record composition of the master file].

> values of fields in master records

3   Given that employees have been added to and deleted from the payroll since the last payroll processing run, the type of transaction which is required is the type which is concerned with changing [values of fields in master records / the record composition of the master file].

> the record composition of the
> master file

4   A third type of transaction is concerned with changing the order of records held in a master file. One way by which such a change can be accomplished is to alter the record to be relocated, write the record on a special _____ file, and eliminate the record from the currently updated master. On the next processing run the (then) old master file his merged with the _____ file from the previous run to form an updated _____.

> transfer; transfer; master file

ACTIVITY RATIOS AND FILE MAINTENANCE

The amount of activity over time is different for the various entries, or items, that constitute a master file. For example, suppose we have a warehouse that stocks 20,000 parts. Some of them will experience daily activity, some may average one transaction a week, while others may have transactions just a few times a year. Let us say that we experience an average of 900 transactions a day and that these transactions are concerned with an average of 400 parts in the inventory system—that is, some parts have more than one transaction. Now suppose we update the master file on a daily basis. Since 400 of the 20,-000 parts were involved in the transactions, we say that the activity ratio is

$$\frac{400}{20,000} = \frac{1}{50} = 0.02$$

Thus, for every 50 records there will be 1 record for which some processing is done and 49 records will simply be copied from the old to the updated file. Obviously the part of the processing concerned with copying is unproductive. As an alternative to updating the file on a daily basis, we might consider processing the file once a week. On the average, there will now be more than 400 active parts per week. However, assuming that there are 5 working days per week, do not be misled into concluding that the number of active parts will be 400 per day × 5 days. Of the 400 average per day, there will be some parts that will be active every day or at least more than once a week. So we may have 1,200 active parts per week, resulting in the activity ratio

$$\frac{1,200}{20,000} = \frac{3}{50} = 0.06$$

The increase in the activity ratio from 0.02 to 0.06 in the above example represents an increase of 300 percent in the value of the ratio. In an extreme case, we may wish to process a batch of records only after a very high percentage —say 98 percent—have had some activity. But this requirement would generally conflict with the need for timely information, since it might well be months before 98 percent of the records experience activity. In a batch-processing system we frequently have to balance information needs against data processing efficiency.

In some files the activity ratio is always high. For example, the payroll file for a manufacturing plant with 5,000 employees will include only a small percentage of "inactive" records on any given day (for those who were absent, on vacation, terminated, etc.). Yet payroll records are not processed daily just because the activity ratio is high. Rather, other factors determine the frequency of updating in this case.

When a file is large and activity variations are great, such a file is often subdivided into two master files, one for "active" items and one for relatively "inactive" items. As a practical matter, it is not easy to specify the difference between these two groups of items. One possible way of making the distinction is to set some parameters on the activity. For example, active items might be defined as those which are involved in at least X transactions per designated period—say, 10 transactions per month. All other items would then be considered inactive by definition. Another approach to distinguishing between active and inactive items is based on the nature of the items themselves. For example, we may know from experience that parts for automobiles that are 8 years old or older are inactive, as are parts for the current model year. Parts for the other model years (1 to 7 years old) would then be considered active.

When two master files are used, some procedure is usually required for exit from one class of items and entry to the other class. The process chart in Figure 8–15 illustrates the basic procedure that is used. There are two types of processing runs, one for the active file and one for the inactive file. Typically, there will be several processing runs for the active file to each run of the inactive file. The input for the updating of the active master file includes the old active master, the transactions, and inactive records that have

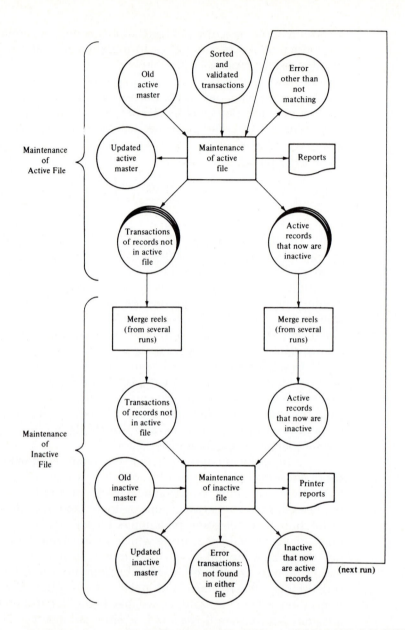

Maintenance of Active File

Maintenance of Inactive File

Old active master

Sorted and validated transactions

Error other than not matching

Updated active master

Maintenance of active file

Reports

Transactions of records not in active file

Active records that now are inactive

Merge reels (from several runs)

Merge reels (from several runs)

Transactions of records not in active file

Active records that now are inactive

Old inactive master

Maintenance of inactive file

Printer reports

Updated inactive master

Error transactions: not found in either file

Inactive that now are active records

(next run)

FIGURE 8-15   FILE MAINTENANCE WITH ACTIVE AND INACTIVE MASTER FILES.

become active. The output consists of the updated active master, those transactions which do not pertain to active records, and those records which have become inactive.

In the maintenance of the inactive file, as portrayed in Figure 8–15, the input is the old inactive master, transactions of records not in the active file, and the (formerly) active records that are now inactive. For each of the latter two inputs several files are typically merged because of there being several processing runs for the active master file for each processing run for the inactive master file. Two types of output are generated in addition to the updated inactive master file. One is concerned with error transactions—that is, transactions not applicable to either file. The other type includes the records that were inactive but now have had increased activity and therefore have been reclassified as being active. These reclassified records will be processed in the next maintenance run for the active master file.

Review

1   If 300 of 1,000 items are involved in transactions during each week, on the average, the weekly activity ratio has the value: _____.

$$300/1{,}000 = 0.30$$

2   For the example above, if the activity ratio is calculated for a typical 2-week period, the value of the ratio is likely to be [less than / equal to / greater than] the value 0.60.

less than

3   When activity variations among the records of a file are great, such a file is frequently subdivided into two master files—one called the _____ master file and the other called the _____ master file.

active; inactive

Exercises

8.1   Consider the master file created by the sample program in Figure 8-5. Transaction records have the following format:

Customer number   in columns 1–5
Transaction code   in column 6
    1 = new name
    2 = new address
    3 = new customer
    4 = delete customer
Customer Name   in columns 7–26
Customer Address   in columns 27–76.

Write a program to update the master file using the following data:

Original Master File Data

12345ADAMS	CUST-10 ADDRESS
14567BROWN	CUST-20 ADDRESS
20050PETERSON	CUST-30 ADDRESS
31020SMITH	CUST-50 ADDRESS
34250JONES	CUST-60 ADDRESS
40000THOMAS	CUST-70 ADDRESS

Transaction Data

145671XAVIER	
300453MATHES	CUST-40 ADDRESS
310003PROVOST	CUST-45 ADDRESS
310204	
330005WRONG CODE EXAMPLE	
400002	CUST-70 NEW-ADDRESS
320204SEQUENCE ERROR	

Your program should output an updated master file both on tape (or disk) and on the printer, for visual inspection. When transaction-code errors are encountered, the program should output an error message along with the transaction record which is in error. When either the transaction file or the master file are out of sequence, then the program should terminate with suitable error messages preceding termination. For the above sample data, the last transaction record is out of sequence and your program should produce the following error messages at that point:

TRANSACTION FILE OUT OF SEQUENCE
TRANSACTION RECORD AT TIME OF ERROR:
   320204
MASTER RECORD AT TIME OF ERROR:
   40000THOMAS   CUST-70 ADDRESS
PREVIOUS TRANS. NO. 40000
PREVIOUS MASTER NO. 40000

Such type error messages help identify clearly the transaction in error and the status of the update process at the time of termination. Apply the general file update model illustrated in Figures 8–9 and 8–10.

8.2   Modify the update program in Exercise 8.1 so that transaction error records are saved on a tape (or disk) file and are printed after the update process has been completed. In a process chart form, we should have:

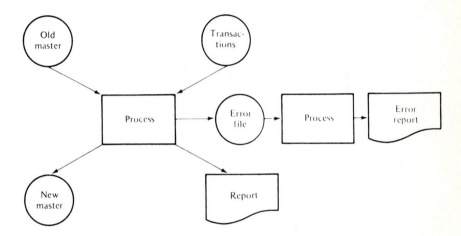

8.3   Modify the update program in Exercise 8.1 so that during the update process only those master records that were in some way altered are output on the printer. Where appropriate, show both the old and the new record for visual reference and comparison. If a record is added or deleted, however, only one master record is relevant. The report should have the following format:

CHANGES TO CUSTOMER MASTER MM/DD/YR	
RECORD	**ACTION**
OLD: xxxxxxxxxxxxx	CHANGED ADDRESS
NEW: xxxxxxxxxxxxx	
NEW: xxxxxxxxxxxxx	NEW RECORD ADDED
OLD: xxxxxxxxxxxxx	DELETED RECORD
OLD: xxxxxxxxxxxxx	CHANGED NAME
NEW: xxxxxxxxxxxxx	

8.4   A company maintains inventory data on a master file which is sorted on part number and contains the following types of data for each item held in inventory:

FIELD	SIZE
Part number	5 numeric positions
Part name	15 alphanumeric positions
Quantity	5 numeric positions

For the sake of simplicity, there are two types of transactions: receipts and issues. Each transaction is recorded on a record of the following format:

FIELD	SIZE
Part number	5 numeric positions
Transaction code	1 numeric position
1 = receipt	
2 = issue	
Quantity	5 numeric positions

Batches of transaction records are accumulated and then processed to update the master file and to print a report that lists each part number, name, previous quantity balance, and new balance. When the transaction code is 1, the quantity is added; if the code is 2, the quantity is subtracted.

a   Write a program to create the master file.

b   Write a program to update the master file, given a file of transaction records. The program should perform a sequence check to see that the transactions are in the same sequence as the master records. It is possible that some items may have no corresponding transactions, but no transactions are present for items not on the master file.

8.5   The county assessor's office maintains a file of property owners, in the following (simplified) format:

Lot number	9-digit code
Owner name	26 alphanumeric characters
Assessed valuation	8-digit field, including 2 decimal places

An update run involves reading records and creating an updated file. The input records have the following format:

Lot number	9-digit code
Code	1-digit code
	1 = change owner name
	2 = change assessed valuation
	3 = change both owner and valuation
	4 = add to tax rolls
	9 = remove from tax rolls
Owner name	26 characters
Assessed valuation	8 digits in dollars and cents

If a code of 1 is used, nothing is written in the assessed valuation field. If a code 2 is used, the owner field is blank. A code of 9 implies that the record is blank from column 11 on.

The printer report should have the following approximate layout:

LOT NUMBER	OWNER	ASSESSED VALUE	NEW OWNER	NEW ASSESSMENT	OFF ROLLS
xxxxxxxxx	xxxxxxxx	$ xxxxxx.xx	xxxxxxxxx	$ xxxxxx.xx	
xxxxxxxxx	xxxxxxxx	xxxx.xx			***

Whenever an item is eliminated, it is signaled by three asterisks in the OFF ROLLS column.

Write a program to update such a file. The program should check for correct sequence in both file records and for possibly erroneous codes in the transaction.

The sample master file is as follows:

LOT NUMBER	OWNER NAME	ASSESSED VALUATION
000150000	JENKING, ANTHONY	10,872.00
000180000	ANDREWS, JULIA	256,237.00
000290000	THOMAS, THEODORE	162,116.00
000350000	MCDONALD, DONNA	769,276.00
000720000	MARTIN, JANE	99,998.00
001050000	RICHARDSON, PETER	820,600.00
001120000	SILVA, ROBIN	959,999.00

Sample transaction records are:

LOT NUMBER	CODE	OWNER NAME	ASSESSED VALUATION
000180000	1	ANDREWS, THOMAS	
000290000	2		300,000.00
000720000	3	STEINMAN, WILLA	100,000.00
001050000	9		

Sample output is as follows:

LOT NUMBER	OWNER	ASSESSED VALUE	NEW OWNER	NEW ASSESSMENT	OFF ROLLS
00015000	JENKING, ANTHONY	$ 10,872.00			
000180000	ANDREWS, JULIA	$256,237.00	ANDREWS, THOMAS		
000290000	THOMAS, THEODORE	$162,116.00		$300,000.00	
000350000	MCDONALD, DONNA	$769,276.00			
000720000	MARTIN, JANE	$ 99,998.00	STEINMAN, WILLA	$100,000.00	
001050000	RICHARDSON, PETER	$820,600.00			* * *
001120000	SILVA, ROBIN	$959,999.00			

9

SORTING AND MERGING

INTRODUCTION

Sorting and merging are very common procedures in data processing, and therefore there are entire books devoted to these subjects. In this chapter we limit our coverage to fundamental concepts and methods as well as presenting COBOL-related features specific to sorting and merging.

INTERNAL SORTING

Internal sorting is concerned with sorting procedures (algorithms) used with tables of data held in central storage. Sorting an internal table is a different task from sorting data recorded on external files, such as disk or tape. There are many internal sort algorithms, and new ones continue to be developed for special cases. In this section we present three *interchange sort algorithms.*

There are several versions of the interchange sort approach. Fundamental to all versions is the interchange of two elements in the table. To interchange data in two fields we need a third field for temporary storage. For instance, if we want to interchange the data in T(X) and T(Y), we could write:

MOVE T(X) TO TEMP
MOVE T(Y) TO T(X)
MOVE TEMP TO T(Y).

Any interchange algorithm involves paired comparisons of table elements. The *adjacent comparison–interchange* approach involves comparison of adjacent table values and may require multiple "passes" through the table. In each pass we interchange adjacent elements that are out of order relative to each other. Specifically, in the first pass the first entry is compared with the second, the second with the third, and so on until the $(N - 1)$th record is compared with the Nth record in the table. The two records being compared each time are interchanged whenever the second record is smaller than the first record, assuming that the table is being sorted into ascending order. If no interchange was necessary during an entire pass, this means that the table is already in order. Otherwise, at least one more pass is required.

By the adjacent comparison approach, at the end of the first pass the largest record is driven to the bottom of the table. Thus in the second pass through the table $N - 1$ table entries are considered, in the third pass $N - 2$ are considered, and so forth. Thus the table is sorted from the last entry up, and every pass through the table involves a smaller table for comparisons and interchanges. Eventually only two elements remain to be considered— the first and the second.

Typically, however, the table will come to be sorted correctly before all possible passes through the table are made by the adjacent comparison approach. As indicated above, the fact that no interchange is necessary during a pass through the table serves to indicate that the table is already correctly sorted. In order to avoid unnecessary passes through the table, it is useful to incorporate a procedure by which such a situation can be detected. One way of doing this is to initialize a data-name with a value such as zero and to change the value to 1 with the occurrence of any interchange. At the end of each pass the value of the data-name is tested. If the value is zero, the table is sorted. If the value is 1, at least one more pass is required.

The procedure associated with the adjacent comparison–interchange algorithm will now be illustrated by means of a COBOL program, which is presented in Figure 9–1.

The input consists of records, each of which consists of two fields. NAME-IN and FILLER. The NAME-IN will be used as the sort key while FILLER is assumed to contain other data. Data is read in by execution of the

```
IDENTIFICATION DIVISION.
PROGRAM-ID. INSORT.
*
ENVIRONMENT DIVISION.
CONFIGURATION SECTION.
SOURCE-COMPUTER. ABC-480.
OBJECT-COMPUTER. ABC-480.
INPUT-OUTPUT SECTION.
FILE-CONTROL.
    SELECT INPUT-FILE  ASSIGN TO READER.
    SELECT OUTPUT-FILE ASSIGN TO PRINTER.
*
DATA DIVISION.
FILE SECTION.
*
FD  INPUT-FILE LABEL RECORD OMITTED
               DATA RECORD INPUT-RECORD.
01  INPUT-RECORD.
    02 NAME-IN        PIC X(15).
    02 FILLER         PIC X(65).
*
FD  OUTPUT-FILE LABEL RECORD OMITTED
               DATA RECORD PRINT-RECORD.
01  PRINT-RECORD      PIC X(132).
*
WORKING-STORAGE SECTION.
*
01  ENTIRE-TABLE.
    02 TABLE-REC OCCURS 50 TIMES.
       03 NAME        PIC X(15).
       03 FILLER      PIC X(65).
01  DATA-END          PIC XXX VALUE 'NO '.
    88 DATA-ENDED              VALUE 'YES'.
01  TEST              PIC X(8).
01  N                 PIC 99.
01  I                 PIC 99.
01  J                 PIC 99.
01  K                 PIC 99.
01  M                 PIC 99.
01  TEMP-STORE        PIC X(80).
/
PROCEDURE DIVISION.
*
MAIN-ROUTINE.
    OPEN INPUT INPUT-FILE
         OUTPUT OUTPUT-FILE
*
    PERFORM READ-DATA-IN
*
    PERFORM SORT-DATA
*
    PERFORM PRINT-DATA
```

FIGURE 9-1   COBOL INTERNAL SORT PROGRAM UTILIZING THE ADJACENT COMPARISON-INTERCHANGE ALGORITHM.

```
                CLOSE INPUT-FILE, OUTPUT-FILE
                STOP RUN.
      *
        READ-DATA-IN SECTION.
      *
        SET-UP-TO-READ.
                MOVE 'NO' TO DATA-END.
                MOVE ZERO TO N.
                PERFORM READ-DATA
      *
                PERFORM STORE-READ
                          UNTIL DATA-ENDED
                             OR N = 50.
                GO TO EXIT-READ.
      *
        READ-DATA.
                READ INPUT-FILE AT END SET DATA-ENDED TO TRUE.
      *
        STORE-READ.
                ADD 1 TO N
                MOVE INPUT-RECORD TO TABLE-REC (N)
                PERFORM READ-DATA.
      *
        EXIT-READ.
                EXIT.
      *
        SORT-DATA SECTION.
      *
        SET-UP-TO-SORT.
                MOVE 'UNSORTED' TO TEST
                MOVE N TO M
      *
                PERFORM OUTER-LOOP VARYING I FROM 1 BY 1
                                UNTIL TEST = 'SORTED'
                                    OR I = N - 1.
                GO TO SORT-ENDED.
      *
        OUTER-LOOP.
                MOVE 'SORTED' TO TEST
                COMPUTE M = M - 1
                PERFORM PAIRED-COMPARISONS VARYING J FROM 1 BY 1
                                UNTIL J > M.
      *
        PAIRED-COMPARISONS.
                COMPUTE K = 1 + J
      *
                IF NAME (J) IS GREATER THAN NAME (K)
                    MOVE TABLE-REC (J) TO TEMP-STORE
                    MOVE TABLE-REC (K) TO TABLE-REC (J)
                    MOVE TEMP-STORE TO TABLE-REC (K)
                    MOVE 'UNSORTED' TO TEST
                ELSE
                    NEXT SENTENCE.
```

FIGURE 9-1   COBOL INTERNAL SORT PROGRAM UTILIZING THE ADJACENT COMPARISON-INTERCHANGE ALGORITHM.   (Continued)

```
SORT-ENDED.
    EXIT.
*
 PRINT-DATA SECTION.
*
 PRINT-ROUTINE.
    PERFORM  VARYING I FROM 1 BY 1
                UNTIL I > N
*
    MOVE TABLE-REC (I) TO PRINT-RECORD
    WRITE PRINT-RECORD AFTER ADVANCING 1 LINE
*
 END-PERFORM.
*
 PRINT-END.
    EXIT.
```

FIGURE 9-1   COBOL INTERNAL SORT PROGRAM UTILIZING THE ADJACENT COMPARISON-INTERCHANGE ALGORITHM.   (Continued)

READ-DATA-IN SECTION, which stores the records in a table called EN-TIRE-TABLE. Notice that N is a counter that represents the number of records read (maximum of 50).

The sorting operation takes place in the SORT-DATA SECTION. The PERFORM OUTER-LOOP is executed as long as TEST is not equal to SORTED and as long as I is not equal to N − 1. In essence, this instruction says to keep going through the table as long as it is not sorted after each pass through, but in any case not to go through the table more than N − 1 times. In the OUTER-LOOP paragraph, TEST is set to the value "SORTED" so that if no interchange takes place, that value will stay as such and will terminate execution of the OUTER-LOOP paragraph. Each time through, M is decreased by 1, since the table is effectively shortened as the largest value floats to the bottom. The PERFORM PAIRED-COMPARISONS instruction allows us to compare M − 1 pairs and interchange their values as needed. The PRINT-DATA SECTION simply lists the data on the printer for visual review.

Another version of the interchange sort algorithm is the *bubble sort–interchange algorithm*. Use of this method results in the first part of the table being sorted first. By the bubble sort–interchange method the first step is that the second record is compared with the first, and if necessary, they are interchanged. Then the third record is compared with the second. If these two records are interchanged, the (new) second record is compared with the first, interchanging if necessary. Next, the fourth and third record are compared for possible interchange. Again, if an interchange occurs, we go "upward" and compare the third with the second record and then possibly the second with the first record. Thus, at each stage a record rises like a bubble to find its proper place, and hence the name "bubble sort" which is applied to this algorithm.

As an example of using the bubble sort–interchange algorithm, consider the following set of six records with sort keys as indicated:

5

8

10

11

9

15

Comparison of the second and first records results in no interchange. Similarly, comparison of the third and second and of the fourth and third records results in no interchange. However, when the fifth and fourth records are compared (9 and 11), an interchange results. Following this, comparison of the fourth and third records (9 and 10) results in another interchange, but then the comparison of the third and second records (9 and 8) results in no further interchange. Finally, the sixth and fifth records are compared (15 and 11). Since this is the last pair of records and no interchange is required, the sort routine is completed.

Another internal sort procedure is one devised by D. L. Shell in 1959 and that bears his name. The main improvement associated with the Shell sort is that it has the property of moving records that are far removed from their proper position in fewer steps than either the adjacent comparisons–interchange algorithm or the bubble sort–interchange algorithm. To achieve this result, the procedure uses a distance parameter. Initially, the distance parameter is set to half the table length, thereby comparing the first element with the "middle" element in the table and exchanging the elements if appropriate. The procedure involves multiple passes, as all sorts do; and on each pass, the distance factor is reduced by half until the distance is 1, which is then the last pass. When an exchange occurs, the procedure followed is to examine whether or not additional exchanges should occur by "backing up" in distance-factor increments. A brief illustration will help to explain the procedure. Suppose that we have the following list of values in a table:

6   2   15   1   3   8   18   10   7   20

Initially, the distance factor is set to 5, resulting in comparison of 6 and 8, 2 and 18, 15 and 10, and so on. When the 15 and 10 are compared, they are interchanged, resulting in the following revised list after the first pass:

6   2   10   1   3   8   18   15   7   20

On the second pass, the distance factor is reduced by half, from 5 to 2 (truncating the fractional quotient), resulting in comparison of 6 and 10, 2 and 1 (and interchange), 10 and 3 (and interchange). At this point in the second pass, the listed order is:

6   1   3   2   10   8   18   15   7   20

Now we back up and compare 3 to 6, since the procedure backs up by the distance factor after an exchange has occurred, when possible. Thus, 6 and 3 would be interchanged and the procedure then would resume with a comparison of 2 and 8, which is where it left off before the backing up. The reason that we did not consider the "backing up" concept earlier in this example is there was no previous occasion in which there was an interchange for which the distance factor allowed us to back up and still be within the limits of the table.

Figure 9–2 presents PROCEDURE DIVISION code to implement the Shell sort. The example includes an algorithm for computing an odd-numbered value as the initial distance factor, DIST, since it has been found that use of an odd-numbered value as the initial distance factor generally results in a faster sort than use of an even-numbered value.

Review

1   By "internal sorting" we mean the sorting of a table held in the _____ of the computer.

internal (or central) storage

2   Several versions of the interchange sort algorithm exist. The feature which is common to all these versions is that in each approach _____ (number) records are compared each time for possible interchange.

2

3   By the adjacent comparison–interchange algorithm all adjacent records are compared and interchanged, when necessary, during each pass through the table. The fact that the table is correctly sorted is indicated when _____ (number) interchanges are required during a particular pass through the table.

0

Definition of variables:

TS = Table size
DIST = Distance factor
L = Controls the number of comparisons in the current pass
I = Current record position
K (J) = Key value of record at location J
R (J) = Record at location J
KEEP-COMPARING = A condition-name used to control the back-up process
STOP-COMPARING = A condition-name used to control the back-up process
TEMP = A temporary record storage field for the exchange

```
MOVE 1 TO DIST
IF TS > 3
   PERFORM UNTIL DIST > TS
      COMPUTE DIST=DIST * 2
   END-PERFORM
   COMPUTE DIST = (DIST / 2) - 1
END-IF
PERFORM UNTIL DIST < 1
   COMPUTE L = TS - DIST
   MOVE 1 TO J
   PERFORM UNTIL I > L
      MOVE I TO J   COMPUTE  M = J + DIST
      IF K (J) > K (M)
         SET KEEP-COMPARING TO TRUE
         PERFORM UNTIL STOP-COMPARING
            MOVE R (J) TO TEMP   COMPUTE M = J + DIST
            MOVE R (M) TO R (J)
            MOVE TEMP TO R (M)
            COMPUTE J = J - DIST
            IF J >= 1
               COMPUTE M = J + DIST
               IF K (J) <= K (M)
                  SET STOP-COMPARING TO TRUE
               ELSE   CONTINUE
               END-IF
            ELSE SET STOP-COMPARING TO TRUE
            END-IF
         END-PERFORM
      END-IF
      ADD 1 TO I
   END-PERFORM
   COMPUTE D = D / 2
END-PERFORM.
```

FIGURE 9-2   PROCEDURE DIVISION CODE FOR A SHELL SORT ROUTINE.

4 Another version of the interchange sort algorithm is the bubble sort–interchange. By this approach, each record is properly placed before subsequent records are considered, resulting in the [first / last] part of the table being sorted first and thereby requiring _____ (number) passes for a table of N records.

first; 1

5 In the Shell sort procedure, the distance parameter used to determine which pairs of items will be compared initially is set at _____ the table length.

one-half

6 In the Shell sort procedure, the distance parameter for the last pass through the table is always equal to _____.

1

COBOL FILE-SORT FEATURE

File sorting differs from internal sorting. Files are generally too large to store as tables in central storage. Therefore, sort algorithms for files proceed in stages, with each successive stage operating internally on part of the data. File-sorting algorithms are complex procedures, and most of them are proprietary products that can be bought or leased. While their specific algorithms are often trade secrets, the general principles of file sorting are common to most algorithms and involve combinations of internal sorting and file merging.

Since file sorting frequently is required in maintaining an information system, the COBOL language incorporates a sort feature that makes it possible to accomplish this operation with minimal programming. The programmer need not be concerned with the details of the sort algorithm in using this feature, but may simply specify the files to be sorted, the sort key (or keys) to be used, and any special procedures for the handling of files before or after the sort. We illustrate here the COBOL file-sort feature by means of two examples.

Example 1

Assume that we have a sequential file with the following record description in the DATA DIVISION:

```
01  INPUT-RECORD.
    02  ACCOUNT-NUMBER      PICTURE 9(8).
    02  NAME                PICTURE X(20).
    02  TRANSACTION-DATE.
        03  DAY-OF-YEAR     PICTURE 999.
        03  YEAR            PICTURE 99.
    02  OTHER-DATA          PICTURE X(47).
```

Suppose we wish to sort the file in ascending sequence according to ACCOUNT-NUMBER and in descending sequence according to YEAR. That is, for each account, all records are to be arranged from the most recent to the least recent YEAR. Also assume that the sorted file is to be called SORTED-FILE. The sorting process can be portrayed as involving three files. INPUT-FILE, SORT-FILE, and SORTED-FILE, as follows:

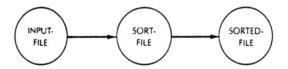

Because the sorting procedure is preprogrammed, you need not be concerned about the detail of the SORT-FILE.

In concept, SORT-FILE represents a preprogrammed file whose description has been embedded in the sorting routine. As the above diagram illustrates, data from the INPUT-FILE are transferred to the SORT-FILE where they are sorted; and the sorted data are then output onto the SORTED-FILE (these specific file-names are, of course, arbitrary choices).

The SORT-FILE is a conceptual file which may involve several physical files. Typically, the sort routine uses several sequential files in order to execute the sort. Since the sort routine is automated, however, the COBOL programmer describes the file as if it were one physical file; and it is through JCL statements that we describe the physical structure of the file.

Figure 9–3 presents the COBOL program that can be used to sort the file described in this example problem. In the ENVIRONMENT DIVISION, three files are identified in the SELECT statements. Notice that SORT-FILE has been ASSIGNed as if it were one physical file.

In the DATA DIVISION, the INPUT-FILE is described in the usual fashion. However, the SORT-FILE is introduced with the special SD level indicator (which stands for Sort Descriptor). The SD level indicator specifies that this is a file to be used in conjunction with the sort routine. Notice that there is no LABEL clause given for such a file.

As far as the record description for the SORT-FILE is concerned, it is just like any other such description. We used the same description as we used for the INPUT-FILE, and qualification is used to differentiate between the two records.

```
 IDENTIFICATION DIVISION.
 PROGRAM-ID. SORT1.
*
*    This program illustrates sorting a sequential
        file called INPUT-FILE and making the sorted file
        available in SORTED-FILE.
*
 ENVIRONMENT DIVISION.
*
 CONFIGURATION SECTION.
 SOURCE-COMPUTER. ABC-480.
 OBJECT-COMPUTER. ABC-480.
*
 INPUT-OUTPUT SECTION.
 FILE-CONTROL.
      SELECT INPUT-FILE   ASSIGN TO READER.
      SELECT SORT-FILE    ASSIGN TO SORTWORK.
      SELECT SORTED-FILE ASSIGN TO PRINTER.
*
 DATA DIVISION.
*
 FILE SECTION.
 FD   INPUT-FILE LABEL RECORD OMITTED
                DATA RECORD IS INPUT-RECORD.
*
 01   INPUT-RECORD.
      02   ACCOUNT-NUMBER     PIC 9(8).
      02   NAME               PIC X(20).
      02   TRANSACTION-DATE.
           03   DAY-OF-YEAR   PIC 999.
           03   YEAR          PIC 99.
      02   OTHER-DATA         PIC X(47).
*
 SD   SORT-FILE DATA RECORD IS SORT-RECORD.
*
 01   SORT-RECORD.
      02   ACCOUNT-NUMBER     PIC 9(8).
      02   NAME               PIC X(20).
      02   TRANSACTION-DATE.
           03   DAY-OF-YEAR   PIC 999.
           03   YEAR          PIC 99.
      02   OTHER-DATA         PIC X(47).
*
 FD   SORTED-FILE LABEL RECORD OMITTED
           DATA RECORD IS SORTED-RECORD.
*
 01   SORTED-RECORD          PIC X(80).
```

FIGURE 9-3   SAMPLE SORT PROGRAM FOR EXAMPLE 1.

```
     PROCEDURE DIVISION.
*
     SORTING-PARAGRAPH.
         SORT SORT-FILE
*
                ON ASCENDING KEY ACCOUNT-NUMBER OF SORT-RECORD
                   DESCENDING KEY YEAR OF SORT-RECORD
*
                USING INPUT-FILE
*
                GIVING SORTED-FILE.
*
         STOP RUN.
```

**FIGURE 9-3   SAMPLE SORT PROGRAM FOR EXAMPLE 1.
(Continued)**

Finally, the SORTED-FILE record has been described as one field of 80 characters to illustrate one possible variation. Since the program is concerned only with the sorting of the file, there is no need to describe the records that constitute this file.

The relevant PROCEDURE DIVISION is simple and consists of just one paragraph. The SORT verb is very powerful in that the programmer need only specify the sort keys and the source and destination of the file records. The statement SORT SORT-FILE identifies the name of the file to be sorted—which should be the same file introduced by an SD entry in the DATA DIVISION. The ASCENDING KEY ACCOUNT-NUMBER OF SORT-RECORD clause specifies that the file is to be sorted in ascending AC-COUNT-NUMBER OF SORT-RECORD sequence. The DESCENDING KEY YEAR OF SORT-RECORD clause specifies that, within each ACCOUNT-NUMBER OF SORT-RECORD, we wish to sort in descending sequence with respect to the values contained in the YEAR OF SORT-RECORD field. The key written first is the principal basis for the sort. Other keys are of decreasing sorting significance as we proceed from one to the next. For example, consider the following KEY clauses:

```
ASCENDING KEY STATE-NAME
ASCENDING KEY COUNTY-NAME
ASCENDING KEY CITY-NAME
```

The order of listing of these clauses indicates that STATE-NAME is the principal basis for the sort. Put another way, CITY-NAME will be sorted within COUNTY-NAME, and COUNTY-NAME, will be sorted within STATE-NAME. The fields used for the sort order are often referred to as "sort keys," and the terms "major," "intermediate," and "minor" sort keys are used to describe multiple sort keys. Thus in the above example, STATE-NAME is the major sort key, COUNTY-NAME is the intermediate sort key, and CITY-NAME is the minor key. Of course if we have more than three sort keys, then this three-level terminology is not applicable.

Note that the sort keys are written according to the desired order of the sort and not according to the order in which the keys appear in the record. For this example, it could very well be that the three fields used as sort keys are in the following physical order in the record: CITY-NAME, STATE-NAME, COUNTY-NAME.

The USING INPUT-FILE clause in Figure 9–3 specifies the file that is the source of the record, while the GIVING SORTED-FILE clause simply specifies the file on which the sort output is to be recorded. Finally, note that in the present example the programmer does not OPEN or CLOSE any of the three files involved. The use of the SORT verb automatically takes care of such procedures.

In the above example, the whole function of the PROCEDURE DIVISION is to sort a file. This need not be the case. The SORT is simply one of the COBOL verbs and, as such, it comprises only one statement in the program. The following example illustrates the point:

```
IF   TIME-TO-SORT
       PERFORM ROUTINE-A
       SORT   CUST-SORT-FILE
               ON ASCENDING KEY NAME
         USING CUSTOMER-SOURCE-FILE
         GIVING CUSTOMER-SORTED-FILE
       PERFORM ROUTINE-B
ELSE
       PERFORM ROUTINE-C.
```

Example 2

We now illustrate use of the INPUT PROCEDURE . . . and OUTPUT PROCEDURE . . . features of the SORT statement. Suppose we want to read a set of records, add a field to each record to indicate its sequential order, sort the file, store the sorted file on magnetic tape, and, finally, print the sorted file as the output of the program. Figure 9–4 presents the COBOL program designed to accomplish this task. Notice that there are four files, called INPUT-FILE, SORT-FILE, SORTED-FILE, and PRINT-FILE. DATA DIVISION entries follow the usual format, except for the use of SD to identify the SORT-FILE as the sort file, as was the case in the preceding example. In the present example, the WORKING-STORAGE SECTION is used to form the SEQUENCE-NUMBER.

Figure 9–5 presents the program logic in flowchart form. Comparing the SORT statement in the PROCEDURE DIVISION in Figure 9–4 with the

```
        IDENTIFICATION DIVISION.
        PROGRAM-ID. SORT2.
*
*    This program illustrates use of the INPUT PROCEDURE
        and OUTPUT PROCEDURE features of the SORT verb.
*
    ENVIRONMENT DIVISION.
*
    CONFIGURATION SECTION.
    SOURCE-COMPUTER. ABC-480.
    OBJECT-COMPUTER. ABC-480.
*
    INPUT-OUTPUT SECTION.
*
    FILE-CONTROL.
        SELECT  INPUT-FILE ASSIGN TO READER.
*
        SELECT SORT-FILE   ASSIGN TO SORTWORK.
*
        SELECT SORTED-FILE ASSIGN TO SORTOUT.
*
        SELECT  PRINT-FILE ASSIGN TO PRINTER.
*
    DATA DIVISION.
    FILE SECTION.
*
    FD   INPUT-FILE LABEL RECORD OMITTED
         DATA RECORD IS INPUT-RECORD.
    01   INPUT-RECORD.
         02  FILLER                 PICTURE X(10).
         02  NAME                   PICTURE X(15).
         02  FILLER                 PICTURE X(51).
         02  DATA-TO-BE-INSERTED    PICTURE 9999.
*
    SD   SORT-FILE DATA RECORD IS SORT-RECORD.
    01   SORT-RECORD.
         02  FILLER                 PICTURE X(10).
         02  NAME                   PICTURE X(15).
         02  FILLER                 PICTURE X(55).
*
    FD   SORTED-FILE LABEL RECORD STANDARD
         BLOCK CONTAINS 77 RECORDS
         DATA RECORD IS SORTED-RECORD.
*
    01   SORTED-RECORD             PICTURE X(80).
*
    FD   PRINT-FILE LABEL RECORD OMITTED
         DATA RECORD IS PRINT-LINE.
*
    01   PRINT-LINE               PICTURE X(132).
```

FIGURE 9-4   SAMPLE SORT PROGRAM FOR EXAMPLE 2.

```
WORKING-STORAGE SECTION.
*
01   END-OF-DATA          PIC XXX.
*
01   SEQUENCE-NUMBER      PIC 9(4) VALUE ZEROS.
/
PROCEDURE DIVISION.
*
MAIN-SORT-ROUTINE.
     MOVE ZERO TO SEQUENCE-NUMBER.
*
     SORT SORT-FILE ASCENDING KEY NAME OF SORT-RECORD
*
           INPUT    PROCEDURE IS READING-SEQUENCING
*
           OUTPUT   PROCEDURE IS RETURNING-PRINTING.
*
     STOP RUN.
*
READING-SEQUENCING SECTION.
*
INPUT-SET-UP.
     OPEN INPUT INPUT-FILE.
     MOVE 'NO' TO END-OF-DATA.
*
     PERFORM READ-DATA
*
     PERFORM SEQ-RELEASE
             UNTIL END-OF-DATA = 'YES'
     CLOSE INPUT-FILE
     GO TO END-OF-INPUT-SECTION.
*
READ-DATA.
     READ INPUT-FILE RECORD
           AT END MOVE 'YES' TO END-OF-DATA.
*
SEQ-RELEASE.
     ADD 1 TO SEQUENCE-NUMBER.
     MOVE SEQUENCE-NUMBER TO DATA-TO-BE-INSERTED
*
     RELEASE SORT-RECORD FROM INPUT-RECORD
*
     PERFORM READ-DATA.
*
END-OF-INPUT-SECTION.
     EXIT.
```

**FIGURE 9-4   SAMPLE SORT PROGRAM FOR EXAMPLE 2.
(Continued)**

```
.RETURNING-PRINTING SECTION.
*
  OUTPUT-SET-UP.
       OPEN OUTPUT SORTED-FILE
                  PRINT-FILE
       MOVE 'NO' TO END-OF-DATA
*
       PERFORM RETURN-DATA
*
       PERFORM WRITE-DATA
              UNTIL END-OF-DATA = 'YES'.
       CLOSE SORTED-FILE PRINT-FILE
       GO TO END-OF-OUTPUT-SECTION.
*
  RETURN-DATA.
       RETURN SORT-FILE RECORD INTO SORTED-RECORD
              AT END MOVE 'YES' TO END-OF-DATA.
*
  WRITE-DATA.
       WRITE PRINT-LINE FROM SORTED-RECORD
       WRITE SORTED-RECORD.
*
       PERFORM RETURN-DATA.
*
  END-OF-OUTPUT-SECTION.
       EXIT.
```

**FIGURE 9-4   SAMPLE SORT PROGRAM FOR EXAMPLE 2.
(Continued)**

flowchart, notice that even though the SORT statement is one statement in form, it consists of three executable steps in function. These three steps are:

1   Execute the section identified by INPUT PROCEDURE IS.

2   Execute the SORT itself.

3   Execute the section identified by OUTPUT PROCEDURE IS.

In the PROCEDURE DIVISION, we first specify that we wish to sort the SORT-FILE on ASCENDING KEY NAME OF SORT-FILE. Thus, the NAME field is the sort key. INPUT PROCEDURE IS READING-SEQUENCING indicates that records will become available to the SORT-FILE according to instructions contained in a section called READING-SEQUENCING. The first paragraph in the READING-SEQUENCING SECTION, called INPUT-SET-UP, serves to open the INPUT-FILE as input. Then we enter a loop involving the SEQ-RELEASE paragraph. Each record is read, and in each case a 4-digit sequence number is assigned to the field called DATA-TO-BE-INSERTED. Then we use the RELEASE SORT-RECORD FROM INPUT-RECORD statement. This simply says to move the contents of INPUT-RECORD to SORT-RECORD and

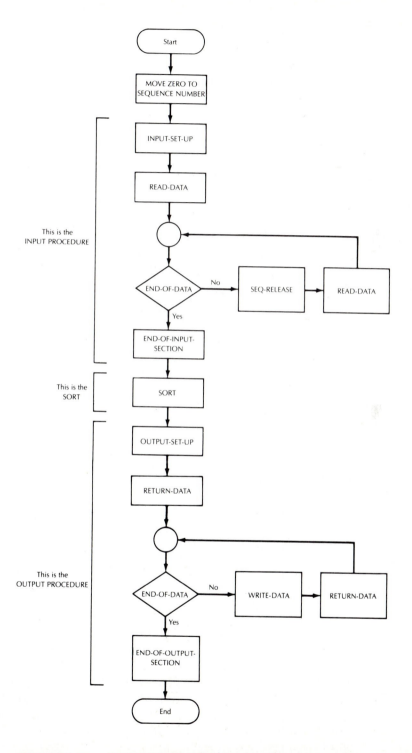

FIGURE 9-5   FLOWCHART REPRESENTATION OF SAMPLE SORT PROGRAM.

then to write the SORT-RECORD on its file. The RELEASE command thus can be thought of as a specialized form of the WRITE instruction.

The loop terminates when the last record is read, at which point the program branches to END-OF-INPUT SECTION, after INPUT-FILE is closed. The END-OF-INPUT-SECTION paragraph is the last paragraph of the READING-SEQUENCING SECTION, and is indicated by the EXIT verb. Recall that the execution of the READING-SEQUENCING SECTION was initiated by execution of the INPUT PROCEDURE statement in the SORT statement. In fact, the INPUT PROCEDURE statement has the same effect as if we had written PERFORM READING-SEQUENCING. Program execution branches to that section, and, when it is completed, the next statement is executed. The next statement in the present example is the SORT itself, which is then followed by OUTPUT PROCEDURE IS RETURNING-PRINTING, the name of another section: therefore, program execution then branches to the RETURNING-PRINTING SECTION.

The first paragraph of the RETURNING-PRINTING SECTION is the OUTPUT-SET-UP, which opens two output files. Then we PERFORM RETURN-DATA and enter a loop involving WRITE-DATA. The RETURN SORT-FILE RECORD INTO SORTED-RECORD statement is simply a special form of saying, "Read a record from the SORT-FILE and move it to the SORTED-RECORD." Notice the use of AT END, which parallels the same clause in the READ verb. After each record is RETURNed, we employ an implicit move (FROM SORTED-RECORD) and we WRITE PRINT-LINE. Finally, we WRITE SORTED-RECORD on the output file. The process is repeated until the END-OF-DATA = 'YES' condition holds. The OUTPUT-SET-UP paragraph closes the files and END-OF-OUTPUT-SECTION is executed next. Program control then returns to the statement that follows the statement, OUTPUT PROCEDURE IS RETURNING-PRINTING, because this is where the branching occurred. The statement in question is STOP RUN and signifies the logical end of the program.

Thus, in this example we have demonstrated that, by using the INPUT PROCEDURE and the OUTPUT PROCEDURE options of the SORT verb, we can specify the procedure to be executed both before the sort takes place and after the sort takes place. Within these procedures we can execute any COBOL statements, but in addition we must use two specialized I/O verbs:

1   When data is ready to be written onto the sort file (the one with the SD level indicator), we use the RELEASE instead of the WRITE verb.

2   When data is ready to be read from the sort file, we use the RETURN instead of the READ verb.

The reader may question why the SORT statement was written with this second format. We could reason that if we want to execute some procedure before and/or after the data is sorted we could do something like the following:

```
PERFORM INPUT-PROC
SORT   file-name-1 ASCENDING KEY key-name
         USING file-name-2
         GIVING file-name-3
PERFORM OUTPUT-PROC.
```

In the above example, we assume that INPUT-PROC executes some procedure that generates the presorted-data in file-name-2. We SORT ... using file-name-2 and obtain the sorted output in file-name-3 (GIVING file-name-3). Then the OUTPUT-PROC can execute whatever procedure we want to do with the sorted output.

The above approach is correct, but it has the disadvantage that it will consume more I/O processing time than the use of the INPUT PROCEDURE and OUTPUT PROCEDURE options included in Figure 9–4. In the above approach we read the input file once in INPUT-PROC and then read it a second time during the USING file-name-2 routine. Also, the sorted data are read and possibly written twice, once during the GIVING phase and a second time during the OUTPUT-PROC. In summary, the example in Figure 9–4 has the advantage that the INPUT PROCEDURE is executed *while* the data are being transferred from the source file to the sort file. Similarly, the OUTPUT PROCEDURE is executed *while* the data are transferred from the sort file.

Review

1   The COBOL language feature by which a file can be sorted without having to write a sorting algorithm as such is called the _____ feature.

sort

2   In order to use the sort feature, the programmer must specify the _____ to be sorted and the _____ to be used as the basis for the sort.

file; key (or keys)

3   If a file is to be sorted on the basis of more than one key, the key that is written [first / last] is the principal basis for the sort.

first

4   In the second example problem in this section, two options of the SORT verb were used to branch to other parts of the program in order to perform required processing tasks. These were the _____ and _____ options of the SORT verb.

INPUT PROCEDURE; OUTPUT
PROCEDURE

SORT STATEMENT FORMATS

We now consider the COBOL format specifications that enable a programmer to use the sort feature.

DATA DIVISION

In the DATA DIVISION, the relevant format is presented in Figure 9–6. The level indicator SD identifies the beginning of a sort file sort description. Notice that, other than the SD, the file description has the usual format. Notice also that there is no BLOCK CONTAINS option. Whether or not any blocking is possible or desirable is determined automatically by the preprogrammed sort routine.

The first two options of the RECORD clause are only applicable in the 1985 COBOL standard. The RECORD CONTAINS integer-1 CHARACTERS specifies fixed-length records, while the RECORD IS VARYING IN SIZE . . . specifies variable-length records. In the 1974 version of the language, variable-length records are specified by RECORD CONTAINS integer-4 to integer-5 CHARACTERS.

Note that in Figure 9–6 both the RECORD and the DATA clauses are

```
SD     file-name-1

       ┌                                                                    ┐
       │            ┌ CONTAINS integer-1 CHARACTERS                       ┐ │
       │            │ IS VARYING IN SIZE                                  │ │
       │ RECORD  ───┤    [[FROM integer-2]  [TO integer-3]  CHARACTERS]   │ │
       │            │    [DEPENDING on data-name-1]                       │ │
       │            └ (CONTAINS [integer-4 TO] integer-5 CHARACTERS       ┘ │
       └                                                                    ┘

       ┌        ┌ RECORD IS    ┐                    ┐
       │ DATA  ─┤              │  {data-name-2} . . .│
       │        └ RECORDS ARE  ┘                    │
       └                                             ┘
```

FIGURE 9–6   SORT FILE DESCRIPTION ENTRY.

optional. Usually the function of these clauses is embedded in the sort routine itself, and there is no need for the program to specify what has already been preprogrammed.

PROCEDURE DIVISION

The SORT verb is the basic verb in the SORT option. The format is presented in Figure 9–7. The verb SORT always is required. File-name-1 is the file designated in an SD entry in the DATA DIVISION. At least one KEY has to be specified. If more than one sort key is used and all are ascending (or all descending), they can be written in the following form:

SORT file-name ON ASCENDING KEY ACCOUNT, NAME, YEAR.

Here we have specified an ascending sort by ACCOUNT, by NAME within ACCOUNT, and by YEAR within NAME. Or, we could have used the word ASCENDING (or DESCENDING) in conjunction with each KEY, as follows:

SORT file-name ON ASCENDING KEY ACCOUNT
    ON ASCENDING KEY NAME
    ON ACENDING KEY YEAR.

The WITH DUPLICATES IN ORDER clause can be used to specify that if there are records with duplicate sort-keys, they should be kept in their original order with respect to each other. Thus if the source file contains 10

```
SORT file-name-1

    {ON  {ASCENDING }  KEY  {data-name-1} . . . } . . .
         {DESCENDING}

    [COLLATING SEQUENCE IS alphabet-name-1]
    [WITH DUPLICATES IN ORDER]

    ( INPUT PROCEDURE IS  {section-name-1  } [{THROUGH} {section-name-2  }] )
    (                     {procedure-name-1}  {THRU   } {procedure-name-2} )

    ( USING   {file-name-2} . . .                                          )

    ( OUTPUT PROCEDURE IS {section-name-3  } [{THROUGH} {section-name-4  }] )
    (                     {procedure-name-3}  {THRU   } {procedure-name-4} )

    ( GIVING {file-name-3} . . .                                           )
```

FIGURE 9–7   THE SORT STATEMENT.

records whose name-field contains SMITH, these 10 records will be in their original order relative to each other.

The INPUT PROCEDURE and the OUTPUT PROCEDURE options refer to a section-name or a set of consecutive sections where the THRU option is used. The paragraphs in such sections specify the processing tasks to be performed prior to the sort (INPUT PROCEDURE) or after the sort (OUTPUT PROCEDURE). If the INPUT PROCEDURE is used, the verb RELEASE must be used somewhere in that procedure. If the OUTPUT PROCEDURE is used, the verb RETURN must be used somewhere in that procedure. The USING file-name-2 option is used when records are made available to the sort from file-name-2 without any processing. The GIVING file-name-3 option specifies that the sorted file is to be recorded on file-name-3.

In the 1985 version of COBOL, INPUT PROCEDURE and OUTPUT PROCEDURE need not refer to section-names. They can be either paragraphs or sections, thus allowing for greater flexibility. In the example in Figure 9–4 we used the section choice, and as a result we had to use the GO TO verb to reach the end-paragraph in the section. The revised version allows us to eliminate the END-OF-INPUT-SECTION and the END-OF-OUTPUT-SECTION paragraphs as well as the two GO TO statements in Figure 9–4.

RELEASE record-name [FROM identifier].

The RELEASE verb can be used only in a section referenced by the INPUT PROCEDURE. The record-name in this format refers to a record in the sort file. If the FROM option is used, the effect is to move the contents of identifier to the record-name and then to RELEASE. In effect, RELEASE is a specialized form of the WRITE verb.

The RETURN verb, which is used in conjunction with the OUTPUT PROCEDURE of a SORT verb, has the format presented in Figure 9–8.

The RETURN verb has the effect of a READ verb. The file-name is the name of the sort file. When the INTO option is used, the effect is the same as execution of the two statements RETURN file-name MOVE record-name TO identifier. The AT END clause is required.

Notice that in the 1985 standard we can use the NOT AT END and the END-RETURN options in the RETURN statement for handling conditionals more easily. For example, we could modify the RETURNING-PRINTING-

---

```
RETURN  file-name-1 RECORD [INTO  identifier]
    AT END  imperative-statement-1
    [NOT AT END imperative-statement-2]
    [END-RETURN]
```

FIGURE 9–8   THE RETURN STATEMENT.

SECTION of Figure 9–4 as follows (including omission of the SECTION requirements):

```
RETURNING-PRINTING.
    OPEN OUTPUT SORTED FILE
                PRINT-FILE
    MOVE 'NO' TO END-OF-DATA
    PERFORM UNTIL END-OF-DATA = 'YES'
        RETURN SORT-FILE RECORD INTO SORTED-RECORD
            AT END
                MOVE 'YES' TO END-OF-DATA
            NOT AT END
                WRITE PRINT-LINE FROM SORTED-RECORD
                WRITE SORTED-RECORD
        END-RETURN
    END-PERFORM
    CLOSE SORTED-FILE
        PRINT-FILE.
```

Review

1   In the DATA DIVISION, the file to be sorted is identified by the level indicator _____.

    SD (standing for Sort Description)

2   The option of specifying a variable-length record depending on a data-name in the sort description is available only in the [1974 version / 1985 version] of COBOL.

    1985 version

3   If the INPUT PROCEDURE option is used in conjunction with the SORT verb, designated processing is performed [before / after] the sort, and the verb _____ must be used somewhere in the procedure.

    before; RELEASE

4   If the OUTPUT PROCEDURE option is used in conjunction with the SORT verb, designated processing is performed [before / after] the

sort, and the verb _____ must be used somewhere in the procedure.

after; RETURN

5   The RELEASE verb can be considered a specialized form of the _____ verb, while the RETURN verb can be considered a form of the _____ verb.

WRITE; READ

6   In order to handle conditionals more easily, the NOT AT END and the END-RETURN options can be used in a RETURN statement that utilizes the [1974 version / 1985 version] of COBOL.

1985 version

FILE MERGING

Essentially, *merging* refers to the process by which two or more files, which are already sorted, are combined to form one file. Merging is often a required step in the process of sorting. Merging is also often used simply to combine two or more files without any further sorting activity. For example, the sales transactions in a department store might be processed on a daily basis, thus creating a daily sales tape sorted by item number. Then, at the end of each week it may be desirable to merge the several daily tapes to form a weekly sales tape for batch processing use. The procedure of combining the several daily tapes to form one weekly tape exemplifies the merging process.

The simplest case of merging is the one in which there are two sorted files A and B, and they are merged to form one file. The process consists of reading a record from each input file, comparing the two records, and writing the "smaller" of the two onto the output file, based on a reference, or "sort key," field. Then another record is read from the file that supplied the last smaller record and the comparison is repeated.

Suppose, however, that five daily transactions tapes are to be merged to form one tape. In such a case the process of merging requires a more complex logic. In each comparison five records are involved, one from each respective daily tape, and the smallest of the five is to be written on the output tape. The flowchart in Figure 9–9 indicates the essential logic of the comparisons which are required to find the smallest record. In this figure, A, B, C, D, and E are the five records from the five input files. File F is the output

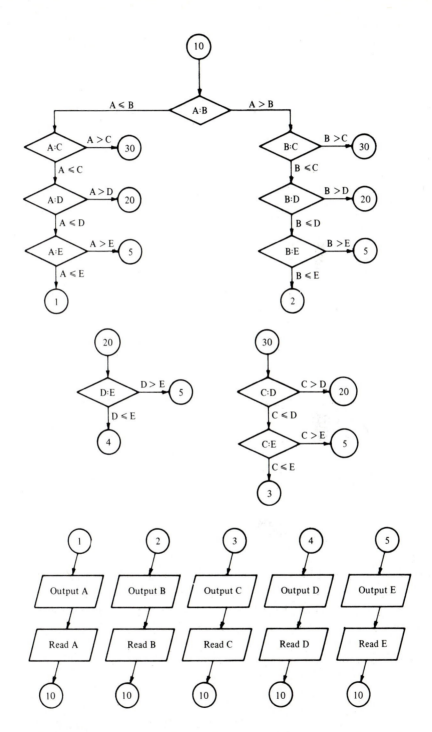

FIGURE 9-9   FLOWCHART FOR THE PROCESS OF MERGING FIVE FILES.

file. Notice that the process described in Figure 9-9 ignores end-of-file conditions. Incorporation of end-of-file condition processing would add considerable complexity to the logic of the procedure, as some reflection will reveal.

When merging multiple files on magnetic tape the number of tape drives available is an important factor. In general we prefer to use all available drives, since merging is more efficient with a greater number of tape drives. Still, when the number of files is larger than the number of tape drives, we may have to choose the right merging sequence to avoid unnecessary processing. For example, suppose that we have 12 files to be merged. These files are identified by the letters A through L in Figure 9-10. If four tape transport units are available, three units would be used for input and one would be used for output. As illustrated in Figure 9-10, in such a case we could merge A, B, and C to form file 1, D, E, and F to form file 2, and G, H, and I to form file 3. Next we could merge files J and K to form file 4. Then files 3, 4, and L can be merged to form file 5, and finally, files 1, 2, and 5 can be merged to form file 6.

An alternative way of merging the 12 files, which is not as efficient, would be to merge files J, K and L to form 1 file, as illustrated in Figure 9-11. Notice, however, that this alternative merging procedure would take longer to accomplish. To see this, let us count the number of file passes that are required by each approach. By "file pass" we mean the process of inputting and merging the contents of a file with the contents of 1 or more other files. Thus, by the procedure portrayed in Figure 9-11 the formation of files 1, 2, 3, and 4 requires 3 file passes each. The formation of file 5 requires 9 file passes because the contents of 9 original input files are involved. Similarly, the formation of file 6 requires 12 file passes. Thus, in total 33 file passes are required to merge the files by the procedure portrayed in Figure 9-11.

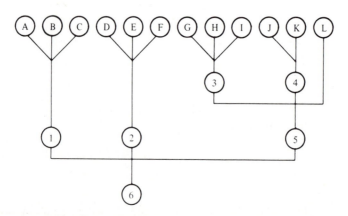

FIGURE 9-10   SCHEMATIC DIAGRAM FOR THE PROCESS OF MERGING 12 TAPE FILES BY THE USE OF FOUR TAPE TRANSPORT UNITS.

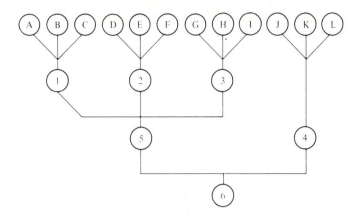

FIGURE 9-11   SCHEMATIC DIAGRAM FOR AN ALTERNATIVE WAY OF MERGING 12 TAPE FILES BY THE USE OF FOUR TAPE TRANSPORT UNITS.

However, by the procedure portrayed in Figure 9–10 only 29 file passes are required. As it happens, given the 12 input files and four tape units the 29 file passes associated with the procedure in Figure 9–10 is the optimum result. A computational procedure, or algorithm, is available to determine the optimum merge configuration given the number of files to be merged and the tape units available. The algorithm is included in most merge program packages, so that its application is automatic without the user having to determine the optimum merging routine for each situation.

Frequently, the files to be merged are not stored on magnetic tape. Rather, it may be that designated disk areas constitute files. In such a case, the limitation of the number of available input-output units does not apply and the need to merge, say, 50 files could conceivably be accomplished by one merge operation.

Review

1   When two or more sequential files are combined to form one sequential file, the process is called _____.

merging

2   The simplest case of merging is the one in which _____ (number) files are merged.

3   In most computer installations, if all the tape transport units available are used to merge a relatively large number of tape files, the system is likely to be [input-output / processing] bound.

input-output

4   The optimum merge configuration to be used in merging several tape files generally is determined [by each user / by the merge program package].

by the merge program package

FILE MERGING IN COBOL

Merging is implemented in COBOL as a very-high-level language feature, in the form of the MERGE statement.

Let us consider an example. A business firm generates a sales history file at the end of the quarter. Each record in the file contains a department number and a product number, as well as many other fields. This quarterly file is sorted, with department number being the major sort key and product number being the minor sort key. At the end of the year we are interested in merging the four quarterly sales history files into one. Figure 9-12 presents an outline of the relevant parts of the program. Four files are introduced with an FD entry, one for each quarter. The fifth FD entry is for the output file. Then the SD introduces the file to be used for the merge, which in this example is called MERGE-FILE. Notice that the data record description for this file corresponds to the record description of the four quarterly files. The merge statement in the PROCEDURE DIVISION references the SD file and specifies that the merge will proceed on the basis of DEPARTMENT being the major key and PRODUCT being the minor key. As is the case with the SORT verb, the keys decrease in significance in the order written. The AS-CENDING option specifies that the next record of each of the four quarterly files will be examined; and the record sent to the output file next is the one that has the highest department number, or the highest product number if the department numbers are equal. If all four records have identical department and product values, then the records will be sent to the output file in the order in which the file names are written in the merge statement.

The USING clause specifies the files to be merged, which are the input files. These files must be closed at the time of merging. Opening is carried out by the MERGE statement in an implicit fashion.

The GIVING clause specifies the output file. This file will contain the combined set of the four quarterly files. This new file will be in the same sort order as the quarterly files. Note that in order for the merge process to take

```
FD    FIRST-QUARTER LABEL RECORDS STANDARD
                        DATA RECORD    SALES-HISTORY.
01    SALES-HISTORY.
      02    DEPT-NO       PIC 999.
      02    PROD-NO       PIC 99999.
      .
      .
      .


FD    SECOND-QUARTER . . .
      .
      .
      .

FD    THIRD-QUARTER . . .
      .
      .
      .

FD    FOURTH-QUARTER . . .
      .
      .
      .

FD    YEARLY LABEL RECORDS STANDARD
                    DATA RECORD    CUMULATIVE-SALES.
01    CUMULATIVE-SALES.
      02    DEPT-NO       PIC 999.
      02    PROD-NO       PIC 99999.
      .
      .
      .


SD    MERGE-FILE DATA RECORD    MERGE-RECORD.
01    MERGE-RECORD.
      02    DEPARTMENT    PIC 999.
      02    PRODUCT       PIC 99999.
      .
      .
      .

PROCEDURE DIVISION.
      .
      .
      .


      MERGE MERGE-FILE ON ASCENDING KEY DEPARTMENT
                      ON ASCENDING KEY PRODUCT
            USING FIRST-QUARTER, SECOND-QUARTER,
                    THIRD-QUARTER, FOURTH-QUARTER
            GIVING YEARLY.
```

FIGURE 9–12   OUTLINE FOR A MERGE PROGRAM.

place correctly, the input files must be in the sort order indicated by the KEY specifications.

The general format of the MERGE statement is presented in Figure 9–13.

The OUTPUT PROCEDURE option parallels the one available with the SORT verb. A RETURN statement is used within the output procedure to make merged records available for processing, just as is the case with SORT. Unlike SORT, MERGE does not include any input procedure options; thus, the input files must be in proper form for merging before a MERGE instruction is executed.

Review

1   The COBOL languge feature by which monthly summaries of transactions can be combined to create an annual summary is the _____ statement.

MERGE

2   If 12 monthly summaries are to be combined to form an annual summary, then the number of FD entries required in the associated MERGE program is _____ (number).

13

3   In order for the merge process to take place correctly, it [is /is not] necessary that each input file be in the exact sort order indicated by the KEY specifications.

is

MERGE   file-name-1

$\left\{\text{ON} \quad \dfrac{\underline{\text{ASCENDING}}}{\underline{\text{DESCENDING}}} \quad \text{KEY} \quad \{\text{data-name-1}\} \dots \right\} \dots$

[COLLATING SEQUENCE IS alphabet-name-1]

USING file-name-2 {file-name-3} . . .

$\left(\underline{\text{OUTPUT}} \; \underline{\text{PROCEDURE}} \; \text{IS} \; \begin{Bmatrix} \text{section-name-1} \\ \text{procedure-name-1} \end{Bmatrix} \; \begin{bmatrix} \begin{Bmatrix} \underline{\text{THROUGH}} \\ \underline{\text{THRU}} \end{Bmatrix} \begin{Bmatrix} \text{section-name-2} \\ \text{procedure-name-2} \end{Bmatrix} \end{bmatrix} \right)$

$\underline{\text{GIVING}} \quad \{\text{file-name-4}\} \dots$

FIGURE 9–13   THE MERGE STATEMENT.

Exercises

9.1   Write suitable COBOL statements to sort a table of N ($N \leqslant 100$) numeric values using the bubble sort–interchange algorithm.

9.2   Suppose that we have a table that contains the following data:

10	12	04	08	03

If we were using the adjacent comparison–interchange algorithm and if a pair comparison takes 1 microsecond and a pair interchange takes 5 microseconds, what would be the total comparison time and what would be the total interchange time? Be sure to justify your results.

9.3   A sort file has been defined as SORT-FILE, and, in part, its data division entries include:

```
02   COURSE-CODE    PIC XXX.
02   COLLEGE        PIC 99.
02   COURSE-NAME    PIC X(6).
```

Using the following data, write a SORT statement that could cause the sorted data shown. The original data come from SOURCE-FILE, and we want to have the sorted data in SORTED-FILE. Be sure to specify which are the major, intermediate, and minor sort keys.

ORIGINAL DATA	SORTED DATA
CIS20BILL	MGT10JILL
CIS30LINDA	QBA10BRENDA
QBA10BRENDA	CIS20MARY
CIS30XAVIER	CIS20JOHN
MGT10JILL	CIS20BILL
CIS20JOHN	CIS30XAVIER
CIS20MARY	CIS30LINDA

9.4   A file contains data about students and has the following record format:

```
FIRST-NAME  PIC  X(10).
LAST-NAME   PIC  X(15).
YEAR        PIC  X(2).
```

MAJOR	PIC	X(93).
GPA	PIC	9V99.

Write a program to sort the file so that student records are in order by year of studies (YEAR) within major field of study (MAJOR) and in descending order of GPA. In addition, the sorted file must have a different format from the original file: the FIRST-NAME and LAST-NAME fields must be reversed.

LAST-NAME	PIC	X(15).
FIRST-NAME	PIC	X(10).
YEAR	PIC	X(2).
MAJOR	PIC	X(3).
GPA	PIC	9V99.

The sorted file is to be saved as a separate file as shown below:

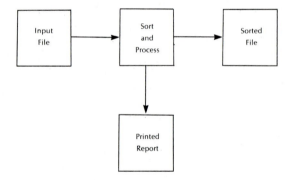

It is also desired to produce a report from the newly sorted file as presented in Figure 9–14 on page 355.

9.5   Consider the following to be the contents of the four quarterly files discussed in the merging example in this chapter. Show the content of the output file.

FIRST QUARTER	SECOND QUARTER	THIRD QUARTER	FOURTH QUARTER
345 12345	123 00112	345 56111	931 00001
345 25936	987 56111		999 99999
619 01110			

```
┌──────────────────────────────────────────────────────┐
│                                                        │
│  MAJOR FIELD: XXX [New page for each new field]        │
│                                                        │
│  STUDENT NAME     YEAR      GPA      AVG. GPA           │
│     L1   F1        FR       3.40                        │
│     L2   F2        FR       2.00                        │
│     L3   F3        FR       1.90                        │
│                                      2.43               │
│                                                        │
│     L4   F4        SO                                   │
│                    )                                    │
│                    JR                                   │
│                    )                                    │
│                    SR                                   │
│                    )                                    │
│  AVG. GPA FOR XXX MAJOR FIELD  = X.XX                   │
│                                                        │
└──────────────────────────────────────────────────────┘
```

FIGURE 9–14   REPORT FORMAT FOR EXERCISE 9.4.

9.6   Using any two sorted data files, write a program incorporating the MERGE feature to combine the two files into one file.

10

INDEXED FILES

INTRODUCTION

In Chapter 8 we introduced the three methods of file organization: *sequential*, *indexed*, and *relative*, and discussed sequential file organization in some detail. This chapter is devoted to indexed file processing.

Indexed files represent something of a balance between sequential and relative files, because they allow for sequential storage as well as random access and random processing. The essential feature of an indexed file is that it consists of two parts: the *data file* and the *index(es)*. As the name implies, the data file contains the data records. Each record in the data file is identified uniquely on the basis of one or more keys within the record. When such a file is first created, the data records are written in ascending order of the unique identifying key(s). On the other hand, the index is some kind of "table" structure that facilitates random access. When looking for a particular record, as identified by its key, the index is used to find the (general) location of the record in the file so that the record can be accessed directly.

Indexed files can have multiple indexes. For example, one index could be based on a unique employee-number key in each employee record, while another index could be based on a possibly nonunique employee-name. In such a case we could achieve random access to the file as exemplified by the cases: "Get the record of Employee 1057" or "Get the record of Dorothy Gonzales."

Indexed files are also sequential files with respect to the unique identifier field in each record. For example, we can designate employee-number as the unique identifier field in employee records, create an indexed file, and then use that file as if it were a sequential file. In other words, records can be accessed in ascending order of employee-number just as they would be accessed with a sequential file. However, there are also added flexibilities for indexed files. For one thing, unlike a sequential file, we can do a random access to a particular record, say to employee-number 1057, and then do a sequential access to the following records, thus being able to bypass the records preceding the record for employee 1057. Another significant difference between indexed and sequential files is that for indexed files both selective and exhaustive updating can be done. Such an option is very useful in applications in which there is natural batch processing as well as a need for occasional selective access to individual records. Payroll, for example, is a natural batch application. All the records in the file need to be processed for each pay period. Yet individual records often need to be accessed between pay periods for such purposes as changing a pay rate, changing a tax deduction, or adding a new employee. Indexed files are an ideal form of file organization to fulfill such needs; however, indexed files can be slower to process than files that are strictly sequential. Therefore, indexed files should be used only when their versatility justifies the potentially slower processing time and the more complex environment that is required for the operating system to support such files.

Review

1   The type of file organization that allows sequential storage but also facilitates random accessing or processing is called _____ file organization.

indexed

2   Every indexed file consists of two parts: a _____ file and at least one _____ file.

data; index

3   Comparing the two, faster processing time is associated with [indexed / sequential] files.

sequential

INDEXING METHODS

There is no standard indexing method. Language implementors are responsible for providing their own methods. As far as COBOL is concerned, the language defines the functional aspects of indexing, or the "what." The "how" part of indexing is not part of COBOL. Still, it is useful for the applications programmer to have a basic understanding of common indexing methods. The details of indexing are too complex to be covered in this book; however, we present the main concepts associated with two common methods: the *Indexed Sequential Access Method (ISAM)* and the *Virtual Storage Access Method (VSAM)*. Both the names and the basic ideas represent specific IBM products; however, they are generic descriptors as well, and therefore their applicability is quite wide.

The ISAM Indexing Method

The essential features of ISAM are illustrated in Figure 10–1. The illustration includes use of the same physical file for both the data records and the index records. This example does not imply that this is the way an ISAM file must be constructed, but it does serve to illustrate one possible implementation.

At the top of Figure 10–1 there is the *cylinder index* for the file. Each record in the index consists of two fields. The *key* field contains the largest key value in the respective cylinder, while the *address* field contains the address of the *track index* for that cylinder. In the figure, 68 is the highest key value in cylinder 0 while 01 (cylinder 0 track 1) is the address of the track index for the first cylinder. Notice that the convention generally used is to number both the cylinders and the tracks consecutively with 0, 1, 2, and so forth.

The track index for cylinder 0 is in track 1 because track 0 of that cylinder is taken up by the cylinder index. Directing our attention to the track index for cylinder 0, we see that there are two index entries: the *prime index* and the *overflow index*. Asterisks are used in the example to signify unused entries. Thus, there is no overflow data for the first track index entry. The first track index entry consists only of the prime index record, which signifies that the highest key in track 2 of cylinder 0 (address = 02) is 68, with the overflow index being unused in this case. The second pair of prime-overflow index records in track 1 is unused because it would be in reference to the next track of the cylinder (track 03), which does not exist. In this simplified example it is assumed that there are only three tracks per cylinder and, in the case of the first cylinder (0), that the first two tracks are taken up by the cylin-

KEY	ADDRESS	KEY	ADDRESS	. . .
68	01	460	10	

Cylinder Index For Entire File } Track 0

PRIME INDEX		OVERFLOW INDEX		PRIME INDEX		OVERFLOW INDEX	
KEY	ADDRESS	KEY	ADDRESS	KEY	ADDRESS	KEY	ADDRESS
68	02	*	*	*	*	*	*

Track Index For Cylinder 0 } Track 1

40	50	54	55	68

Data Records } Track 2

Cylinder 0

125	11	200	901	369	12	460	913

Track Index For Cylinder 1 } Track 0

100	101	119	120	125
210	250	260	271	369

Data Records } Track 1
Data Records } Track 2

Cylinder 1

Record 1		Record 2		Record 3		Record 4		Record 5	
132	903	190	912	189	902	380	905	382	911
390	914	200	0	375	904	460	0		

Track 0
Track 1
Track 2
Cylinder 9
(Overflow) Data Records

FIGURE 10-1   SAMPLE INDEXED FILE (ISAM METHOD).

der index and the track index, respectively, thereby leaving only one track available for data records.

The second cylinder is a somewhat more typical case. First referring to the top of Figure 10-1, note that the second record in the cylinder index indicates that the highest record key in the second cylinder has the value 460 and that the address of the track index for that cylinder is cylinder 1, track 0 (10).

Next, consider the data in track 0 of cylinder 1, which is the track index for that cylinder. There are no headings shown for this track in Figure 10-1, but they are the same headings as for track 1 of cylinder 0. The first entry, 125, indicates that the highest prime key is 125 for cylinder 1, track 1 (address 11 in the following entry). The next entry, 200, indicates that the highest overflow key is 200; while the address, 901, indicates that the first record in overflow for this track is located in cylinder 9, track 0, at record 1.

Overflow records are records that have been added to a file after the file was created. Consider the record at address 901, which is an overflow record for cylinder 1, track 1. Notice that its value, 132, is larger than the last record already included in cylinder 1, track 1 (125), but smaller than the first record in cylinder 1, track 2 (210). A record with a key value such as 132 must precede the first entry in track 2 and, therefore, is placed in overflow for track 1.

Now consider the overflow cylinder, cylinder 9. Each record includes the record value followed by a *pointer field*, which contains the address of the next logical record. For example, the pointer for the first record in cylinder 9, track 0 is 903, meaning that the next logical record is at cylinder 9, track 0, record 3. Following the chain of pointers, we can observe that the last record in overflow for cylinder 1, track 1 is the record with a key value of 200, located at cylinder 9, track 1, record 2. Its pointer value of 0 indicates the end of the chain. If the file included in Figure 10-1 were accessed sequentially by key value, the records would be retrieved in the following order:

40, 50, 54, 55, 68, 100, 101, 119, 120, 125, 132, 189, 190, 200, 210, 250, 260, 271, 369, 375, 380, 382, 390, 460

Figure 10-2 presents a flowchart which indicates the accessing logic associated with sequential processing. Briefly, we begin with the cylinder index, which directs us to the first track index. From the track index we process all the records, both prime and overflow, for the cylinder. These processing steps are repeated for all the cylinders contained in the file. When the last record in the last cylinder and track is processed, the overall processing of the file is completed.

The main appeal of an indexed file, however, is the capability of processing such a file randomly. Figure 10-3 presents a flowchart that indicates the accessing logic associated with random access. Given the key associated with a record, the cylinder index is searched. The search may be sequential or binary. We then access the corresponding track index, which indicates whether the record is located in the prime or overflow area. The appropriate area is searched for a key-equal condition and the record is accessed.

Review

1   In the Indexed Sequential Access Method (ISAM), the two types of indexes are the _____ index and the _____ index.

cylinder; track

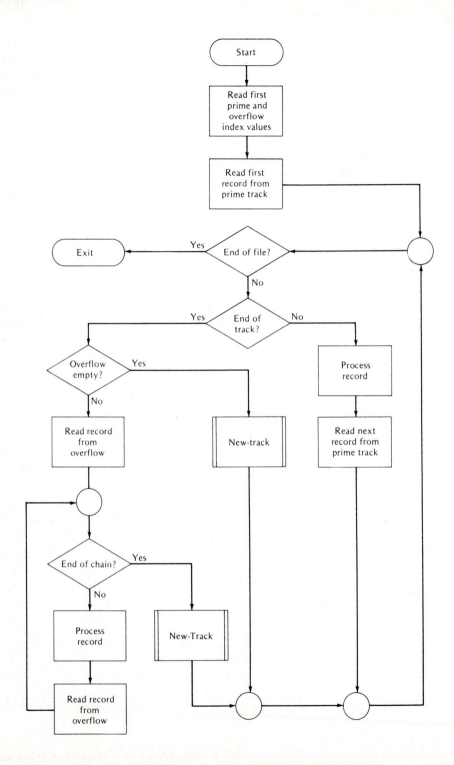

FIGURE 10-2   SEQUENTIAL ACCESS WITH AN INDEXED FILE.

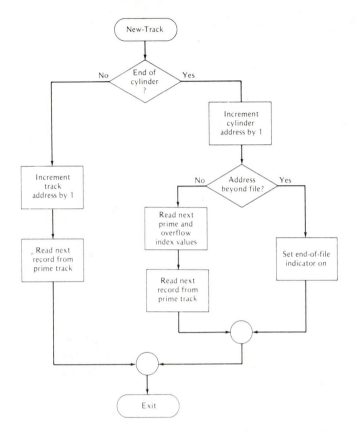

FIGURE 10-2   SEQUENTIAL ACCESS WITH AN INDEXED FILE.
(Continued)

2   Each record in a track index consists of four fields: the prime key, the prime address, the _____, and the _____.

> overflow key; overflow address

3   When a record which is to be added to an indexed file should logically be located within a prime track, [the record is placed in that track and the last record is "bumped" into overflow / the record in question is entered directly into overflow].

> the record is placed in that track
> and the last record is "bumped"
> into overflow

4   When a record which is to be added to an indexed file should logically be located within a particular track in overflow, [it is located in the ap-

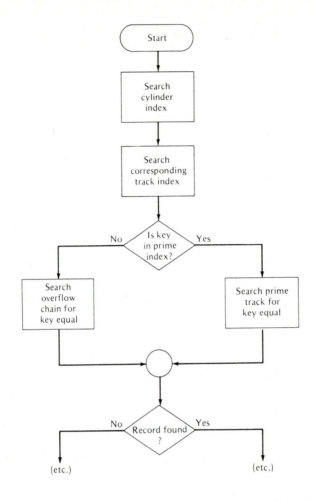

FIGURE 10-3   RANDOM ACCESS WITH AN INDEXED FILE.

propriate position and other records are "bumped" / it is located in the next available position in overflow].

it is located in the next available
position in overflow

5   In order to achieve logical contiguity of the records in overflow for records which may be physically separated, a(n) _____ field is included with each record to identify the location of the next sequential record, if it is located in overflow.

pointer

6   The concept of file chaining is particularly concerned with identifying the appropriate sequencing of records in the [prime / overflow] area of the data file.

overflow

VSAM—An Alternate Index Structure

The indexed file structure described in the preceding section represents a widely used approach. However, it has one major shortcoming: as the number of records added to the file increases, the average access time grows rather quickly. As you will recall, additions to the file go in overflow space and are no longer in physical sequential order. In recent years other indexing methods have been developed which are more efficient in accommodating additions. One of these methods is IBM's VSAM—Virtual Storage Access Method, which, among other features, incorporates an alternate index structure and can be used with COBOL indexed files. We describe some basic concepts in VSAM so that the reader has a sufficient background in this widely used index structure.

One of the options in VSAM is to build a *key-sequenced* indexed file which corresponds to COBOL indexed sequential files. In such a file the records are written in storage areas called *control intervals.* A control interval is similar to the concept of a *block* of records and may be a track in disk storage. A group of control intervals comprise a *control* area. We could think of the control interval as a track and the control area as a cylinder. However, VSAM is a logical method of file structure that is not dependent directly on the physical storage medium in use. For instance, one could have several control intervals per track or two cylinders per control area. Further, VSAM would be, in concept, applicable to non-disk-storage devices, such as bubble memories etc.

Figure 10-4 illustrates the conceptual structure of a VSAM key-sequenced file. Two control areas are shown, each control area having three control intervals, and each control interval having space for five data records. It should be noted that control intervals, A3, B1, and B2 contain some vacant record spaces, while B3 is wholly vacant. VSAM deliberately leaves vacant spaces to facilitate the addition of new records, as will be explained below.

There are two index levels used. The higher level is called the *index* set while the lower level is called the *sequence* set. These two index levels parallel the cylinder and track indexes discussed earlier in the chapter, but they are more flexible constructs since they are device-independent. Each record in the sequence set contains the value of the highest key in a control interval and the address of that control interval. For instance, the highest key in the A1 interval is the record key 61. In addition to these index values, each sequence set contains the address of the next sequence set. Thus, if we were processing such a VSAM file sequentially, after all records in control area 1

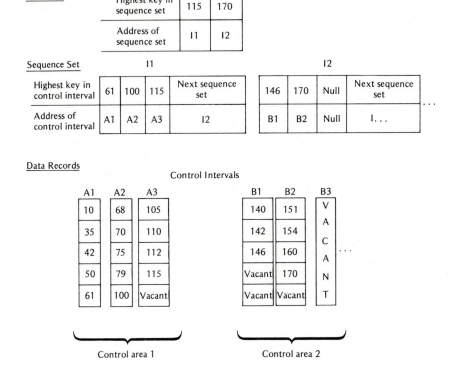

FIGURE 10-4   SAMPLE CONCEPTUAL VSAM STRUCTURE.

were accessed we would move to sequence set I2 next, which indexes the control intervals in control area 2.

As an illustration of using the VSAM structure in Figure 10–4, suppose that we wanted to access record 154. The first record in the index set would be accessed and would indicate that record 154 is not in the first control area since the highest key there is 115. The next record in the index set would then be accessed and it would indicate that record 154, if it exists, is in the control area indexed by this record (control area 2). The address of the corresponding sequence set is I2 and the first record in sequence I2 would be accessed next. Since the highest key in the first record of I2 is 146, it would be known that record 154 is not in the first control interval indexed by I2. The next record is I2 and has a key value of 170, and therefore record 154 should be in the control interval whose address is B2. Sequential access of the records in control interval B2 would result in retrieval of record 154, which happens to be the second record in the interval. Thus, random access to records can be achieved using the VSAM index structure.

When records are added to a VSAM file the resultant action depends on the availability of vacant space. For instance, if record 114 were to be added, record 115 would be moved down one place to the vacant space in control interval A3 and the new record 114 would be written in the space where 115 was; no change in the index structure takes place.

Suppose now that records 162 and 163 are to be added. Logically, they both belong in control interval B2. However, when it would be time to add record 163 there would be no room left in that control interval. VSAM would now cause a *control interval split* as illustrated in Figure 10–5. The formerly vacant interval B3 is now partially occupied and the records have been split across intervals B2 and B3, both of which now have some vacant spaces in them. Notice that a third record was added to sequence set I2 but the index set was not affected since 170 remains the highest record in that control area.

Addition of record 80 causes a *control area split* as illustrated also in Figure 10–5. Record 80 belongs in control interval A2 which happened to have no vacant space in Figure 10–4. Further, no interval in this control area is vacant after the addition of record 114, and therefore an interval split cannot take place as when we added record 163 in the preceding example. VSAM causes an *area split* by adding another control area, control area 3, and splitting the records across control area 1 and 3. Notice that intervals A3 and C3 are left vacant so that there will be some time before another split is caused by addition of records in the intervals A1–A3 and C1–C3. As a result of the control area split a new sequence set, I3, has been created and a new record has been added to the index set to index the new sequence set. Also, notice that if the records were processed sequentially, the next sequence set

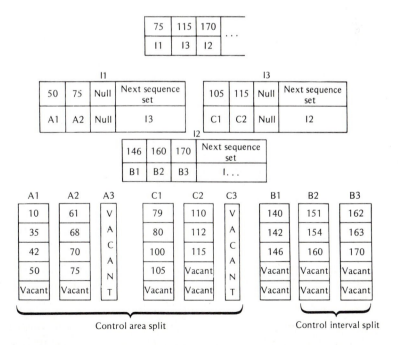

FIGURE 10-5   MODIFICATION OF THE FIGURE 10-4 VSAM STRUCTURE TO REFLECT ADDITION OF RECORDS 162, 163, AND 80.

after I1 is I3, as designated by the last field in I1. Of course, identifiers such as I3, C1, etc., are used arbitrarily in these illustrations to emphasize the fact that these are new sequence sets and control intervals.

Overall, VSAM avoids creation of overflow record chains by leaving vacant spaces within control intervals and areas and by the use of "splits" as discussed above. These techniques make VSAM a flexible, highly efficient index structure. The name "VSAM" is used by IBM, but the general method represented by VSAM is in use by many vendors.

Both ISAM- and VSAM-type index structures are more or less transparent to the COBOL programmer. The software needed to create, maintain, and use the indexed file structure is provided as part of the COBOL language processor. Still, it is useful for the COBOL programmer to be familiar with the basic concepts of these methods.

Review

1   In the Virtual Storage Access Method (VSAM), data records are written in physical groups called control intervals. Then, control intervals are grouped into units called _____ .

control areas

2   There are two index levels in VSAM. The higher-level index references the highest records in the control areas and it is called the _____ ; the other index references records in each control interval and it is called the _____ .

index set; sequence set

3   When a VSAM key-sequenced file is created, disk storage space is [packed/deliberately left vacant].

deliberately left vacant

4   When records are added to a VSAM file, a control interval split takes place when _____ .

no vacancy remains in the appro-
priate control interval and no
vacant interval remains in the
area

AN EXAMPLE OF THE CREATION OF AN INDEXED FILE

An indexed file can be created with minimal effort on the part of the programmer. The source records first must have been sorted in ascending sequence on a data field that will serve as the primary key for the file. Because an indexed file is a sequential file, the records are positioned in ascending order. We now consider an example to illustrate the process.

Suppose that we have source records that contain data about vendors. Columns 1–8 contain an identifier that is unique for each vendor and columns 9–80 contain other relevant data. We want to copy these records on disk, forming an indexed file sorted on the basis of the data in columns 1–8. Each disk record will consist of 68 characters, and the source records must have been sorted on columns 1–8.

Figure 10–6 presents a COBOL program written to create an indexed file. Notice the SELECT statement. ORGANIZATION IS INDEXED specifies that this is an indexed file, while ACCESS IS SEQUENTIAL specifies that the access mode for this file is sequential. RECORD KEY IS VENDOR-NUMBER specifies that there is a field called VENDOR-NUMBER that is a field in the file record and that serves as the primary key for the file. In other words, the file will be in ascending order of VENDOR-NUMBER values.

In the DATA DIVISION included in Figure 10–6, observe that VENDOR-NUMBER is a field in the record description of the indexed file (VENDOR-FILE). The RECORD KEY must be a field in the file record, and it must be an alphanumeric field.

In the PROCEDURE DIVISION of Figure 10–6, in the FILE-CREATE paragraph, we move VENDOR-IDENT, a field in the source record, to VENDOR-NUMBER, which was declared to be the RECORD KEY in the SELECT statement. The move of VENDOR-DATA simply transfers the other fields of the source record to the output record. The WRITE statement now includes the INVALID KEY condition. This condition is true whenever the record key of the record about to be written is not greater than the key of the preceding record in the file. If the INVALID KEY condition is true, the imperative statements that follow are executed. In the example, we print an error message and the source record associated with the error condition.

The INVALID KEY test is nonspecific. It could be true because the records are out of order with respect to the values of the RECORD KEY field (including records with duplicate key values), or it could be true because the file is full. As an alternative to the INVALID KEY test, we can use the FILE STATUS feature, as explained in Chapter 8, "Sequential Files."

Creation of an indexed file is a complex task, yet the language is very high level with respect to this task. The programmer need write very few instructions to invoke the procedure necessary for the task. In review, these instructions involve a few clauses in the SELECT statement, provision for a record key in the record description of the file, and moving data to the output record in the PROCEDURE DIVISION. In the following section, we study these specialized instructions in a more thorough and comprehensive framework.

```
IDENTIFICATION DIVISION.
PROGRAM-ID. INDEXFILE.
*
ENVIRONMENT DIVISION.
CONFIGURATION SECTION.
SOURCE-COMPUTER. ABC-480.
OBJECT-COMPUTER. ABC-480.
INPUT-OUTPUT SECTION.
*
FILE-CONTROL.
    SELECT VENDOR-FILE ASSIGN TO OLDMSTR
                    ORGANIZATION IS INDEXED
                    ACCESS IS SEQUENTIAL
                    RECORD KEY IS VENDOR-NUMBER.
*
    SELECT SOURCE-FILE ASSIGN TO READER.
*
    SELECT PRINT-FILE ASSIGN TO PRINTER.
*
DATA DIVISION.
FILE SECTION.
FD    VENDOR-FILE LABEL RECORDS ARE STANDARD
                    DATA RECORD IS VENDOR-RECORD.
*
01    VENDOR-RECORD.
      02 VENDOR-NUMBER              PIC X(8).
      02 VENDOR-DATA                PIC X(60).
*
FD    SOURCE-FILE LABEL RECORDS ARE STANDARD
                    DATA RECORD IS SOURCE-RECORD.
*
01    SOURCE-RECORD.
      02 VENDOR-IDENT              PIC 9(8).
      02 VENDOR-DATA              PIC X(72).
*
FD    PRINT-FILE LABEL RECORDS OMITTED
                    DATA RECORD IS PRINT-RECORD.
*
01    PRINT-RECORD              PIC X(132).
*
WORKING-STORAGE SECTION.
*
01    END-OF-DATA-INDICATOR    PIC 9 VALUE ZERO.
      88 INPUT-ENDED    VALUE 1.
```

FIGURE 10-6   A COBOL PROGRAM TO CREATE AN INDEXED FILE.

```
PROCEDURE DIVISION.
*
 MAIN-ROUTINE.
     OPEN INPUT    SOURCE-FILE
          OUTPUT  VENDOR-FILE, PRINT-FILE.
     READ SOURCE-FILE RECORD
          AT END SET INPUT-ENDED TO TRUE
     END-READ
*
     PERFORM FILE-CREATE UNTIL INPUT-ENDED.
*
     CLOSE SOURCE-FILE, VENDOR-FILE, PRINT-FILE.
     STOP RUN.
*
 FILE-CREATE.
*
     MOVE VENDOR-IDENT TO VENDOR-NUMBER
*
     MOVE VENDOR-DATA OF SOURCE-RECORD
          TO VENDOR-DATA OF VENDOR-RECORD
*
     WRITE VENDOR-RECORD
        INVALID KEY
           MOVE ' INVALID KEY CONDITION FOR THIS RECORD'
                TO PRINT-RECORD
           WRITE PRINT-RECORD AFTER ADVANCING 1 LINE
           WRITE PRINT-RECORD FROM SOURCE-RECORD AFTER 1 LINE
     END-WRITE
*
     READ SOURCE-FILE RECORD
          AT END SET INPUT-ENDED TO TRUE
     END-READ.
```

FIGURE 10-6   A COBOL PROGRAM TO CREATE AN INDEXED FILE. (Continued)

Review

1   An indexed file essentially is a [sequential / direct] file.

sequential

2   In the ENVIRONMENT DIVISION, after the file is described as being SEQUENTIAL and INDEXED, the basis on which the file is sorted is identified by the COBOL reserved words _____.

RECORD KEY

3   The RECORD KEY field must be [alphabetic / alphanumeric] and it [must / need not] be a field in the file record.

alphanumeric; must

4   The fact that one or more records to be written in an indexed file are not in the appropriate sequence can be detected and identified by using the _____ option in conjunction with the WRITE statement.

INVALID KEY

COBOL LANGUAGE INSTRUCTIONS FOR INDEXED FILES

There are two divisions of a COBOL program that involve special instructions for indexed files—The ENVIRONMENT DIVISION and the PROCEDURE DIVISION.

ENVIRONMENT DIVISION

Figure 10–7 presents the general format for the SELECT statement. Note that in the ASSIGN portion of the statement the 1985 version of COBOL provides for a literal option as a means for referencing the physical file, just as is true for the sequential file format, as explained in Chapter 8.

The ORGANIZATION statement specifies that this is an indexed file.

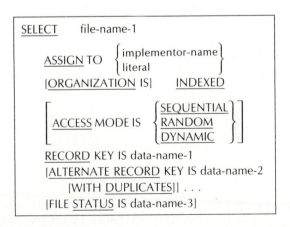

FIGURE 10-7   GENERAL FORMAT FOR THE SELECT STATEMENT FOR INDEXED FILES.

The ACCESS MODE clause specifies the way records in the file will be accessed. ACCESS MODE IS SEQUENTIAL specifies that records will be accessed in ascending order of the record key. Omission of the ACCESS clause defaults to the SEQUENTIAL option. The RANDOM option specifies that the order in which records are accessed will be controlled by the programmer. This control is accomplished by moving the value of the key of the desired record into the RECORD KEY field and then issuing an input/output command (READ, WRITE, REWRITE, DELETE).

The DYNAMIC option allows the programmer to change at will from sequential access to random access, using appropriate forms of input/output statements. In its absence, the file for a given program must be declared to be either in SEQUENTIAL or in RANDOM access mode, but not in both modes in the same program.

We repeat here a point made in the previous section on creating an indexed file. When the file is first being created, it *must* be in sequential access mode. In subsequent uses, it may be in any of the three options, SEQUENTIAL, RANDOM, or DYNAMIC.

RECORD KEY references a data-name that must be a field within the record description of the file. In case of multiple records, a field from any record description may be given. RECORD KEY specifies the *primary* key field, on the basis of which the file is sorted. The ALTERNATE RECORD option specifies a *secondary* key that is an alternate record key for the file. When alternate keys are used, we can access records either on the basis of the primary key specified in the RECORD KEY clause or on the basis of another ALTERNATE RECORD KEY. The file, of course, is always sorted on the basis of the primary record key. The DUPLICATES phrase specifies that the value of the associated alternate record key may be duplicated within any of the records in the file. In the absence of this phrase, the presence of duplicate key values is an error condition. Notice that duplicate key values are permitted for alternate keys only. Each record must have a unique primary key. An example of alternate key values that are duplicates may be the postal code in an address record, where the postal code was specified as an alternate record key. Such a key allows the accessing of a record with a specified postal code—with recognition that the record so accessed will not be unique with respect to this (alternate) key value.

If the indexed file contains variable-length records, the primary RECORD KEY field must be in the fixed portion of the record. For example, consider the following record description:

```
FD    INDEXED-FILE . . .
      RECORD IS VARYING IN SIZE
            FROM 20 TO 200 CHARACTERS . . .
```

With respect to the record description above, the RECORD KEY field must be a field within the first 20 bytes in the record.

SELECTED FILE STATUS CODES	EXPLANATION
00	Successful completion.
02	Successful completion but a duplicate key is detected.
04	A READ statement was executed but the length of the record is inconsistent with the record description.
21	Sequence error exists. The program changed the primary key between a READ and a REWRITE statement.
23	Attempt to read a nonexistent record.
24	An attempt is made to write beyond the boundaries of the file, such as when the file is full.
41	Attempt to OPEN file that is already open.
42	Attempt to CLOSE a file that has not been opened.
43	Attempt to DELETE or REWRITE without the prior execution of a corresponding successful READ.
47	Attempt to READ or START on a file not open in the INPUT or I/O mode.
49	Attempt to DELETE or REWRITE on a file not open in the I/O mode.

FIGURE 10-8   SELECTED FILE STATUS CODES.

The FILE STATUS option operates just as explained for sequential files in Chapter 8. Figure 10–8 presents some selected status codes and their explanation. For a complete set of codes it is advisable to refer to your own operating system, since many codes are specific to the implementor.

As an illustration, the sample program in Figure 10–6 can be modified with the following addition of the FILE STATUS clause:

```
SELECT VENDOR-FILE ASSIGN TO OLDMSTR
            ORGANIZATION IS INDEXED
            ACCESS IS SEQUENTIAL
            RECORD-KEY IS VENDOR-NUMBER
            FILE STATUS IS VENDOR-FILE-STATUS.
```

Consistent with the above, the WRITE statement in the FILE-CREATE paragraph of Figure 10–6 can be modified to make use of the FILE STATUS as follows:

```
WRITE VENDOR-RECORD
IF VENDOR-FILE-STATUS NOT = '00' . . .
```

In the above program segment, the IF statement is used in lieu of the IN-VALID KEY test.

Review

1   In the SELECT statement in the ENVIRONMENT DIVISION, the fact that a file is to be set up as an indexed file is specified by the _____ statement.

ORGANIZATION

2   A file organized as an indexed file [can /cannot] be accessed in a sequential manner.

can

3   Omission of the ACCESS clause in the SELECT statement for an indexed file results in the file having to be accessed by the [sequential / random] mode.

sequential

4   The ACCESS MODE option that allows the programmer to change at will from sequential access to random access is called the _____ mode.

DYNAMIC

5   When the ALTERNATE RECORD KEY is used to access a record in a file, the file has to be sorted on the basis of the [prime / alternate] key.

prime

6   The ALTERNATE KEY associated with a record [must / need not] be a unique key value in the file.

need not

		OPEN MODE		
FILE ACCESS MODE	STATEMENT	INPUT	OUTPUT	I-O
Sequential	READ	X		X
	WRITE		X	
	REWRITE			X
	START	X		X
	DELETE			X
Random	READ	X		X
	WRITE		X	X
	REWRITE			X
	START			
	DELETE			X
Dynamic	READ	X		X
	WRITE		X	X
	REWRITE			X
	START	X		X
	DELETE			X

FIGURE 10-9   PERMISSIBLE INPUT-OUTPUT STATEMENT.

PROCEDURE DIVISION

An indexed file can be opened as INPUT, OUTPUT, or I-O (input-output). Figure 10-9 summarizes the permissible input-output statements for each of these options, depending on the access mode specified.

Reading records from an indexed file is done by using one of the two formats presented in Figure 10–10. The first format must be used if the SE-

```
Format 1:
    READ file-name-1   [NEXT] RECORD [INTO identifier-1]
        [AT END imperative-statement-1]
        [NOT AT END imperative-statement-2]
    [END-READ]
Format 2:
    READ file-name-1 RECORD [INTO identifier-1]
        [INVALID KEY imperative-statement-3]
        [NOT INVALID Key imperative-statement-4]
    [END-READ]
```

FIGURE 10-10   GENERAL FORMATS FOR THE READ STATEMENT FOR INDEXED FILES.

QUENTIAL access mode has been specified either explicitly or implicitly (by default). The NEXT phrase must be specified when a file is declared to be in the DYNAMIC access mode and records are to be retrieved sequentially. Execution of READ . . . NEXT RECORD retrieves from the file the next record whose record key is higher than the one accessed previously. From a logical standpoint, READ . . . NEXT operates identically to READ in a sequential file. We use the qualification "from a logical standpoint" because in an indexed file the physical and logical order may not be in direct correspondence. This happens when an indexed file has new records added to it. Instead of being "squeezed" in between existing records, they are put in a physically separate location (overflow) and connected by address pointers to the records that logically precede and follow them.

Format 2 is used for files in RANDOM access mode; it also is used when records are to be retrieved randomly from a file in DYNAMIC access mode. The KEY clause references the data-name specified as a key either in the RECORD KEY or the ALTERNATE RECORD KEY clauses. If the KEY clause is omitted in the Format 2 READ statement, the prime key (RECORD KEY) of the file is assumed by default. The INVALID KEY condition holds when no record can be located whose record key matches the value of the data-name specified or implied by the KEY IS clause. For instance, we may have:

```
MOVE '123456789' TO SOC-SEC-NO.
READ STUDENT-MASTER RECORD
      KEY IS SOC-SEC-NO
      INVALID KEY PERFORM READ-ERROR
      NOT INVALID KEY PERFORM ROUTINE-A
                      PERFORM ROUTINE-B
END-READ
PERFORM ROUTINE-C.
```

In the above program segment. READ-ERROR will be executed if no record in the file has a SOC-SEC-NO key equal to 123456789. If such a record does exist, then ROUTINE-A and ROUTINE-B are executed. ROUTINE-C is executed regardless of the outcome of the READ because of the END-READ scope terminator. Also, SOC-SEC-NO is of course a key field. Therefore, one of the following two clauses is assumed to have been written in the SELECT statement:

```
RECORD KEY IS SOC-SEC-NO
or
ALTERNATE RECORD KEY IS SOC-SEC-NO.
```

It is instructive also to consider rewriting the above example using the FILE STATUS construct. Assume that in the SELECT statement, we had written the clause:

FILE STATUS IS STUD-MAST-STATUS.

Then the example could be rewritten as follows:

```
MOVE '123456789' TO SOC-SEC-NO
READ STUDENT-MASTER RECORD
     KEY IS SOC-SEC-NO
     INVALID KEY PERFORM CHECK-STATUS-CODE
     NOT INVALID KEY PERFORM ROUTINE-A
                      PERFORM ROUTINE-B
END-READ
PERFORM ROUTINE-C.
CHECK-STATUS-CODE.
   IF STUD-MAST-STATUS = '23'
        PERFORM READ-ERROR
   ELSE
        IF STUD-MAST-STATUS = . . .
```

When a FILE STATUS clause has been specified, and prior to the execution of the INVALID . . . and NOT INVALID . . . tests, the system places the appropriate status code in the FILE STATUS field. Making reference to the codes in Figure 10–8, we see that a code of 00 signifies successful completion. When a read instruction has been successful in the example above, STUD-MAST-STATUS would contain 00 and the NOT INVALID KEY branch would be executed. Within that branch we could look at the contents of STUD-MAST-STATUS, but since it is known to be 00 there is no point in doing so.

When the read operation is not successful, the INVALID KEY clause applies, and we execute CHECK-STATUS-CODE in which we proceed to test for the specific error condition. A code of 23 signifies attempt to read a non-existent record, as shown in Figure 10–8. Other status codes could also be tested in order to ascertain the specific cause of the INVALID KEY condition.

As a summary statement, the INVALID KEY condition is generic, whereas the FILE STATUS construct allows us to identify the specific invalid condition.

We take the opportunity here to suggest a more documentative presentation of the file-status specification. Assuming, as above, that we had written FILE STATUS IS STUD-MAST-STATUS, we could write:

```
01   STUD-MAST-STATUS      PIC     XX.
     88   VALID-READ       VALUE '00'.
     88   NONEXISTENT-RECORD VALUE '23'.
     88   (etc.)
      .
      .
      .
```

Such a specification would allow replacing statements like IF STUD-MAST-STATUS = '23' by IF NONEXISTENT-RECORD and would remove the hard-to-remember numeric codes from the PROCEDURE DIVISION.

The INVALID KEY and the AT END clauses in the READ statement are shown to be optional in the general format in Figure 10–10. If the INVALID KEY and the AT END are omitted, then there must be a USE AFTER STANDARD EXCEPTION PROCEDURE specified for the corresponding file-name. This rule applies to all of the input/output verbs WRITE, REWRITE and DELETE, for which the general formats are presented in Figure 10–11. As an example, consider the following PROCEDURE DIVISION statements:

```
PROCEDURE DIVISION.
DECLARATIVES.
I-O-TEST SECTION.
     USE AFTER STANDARD EXCEPTION PROCEDURE ON
          STUDENT-MASTER.
READ-TEST.
     IF STUD-MAST-STATUS = '00'
       NEXT SENTENCE
     ELSE
```

```
WRITE     record-name-1      [FROM identifier-1]
     [INVALID KEY imperative-statement-1]
     [NOT INVALID KEY imperative-statement-2]
[END-WRITE]


REWRITE record-name-1 [FROM identifier-1]
     [INVALID KEY imperative-statement-1]
     [NOT INVALID KEY imperative-statement-2]
     [END-REWRITE]


DELETE file-name-1 RECORD
     [INVALID KEY imperative-statement-1]
     [NOT INVALID KEY imperative-statement-2]
[END-DELETE]
```

FIGURE 10–11   GENERAL FORMATS FOR WRITE, REWRITE, AND DELETE STATEMENTS FOR INDEXED FILES.

```
        IF STUD-MAST-STATUS = '23'
          MOVE 'CODE 23 ERROR WHILE READING STUDENT-MASTER'
            TO PRINT-LINE
        ELSE
          MOVE 'UNSPECIFIED ERROR WHILE READING STUDENT-MASTER'
            TO PRINT-LINE
        END-IF
        WRITE PRINT-LINE
      END-IF.
  END-DECLARATIVES.
```

Because of the EXCEPTION PROCEDURE ON STUDENT-MASTER included in the above code, the READ statement does *not* require the INVALID KEY.

```
  MOVE '123456789' TO SOC-SEC-NO
  READ STUDENT-MASTER RECORD
  PEFORM ROUTINE-C.
```

If an exception occurs during execution of the above READ statement, program control will transfer to the READ-TEST paragraph in the DECLARA-TIVES portion of the program before resuming with execution of the PERFORM ROUTINE-C statement that follows the READ.

The choice of using INVALID KEY and AT END clauses versus the USE AFTER EXCEPTION construct in the DECLARATIVES portion of the program should depend on the intended focus of program logic with respect to input/output exceptions. If such exceptions or errors can be viewed as unusual or parenthetical to the task at hand, use of DECLARATIVES is the recommended approach, because it removes these unusual cases from the mainline code. On the other hand, if treatment of errors or exceptions is an integral part of the task logic, then use of the INVALID KEY and the AT END clauses is the recommended approach, because up-front visibility is then given to the logic of handling such exceptions.

New records are written in the file by use of the WRITE statement presented in the first portion of Figure 10–11. When a file is being created, WRITE is used as illustrated in the example included in the preceding section of this chapter.

After a file has been created, WRITE is used to add new records to the file. As always, the proper value is moved to the primary record key, and the execution of WRITE causes the new record to be inserted in the correct logical position within the file. The INVALID KEY condition is true under the following circumstances: (1) when the file has been opened as OUTPUT, and the value of the primary record key is not greater than the value of the primary record key of the previous record; (2) when the file has been opened as I-O, and the value of the primary record key is equal to the value of the primary record key of a record already existing in the file; (3) when an attempt is being made to write more records than can be accommodated by the available disk storage.

As with the READ verb, the WRITE allows for NOT INVALID . . . END-WRITE options. Further, both the INVALID . . . and NOT INVALID clauses are optional and can be replaced by corresponding FILE STATUS related statements in the DECLARATIVES portion, as illustrated in the preceding program segment for the READ statement.

In updating tasks, REWRITE is used to replace a record that exists in the file. The general format is included in the middle portion of Figure 10–11.

At the time of execution of REWRITE, the file must be open in the I-O mode. The record being replaced is the one whose key matches the value of the primary record key. The INVALID KEY holds when the value of the record key in the record to be replaced does not match the value of the record key of the last record read, or the value of the record key does not equal the record key of any record existing in the file.

The DELETE statement logically removes a record from an indexed file. The general format is shown in the last portion of Figure 10–11.

A DELETE command can be executed only if the file has been opened in the I-O mode. Notice the explanations associated with codes 43 and 49 in Figure 10–8, which are file-status codes for invalid DELETE operations.

If the file has been declared to be in RANDOM or DYNAMIC access mode, INVALID KEY is true when the file does not contain a record whose prime record key value matches the value of the record key. Thus, the programmer is responsible for moving the key value of the record to be deleted to RECORD KEY.

If the file is in the SEQUENTIAL access mode, then a successful READ must precede the execution of a DELETE. In such a case, it is understood that we are deleting the record previously read. If the access mode is RANDOM, then the value placed in the RECORD KEY determines the record to be deleted.

The START verb allows sequential retrieval of records from a point other than the beginning of the file. Thus, it is possible to retrieve records sequentially starting with some record in the "middle" of the file, as shown in the general format for the START statement in Figure 10–12.

The file must be in SEQUENTIAL or DYNAMIC access mode and must be open in the INPUT or I-O mode at the time START is executed. The KEY phrase may be omitted, in which case EQUAL is implied. In essence, the START statement means to position the file to that record whose record key satisfies the explicit or implicit KEY condition. If we simply write:

START CUSTOMER FILE   INVALID KEY PEFORM CANT-START

we specify that the file is to be positioned at the record whose primary key has a value equal to the current content of the RECORD KEY field. Thus, it

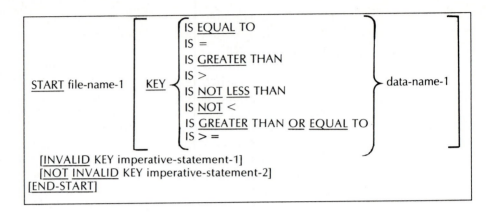

FIGURE 10-12   GENERAL FORMAT FOR THE START STATEMENT FOR INDEXED FILE.

would be important to have ascertained that the RECORD KEY has an appropriate value. For instance if the RECORD KEY field contained the value of a deleted record, we would execute CANT-START, since the INVALID KEY condition would be true.

 A more typical example would involve use of the KEY clause to specify the key-name (date-name-1) and the condition for determining the "match." For example, if CUSTOMER-NAME is a record key and we want to retrieve the records of customers whose names begin with M or higher, we can write:

MOVE 'M' TO CUSTOMER-NAME
START CUSTOMER-FILE
    KEY IS NOT LESS THAN CUSTOMER-NAME
        INVALID KEY PERFORM START-ERROR.

In this program segment, MOVE is an alphanumeric move resulting in CUS-TOMER-NAME containing the letter M and blanks to the right of M. The KEY IS NOT LESS condition specifies that we want to position the file at the first record whose key is not less than the letter M; in other words, it will be the first name that begins with the letter M. A READ statement then retrieves that record, and subsequent READ statement execution retrieves the following records sequentially.

 The data-name in the KEY phrase can be either a record key (specified as RECORD KEY, or ALTERNATE RECORD KEY) or a data item subordinate to a record key, provided that the data item is the first (leftmost) field in the record key. In other words we can specify the "first part" of a record key. For the above example, we could have:

```
...RECORD KEY IS CUSTOMER-NAME...
   .
   .
   .
02  CUSTOMER-NAME.
    03  STARTING-LETTER-OF-NAME   PIC X.
    03  REST-OF-NAME              PIC X(19).
   .
   .
   .

    MOVE 'M' TO STARTING-LETTER-OF-NAME
    START CUSTOMER-FILE
      KEY IS GREATER THAN OR EQUAL TO STARTING-LETTER-OF-NAME
      INVALID KEY PERFORM START-ERROR.
```

The INVALID condition is true if the KEY condition cannot be met. For example, consider the following program segment:

```
MOVE 'MICHENER' TO CUSTOMER-NAME.
START CUSTOMER-FILE
    KEY IS EQUAL TO CUSTOMER-NAME
    INVALID KEY PERFORM ERROR-START.
```

ERROR-START will be executed if there is no customer in the file whose record key is equal to 'MICHENER'.

As with all I-O verbs (OPEN, CLOSE, READ, WRITE, REWRITE, DE-LETE, and START), the FILE STATUS may be used as a more descriminating alternative to the generic INVALID KEY ... NOT INVALID KEY ..., and the USE AFTER STANDARD EXCEPTION PROCEDURE may be used in lieu of the INVALID KEY approach.

Review

1   In the PROCEDURE DIVISION, reading records from an indexed file is accomplished by using the _____ verb.

READ

2   Whenever records in an indexed file are to be retrieved randomly, the _____ clause indicates the data-name to be used to identify each record.

KEY

3   If the KEY clause is omitted in conjunction with random retrieval of records, the basis for identifying each record is the [RECORD KEY / ALTERNATE RECORD KEY].

RECORD KEY

4   There must be a USE AFTER STANDARD EXCEPTION PROCEDURE specified for the corresponding file-name if the READ statement omits use of both the _____ and _____ clauses.

INVALID KEY; AT END

5   In the PROCEDURE DIVISION, records are added to an indexed file by using the _____ verb.

WRITE

6   Execution of a WRITE statement to add a record to an indexed file results in the record being added [at the end of the file / in the correct logical position within the file].

in the correct logical position
within the file

7   The verb that is used to modify a record held in an indexed file is _____.

REWRITE

8   In order for a REWRITE instruction to be executed, the file must be open in _____ mode.

I/O

9   The verb used to remove a record from an indexed file is _____.

DELETE

10   A DELETE command can be executed only if the file has been opened in _____ mode.

I-O

11   The verb that makes possible the sequential retrieval of records from a point other than the beginning of the file is _____.

START

12   In conjunction with executing a START statement, the data-name used as the key [must / need not] have been specified previously as RECORD KEY or ALTERNATE RECORD KEY.

need not

AN EXAMPLE OF PROCESSING AN INDEXED FILE

We present an example here that illustrates the use of most of the language statements and options described in the preceding section. The example involves processing the vendor file created by the example program that is given in Figure 10–6. We now give the following record description to the file.

```
FD   VENDOR-FILE LABEL RECORDS ARE STANDARD
     DATA RECORD IS VENDOR-RECORD.
01   VENDOR-RECORD.
     02   VENDOR-NUMBER    PIC X(8).
     02   VENDOR-NAME      PIC X(15).
     02   VENDOR-ADDRESS   PIC X(45).
```

Transaction records are submitted through a TRANS-FILE and have the record description that follows (shown at the top of page 386):

```
01  TRANS-RECORD.
    02  TRANS-CODE              PIC 9.
        88  CHANGE-ADDRESS      VALUE 1.
        88  ADD-VENDOR          VALUE 2.
        88  DELETE-VENDOR       VALUE 3.
        88  ERROR-CODE VALUES ARE ZERO, 4 THRU 9.
    02  VENDOR-IDENT           PIC 9(8).
    02  VENDOR-NAME            PIC X(15).
    02  VENDOR-ADDRESS         PIC X(45).
    02  FILLER                 PIC X(11).
```

It is apparent from the self-documenting nature of this record description that we are interested in changing the address of a vendor and in adding or deleting vendors.

Figure 10–13 presents the complete program. Notice in the EN-VIRONMENT DIVISION that VENDOR-FILE is in DYNAMIC access mode and that VENDOR-NUMBER is the record key. The PROCEDURE DIVISION is self-documenting and consists of three control portions that illustrate random updating, sequential retrieval, and use of the START verb, respectively. The first portion illustrates random access and updating.

The first portion of the MAIN-ROUTINE paragraph in the PROCE-DURE DIVISION illustrates random updating of an indexed file. By studying Figure 10–13 we can observe that the 020-UPDATE paragraph analyzes the transaction code. Then we execute the 030-CHANGE-ADDRESS, 040-ADD-VENDOR, 050-DELETE-VENDOR, or 060-TRANS-ERROR paragraph. Each of these paragraphs illustrates, respectively: the replacing of a record (RE-WRITE), the addition of a record (WRITE), the deletion of a record (DELETE), and the handling of INVALID KEY conditions.

The second portion of the MAIN-ROUTINE procedure illustrates se-quential retrieval. When OPEN INPUT VENDOR-FILE is executed, the open instruction causes the file to be positioned at the beginning, so that when the first READ VENDOR-FILE NEXT RECORD is executed, the first record is retrieved.

The third portion of the MAIN-ROUTINE illustrates use of the START verb:

```
MOVE '35290001' TO VENDOR-NUMBER
    :
    :
START VENDOR-FILE KEY IS GREATER THAN VENDOR-NUMBER
    INVALID KEY SET INPUT-ENDED TO TRUE.
```

In this illustration, we want to retrieve sequentially all records whose key is greater than 35290001. Since the GREATER THAN option is used, the record whose key equals 35290001 will not be retrieved.

```
      IDENTIFICATION DIVISION.
      PROGRAM-ID. UPDATEINDEX.
*
      ENVIRONMENT DIVISION.
      CONFIGURATION SECTION.
      SOURCE-COMPUTER. ABC-480.
      OBJECT-COMPUTER. ABC-480.
*
      INPUT-OUTPUT SECTION.
      FILE-CONTROL.
          SELECT VENDOR-FILE ASSIGN TO OLDMSTR
                              ORGANIZATION IS INDEXED
                              ACCESS MODE IS DYNAMIC
                              RECORD KEY IS VENDOR-NUMBER.
*
          SELECT TRANS-FILE ASSIGN TO TRANS.
*
          SELECT PRINT-FILE ASSIGN TO PRINTER.
*
      DATA DIVISION.
      FILE SECTION.
*
      FD  VENDOR-FILE LABEL RECORDS ARE STANDARD
                      DATA RECORD IS VENDOR-RECORD.
      01  VENDOR-RECORD.
          02 VENDOR-NUMBER       PIC X(8).
          02 VENDOR-NAME         PIC X(15).
          02 VENDOR-ADDRESS      PIC X(45).
*
      FD  TRANS-FILE LABEL RECORDS ARE OMITTED
                      DATA RECORD IS TRANS-RECORD.
      01  TRANS-RECORD.
          02 TRANS-CODE          PIC 9.
             88 CHANGE-ADDRESS    VALUE 1.
             88 ADD-VENDOR        VALUE 2.
             88 DELETE-VENDOR     VALUE 3.
             88 ERROR-CODE        VALUES ARE ZERO, 4 THRU 9.
          02 VENDOR-IDENT        PIC 9(8).
          02 VENDOR-NAME         PIC X(15).
          02 VENDOR-ADDRESS      PIC X(45).
          02 FILLER              PIC X(11).
*
      FD  PRINT-FILE LABEL RECORD OMITTED
                      DATA RECORD PRINTLINE.
      01  PRINTLINE              PIC X(132).
*
      WORKING-STORAGE SECTION.
      01  END-OF-DATA-INDICATOR   PIC 9 VALUE ZERO.
          88 INPUT-ENDED          VALUE 1.
          88 INPUT-NOT-ENDED      VALUE 0.
```

FIGURE 10-13   SAMPLE PROGRAM TO ILLUSTRATE PROCESSING OF AN INDEXED FILE.

```
/
 PROCEDURE DIVISION.
 MAIN-ROUTINE.
*
*   THIS PORTION ILLUSTATES RANDOM UPDATING OF INDEXED FILE
*
      OPEN INPUT TRANS-FILE
          OUTPUT PRINT-FILE
           I-O   VENDOR-FILE.
      MOVE ' LISTING FROM UPDATE PORTION' TO PRINTLINE
      WRITE PRINTLINE AFTER ADVANCING PAGE.
      PERFORM READ-TRANS.
      PERFORM UPDATE UNTIL INPUT-ENDED.
      CLOSE VENDOR-FILE.
*
*   THIS PORTION ILLUSTRATES SEQUENTIAL RETRIEVAL.
*
      MOVE ZERO TO END-OF-DATA-INDICATOR.
      MOVE ' LISTING FROM SEQUENTIAL RETRIEVAL' TO PRINTLINE
      WRITE PRINTLINE AFTER ADVANCING 5 LINES.
      OPEN INPUT VENDOR-FILE
      PERFORM READ-VENDOR.
*
      PERFORM LISTING UNTIL INPUT-ENDED.
      CLOSE VENDOR-FILE.
*
*   THIS PORTION ILLUSTRATES USE OF THE START VERB.
*
      MOVE ZERO TO END-OF-DATA-INDICATOR
      OPEN INPUT VENDOR-FILE
      MOVE 35290001 TO VENDOR-NUMBER
*
      START VENDOR-FILE KEY IS GREATER THAN VENDOR-NUMBER
              INVALID KEY MOVE 1 TO END-OF-DATA-INDICATOR.
*
      MOVE ' LISTING FROM USE OF START VERB' TO PRINTLINE.
      WRITE PRINTLINE AFTER ADVANCING 5 LINES.
      PERFORM READ-VENDOR
      PERFORM LISTING UNTIL INPUT-ENDED
      CLOSE VENDOR-FILE.
*
      CLOSE TRANS-FILE.
      STOP RUN.
*
 READ-TRANS.
      READ TRANS-FILE RECORD
              AT END MOVE 1 TO END-OF-DATA-INDICATOR.
```

**FIGURE 10-13   SAMPLE PROGRAM TO ILLUSTRATE PROCESSING OF AN
INDEXED FILE.   (Continued)**

```
020-UPDATE.
    MOVE VENDOR-IDENT OF TRANS-RECORD TO VENDOR-NUMBER
*
    EVALUATE TRUE
        WHEN CHANGE-ADDRESS
            PERFORM 030-CHANGE-ADDRESS
        WHEN ADD-VENDOR
            PERFORM 040-ADD-VENDOR
        WHEN DELETE-VENDOR
            PERFORM 050-DELETE-VENDOR
        WHEN OTHER
            PERFORM 060-TRANS-ERROR
    END-EVALUATE
*
    READ TRANS-FILE RECORD
        AT END SET INPUT-ENDED TO TRUE
    END-READ.
*
 030-CHANGE-ADDRESS.
    READ VENDOR-FILE RECORD
        INVALID KEY
            MOVE ' CANNOT FIND VENDOR FOR THIS TRANS '
                TO PRINTLINE
            WRITE PRINTLINE AFTER 1
            WRITE PRINTLINE FROM TRANS-RECORD AFTER 1
        NOT INVALID KEY
            MOVE VENDOR-ADDRESS OF TRANS-RECORD
                TO VENDOR-ADDRESS OF VENDOR-RECORD
            REWRITE VENDOR-RECORD
                INVALID KEY
                    MOVE ' CANNOT REWRITE THIS RECORD'
                        TO PRINTLINE
                    WRITE PRINTLINE AFTER 1
                    WRITE PRINTLINE FROM VENDOR-RECORD AFTER 1
            END-REWRITE
    END-READ.
*
 040-ADD-VENDOR.
    MOVE VENDOR-NAME OF TRANS-RECORD
            TO VENDOR-NAME OF VENDOR-RECORD
    MOVE VENDOR-ADDRESS OF TRANS-RECORD
            TO VENDOR-ADDRESS OF VENDOR-RECORD.
    WRITE VENDOR-RECORD
        INVALID KEY
            MOVE ' CANNOT CREATE A RECORD FROM THIS TRANS'
                TO PRINTLINE
            WRITE PRINTLINE AFTER 1
            WRITE PRINTLINE FROM TRANS-RECORD AFTER 1
    END-WRITE.
```

FIGURE 10-13   SAMPLE PROGRAM TO ILLUSTRATE PROCESSING OF AN INDEXED FILE.   (Continued)

```
   050-DELETE-VENDOR.
       DELETE VENDOR-FILE RECORD
           INVALID KEY
               CONTINUE
           NOT INVALID KEY
               MOVE ' CANNOT DELETE RECORD SPECIFIED BY THIS TRANS'
                   TO PRINTLINE
               WRITE PRINTLINE AFTER 1
               WRITE PRINTLINE FROM TRANS-RECORD AFTER 1
       END-DELETE.
*
   060-TRANS-ERROR.
       MOVE 'WRONG TRANSACTION CODE IN ' TO PRINTLINE
       WRITE PRINTLINE AFTER 1
       WRITE PRINTLINE FROM TRANS-RECORD AFTER 1.
*
   070-SEQUENTIAL-LISTING.
       READ VENDOR-FILE NEXT RECORD
           AT END
               SET INPUT-ENDED TO TRUE
*          NOT AT END
               WRITE PRINTLINE FROM VENDOR-RECORD AFTER 1
       END-READ.
```

FIGURE 10-13   SAMPLE PROGRAM TO ILLUSTRATE PROCESSING OF AN INDEXED FILE.   (Continued)

Exercises

10.1 Outline a program to re-create an indexed sequential file. Assume that the original file has too many overflow records and that we therefore want to create a new version of the file to eliminate all overflow. Include in your outline the FILE-CONTROL paragraph of the ENVIRONMENT DIVISION and the complete PROCEDURE DIVISION. Assume that OLD-FILE, OLD-REC, NEW-FILE, and NEW-REC are the corresponding file- and record-names.

10.2 Refer to Exercise 8.4 for the program description.

a Create the master file as an indexed file, using the part number as the RECORD KEY.

b Update the master file on a random basis, using the part number as the RECORD KEY.

10.3 Refer to Exercise 8.5 for the program description.

a Create the master file as an indexed file, using the lot number as the RECORD KEY.

b Update the master file on a random basis, using the lot number as the RECORD KEY.

11

RELATIVE FILE PROCESSING

RELATIVE FILE ORGANIZATION

A relative file is one in which records are accessed by reference to their relative position in the file. If we think of a file that can hold 100 records, the first record has a *relative key* of 1, while the last one has a relative key of 100. Access to records in a file organized as relative is by reference to the relative key of each record. For instance, we may use the following two types of commands:

1   Write this record as the 20th record in the file.
2   Read the 68th record in the file.

As this shows, reference is made to the relative location of a record. We say "relative" as distinguished from the *absolute* location of a given record. An absolute location would be specified in terms of the address of the record within a specific disk volume, within a specific cylinder, within a specific track, and the record number in that track.

Relative file organization is ideal for a case where records are identified by consecutive numbers. For instance, suppose that invoice records are numbered 0001, 0002, 0003 . . . We can use relative organization and store the records in the order of the invoice number. If we want to access invoice number 0050, we can do so simply by accessing the record whose relative key is 50. It is rare, however, that records can be numbered exactly consecutively as in this example, and relative file organization requires some specific techniques in order to utilize this method of file organization.

There are several key-to-address transformation methods that can be used to transform record keys (identifiers) to relative location addresses. All such methods have one common property: they enable us to transform record identifiers, such as social security numbers, product numbers, and customer names, to relative key values. Thus, if we want the record of product number 1234, we would apply a key-to-address transformation procedure that would transform product number 1234 into a relative key value, say 371. Then we would retrieve the 371st record in the relative file, with the expectation that it would be the record of product number 1234.

As the preceding example illustrates, a relative file can be a high-performance file. We can compute the address of a record without having to use index structures, as is required with indexed files. It generally is true that relative files can provide fast, direct access to records, but it should be added that the level of performance depends on the specific file and the specific method chosen. Good performance in a relative file often requires some analysis and experimentation. The main reason for variability in performance is that all known key-to-address methods produce *synonyms*, which are said to occur when the key-to-address method generates the same relative key for two or more data records. For instance, it may be that product numbers 1234 and 4965 both generate the same relative key; therefore, we need additional processing beyond the key-to-address methods.

There are many ways to handle the occurrence of synonyms, but we illustrate here one procedure that is successful. At file creation time, go through the file and mark each record as a vacant record, using a special field in the record for this purpose. Then, as each data record is being stored in the file, we apply the chosen key-to-address method and compute a *home-address* relative key value. We now read that record space, and, if it is marked as vacant, we record the data in that space and then mark it as occupied. If we previously stored a data record in the home-address space, we look at the next record space to see if it is vacant and, if it is, we write the data record there. If it is occupied, we continue looking for a vacancy in consecutive record spaces, and either we find a vacancy or we come full circle in the case of a file that is completely filled. For example, suppose that V = vacant, and O = occupied. Let us assume that we want to store a product record for product number 2645 in the file. Further, let us assume that the chosen key-to-address method computes a relative key of 132. As can be observed in the following, the product record will be stored in relative record location 134, which is the first available vacancy.

RECORD RELATIVE KEY	130		131		132		133		134		135	
Content	V		O	7391	O	0935	O	5383	V		V	

If we wanted to retrieve the record of product number 2645 after it had been loaded into the file, we would compute its home address as 132 as before. We would attempt to retrieve the record at location 132 by comparing the record key of 2645 to the record key at location 132, which happens to be 0935. This comparison indicates that record 2645 is a synonym, and we would continue searching sequentially until the record was found at location 134. Notice that if we were trying to retrieve a record that in fact did not exist in the file, we would know that the record did not exist as soon as we came upon the first vacancy. We could conclude that the record did not exist, because if a record is a synonym, it is stored in the *first* available vacancy past the home address.

This procedure needs to be expanded to take account of deletion of records from the file. If we desire to free up the record space when a record is deleted, we recommend that the space be marked as deleted. If we want to add a new record, a deleted record then constitutes a vacancy. If we are retrieving a record and it is not at its home address, however, we should continue looking for it until we encounter the first vacancy, *not* counting deleted records as vacancies. In the preceding example of record 2645, whose home address was 132 but which was written at 134 due to synonyms, suppose that the record at location 133 was later deleted. To retrieve record 2645 from location 134, we would have to continue looking past the deleted record at location 133. Of course, if the record at location 133 were deleted *before* record 2645 was added to the file, then record 2645 would have been written at location 133.

This procedure for handling synonyms is incorporated into the program illustration in Figure 11–7, later in this chapter.

Review

1   In a relative file, the location of a record is described relative to the other _____ in the file.

records

2   Key-to-address transformation methods are concerned with converting a record key (identifier) into a relative _____.

location address

3   When two different record keys result in the same relative location address, it is said that a _____ has been produced.

synonym

4   When a synonym has occurred, a common solution is to store the synonym in the first vacant record space [preceding/following] the home-address space.

following

5   When records are deleted from a relative file and are marked as deleted, such record spaces then [are / are not] available for the storage of new records.

are

6   If a record is neither at its home address nor at the first vacancy after that address (not counting deleted records), then we can conclude that _____.

the record does not exist

THE DIVISION REMAINDER METHOD

In the preceding section, we saw that use of relative file organization is predicated on a key-to-address transformation capability. There are several

key-to-address methods available. One that is in wide use is the division remainder method.

In order to apply the division remainder method, we first must choose
the file size. A rule of thumb to determine the file size is to divide the number of records in the file by 0.80, so that 80 percent of the file will be filled
and 20 percent of the file will be unused.* This unused space serves two
purposes: it cuts down the incidence of synonyms and it also allows for file
expansion. The term *packing factor* or *file density* is used to denote the percent of filled space in a relative file. If we divide the number of data records
by 0.80, the result is an 80 percent packing factor, or density. In general, the
lower the packing factor, the fewer the synonyms but the greater the unused
file space. We can see now why relative files require analysis and experimentation. For instance, record size and frequency of access are factors
that would be considered in the analysis for choosing a suitable packing
factor.

Once the file size has been chosen, we select the prime number closest to the file size. A prime number is divisible only by itself and the number
1. For instance, the numbers 3 and 7 are prime numbers. There are tables of
prime numbers available in mathematical handbooks. Use of a prime number is not critical, however. We also can use the file size instead of the prime
number closest to it, and in most cases there is little difference in the number of synonyms generated. In general, however, the use of a prime number
is likely to result in fewer synonyms.

Suppose a customer file contains 9,600 records. We decide on a packing factor of 80 percent; therefore, the allocated file size is 9,600 ÷ 0.80 =
12,000 record spaces. The prime number closest to 12,000 is 11,987. The customers are identified by a 6-digit customer number. The first step in the division remainder method is to divide the record identifier by the prime
number (or the file size itself). Thus, if we want to compute the location address of customer 123456, we divide this record identifier by the prime number 11987, obtaining a whole-number quotient of 10 and a remainder of
3586. By the division remainder method, the remainder plus 1 is the computed home address. For our example, the address is thus 3586 + 1 = 3587. If
we had used the file size instead of the prime number as the divisor, we
would have divided 123456 by 12000, giving a whole-number quotient of 10
and a remainder of 3456. The home address in this case would have been
3456 + 1 = 3457.

It should be noted that, when we divide a number by any divisor, the
remainder from the division can range from 0 to the value of the divisor
minus 1. Thus, if we are dividing by 12000, the smallest possible remainder is
0 and the largest possible remainder is 11999. Since we add 1 to the remainder in the division remainder method, we can see that division by the file

---

* Where X = file size

If No. Records = .80X

Then $X = \dfrac{\text{No. Records}}{.80}$

size results in the smallest computed value being 1 and the largest value being the file size itself. Thus, by taking the remainder plus 1, we generate addresses that correspond to the relative addresses in the file. In the case where a prime number is used that is smaller than the file size itself, a few addresses would be impossible to generate. For example, with a prime number of 11987 as a divisor and a file size of 12000, we would never generate addresses 11988, 11989, 11990, . . . 12000. Still, those addresses could be occupied by records if we happened to have enough synonyms in the addresses 11987 and before.

As indicated by this example, the division remainder method is rather easy to apply. In the same program given later in the chapter (Figure 11–7), the procedure is implemented as follows:

```
MOVE ITEM-NUMBER OF SOURCE-RECORD TO WORKFIELD
DIVIDE PRIME-NUMBER INTO WORKFIELD GIVING QUOTIENT
COMPUTE LOCATION-ADDRESS =
    WORKFIELD − (PRIME-NUMBER * QUOTIENT) + 1.
```

The QUOTIENT field must be defined as an integer field, of course. Then the remainder is computed by multiplying the divisor by the interger quotient and then subtracting the result from the dividend. The address is stored in LOCATION-ADDRESS as the remainder plus 1.

The division remainder method, as well as other methods for transforming record identifiers into file addresses, has the property of giving about an equal chance to every possible file address. The general relationship between the record identifier and the address computed is random, and this is the reason that key-to-address methods are referred to as *randomizing* methods. The term *hashing* also is used very widely to describe such randomizing key-to-address methods.

Review

1   A key-to-address transformation is required for relative files in order to convert a record key (identifier) into a relative file address. The widely used method described in this section is the _____ method.

division remainder

2   The percentage of filled space in a relative file is identified by the term
_____.

packing factor (or file density)

3   Suppose an accounts payable file includes 2,100 records. If a 70 percent packing factor is to be used, the allocated field size would be _____ record spaces.

$$2,100 \div 0.70 = 3,000$$

4   Given a file size of 3,000, transform Account No. 4211 into a file address by using the file size as the divisor.

Integer quotient: 1
Remainder: 1211
File Address: 1211 + 1 = 1212

5   Given a file size of 3,000, transform Account No. 911 into a file address by using the file size as the divisor.

Integer quotient: 0
Remainder: 911
File Address: 911 + 1 = 912

6   Key-to-address methods are called randomizing methods because the possible [record identifiers/file addresses] have about an equal chance of occurring.

file addresses

OTHER KEY-TO-ADDRESS TRANSFORMATION METHODS

Digit Analysis Method

By this method a frequency count is performed in regard to the number of times each of the 10 digits occurs in each of the positions included in the record key. For example, Table 11–1 presents a frequency count for the number of times each digit occurred in a five-position numeric key for 2,800

TABLE 11-1   FREQUENCY OF OCCURRENCE OF THE DIGITS 169 FOR 2,800 FIVE-POSITION KEYS

	KEY POSITION				
DIGIT	1	2	3	4	5
0	2026				
1	618	250	218	1012	260
2	128	395	391	185	382
3	23	263	389	299	271
4	5	298	330	52	302
5		335	299	101	387
6		303	339	18	299
7		289	308	134	301
8		267	267	999	245
9		400	259		353

records. In this tabulation we can observe that digits 0–9 occur with approximately uniform distribution in key positions 2, 3, and 5; therefore, if a 3-digit address were required, the digits in these three positions in the record keys could be used. Given that there are 2,800 records, however, a 4-digit address would be required. Suppose we desire the first digit to be a 0, 1, 2, or 3 only. Such assignment can be made with about equal frequency for each digit by using a rule such as the following: assign a "0" when digits in positions 2 and 3 both contain odd numbers, a "1" if position 2 is odd and position 3 is even, a "2" if position 2 is even and position 3 is odd, or a "3" if positions 2 and 3 both contain even numbers. Thus, the address for key 16258 would be 3628: the "3" from the fact that positions 2 and 3 both contain even numbers and the "628" from key positions 2, 3, and 5. Other rules for prefixing additional digits can be formulated for different circumstances. In any event, the digit analysis method relies on the digits in some of the key positions being approximately equally distributed. If such is not the case, the method cannot be used with good results.

Mid-Square Method

The record key is multiplied by itself, and the product is truncated from both left and right so as to form a number equal to the desired address length. Thus, key 36258 would be squared to give 1314642564. To form a 4-digit address, this number would be truncated from both the left and right, resulting in the address 4642.

Folding

The key is separated into two parts which then are added together to form the address. For example, suppose key 1234567 is to be transformed into a 4-digit address. We can add the first four positions to the last three positions to form the address; in this case: 1234 + 567 = 1801. As another possibility, we can begin with the middle 4 digits and add the other digits as follows:

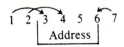

In general, the concept of folding does not refer to one standard method but to a general class of possibilities.

Alphabetic Keys

It is possible and sometimes common that the key is alphabetic, as in the case of a student file that utilizes an alphabetic key. In order to determine a numeric address, a procedure is defined by which letters are transformed into numbers. These numbers then might be used as addresses or, more likely, might be used in conjunction with one of the randomizing techniques discussed previously. Thus, if the transformation rule is that A = 00, B = 01, . . . Z = 25, then ADAM would become 00030012.

The key-to-address transformation methods that have been discussed are not the only ones that can be used, but they do represent the principal techniques. As indicated previously, the division remainder technique is used most frequently and generally works at least as well as other methods, but special circumstances may make some other method desirable for a given file.

Review

1   The transformation method for which the digits in at least some of the key positions must be dispersed about equally in terms of value is the _____ method.

digit analysis

2   The transformation method in which the key is multiplied by itself as part of the procedure for determining the address for the record is the _____ method.

mid-square

3   The transformation method in which one part of a key number is added to another part of the number to form the address is the _____ method.

folding

4   Alphabetic keys generally are transformed [directly into a numeric address/into a numeric code for subsequent determination of an address].

into a numeric code for
subsequent determination of an
address

5   The transformation technique most frequently used in conjunction with relative file organization is the _____ method.

division remainder

COBOL STATEMENTS FOR RELATIVE FILES

The SELECT Statement

Matters such as key-to-address transformations and handling of synonyms are not acknowledged by the language. COBOL assumes that the programmer handles these. The language provides only the basic mechanism by which relative files can be created and processed.

The general format for the SELECT statement is presented in Figure 11-1. ORGANIZATION IS RELATIVE has the obvious meaning. The ACCESS MODE clause has the same meaning as discussed for indexed files. Notice, however, RELATIVE KEY as contrasted to RECORD KEY. The data-name specified as RELATIVE KEY must be a WORKING-STORAGE unsigned integer item. Its function is to contain the location address for the record about to be accessed, or the location of the record that was just accessed.

The reader should understand clearly the role of RELATIVE KEY,

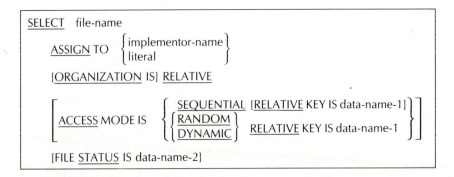

FIGURE 11-1   GENERAL FORMAT FOR THE SELECT STATEMENT.

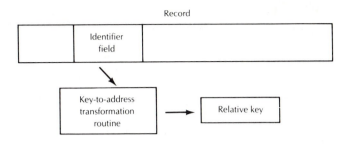

FIGURE 11–2   ILLUSTRATION OF THE ROLE OF RELATIVE KEY.

which is different from the RECORD KEY of indexed files. RECORD KEY is part of the file record. RELATIVE KEY is an item apart from the record. When we want to access the 3rd record we move the value 3 to the RELATIVE KEY field and then we issue an I/O verb such as READ, WRITE, REWRITE, or DE-LETE. The system then uses the RELATIVE KEY value to determine where the I/O verb applies in the file.

Typically, rather than wanting the 3rd or some other record referenced by its location, a record whose key field has some particular value is desired. Given a record, the value of its identifier field is taken by the programmer and transformed through a key-to-address routine to a location address. Figure 11–2 illustrates the process.

The FILE STATUS clause in Figure 11–1 is identical to its counterpart in sequential and indexed files. Figure 11–3 is a list of selected status codes. For a complete list, the reader should consult the appropriate manual for the computer system used.

STATUS CODE	DESCRIPTION
00	Successful execution.
04	Record length does not conform to file description.
10	End of file while attempting a sequential read.
22	Attempt to write a record where a record is already written (perhaps, a REWRITE should have been used).
23	Attempt to read a record that does not exist.
24	Attempt to write beyond the boundaries of the file.
41	Attempt to OPEN a file that is already opened.
42	Attempt to CLOSE a file that is not open.
43	Attempt to DELETE or REWRITE while in the sequential access mode, yet no preceding successful READ has been executed.
47	Attempt to READ or START a file not in the I-O mode.
48	Attempt to WRITE in a file not open in the OUTPUT, I-O, or EXTEND mode.
49	Attempt to DELETE or REWRITE in a file not in the I-O mode.

FIGURE 11–3   SELECTED FILE STATUS CODES AND THEIR MEANING.

Creating a Relative File

A relative file may be created either sequentially or randomly. If it is to be created sequentially, we may omit the RELATIVE KEY clause, an option shown in Figure 11–1. In the format, observe that the RELATIVE KEY clause is required if the access mode is RANDOM or DYNAMIC. To create the file sequentially, we can write:

```
SELECT file-name ASSIGN TO ...
    ORGANIZATION IS RELATIVE
    ACCESS MODE IS SEQUENTIAL.
```

In the PROCEDURE DIVISION, we then open the file as OUTPUT and we WRITE record-name. The first execution of WRITE results in writing in the first record location, the second execution results in writing in the second location, and so on.

The above procedure is used to create the file in the sequential mode. It is also possible to declare the file as ACCESS MODE IS RANDOM, in which case each WRITE execution results in writing a record in the location specified by the relative key. To illustrate the concept, consider this example:

```
SELECT CUSTOMER-FILE ASSIGN TO ...
    ORGANIZATION IS RELATIVE
    ACCESS MODE IS RANDOM
    RELATIVE KEY IS CUST-KEY.
    .
    .
    .

OPEN OUTPUT CUSTOMER-FILE
PERFORM WRITE-SAMPLE VARYING CUST-KEY FROM 1 BY 2
                        UNTIL CUST-KEY > 9.
    .
    .
    .
WRITE-SAMPLE.
    MOVE SPACES TO CUSTOMER-RECORD
    WRITE CUSTOMER-RECORD.
```

The above example writes (blank) records in record-locations 1, 3, 5, 7, and 9; all other record-locations do not contain data records at this point. If we attempted to read the 6th record, we would be attempting to read a nonexistent record. Also, if subsequent to the above example we accessed all the records sequentially, there would be five records accessed. In other words, the system keeps track of used and vacant record-locations. Still, we recommend that the programmer initialize all the records in the file with a distinguishing code in a special field. This method allows a more convenient control method for sensing vacant and used record-locations. The following example illustrates the procedure:

```
        SELECT DISK-FILE ASSIGN TO . . .
                ORGANIZATION IS RELATIVE
                ACCESS MODE IS RANDOM
                RELATIVE KEY IS LOCATION-ADDRESS.
01  DISK-RECORD.
    02  REC-STATUS-CODE      PIC 9.
        88  VACANT-RECORD    VALUE ZERO.
        88  USED-RECORD      VALUE 1.
            .
            .
            .

        OPEN OUTPUT DISK-FILE
        PERFORM ZERO-DISK
            VARYING I FROM 1 BY 1 UNTIL I > MAX-NO-OF-LOCATIONS.
            .
            .
            .

ZERO-DISK.
        MOVE I TO LOCATION-ADDRESS
        MOVE ZERO TO REC-STATUS CODE
        WRITE DISK-RECORD
            INVALID KEY PERFORM . . .
```

Notice that the first field in the disk record is used to identify whether the record is vacant or occupied, as explained in the first section of this chapter. MAX-NO-Of-LOCATIONS is assumed to contain the number of record-locations in the file. The PERFORM ZERO-DISK loop writes a zero in all the records as a means of initializing the file.

In the above example, the file was declared to be in RANDOM access mode. However, since the VARYING clause varies I through all the values, we could just as well have used sequential access.

I/O Verbs Used With Relative Files

Input/output verbs used with relative files are similar to the ones discussed in the preceding chapter on indexed files. Figure 11–4 presents the two general formats for the READ statement.

Format 1 must be used if records are retrieved in sequential mode. NEXT must be used if DYNAMIC access mode is specified and records are retrieved sequentially.

Format 1 (for Sequential Access):
>   READ file-name-1 [NEXT] RECORD [INTO identifier-1]
>   AT END imperative-statement-1]
>   [NOT AT END imperative-statement-2]
>   [END-READ]

Format 2 (for Random Access):
>   READ file-name-1 RECORD [INTO identifier-1]
>   [INVALID KEY imperative-statement-1]
>   [NOT INVALID KEY imperative-statement-2]
>   [END-READ]

FIGURE 11–4   GENERAL FORMATS FOR THE READ STATEMENT.

Format 2 is used when the access mode is RANDOM, or when the access mode is DYNAMIC and records are retrieved in random order. The IN-VALID KEY condition occurs when RELATIVE KEY contains an address pointing to a record that was deleted previously (see DELETE verb, following) or to an address beyond the boundaries of the file.

The WRITE, REWRITE, DELETE, and START statements parallel the ones discussed in Chapter 10 with respect to indexed files. Figures 11–5 and 11–6 present the general format for these statements. In all cases, if the effective access mode is random, the RELATIVE KEY field must contain the record number of the record involved in the I/O operation. For instance, to DELETE a record, we must first determine its location address, put that ad-

WRITE   record-name-1   [FROM identifier-1]
>   [INVALID KEY imperative-statement-1]
>   [NOT INVALID KEY imperative-statement-2]
>   [END-WRITE]

REWRITE   record-name-1   [FROM identifier-1]
>   [INVALID KEY imperative-statement-1]
>   [NOT INVALID Key imperative-statement-2]
>   [END-REWRITE]

DELETE file-name-1 RECORD
>   [INVALID KEY imperative-statement-1]
>   [NOT INVALID KEY imperative-statement-2]
>   [END-DELETE]

FIGURE 11–5   GENERAL FORMAT FOR THE WRITE, REWRITE, AND DELETE STATEMENTS.

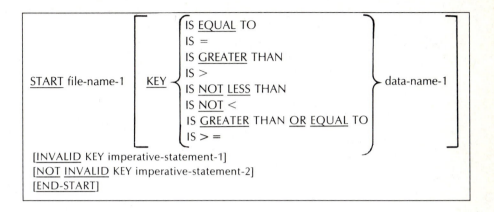

FIGURE 11–6   GENERAL FORMAT FOR THE START VERB.

dress value in the RELATIVE KEY field, and then issue a DELETE command.

Sequential retrieval of records may be accomplished using the SE-QUENTIAL or DYNAMIC access mode, the issuance of an OPEN INPUT instruction, and repetitive execution of READ or READ NEXT. Whenever sequential retrieval is desired from a point other than the beginning of a file, then the START command can be used. The same format applies as for indexed files, except that the starting record location is placed in the RELATIVE KEY field.

As was explained in Chapter 10 in connection with indexed files, the INVALID KEY and AT END options in the respective verb formats in Figures 11–4, 11–5, and 11–6 are optional. However, if these options are omitted, then the program must contain a DECLARATIVES portion with an appropriate USE AFTER STANDARD EXCEPTION PROCEDURE specification.

Review

1   The location address determined by a key-to-address routine is stored in the _____ field.

RELATIVE KEY

2   For an indexed file, the RECORD KEY [is/is not] part of the original file record. For a relative file, the RELATIVE KEY [is/is not] part of the original file record.

is; is not

3 In the SELECT statement of the ENVIRONMENT DIVISION, the RELA-
TIVE KEY clause is not needed and may be omitted if the file is to be
created [sequentially/randomly].

sequentially

4 Records stored sequentially in a relative file [can/cannot] be accessed
randomly.

can

5 Records stored randomly in a relative file [can/cannot] be accessed
sequentially.

can

AN EXAMPLE OF CREATING A RELATIVE FILE

A source file is to be transferred to disk, organized as a relative file. For simplicity, we assume that there will be no more than 50 records. Each record
contains an ITEM-NUMBER in columns 1–5 and an ITEM-NAME in columns
6–25. We shall use ITEM-NUMBER as the identifier for each record and we
shall compute disk addresses using this identifier and the prime number 47.
By using the division remainder technique, we convert each ITEM-NUMBER
value to a (relative) disk address in the range 1–50.

Figure 11–7 presents a program written to create such a relative file.
In the 010-MAIN ROUTINE we perform 020-ZERO-DISK as many times as
the value of MAX-NO-OF-LOCATIONS, which was set to 50 in the DATA
DIVISION. The function of 020-ZERO-DISK is to initialize to zero the REC-
STATUS-CODE of each record space, thereby indicating a vacant record
space.

The second main task in 010-MAIN-ROUTINE is the in-line PER-
FORM, which iteratively reads a record from SOURCE-FILE and invokes execution of 030-LOAD-RECORD in order to "load" the record into the file.
Loading involves execution of 040-RANDOMIZE-READ, which computes
LOCATION-ADDRESS and executes 060-READ-DISK-REC in order to read
the record at that LOCATION-ADDRESS. Continuing with the 030-LOAD-
RECORD paragraph, following execution of 040-RANDOMIZE-READ we
check to determine if the record read is already occupied (USED-RECORD),
in which case the 050-HANDLE-SYNONYMS paragraph is executed. In either
case, if there is a VALID-READ and VACANT-RECORD condition, we proceed to load the data into the disk. Notice that we use the REWRITE rather
than the WRITE verb. This is so because the 020-ZERO-DISK procedure did

```
IDENTIFICATION DIVISION.
PROGRAM-ID. RELATIVE-CREATE.
*
ENVIRONMENT DIVISION.
CONFIGURATION SECTION.
SOURCE-COMPUTER. ABC-480.
OBJECT-COMPUTER. ABC-480.
INPUT-OUTPUT SECTION.
FILE-CONTROL.
    SELECT DISK-FILE    ASSIGN TO DISK
                        ORGANIZATION IS RELATIVE
                        ACCESS MODE IS RANDOM
                        RELATIVE KEY IS LOCATION-ADDRESS.
*
    SELECT SOURCE-FILE  ASSIGN TO READER.
    SELECT PRINT-FILE   ASSIGN TO PRINTER.
*
DATA DIVISION.
FILE SECTION.
*
FD  DISK-FILE       LABEL RECORDS OMITTED
                    DATA RECORD IS DISK-RECORD
                    RECORD CONTAINS 26 CHARACTERS.
01  DISK-RECORD.
    02 REC-STATUS-CODE     PIC 9.
       88 VACANT-RECORD    VALUE ZERO.
       88 USED-RECORD      VALUE 1.
    02 ITEM-NUMBER         PIC 9(5).
    02 ITEM-NAME           PIC X(20).
*
FD  SOURCE-FILE     LABEL RECORDS OMITTED
                    DATA RECORD IS SOURCE-RECORD.
01  SOURCE-RECORD.
    02 ITEM-NUMBER         PIC 9(5).
    02 ITEM-NAME           PIC X(20).
    02 FILLER              PIC X(55).
*
FD  PRINT-FILE      LABEL RECORDS OMITTED
                    DATA RECORD IS PRINT-RECORD.
01  PRINT-RECORD           PIC X(132).
*
WORKING-STORAGE SECTION.
*
01  END-OF-DATA-FLAG       PIC XXX.
    88 END-OF-SOURCE       VALUE 'YES'.
    88 NOT-END-OF SOURCE   VALUE ' NO'.
*
01  LOOP-FLAG              PIC XXX.
    88 FILE-IS-FULL        VALUE 'YES'.
    88 FILE-IS-NOT-FULL    VALUE 'NO '.
```

FIGURE 11-7   SAMPLE PROGRAM FOR CREATING A RELATIVE FILE.

```
01   READ-VALIDITY-FLAG      PIC XXX.
     88 VALID-READ           VALUE 'YES'.
     88 INVALID-READ         VALUE 'NO '.
*
01   LOCATION-ADDRESS        PIC 999.
01   STARTING-ADDRESS        PIC 999.
*
01   PRIME-NUMBER            PIC 99        VALUE 47.
01   WORKFIELD               PIC S99999 USAGE COMP.
01   QUOTIENT                PIC S999 USAGE COMP.
01   MAX-NO-OF-LOCATIONS     PIC 999 VALUE 50.
01   I                       PIC 999.
*
01   ERROR-RECORD.
     02 FILLER               PIC X VALUE SPACE.
     02 ERROR-LOCATION       PIC ZZ999.
     02 FILLER               PIC XX VALUE SPACE.
     02 ERR-MESSAGE          PIC X(50).
/
 PROCEDURE DIVISION.
*
 010-MAIN-ROUTINE.
     OPEN INPUT  SOURCE-FILE
     OPEN OUTPUT DISK-FILE
                 PRINT-FILE.
*
     PERFORM 020-ZERO-DISK
        VARYING I FROM 1 BY 1 UNTIL I > MAX-NO-OF-LOCATIONS.
*
     CLOSE DISK-FILE.
*
     OPEN I-O DISK-FILE
     SET NOT-END-OF-SOURCE TO TRUE
     SET FILE-IS-NOT-FULL  TO TRUE
     SET VALID-READ        TO TRUE
*
     PERFORM
           UNTIL END-OF-SOURCE
              OR FILE-IS-FULL
              OR INVALID-READ
        READ SOURCE-FILE RECORD
          AT END
              SET END-OF-SOURCE TO TRUE
          NOT AT END
              PERFORM 030-LOAD-RECORD
        END-READ
     END-PERFORM
*
     CLOSE SOURCE-FILE
           PRINT-FILE
           DISK-FILE.
     STOP RUN.
```

**FIGURE 11-7   SAMPLE PROGRAM FOR CREATING A RELATIVE FILE.
(Continued)**

```
020-ZERO-DISK.
    MOVE I TO LOCATION-ADDRESS
    MOVE ZERO TO REC-STATUS-CODE
*
    WRITE DISK-RECORD
        INVALID KEY
            MOVE 'INVALID KEY WHILE IN ZERO-DISK'
                TO ERR-MESSAGE
            PERFORM 070-CANT-ACCESS
    END-WRITE.
*
 030-LOAD-RECORD.
    PERFORM 040-RANDOMIZE-READ
    IF VALID-READ AND USED-RECORD
        MOVE LOCATION-ADDRESS TO STARTING-ADDRESS
        MOVE 'NO' TO LOOP-FLAG
        PERFORM 050-HANDLE-SYNONYMS
            UNTIL VACANT-RECORD
                OR INVALID-READ
                OR FILE-IS-FULL.
*
    IF VALID-READ AND VACANT-RECORD
        MOVE 1 TO REC-STATUS-CODE
        MOVE ITEM-NUMBER OF SOURCE-RECORD
            TO ITEM-NUMBER OF DISK-RECORD
        MOVE ITEM-NAME OF SOURCE-RECORD
            TO ITEM-NAME OF DISK-RECORD
*
        REWRITE DISK-RECORD
            INVALID KEY
                MOVE 'ERROR DURING REWRITE OPERATION'
                    TO ERR-MESSAGE
                PERFORM 070-CANT-ACCESS
                MOVE SPACES TO PRINT-RECORD
                STRING 'SOURCE RECORD INVOLVED = '
                        SOURCE-RECORD DELIMITED BY SIZE
                    INTO PRINT-RECORD
                WRITE PRINT-RECORD AFTER 2
        END-REWRITE
*
    END-IF.
```

**FIGURE 11-7   SAMPLE PROGRAM FOR CREATING A RELATIVE FILE.
(Continued)**

```
040-RANDOMIZE-READ.
    MOVE ITEM-NUMBER OF SOURCE-RECORD TO WORKFIELD
    DIVIDE PRIME-NUMBER INTO WORKFIELD GIVING QUOTIENT
    COMPUTE LOCATION-ADDRESS =
        WORKFIELD - (PRIME-NUMBER * QUOTIENT) + 1
*
*COULD ALSO WRITE THE FOLLOWING INSTEAD OF COMPUTE:
*   DIVIDE PRIME-NUMBER INTO WORKFIELD GIVING QUOTIENT
*       REMAINDER LOCATION-ADDRESS
*   ADD 1 TO LOCATION-ADDRESS
*
    PERFORM 060-READ-DISK-REC.
*
050-HANDLE-SYNONYMS.
    ADD 1 TO LOCATION-ADDRESS
    IF LOCATION-ADDRESS > MAX-NO-OF-LOCATIONS
        MOVE 1 TO LOCATION-ADDRESS.
    IF LOCATION-ADDRESS = STARTING-ADDRESS
        MOVE SPACES TO PRINT-RECORD
        STRING 'FILE IS FULL; NEW RECORD IS = '
                SOURCE-RECORD DELIMITED BY SIZE
            INTO PRINT-RECORD
        WRITE PRINT-RECORD AFTER 2
        SET FILE-IS-FULL TO TRUE
    ELSE
        SET FILE-IS-NOT-FULL TO TRUE
        PERFORM 060-READ-DISK-REC.
*
060-READ-DISK-REC.
    READ DISK-FILE RECORD
        INVALID KEY
            SET INVALID-READ TO TRUE
            MOVE 'ERROR WHILE READING' TO ERR-MESSAGE
            PERFORM 070-CANT-ACCESS
        NOT INVALID KEY
            SET VALID-READ TO TRUE
    END-READ.
*
070-CANT-ACCESS.
        MOVE LOCATION-ADDRESS TO ERROR-LOCATION
        WRITE PRINT-RECORD FROM ERROR-RECORD AFTER 2.
```

**FIGURE 11-7   SAMPLE PROGRAM FOR CREATING A RELATIVE FILE.
(Continued)**

WRITE all 50 records. From the standpoint of the language, records are being updated (REWRITE) in the 030-LOAD-RECORD paragraph.

As a final point, notice the two special cases handled in the 050-HANDLE-SYNONYMS paragraph. By the IF LOCATION-ADDRESS > MAX-NO-OF-LOCATIONS we MOVE 1 to LOCATION-ADDRESS in order to "wrap around" the file. Also, by the IF LOCATION-ADDRESS = STARTING-ADDRESS we recognize the FILE-IS-FULL condition, and the program then terminates execution because of the PERFORM UNTIL . . . OR FILE-IS-FULL in 010-MAIN-ROUTINE.

AN EXAMPLE OF UPDATING A RELATIVE FILE

We illustrate the use of relative file organization by a sample program that updates the file created by the program in Figure 11–7. Figures 11–8 and 11–9 present the structure chart and the corresponding program for the update task.

Transaction records are submitted through a TRANS-FILE. In each transaction record, there is a code indicating the type of transaction:

```
01   TRANS-REC.
     02   TRANS-CODE          PIC 9.
          88   ADD-TRANS       VALUE ZERO.
          88   DELETE-TRANS    VALUE 1.
          88   MODIFY-TRANS    VALUE 2.
          88   ERROR-TRANS     VALUES 3 THRU 9.
     02   ITEM-NUMBER         PIC 9(5).
     02   ITEM-NAME           PIC X(20).
     02   FILLER              PIC X(54).
```

An ADD-TRANS indicates the addition of a new record to the disk file, a DELETE-TRANS indicates the deletion of a record existing in the file, while a MODIFY-TRANS represents a change in the ITEM-NAME of the disk record.

It should be noted that disk records are specified by the following description:

```
01   DISK-RECORD.
     02   REC-STATUS-CODE     PIC 9.
          88   VACANT-RECORD    VALUE ZERO.
          88   USED-RECORD      VALUE 1.
          88   DELETED-RECORD   VALUE 2.
     02   ITEM-NUMBER         PIC 9(5).
     02   ITEM-NAME           PIC X(20).
```

When a record is deleted, the REC-STATUS-CODE for that record space is set equal to 2. On any subsequent occasion, we can identify the fact

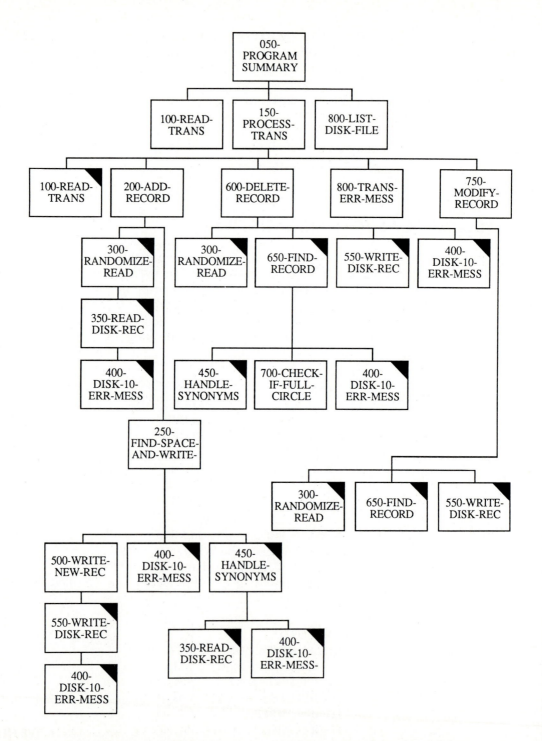

FIGURE 11-8 **STRUCTURE CHART FOR THE RELATIVE FILE UPDATE PROGRAM.**

```
       IDENTIFICATION DIVISION.
       PROGRAM-ID. REL-UPDATE.
*
       ENVIRONMENT DIVISION.
       CONFIGURATION SECTION.
       SOURCE-COMPUTER. ABC-480.
       OBJECT-COMPUTER. ABC-480.
*
       INPUT-OUTPUT SECTION.
       FILE-CONTROL.
           SELECT DISK-FILE   ASSIGN TO DISK
                              ORGANIZATION IS RELATIVE
                              ACCESS MODE IS RANDOM
                              RELATIVE KEY IS LOCATION-ADDRESS.
*
           SELECT TRANS-FILE ASSIGN TO READER.
           SELECT PRINT-FILE ASSIGN TO PRINTER.
*
       DATA DIVISION.
       FILE SECTION.
*
       FD   DISK-FILE      LABEL RECORDS OMITTED
                           DATA RECORD IS DISK-RECORD
                           RECORD CONTAINS 26 CHARACTERS.
       01   DISK-RECORD.
            02   REC-STATUS-CODE PIC 9.
                 88 VACANT-RECORD  VALUE ZERO.
                 88 USED-RECORD    VALUE 1.
                 88 DELETED-RECORD VALUE 2.
            02 ITEM-NUMBER    PIC 9(5).
            02 ITEM-NAME      PIC X(20).
*
       FD   TRANS-FILE     LABEL RECORDS OMITTED
                           DATA RECORD IS TRANS-REC.
       01   TRANS-REC.
            02 TRANS-CODE      PIC 9.
               88 ADD-TRANS     VALUE ZERO.
               88 DELETE-TRANS VALUE 1.
               88 MODIFY-TRANS VALUE 2.
               88 ERROR-TRANS  VALUES 3 THRU 9.
            02 ITEM-NUMBER     PIC 9(5).
            02 ITEM-NAME       PIC X(20).
            02 FILLER          PIC X(54).
*
       FD   PRINT-FILE     LABEL RECORDS OMITTED
                           DATA RECORD IS PRINT-REC.
       01   PRINT-REC         PIC X(132).
*
       WORKING-STORAGE SECTION.
*
       01   FLAGS.
            02 END-OF-TRANS-FLAG   PIC XXX VALUE 'NO'.
               88 END-OF-TRANS     VALUE 'YES'.
```

FIGURE 11-9   SAMPLE PROGRAM FOR UPDATING A RELATIVE FILE.

```
        02 SYNONYM-LOOP-FLAG    PIC XXX VALUE 'NO'.
           88 FILE-IS-FULL       VALUE 'YES'.
           88 FILE-IS-NOT-FULL  VALUE 'NO '.
*
        02 READ-VALIDITY-FLAG   PIC 9.
           88 VALID-READ         VALUE 0.
           88 INVALID-READ       VALUE 1.
*
        02 WRITE-VALIDITY-FLAG  PIC 9.
           88 VALID-WRITE        VALUE ZERO.
           88 INVALID-WRITE      VALUE 1.
*
        02 RECORD-FOUND-FLAG    PIC 9.
           88 RECORD-FOUND       VALUE ZERO.
           88 RECORD-NOT-FOUND  VALUE 1.
           88 STILL-LOOKING      VALUE 2.
*
        02 ADD-REC-FLAG         PIC 9.
           88 RECORD-ADDED       VALUE ZERO.
           88 RECORD-NOT-ADDED  VALUE 1.
*
   01  LOCATION-ADDRESS    PIC 9(3).
   01  MAX-NO-OF-LOCATIONS PIC 9(3) VALUE 50.
   01  STARTING-ADDRESS    PIC 9(3).
   01  PRIME-NUMBER        PIC 99 VALUE 57.
   01  WORKFIELD           PIC S9(5).
   01  QUOTIENT            PIC S9(3).
*
   01  ERROR-RECORD.
       02 FILLER           PIC X VALUE SPACE.
       02 ERROR-LOCATION   PIC ZZ999.
       02 ERR-MESSAGE      PIC X(50).
/
   PROCEDURE DIVISION.
*
   050-PROGRAM-SUMMARY.
       OPEN INPUT    TRANS-FILE
       OPEN OUTPUT   PRINT-FILE
       OPEN I-O      DISK-FILE.
*
       PERFORM 100-READ-TRANS
*
       PERFORM 150-PROCESS-TRANS
            UNTIL END-OF-TRANS OR FILE-IS-FULL.
*
*  FOLLOWING IS SEQUENTIAL LISTING OF DIRECT FILE
*
       MOVE ZERO TO READ-VALIDITY-FLAG
       PERFORM 800-LIST-DISK-FILE
            VARYING LOCATION-ADDRESS FROM 1 BY 1
               UNTIL LOCATION-ADDRESS > MAX-NO-OF-LOCATIONS
                  OR INVALID-READ
```

FIGURE 11-9   SAMPLE PROGRAM FOR UPDATING A RELATIVE FILE.
(Continued)

```
        CLOSE DISK-FILE  PRINT-FILE  TRANS-FILE
*
        STOP RUN.
*
  100-READ-TRANS.
        READ TRANS-FILE RECORD
             AT END SET END-OF-TRANS TO TRUE.
*
  150-PROCESS-TRANS.
        EVALUATE TRUE
        WHEN ADD-TRANS
             PERFORM 200-ADD-RECORD
        WHEN DELETE-TRANS
             PERFORM 600-DELETE-RECORD
        WHEN MODIFY-TRANS
             PERFORM 750-MODIFY-RECORD
        WHEN OTHER
             PERFORM 800-TRANS-ERR-MESS.
*
        PERFORM 100-READ-TRANS.
*
  200-ADD-RECORD.
*
        PERFORM 300-RANDOMIZE-READ
        MOVE 1 TO ADD-REC-FLAG
        MOVE ZERO TO READ-VALIDITY-FLAG.
*
        PERFORM 250-FIND-SPACE-AND-WRITE
                UNTIL RECORD-ADDED
                     OR INVALID-READ
                     OR FILE-IS-FULL.
*
  250-FIND-SPACE-AND-WRITE.
        IF VACANT-RECORD OR DELETED-RECORD
           PERFORM 500-WRITE-NEW-REC
           MOVE ZERO TO ADD-REC-FLAG
        ELSE
           IF ITEM-NUMBER OF TRANS-REC = ITEM-NUMBER OF DISK-RECORD
              MOVE 'ATTEMPT TO ADD DUPLICATE RECORD' TO ERR-MESSAGE
              PERFORM 400-DISK-IO-ERR-MESS
              SET INVALID-READ TO TRUE
           ELSE
              PERFORM 450-HANDLE-SYNONYMS.
*
  300-RANDOMIZE-READ.
        MOVE ITEM-NUMBER OF TRANS-REC TO WORKFIELD
        DIVIDE PRIME-NUMBER INTO WORKFIELD GIVING QUOTIENT
        COMPUTE LOCATION-ADDRESS =
                WORKFIELD - (QUOTIENT * PRIME-NUMBER) + 1
```

FIGURE 11-9   SAMPLE PROGRAM FOR UPDATING A RELATIVE FILE.
(Continued)

```
         SET FILE-IS-NOT-FULL TO TRUE
         MOVE LOCATION-ADDRESS TO STARTING-ADDRESS
 *
         PERFORM 350-READ-DISK-REC.
 *
  350-READ-DISK-REC.
         READ DISK-FILE RECORD
             INVALID KEY
                 SET INVALID-READ TO TRUE
                 MOVE 'THIS RECORD LOCATION CANNOT BE READ'
                     TO ERR-MESSAGE
                 PERFORM 400-DISK-IO-ERR-MESS
             NOT INVALID KEY
                 SET VALID-READ TO TRUE
         END-READ.
 *
  400-DISK-IO-ERR-MESS.
         MOVE LOCATION-ADDRESS TO ERROR-LOCATION
         WRITE PRINT-REC FROM ERROR-RECORD AFTER 2 LINES
         MOVE SPACES TO ERROR-RECORD
         MOVE 'TRANSACTION RECORD IS' TO ERR-MESSAGE
         WRITE PRINT-REC FROM ERROR-RECORD AFTER 2 LINES
         MOVE TRANS-REC TO ERR-MESSAGE
         WRITE PRINT-REC FROM ERROR-RECORD AFTER 2 LINES.
 *
  450-HANDLE-SYNONYMS.
         SET FILE-IS-NOT-FULL TO TRUE
         ADD 1 TO LOCATION-ADDRESS
         IF LOCATION-ADDRESS GREATER THAN MAX-NO-OF-LOCATIONS
             MOVE 1 TO LOCATION-ADDRESS
         END-IF
 *
         IF LOCATION-ADDRESS = STARTING-ADDRESS
             MOVE 'ENTIRE FILE READ FULL CIRCLE' TO ERR-MESSAGE
             PERFORM 400-DISK-IO-ERR-MESS
             SET FILE-IS-FULL TO TRUE
         ELSE
             PERFORM 350-READ-DISK-REC.
 *
  500-WRITE-NEW-REC.
         MOVE 1 TO REC-STATUS-CODE
         MOVE ITEM-NUMBER OF TRANS-REC
             TO ITEM-NUMBER OF DISK-RECORD
         MOVE ITEM-NAME OF TRANS-REC
             TO ITEM-NAME OF DISK-RECORD
 *
         PERFORM 550-WRITE-DISK-REC.
```

**FIGURE 11-9   SAMPLE PROGRAM FOR UPDATING A RELATIVE FILE.
(Continued)**

```
    550-WRITE-DISK-REC.
        REWRITE DISK-RECORD
            INVALID KEY
                SET INVALID-WRITE TO TRUE
                MOVE 'THIS RECORD LOCATION CANNOT BE WRITTEN'
                    TO ERR-MESSAGE
                PERFORM 400-DISK-IO-ERR-MESS
            NOT INVALID KEY
                SET VALID-WRITE TO TRUE
        END-REWRITE.
*
    600-DELETE-RECORD.
        SET STILL-LOOKING TO TRUE
        SET VALID-READ TO TRUE
*
        PERFORM 300-RANDOMIZE-READ
*
        PERFORM 650-FIND-RECORD
                UNTIL RECORD-FOUND
                    OR RECORD-NOT-FOUND
                    OR INVALID-READ.
        IF RECORD-FOUND
            MOVE 1 TO REC-STATUS-CODE
            PERFORM 550-WRITE-DISK-REC
        ELSE
            IF RECORD-NOT-FOUND
                MOVE 'ATTEMPT TO DELETE NONEXISTENT RECORD'
                    TO ERR-MESSAGE
                PERFORM 400-DISK-IO-ERR-MESS.
    650-FIND-RECORD.
        IF VALID-READ AND USED-RECORD
            IF ITEM-NUMBER OF TRANS-REC = ITEM-NUMBER OF DISK-RECORD
                SET RECORD-FOUND TO TRUE
            ELSE
                PERFORM 450-HANDLE-SYNONYMS
                PERFORM 700-CHECK-IF-FULL-CIRCLE
        ELSE
            IF VALID-READ AND DELETED-RECORD
                PERFORM 450-HANDLE-SYNONYMS
                PERFORM 700-CHECK-IF-FULL-CIRCLE
            ELSE
                IF VALID-READ AND VACANT-RECORD
                    SET RECORD-NOT-FOUND TO TRUE
                ELSE
                    SET RECORD-NOT-FOUND TO TRUE
                    MOVE 'STATUS CODE OF DISK-REC IS INVALID'
                        TO ERR-MESSAGE
                    PERFORM 400-DISK-IO-ERR-MESS.
*
    700-CHECK-IF-FULL-CIRCLE.
        IF FILE-IS-FULL
            MOVE 'CAME FULL CIRCLE' TO ERR-MESSAGE
            PERFORM 400-DISK-IO-ERR-MESS
            SET RECORD-NOT-FOUND TO TRUE.
```

**FIGURE 11-9   SAMPLE PROGRAM FOR UPDATING A RELATIVE FILE.
(Continued)**

```
*
 750-MODIFY-RECORD.
      SET STILL-LOOKING TO TRUE
      SET VALID-READ TO TRUE
      PERFORM 300-RANDOMIZE-READ.
*
      PERFORM 650-FIND-RECORD
              UNTIL RECORD-FOUND
                    OR RECORD-NOT-FOUND
                    OR INVALID-READ.
*
      IF RECORD-FOUND
         THEN
            MOVE ITEM-NAME OF TRANS-REC TO ITEM-NAME OF DISK-RECORD
            PERFORM 550-WRITE-DISK-REC
         ELSE
            IF RECORD-NOT-FOUND
               THEN
                  MOVE 'ATTEMPT TO MODIFY NONEXISTENT RECORD'
                       TO ERR-MESSAGE
                  PERFORM 400-DISK-IO-ERR-MESS
               ELSE
                  NEXT SENTENCE
            END-IF
      END-IF.

 800-TRANS-ERR-MESS.
      MOVE SPACES TO ERROR-RECORD
      MOVE 'THIS TRANSACTION HAS INVALID-CODE' TO ERR-MESSAGE
      WRITE PRINT-REC FROM ERROR-RECORD AFTER 2 LINES
      MOVE TRANS-REC TO ERR-MESSAGE
      WRITE PRINT-REC FROM ERROR-RECORD AFTER 2 LINES.
*
 850-LIST-DISK-FILE.
      READ DISK-FILE RECORD
         INVALID KEY
              SET INVALID-READ TO TRUE
         NOT INVALID KEY
              WRITE PRINT-REC FROM DISK-RECORD AFTER 1.
```

**FIGURE 11-9   SAMPLE PROGRAM FOR UPDATING A RELATIVE FILE.
(Continued)**

that the record space is available for a new record, and we ignore it when looking for synonyms, as explained in the first section of this chapter. For instance, suppose that a transaction record specifies deletion of an item-number. In the 600-DELETE-RECORD paragraph of Figure 11–9, we see that we PERFORM 300-RANDOMIZE-READ to compute the home address of the item record and then read the record at the home address. Then we say:

PERFORM 650-FIND-RECORD
    UNTIL RECORD-FOUND OR RECORD-NOT-FOUND
    OR INVALID-READ.

In the 650-FIND-RECORD paragraph, we first check to determine if the record space at the home address is occupied (IF USED-RECORD). If it is occupied, we check to determine if the ITEM-NUMBER in the transaction record matches the one in the disk record, in which case that is the record to be deleted. If the record space is occupied but does not contain the record that we want, then the 650-FIND-RECORD paragraph PERFORMs 450-HANDLE-SYNONYMS. As a result, the next disk record is read and we repeat the process under control of the PERFORM 650-FIND-RECORD UNTIL . . . loop in the 600-DELETE-RECORD paragraph.

Continuing our analysis of the 650-FIND-RECORD paragraph, note that we say IF VALID-READ AND DELETED-RECORD PERFORM 450-HANDLE-SYNONYMS PERFORM 700-CHECK-IF-FULL-CIRCLE. If there is a deleted record, we simply PERFORM 450-HANDLE-SYNONYMS in order to move to the next disk record space on the relative file. The 700-CHECK-IF-FULL-CIRCLE procedure prevents us from searching the entire file repeatedly for a nonexisting record, in the case where all the records are occupied or vacant from deletions only. Notice that the 650-FIND-RECORD terminates SET RECORD-NOT-FOUND TO TRUE when a vacant record is encountered (IF VALID-READ AND VACANT-RECORD), since such an occurrence indicates that the record does not exist.

The program is substantially self-documenting, and the reader should be able to review it and follow the details. The overall task is typical of most such update programs, and the sample program can be used as the basic structure for most of them.

USING BUCKETS WITH RELATIVE FILES

Relative files can be very efficient for the purpose of achieving direct access to records. However, such files can be associated with serious inefficiencies if synonym chains are very long, thereby causing multiple disk access for each logical I/O operation. As we have discussed, choice of an appropriate hashing procedure is one critical factor that affects synonyms. A second factor under our control is the file density; by decreasing the packing factor and allowing more unused space, the probability of generating synonyms is decreased.

A third tool for controlling synonyms is the use of the concept of a "bucket." A bucket is really a block of records. From the standpoint of this approach, a file is considered to consist of a number of buckets, with each bucket capable of holding a certain number of records. The hashing procedure is based on buckets rather than individual records. As a result, the incidence of effective synonyms is reduced. For example, if a bucket size of five records is defined, a synonym would be generated only when six or more records hashed to the same bucket.

The concept of using buckets works (1) because of the difference in speed between accessing a record on disk versus processing records in central storage, and (2) because once an I/O operation begins, data transfer rates are high compared to the time that it takes to get ready to carry out an I/O operation.

Let us consider an example to help explain how these concepts work. Suppose that a bucket size of five records is defined for a file that has already been created. We are about to read a record. The home address of the record is computed as a bucket number, and the entire bucket of five records is read from the disk in one READ operation. The bucket is a table in central storage, and it is searched to determine if it contains the desired record. Searching a table in central storage is very fast compared with reading multiple times from a disk. For example, if the given record and three other records happen to be synonyms, all four records would be in the same bucket and be accessed by one disk operation. On the other hand, in the absence of a bucket, as many as four disk reads could be required to access one particular record when there are four synonyms. It is true that with a bucket size of five, every disk read (or write) requires five times the number of bytes as accessing an individual record does. However, data transfer rates are very high. What is relatively slow is the time needed for initiating a read operation, due to the rotational delay of the disk and the time required to move from one cylinder or track to the next cylinder or track.

If the use of buckets is a good thing, the question then is how large a bucket should be in terms of number of records. Conceptually, we might try to balance the opposing factors of data transfer rates as contrasted to access times to disk. However, a practical approach is to consider the track size of the disks being used and aim for a bucket size that approaches the track size. Remember, though, that file I/O areas are double-buffered in most operating systems, so that for each relative file in use, the total I/O buffer size will be double the bucket size. This consideration may lead to the conclusion that the bucket size should be smaller than the track size. Finally, it is a general rule that a bucket size divided into a track size should yield an integer, to avoid unused track portions or spanned records across tracks.

In order to illustrate use of the bucket concept, Figure 11–10 is a mod-

```
IDENTIFICATION DIVISION.
PROGRAM-ID. RELATIVE-CREATE.
*
ENVIRONMENT DIVISION.
CONFIGURATION SECTION.
SOURCE-COMPUTER. ABC-480.
OBJECT-COMPUTER. ABC-480.
INPUT-OUTPUT SECTION.
FILE-CONTROL.
    SELECT DISK-FILE    ASSIGN TO DISK
                        ORGANIZATION IS RELATIVE
                        ACCESS MODE IS RANDOM
                        RELATIVE KEY IS LOCATION-ADDRESS.
*
    SELECT SOURCE-FILE  ASSIGN TO READER.
    SELECT PRINT-FILE   ASSIGN TO PRINTER.
*
DATA DIVISION.
FILE SECTION.
*
FD  DISK-FILE       LABEL RECORDS STANDARD
                    DATA RECORD IS DISK-RECORD
                    RECORD CONTAINS 127 CHARACTERS.
01  DISK-RECORDS-BUCKET.
    02  BUCKET-STATUS-CODE  PIC 9.
        88 VACANT-BUCKET     VALUE ZERO.
        88 USED-BUCKET       VALUE 1.
    02  NO-OF-RECS-IN-BUCKET PIC 9.
        88 FULL-BUCKET       VALUE 5.
*
    02  DISK-RECORD  OCCURS 5 TIMES.
        03 ITEM-NUMBER       PIC 9(5).
        03 ITEM-NAME         PIC X(20).
*
FD  SOURCE-FILE     LABEL RECORDS OMITTED
                    DATA RECORD IS SOURCE-RECORD.
01  SOURCE-RECORD.
    02 SOURCE-ITEM-NUMBER   PIC 9(5).
    02 SOURCE-ITEM-NAME     PIC X(20).
    02 FILLER               PIC X(55).
*
FD  PRINT-FILE      LABEL RECORDS OMITTED
                    DATA RECORD IS PRINT-RECORD.
01  PRINT-RECORD            PIC X(132).
*
WORKING-STORAGE SECTION.
*
01  END-OF-DATA-FLAG        PIC XXX.
    88 END-OF-SOURCE        VALUE 'YES'.
    88 NOT-END-OF-SOURCE    VALUE 'NO '.
```

FIGURE 11-10   SAMPLE PROGRAM TO CREATE A RELATIVE FILE WITH THE USE OF THE BUCKET CONCEPT.

```
01    READ-VALIDITY-FLAG      PIC XXX.
      88 VALID-READ           VALUE 'YES'.
      88 INVALID-READ         VALUE 'NO '.
*
01    LOOP-FLAG               PIC XXX.
      88 FILE-IS-FULL         VALUE 'YES'.
      88 FILE-IS-NOT-FULL     VALUE 'NO '.
*
01    LOCATION-ADDRESS        PIC 999.
01    STARTING-ADDRESS        PIC 999.
01    PRIME-NUMBER            PIC 9         VALUE 7.
01    WORKFIELD               PIC S99999 USAGE COMP.
01    QUOTIENT                PIC S999    USAGE COMP.
01    MAX-NO-OF-LOCATIONS     PIC 999       VALUE 10.
01    I                       PIC 999.
*
01    ERROR-RECORD.
      02 FILLER               PIC X VALUE SPACE.
      02 ERROR-LOCATION       PIC ZZ999.
      02 FILLER               PIC XX VALUE SPACE.
      02 ERR-MESSAGE          PIC X(50).
/
 PROCEDURE DIVISION.
*
 010-MAIN-ROUTINE.
     OPEN INPUT  SOURCE-FILE
     OPEN OUTPUT DISK-FILE
                 PRINT-FILE.
*
     PERFORM 020-ZERO-DISK
         VARYING I FROM 1 BY 1 UNTIL I > MAX-NO-OF-LOCATIONS.
*
     CLOSE DISK-FILE.
*
     OPEN I-O DISK-FILE
     SET NOT-END-OF-SOURCE TO TRUE
     SET FILE-IS-NOT-FULL  TO TRUE
     SET VALID-READ        TO TRUE
     PERFORM  UNTIL END-OF-SOURCE
                 OR INVALID-READ
                 OR FILE-IS-FULL
         READ SOURCE-FILE RECORD
            AT END
                SET END-OF-SOURCE TO TRUE
            NOT AT END
                PERFORM 030-LOAD-RECORD
         END-READ
     END-PERFORM.
*
     CLOSE SOURCE-FILE
           PRINT-FILE
           DISK-FILE.
     STOP RUN.
```

FIGURE 11-10   SAMPLE PROGRAM TO CREATE A RELATIVE FILE WITH THE USE OF THE BUCKET CONCEPT.   (Continued)

```
 020-ZERO-DISK.
      MOVE I TO LOCATION-ADDRESS
      MOVE SPACES TO DISK-RECORDS-BUCKET
      MOVE ZERO TO BUCKET-STATUS-CODE
      MOVE ZERO TO NO-OF-RECS-IN-BUCKET
*
      WRITE DISK-RECORD
          INVALID KEY
              MOVE 'INVALID KEY DURING ZERO-DISK' TO ERR-MESSAGE
              PERFORM 070-CANT-ACCESS
      END-WRITE.
*
 030-LOAD-RECORD.
      PERFORM 040-RANDOMIZE-READ
*
      IF VALID-READ AND USED-BUCKET
          MOVE LOCATION-ADDRESS TO STARTING-ADDRESS
          SET FILE-IS-NOT-FULL TO TRUE
          PERFORM 050-HANDLE-SYNONYMS
              UNTIL INVALID-READ
                  OR VACANT-BUCKET
                  OR FILE-IS-FULL.
*
      IF VALID-READ AND VACANT-BUCKET
          ADD 1 TO NO-OF-RECS-IN-BUCKET
          IF FULL-BUCKET
              MOVE 1 TO BUCKET-STATUS-CODE
          END-IF
          MOVE SOURCE-ITEM-NUMBER
              TO ITEM-NUMBER (NO-OF-RECS-IN-BUCKET)
          MOVE SOURCE-ITEM-NAME
              TO ITEM-NAME (NO-OF-RECS-IN-BUCKET)
          REWRITE DISK-RECORD
              INVALID KEY
                  MOVE 'ERROR DURING REWRITE' TO ERR-MESSAGE
                  PERFORM 070-CANT-ACCESS
                  STRING 'SOURCE RECORD INVOLVED = '
                      SOURCE-RECORD DELIMITED BY SIZE
                  INTO PRINT-RECORD
                  WRITE PRINT-RECORD AFTER 2
          END-REWRITE
      ELSE
          NEXT SENTENCE.
*
 040-RANDOMIZE-READ.
      MOVE SOURCE-ITEM-NUMBER TO WORKFIELD
      DIVIDE PRIME-NUMBER INTO WORKFIELD GIVING QUOTIENT
      COMPUTE LOCATION-ADDRESS =
          WORKFIELD - (PRIME-NUMBER * QUOTIENT) + 1
*
      PERFORM 060-READ-DISK-REC.
```

FIGURE 11-10   SAMPLE PROGRAM TO CREATE A RELATIVE FILE WITH THE USE OF THE BUCKET CONCEPT.   (Continued)

```
050-HANDLE-SYNONYMS.
    ADD 1 TO LOCATION-ADDRESS
    IF LOCATION-ADDRESS > MAX-NO-OF-LOCATIONS
       MOVE 1 TO LOCATION-ADDRESS
    END-IF
    IF LOCATION-ADDRESS = STARTING-ADDRESS
       THEN
           MOVE SPACES TO PRINT-RECORD
           STRING 'FILE IS FULL; NEW RECORD IS = '
               SOURCE-RECORD DELIMITED BY SIZE
           INTO PRINT-RECORD
           WRITE PRINT-RECORD AFTER 2
           SET FILE-IS-FULL TO TRUE
       ELSE
           SET FILE-IS-NOT-FULL TO TRUE
           PERFORM 060-READ-DISK-REC
    END-IF.
*
060-READ-DISK-REC.
    READ DISK-FILE RECORD
       INVALID KEY
          MOVE 'ERROR WHILE READING ' TO ERR-MESSAGE
          PERFORM CANT-ACCESS
          SET INVALID-READ TO TRUE
       NOT INVALID KEY
          SET VALID-READ TO TRUE
    END-READ.
*
070-CANT-ACCESS.
    MOVE LOCATION-ADDRESS TO ERROR-LOCATION
    WRITE PRINT-RECORD FROM ERROR-RECORD AFTER 2.
```

**FIGURE 11-10   SAMPLE PROGRAM TO CREATE A RELATIVE FILE WITH THE
USE OF THE BUCKET CONCEPT.   (Continued)**

ification of the program presented in Figure 11-7 to create a relative file. For
ease of reference, repeated below is the file description that is concerned
with the bucket:

FD	DISK-FILE LABEL RECORDS STANDARD	
	DATA RECORD IS DISK-RECORD	
	RECORD CONTAINS 127 CHARACTERS.	
01	DISK-RECORDS-BUCKET.	
02	BUCKET-STATUS-CODE	PIC 9.
	88 VACANT-BUCKET	VALUE ZERO.
	88 USED-BUCKET	VALUE 1.
02	NO-OF-RECS-IN-BUCKET	PIC 9.
	88 FULL-BUCKET	VALUE 5.
02	DISK-RECORD OCCURS 5 TIMES.	
	03 ITEM-NUMBER	PIC 9(5).
	03 ITEM-NAME	PIC X(20).

The BUCKET-STATUS-CODE refers to the entire bucket. A bucket has a vacancy if there are four or fewer records stored in it, and it is full if it contains five records. The field NO-OF-RECS-IN-BUCKET is used to keep track of how many records are in the bucket. The FULL-BUCKET and USED-BUCKET condition-names are apparently redundant, leading to the thought that NO-OF-RECS-IN-BUCKET with suitable condition-names could serve the role of BUCKET-STATUS-CODE as well. While such is the case for this program, it would not be true for an updating program, such as the one in Figure 11–9. Because of the need to know "delete" status codes for a bucket when files are being updated, it makes sense to use two "marker" fields in each bucket.

Again, keep in mind that the bucket *is* the record from the standpoint of the COBOL language and the operating system. It is up to the programming logic to "split" the bucket into five records during processing. Accordingly, in the DATA DIVISION included in Figure 11–10 notice that PRIME-NUMBER is initialized to 7 and MAX-NO-OF-LOCATIONS is initialized to 10. This corresponds to the total of 50 records in Figure 11–7 (10 buckets x 5 records = 50).

In order to initialize each bucket to an empty state, the 020-ZERO-DISK paragraph in Figure 11–10 moves a zero value to both the BUCKET-STATUS-CODE and the NO-OF-RECS-IN-BUCKET fields.

Finally, in the 030-LOAD-RECORD paragraph, notice that we ADD 1 TO NO-OF-RECS-IN-BUCKET as we are about to add a new record, and then that incremented value is used as a subscript. Also, if the bucket is full, we set BUCKET-STATUS-CODE to the appropriate value so that the bucket will be sensed as being full on any subsequent occasion. Again, a bucket is not full until all five record locations are filled.

Incorporating the bucket concept in an update procedure is described in Exercise 11.7.

Review

1   A "bucket" essentially is a block, or group, of _____.

records

2   When a bucket of, say, five records is read, it is entered into central _____ where a search is then made for the particular _____ that is desired.

storage; record

3   The size of the bucket that is used should generally be [smaller/larger] than the track size.

smaller

4   In program processing, a bucket with a record size of five records is full only when there are _____ records stored in it.

five

EXERCISES

11.1   Do a digit analysis of the following set of customer account numbers: 8023, 9178, 9034, 8187, 8056, 9162, 9019.

11.2   Based on the digit analysis in Exercise 11.1, above, describe a key-to-address transformation method for a file that consists of 100 customer accounts. Demonstrate the procedure by computing the address for account numbers 8023 and 3456.

11.3   Outline what changes would be needed in the sample program for creating a relative file in Figure 11-7 to guarantee that there will be no duplicate records in the file. A duplicate record is one that has the same key as another record in the file.

11.4   Outline what changes would be needed in the sample program for creating and updating a relative file in Figure 11-9 to guarantee that there will be no duplicate records in the file. A duplicate record is one that has the same key as another record in the file.

11.5   Refer to Exercise 8-4 for the program description.
   a   Create the master file as a relative file, using the part number as the RELATIVE KEY.
   b   Update the master file on a random basis, using the part number as the RELATIVE KEY.

11.6   A manufacturer of three product classes has a sales force consisting of 100 salespeople, each person assigned a unique salesperson number of 5 digits. Salespeople are paid on commission, receiving monthly commission benefits as well as an annual bonus based on monthly performance. We want to maintain commission data for each salesperson, by product class and by month, on a disk file.
   a   Create a relative file that will contain a record of the commission data for each salesperson in the following form. Salesperson number will serve for the RELATIVE KEY.

FIELD	FIELD SIZE
Salesperson number	5 digits
Salesperson-name	
Last name	15 characters
First name	10 characters
Middle initial	1 character
Commission totals by product class (3 classes) and by month (12 months).	Each total can be as large as 999,999.99. Note: There will be 36 totals.

The file is created by reading one record per salesperson, containing the salesperson-number and salesperson-name fields. After the randomizing technique has been employed to determine the disk location, all commission totals (36 fields) are set to zero. Then the record is written on the disk.

b   Update this file, using sales transaction data. Use the salesperson number as the RELATIVE KEY.

The transaction records have the following layout:

COLUMNS	FIELD
1-5	Salesperson number
6	Commission code (based on product class)
	1 = 0.02 of sales
	2 = 0.03 of sales
	3 = 0.05 of sales
7-8	Month code (from 01 to 12)
9-14	Sales values in dollars and cents

Assume that the transaction records are sorted by salesperson number; therefore, we need to access the relevant master record only once for each set of records corresponding to one salesperson. Of course, we may have transactions for only *some* of the salespeople.

As each salesperson is processed, we want to print on the printer a report, as follows:

CURRENT COMMISSION DATA			
		TOTALS	
SALESPERSON NUMBER	SALESPERSON-NAME	THIS MONTH	YEAR-TO-DATE
12345	LAST, FIRST, M.	$ 870.35	$18,562.40
24966	LAST, FIRST, M.	1020.20	12,112.96
.	.	.	.
.	.	.	.
.	.	.	.

In other words, we want to accumulate the commissions, regardless of product class, for the current month; as well as the year-to-date totals for all months through the present one.

11.7   Modify the sample program for updating a relative file in Figure 11.9 to incorporate the concept of a bucket. Use a bucket size of five records.

When a record is deleted from a bucket and it is not the last record in the table, shift the remaining records so that the "top" of the table is packed. In other words, do not leave any gaps in the table of records that constitutes a bucket.

IV Special topics

12

SUBPROGRAMS AND NESTED PROGRAMS

INTRODUCTION

The PERFORM verb is one basic control mechanism for implementing modular program structure. Still, it is often desirable to program a task in terms of one main program and one or more subprograms. In such a structure, the main program is the executable program. Subprograms can be written and compiled independently, but they can be executed only in conjunction with a main program. There are three basic reasons why subprograms are desirable:

1   Whenever a task is either too large for one person or the time available requires the formation of a project team, subprograms are a natural way of partitioning one task among several per-

sons. Because subprograms can be compiled independently, each team member can work individually to develop and test a portion of the total task. Communication among the team members is limited to brief coordinative activities assigned to a chief programmer who is responsible for the overall project design and for effective and efficient interfacing between subtasks partitioned out as a subprograms.

2   There is a frequent need to incorporate the same task into more than one program. In such a case, a subprogram that is written and tested once can be recorded in a program library and can be used by several programs, thus avoiding the "reinvention-of-the-wheel" syndrome.

3   When using subprograms we can identify the data items specifically involved with the functions performed by each individual subprogram. In contrast, there is only one DATA DIVISION in each program, and it contains a description of the data for all modules in the program, as a group.

When using subprograms, there is one main program and one or more subprograms. The main program initiates and controls execution of the entire job, including the execution of subprograms, and eventually terminates the job. A given subprogram may be called into execution by the main program or it may be called by another subprogram; however, in a given program there must be at least one call issued by the main program, and that must be the first call. After that point, subprograms may call each other—although they cannot call themselves (recursion is not allowed). You may have noticed the use of the word "call." It is standard terminology in reference to subprogram execution, and it is implemented in COBOL through the verb CALL.

Review

1   In lieu of using the PERFORM verb, modular program structure can be implemented by writing separate _____.

subprograms

2   The use of subprograms makes the partitioning of a programming task among several individuals [easier/more difficult].

easier

3   A subprogram [can/cannot] be used easily in conjunction with different programs.

can

4   When a subprogram is written, the data involved in that subprogram are described specifically in the DATA DIVISION of the [main program / subprogram].

subprogram

CALLING AND CALLED PROGRAMS

Whenever subprograms are in use we have one so-called *main* program and one or more subprograms. The main program is the executable program; execution of all subprograms is under the explicit or implicit control of the main program. Figure 12-1 illustrates the program execution process. Execution begins with the first executable statement in the main program and continues in that program until a CALL statement is encountered. The CALL statement transfers control to the subprograms referenced in the CALL statement, such as CALL A in Figure 12-1.

After the CALL is encountered, program execution continues within

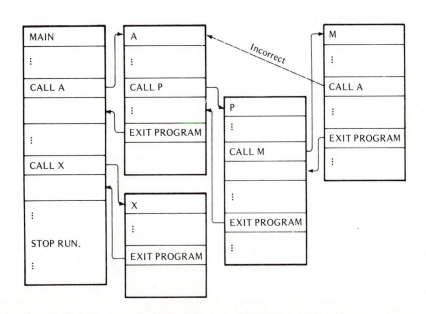

FIGURE 12-1   CORRECT AND INCORRECT SUBPROGRAM CALLS.

the called subprogram until an EXIT PROGRAM command is encountered, which then returns program execution and control to the statement immediately following the original CALL. EXIT PROGRAM is a COBOL statement that has the meaning "return to the calling program." A CALL is in essence a "Go to and Return" command.

As shown in Figure 12–1, a subprogram such as A may contain CALL statements to other subprograms, such as P in the example. In such a case A is the *calling* program and P is the *called* program. These two terms are more appropriate general terminology than the terms *main* and *subprogram*, since often a subprogram may serve as the controlling program for another subprogram. Of course, in any executable *run unit* (or *job*) there must be one main (calling) program which must not be called. It initiates and terminates the run unit, and all subprograms are controlled by it, either directly or indirectly. In Figure 12–1 notice that after every CALL in the main program there is a return arrow to that program, and the main program is the only one that contains a STOP RUN statement.

In Figure 12–1 the combination of the CALL M statement in subprogram P and the CALL A statement in subprogram M illustrate an improper calling structure, as designated by the broken line. A subprogram may not be called by its dependents even directly, as in the case in the example.

Subprograms are *linked-edited* with the main program to form a run unit, or job. A COBOL subprogram is compiled and translated into object-program form, and can be used immediately after compilation or can be saved in a *load library* for future use. In either case, the link-edit processor will combine object-form subprograms together with the main program to form an executable job. The process is specified via Job Control Language statements.

One type of job control setup is to submit the main program and the subprograms in source language form, compile each one into object form, use the link-edit processor to build an executable module (also called *load module*), and then execute the job. This approach is not common, and it is not recommended because it involves recompilation of every program (calling and called) every time.

Another, more common, job stream setup is to compile subprograms and save them in a library in object form. Then job control statements include reference to this library so that the link-editor can access the modules needed. Most systems have facilities to create a load module library that contains the result of the link-edit process, which is, in turn, an executable job stream. Modules (subprograms) then may be added or deleted in such a load library without the need to recompile and link-edit the whole job.

The procedures for handling subprograms are specific to each system and each computer site, and the reader will need to obtain specific instruction with respect to any given computer system.

Considering the job execution phase, the main program and the subprograms are loaded into storage, as illustrated conceptually in Figure 12–2. The link-editor builds a storage layout where the main and the subprograms then are located relative to one other. (The actual physical storage layout is dependent on the operating system and will be dynamically varied

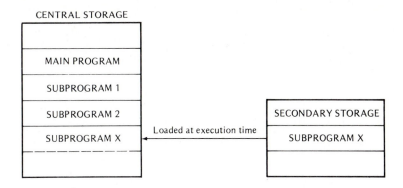

FIGURE 12–2   STORAGE LAYOUT OF SUBPROGRAMS.

during program execution due to *swapping* and/or *virtual storage paging* operations.)

As Figure 12–2 also illustrates, a subprogram may not be physically loaded into main storage until it is needed. The subprogram is held in secondary storage and is brought into and out of main storage dynamically, in order to save central storage space. This is accomplished by writing the CALL statements so that they have the format "CALL identifier." The identifier will have a value during execution which refers to a specific subprogram. By this procedure, at link-edit time the processor does not know which subprogram to actually link into the run unit. Linkage is instead performed dynamically during execution. To illustrate this concept, suppose that there are two subprograms for payroll processing: HOURLY and SALARIED. In a calling program we may have:

```
IF condition
     MOVE 'HOURLY' TO SUB-NAME
ELSE
     MOVE 'SALARIED' TO SUB-NAME.
CALL SUB-NAME . . .
```

The call statement does not specify explicitly the subprogram to be called. The value in SUB-NAME is dependent on specific conditions during program execution.

We conclude this section by providing an outline of COBOL statements and program layouts used in subprograms. Figure 12–3 provides such an overview. In the calling program (which may or may not be a main program) there is a CALL statement that references a subprogram and the data names used to pass data to and from the subprogram. In the called program the PROGRAM-ID contains the name by which the calling program calls the called program ('SUBPR' in this example). In the DATA DIVISION, there is a LINKAGE SECTION that contains data descriptions for the data-names that are used to pass data to and from the subprogram. The PROCEDURE DIVISION header involves the USING clause followed by a list of data-names

Calling Program	Called Program
IDENTIFICATION DIVISION.	IDENTIFICATION DIVISION.
PROGRAM-ID. MAINPROG.	PROGRAM-ID. SUBPR.
ENVIRONMENT DIVISION.	ENVIRONMENT DIVISION.
.	.
.	.
.	.
DATA DIVISION.	DATA DIVISION.
FILE SECTION.	FILE SECTION.
.	.
.	.
.	.
FD FILE-1 . . .	FD FILE-M . . .
01 F-REC . . .	.
.	.
.	.
.	.
WORKING-STORAGE SECTION.	WORKING-STORAGE SECTION.
.	.
.	.
.	.
77 ABC . . .	77 FIELD-A . . .
01 XYZ . . .	.
LINKAGE SECTION.	01 FIELD-B . . .
[only if a subprogram]	LINKAGE SECTION.
.	77 PART-NO . . .
.	01 V-CODE . . .
PROCEDURE DIVISION.	01 DATA-REC . . .
.	
.	PROCEDURE DIVISION USING DATA-REC
CALL 'SUBPR' USING F-REC	PART-NO
ABC	V-CODE.
XYZ.	.
	.
	RETURN-P.
.	EXIT PROGRAM.
.	

FIGURE 12-3   CALLING-CALLED PROGRAM OUTLINE.

that correspond to the ones in the CALL statement of the calling program (possibly using different names, as in the example). Finally, there is an EXIT PROGRAM statement that serves to return control to the calling program.

Review

1   When subprograms are used there are always only one _____ program and one or more _____.

main; subprograms

2   The command that transfers program control from the main program to the subprogram is the _____ statement.

CALL

3   The command that returns program execution and control from the subprogram back to the main program is the _____ statement.

EXIT PROGRAM

4   A subprogram that has been called by a main program [may/may not] contain CALL statements to other subprograms.

may

5   When subprogram B includes a CALL to subprogram C, B is referred to as the _____ program and C is referred to as the _____ program.

calling; called

6   With respect to the relationship among the main program and several subprograms, the main program itself can [sometimes/never] be the object of a CALL statement.

never

7   With respect to the relationship between a subprogram that is a calling program and the other called programs, the calling program can [sometimes / never] be called by its dependents.

never

8   Object-form subprograms are combined with the main program to form an executable job by the _____ processor.

link-edit

9   Linkage of a subprogram with a main program is said to be performed dynamically during program execution when the CALL statement [does/does not] specify explicitly the subprogram to be called.

does not

SUBPROGRAM DATA LINKAGE

A subprogram may contain a FILE and a WORKING-STORAGE SECTION in its DATA DIVISION. In addition, there may be a LINKAGE SECTION which contains data descriptions for items that serve as arguments in a subprogram call. In the typical case, arguments are data items that send data to a subprogram or receive data from a subprogram. For example, assume that we have a simplified subprogram whose function is to receive two numbers and return their sum to the calling program. The CALL will need as arguments the two fields containing the numbers and a third field to return the sum. Further, there could be a fourth argument which is used to indicate whether some wrong condition exists, such as nonnumeric data in the incoming values or an arithmetic overflow condition.

The list of arguments both in the CALL statement and in the PROCEDURE DIVISION header of the subprogram. For example, we could have:

Calling program: CALL 'SUM-SUB' USING AMT-1, AMT-2, TOTAL, OK-FLAG

Called program: PROCEDURE DIVISION USING A, B, TOT, FLAG.

The lines inserted above serve to clarify the correspondence between arguments. For example, a reference to AMT-1 in the calling program and a reference to A in the called program are references to the same storage area. If either the calling program specifies MOVE ZERO TO AMT-1 or the called program specifies MOVE ZERO TO A the field represented will be set to zero. It is important to write the arguments in the CALL and in the PROCEDURE DIVISION header of the subprogram in the right order, so that correct references are made.

When a subprogram is compiled, statements that involve items in the LINKAGE SECTION are not translated to addresses in the usual way. For instance, for the example we have been discussing, MOVE ZERO TO TOT in the subprogram would in concept be translated to: "Move zero to the field whose beginning address will be identified by the third argument in the CALL statement and whose data description is provided in the LINKAGE SECTION under the name TOT." One of the functions of the link-editor is to specify the address of linkage items. For example, if the CALL was written as CALL 'SUM-SUB' USING AMT-1, AMT-2, TOTAL, OK-FLAG, and if TOTAL was stored beginning with location 1,000, the MOVE ZERO TO TOT statement in the subprogram would be modified to: "Move zero to the field be-

ginning at address 1,000, whose data description is under TOT in the LINK-
AGE SECTION."

It is important to keep in mind that the (beginning) address of the arguments is passed by the calling program, but it is the LINKAGE SECTION
that describes the size and the data characteristics of the fields. Consider the
illustration in Figure 12–4 as to why it is important to have consistent data
definitions.

In Figure 12–4, notice that A has PIC X(4) but X has PIC X(5). If we assume that A and B were stored by the compiler next to each other, the
MOVE X TO . . . in the subprogram would move 'MARY3', since it refers to a
move of 5 characters. However, the second move, MOVE Y TO . . . would
correctly move '321', since the data descriptions in the calling and the called
programs are consistent.

The important point to observe is that it is the size of the data involved that is crucial to maintain consistency between the calling and the
called program. The specific descriptions can vary according to the needs in
each case. Figure 12–5 illustrates the point. Notice that X has PIC X(20) in the
calling program, but A is broken down into several subfields whose PIC sizes
add up to 20. Also notice that table data may be specified in either program
with or without OCCURS descriptors. As a general rule, however, it is a good
idea to use identical data descriptions in both calling and called programs in
order to avoid errors.

COBOL offers two options for associating argument fields in the calling and called programs. As explained in the next section of this chapter, the
CALL statement provides a choice between BY REFERENCE and BY CON-
TENT. An argument field BY REFERENCE is treated as described in the discussion above. After its address is passed to the called program, that program
can refer to the field by its corresponding name, with such use including the

Calling Program

```
01   A    PIC    X(4) VALUE 'MARY'.
01   B    PIC    9(3) VALUE 321
  .
  .
CALL 'SUB' USING A, B.
```

Called Program

```
LINKAGE SECTION.
01   X    PIC    X(5).
01   Y    PIC    9(3).
  .
  .
PROCEDURE DIVISION USING X, Y.
  .
  .
      MOVE X TO . . .
  .
  .
      MOVE Y TO . . .
```

FIGURE 12–4   ILLUSTRATION OF ARGUMENT DEFINITIONS.

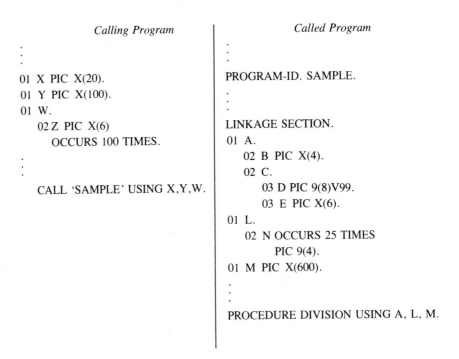

FIGURE 12–5   ILLUSTRATION OF LINKAGE SECTION DATA DESCRIPTIONS.

possibility of changing the content of the field. In the 1985 standard, however, it is possible to use an argument BY CONTENT, in which case the calling program cannot alter the content of the field in the called program. An argument declared BY CONTENT is used by the called program in a routine fashion during execution of the called program, including changing the original value. But when control returns to the calling program, the content of the BY CONTENT argument is unaltered. This option allows the programmer to provide certain immunity from contamination of data included in arguments because of errors in the subprogram.

In the 1974 standard, you need to use two fields in order to achieve the BY CONTENT effect. The original data is moved to a field that is then used as an argument in the CALL, thus preserving the original data by saving it as a separate field.

Another point to observe is that in the 1974 standard, arguments must refer to fields described at the 01 or 77 level. In the 1985 standard, on the other hand, arguments can also be elementary items.

The LINKAGE SECTION may not contain a VALUE clause except one associated with a condition-name (level 88). Since arguments in the subprogram represent fields that are only identified by the CALL, it would make no sense to specify contents via a VALUE clause. This point is further reinforced when we consider that there may be several calls to the same subprogram with different sets of arguments. For instance, we could have in the same calling program:

CALL 'SUM-SUB' USING AMT-1, AMT-2, TOTAL, OK-FLAG
.
.
.
CALL 'SUM-SUB' USING M, N, P, OK-FLAG.

The link-editor would associate these two different sets of arguments with the corresponding set in the PROCEDURE DIVISION header of SUM-SUB.

A special note should be added regarding INDEX items. Index items cannot be shared between calling and called programs. Rather, they are treated separately. Thus an index item defined in the subprogram is different from one in the main program, even if both items are associated with the same table. This makes sense, since index items do not represent defined storage locations, being registers used during processing of a table.

Arguments may be literals instead of data-names. Let us consider an example. Suppose that there is a subprogram designed to perform any of three functions on a 60-character field. These functions are identified by the following names: CENTER TITLE, CHECK, FORMAT. These names are included in Figure 12–6 as arguments in the sample CALL statements of the calling program.

In the LINKAGE SECTION of the subprogram, RENAMES is used to subdivide the first argument into 5-, 6-, and 12-character fields, which correspond to the lengths of the names of the three functions. It is important to recognize that if we issued a CALL 'CHR-PROC' USING 'FORMAT' DATA-FIELD and we wrote IF FUNCTION-CODE = 'FORMAT' in the subprogram, the condition would be false! Since FUNCTION-CODE is a 12-character field, we check the 12 characters that start with the 'F' of the literal 'FOR-MAT' to determine if they equal 'FORMAT'. The equality condition would be true only if, by coincidence, the 6 characters following FORMAT in storage happened to be spaces. Recall that the arguments are passed to a subprogram as storage addresses, not as content. Thus, it is necessary to check the first 6 characters of the 12-character FUNCTION-CODE to determine if they are equal to 'FORMAT', and the RENAMES provides a convenient mechanism for handling the task.

Generally, it is preferable not to pass literals as arguments. However, it is sometimes appropriate to use literals in order to make the CALL statement more understandable, as in the above example. As an alternative to the use of RENAMES, we could use the approach illustrated in Figure 12–7. In this figure, three 12-character fields are defined which contain the desired literals. Then each CALL specifies the data-name that contains the appropriate literal in each case. In the calling program we use 88-level condition-names to designate the five possibilities, and then the IF statement is used to identify the value in FUNCTION-CODE.

Calling Program
.
.
01 DATA-FIELD PIC X(60).
.
.
  CALL 'CHR-PROC' USING 'CHECK' DATA-FIELD ...
.
.
    CALL 'CHR-PROC' USING 'CENTER TITLE' DATA-FIELD ...
.
.

Called Program
  PROGRAM-ID. CHR-PROC.
  LINKAGE SECTION.
  01 FUNCTION-CODE.
     02 A1 PIC X(5).
     02 A2 PIC X.
     02 A3 PIC X(6).
  66 CHAR-5 RENAMES A1.
  66 CHAR-6 RENAMES A1 THRU A2.
  66 CHAR-12 RENAMES A1 THRU A3.
  01 DATA-FIELD PIC X(60).
  PROCEDURE DIVISION USING
     FUNCTION-CODE, DATA-FIELD.
  A. IF CHAR-5 = 'CIIECK'
    PERFORM CHECK-ROUTINE
    ELSE
     IF CHAR-6 = 'FORMAT'
      PERFORM FORMAT-ROUTINE
     ELSE ...

FIGURE 12-6   **ILLUSTRATION OF LITERALS AS ARGUMENTS.**

    As another approach, we could define one field in the calling program, such as 01 FUNCTION-CODE-PIC X(12), and then precede each call by a MOVE-literal statement:

MOVE 'FORMAT' TO FUNCTION-CODE
CALL 'CHR-PROC' USING FUNCTION-CODE, DATA-FIELD
.
.
MOVE 'CENTER TITLE' TO FUNCTION-CODE
CALL 'CHR-PROC' USING FUNCTION-CODE, DATA-FIELD
.
.

Calling Program
```
01 CHECK          PIC X(12) VALUE 'CHECK'.
01 FORMAT         PIC X(12) VALUE 'FORMAT'.
01 CENTER-TITLE   PIC X(12) VALUE 'CENTER-TITLE'.
```

```
    CALL 'CHR-PROC' USING CHECK, DATA-FIELD
    .
    .

    CALL 'CHR-PROC' USING CHECK, DATA-FIELD
    .
    .

    CALL 'CHR-PROC' USING CENTER-TITLE, DATA-FIELD
```

Called Program
```
  PROGRAM-ID. CHR-PROC.
  .
  .

  LINKAGE SECTION.
  01 FUNCTION-CODE PIC X(12).
     88 CHECK VALUE 'CHECK'.
     88 FORMAT VALUE 'FORMAT'.
     .
     .

  01 DATA-FIELD PIC X(12).
  .
  .

PROCEDURE DIVISION USING
     FUNCTION-CODE, DATA-FIELD.

A.
   IF CHECK PERFORM CHECK-ROUTINE
   ELSE
      IF FORMAT PERFORM. . .
      .
      .
```

FIGURE 12-7   ALTERNATE METHOD OF HANDLING LITERALS AS ARGUMENTS.

In conclusion, it can be stated that improper argument definition is often a source of errors in conjunction with the use of subprograms. As a general rule, document clearly the meaning and description of each argument and avoid "tricks." For instance, never use an argument for different purposes. If a subprogram is designed to take the square root of a number, provide a separate argument for the original number and for its square root. If the square root is stored in the same location as the original number, then by such an approach we destroy the original number. Further, always provide for some way of communicating error conditions back from a subprogram. What if there is an error in the input data? What should the subprogram do in such a case?

Another form of a confusing argument specification is the use of group items when elementary items would be more meaningful. If we write one item at the 01 level which includes all the arguments involved in the CALL, the item is not very meaningful in itself because we have to refer to the DATA DIVISION to determine what arguments are actually involved. Writing 5 to 10 argument names with each CALL is not really as time-consuming as the confusion which might result from using 1 or 2 group items that "hide" the arguments. On the other hand, if we have 30 arguments, it does make good sense to treat them as a group. It would be confusing to write them all every time a CALL is needed.

Sometimes arguments may not be used at all. For instance, a program may create a file that is to be processed further by a subprogram. The file is CLOSEd by the calling program and then it is OPENed as input by the called program. In such a case the file in essence serves as the means of data linkage, but in a totally different form from the use of arguments. We should add that files cannot be shared by calling and called programs. If the same file is to be used by both types of programs, it must be closed by the calling program before it can be opened by the called program, and vice-versa.

Review

1   The data items that send data to a subprogram or receive data from a subprogram are called _____.

arguments

2   The list of arguments appears in the _____ statement of the main program and in the _____ header of the subprogram.

CALL; PROCEDURE DIVISION

3   The data-name for an argument [need not be/must be] the same in both the main program and the subprogram.

need not be

4   The overall PICTURE description associated with an argument [need

not be/should be] the same in both the main program and the sub-program.

should be

5 Arguments essentially are passed from a main program to a subprogram as [content/storage addresses].

storage addresses

6 In the 1985 standard, the calling program cannot alter the content of the field in the called program when the _____ option is used.

BY CONTENT

7 In the 1974 standard, the data items to be used as an argument should be described at the _____ or _____ level in the DATA DIVISION of the calling program.

01; 77

8 Although data names generally serve as arguments, in order to make the CALL statement more understandable _____ can be used as arguments.

literals

9 In order to avoid argument specifications that are confusing, it is generally advisable that [elementary items/group items] serve as arguments.

elementary items

10 If a file, rather than a set of arguments, serves as the means of data linkage, it is CLOSEd by the [calling/called] program and OPENed as input by the [calling/called] program.

calling; called

TRANSFER OF CONTROL

As explained previously in this chapter, a run unit or job that includes subprograms consists of one main program and one or more subprograms. Program execution is initiated by the main program and should also be terminated via a STOP RUN command in the main program. This main program transfers control to a subprogram via a CALL statement, while the subprogram transfers control back to the calling program via an EXIT PROGRAM command.

The main program may contain more than one CALL statement to one or several subprograms. The subprograms may, in turn, contain CALL statements to other subprograms. Transfer of control from the calling to the called programs and back is very much like a procedure in a program which invokes execution of another procedure via the PERFORM verb. The PERFORMed procedure may in turn PERFORM one or more other procedures, and so on, but no procedure may PERFORM the one that PERFORMed it, either directly or indirectly. Of course, the EXIT PROGRAM command has no explicit counterpart in PERFORM structures, but it is understood that this return function is implied by the end of the procedure being PERFORMed.

Figure 12-1 earlier in this chapter illustrates correct and incorrect calling sequences.

Figure 12-8 presents the two formats of the CALL statement. Identifier-1 must be an alphanumeric field capable of storing a valid program-name. The identifier-1 option often is not available in small-system compilers. This option is designed to provide for dynamic specification of the subprogram name during execution. When the identifier-1 option is used, it is not known which subprogram is being called until the CALL statement is actually executed. At the time of CALL execution the content of identifier-1 is used to determine the subprogram name. For example, if we have: CALL SUBNAME USING ARG-1, ARG-2, the calling program will need to move a subprogram name into SUBNAME. The move may be explicit, such as MOVE 'CHECK-NAME' TO SUBNAME, or it may be indirect, as in the following example:

```
DISPLAY 'DO YOU WANT NAMES OR ADDRESSES' UPON terminal
DISPLAY 'TYPE IN EITHER NAME OR ADDR' UPON terminal
ACCEPT SUBNAME FROM terminal
CALL SUBNAME USING ARG-1 . . .
```

In this example we assume that 'NAME' and 'ADDR' are the names of two subprograms, and that the terminal user specifies the appropriate subprogram.

When the identifier-1 option is used, the link-edit process cannot resolve the program being called, but it provides code to do that at execution

Format 1

CALL $\begin{Bmatrix} \text{identifier-1} \\ \text{literal-1} \end{Bmatrix}$

$\left[\underline{\text{USING}} \quad \begin{Bmatrix} [\ \text{BY } \underline{\text{REFERENCE}}\ ] \text{identifier-2} \dots \\ \text{BY } \underline{\text{CONTENT}} \qquad \text{identifier-2} \end{Bmatrix} \dots \right]$

[ON <u>OVERFLOW</u> imperative-statement-1]   [<u>END-CALL</u>]

Format 2

CALL $\begin{Bmatrix} \text{identifier-1} \\ \text{literal-1} \end{Bmatrix}$

$\left[\underline{\text{USING}} \quad \begin{Bmatrix} [\ \text{BY } \underline{\text{REFERENCE}}\ ] \text{ identifier-2} \dots \\ \text{BY } \underline{\text{CONTENT}} \qquad \text{identifier-2} \dots \end{Bmatrix} \dots \right]$

[ON <u>EXCEPTION</u> imperative-statement-1]

[<u>NOT</u> ON <u>EXCEPTION</u> imperative-statement-2]

[<u>END-CALL</u>]

FIGURE 12–8   GENERAL FORMATS FOR THE CALL STATEMENT.

time. When such a CALL is executed, the system looks for the subprogram in the object program library and loads the subprogram into main storage. Subsequently that subprogram is available in central storage. Therefore, the subprogram is not copied every time that it is CALLed, but only once, when the first CALL for that subprogram is executed.

Literal-1 must be an alphanumeric literal corresponding to a program-name; that is, it specifies the name of a subprogram as given in the PROGRAM-ID paragraph of the subprogram being called.

The BY REFERENCE clause may be omitted, in which case it is specified by default. BY REFERENCE means to associate subprogram data-names in the LINKAGE and PROCEDURE DIVISION USING . . . specifications with the address of the corresponding data-names in the calling program.

When the BY CONTENT clause is used, the CALL statement makes available the content of the data-names listed in the CALL statement to the subprogram. The subprogram then does not make reference to the actual data-name storage locations in the calling program. In essence, the calling program passes data, not references, to the called program. As an example, we could write:

CALL 'STATS' USING BY CONTENT NO-OF-RECS, SALES-DATA
                     BY REFERENCE SALES-STATS, COMPLETION-CODE.

The ON OVERFLOW in Format 1 and the [NOT] ON EXCEPTION clauses in Format 2 are designed for exception processing when it is determined, at the time of the CALL, that the program specified by the CALL statement cannot be made available for execution. The OVERFLOW in Format 1 and the ON EXCEPTION in Format 2 perform the same function. The difference in the two formats is the NOT ON EXCEPTION option in Format 2. The latter option allows for a more flexible structure, as in the following example, which also includes use of the END-CALL:

IF N > ZERO
    THEN CALL 'STATS' USING . . .
                    ON EXCEPTION
                        PERFORM CANT-CALL-STATS
                    NOT ON EXCEPTION
                        PERFORM AFTER-STATS
            END-CALL
ELSE . . .

Referring to the example above, if the CALL is successful, we PERFORM AFTER-STATS; if it is not successful, then we PERFORM CANT-CALL-STATS. If Format 1 is used, we have to establish a flag type of field, set it to a specific value with the ON OVERFLOW condition, and then test whether an "overflow" condition occurs after the CALL.

A subprogram that is declared with the INITIAL option, which is described in a later section, The COMMON and INITIAL Options, is initialized every time it is CALLed. Therefore, each CALL to such a subprogram is like the first CALL, and the INITIAL option enables the CALL to act as if a CANCEL verb, described below, preceded each CALL.

It is apparent that use of identifier-1 can be a useful tool in saving storage by loading subprograms only when needed. This capability is further enhanced by the CANCEL verb:

$$\text{CANCEL} \left\{ \begin{array}{l} \text{identifier-1} \\ \text{literal-1} \end{array} \right\} \; \ldots$$

Use of this verb in a calling program releases the memory areas occupied by the subprogram(s) referenced in the CANCEL statement. Thus, a subprogram can be brought into storage by the use of CALL and can be removed by use of CANCEL. A subsequent CALL after a CANCEL will initiate the subprogram in its original state. Thus we must be careful not to assume resumption of the subprogram in its previous state. If the subprogram contained WORKING-STORAGE fields which had accumulated data as a result of previous CALLs, we should recognize that a CANCEL "erases" such accumulations and a subsequent CALL will restore the subprogram as if it were the first CALL issued.

Care must be taken in using CANCEL whenever several subprograms in a job call a given subprogram which is CANCELed by one of them. Regardless of which subprogram cancels the subprogram, the action takes effect for that subprogram in general and affects all its calling programs.

The identifiers and literals in the format for the CANCEL statement refer to subprogram names in the same way as they are used in the CALL statement.

The CANCEL also provides an explicit mechanism for setting a subprogram to its initial state if it precedes a subsequent CALL. A CALL that follows a CANCEL for a given subprogram causes that subprogram to be executed as if it were the first execution during the job. Thus a CALL ... CANCEL ... CALL sequence has the same effect as achieved by each CALL for a subprogram that is declared with the INITIAL option.

The EXIT PROGRAM is a specialized verb for subprograms, and transfers control to the calling program. It must be written as the last executable statement in a paragraph. Although a subprogram may contain several EXIT PROGRAM paragraphs, it is recommended that only one such command be used in order to preserve the one-entry one-exit principle of good program structure.

If an EXIT PROGRAM is executed for a subprogram that possesses the INITIAL attribute, the EXIT PROGRAM serves as an equivalent of a CANCEL statement. In other words, when a subsequent CALL is executed for that subprogram, the subprogram will be the same as it was at the first execution of the CALL verb.

Review

1   Transfer of control to a subprogram by use of the CALL command is very similar to transfer of control to another procedure *within* a program by use of the _____ verb.

PERFORM

2   When the object of the CALL command is a literal, what is specified is an alphanumeric name of a subprogram as given in the PROGRAM-ID paragraph of the [calling/called] program.

called

3   Dynamic specification of the subprogram name is accomplished by use of the [identifier-1/literal-1] option associated with the CALL verb.

identifier-1

4   The option associated with the CALL verb which allows the calling program to specify the procedure to be executed for the specific case in which insufficient central storage space is encountered for a called program is the _____ option.

ON OVERFLOW

5   The option associated with the CALL verb that is similar to the ON OVERFLOW option but is concerned with any situation in which the called program cannot be made available for execution and also allows for a more flexible programming structure is the [NOT] _____ option.

ON EXCEPTION

6   A subprogram declared with the INITIAL option is initialized [only the first time/each time] that it is CALLed.

each time

7   Whereas a subprogram is brought into central storage by use of the CALL command, it can be removed from central storage by use of the _____ command in the calling program.

CANCEL

8   If a subprogram contains WORKING-STORAGE fields with accumulated data, use of the CANCEL command [does not affect the WORKING-STORAGE fields/deletes all accumulated values in the WORKING-STORAGE fields].

Deletes all accumulated values in
the WORKING-STORAGE fields

9   If a CALL is executed after an EXIT PROGRAM for a subprogram with the INITIAL attribute, the content of the CALLed program will be as it was [before/after] a previous CALL execution.

before

SAMPLE PROGRAM WITH A SUBPROGRAM

Figures 12–9 and 12–10 illustrate a main program and a subprogram. These sample program s were written as follows:

MAIN PROGRAM. The main program reads source records containing sales data and stores them in a table. In the process, the program counts the number of data items, up to a maximum of 100 items. When all the data are input, the main program calls a subprogram and provides the subprogram with the table of sales data and the number of items. If the indication from the subprogram is that there were no errors, the main program prints the data processed by the subprogram; otherwise, the main program sets the results data to zero to indicate the presence of errors.

SUBPROGRAM. This program finds the minimum and maximum value in the table of sales data and computes the average. If a SIZE ERROR condition occurs during accumulation of the total sales value, then the subprogram indicates the occurrence of such an error by putting spaces in a status field and then returns to the calling (main) program. If no error occurs, then the subprogram places the literal value 'O.K.' in the status field and returns to the main program.

Notice that the list of arguments includes a table and that different names have been used for some of the arguments in the main program and the subprogram. The corresponding arguments are illustrated in the following arrangement, on page 454:

```
 IDENTIFICATION DIVISION.
 PROGRAM-ID.  SALESTATS.
*
 ENVIRONMENT DIVISION.
*
 CONFIGURATION SECTION.
 SOURCE-COMPUTER. ABC-480.
 OBJECT-COMPUTER. ABC-480.
*
 INPUT-OUTPUT SECTION.
 FILE-CONTROL.
     SELECT SOURCE-FILE   ASSIGN TO SOURCE.
     SELECT OUTPUT-FILE   ASSIGN TO PRINTER.
*
 DATA DIVISION.
*
 FILE SECTION.
*
 FD   SOURCE-FILE             LABEL RECORDS STANDARD
                              DATA RECORD IS SOURCE-REC.

 01   SOURCE-REC.
      02   SALES-AMOUNT       PIC 9(4)V99.
      02   FILLER            PIC X(74).
*
 FD   OUTPUT-FILE             LABEL RECORDS OMITTED
                              DATA RECORD IS OUTPUT-REC.

 01   OUTPUT-REC             PIC X(132).
*
 WORKING-STORAGE SECTION.
*
 01   END-OF-FILE-TEST       PIC XXX VALUE 'NO '.
      88 END-OF-FILE          VALUE 'YES'.
*
 01   COMPLETION-CODE        PIC X(4).
*
 01   NO-OF-RECS             PIC 9(3) VALUE ZERO.
 01   RECORD-COUNTERS.
      02   N-GOOD            PIC 9(3) VALUE ZERO.
      02   N-TOTAL           PIC 9(3) VALUE ZERO.
*
 01    SALES-TABLE.
       02    SALES   OCCURS 100 TIMES PIC 9(4)V99.
*
 01   SALES-STATS.
      02   MIN               PIC 9(4)V99.
      02   MAX               PIC 9(4)V99.
      02   AVG               PIC 9(4)V99.
```

FIGURE 12-9   SAMPLE MAIN PROGRAM.

```
01   WS-OUTPUT-REC.
     02   FILLER              PIC X(6) VALUE 'MIN = '.
     02   MIN-OUT             PIC Z(4)9.99.
     02   FILLER              PIC X(8) VALUE '  MAX = '.
     02   MAX-OUT             PIC Z(4)9.99.
     02   FILLER              PIC X(8) VALUE '  AVG = '.
     02   AVG-OUT             PIC Z(4)9.99.
     02   FILLER              PIC X(6) VALUE ' N = '.
     02   N-OUT               PIC ZZ9.
/
 PROCEDURE DIVISION.
*
 PROGRAM-SUMMARY.
     OPEN INPUT SOURCE-FILE  OUTPUT OUTPUT-FILE
*
     PERFORM READ-SOURCE-RECORDS
*
     IF N-GOOD > ZERO
        THEN
           MOVE N-GOOD TO NO-OF-RECS
           CALL 'STATS' USING NO-OF-RECS,
                              SALES-TABLE,
                              SALES-STATS,
                              COMPLETION-CODE
           IF COMPLETION-CODE = 'O.K.'
              THEN
                 CONTINUE
              ELSE
                 MOVE ZEROS TO SALES-STATS
           END-IF
        ELSE
           MOVE ZEROS TO SALES-STATS
     END-IF
*
     PERFORM PRINT-STATS
*
     CLOSE SOURCE-FILE OUTPUT-FILE
     STOP RUN.
*
 READ-SOURCE-RECORDS.
*
     PERFORM WITH TEST AFTER UNTIL END-OF-FILE
                              OR  N-GOOD = 100
```

FIGURE 12-9   SAMPLE MAIN PROGRAM.   (Continued)

```
            READ SOURCE-FILE
                AT END SET END-OF-FILE TO TRUE
                NOT AT END
                    ADD 1 TO N-TOTAL
                    IF SALES-AMOUNT IS NUMERIC
                        THEN
                            ADD 1 TO N-GOOD
                            MOVE SALES-AMOUNT TO SALES (N-GOOD)
                        ELSE
                            STRING 'RECORD ' N-TOTAL
                                    ' CONTAINS NONUMERIC DATA: '
                                   SALES-AMOUNT
                                DELIMITED BY SIZE
                                INTO OUTPUT-REC
                            WRITE OUTPUT-REC
                    END-IF
                END-READ
    *
            END-PERFORM.
    *
        PRINT-STATS.
            MOVE MIN TO MIN-OUT
            MOVE MAX TO MAX-OUT
            MOVE AVG TO AVG-OUT
            MOVE NO-OF-RECS TO N-OUT
            WRITE OUTPUT-REC FROM WS-OUTPUT-REC.
```

FIGURE 12-9   SAMPLE MAIN PROGRAM.   (Continued)

```
CALL 'STATS'                       PROCEDURE  DIVISION
    USING NO-OF-RECS                  USING NO-OF-VALUES
          SALES-TABLE                       INPUT-TABLE
          SALES-STATS                       OUTPUT-STATS
          COMPLETION-CODE.                  STATUS-CODE.
```

The sample subprogram could be thought of as having the following function: Receive a table of data and compute the minimum, maximum, and average values; if no error occurs in the process, indicate so by placing 'O.K.' in a status field, otherwise put spaces in that field. This description makes no reference to sales data or any particular type of data. Thus, generic data-names such as INPUT-TABLE and OUTPUT-STATS are reasonable choices and serve to emphasize the point that a subprogram may be designed to perform a general-purpose function and could therefore be used (CALLED) by *many* programs needing execution of that same function.

Incidentally, the . . . OCCURS DEPENDING ON could have been used

```
IDENTIFICATION DIVISION.
PROGRAM-ID.  STATS.
*
ENVIRONMENT DIVISION.
*
CONFIGURATION SECTION.
SOURCE-COMPUTER. ABC-480.
OBJECT-COMPUTER. ABC-480.
*
DATA DIVISION.
WORKING-STORAGE SECTION.
01   SALES-TOTAL            PIC 9(5)V99 VALUE ZERO.
01   I                      PIC 999.
*
LINKAGE SECTION.
*
01   NO-OF-VALUES           PIC 9(3).
01   INPUT-TABLE.
     02   DATA-VALUE   OCCURS 100 TIMES PIC 9(4)V99.
*
01   OUTPUT-STATS.
     02   MIN               PIC 9(4)V99.
     02   MAX               PIC 9(4)V99.
     02   AVG               PIC 9(4)V99.
*
01   STATUS-CODE            PIC X(4).
*
PROCEDURE DIVISION USING NO-OF-VALUES, INPUT-TABLE
                        OUTPUT-STATS, STATUS-CODE.

*
PROGRAM-SUMMARY.
     MOVE 'O.K.' TO STATUS-CODE
     MOVE DATA-VALUE (1) TO MIN, MAX, SALES-TOTAL.
     PERFORM STATISTICS VARYING I FROM 2 BY 1
                   UNTIL I > NO-OF-VALUES
                   OR STATUS-CODE = SPACES.
     DIVIDE SALES-TOTAL BY NO-OF-VALUES GIVING AVG
            ON SIZE ERROR MOVE SPACES TO STATUS-CODE.
*
RETURN-TO-CALL.
     EXIT PROGRAM.
*
STATISTICS.
     IF MIN > DATA-VALUE (I)
        MOVE DATA-VALUE (I) TO MIN.
     IF MAX < DATA-VALUE (I)
        MOVE DATA-VALUE (I) TO MAX.
     ADD DATA-VALUE (I) TO SALES-TOTAL
        ON SIZE ERROR MOVE SPACES TO STATUS-CODE.
```

FIGURE 12-10   SAMPLE SUBPROGRAM.

in the table description of either the main program or the subprogram. It was not used here because the SEARCH verb, which takes direct advantage of this feature, was not included in the program.

THE CONCEPT OF NESTED COBOL PROGRAMS

In the 1985 version of COBOL it is possible to write programs that contain other programs. Of course, a subprogram logically is a program contained within its calling program. However, the current version of COBOL makes available an additional technique by which programs can be contained, or nested, within another program. One advantage of nested programs is that they not only allow the modularity benefits of subprograms but also further facilitate data sharing among programs.

Figure 12–11 illustrates a sample outline of nested programs. Each program begins with the keywords IDENTIFICATION DIVISION and ends with the keywords END PROGRAM.... The outer *containing* program in Figure 12–11 is called MASTER-PROGRAM. It is shown as having all four divisions of a COBOL program. The MASTER-PROGRAM contains PROGRAM-A, which in turn contains PROGRAM-B. The latter two programs contain IDENTIFICATION AND PROCEDURE divisions, and they could include the ENVIRONMENT and/or the DATA divisions as well, as required by the specific data processing circumstances. The fact that a nested program need not include the ENVIRONMENT and DATA divisions is consistent with these two divisions being optional for any COBOL program.

Each program terminates with the special END PROGRAM terminator, followed by the program-name that was given in the respective PROGRAM-ID. The large vertical brackets in Figure 12–11 identify the scope of each program.

Figure 12–12 further illustrates the concept of nested programs by showing a more extensive example of nesting. The name of the containing program in Figure 12–12 is MASTER-PROGRAM. This program directly contains two other programs: PROGRAM-A and PROGRAM-X. In turn, PROGRAM-A is the containing program for PROGRAM-B, which is the containing program for PROGRAM-C.

A program such as PROGRAM-C in Figure 12–12 is directly contained by PROGRAM-B and indirectly contained by PROGRAM-A and MASTER-PROGRAM. On the other hand, PROGRAM-Y is directly contained by PROGRAM-X and indirectly contained by MASTER-PROGRAM. It is important to have a clear understanding of the direct and indirect containment of specific programs in a given nested structure, because several rules of the language apply according to whether a program is or is not contained by another program in the structure. For example, the GLOBAL clause (discussed in a subsequent section) can be used to declare data-names, which then become available to all programs contained directly or indirectly within the declaring

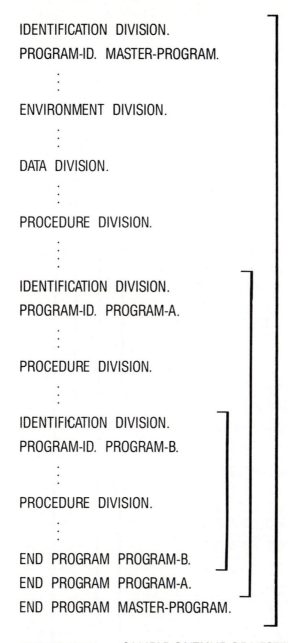

IDENTIFICATION DIVISION.
PROGRAM-ID. MASTER-PROGRAM.
.
.
ENVIRONMENT DIVISION.
.
.
DATA DIVISION.
.
.
PROCEDURE DIVISION.
.
.
.
IDENTIFICATION DIVISION.
PROGRAM-ID. PROGRAM-A.
.
.
PROCEDURE DIVISION.
.
.
IDENTIFICATION DIVISION.
PROGRAM-ID. PROGRAM-B.
.
.
PROCEDURE DIVISION.
.
.
END PROGRAM PROGRAM-B.
END PROGRAM PROGRAM-A.
END PROGRAM MASTER-PROGRAM.

FIGURE 12–11   SAMPLE OUTLINE OF NESTED PROGRAMS.

program. In Figure 12–12, if PROGRAM-A declared item XYZ as GLOBAL, it
would be GLOBAL for PROGRAM-B and PROGRAM-C, but it would not be
GLOBAL for MASTER-PROGRAM, PROGRAM-X, or PROGRAM-Y.

A set of nested programs constitutes a *run unit*. Thus, the run unit in
Figure 12–12 consists of six programs. The concept of the run unit is used in

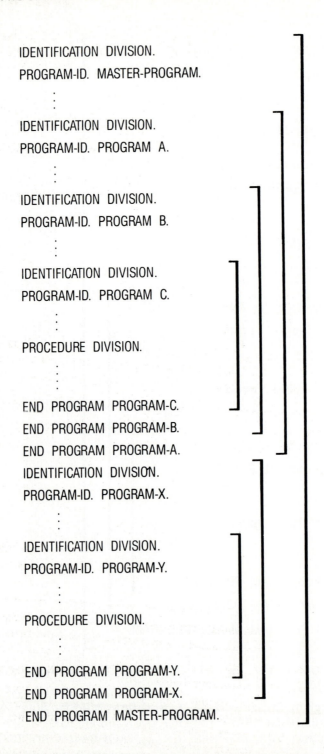

```
IDENTIFICATION  DIVISION.
PROGRAM-ID.  MASTER-PROGRAM.
          .
          .
IDENTIFICATION  DIVISION.
PROGRAM-ID.  PROGRAM  A.
          .
          .
IDENTIFICATION  DIVISION.
PROGRAM-ID.  PROGRAM  B.
          .
          .
IDENTIFICATION  DIVISION.
PROGRAM-ID.  PROGRAM  C.
          .
          .
PROCEDURE  DIVISION.
          .
          .
          .
END  PROGRAM  PROGRAM-C.
END  PROGRAM  PROGRAM-B.
END  PROGRAM  PROGRAM-A.
IDENTIFICATION  DIVISION.
PROGRAM-ID.  PROGRAM-X.
          .
          .
IDENTIFICATION  DIVISION.
PROGRAM-ID.  PROGRAM-Y.
          .
          .
PROCEDURE  DIVISION.
          .
          .
END  PROGRAM  PROGRAM-Y.
END  PROGRAM  PROGRAM-X.
END  PROGRAM  MASTER-PROGRAM.
```

FIGURE 12-12   SAMPLE OUTLINE OF MULTIPLE-NESTED PROGRAMS.

the next two sections of this chapter in connection with the COMMON, IN-ITIAL, EXTERNAL, and GLOBAL options. A sample complete nested program illustration is presented in the concluding section of this chapter.

Review

1 In addition to the use of subprograms, the current version of COBOL makes it possible to have programs that are contained *within* another program through the process of _____.

nesting

2 In the context of nesting, the main program is called the *containing* program while the nested programs are called the _____ programs.

contained

3 When nesting is used, detailed DATA DIVISION specifications [need to/need not] be included in the contained programs.

need not

4 A set of nested source programs is said to constitute a _____ unit.

run

THE COMMON AND INITIAL OPTIONS

A set of nested source programs constitutes a run unit. In such a run unit, programs may be declared as being COMMON and/or INITIAL by the following format:

PROGRAM-ID. program-name $\left[\text{IS} \left\{ \begin{array}{l} \underline{\text{COMMON}} \\ \underline{\text{INITIAL}} \end{array} \right\} \text{PROGRAM} \right]$.

The straight vertical lines in the above format specify "choice indicators" that require that one or more of the unique options contained within the choice indicators must be specified, but any one option may only be specified once. Thus, either COMMON or INITIAL, or both, may be written for the same program.

A COMMON program may be called by any program contained within a nested program structure. For example, if PROGRAM-C had been declared COMMON in Figure 12–12, then PROGRAM-Y could call PROGRAM-C, as one particular possibility.

An INITIAL program is initialized to its original state each time that such a program is called. Thus, the state of an INITIAL program is the same on the tenth time that it is called, for example, as it was on the first call. The INITIAL option can be thought of as a shorthand way of initializing the data fields that are "local" to a given program. As explained in the next section of this chapter, the INITIAL option may be combined with the EXTERNAL option to effect selective initialization.

Review

1 A program that can be called by any program contained within a nested program structure is declared as being _____ in the PROGRAM-ID paragraph.

COMMON

2 The option used in the PROGRAM-ID paragraph for a nested program that is to be initialized to its original state each time it is called is the _____ option.

INITIAL

EXTERNAL AND GLOBAL ITEMS

In a nested program structure it is possible to define a file or a record as being EXTERNAL, GLOBAL, or both. The general format for such file description is presented in Figure 12–13.

The storage associated with an EXTERNAL object is not part of any particular program in the run unit. Rather, EXTERNAL item storage is associated with the run unit itself. Figure 12–14 illustrates the point. The run unit consists of three programs, each of which occupies a certain storage area. For

```
FD    file-name
      [ IS EXTERNAL ]
      [ IS GLOBAL ]


01    ⎡data-name-1⎤
      ⎣FILLER     ⎦
      [ IS EXTERNAL ]
      [ IS GLOBAL ]
```

FIGURE 12-13   GENERAL FORMATS FOR EXTERNAL AND GLOBAL CLAUSES.

instance, data items declared in PROGRAM-A that are *not* EXTERNAL are contained in the storage area for PROGRAM-A. However, any items declared to be EXTERNAL are not in that area. Rather, they are stored separately and may be referenced by any program that belongs to the run unit and includes the same description of the item. Thus, several programs can make reference to the same storage area without that area being exclusively asso-

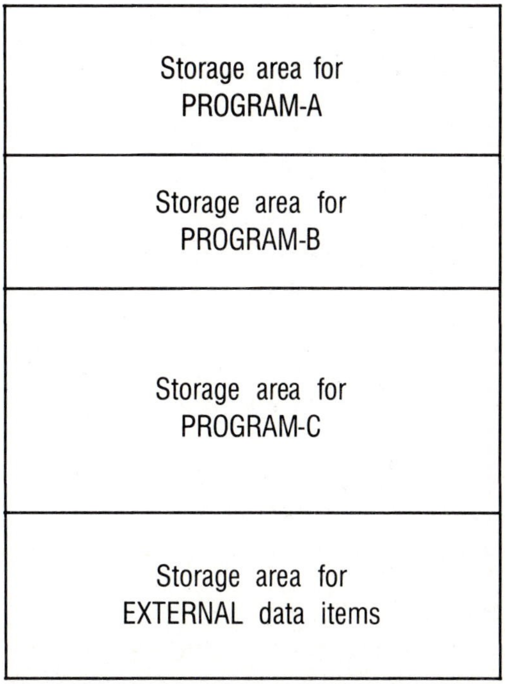

Storage area for
PROGRAM-A

Storage area for
PROGRAM-B

Storage area for
PROGRAM-C

Storage area for
EXTERNAL data items

FIGURE 12-14   ILLUSTRATION OF EXTERNAL STORAGE.

ciated with any one program. As a result, a program whose PROGRAM-ID is declared as INITIAL will not have its EXTERNAL items (if any) affected by the INITIAL attribute upon a CALL.

As a specific example, consider Figure 12–15. The WORKING-STOR-AGE item CUST-REC is declared EXTERNAL in both PROGRAM-B and in PROGRAM-C and is given identical descriptions in each program. Either of these programs can make reference to the same storage location via CUST-REC or either of the two subordinate data items in CUST-REC. Thus, CUST-REC is "shared" by these two programs. However, it is not so shared by PROGRAM-A, which did not declare that item as EXTERNAL. Also, notice that PROGRAM-C is INITIAL. Nevertheless, when PROGRAM-C is CALLed by one of the other two programs, CUST-REC is *not* set to the initial state, because of having been declared as EXTERNAL.

The EXTERNAL option requires that each program describe the EX-TERNAL item by the same data-name and general data description. How-ever, any program so describing an EXTERNAL item may also use the REDEFINES clause to alter the description of that item to fit the needs of that program. Such use is illustrated in the example on the following page.

```
IDENTIFICATION DIVISION.
PROGRAM-ID.   PROGRAM-A.
 :
IDENTIFICATION DIVISION.
PROGRAM-ID.   PROGRAM-B.
 :
DATA DIVISION.
 :
WORKING-STORAGE SECTION.
01   CUST-REC IS EXTERNAL.
     02   CUST-NO PIC X(5).
     02   CUST-NAME PIC X(15).
 :
IDENTIFICATION DIVISION.
PROGRAM-ID.   PROGRAM-C IS INITIAL.
 :
01   CUST-REC IS EXTERNAL.
     02   CUST-NO PIC X(5).
     02   CUST-NAME PIC X(15).
 :
END PROGRAM PROGRAM-C.
END PROGRAM PROGRAM-B.
END PROGRAM PROGRAM-A.
```

FIGURE 12–15   ILLUSTRATION OF EXTERNAL ITEMS.

```
01  CUST-REC IS EXTERNAL.
    02  CUST-NO      PIC X(5).
    02  CUST-NAME    PIC X(15).
01  CUSTOMER REDEFINES CUST-REC.
    02  REGION-CODE  PIC X.
    02  FILLER       PIC X(19).
```

We now consider the GLOBAL option. This option allows us to describe items in one program and have them referenced in that program or in any program contained in the program that declared the GLOBAL option. GLOBAL names provide a means of avoiding duplicate definitions for data items that need to be used by more than one program. When a name is declared as GLOBAL in a program, that item need not be described again in any of the contained programs.

An item may be declared as being both GLOBAL and EXTERNAL. In such a case the name is GLOBAL and the storage is EXTERNAL. As a GLOBAL item, it is available to every program contained within the program that describes the item. As an EXTERNAL item, it is available only to programs in the run unit that include the same description for that item.

Figure 12–16 presents an example of nested programs that include the use of both the GLOBAL and EXTERNAL options. Notice, for instance, that COMPLETION-CODE and SALES-DATA in the first program are GLOBAL. Thus, in the second program, called STATS, COMPLETION-CODE and SALES are used in the PROGRAM-SUMMARY paragraph without having been described in that (contained) program. Note also that SALES is a field within SALES-DATA in the containing program. The nested program structure in this figure is discussed further in the next section of this chapter.

A data-item that is not declared as being GLOBAL is thereby local, and its name has meaning only in the program that describes it. For example, in Figure 12–16 WS-OUTPUT-REC is a local item in the first program and SALES-TOTAL is a local item in the second program. Local items that are not EXTERNAL have storage associated with their defining program, as is true for GLOBAL items that are not EXTERNAL. Similarly, local items that are declared EXTERNAL have storage associated with the run unit and not with any individual program.

Review

1   When a file is to be stored separately from any particular program in a run unit and may be referenced by any program that belongs to that unit, then it is declared as being _____ in the file description.

EXTERNAL

```
       IDENTIFICATION DIVISION.
       PROGRAM-ID. SALESTATS.
       ENVIRONMENT DIVISION.
       CONFIGURATION SECTION.
       SOURCE-COMPUTER. ABC-480.
       OBJECT-COMPUTER. ABC-480.
       INPUT-OUTPUT SECTION.
       FILE-CONTROL.
           SELECT SOURCE-FILE    ASSIGN TO 'SOURCE'.
           SELECT OUTPUT-FILE    ASSIGN TO 'PRINTER'.
      *
       DATA DIVISION.
       FILE SECTION.
      *
       FD   SOURCE-FILE               LABEL RECORDS STANDARD
                                      DATA RECORD IS SOURCE-REC.
       01   SOURCE-REC.
            02   SALES-AMOUNT         PIC 9(4)V99.
            02   FILLER               PIC X(74).
      *
       FD   OUTPUT-FILE               LABEL RECORDS OMITTED
                                      DATA RECORD IS OUTPUT-REC.
       01   OUTPUT-REC                PIC X(132).
      *
       WORKING-STORAGE SECTION.
      *
       01   END-OF-FILE-TEST          PIC XXX VALUE 'NO '.
            88 END-OF-FILE            VALUE 'YES'.
      *
       01   COMPLETION-CODE  IS  GLOBAL.
            02    PIC X(4).
      *
       01   SALES-DATA  IS  GLOBAL.
            02   N-GOOD               PIC 9(3).
            02   N-TOTAL              PIC 9(3).
            02   SALES-TABLE.
                 03   SALES           OCCURS 100 TIMES
                                      PIC 9(4)V99.
      *
       01   SALES-STATS  IS  EXTERNAL  GLOBAL.
            02   MIN                  PIC 9(4)V99.
            02   MAX                  PIC 9(4)V99.
            02   AVG                  PIC 9(4)V99.
      *
       01   WS-OUTPUT-REC.
            02   FILLER               PIC X(6) VALUE 'MIN = '.
            02   MIN-OUT              PIC Z(4)9.99.
            02   FILLER               PIC X(8) VALUE '  MAX = '.
            02   MAX-OUT              PIC Z(4)9.99.
            02   FILLER               PIC X(8) VALUE '  AVG = '.
            02   AVG-OUT              PIC Z(4)9.99.
            02   FILLER               PIC X(6) VALUE '  N = '.
            02   N-OUT                PIC ZZ9.
```

FIGURE 12-16   SAMPLE NESTED PROGRAMS.

```
      PROCEDURE DIVISION.
 *
      PROGRAM-SUMMARY.
          OPEN INPUT SOURCE-FILE  OUTPUT OUTPUT-FILE
          INITIALIZE SALES-DATA
 *
          PERFORM READ-SOURCE-RECORDS
 *
          IF N-GOOD > ZERO
             THEN
               CALL 'STATS'
               IF COMPLETION-CODE = 'O.K.'
                   THEN
                       CONTINUE
                   ELSE
                       MOVE ZEROS TO SALES-STATS
               END-IF
             ELSE
               MOVE ZEROS TO SALES-STATS
          END-IF
 *
          PERFORM PRINT-STATS
 *
          CLOSE SOURCE-FILE OUTPUT-FILE
          STOP RUN.
 *
      READ-SOURCE-RECORDS.
          PERFORM WITH TEST AFTER
                  UNTIL END-OF-FILE OR N = 100
 *
            READ SOURCE-FILE
 *
              AT END SET END-OF-FILE TO TRUE
              NOT AT END
                ADD 1 TO N-TOTAL
                IF SALES-AMOUNT IS NUMERIC
                   THEN
                       ADD 1 TO N-GOOD
                       MOVE SALES-AMOUNT TO SALES (N-GOOD)
                   ELSE
                       STRING 'RECORD ', N-TOTAL,
                              ' CONTAINS NONNUMERIC DATA: '
                              SOURCE-REC(1:6)
                              DELIMITED BY SIZE
                          INTO OUTPUT-REC
                       WRITE OUTPUT-REC
                END-IF
 *
            END-READ
 *
          END-PERFORM.
```

FIGURE 12-16   SAMPLE NESTED PROGRAMS.   **(Continued)**

```
     PRINT-STATS.
          MOVE MIN TO MIN-OUT
          MOVE MAX TO MAX-OUT
          MOVE AVG TO AVG-OUT
          MOVE N TO N-OUT
          WRITE OUTPUT-REC FROM WS-OUTPUT-REC.
 *
 * The following program is a contained program
 *
  IDENTIFICATION DIVISION.
  PROGRAM-ID. STATS.
 *
  DATA DIVISION.
  WORKING-STORAGE SECTION.
  01   SALES-TOTAL              PIC 9(5)V99 VALUE ZERO.
  01   I                        PIC 999.
 *
  PROCEDURE DIVISION.
 *
  PROGRAM-SUMMARY.
          MOVE 'O.K.' TO COMPLETION-CODE
          MOVE SALES (1) TO MIN, MAX, SALES-TOTAL.
          PERFORM   VARYING I FROM 2 BY 1
                               UNTIL I > N-GOOD
                               OR COMPLETION-CODE = SPACES
          IF MIN > SALES (I)
              THEN
                MOVE SALES (I) TO MIN
              ELSE
                IF MAX < SALES (I)
                    THEN
                       MOVE SALES (I) TO MAX
                    ELSE
                       CONTINUE
                END-IF
          END-IF
 *
          ADD SALES (I) TO SALES-TOTAL
              ON SIZE ERROR MOVE SPACES TO COMPLETION-CODE
          END-ADD
 *
      END-PERFORM
 *
      DIVIDE SALES-TOTAL BY N-GOOD GIVING AVG
              ON SIZE ERROR MOVE SPACES TO COMPLETION-CODE.
 *
  RETURN-TO-CALL.
      EXIT PROGRAM.
 *
  END PROGRAM STATS.
 *
  END PROGRAM SALESTATS.
```

FIGURE 12-16   SAMPLE NESTED PROGRAMS.   **(Continued)**

2   When the EXTERNAL option is used, each program that is to make reference to the file [must/need not] describe the file by the same data-name and data description.

must

3   In order to fit the needs of a particular nested program, the description of an EXTERNAL data item can be altered by use of the _____ clause in that nested program.

REDEFINES

4   The declaration in the WORKING-STORAGE SECTION of the containing program that makes it possible to reference the data-names in the contained programs is the _____ declaration.

GLOBAL

5   The DATA DIVISION of a contained program can include data-names that are not defined in the containing program. As opposed to global data-names, such data-names are called _____ data-names.

local

SAMPLE NESTED PROGRAMS

Continuing with discussion of Figure 12–16, the figure includes a sample nested program structure consisting of two programs. The outer, or containing, program is called SALESTATS and contains the STATS program nested within it. The programs perform the following tasks:

Sales data are read from SOURCE-FILE and stored in SALES-TABLE. We READ SOURCE-FILE once, and we continue to execute STORE-SALES, which reads and stores data until the END-OF-FILE or until the number of valid data items (N-GOOD) is equal to 100.

If one or more valid (N-GOOD > ZERO) data items have been stored, then the second program, STATS, is called. The STATS program determines the minimum, maximum, and average values for the data in SALES-TABLE. If no errors occur during execution of the STATS program, then COMPLETION-CODE is set to 'O.K.' Otherwise, COMPLETION-CODE is set to SPACES.

The outer program continues by executing the PRINT-STATS routine, closing the files, and terminating the run unit.

EXERCISES

12.1   Discuss three main reasons for using externally compiled subprograms rather than using PERFORM structures within a large program.

12.2   Consider the following:

Main Program
CALL 'CHR-PROC' USING X, 'SAMPLE'.
.
.
Subprogram
LINKAGE SECTION.
01   A   PIC   X(5).
01   B   PIC   X(3).
PROCEDURE DIVISION USING B, A.
.
.
MOVE SPACES TO A.

What will happen as a result of the MOVE statement in the subprogram?

12.3   Consider the following:

Main Program
    CALL 'A' USING ARG-A, ARG-B.
Subprogram A
    PROCEDURE DIVISION USING P, R.

    .
    .

        CALL 'B' USING L, P, N.
        CANCEL 'B'.
    LAST-PAR. EXIT PROGRAM.
Subprogram B
    PROCEDURE DIVISION USING X, Y, Z.

    .
    .

        MOVE SPACES TO Y.
    LAST-PAR. EXIT PROGRAM.

What will be stored in ARG-A immediately after execution of the CALL statement in the main program?

12.4 Employees pay FICA-RATE percent of their FICA-LIMIT annual earnings as FICA tax. We wish to write a subprogram that will compute the FICA tax for each employee. Outline a skeleton program structure for a main program and the subprogram. The main program CALLs the subprogram to compute the FICA tax. Be sure to include argument definition and PROCEDURE DIVISION statements for both the main program and the subprogram.

12.5 A subprogram is to be written that can perform the following functions:

Open the printer file

Close the printer file

Write a record, leaving a specified number of blank lines before printing

Design such a subprogram by responding to the following requirements:
a Write the LINKAGE SECTION of the subprogram (named PRINTER).
b Write the entire PROCEDURE DIVISION of the subprogram.
c Write sample CALL statements for the main program.

12.6 A subprogram is to be written that receives data in a table and produces the sum, average, minimum, and maximum values in the table.

Data in the table have PIC S9(4)V99 and there can be a maximum of 100 values. However, not all 100 values are used every time the subprogram is called. The calling program indicates to the subprogram how many values to use (starting from the beginning of the table). Design such a subprogram by answering the following:

a What error possibilities exist?
b Write the LINKAGE SECTION of the subprogram.
c Write the entire PROCEDURE DIVISION of the subprogram.
d Write sample CALL statements for the main program.

12.7 Your task is to prepare a program to check for errors in transaction data pertaining to inventory. The source data items have the following format:

COLUMN	FIELD-NAME
1–5	Item-number
6–20	Item-name
21	Item-code
22–26	Quantity

The basic checking procedure is concerned with the value of ITEM-CODE, because this signifies the type of record. The value 1 means that the QUANTITY field contains the previous balance for the item specified by ITEM-NUMBER; the value 2 indicates the receipt of goods; and 3 indicates the issue of goods from inventory. Any other code is an error. We assume that the records are sorted so that all records of the same item number are grouped together and the record with a 1 in column 21 leads the group. We recognize four types of error conditions:

Duplicate balance record: This condition arises whenever more than one record in a group of the same item number has a code of 1.

Misplaced balance record: A record with a code of 1 exists, but it is not the first in the group.

Balance record missing: The first record in a group is not a code 1 record.

Incorrect code: A code other than 1, 2, or 3 exists.

On detection of a record meeting one of these conditions, the record is printed with the corresponding explanatory error message so that it can be corrected.

In addition to the error messages, we also desire a summary of totals. Figure 12–17 illustrates a set of sample input records and the resulting sample output.

We proceed to define the function of the main program and the subprogram as follows:

Main program: This reads each transaction and gives each record to the subprogram to check for data validity. If execution of the subprogram indicates that the data are not valid, the record is printed along with an error message. If execution of the subprogram indicates that the data are valid, then we accumulate the proper totals. We then proceed to read another record. When all the records have been read, we print a summary of the accumulated totals and terminate the program.

Subprogram: The subprogram receives a transaction record from the main program. It checks for errors. If an error is found, an appropriate error message is supplied to the main program. If no error is found, a blank error message is supplied to the main program. Then the subprogram terminates.

The four error messages are:

DUPLICATE BALANCE CARD
MISPLACED BALANCE CARD
BALANCE CARD MISSING
INCORRECT CODE

Figure 12–18 is a *decision table* that facilitates complete enumeration of the possibilities.

```
Sample Input


12345TEST-ITEM-1      100100
12345TEST-ITEM-1      200100
12345TEST-ITEM-1      300200
23456TEST-ITEM-2      300010
34567TEST-ITEM-3      100020
34567TEST-ITEM-3      200100
34567TEST-ITEM-3      300050
45678TEST-ITEM-4      200100
45678TEST-ITEM-4      100100
45678TEST-ITEM-4      300100
45678TEST-ITEM-4      100200
56789TEST-ITEM-5      100100
56789TEST-ITEM-5      40050
56789TEST-ITEM-5      300020
67890TEST-ITEM-6      100300
67890TEST-ITEM-6      300100
78901TEST-ITEM-7      100400
78901TEST-ITEM-7      100300
89012TEST-ITEM-8      100200



Sample Output


23456TEST-ITEM-2      300010    BALANCE CARD MISSING
45678TEST-ITEM-4      200100    BALANCE CARD MISSING
45678TEST-ITEM-4      100100    MISPLACED BALANCE CARD
45678TEST-ITEM-4      300100    BALANCE CARD MISSING
45678TEST-ITEM-4      100200    MISPLACED BALANCE CARD
56789TEST-ITEM-5      40050     INCORRECT CODE
78901TEST-ITEM-7      100300    DUPLICATE BALANCE CARD


VALID RECORDS   =                  012

INVALID RECORDS =                  007

BALANCE TOTAL   =                  1120

RECEIPTS TOTAL  =                  200

ISSUES TOTAL    =                  370
```

FIGURE 12-17   SAMPLE INPUT AND OUTPUT FOR THE INVENTORY EXAMPLE.

	POSSIBILITY							
CONDITION	1	2	3	4	5	6	7	8
PREVIOUS-ITEM = CURRENT-ITEM	X	X	X					
PREVIOUS-ITEM NOT = CURRENT-ITEM				X	X	X	X	X
KODE = 1	X			X	X			
KODE = 2 OR 3		X				X		X
KODE NOT = 1 OR 2 OR 3				X			X	
BALANCE-CODE = 1				X	X			
BALANCE-CODE = 2					X			X
ACTION	1	2	3	4	5	6	7	8
BLANK ERROR MESSAGE	X					X		
DUPLICATE BALANCE CARD				X				
MISPLACED BALANCE CARD					X			
BALANCE CARD MISSING		X	X					X
INCORRECT CODE							X	

FIGURE 12-18   DECISION TABLE FOR THE INVENTORY EXAMPLE.

12.8   Discuss the concept of nested COBOL programs and sketch an outline structure of two nested programs.

12.9   When would you use the EXTERNAL attribute with a subprogram whose PROGRAM-ID has the INITIAL option?

12.10   Explain and contrast the GLOBAL and INITIAL options.

12.11   Restructure the program/subprogram answer to Exercise 12.7 above, using a nested program structure.

13
REPORT GENERATION

INTRODUCTION

Report generation constitutes a common and extensive activity in computer use. People use computer data through reports. A *report* is a formatted collection of data recorded on paper, on a display screen, on microfilm, etc., and it is intended for human reading.

Figure 13–1 presents the general structure of a report. There may be a *report heading* at the beginning of the report which typically contains a title, date, and information like authorship, recipients, and the like. Then the *report body* consists of one or more pages. A *page* is a formatted collection of lines. Usually, pages are defined on the basis of some physical characteristics of the recording medium. For instance, paper reports are conventionally printed on 11-inch pages, while display screen reports tend to be equal to the size of the screen (about 24 lines). A page is subdivided into five parts: a *page heading, control heading(s), report detail lines, control footing(s),* and a *page footing.* A *page heading* is included to enhance the readability of long reports by including such information as page numbers and column

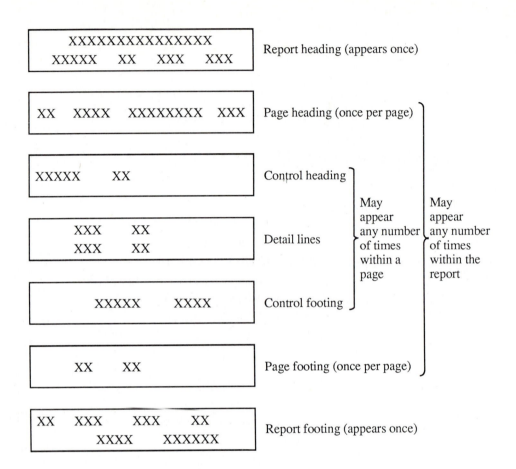

FIGURE 13-1   GENERAL REPORT STRUCTURE.

headings. The report data are included in *detail lines* of one or more formats. A *control heading* introduces a new category of data, such as a new department or a new salesperson. A *control footing* typically is used to summarize the data presented in the preceding group of detail lines, as, for instance, the total sales for the salesperson whose detail sales were just reported. Finally, the end of each page may include a *page footing* that includes summary data for the page or simply serves as an alternate page-numbering position. After all pages have been presented, a *report footing* may be included to designate the end of the report or to provide summary data about the report as a whole.

Report generation is characterized by common logical program procedures. Because of the common characteristics and the frequent need for report programs, a large number of *report writer* program products have been developed. These proprietary report writers are of two types. One type uses a specialized language that the programmer can use to compose a report-generating program. Such specialized languages are of course nonstandard and are unique to each program product. Many are "user-friendly" languages that can be used by "layman" users with just a few hours of training. A second type of report writer is the parameter-driven report writer. The program requires specifications about headings, totals, etc., as parameters, and then is used to generate the desired report.

In the context of COBOL programming many report-generating programs are coded in the usual fashion. However, a special *report writer feature* which facilitates report programming, and also has the property of being standardized, is available. This COBOL feature is a language type of report writer. In essence, the report writer feature is a specialized language embedded in the COBOL framework for use in report-generating programs. The report writer is described in the last four sections of this chapter, after some general concepts on report generation are discussed.

Review

1   In general, a report may consist of a report heading, a report body, and a report _____.

footing

2   Of the subdivisions in a page of a report, the type of heading that introduces a new category of data is the _____ heading.

control

3   Data that have been presented in the preceding group of data lines are summarized in the control _____.

footing

4   With respect to commercially available report writer programs, one type is based on the use of specialized _____ while the second type requires that the _____ of the desired report be input.

languages; parameters

5   The COBOL feature which facilitates the programming of report-generating programs, is called the _____ feature.

report writer

CONTROL BREAKS IN REPORT WRITING

Most reports pertain to data that are associated with categories which bear a hierarchical relation to each other. Very often, the categories correspond to organizational departments or groupings. For instance, suppose that we are producing a report listing alphabetically the enrollment for a college. We have students enrolled in a section, sections belonging to a course, courses belonging to a department, and departments belonging to a college. Suppose that we are interested in having the enrollment reported in a way that makes these relationships meaningful. To achieve this objective, we designate that each section begin on a new page with a header, that there be a header for each course, and that there be a header for each department. Further, we designate that total enrollment be reported for each section, for each course, for each department, and for the entire college.

In the context of the recurring control breaks in this example, we would say that we have three control breaks: section, course, and department. We speak of department as the *major* control, course as the *intermediate*, and section as the *minor* control. Of course, we may have more than three control levels, each subordinate to its superior and all subordinates to one—the major control.

As the report is being produced we want to *break* the routine whenever a new section, a new course, or a new department begins. The *control* is based on the content of the fields that designate the section, course, and department. We would expect that the report writer would check the section, for instance; and, if it changed, we would want to print the total enrollment for the section just listed. But it may be that the section did not change (say section 1 of a one-section course), but the course number changed from CIS-302 to CIS-402. The report writer then also must be checking the course designation to capture the change. A similar checking procedure is required for department designation.

The highest level of control break is called the *final* control, which is of course nonrecurring. In essence, it is a means of controlling the report writer action when all the detail data have been processed. In the registration example, a final control break would occur when the last department in the college had been processed and we were ready to report the enrollment for the entire college.

A point that relates to the control breaks is the fact that they enable the user to present report groups that are called control headings and control footings. A *control heading* is a report group (one or more lines of output) that is presented when a control break occurs. For example, a control heading specified for the department field could be used to print the department-name and start a new page. As the name implies, a *control footing* is a report group that is presented at the end of a group and before the next category begins. In our example, at the end of each course we might desire a control footing to write the accumulated total enrollment of all the sections in that course. Typically, control footings are used for accumulating and reporting totals, while control headings are used for printing headers.

It should be noted that the control fields and the sort order of the input file are related. In our example, we would expect that the data have been sorted by student within section, by section within course, by course within department, and by department within the college. This sorting would be appropriate to establishing control breaks that treat department as a more inclusive control than course, course as more inclusive than section, and so forth.

Review

1   When control breaks are used in conjunction with a report writer, the category that is at the highest hierarchical level compared with the other categories is termed the _____ control.

major

2   In addition to the major control breaks, other levels of such breaks are _____ and _____ controls.

intermediate; minor

3   When all data have been processed, the last break is associated with the output of grand totals for all of the categories and is called the _____ control break.

final

4   A heading (or footing) that is printed just before (or just after) a data group that is associated with a control break is called a(n) _____ heading (or footing).

control

LOGIC OF REPORT PROGRAMS

The logical structure of report-generating programs tends to be similar regardless of the specific characteristics of the individual report. Figure 13–2 outlines this general logic in flowchart form. The figure is based on a report with three control breaks that are associated with the three fields: Dept.,

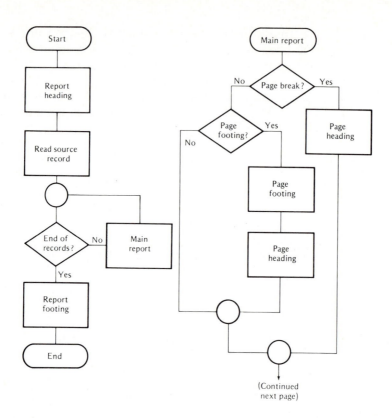

FIGURE 13-2   SAMPLE REPORT LOGIC FLOWCHART FOR THREE CONTROL BREAKS.

Month, and Part. Although the flowchart references these three control breaks, it is easy to see that it applies in concept to any report program with three levels of control breaks. Also, if we have a different number of control breaks, the flowchart can be easily adapted to that need.

We illustrate report program logic with an example. Figure 13-3 presents sample output from a report with two control breaks: Salesman Name and Product No. A generalized structure chart is presented in Figure 13-4, while Figure 13-5 presents the structure chart for a specific example program. In this case there is no report heading, but such a module could be easily added without affecting the existing structure. The sample program that corresponds to the structure chart in Figure 13-5 is presented in Figure 13-6.

Reviewing Figure 13-5, notice the module labeled 030-DETERMINE-CONTROL-BREAK-LEVEL. What was the basis for including this module in the chart? We asked the question: "What is needed in order to select execution of particular control headings and footings?" We then realized that their execution is dependent on the *particular* control break. So, we concluded that a black box is needed to do the task of "sorting out" the control break situation.

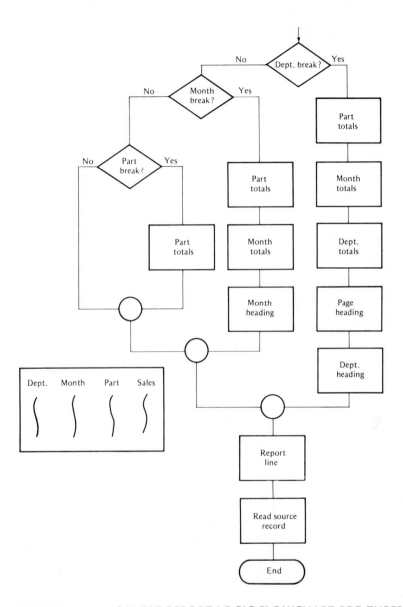

FIGURE 13-2   SAMPLE REPORT LOGIC FLOWCHART FOR THREE CONTROL BREAKS.   (Continued)

The 100-PRINT-LINE module(s) in Figure 13-5 do not show subordinates, unlike the counterpart in Figure 13-4. Since no page footing is needed in this case, and since the page heading is a minor task, we chose to combine those functions in one module. However, should we later need to add more elaborate page heading and/or page footing functions, it would be easy to add both to the chart and to the program.

```
SALESMAN NAME       PRODUCT NO.     SALES AMOUNT     TOTAL SALES

ADAMSON, JOHN       123               125.27
                                      100.00

    *  TOTAL FOR PRODUCT   123                          $225.27

ADAMSON, JOHN       345                50.00
                                      110.25
                                       10.29

    *  TOTAL FOR PRODUCT   345                          $170.54

   **  TOTAL FOR SALESMAN    ADAMSON, JOHN             $395.81

ROSELLE, LINDA      123             4,000.00

    *  TOTAL FOR PRODUCT   123                        $4,000.00

   **  TOTAL FOR SALESMAN    ROSELLE, LINDA           $4,000.00

WILLIAMS, MARY      123               200.00
                                      500.00
                                      300.00
                                    1,125.00


SALESMAN NAME       PRODUCT NO.     SALES AMOUNT     TOTAL SALES

    *  TOTAL FOR PRODUCT   123                        $2,125.00

   **  TOTAL FOR SALESMAN    WILLIAMS, MARY           $2,125.00

      ***  TOTAL SALES FOR REPORT                     $6,520.81
```

FIGURE 13-3   SAMPLE OUTPUT FOR A PROGRAM WITH TWO CONTROL BREAKS.

Review

1   The logical structure of different report-generating programs generally is [very similar/quite different].

very similar

2   In a flowchart, control breaks are always represented by _____ symbols.

decision

WRITE WITH THE LINAGE CLAUSE

The WRITE verb has some specialized options in order to facilitate report generation for sequential files. Figure 13–7 presents the expanded format for the WRITE verb. We observe the AT END-OF-PAGE conditional statement.

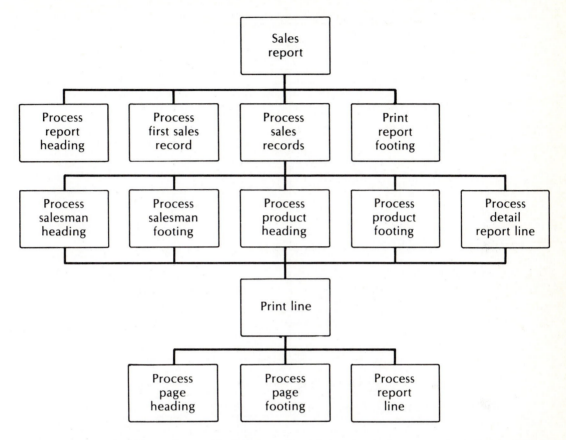

FIGURE 13-4   STRUCTURE CHART FOR TWO-LEVEL CONTROL BREAK LOGIC.

When specified, a check is made to determine if the END-OF-PAGE (abbreviated EOP) condition is met. If it is, then the imperative statement is executed.

The END-OF-PAGE condition is defined by means of the LINAGE clause in the DATA DIVISION, which has the format presented in Figure 13–8.

Let us consider an example. We want to produce a report with the following format:

LINE NUMBER	CONTENTS
1–5	Not used
6	The page header
7–56	The body of the report
57–59	The page totals
60–66	Not used

Text continues on page 487.

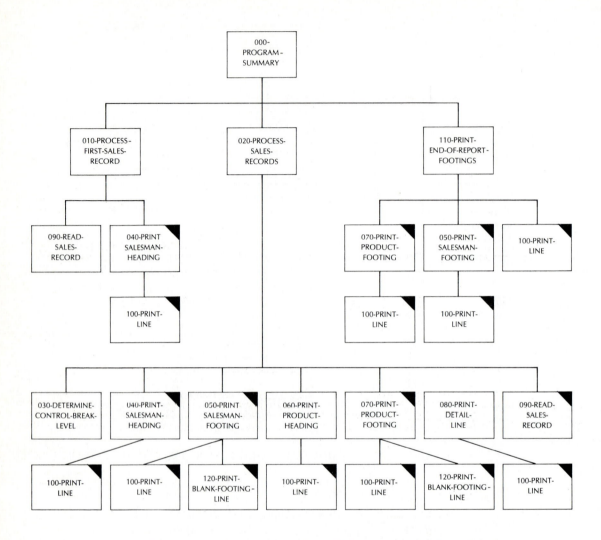

FIGURE 13-5   STRUCTURE CHART FOR SAMPLE REPORT PROGRAM.

```
IDENTIFICATION DIVISION.
PROGRAM-ID. CONTROL-BREAKS.
*
ENVIRONMENT DIVISION.
*
CONFIGURATION SECTION.
SOURCE-COMPUTER. ABC-480.
OBJECT-COMPUTER. ABC-480.
*
INPUT-OUTPUT SECTION.
*
FILE-CONTROL.
    SELECT SALES-FILE  ASSIGN TO  file name/device.
    SELECT REPORT-FILE ASSIGN TO  printer name.
*
DATA DIVISION.
*
FILE SECTION.
*
FD   SALES-FILE     LABEL RECORDS ARE OMITTED
                    RECORD CONTAINS 80 CHARACTERS
                    DATA RECORD IS SALES-RECORD.
01   SALES-RECORD.
     02 SALESMAN-NAME          PIC X(15).
     02 PRODUCT-NUMBER         PIC 9(3).
     02 SALES-AMOUNT           PIC 9(4)V99.
     02 FILLER                 PIC X(56).
*
FD   REPORT-FILE    LABEL RECORDS ARE OMITTED
                    DATA RECORD IS REPORT-RECORD.
01   REPORT-RECORD             PIC X(132).
*
WORKING-STORAGE SECTION.
*
01   PREVIOUS-VALUES.
     02 PREVIOUS-SALESMAN-NAME  PIC X(15).
     02 PREVIOUS-PRODUCT-NUMBER PIC 9(3).
*
01   PROGRAM-FLAGS.
     02 END-OF-FILE-INDICATOR   PIC XXX    VALUE 'NO'.
        88  END-OF-FILE                    VALUE IS 'YES'.
*
     02 CONTROL-BREAK-LEVEL     PIC 9.
        88  NO-BREAK                       VALUE ZERO.
        88  PRODUCT-BREAK                  VALUE 1.
        88  SALESMAN-BREAK                 VALUE 2.
*
     02 FOOTING-INDICATOR       PIC XXX    VALUE 'NO'.
        88  NO-FOOTING                     VALUE 'NO'.
        88  YES-FOOTING                    VALUE 'YES'.
*
01   PAGE-SIZE                  PIC 99     VALUE 25.
```

FIGURE 13-6   LISTING OF PROGRAM WITH CONTROL BREAKS.

```
01   PAGE-LINE-COUNTER              PIC 99     VALUE 25.
*
01   PAGE-HEADING.
     02 FILLER                      PIC X(10) VALUE SPACE.
     02 FILLER                      PIC X(13) VALUE 'SALESMAN NAME'.
     02 FILLER                      PIC X(4)  VALUE SPACES.
     02 FILLER                      PIC X(11) VALUE 'PRODUCT NO.'.
     02 FILLER                      PIC X(3)  VALUE SPACES.
     02 FILLER                      PIC X(12) VALUE 'SALES AMOUNT'.
     02 FILLER                      PIC X(4)  VALUE SPACES.
     02 FILLER                      PIC X(11) VALUE 'TOTAL SALES'.
*
01   REPORT-LINE.
     02 FILLER                      PIC X(10) VALUE SPACES.
     02 SALESMAN-NAME-OUT           PIC X(15).
     02 FILLER                      PIC X(2)  VALUE SPACES.
     02 PRODUCT-NUMBER-OUT          PIC 999.
     02 FILLER                      PIC X(11) VALUE SPACES.
     02 SALES-AMOUNT-OUT            PIC Z,ZZ9.99.
     02 FILLER                      PIC X(8)  VALUE SPACES.
     02 TOTAL-SALES-OUT             PIC $$$,$$9.99.
*
01   SALESMAN-FOOTING.
     02 FILLER                      PIC X(12) VALUE SPACES.
     02 FILLER                      PIC X(24)
          VALUE '** TOTAL FOR SALESMAN   '.
     02 SALESMAN-NAME-FOOTING       PIC X(15).
     02 FILLER                      PIC X(3)  VALUE SPACES.
     02 TOTAL-SALESMAN-FOOTING      PIC $$,$$$,$$9.99.
*
01   PRODUCT-FOOTING.
     02 FILLER                      PIC X(14) VALUE SPACES.
     02 FILLER                      PIC X(21)
          VALUE '* TOTAL FOR PRODUCT   '.
     02 PRODUCT-NUMBER-FOOTING      PIC 999.
     02 FILLER                      PIC X(16) VALUE SPACES.
     02 TOTAL-PRODUCT-FOOTING       PIC $$,$$$,$$9.99.
*
01   REPORT-FOOTING.
     02 FILLER                      PIC X(18) VALUE SPACES.
     02 FILLER                      PIC X(26)
          VALUE '*** TOTAL SALES FOR REPORT'.
     02 FILLER                      PIC X(10) VALUE SPACES.
     02 TOTAL-REPORT-FOOTING        PIC $$,$$$,$$9.99.
*
01   SALES-TOTALS.
     02 PRODUCT-TOTAL-SALES         PIC 9(6)V99 VALUE ZERO.
     02 SALESMAN-TOTAL-SALES        PIC 9(6)V99 VALUE ZERO.
     02 REPORT-TOTAL-SALES          PIC 9(7)V99 VALUE ZERO.
```

**FIGURE 13-6   LISTING OF PROGRAM WITH CONTROL BREAKS.
(Continued)**

```
    PROCEDURE DIVISION.
*
000-PROGRAM-SUMMARY.
    OPEN INPUT SALES-FILE.
    OPEN OUTPUT REPORT-FILE.
*
    PERFORM 010-PROCESS-FIRST-SALES-RECORD.
*
    PERFORM 020-PROCESS-SALES-RECORDS
        UNTIL END-OF-FILE.
*
    PERFORM 110-END-OF-REPORT-FOOTING.
*
    CLOSE SALES-FILE
          REPORT-FILE.
*
    STOP RUN.
*
010-PROCESS-FIRST-SALES-RECORD.
    PERFORM 090-READ-SALES-RECORD.
*
    IF NOT END-OF-FILE
        MOVE SALESMAN-NAME TO PREVIOUS-SALESMAN-NAME
        MOVE PRODUCT-NUMBER TO PREVIOUS-PRODUCT-NUMBER
        PERFORM 040-PRINT-SALESMAN-HEADING
        PERFORM 090-READ-SALES-RECORD.
*
020-PROCESS-SALES-RECORDS.
*
    PERFORM 030-DETERMINE-CNTRL-BRK-LEVEL.
*
    IF CONTROL-BREAK-LEVEL > 0
        PERFORM 070-PRINT-PRODUCT-FOOTING.
    IF CONTROL-BREAK-LEVEL > 1
        PERFORM 050-PRINT-SALESMAN-FOOTING.
*
  EVALUATE CONTROL-BREAK-LEVEL
        WHEN ZERO PERFORM 080-PRINT-DETAIL-LINE
        WHEN 1    PERFORM 060-PRINT-PRODUCT-HEADING
        WHEN 2    PERFORM 040-PRINT-SALESMAN-HEADING.
*
    MOVE SALESMAN-NAME TO PREVIOUS-SALESMAN-NAME.
    MOVE PRODUCT-NUMBER TO PREVIOUS-PRODUCT-NUMBER.
    PERFORM 090-READ-SALES-RECORD.
*
030-DETERMINE-CNTRL-BRK-LEVEL.
*
    IF SALESMAN-NAME NOT = PREVIOUS-SALESMAN-NAME
        MOVE 2 TO CONTROL-BREAK-LEVEL
    ELSE
        IF PRODUCT-NUMBER NOT = PREVIOUS-PRODUCT-NUMBER
            MOVE 1 TO CONTROL-BREAK-LEVEL
        ELSE
            MOVE 0 TO CONTROL-BREAK-LEVEL.
```

**FIGURE 13-6   LISTING OF PROGRAM WITH CONTROL BREAKS.
(Continued)**

```
 040-PRINT-SALESMAN-HEADING.
*
     MOVE SPACES TO REPORT-LINE.
     MOVE SALESMAN-NAME TO SALESMAN-NAME-OUT.
     MOVE PRODUCT-NUMBER TO PRODUCT-NUMBER-OUT.
     MOVE SALES-AMOUNT TO SALES-AMOUNT-OUT.
     PERFORM 100-PRINT-LINE.
     ADD SALES-AMOUNT TO PRODUCT-TOTAL-SALES.
*
 050-PRINT-SALESMAN-FOOTING.
*
     MOVE PREVIOUS-SALESMAN-NAME TO SALESMAN-NAME-FOOTING.
     MOVE SALESMAN-TOTAL-SALES TO TOTAL-SALESMAN-FOOTING.
     MOVE SALESMAN-FOOTING TO REPORT-LINE.
     MOVE 'YES' TO FOOTING-INDICATOR.
     PERFORM 100-PRINT-LINE.
     MOVE 'NO' TO FOOTING-INDICATOR.
     PERFORM 120-PRINT-BLANK-FOOTING-LINE.
     ADD SALESMAN-TOTAL-SALES TO REPORT-TOTAL-SALES.
     MOVE ZERO TO SALESMAN-TOTAL-SALES.
*
 060-PRINT-PRODUCT-HEADING.
*
     MOVE SPACES TO REPORT-LINE.
     MOVE SALESMAN-NAME TO SALESMAN-NAME-OUT.
     MOVE PRODUCT-NUMBER TO PRODUCT-NUMBER-OUT.
     MOVE SALES-AMOUNT TO SALES-AMOUNT-OUT.
     PERFORM 100-PRINT-LINE.
     ADD SALES-AMOUNT TO PRODUCT-TOTAL-SALES.
*
 070-PRINT-PRODUCT-FOOTING.
*
     PERFORM 120-PRINT-BLANK-FOOTING-LINE.
     MOVE PREVIOUS-PRODUCT-NUMBER TO PRODUCT-NUMBER-FOOTING.
     MOVE PRODUCT-TOTAL-SALES TO TOTAL-PRODUCT-FOOTING.
     MOVE PRODUCT-FOOTING TO REPORT-LINE.
     MOVE 'YES' TO FOOTING-INDICATOR.
     PERFORM 100-PRINT-LINE.
     MOVE 'NO' TO FOOTING-INDICATOR.
     PERFORM 120-PRINT-BLANK-FOOTING-LINE.
     ADD PRODUCT-TOTAL-SALES TO SALESMAN-TOTAL-SALES.
     MOVE ZERO TO PRODUCT-TOTAL-SALES.
*
 080-PRINT-DETAIL-LINE.
     MOVE SPACES TO REPORT-LINE.
     MOVE SALES-AMOUNT TO SALES-AMOUNT-OUT.
     PERFORM 100-PRINT-LINE.
     ADD SALES-AMOUNT TO PRODUCT-TOTAL-SALES.
*
 090-READ-SALES-RECORD.
*
   READ SALES-FILE RECORD
       AT END SET END-OF-FILE TO TRUE.
```

**FIGURE 13-6   LISTING OF PROGRAM WITH CONTROL BREAKS.
(Continued)**

```
  100-PRINT-LINE.
*
      IF PAGE-LINE-COUNTER > PAGE-SIZE OR
         PAGE-LINE-COUNTER = PAGE-SIZE
         WRITE REPORT-RECORD FROM PAGE-HEADING
            AFTER ADVANCING PAGE
         MOVE SPACES TO REPORT-RECORD
         WRITE REPORT-RECORD AFTER ADVANCING 1
         MOVE 2 TO PAGE-LINE-COUNTER
*
         IF NO-FOOTING
            MOVE SALESMAN-NAME TO SALESMAN-NAME-OUT
            MOVE PRODUCT-NUMBER TO PRODUCT-NUMBER-OUT.
*
      WRITE REPORT-RECORD FROM REPORT-LINE
         AFTER ADVANCING 1.
      ADD 1 TO PAGE-LINE-COUNTER.
*
  110-END-OF-REPORT-FOOTING.
*
      PERFORM 070-PRINT-PRODUCT-FOOTING.
      PERFORM 050-PRINT-SALESMAN-FOOTING.
      MOVE REPORT-TOTAL-SALES TO TOTAL-REPORT-FOOTING.
      MOVE REPORT-FOOTING TO REPORT-LINE.
      MOVE 'YES' TO FOOTING-INDICATOR.
      PERFORM 100-PRINT-LINE.
*
  120-PRINT-BLANK-FOOTING-LINE.
      IF PAGE-LINE-COUNTER < PAGE-SIZE
         MOVE SPACES TO REPORT-LINE
         PERFORM 100-PRINT-LINE.
```

**FIGURE 13-6   LISTING OF PROGRAM WITH CONTROL BREAKS.
(Continued)**

We could proceed as follows:

DATA DIVISION.
 :
 :
 :
FD PRINT-FILE LABEL RECORD OMITTED
            DATA RECORD IS PRINT-REC
            LINAGE IS 54 LINES
                WITH FOOTING AT 51
                LINES AT TOP 5
                LINES AT BOTTOM 7.

The page will consist of 66 lines, which is the sum of the values referenced in each phrase except for the FOOTING phrase. Five lines are unused at the top, and 7 at the bottom.

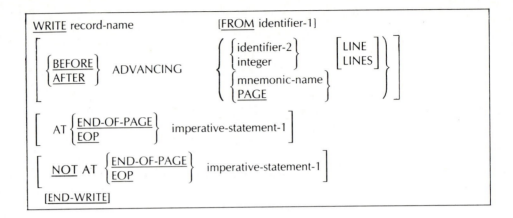

FIGURE 13-7   GENERAL FORMAT FOR THE WRITE VERB.

In the PROCEDURE DIVISION, the statement:

WRITE PRINT-REC FROM TOP-HEADER AFTER ADVANCING PAGE

will cause printing of the header on line 6 because now PAGE is associated with line 6, since LINES AT TOP 5 specifies that 5 lines be left blank at the top of the page. (TOP-HEADER in this example is assumed to contain the desired header.)

Now consider these statements:

```
        WRITE PRINT-REC FROM BODY-OF-REPORT-LINE
            AFTER ADVANCING 1 LINE
            AT END-OF-PAGE PERFORM TOTALS.
TOTALS.
        WRITE PRINT-REC FROM TOTALS-LINE
            AFTER ADVANCING 3 LINES
        WRITE PRINT-REC FROM TOP-HEADER
            AFTER ADVANCING PAGE.
```

We will keep printing data from BODY-OF-REPORT-LINE until we have reached line 56 (51 + 5), which is defined as the footing: WITH FOOTING AT 51. At that point, the END-OF-PAGE condition will hold and we will PERFORM TOTALS, in which we print data on line 59 (triple-spacing) and then skip to the next page (line 6 of the next page) to print the page header TOP-HEADER.

$$\boxed{\begin{array}{l} \underline{\text{LINAGE}} \text{ IS } \left\{\begin{array}{l} \text{data-name-1} \\ \text{integer-1} \end{array}\right\} \text{ LINES } \left[\text{WITH } \underline{\text{FOOTING}} \text{ AT } \left\{\begin{array}{l} \text{data-name-2} \\ \text{integer-2} \end{array}\right\}\right] \\ \left[\text{LINES AT } \underline{\text{TOP}} \ \left\{\begin{array}{l} \text{data-name-3} \\ \text{integer-3} \end{array}\right\}\right] \quad \left[\text{LINES AT } \underline{\text{BOTTOM}} \ \left\{\begin{array}{l} \text{data-name-4} \\ \text{integer-4} \end{array}\right\}\right] \end{array}}$$

FIGURE 13-8   GENERAL FORMAT FOR THE LINAGE CLAUSE.

A special counter is used whenever LINAGE is specified. It is called LINAGE-COUNTER, a COBOL reserved word. It is set to 1 when a print file is opened or when an ADVANCING PAGE is encountered. Afterward, the counter is automatically incremented the appropriate number of lines implied in each WRITE statement. When LINAGE-COUNTER is equal to the value of the FOOTING phrase, then an END-OF-PAGE condition occurs. The LINAGE-FOOTER may not be modified by the program, but it may be accessed. Thus, it is legitimate to write: IF LINAGE-COUNTER = 25 PERFORM MID-PAGE ROUTINE.

Review

1   When an END-OF-PAGE (EOP) condition is specified in conjunction with a WRITE statement, then the description of the number of lines and their use has to be defined in a(n) _____ clause in the DATA DIVISION.

LINAGE

2   The special counter that is a reserved word and is used implicitly whenever the LINAGE option is specified is the _____.

LINAGE-COUNTER

3   Assume these entries for the figure shown on page 490:

LINAGE IS 25 LINES
WITH FOOTING AT 21
LINES AT TOP 2
LINES AT BOTTOM 3

Fill in the missing members:

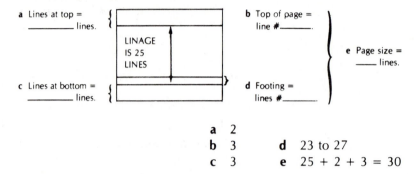

a Lines at top =
_____ lines.

b Top of page =
line #_____.

c Lines at bottom =
_____ lines.

d Footing =
lines #_____.

e Page size =
_____ lines.

LINAGE
IS 25
LINES

a 2
b 3   **d** 23 to 27
c 3   **e** 25 + 2 + 3 = 30

THE REPORT WRITER FEATURE—A BASIC EXAMPLE

The report writer module provides the facility for producing reports by specifying the physical appearance of a report through the use of special instructions rather than by requiring specification of the detailed procedures necessary to produce the report. For most reports, the report writer facility will prove an advantage by reducing program logic requirements and by reducing errors. The report writer is part of the COBOL language, and it can be incorporated into any program except in cases of small-system compilers which do not include this feature.

Our description of the report writer begins with a basic example, in an attempt to impart an overall view of the use of this language feature. Then additional capabilities are discussed in the context of a more advanced example. Finally, the formal language skeleton is presented along with explanations.

Figure 13-9 presents the desired report format for the basic example. In this case, there are five parts to the report. The first one is a *report heading*, a title for the report. Such a heading will appear only once in a report, and, in this example, we desire it to be on a separate page. Then there is the *page heading*. This is a heading that we want to have printed at the beginning of each page of the report. The report *detail* consists of the actual data of the report. In this case, we require four fields for each line of report detail. The first field includes 18 alphanumerics in columns 4–21, the second field includes 2 numerics in columns 27–28, the third field includes 4 alphanumerics in columns 39–42, and the fourth field is a numeric edited field in columns 52–61. A *page footing* is desired that consists of the literal PAGE and a Z9 field to print the page number. Finally, corresponding to the report heading, we desire a *report footing*, which will be printed at the very end of the report. In the report writer terminology, the report heading, the page heading, the detail, the page footing, and the report footing are called *report groups*. Additional report groups will be described later.

Now that we have described the horizontal format for each report group, we turn our attention to the vertical format of the report. Most re-

AMERICAN SALES CORPORATION

INVOICE TOTALS REPORT

********** }
******** } Report Heading lines 12 - 19 on separate page
***

| DEPARTMENT | MONTH | PRODUCT CODE | INVOICE TOTALS |

} Page Heading on line 5

XXXXXXXXXXXXXXXXX   99   XXXX   ZZZ,ZZ9.99   } Report Detail on lines 7-19

PAGE 29   } Page Footing on line 23

** END OF REPORT**   } Report Footing on line 25

FIGURE 13-9   DESIRED REPORT FORMAT.

ports consist of pages. For this example, we assume that a page consists of 25 lines. Within the per-page limit of 25 lines, we define the desired vertical layout, as shown in Figure 13–9. Notice that the report heading will start on line 12 of the first page and will end on line 18. No other data will be presented on that page. The page heading will appear on line 5, and, since in this case it consists of only 1 line, it will also end on line 5. The first detail line will start on line 7 (we double-space between it and the page heading), while the last detail line will be printed on line 19. Then the page footing will appear on line 23, while the report footing will appear on line 25 of the last page only.

Figure 13–10 presents the header page, the second page, and the last page of the report. The design of the report format constitutes the major conceptual effort in report writing. The next step consists of translating the two-dimensional layout to COBOL instructions.

Let us assume that our task is defined as follows. We desire to read data from a file and to produce a report with the format presented in Figure 13–9. The input file records have the record description on the following page.

```
               AMERICAN SALES CORPORATION
               INVOICE TOTALS REPORT
                    ***************
                       *******
                         ***


      DEPARTMENT      MONTH    PRODUCT CODE      INVOICE-TOTALS
   APPLIANCES           01        A-10             100.25
   APPLIANCES           01,       A-11              25.25
   APPLIANCES           01        A-15             250.00
   APPLIANCES           01        B-13              83.00
   APPLIANCES           01        B-20           9,008.30
   APPLIANCES           01.       B-21             150.50
   APPLIANCES           01        B-22             326.60
   APPLIANCES           01        C-10               8.90
   APPLIANCES           02        A-10              90.20
   APPLIANCES           02        A-15              85.37
   APPLIANCES           02        A-25             654.92
   APPLIANCES           02        B-18             870.00
   APPLIANCES           02        B-20              50.00


                      PAGE    2


      DEPARTMENT      MONTH    PRODUCT CODE      INVOICE-TOTALS
   CHILDRENS CLOTHING   03        1-16             118.42
   CHILDRENS CLOTHING   03        1-17             100.00
   CHILDRENS CLOTHING   03        1-18              20.00
   CHILDRENS CLOTHING   03        1-19              70.00
   CHILDRENS CLOTHING   03        1-20              79.85
   CHILDRENS CLOTHING   03        1-21              85.42
   CHILDRENS CLOTHING   03        1-22             160.66
   CHILDRENS CLOTHING   03        1-23             158.18
   CHILDRENS CLOTHING   03        1-24             750.00


                    PAGE    6

                 **END OF REPORT**
```

FIGURE 13–10   HEADER PAGE, PAGE 2, AND LAST PAGE OF THE REQUIRED REPORT.

COLUMN	DATA-NAME	PICTURE
1–18	DEPARTMENT-IN	X(18)
19–20	MONTH-IN	99
21–24	PRODUCT-CODE-IN	X(4)
25–32	INVOICE-TOTALS-IN	9(6)V99
33–80	FILLER	X(48)

Our task will involve printing a report with appropriate page headings, specified horizontal and vertical spacing, and page and report footings. The data for the report will be provided from a file. For each record read in there will be a report line printed. Figure 13-11 presents the first part of a program written to accomplish this task. It will be noted that it is just like any COBOL program so far, with one file assigned to SOURCE and another file assigned to the PRINTER. The FD entry and the record description for SOURCE-REC are typical of COBOL programs in general.

We want to produce the report on the device called PRINTER (as indicated by the SELECT statement in the ENVIRONMENT DIVISION). Since this will be a report produced by the report writer, the FD for REPORTFILE is as given on the following page.

```
IDENTIFICATION DIVISION.
PROGRAM-ID. REPGEN1.
*
ENVIRONMENT DIVISION.
CONFIGURATION SECTION.
SOURCE-COMPUTER. ABC-480.
OBJECT-COMPUTER. ABC-480.
INPUT-OUTPUT SECTION.
FILE-CONTROL.
     SELECT SOURCE-FILE   ASSIGN TO SOURCE-READER.
     SELECT REPORTFILE    ASSIGN TO PRINTER.
*
DATA DIVISION.
FILE SECTION.
FD   SOURCE-FILE
        LABEL RECORDS ARE OMITTED
        DATA RECORD IS SOURCE-REC.
01   SOURCE-REC.
     02 DEPARTMENT-IN        PIC X(18).
     02 MONTH-IN             PIC 99.
     02 PRODUCT-CODE-IN      PIC X(4).
     02 INVOICE-TOTALS-IN    PIC 9(6)V99.
     02 FILLER              PIC X(48).
```

FIGURE 13-11   FIRST PART OF THE COBOL PROGRAM FOR THE BASIC EXAMPLE.

```
FD REPORTFILE
        LABEL RECORDS ARE OMITTED
        REPORT IS INVOICE-REPORT.
```

The terms REPORTFILE and INVOICE REPORT are arbitrary choices of the program author. That the LABEL RECORDS ARE OMITTED is no surprise, since this is a printer file, but they could have been STANDARD if, for example, the report were to be produced on tape (for eventual transmission to printer or display terminal). What is new is the REPORT IS clause. Instead of saying DATA RECORDS IS, as is the case for other files, we now use the reserved word REPORT IS.

Figure 13–12 presents the complete COBOL program. Notice that, following the FILE SECTION of the DATA DIVISION and the WORKING-STORAGE SECTION, we write the REPORT SECTION.

The report description (RD) entry parallels the file description (FD) entry of an ordinary file. The report-name in RD INVOICE-REPORT must be the same as in the FD entry of the report file, where the REPORT IS clause gives the report-name. The PAGE clause is optional, but it is commonly used unless we simply desire a report that is continuous and not broken into pages (in other words, a report consisting of one long page). In the example, we have:

```
RD INVOICE-REPORT
        PAGE LIMIT IS 25 LINES
        HEADING 5
        FIRST DETAIL 7
        LAST DETAIL 19.
```

The indentations and the separate lines are used here for visual clarity. The RD must appear on columns 8–9, and the other clauses must be in column 12 or to the right of 12. PAGE LIMIT IS 25 LINES defines the page size in terms of vertical lines. This page size has nothing to do with the physical size of the paper, which is defined by the crease. It should be kept in mind that the space between pages is controlled by the printer carriage control tape, which is designated by the operator or reflects the convention of each computer installation.

The HEADING 5 entry in Figure 13–12 means that page or report headings will start on line 5. The entries for FIRST DETAIL and LAST DETAIL define the inclusive range of lines on which detail report lines can be written.

It will be noted that in this example no mention is made in the PAGE entry about the page and report footing. The omission is intentional, so that the example can provide an illustration of defining vertical positioning apart

```
IDENTIFICATION DIVISION.
PROGRAM-ID. REPGEN1.
*
ENVIRONMENT DIVISION.
CONFIGURATION SECTION.
SOURCE-COMPUTER. ABC-480.
OBJECT-COMPUTER. ABC-480.
INPUT-OUTPUT SECTION.
FILE-CONTROL.
    SELECT SOURCE-FILE    ASSIGN TO SOURCE-READER.
    SELECT REPORTFILE     ASSIGN TO PRINTER.
*
DATA DIVISION.
FILE SECTION.
FD  SOURCE-FILE
        LABEL RECORDS ARE OMITTED
        DATA RECORD IS SOURCE-REC.
01  SOURCE-REC.
    02 DEPARTMENT-IN       PIC X(18).
    02 MONTH-IN            PIC 99.
    02 PRODUCT-CODE-IN     PIC X(4).
    02 INVOICE-TOTALS-IN   PIC 9(6)V99.
    02 FILLER              PIC X(48).
*
FD  REPORTFILE
        LABEL RECORDS ARE OMITTED
        REPORT IS INVOICE-REPORT.
*
WORKING-STORAGE SECTION.
01  END-OF-DATA        PIC XXX.
*
REPORT SECTION.
RD  INVOICE-REPORT
        PAGE LIMIT IS 25 LINES
            HEADING 5
            FIRST DETAIL 7
            LAST DETAIL 19.
*
01  TYPE IS REPORT HEADING
      NEXT GROUP NEXT PAGE.
    02 LINE NUMBER IS 12
       COLUMN NUMBER IS 24
       PICTURE IS A(26)
       VALUE IS 'AMERICAN SALES CORPORATION'.
    02 LINE NUMBER IS PLUS 2
       COLUMN NUMBER IS 28
       PICTURE IS X(21)
       VALUE IS 'INVOICE TOTALS REPORT'.
```

FIGURE 13-12   THE COMPLETE COBOL PROGRAM FOR THE BASIC
EXAMPLE.

```
        02 LINE NUMBER IS PLUS 2
           COLUMN NUMBER IS 32
           PICTURE IS X(13)
           VALUE IS ALL '*'.
        02 LINE NUMBER IS PLUS 1
           COLUMN NUMBER IS 35
           PICTURE IS X(7)
           VALUE ALL '*'.
        02 LINE NUMBER IS PLUS 1
           COLUMN NUMBER IS 37
           PICTURE IS XXX
           VALUE '***'.
*
  01   TYPE PAGE HEADING
     LINE NUMBER IS 5.
        02 COLUMN NUMBER IS 11
           PICTURE IS X(20)
           VALUE IS 'DEPARTMENT      MONTH'.
        02 COLUMN NUMBER IS 35
           PICTURE IS X(30)
           VALUE IS 'PRODUCT CODE     INVOICE-TOTALS'.
*
  01   INVOICE-DATA
           TYPE IS DETAIL
           LINE NUMBER IS PLUS 1.
        02 COLUMN NUMBER IS 4
           PICTURE IS X(18)
           SOURCE IS DEPARTMENT-IN.
        02 COLUMN NUMBER IS 27
           PICTURE IS 99
           SOURCE IS MONTH-IN.
        02 COLUMN NUMBER IS 39
           SOURCE IS PRODUCT-CODE-IN
           PICTURE IS X(4).
        02 COLUMN NUMBER IS 52
           PICTURE IS ZZZ,ZZ9.99
           SOURCE IS INVOICE-TOTALS-IN.
*
  01   TYPE PAGE FOOTING.
        02 LINE 23.
           03 COLUMN 34
              PIC AAAA
              VALUE 'PAGE'.
           03 COLUMN 40
              PIC Z9
              SOURCE IS PAGE-COUNTER.
  01   TYPE REPORT FOOTING
       LINE 25.
       02 COLUMN 30
       VALUE '**END OF REPORT**'
       PIC X(17).
```

**FIGURE 13-12   THE COMPLETE COBOL PROGRAM FOR THE BASIC
EXAMPLE.   (Continued)**

*

```
PROCEDURE DIVISION.
SET-UP.
    OPEN INPUT  SOURCE-FILE
          OUTPUT REPORTFILE.
    MOVE 'NO' TO END-OF-DATA
    READ SOURCE-FILE RECORD
        AT END MOVE 'YES' TO END-OF-DATA.
    INITIATE INVOICE-REPORT.
    PERFORM READ-PRINT
       UNTIL END-OF-DATA = 'YES'.
    TERMINATE INVOICE-REPORT
    CLOSE SOURCE-FILE REPORTFILE
    STOP RUN.
 READ-PRINT.
    GENERATE INVOICE-DATA.
    READ SOURCE-FILE RECORD
        AT END MOVE 'YES' TO END-OF-DATA.
```

FIGURE 13-12   THE COMPLETE COBOL PROGRAM FOR THE BASIC EXAMPLE.   (Continued)

from the PAGE option. A later example will include another option (FOOTING) in the PAGE description.

After the RD entry, it will be noted that there are five report groups described, each at the 01 level:

01   TYPE PAGE HEADING...
     :
     :
01   INVOICE-DATA TYPE IS DETAIL...
     :
     :
01   TYPE PAGE FOOTING...
     :
     :
01   TYPE REPORT FOOTING...

Each 01 level in Figure 13-12 introduces a report group in a fashion analogous to the record descriptions in an ordinary file. A report group may consist of one or several lines of output, and within each line there may be one or several fields. Following is a description of each report group and an explanation of the options used.

The first report group is:

01   TYPE IS REPORT HEADING
     NEXT GROUP NEXT PAGE.

```
02   LINE NUMBER IS 12
     COLUMN NUMBER IS 24
     PICTURE IS A(26)
     VALUE IS 'AMERICAN SALES CORPORATION'.
02   LINE NUMBER IS PLUS 2
     COLUMN NUMBER IS 28
     PICTURE IS X(21)
     VALUE IS 'INVOICE TOTALS REPORT'.
02   LINE NUMBER IS PLUS 2
     COLUMN NUMBER IS 32
     PICTURE IS X(13)
     VALUE ALL '*'.
02   LINE NUMBER IS PLUS 1
     COLUMN NUMBER IS 35
     PICTURE IS X(7)
     VALUE ALL '*'.
02   LINE NUMBER IS PLUS 1
     COLUMN NUMBER IS 37
     PICTURE IS XXX
     VALUE '***'.
```

The 01 level number introduces a new report group. The reserved words TYPE IS REPORT HEADING declare the type of report group about to be described. The NEXT GROUP specifies the positioning of the next group, and NEXT PAGE specifies that it should be on the next page. It will be recalled that the report heading was to be on a page by itself.

At the 02 level, there are five entries. In this case each represents 1 line. The level numbers used are in the range 01–49, as usual. The first level-02 entry reads:

```
02   LINE NUMBER IS 12
     COLUMN NUMBER IS 24
     PICTURE IS A(26)
     VALUE IS 'AMERICAN SALES CORPORATION'.
```

The LINE NUMBER IS 12 specifies that we want this item to be printed on line 12. Then, in column 24 (COLUMN NUMBER IS 24), we want to print a field whose PICTURE IS A(26) and whose content is supplied by the VALUE clause.

The second level-02 entry illustrates what is called *relative* line spacing with the option LINE NUMBER IS PLUS 2, meaning to double-space from the previous line. In our example, the previous line was number 12, which was specified by *absolute* line spacing; therefore, the PLUS 2 in this case has the same effect as having said LINE NUMBER IS 14.

The remaining three level-02 entries of this report group are similar to the first two and have the purpose of printing three lines of asterisks for visual effect.

The second report group in Figure 13–12—remember, a report group is introduced by an 01 level—is TYPE PAGE HEADING, which implies that this information will be printed once for each page as a heading on the page. The LINE NUMBER IS 5 specifies that the page heading will be printed on line 5. Notice that, for this report group, the LINE clause is not given at the 02 level, unlike the previous report group (the REPORT HEADING). The reason for the difference is that the PAGE HEADING will consist of one line only and so the LINE clause can be included in the 01 level.

Two level-02 entries now introduce two fields, one starting in column 11, the other starting in column 35. They both contain literals specified by VALUE clauses. The presence of two fields is simply for illustration. One longer field would have the same effect as two shorter ones, since the intent is simply to print a heading.

The third report group described is given a data-name (INVOICE-DATA) and is TYPE DETAIL. The data-name is optional for the other report groups but is required for this one because later on, in the PROCEDURE DIVISION, we will want to make direct reference to this report group. The first field of this group is:

```
02   COLUMN NUMBER IS 4
     PICTURE IS X(18)
     SOURCE IS DEPARTMENT-IN.
```

The SOURCE clause specifies the source of the contents of this field. It is analogous in effect to a MOVE DEPARTMENT-IN TO the X(18) field starting in column 4. Whenever this report group is to be printed, the data contained in the field DEPARTMENT-IN will be moved to the current field. (It will be recalled that DEPARTMENT-IN was a field in the input file, in this example.)

The remaining three fields of the INVOICE-DATA report group specify the location and source for the remainder of the line.

The next level-01 entry in Figure 13–12 introduces a TYPE PAGE FOOTING, which will be printed once for each page. The page footing will consist of one line of output as specified by 02 LINE 23. Notice that, for illustration of the available options, the LINE clause has been given its own 02 level and that the IS has been omitted, being optional in all cases. There are two fields in that line, each introduced at the 03 level (it could have been 04 or higher just as well). The first field starts at column 34 and has the VALUE clause, the second field is in columns 40–41 and has the SOURCE IS PAGE-COUNTER clause. The PAGE-COUNTER is a COBOL reserved word. It is a counter that contains an integer value indicating the page number of the current page. The counter is updated automatically each time a new page is to be printed, and so no special instructions along this line are required.

However, the programmer may access (but not alter) the content of PAGE-COUNTER both in the REPORT SECTION and in the PROCEDURE DIVISION. The effect of this page footing report group will be to print the page number at the bottom of each page, as can be observed in Figure 13–10.

The final report group described in Figure 13–12 is TYPE REPORT FOOTING, which indicates that the report footing will be printed at the end of the report at the bottom of the last page, on line 25.

Completion of the REPORT SECTION constitutes the end of the major task in the use of the report writer. The PROCEDURE DIVISION for this example is rather simple:

```
PROCEDURE DIVISION.
SET-UP.
    OPEN INPUT SOURCE-FILE
        OUTPUT REPORTFILE.
    MOVE 'NO' TO END-OF-DATA
    READ SOURCE-FILE RECORD
        AT END MOVE 'YES' TO END-OF-DATA.
    INITIATE INVOICE-REPORT.
    PERFORM READ-PRINT
        UNTIL END-OF-DATA = 'YES'
    TERMINATE INVOICE-REPORT
        CLOSE SOURCE-FILE REPORTFILE
        STOP RUN.
READ-PRINT.
        GENERATE INVOICE-DATA.
        READ SOURCE-FILE RECORD
            AT END MOVE 'YES' TO END-OF-DATA.
```

First the files are opened and the first input record is read. Then comes the INITIATE INVOICE-REPORT which is an instruction that is analogous to OPEN for files. For instance, the INITIATE will cause the PAGE-COUNTER to be set to zero. Other actions resulting from the INITIATE will be described later. For now, it will suffice to say that before a report can be written the INITIATE command must be issued once—and only once.

In the READ-PRINT paragraph, the procedure consists of reading a record from the SOURCE-FILE and then generating INVOICE-DATA. It will be recalled that INVOICE-DATA was the data-name that we gave to the TYPE IS DETAIL report group. As a result of executing the GENERATE instruction, the report writer will control the printing of all other report groups (REPORT HEADING, PAGE HEADING, PAGE FOOTING) used in this example. Thus, the report writer is concerned mainly with report format specifications, not with procedure specifications.

When all the records from SOURCE-FILE have been processed, we TERMINATE INVOICE-REPORT in the JOB-END paragraph. As a result of the

```
MONTH   PRODUCT CODE   INVOICE-TOTALS          MONTH TOTAL   DEPT. TOTAL

03      1-19                70.00
        1-20                79.85
        1-21                85.42
        1-22               160.66
        1-23               158.18
        1-24               750.00

                                                  2,041.16      5,157.10

***************************************************************************
***************************************************************************

        GRAND TOTAL FOR INVOICE REPORT          19,289.69


                    PAGE    7

                 **END OF REPORT**

                      (c)
```

FIGURE 13-13   (a) FIRST PAGE OF THE REPORT. (b) SECOND PAGE OF THE REPORT. (c) LAST PAGE OF THE REPORT.   (Continued)

AMERICAN SALES CORPORATION
INVOICE TOTALS REPORT

DEPARTMENT: APPLIANCES

MONTH	PRODUCT CODE	INVOICE-TOTALS	MONTH TOTAL	DEPT. TOTAL
01	A-10	100.25		
	A-11	25.25		
	A-15	250.00		
	B-13	83.00		
	B-20	9,008.30		
	B-21	150.50		
	B-22	326.60		
	C-10	8.90		
			9,952.80	

PAGE 1

(a)

MONTH	PRODUCT CODE	INVOICE-TOTALS	MONTH TOTAL	DEPT. TOTAL
02	A-10	90.20		
	A-15	85.37		
	A-25	654.92		
	E-18	870.00		
	F-20	50.00		
			1,750.49	
03	A-15	15.00		
	E-20	182.18		
			197.18	11,900.47

****

PAGE 2

(b)

FIGURE 13-13 (a) FIRST PAGE OF THE REPORT. (b) SECOND PAGE OF THE REPORT. (c) LAST PAGE OF THE REPORT.

A new report group appears that consists of the fixed header, DE-PARTMENT:, and the department name (in the case of the first page it is AP-PLIANCES). This type of header is absent from the second page, part (b), because we want department name to be printed only at the start of a new department listing.

The page footing remains the same as in the previous example.

Part (b) of Figure 13–13 presents the second page of the report and serves to illustrate the accumulation of month and department totals. The page is short because the end of the first department (APPLIANCES) occurs on this page and we want to start each department at the top of a new page. The line of asterisks is used for visual effect.

Part (c) of Figure 13–13 presents the last page of the report. One item deserves special attention: the line GRAND TOTAL FOR INVOICE REPORT. The purpose is to show the grand total of all invoice totals processed in this report. It is, therefore, produced as a *final* control footing.

Now that we have a clear visualization of the desired report, let us consider the programming aspects. Figure 13–14 presents the entire program from which the sample report pages were produced. Up to the REPORT SECTION, the program is identical to the one used in the basic example.

The Report Description (RD) entry specifies the fields that will be used for control break purposes:

```
RD INVOICE-REPORT
        CONTROLS ARE FINAL
                    DEPARTMENT-IN
                    MONTH-IN
```

There are three control breaks specified. One is declared with the reserved word FINAL. This is always the most inclusive control in the hierarchy. The next control field is DEPARTMENT-IN, which is a field in the input record. The minor control is MONTH-IN, which is also a field in the input record. The order of writeup establishes the hierarchy. The FINAL must be the first control (if used); then the remaining order is established. Thus, if instead of having written MONTH-IN as the last item we had written it as the second, we would have established DEPARTMENT-IN as the minor control.

In the present example, we want control footings for month and department. Referring back to Figure 13–13, it should be noted that the data presented to the report writer were sorted by month within department. If the data were sorted by department within month and given the hierarchy of FINAL, DEPARTMENT-IN, MONTH-IN, then the report would be different. The difference would be that department totals would be produced for all departments for each month. Thus, it is important to relate the input file sort order with the control breaks desired and, when required, sort the input file in a different order or change the format of the report.

The PAGE clause in the RD entry in Figure 13–14 is similar in form to the basic example. The FOOTING 20 clause specifies that line 20 will be the

```
     IDENTIFICATION DIVISION.
     PROGRAM-ID. REPGEN2.
*
     ENVIRONMENT DIVISION.
     CONFIGURATION SECTION.
     SOURCE-COMPUTER. ABC-480.
     OBJECT-COMPUTER. ABC-480.
     INPUT-OUTPUT SECTION.
     FILE-CONTROL.
         SELECT SOURCE-FILE   ASSIGN TO SOURCE-READER.
         SELECT REPORTFILE ASSIGN TO PRINTER.
*
     DATA DIVISION.
     FILE SECTION.
     FD  SOURCE-FILE
             LABEL RECORDS ARE OMITTED
             DATA RECORD IS SOURCE-REC.
     01  SOURCE-REC.
         02 DEPARTMENT-IN        PIC X(18).
         02 MONTH-IN             PIC 99.
         02 PRODUCT-CODE-IN      PIC X(4).
         02 INVOICE-TOTALS-IN    PIC 9(6)V99.
         02 FILLER               PIC X(48).
*
     FD  REPORTFILE
             LABEL RECORDS ARE OMITTED
             REPORT IS INVOICE-REPORT.
     WORKING-STORAGE SECTION.
     01  END-OF-DATA        PIC XXX.
*
     REPORT SECTION.
     RD  INVOICE-REPORT
             CONTROLS ARE FINAL
                         DEPARTMENT-IN
                         MONTH-IN
             PAGE LIMIT IS 25 LINES
                 HEADING 2
                 FIRST DETAIL 8
                 LAST DETAIL 18
                 FOOTING 20.
*
     01  TYPE IS REPORT HEADING.
         02 LINE IS 2
            COLUMN NUMBER IS 35
            PICTURE IS A(26)
            VALUE IS 'AMERICAN SALES CORPORATION'.
         02 LINE NUMBER IS PLUS 2
            COLUMN NUMBER IS 38
            PICTURE IS X(21)
            VALUE IS 'INVOICE TOTALS REPORT'.
```

FIGURE 13-14   COBOL PROGRAM FOR THE EXAMPLE WITH CONTROL BREAKS.

```
01    PAGE-TOP TYPE IS PAGE HEADING
         LINE NUMBER IS PLUS 2.
      02 COLUMN NUMBER IS 25
         PICTURE IS XXXXX
         VALUE IS 'MONTH'.
      02 COLUMN NUMBER IS 35
         PICTURE IS X(30)
         VALUE IS 'PRODUCT CODE     INVOICE-TOTALS'.
        03 COLUMN NUMBER IS 72
           VALUE IS 'MONTH TOTAL    DEPT. TOTAL'
           PICTURE IS X(25).
*
 01   TYPE IS CONTROL HEADING DEPARTMENT-IN
         LINE NUMBER IS PLUS 2.
         NEXT GROUP IS PLUS 2.
      02 COLUMN 6
         PICTURE X(11)
         VALUE 'DEPARTMENT:'.
      02 COLUMN 18
         PICTURE X(18)
         SOURCE DEPARTMENT-IN.
*
 01   INVOICE-DATA
         TYPE IS DETAIL
         LINE NUMBER IS PLUS 1.
      02 COLUMN NUMBER IS 4
         PIC IS X(18)
         SOURCE IS DEPARTMENT-IN
         GROUP INDICATE.
      02 COLUMN NUMBER IS 27
         PICTURE IS 99
         SOURCE IS MONTH-IN
         GROUP INDICATE.
         02 COLUMN NUMBER IS 39
         SOURCE IS PRODUCT-CODE-IN
         PIC X(4).
      02 COLUMN NUMBER IS 52
         PIC IS ZZZ,ZZ9.99
         SOURCE IS INVOICE TOTALS-IN.
*
 01   TYPE IS CONTROL FOOTING MONTH-IN
         LINE NUMBER IS PLUS 1.
      02 MONTH-TOTAL
         COLUMN NUMBER IS 69
         PICTURE IS Z,ZZZ,ZZ9.99
         SUM INVOICE-TOTALS-IN.
```

FIGURE 13-14   COBOL PROGRAM FOR THE EXAMPLE WITH CONTROL BREAKS.   (Continued)

```
01   DEPT-TOTAL TYPE IS CONTROL FOOTING DEPARTMENT-IN
          NEXT GROUP NEXT PAGE.
     02 LINE NUMBER PLUS 1
        COLUMN NUMBER IS 82
        PICTURE IS ZZ,ZZZZ,ZZ9.99
        SUM MONTH-TOTAL.
     02 LINE NUMBER IS PLUS 2
        PICTURE IS X(95)
        VALUE ALL '*'
        COLUMN NUMBER IS 2.
*
01   TYPE IS CONTROL FOOTING FINAL.
     02 LINE NUMBER IS PLUS 2
        COLUMN NUMBER 2
        PICTURE X(95)
        VALUE ALL '*'.
     02 LINE NUMBER PLUS 2.
        03 COLUMN NUMBER 36
           PIC X(30)
           VALUE 'GRAND TOTAL FOR INVOICE REPORT'.
        03 COLUMN NUMBER 66
           PIC ZZZ,ZZZ,ZZ9.99
        SUM INVOICE-TOTALS-IN.
*
01   TYPE PAGE FOOTING.
     02 LINE 23.
        03 COLUMN 46
           PIC AAAA
           VALUE 'PAGE'.
        03 COLUMN 54
           PIC Z9
           SOURCE IS PAGE-COUNTER.
*
01   TYPE REPORT FOOTING
        LINE NUMBER IS PLUS 2.
     02 COLUMN NUMBER IS 41
        PICTURE X(17)
        VALUE '**END OF REPORT**'.
*
PROCEDURE DIVISION.
*
SET-UP.
    OPEN INPUT  SOURCE-FILE
         OUTPUT REPORTFILE.
    MOVE 'NO' TO END-OF-DATA
*
    INITIATE INVOICE-REPORT
```

FIGURE 13-14   COBOL PROGRAM FOR THE EXAMPLE WITH CONTROL BREAKS.   (Continued)

```
        READ SOURCE-FILE RECORD
            AT END MOVE 'YES' TO END-OF-DATA.
*
        PERFORM READ-PRINT
           UNTIL END-OF-DATA = 'YES'.
*
        TERMINATE INVOICE-REPORT
*
        CLOSE SOURCE-FILE REPORTFILE
        STOP RUN.
*
   READ-PRINT.
*
        GENERATE INVOICE-DATA.
*

        READ SOURCE-FILE RECORD
            AT END MOVE 'YES' TO END-OF-DATA.
```

**FIGURE 13-14   COBOL PROGRAM FOR THE EXAMPLE WITH CONTROL
BREAKS.   (Continued)**

last line number on which a CONTROL FOOTING report group may be presented. PAGE FOOTING and REPORT FOOTING report groups must follow line 20.

The REPORT HEADING group is specified to begin on LINE 2. The absence of NEXT GROUP NEXT PAGE (as contrasted to Figure 13–12) implies that this heading will be on the first page of the report, along with the page heading.

The next report group is:

```
01  PAGE-TOP TYPE IS PAGE HEADING
        LINE NUMBER IS PLUS 2.
        .
        .
        .
```

For illustration, a data-name (PAGE-TOP) has been assigned to this TYPE PAGE HEADING report group, and this heading begins two lines below the previous line printed. Referring back to the REPORT HEADING description, it will be observed that the report heading begins on line 2 and consists of 2 lines with double spacing (PLUS 2). Thus, the report heading will be printed on lines 2–4, and the page heading will begin on line 6 of the first page. On subsequent pages, however, the report heading will not be printed. Then the page heading will start on line 4, which is determined as follows: the PAGE clause established line 2 as the first line on which a heading (HEADING 2) can be printed. Since the PAGE HEADING has relative spacing (LINE NUMBER IS PLUS 2), it follows that the page heading will start on line 4 of the second and subsequent pages.

The next report group in Figure 13–14 is:

```
01   TYPE IS CONTROL HEADING DEPARTMENT-IN
         LINE NUMBER IS PLUS 2
         NEXT GROUP IS PLUS 2.
     02   COLUMN 6
         PICTURE X(11)
         VALUE 'DEPARTMENT:'.
     02   COLUMN 18
         PICTURE X(18)
         SOURCE DEPARTMENT-IN.
```

This is a CONTROL HEADING group, and it will be printed every time the DEPARTMENT-IN field changes value. Referring to Figure 13–13, the header DEPARTMENT: XXXXXXXXXXXXXXXXXX (where the X's stand for the department name) is printed only when a new department is introduced in the input stream. (The fact that the DEPARTMENT-IN field is used both as a control heading break and as a source field is just a coincidence in this example.)

The clauses LINE NUMBER IS PLUS 2, and NEXT GROUP IS PLUS 2 specify that this report group will be printed 2 lines after the previous report group (the page header) and that the next group (which is a detail report group in this example) will be presented 2 lines below, thus double spacing before and after. The two 02 fields are similar to the type we have discussed already in the basic example.

Reviewing Figure 13–13, you will notice that DEPARTMENT: APPLI-ANCES is single-spaced after the page header, seemingly contradicting the LINE NUMBER PLUS 2 clause. The explanation for this lies in the complicated rules by which the report writer operates. If no previous report body group has been presented on the page, then the single spacing prevails; otherwise, the relative spacing specified in the CONTROL HEADING takes effect. Thus, in this case, single spacing resulted from DEPARTMENT: APPLIANCES being the first report body group. If we had another control break based on DEPARTMENT-IN, there would have been double spacing.

The next report group specified in Figure 13–14 is 01 INVOICE-DATA TYPE IS DETAIL LINE NUMBER IS PLUS 1. As in the previous sample, this will be the report group referenced in the GENERATE statement in the PROCEDURE DIVISION. The only difference between this and the corresponding group in the basic example is the use of the GROUP INDICATE clause. Specifically, we have:

```
02   COLUMN NUMBER IS 27
     PICTURE IS 99
     SOURCE IS MONTH-IN
     GROUP INDICATE.
```

The effect of the GROUP INDICATE is to print the data only at the beginning of a report, at the beginning of each page, and after each control break. A glance at the sample report output in Figure 13–13 will show the effect of the GROUP INDICATE. A good contrast is provided by the absence of this clause in the description of the detail group of the basic (first) example.

The next report group in Figure 13–14 is:

```
01   TYPE IS CONTROL FOOTING MONTH-IN
            LINE NUMBER IS PLUS 1.
      02   MONTH-TOTAL
           COLUMN NUMBER IS 69
           PICTURE IS Z,ZZZ,ZZ9.99
           SUM INVOICE-TOTALS-IN.
```

The TYPE clause specifies this to be a CONTROL FOOTING associated with the data-name MONTH-IN, which is a data-name in the input file record. The meaning of this control footing is that whenever the value of the data-name MONTH-IN changes, a control break will occur which will, in turn, result in printing the edited sum of the values of the data-name INVOICE-TOTALS-IN in column 69 of the next line. As each detail group is presented, the sum of the INVOICE-TOTALS-IN fields is formed in the MONTH-TOTAL field.

The ability to specify summation fields whose data are printed as a result of control breaks is a fundamental capability of the report writer. A sum counter is set initially to zero by the report writer. Then, as each detail line is presented, the specified data are added to this sum counter. When a control break occurs, the value of the sum counter is printed and then it is reset to zero. In the present example, a name has been given to the accumulator: MONTH-TOTAL. As each input record is read and a detail report line is printed, MONTH-TOTAL is incremented by the value of INVOICE-TOTALS-IN. Then, when MONTH-IN changes value, the edited value of MONTH-TOTAL will be printed, starting in column 69. Referring to part (a) of Figure 13–13, it will be observed that when the month changed from 01 to 02 a month total of 9,952.80 was printed.

The next report group introduced in Figure 13–14 is:

```
01   DEPT-TOTAL TYPE IS CONTROL FOOTING DEPARTMENT-IN
            NEXT GROUP NEXT PAGE.
```

The effect of this control footing is to sum the values of the MONTH-TOTAL sum counter (SUM MONTH-TOTAL) and to print the edited sum, starting in column 82 of the next line. Reference to Figure 13–13 reveals that this sum counter is printed only when the department changes; thus, all the month totals for a given department are printed before the department total. Referring back to CONTROLS ARE FINAL DEPARTMENT-IN MONTH-IN serves to remind us that in this hierarchy of control breaks the MONTH-IN is subordinate to DEPARTMENT-IN. Thus, the expected order of control footings is that several MONTH-TOTALS will be printed for each DEPT-TOTAL.

Incidentally, the order in which the control footing report groups are written is immaterial. The logic of report presentation is not related to the order in which the report groups are specified in the program.

Two additional features of the DEPT-TOTAL report group deserve attention. The NEXT GROUP NEXT PAGE clause specifies that, after this group, we want to start a new page. The second feature is that this group consists of two lines. The first one prints the value of the sum counter while the second line consists of asterisks.

The next group is:

```
01   TYPE IS CONTROL FOOTING FINAL.
```

No name is given to this report group (names are optional). This kind of control footing will be printed after all control breaks have occurred, since it is the highest in the control hierarchy. Thus, after the last detail group has been presented and after all the control footings have been presented, the final control footing is presented in the report. In a sense it resembles a report footing, except that SUM clauses can appear only in control footing groups; therefore, a CONTROL FOOTING FINAL is necessary.

The SUM INVOICE-TOTALS-IN specifies that this sum counter (and we have given it no name) will accumulate the sums of the INVOICE-TOTALS-IN values. Actually, it would be advisable to have said SUM DEPT-TOTAL to reduce the required number of additions, in a fashion similar to the SUM MONTH-TOTAL specified for the DEPT-TOTAL group. This inadvisable variation is shown here to illustrate the options available. If the report consisted of thousands of lines, the extra additions might be considered somewhat inefficient.

One point needs clarification. Referring to part (c) of Figure 13–13, the question may be raised: Why is the final control footing not printed on a new page, since the previous control footing (DEPT-TOTAL) contained the NEXT GROUP NEXT PAGE clause? The reason is that the NEXT GROUP clause is ignored when it is specified on a control footing report group that is at a level other than the highest level at which a control break is detected. In this case, a final control footing is at a higher level; therefore, the NEXT GROUP clause associated with the DEPT-TOTAL control footing group is ignored.

The PAGE FOOTING and REPORT FOOTING groups in Figure 13–14 are similar to the ones in the basic example in Figure 13–12.

The PROCEDURE DIVISION is identical to the one in the basic example, illustrating that the differences in the resulting report are attributable to the differences in the report description, rather than in the procedures specified.

Review

1 In the RD entry in the REPORT SECTION of the DATA DIVISION, if the FINAL control break is used then it must be the [first one/last one] listed.

first one

2 When the major report groups are described at the 01 level in the DATA DIVISION, then the CONTROL HEADING and CONTROL FOOTING groups are described at the [01/02] level.

01

3 The effect of the GROUP INDICATE clause in the description of a report group is to print the associated information only at the beginning of the report, at the beginning of each _____, and after each _____.

page; control break

4 A CONTROL HEADING report group typically involves the specification of descriptive _____ headings.

column (or report)

5 A CONTROL FOOTING report group typically involves the specification of various _____ which are to be reported.

sums (or totals)

6 Even though a report footing has been specified, it also is necessary to specify a FINAL control footing if the output of a(n) _____ clause is desired at the end of the report.

SUM

REPORT WRITER USING DECLARATIVES

Figure 13–15 illustrates the output of what appears similar to the report discussed in the preceding example, with one main exception: The line PAGE TOTAL = 10,783.29 is new. Suppose then that we are interested in showing a PAGE TOTAL for the INVOICE-TOTALS printed on that page. This example will serve as a vehicle to illustrate how the programmer can specify procedures other than those made possible by the standard report groups.

What we desire is to have the INVOICE-TOTALS summarized and printed at the bottom of the page above the page footing. In a sense, we desire a control break associated with the end of a page, but the rules of the CONTROLS clause specify that we must not use control breaks associated with data-names defined in the REPORT SECTION. Further, a SUM counter cannot be used except with CONTROL FOOTING report groups.

In order to proceed directly to the illustration, consider the modification to the preceding example in Figure 13–16. A WORKING-STORAGE field has been added, called PAGE-ACCUMULATOR. Then, in the PROCEDURE DIVISION, the reserved word DECLARATIVES introduces a special-purpose section; in this example, it is the PAGE-END SECTION. The USE verb specifies the condition under which the procedures in the DECLARATIVES portion will be executed; in this case, it is BEFORE REPORTING PAGE-TOP. It will be recalled that PAGE-TOP was the name given to the page heading report group. Thus, the procedures specified in this section will be executed before printing the page header. Now, looking at PAR-A, the simple task of MOVE ZEROS TO PAGE-ACCUMULATOR is the only procedure specified in this section (PAR-B simply contains an EXIT command). In essence, then, we have said: before printing the heading on each page, zero out the WORKING-STORAGE field called PAGE-ACCUMULATOR. The END DECLARATIVES marks the end of the declarative part of the PROCEDURE DIVISION.

In the READ-PRINT paragraph, observe the two statements:

GENERATE INVOICE-DATA.
ADD INVOICE-TOTALS-IN TO PAGE-ACCUMULATOR.

After each report detail group is generated, the value of PAGE-ACCUMULATOR is incremented by the amount of INVOICE-TOTALS-IN. When a page footing is printed, the value of PAGE-ACCUMULATOR serves as the SOURCE. Then, the declarative portion takes effect, before the next page heading is printed, and the PAGE-ACCUMULATOR is set to zero to begin again the new page accumulation.

```
                    AMERICAN SALES CORPORATION
                      INVOICE TOTALS REPORT

DEPARTMENT          MONTH    PRODUCT CODE   INVOICE-TOTALS    MONTH TOTAL    DEPT. TOTAL
APPLIANCES           01         A-10            100.25
                                A-11            125.25
                                A-15            250.00
                                B-13             83.00
                                B-20          9,008.30
                                B-21            150.50
                                B-22            326.60
                                C-10              8.90

                     02         A-10             90.20
                                A-15             85.37                        9,952.80
                                A-25            654.92

                          PAGE TOTAL =      10,783.29

                                     PAGE   1
```

FIGURE 13-15   OUTPUT RESULTING FROM THE MODIFIED PROGRAM
USING DECLARATIVES.

```
IDENTIFICATION DIVISION.
PROGRAM-ID. REPGEN3.
*
ENVIRONMENT DIVISION.
CONFIGURATION SECTION.
SOURCE-COMPUTER. ABC-480.
OBJECT-COMPUTER. ABC-480.
INPUT-OUTPUT SECTION.
FILE-CONTROL.
     SELECT SOURCE-FILE   ASSIGN TO SOURCE-READER.
     SELECT REPORTFILE ASSIGN TO PRINTER.
*
DATA DIVISION.
FILE SECTION.
FD   SOURCE-FILE
         LABEL RECORDS ARE OMITTED
         DATA RECORD IS SOURCE-REC.
01   SOURCE-REC.
     02 DEPARTMENT-IN        PIC X(18).
     02 MONTH-IN             PIC 99.
     02 PRODUCT-CODE-IN      PIC X(4).
     02 INVOICE-TOTALS-IN    PIC 9(6)V99.
     02 FILLER              PIC X(48).
*
FD   REPORTFILE
         LABEL RECORDS ARE OMITTED
         REPORT IS INVOICE-REPORT.
*
WORKING-STORAGE SECTION.
01   END-OF-DATA        PIC XXX.
01   PAGE-ACCUMULATOR PIC 9(7)V99.
*
REPORT SECTION.
RD   INVOICE-REPORT
         CONTROLS ARE FINAL
                      DEPARTMENT-IN
                      MONTH-IN
         PAGE LIMIT IS 25 LINES
             HEADING 2
             FIRST DETAIL 8
             LAST DETAIL 18
             FOOTING 20.
*
01   TYPE IS REPORT HEADING.
     02 LINE IS 2
         COLUMN NUMBER IS 35
         PICTURE IS A(26)
         VALUE IS 'AMERICAN SALES CORPORATION'.
```

**FIGURE 13-16   REVISED PROGRAM FOR THE MODIFIED EXAMPLE
USING DECLARATIVES.**

```
            02 LINE NUMBER IS PLUS 2
                COLUMN NUMBER IS 38
                PICTURE IS X(21)
                VALUE IS 'INVOICE TOTALS REPORT'.
*
  01  PAGE-TOP TYPE IS PAGE HEADING
                LINE NUMBER IS PLUS 2.
            02 COLUMN NUMBER IS 6
                 PICTURE IS X(24)
                 VALUE IS 'DEPARTMENT        MONTH'.
            02 COLUMN NUMBER IS 35
                 PICTURE IS X(30)
                 VALUE IS 'PRODUCT CODE      INVOICE-TOTALS'.
                 03 COLUMN NUMBER IS 72
                     VALUE IS 'MONTH TOTAL    DEPT. TOTAL'
                     PICTURE IS X(25).
*
  01  INVOICE-DATA
                TYPE IS DETAIL
                LINE NUMBER IS PLUS 1.
            02 COLUMN NUMBER IS 4
                PIC IS X(18)
                SOURCE IS DEPARTMENT-IN
                GROUP INDICATE.
            02 COLUMN NUMBER IS 27
                PICTURE IS 99
                SOURCE IS MONTH-IN
                GROUP INDICATE.
                02 COLUMN NUMBER IS 39
                SOURCE IS PRODUCT-CODE-IN
                PIC X(4).
            02 COLUMN NUMBER IS 52
                PIC IS ZZZ,ZZ9.99
                SOURCE IS INVOICE-TOTALS-IN.
*
  01  TYPE IS CONTROL FOOTING MONTH-IN
                LINE NUMBER IS PLUS 1.
            02 MONTH-TOTAL
                COLUMN NUMBER IS 69
                PICTURE IS Z,ZZZ,ZZ9.99
                SUM INVOICE-TOTALS-IN.
*
  01  DEPT-TOTAL TYPE IS CONTROL FOOTING DEPARTMENT-IN
                NEXT GROUP NEXT PAGE.
            02 LINE NUMBER IS PLUS 1
                COLUMN NUMBER IS 82
                PICTURE IS ZZ,ZZZZ,ZZ9.99
                SUM MONTH-TOTAL.
            02 LINE NUMBER IS PLUS 2
                 PICTURE IS X(95)
                VALUE ALL '*'
                COLUMN NUMBER IS 2.
```

FIGURE 13-16   REVISED PROGRAM FOR THE MODIFIED EXAMPLE USING DECLARATIVES.   (Continued)

```
01   TYPE IS CONTROL FOOTING FINAL.
     02 LINE NUMBER IS PLUS 2
         COLUMN NUMBER 2
         PICTURE X(95)
         VALUE ALL '*'.
     02 LINE NUMBER PLUS 2.
         03 COLUMN NUMBER 32
             PIC X(30)
             VALUE 'GRAND TOTAL FOR INVOICE REPORT'.
         03 COLUMN NUMBER 66
             PIC ZZZ,ZZZ,ZZ9.99
         SUM INVOICE-TOTALS-IN.
*
 01   TYPE PAGE FOOTING.
     02 LINE 21.
         03 COLUMN 34
             PIC A(12)
             VALUE 'PAGE TOTAL ='.
         03 COLUMN 49
             PIC ZZ,ZZZ,ZZ9.99
             SOURCE PAGE-ACCUMULATOR.
     02 LINE 23.
         03 COLUMN 46
             PIC AAAA
             VALUE 'PAGE'.
         03 COLUMN 52
             PIC Z9
             SOURCE IS PAGE-COUNTER.
*
 01   TYPE REPORT FOOTING
     LINE NUMBER IS PLUS 2.
     02 COLUMN NUMBER IS 41
         PICTURE X(17)
         VALUE '**END OF REPORT**'.
*
 PROCEDURE DIVISION.
*
 DECLARATIVES.
*
 PAGE-END SECTION.
*

     USE BEFORE REPORTING PAGE-TOP.
*
 PAR-A.
     MOVE ZEROS TO PAGE-ACCUMULATOR.
 PAR-B.
     EXIT.
 END DECLARATIVES.
```

**FIGURE 13-16   REVISED PROGRAM FOR THE MODIFIED EXAMPLE
USING DECLARATIVES.   (Continued)**

```
PROCEDURAL SECTION.
SET-UP.
    OPEN INPUT SOURCE-FILE
         OUTPUT REPORTFILE.
    MOVE 'NO' TO END-OF-DATA
    INITIATE INVOICE-REPORT
    READ SOURCE-FILE RECORD
         AT END MOVE 'YES' TO END-OF-DATA.
    PERFORM READ-PRINT
       UNTIL END-OF-DATA = 'YES'.
    TERMINATE INVOICE-REPORT
    CLOSE SOURCE-FILE REPORTFILE
    STOP RUN.
READ-PRINT.
    GENERATE INVOICE-DATA.
    ADD INVOICE-TOTALS-IN TO PAGE-ACCUMULATOR
    READ SOURCE-FILE RECORD
         AT END MOVE 'YES' TO END-OF-DATA.
```

**FIGURE 13-16   REVISED PROGRAM FOR THE MODIFIED EXAMPLE
USING DECLARATIVES.   (Continued)**

Review

1   The reserved word DECLARATIVES is used to introduce special purpose sections in the _____ DIVISION of a COBOL program.

PROCEDURE

2   The verb that specifies the condition under which the procedures
under DECLARATIVES are to be executed is the _____ verb.

USE

3   When presentation of the DECLARATIVES in the PROCEDURE DIVI-
SION has been completed, this is indicated by the command
_____ .

END DECLARATIVES

LANGUAGE SPECIFICATIONS FOR THE COBOL REPORT WRITER

A complete language specification description is beyond the scope of the present discussion; however, a full list of the language options is included in Appendix C of this book. In the following description, only the main options are highlighted.

One option looks like this:

$$
\left\{
\begin{array}{l}
\underline{\text{CONTROL}} \text{ IS} \\
\underline{\text{CONTROLS}} \text{ ARE}
\end{array}
\right\}
\left\{
\begin{array}{l}
\text{data-name-1 [data-name-2] } \ldots \\
\underline{\text{FINAL}} \text{ [data-name-1 [data-name-2] } \ldots
\end{array}
\right\}
$$

Data-name-1 and data-name-2 must not be defined in the report section. FINAL, if specified, is the highest control; data-name-1 is the major control; data-name-2 is an intermediate control, and so forth. The last data-name specified is the minor control.

A second option is:

$$
\boxed{\underline{\text{GROUP}} \text{ INDICATE}}
$$

The GROUP INDICATE clause specifies that the associated printable item is presented only on the first occurrence of the associated report group, after a control break or page advance.

A third format is as follows:

$$
\underline{\text{LINE}} \text{ NUMBER IS}
\left\{
\begin{array}{l}
\text{integer-1 [ON } \underline{\text{NEXT}} \text{ } \underline{\text{PAGE}}\text{]} \\
\underline{\text{PLUS}} \text{ integer-2}
\end{array}
\right\}
$$

This clause specifies vertical positioning information for the associated report group. The following rules apply:

1   Integer-1 and integer-2 must not be specified in such a way as to cause any line of a report group to be presented outside the vertical subdivisions of the page designated for the report group type, as defined by the PAGE clause (see discussion of the PAGE clause).

2   Within a given report group, an entry that contains a LINE NUMBER clause must not contain a subordinate entry that also contains a LINE NUMBER clause.

3   Within a given report description entry, a NEXT PAGE phrase can appear only once and, if present, must be in the first LINE NUMBER clause in that report group.

4   A LINE NUMBER clause with the NEXT PAGE phrase can appear only in the description of the CONTROL HEADING, DETAIL, CONTROL FOOTING, and REPORT FOOTING groups.

5   The first LINE NUMBER clause specified within a PAGE FOOTING report group must be an absolute LINE NUMBER clause.

A fourth clause is:

$$
\underline{\text{NEXT GROUP IS}} \left\{ \begin{array}{l} \text{integer-1} \\ \underline{\text{PLUS}}\ \text{integer-2} \\ \underline{\text{NEXT PAGE}} \end{array} \right\}
$$

The NEXT GROUP clause specifies information for vertical positioning following presentation of the last line of a report group. However, it is ignored when it is specified on a CONTROL FOOTING report group that is at a level other than the highest level at which a control break is detected. These two rules apply:

1   The NEXT PAGE phrase of the NEXT GROUP clause must not be specified in a PAGE FOOTING report group.

2   The NEXT GROUP clause must not be specified in a REPORT FOOTING or PAGE HEADING report group.

A fifth format is as follows:

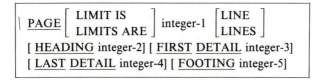

$$
\setminus\ \underline{\text{PAGE}} \left[\begin{array}{l} \text{LIMIT IS} \\ \text{LIMITS ARE} \end{array} \right] \text{integer-1} \left[\begin{array}{l} \text{LINE} \\ \text{LINES} \end{array} \right]
$$
$$
[\ \underline{\text{HEADING}}\ \text{integer-2}]\ [\ \underline{\text{FIRST DETAIL}}\ \text{integer-3}]
$$
$$
[\ \underline{\text{LAST DETAIL}}\ \text{integer-4}]\ [\ \underline{\text{FOOTING}}\ \text{integer-5}]
$$

The PAGE clause defines the length of a page and the vertical subdivisions within which report groups are presented. Use of the PAGE clause defines certain page regions that are described in this format. The integer-1, integer-2, and so on refer to the operands of the PAGE clause. As an illustration of using the format, notice that the CONTROL FOOTING report groups are al-

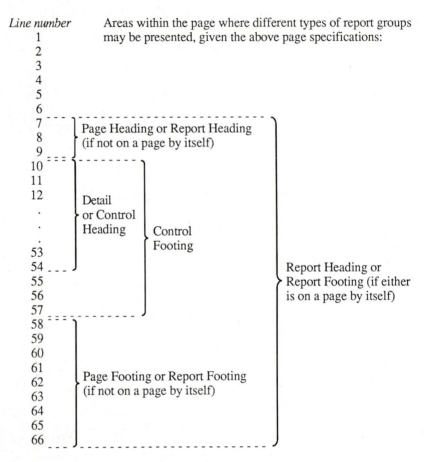

PAGE LIMIT IS   66 LINES
        HEADING   7
        FIRST DETAIL   54
        FOOTING   57

Line number   Areas within the page where different types of report groups
    1   may be presented, given the above page specifications:

FIGURE 13–17   SAMPLE APPLICATION OF THE PAGE CLAUSE.

located the region between integer-3 and integer-5. Thus, if the PAGE clause had contained FIRST DETAIL 6, FOOTING 20, the CONTROL FOOTING report group description should not contain, for example, an absolute LINE NUMBER clause referring to line 22.

Figure 13–17 clarifies the meaning of the PAGE clause with an example that illustrates the different regions defined by integer-1 through integer-5 in the general format.

A sixth option is:

SOURCE IS identifier-1

The SOURCE clause identifies the sending data item that is moved to an associated printable item defined within a report group description entry. Identifier-1 may be defined in any section of the DATA DIVISION. If identifier-1 is a REPORT SECTION item, it can only be PAGE-COUNTER, LINE-COUNTER, or a sum counter.

A seventh clause looks like this:

```
[ SUM identifier-1 [ identifier-2] ...
    [ UPON data-name-1 [ data-name-2] ... ] } ...
[ RESET ON  { data-name-3
              FINAL       } ]
```

The SUM clause establishes a sum counter and names the data items to be summed. When more than one identifier is used, the sum counter is incremented by the sum of the identifiers. Thus:

03   EX-TOTAL PIC Z(6).99 SUM DAT1, DAT2

indicates that EX-TOTAL will be incremented by both the value of DAT1 and DAT2 each time a summation is indicated. If DAT1 and DAT2 are items described in the same report group and on the same line, we refer to this sum as a *crossfooting*, as in this example:

DAT1	DAT2	EX-TOTAL
20	30	50

In contrast to crossfooting, we refer to *rolling forward* as the summation of sum counters at a lower hierarchical level. Thus:

02   DEPT-TOTAL PIC ZZ,ZZZ,ZZ9.99 COLUMN 69
        SUM MONTH-TOTAL

where MONTH-TOTAL was a sum counter specified earlier, represents an example of a *rolling forward* total.

The following rules apply:

1   A SUM clause can appear only in the description of a CONTOL FOOTING report group.

2 The UPON phrase provides the capability to accomplish selective sub-totaling for the detail report groups named in the phrase.

3 The RESET option inhibits automatic resetting to zero upon the occurrence of a control break. Thus the sum counter can be zeroed only when a control break occurs for data-name-3, or on the occurrence of FINAL. The latter case represents an accumulation for the entire report.

An eighth format is:

$$
\underline{\text{TYPE}} \text{ IS}
\begin{cases}
\begin{Bmatrix} \underline{\text{REPORT}} \ \underline{\text{HEADING}} \\ \underline{\text{RH}} \end{Bmatrix} \\[6pt]
\begin{Bmatrix} \underline{\text{PAGE}} \ \underline{\text{HEADING}} \\ \underline{\text{PH}} \end{Bmatrix} \\[6pt]
\begin{Bmatrix} \underline{\text{CONTROL}} \ \underline{\text{HEADING}} \\ \underline{\text{CH}} \end{Bmatrix}
\begin{Bmatrix} \text{data-name-1} \\ \underline{\text{FINAL}} \end{Bmatrix} \\[6pt]
\begin{Bmatrix} \underline{\text{DETAIL}} \\ \underline{\text{DE}} \end{Bmatrix} \\[6pt]
\begin{Bmatrix} \underline{\text{CONTROL}} \ \underline{\text{FOOTING}} \\ \underline{\text{CF}} \end{Bmatrix}
\begin{Bmatrix} \text{data-name-2} \\ \underline{\text{FINAL}} \end{Bmatrix} \\[6pt]
\begin{Bmatrix} \underline{\text{PAGE}} \ \underline{\text{FOOTING}} \\ \underline{\text{PF}} \end{Bmatrix} \\[6pt]
\begin{Bmatrix} \underline{\text{REPORT}} \ \underline{\text{FOOTING}} \\ \underline{\text{RF}} \end{Bmatrix}
\end{cases}
$$

The TYPE clause specifies the particular type of report group that is described by this entry. Each option can be abbreviated in a two-letter reserved COBOL word, as shown.

A ninth option is as follows:

$$\boxed{\underline{\text{INITIATE}} \text{ report-name}}$$

The INITIATE statement causes the system to begin processing a report. As part of the initialization procedure, all sum counters are set to zero, and PAGE-COUNTER and LINE-COUNTER are initialized.

A tenth format is:

The GENERATE statement directs the production of a report in accordance with the report description in the REPORT SECTION of the DATA DIVISION. Data-name is a TYPE DETAIL report group. If report-name is used, no detail report groups are printed; instead, we produce what is called a summary report. The GENERATE statement causes report generation, including handling of control breaks, the start of page procedures, and so forth. A report may contain more than one type of detail report group. In such a case there will be more than one GENERATE statement in the PROCEDURE DIVISION, each referencing the proper detail group.

An eleventh statement is:

TERMINATE report-name

The TERMINATE statement causes the completion of the report processing. All CONTROL FOOTING and REPORT FOOTING groups are produced.

A twelfth format is as follows:

USE BEFORE REPORTING identifier

The USE statement specifies PROCEDURE DIVISION statements that are executed just before a report group named in the REPORT SECTION of the DATA DIVISION is produced. The USE statement, when present, must follow immediately a section header in the declaratives section, and must be followed by a period and a space. The identifier is a report group.

Exercises

13.1   Revise the flowchart in Figure 13–2 for a report program that would also include Division as a control break. A Division consists of departments; thus, the major control break is Division.

13.2   A file contains data pertaining to student grades. Each record consists of:

COLUMN	CONTENT
1–15	Student name
16–27	Course name
28	Credits
29	Grade (A, B, C, D, or F)

Create a program whereby we can print a report as outlined on the following print chart:

The report heading SEMESTER GRADE REPORT will be printed on the first page only.

Each student is enrolled in five courses.

A report footing is printed at the end of the report, as shown.

The grade point average (GPA) is computed by considering A = 4, B = 3, C = 2, D = 1, F = 0 points.

Hint: You may find it useful to use two DECLARATIVES procedures; one to compute the GPA before printing the line containing the GPA, and one to clear the total credits accumulator which you will need to sum up the credits for each student.

13.3 Incorporate the report writer feature into a program that you have already written.

14

INTERACTIVE PROCESSING

INTRODUCTION

Interactive programs are designed to carry on some kind of "dialogue" between the program and an individual utilizing a computer terminal or personal computer. Although such programs are widely used, the COBOL language lacks the specific features that facilitate interactive processing. Consequently, individual vendors have written extensions to COBOL that can be used to write interactive programs. Because each vendor has a different product, it is difficult to present one unified set of concepts and techniques in this chapter. In order to cover this subject, we first present some general concepts and then an interactive program using one particular vendor's approach to providing such a capability.

ACCEPT AND DISPLAY

COBOL provides some interactive processing capability through the use of the ACCEPT and DISPLAY verbs, as represented in the following formats:

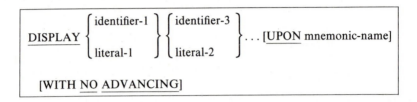

With respect to the above format specifications, when mnemonic names are used, they are defined in the SPECIAL-NAMES paragraph of the ENVIRON-MENT DIVISION. A chosen mnemonic name can be an interactive terminal, and thus we can ACCEPT data from such a terminal and DISPLAY data upon the screen of such a terminal. As a matter of fact, the WITH NO ADVANC-ING clause in the DISPLAY format was added in the 1985 standard specifi-cally to provide control over cursor positioning at a terminal. Thus, if we DISPLAY . . . WITH NO ADVANCING, we can present a message to the user and then ACCEPT input on the same line. In the absence of the NO AD-VANCING clause, a DISPLAY results in an automatic line-feed, thus making it impossible to arrange a simple dialogue such as:

ENTER YOUR NAME:

where the user response is to be entered on the same line as the above mes-sage.

The above example notwithstanding, the ACCEPT and DISPLAY verbs have inadequate features to support interactive programming. As a com-parison of what is needed versus what is available, Figures 14–1 and 14–2 present the extensions of ACCEPT and DISPLAY verbs, respectively, in one of the compilers of the Digital Equipment Corporation. Unfortunately, the variability in terminals and their use has led language designers away from adopting any standard set of specifications for interactive proces-sing.

Review

1   The COBOL verb that provides capability to input data from a com-puter terminal is the _____ verb.

ACCEPT

ACCEPT dest-item

$$\left\{ \begin{array}{l} \text{FROM \underline{LINE} NUMBER} \quad \left\{ \begin{array}{l} \text{line-num} \\ \text{line-id} \; [\; \underline{\text{PLUS}} \; [\; \text{plus-num} \;]] \\ \underline{\text{PLUS}} \; [\; \text{plus-num} \;] \end{array} \right\} \\[2em] \text{FROM \underline{COLUMN} NUMBER} \quad \left\{ \begin{array}{l} \text{column-num} \\ \text{column-id} \; [\; \underline{\text{PLUS}} \; [\; \text{plus-num} \;]] \\ \underline{\text{PLUS}} \; [\; \text{plus-num} \;] \end{array} \right\} \\[2em] \underline{\text{ERASE}} \; [\; \text{TO \underline{END} OF} \;] \quad \left\{ \begin{array}{l} \underline{\text{SCREEN}} \\ \underline{\text{LINE}} \end{array} \right\} \\[1em] \text{WITH \underline{BELL}} \\ \underline{\text{UNDERLINED}} \\ \underline{\text{BOLD}} \\ \text{WITH \underline{BLINKING}} \\ \underline{\text{PROTECTED}} \; [\; \underline{\text{SIZE}} \; \text{protect-length} \;] \\ \text{WITH \underline{CONVERSION}} \\ \underline{\text{REVERSED}} \\ \text{WITH \underline{NO} \underline{ECHO}} \\ \underline{\text{DEFAULT}} \text{ IS} \quad \left\{ \begin{array}{l} \text{def-src-lit} \\ \text{def-src-item} \end{array} \right\} \\ \text{CONTROL \underline{KEY} IN key-dest-item} \end{array} \right\}$$

FIGURE 14–1   DIGITAL EQUIPMENT CORPORATION IMPLEMENTATION OF ACCEPT.

DISPLAY $\left\{ \begin{array}{l} \text{src-item} \end{array} \right.$

$$\left[\left\{ \begin{array}{l} \text{AT \underline{LINE} NUMBER} \quad \left\{ \begin{array}{l} \text{line-num} \\ \text{line-id} \; [\; \underline{\text{PLUS}} \; [\; \text{plus-num} \;]] \\ \underline{\text{PLUS}} \; [\; \text{plus-num} \;] \end{array} \right\} \\[2em] \text{AT \underline{COLUMN} NUMBER} \quad \left\{ \begin{array}{l} \text{column-num} \\ \text{column-id} \; [\; \underline{\text{PLUS}} \; [\; \text{plus-num} \;]] \\ \underline{\text{PLUS}} \; [\; \text{plus-num} \;] \end{array} \right\} \\[2em] \underline{\text{ERASE}} \; [\; \text{TO \underline{END} OF} \;] \quad \left\{ \begin{array}{l} \underline{\text{SCREEN}} \\ \underline{\text{LINE}} \end{array} \right\} \\[1em] \text{WITH \underline{BELL}} \\ \underline{\text{UNDERLINED}} \\ \underline{\text{BOLD}} \\ \text{WITH \underline{BLINKING}} \\ \underline{\text{REVERSED}} \\ \text{WITH \underline{CONVERSION}} \end{array} \right\} \right] \; \ldots$$

[WITH \underline{NO} ADVANCING]

FIGURE 14–2   DIGITAL EQUIPMENT CORPORATION IMPLEMENTATION OF DISPLAY.

2 The COBOL verb that provides the capability to present data at a terminal screen is the _____ verb.

DISPLAY

3 When mnemonic names are used in an ACCEPT or DISPLAY statement, they are defined in the _____ paragraph of the ENVIRONMENT DIVISION.

SPECIAL-NAMES

4 The COBOL language [does/does not] include the features that facilitate the development of programs for interactive processing.

does not

PROGRAMMING CONCEPTS FOR INTERACTIVE PROCESSING

When writing interactive programs, two main characteristic operations concern the programmer:

1. The need for control over the screen display, so that appropriate data and messages can be presented to the user.

2. The need for control over the data entered by the user on the keyboard. Program logic intervenes between the keyboard and the screen display. After the user strikes a key, the program logic decides whether or not anything is displayed on the screen and where it is displayed.

A typical interactive program involves presentation of a "menu" screen to the user, with instructions to enter one or more keystrokes in reply. When the user keys-in a chosen reply, the program analyzes the reply; and depending on its content, the program may do one of several things. For example, it can display a corrective message telling the user to give a different reply, or it can take some other action (including that of terminating the program).

All interactive programs are of the "question-answer" type. The program issues a "question," the user provides a reply, and based upon the reply, the program proceeds to the next question. Such questions may be direct, such as, "Do you want to make a deposit or a withdrawal?"; or they may be indirect, such as, "What do you want me to do next?" Programs that ask explicit questions of the user are called *menu driven*, while programs that ask implicit questions of the "What next?" type are called *command driven*. In either case, the critical programming feature is the ability to examine keyboard input and, based on the input, to take the next step in the program logic. Once a data item has been made available to the program, its further processing is independent of its origin (the keyboard, magnetic disk, or magnetic tape, etc.). For example, given a product number, a routine to validate such a number would be the same whether the program is interactive or batch; thus, the difference lies only in the method by which the data item is entered into the program and not on how it is processed.

As we stated at the beginning of this section, there are two main operations involved in interactive programs: controlling display output on the screen and controlling keyboard input. We now proceed to describe these two operations in turn.

Review

1   In interactive programs, one area of required attention is control over display [input/output] on the screen.

output

2   Another area of concern is control over keyboard _____.

input

3   All interactive programs are "question-_____" types of programs.

answer

4   Interactive programs that ask explicit questions of the user are called _____ driven.

menu

5   Interactive programs that ask implicit questions of "What next?" type are called _____ driven.

command

Writing on the Screen

The screen display typically consists of 24 lines of 80 columns each, for a total of 1,920 characters (24 × 80). There are larger and smaller screens as well (for example, older portable machines often include displays of 16 lines by 40 characters). For a given screen size, the programmer must specify the characters to be displayed in each of the available positions on the screen. For example, we can fill the first line with spaces and the second line with 26 spaces followed by the literal "AMERICAN SALES COMPANY," followed by 30 spaces, and so on.

In addition to determining what to write on the screen and where it is to be written, the programmer must control the special display attributes of the screen. For instance, we can show characters in a particular position on the screen as boldfaced, underscored, or blinking. If color is available, we can display characters in blue, red, etc. To store such display-attribute information, we typically need an additional "attribute" byte for each of the character bytes on the screen. Thus, if we have a 24 × 80 screen, we must define two fields to fully describe and control the screen display: one field of 1,920 (24 × 80) bytes to store the displayed data and another field of 1,920 bytes to describe the display attributes of the character bytes.

In order for a program to "paint" a full screen, the programmer must define two fields, each 1,920 bytes long. In a simple case we could have:

```
01   DAT-SCREEN   PIC X(1920).
01   ATTR-SCREEN  PIC X(1920).
.
.
.
MOVE SPACES TO DAT-SCREEN
MOVE ALL GREEN TO ATTR-SCREEN
```

Assuming that GREEN was defined to contain the data bits that display green color, if we displayed DAT-SCREEN and ATTR-SCREEN, we would get a screen filled with green spaces. We will return to the obvious question as to how we would display those two fields. For the moment, though, we want to emphasize that a full screen display involves defining and displaying two fields, each equivalent to the screen size.

There is often a need to display a message or a field of data in a specific place on the screen, without displaying the entire screen. For instance, to display the message "INVALID CHOICE. TRY AGAIN" on line 20, starting with column 30, define a specific field within the screen defining field. For example:

```
01   DAT-SCREEN.
     02   FILLER          PIC X(1529).
     02   MESSAGE-FIELD   PIC X(26).
     02   FILLER          PIC X(365).
```

If we write MOVE "INVALID CHOICE. TRY AGAIN" to MESSAGE-FIELD and subsequently we display DAT-SCREEN, we have a way of displaying that message in row 20, column 30 [(19 x 80) + 29 = 1,529].

We can also display data in a specific position on the screen by moving the cursor to a specified position and then displaying the desired data. Positioning the cursor is specific to each device type, so we cannot give a standard description. In general terms, we need to define a field containing special codes that mean "move the cursor" followed by the row-column values for the desired location. Thus, to display data on the screen, define the screen as a field and position data within that field; or position the cursor at the desired place on the screen and then display the data.

Another method of handling screen display-attributes, particularly when remote terminals are involved, is to send special codes to the receiving terminal that specify the desired action. The terminal then sorts out the special codes, does what these codes specify, and then displays the (remaining) data. Consider an example, which is hypothetical because the specific procedure and codes depend on both the computer and the terminal.

Assume the following (fictitious) codes:

= the "escape" character. When the terminal receives such a character it is recognized as a special code that marks the beginning of a command string. The escape character plus the one or more characters that follow are not displayed. They are understood to comprise a command to the terminal. The character immediately following the escape character determines the length of the command string.

@ = position the cursor to row/column position designated by the following two 2-digit numbers

? = turn on the normal display mode.

! = turn on the bold-face display mode.

Next we define the following fields:

```
02   CURSOR-POSITION.
        03   ESCAPE-CODE          PIC X        VALUE '#'.
        03   CURSOR-CODE          PIC X        VALUE '@'.
        03   ROW-POSITION         PIC 99.
        03   COLUMN-POSITION      PIC 99.
02   DISPLAY-FIELD.
        03   ESCAPE-CODE          PIC X        VALUE '#'.
        03   PRINT-MODE           PIC X.
        03   MESSAGE-FIELD        PIC X(40).
02   INPUT-FIELD PIC X(20).
```

In order to write the words "Type your NAME:" in row 10, column 20, we would write:

```
MOVE 10 TO ROW-POSITION
MOVE 20 TO COLUMN-POSITION
DISPLAY CURSOR-POSITION WITH NO ADVANCING
MOVE '?' TO PRINT-MODE
MOVE 'Type your NAME:' TO MESSAGE-FIELD
DISPLAY DISPLAY-FIELD.
```

In order to move the cursor to row 11, column 30, and to receive whatever data is entered in the keyboard we would write:

```
MOVE 11 TO ROW-POSITION
MOVE 30 TO COLUMN-POSITION
DISPLAY CURSOR-POSITION WITH NO ADVANCING
ACCEPT INPUT-FIELD.
```

Finally, to print the word 'BOLD' in column 1, row 1, in boldface mode and to leave the cursor on the same line, we would write:

```
MOVE 1 TO ROW-POSITION
MOVE 1 TO COLUMN-POSITION
DISPLAY CURSOR-POSITION WITH NO ADVANCING
MOVE '!' TO PRINT-MODE
MOVE 'BOLD' TO DISPLAY-FIELD
DISPLAY DISPLAY-FIELD WITH NO ADVANCING.
```

The above discussion and illustrations are designed to present the general concept. Each reader will have to use the specific methods and codes applicable on the equipment being used.

Review

1 The screen display typically consists of _____ lines of _____ columns each.

24; 80

2   If particular positions on the screen are to be boldface, underscored, or in color, such required information is called display-_____ information.

attribute

3   Two fields need to be defined for a given screen: one field to store the displayed _____ and another field to describe the display-_____ of the character bytes.

data; attributes

4   Selective display on a given screen can be accomplished by defining a specific field within the _____ field.

screen-defining

5   Data can also be displayed selectively on a screen by moving the _____ to a specified position and then displaying the desired data.

cursor

6   Such special effects as boldface can be obtained on a screen by sending special _____ to the terminal.

codes

7   Each code to be used to achieve a special effect on a screen is defined in the DATA DIVISION, in the _____ clause for the data-item designating that effect.

VALUE

Handling Keyboard Input

When a key is pressed on the keyboard, a signal is sent to the processor representing the key. The program in effect at the time takes that key value and processes it in any desired way. It is important to note that there is no direct connection between the keyboard and the display screen. It is almost universal for programs to show keyboard operations on the screen, so that if we depress the letter A we see an A displayed on the screen. Such a universal convention should not be interpreted as being a hardware function. When the A key is pressed, the program receiving that signal could choose to display a letter other than A, a multiword message, or whatever; therefore, interactive programs must capture keyboard input.

Interactive COBOL programs handle keyboard input in one of two ways: Either the program contains logic to "look at" each incoming keyboard value and process it individually, or we can define a whole field and issue a command to receive from the keyboard a value for the entire field. In the latter case, while the user is keying in the data, our program cannot "see" what is being keyed-in until the entire field value is available. When data for the field is available, then the contents of the field can be examined, just as in batch processing. When a record is read from a disk, for example, the contents of a given field in the record are made available as a unit, not character by character.

If we are able to get character-by-character input, we can provide the user with an opportunity for exception input. For instance, in the middle of entering a customer's name, the user may want to issue a "cancel," or "re-do from start," or "exit" command by pressing a special key. The program that senses each character senses such an exception key and takes immediate action. In contrast, a program that receives field-at-a-time input from the keyboard cannot sense the user's signal immediately. The user must wait until the right occasion comes along before the special command is given. The programmer chooses one method over the other depending on the specific applications and programming ease.

Review

1   It is important to recognize that there [is/is not] a direct hardware connection between the keyboard and the display screen.

                                                                    is not

2   Keyboard entries can be handled character-by-_____ or as an entire _____.

                                                           character; field

3   A user can issue a "cancel" command before completing an input entry for a field only if the input is handled [character by character/as an entire field].

                                                           character by character

```
CUSTOMER FILE MENU


    (1)  ADD A NEW CUSTOMER

    (2)  CHANGE CUSTOMER DATA

    (3)  DELETE CUSTOMER

    (4)  EXIT PROGRAM




    ENTER SELECTION >


*** INVALID CHARACTER - TRY AGAIN ***
```

FIGURE 14-3   SAMPLE MENU SCREEN.

SAMPLE INTERACTIVE PROGRAM

In this section we present a sample interactive program to help illustrate in a specific context the general concepts already discussed. The specifics in the sample program apply *only* to the compiler used (Micro Focus COBOL) and the particular computer system (IBM PC with color graphics).

The overall function of the program is described in Figures 14-3 and 14-4. Initially, the program shows a menu such as the one in Figure 14-3. The ENTER SELECTION > prompt asks the user to enter one of the four designated choices. If the user enters anything other than 1, 2, 3, or 4, the message *** INVALID CHARACTER—TRY AGAIN *** appears at the bottom of the screen as shown in Figure 14-3; otherwise the program does one of the four specified choices. If the user enters choice 1, the program displays the screen shown in Figure 14-4. At that point, the user will enter the name (last, first, and middle) and a telephone number. When the user has finished entering input (or at any time), one of the three special keys, F1, F2, or ESC, is pressed to indicate the desired action.

To describe the sample program in greater detail, a full program listing is presented in Figure 14-5. A file is defined CUST-FILE so that we can write the data entered in the screen, as shown in Figure 14-4. When the user presses F2, the program will save the data displayed on the screen onto the CUST-FILE.

Text continues on page 548.

```
************************************************
*  *  *  *  *  *  *  *  *  *  *  *  *  *  *  * *
*                                             **
*                                             **
*          AMERICAN SALES COMPANY             **
*               CUSTOMER DATA                 **
*                                             **
*                                             **
*  NAME(Last):      (First):      (Middle):   **
*                                             **
*  PHONE:  (    )    -                        **
*                                             **
*                                             **
*      F1=RE-ENTER   F2=INPUT COMPLETE   Esc=BACK TO MENU  **
*                                             **
*  *  *  *  *  *  *  *  *  *  *  *  *  *  *  * *
************************************************
```

FIGURE 14-4   SAMPLE INPUT SCREEN.

```
       IDENTIFICATION DIVISION.
       PROGRAM-ID.  INTERACTIVE.
   *
       ENVIRONMENT DIVISION.
       CONFIGURATION SECTION.
   *
       SPECIAL-NAMES.
           CONSOLE IS CRT.
   *
       SOURCE-COMPUTER. IBM-PC.
       OBJECT-COMPUTER. IBM-PC.
   *
       INPUT-OUTPUT SECTION.
       FILE-CONTROL.
           SELECT CUST-FILE ASSIGN TO "B:CUST.DAT".
   *
       DATA DIVISION.
       FILE SECTION.
   *
       FD  CUST-FILE
           LABEL RECORDS ARE OMITTED
           DATA RECORD IS CUST-RECORD.
       01  CUST-RECORD.
           05   CUST-NAME-OUT.
               10   L-NAME-OUT           PIC X(15).
               10   F-NAME-OUT           PIC X(12).
               10   M-NAME-OUT           PIC X(12).
           05   PHONE-NUM-OUT.
               10   AREA-CODE-OUT        PIC 9(3).
               10   PHONE-1-OUT          PIC 9(3).
               10   PHONE-2-OUT          PIC 9(4).
   *
       WORKING-STORAGE SECTION.
       01  ERROR-MES                     PIC X(37) VALUE
           "*** INVALID CHARACTER - TRY AGAIN ***".
   *
       01  PUT-CHAR                      PIC X VALUE X"82".
       01  GET-CHAR                      PIC X VALUE X"83".
   *
       01  BEEPER                        PIC X VALUE X"E5".
   *
       01  CURSOR-POSITION               PIC X VALUE X"E6".
   *
       01  ROW-COL-POSITION.
           05   CURSOR-ROW               PIC 99 COMP.
           05   CURSOR-COL               PIC 99 COMP.
   *
       01  PARAM                         PIC 99 COMP.
```

FIGURE 14-5   SAMPLE INTERACTIVE COBOL PROGRAM.

```
      01    FUNCTION-KEYS.
            05   FUNCTION-KEY-ROUTINE        PIC X VALUE X"B0".
            05   SET-UP-FUNCTIONS            PIC 99 COMP VALUE O.
            05   FUNCTION-KEY-TABLE.
                 10   FUNCTION-CHAR          PIC 99 COMP.
                      88   ENTER-PRESSED     VALUE 1.
                      88   F1-PRESSED        VALUE 2.
                      88   F2-PRESSED        VALUE 3.
                      88   ESC-PRESSED       VALUE 4.
                 10   LENGTH-ENTER          PIC 99 COMP VALUE 1.
                 10   ENTER-KEY             PIC X       VALUE X"OD".
                 10   LENGTH-F1             PIC 99 COMP VALUE 2.
                 10   F1                    PIC XX      VALUE X"OO3B".
                 10   LENGTH-F2             PIC 99 COMP VALUE 2.
                 10   F2                    PIC XX      VALUE X"OO3C".
                 10   LENGTH-ESC            PIC 99 COMP VALUE 1.
                 10   ESC                   PIC X       VALUE X"1B".
                 10   FILLER                PIC 99 COMP VALUE O.
      *
      01    SCRN-IO                          PIC X VALUE X"B7".
      *
      01    WRITE-ATTR                       PIC 99 COMP.
      *
      01    FORM-PARAMS.
            05   IO-LENGTH                   PIC 9(4) COMP.
            05   SCRN-OFFSET                 PIC 9(4) COMP.
            05   BUFFER-OFFSET               PIC 9(4) COMP.
      *
      01    MAIN-MENU.
            05   FILLER                      PIC X(27) VALUE SPACES.
            05   FILLER                      PIC X(24) VALUE
                 "    CUSTOMER FILE MENU     ".
            05   FILLER                      PIC X(458) VALUE SPACES.
            05   MAIN-0528                   PIC X(22) VALUE
                 "(1) ADD A NEW CUSTOMER".
            05   FILLER                      PIC X(138) VALUE SPACES.
            05   MAIN-0728                   PIC X(24) VALUE
                 "(2) CHANGE CUSTOMER DATA".
            05   FILLER                      PIC X(136) VALUE SPACES.
            05   MAIN-0928                   PIC X(19) VALUE
                 "(3) DELETE CUSTOMER".
            05   FILLER                      PIC X(141) VALUE SPACES.
            05   MAIN-1128                   PIC X(16) VALUE
                 "(4) EXIT PROGRAM".
            05   FILLER                      PIC X(384) VALUE SPACES.
            05   MAIN-1628                   PIC X(16) VALUE
                 "ENTER SELECTION ".
            05   MAIN-1645                   PIC X VALUE ">".
            05   FILLER                      PIC X(515) VALUE SPACES.
      *
      01    MAIN-MENU-ATTR.
            05   FILLER                      PIC X(1920) VALUE ALL X"71".
```

FIGURE 14-5   SAMPLE INTERACTIVE COBOL PROGRAM.
(Continued)

```
01    NEW-CUST-SCREEN.
      05   SCRN-0101                    PIC X VALUE "*".
      05   SCRN-0102                    PIC X(78) VALUE ALL "*".
      05   SCRN-0180                    PIC X VALUE "*".
      05   SCRN-0201                    PIC X VALUE "*".
      05   FILLER                       PIC X(26).
      05   SCRN-0228                    PIC X(24) VALUE
           " AMERICAN SALES COMPANY ".
      05   FILLER                       PIC X(28).
      05   SCRN-0280                    PIC X VALUE "*".
      05   SCRN-0301                    PIC X VALUE "*".
      05   FILLER                       PIC X(32).
      05   SCRN-0329                    PIC X(13) VALUE
           "CUSTOMER DATA".
      05   FILLER                       PIC X(33).
      05   SCRN-0380                    PIC X VALUE "*".
      05   SCRN-0401                    PIC X VALUE "*".
      05   FILLER                       PIC X(78).
      05   SCRN-0480                    PIC X VALUE "*".
      05   SCRN-0501                    PIC X VALUE "*".
      05   FILLER                       PIC X(78).
      05   SCRN-0580                    PIC X VALUE "*".
      05   SCRN-0601                    PIC X VALUE "*".
      05   FILLER                       PIC X(78).
      05   SCRN-0680                    PIC X VALUE "*".
      05   SCRN-0701                    PIC X VALUE "*".
      05   FILLER                       PIC X.
      05   SCRN-0703                    PIC X(52) VALUE
           "NAME(Last):                    (First):
      05   SCRN-0757                    PIC X(23) VALUE
           "(Middle):                   ".
      05   FILLER                       PIC X(2).
      05   SCRN-0780                    PIC X VALUE "*".
      05   SCRN-0801                    PIC X VALUE "*".
      05   FILLER                       PIC X(78).
      05   SCRN-0880                    PIC X VALUE "*".
      05   SCRN-0901                    PIC X VALUE "*".
      05   FILLER                       PIC X(78).
      05   SCRN-0980                    PIC X VALUE "*".
      05   SCRN-1001                    PIC X VALUE "*".
      05   FILLER                       PIC X.
      05   SCRN-1003                    PIC X(21) VALUE
           "PHONE:   (    )    -      ".
      05   FILLER                       PIC X(56).
      05   SCRN-1080                    PIC X VALUE "*".
      05   SCRN-1101                    PIC X VALUE "*".
      05   FILLER                       PIC X(78).
      05   SCRN-1180                    PIC X VALUE "*".
      05   SCRN-1201                    PIC X VALUE "*".
      05   FILLER                       PIC X(78).
      05   SCRN-1280                    PIC X VALUE "*".
```

FIGURE 14-5   SAMPLE INTERACTIVE COBOL PROGRAM.
(Continued)

```
        05    SCRN-1301                 PIC X VALUE "*".
        05    FILLER                    PIC X(78).
        05    SCRN-1380                 PIC X VALUE "*".
        05    SCRN-1401                 PIC X VALUE "*".
        05    FILLER                    PIC X(78).
        05    SCRN-1480                 PIC X VALUE "*".
        05    SCRN-1501                 PIC X VALUE "*".
        05    FILLER                    PIC X(78).
        05    SCRN-1580                 PIC X VALUE "*".
        05    SCRN-1601                 PIC X VALUE "*".
        05    FILLER                    PIC X(78).
        05    SCRN-1680                 PIC X VALUE "*".
        05    SCRN-1701                 PIC X VALUE "*".
        05    FILLER                    PIC X(78).
        05    SCRN-1780                 PIC X VALUE "*".
        05    SCRN-1801                 PIC X VALUE "*".
        05    FILLER                    PIC X(78).
        05    FILLER                    PIC X VALUE "*".
        05    FILLER                    PIC X VALUE "*".
        05    FILLER                    PIC X(78).
        05    SCRN-1980                 PIC X VALUE "*".
        05    SCRN-2001                 PIC X VALUE "*".
        05    FILLER                    PIC X(78).
        05    SCRN-2080                 PIC X VALUE "*".
        05    SCRN-2101                 PIC X VALUE "*".
        05    FILLER                    PIC X(78).
        05    SCRN-2180                 PIC X VALUE "*".
        05    SCRN-2201                 PIC X VALUE "*".
        05    FILLER                    PIC X(13).
        05    SCRN-2228                 PIC X(53) VALUE
       "F1=RE-ENTER      F2=INPUT COMPLETE     Esc=BACK TO MENU".
        05    FILLER                    PIC X(12).
        05    SCRN-2280                 PIC X VALUE "*".
        05    SCRN-2301                 PIC X VALUE "*".
        05    FILLER                    PIC X(78).
        05    SCRN-2380                 PIC X VALUE "*".
        05    SCRN-2401                 PIC X VALUE "*".
        05    SCRN-2402                 PIC X(78) VALUE ALL "*".
        05    SCRN-2480                 PIC X VALUE "*".
   *
   01   L-NAME-SCREEN REDEFINES NEW-CUST-SCREEN.
        05    FILLER                    PIC X(495).
        05    LAST-NAME                 PIC X(15).
        05    FILLER                    PIC X(1410).
   01   F-NAME-SCREEN REDEFINES NEW-CUST-SCREEN.
        05    FILLER                    PIC X(521).
        05    FIRST-NAME                PIC X(12).
        05    FILLER                    PIC X(1387).
   01   M-NAME-SCREEN REDEFINES NEW-CUST-SCREEN.
        05    FILLER                    PIC X(545).
        05    MIDDLE-NAME               PIC X(12).
        05    FILLER                    PIC X(1363).
```

FIGURE 14-5   SAMPLE INTERACTIVE COBOL PROGRAM.
(Continued)

```
01    PHONE-NUM REDEFINES NEW-CUST-SCREEN.
      05   FILLER                     PIC X(731).
      05   AREA-CODE                  PIC 9(3).
      05   FILLER                     PIC X.
      05   PHONE-1                    PIC 9(3).
      05   FILLER                     PIC X.
      05   PHONE-2                    PIC 9(4).
*
01    ADD-SCRN-ATTR.
      05   FILLER                     PIC X(495) VALUE ALL X"1F".
      05   FILLER                     PIC X(15) VALUE ALL X"71".
      05   FILLER                     PIC X(11) VALUE ALL X"1F".
      05   FILLER                     PIC X(12) VALUE ALL X"71".
      05   FILLER                     PIC X(12) VALUE ALL X"1F".
      05   FILLER                     PIC X(12) VALUE ALL X"71".
      05   FILLER                     PIC X(173) VALUE ALL X"1F".
      05   FILLER                     PIC X(13) VALUE ALL X"71".
      05   FILLER                     PIC X(951) VALUE ALL X"1F".
      05   FILLER                     PIC X(53) VALUE ALL X"71".
      05   FILLER                     PIC X(174) VALUE ALL X"1F".
*
01    MENU-CHOICE              PIC X.
      88   VALID-CHOICE VALUES ARE "1", "2", "3", "4".
      88   ADD-CUST      VALUE "1".
      88   CHANGE-CUST   VALUE "2".
      88   DELETE-CUST   VALUE "3".
      88   EXIT-PROGRAM  VALUE "4".
*
01    KEY-IN                   PIC X.
*
01    PROGRAM-END-FLAG         PIC X VALUE "0".
      88   PROGRAM-END         VALUE "1".
01    ADD-CUST-END-FLAG        PIC X.
      88   KEEP-ADDING         VALUE "0".
      88   BACK-TO-MENU        VALUE "1".
*
*
*
PROCEDURE DIVISION.
*
000-MAIN-ROUTINE.
*
    DISPLAY SPACE.
*
    CALL FUNCTION-KEY-ROUTINE USING SET-UP-FUNCTIONS
                                    FUNCTION-KEY-TABLE.
    OPEN OUTPUT CUST-FILE.
```

FIGURE 14-5   SAMPLE INTERACTIVE COBOL PROGRAM.
(Continued)

```
            PERFORM WITH TEST AFTER UNTIL PROGRAM-END
    *
            PERFORM 100-DISPLAY-MENU
    *
            PERFORM 200-GET-MENU-CHOICE WITH TEST AFTER
                    UNTIL VALID-CHOICE
                EVALUATE TRUE
                    WHEN ADD-CUST
                        SET KEEP-ADDING TO TRUE
                        PERFORM 300-ADD-NEW-CUSTOMER
                            UNTIL BACK-TO-MENU
                    WHEN CHANGE-CUST
                        PERFORM 500-CHANGE-CUSTOMER
                    WHEN DELETE-CUST
                        PERFORM 600-DELETE-CUSTOMER
                    WHEN OTHER
                        SET PROGRAM-END TO TRUE
                END-EVALUATE
            END-PERFORM
        END-PERFORM.
    *
        CLOSE CUST-FILE
        DISPLAY SPACE UPON CRT
        STOP RUN.
    *
     100-DISPLAY-MENU.
        MOVE 1920 TO IO-LENGTH.
        MOVE 1 TO SCRN-OFFSET BUFFER-OFFSET.
        MOVE 3 TO WRITE-ATTR.
        CALL SCRN-IO USING WRITE-ATTR FORM-PARAMS MAIN-MENU-ATTR.
        MOVE 1 TO WRITE-ATTR.
    *
        CALL SCRN-IO USING WRITE-ATTR FORM-PARAMS MAIN-MENU.
    *
        MOVE 17 TO CURSOR-ROW.
        MOVE 47 TO CURSOR-COL.
        CALL CURSOR-POSITION USING PARAM  ROW-COL-POSITION.
    *
     200-GET-MENU-CHOICE.
        CALL GET-CHAR USING MENU-CHOICE
        CALL PUT-CHAR USING MENU-CHOICE
        IF VALID-CHOICE
           THEN CONTINUE
           ELSE
               CALL BEEPER
               DISPLAY ERROR-MES AT 2124
               MOVE 17 TO CURSOR-ROW
               MOVE 47 TO CURSOR-COL
               CALL CURSOR-POSITION USING PARAM  ROW-COL-POSITION.
```

**FIGURE 14-5   SAMPLE INTERACTIVE COBOL PROGRAM.
(Continued)**

```
300-ADD-NEW-CUSTOMER.
    MOVE 1920 TO IO-LENGTH.
    MOVE 1 TO SCRN-OFFSET BUFFER-OFFSET
    MOVE 3 TO WRITE-ATTR.
*
    CALL SCRN-IO USING WRITE-ATTR FORM-PARAMS ADD-SCRN-ATTR.
    MOVE 1 TO WRITE-ATTR.
*
    CALL SCRN-IO USING WRITE-ATTR FORM-PARAMS
                     NEW-CUST-SCREEN
*
    ACCEPT L-NAME-SCREEN
    IF ENTER-PRESSED
       ACCEPT F-NAME-SCREEN
        IF ENTER-PRESSED
           ACCEPT M-NAME-SCREEN
            IF ENTER-PRESSED
               ACCEPT PHONE-NUM
                IF ENTER-PRESSED
                   PERFORM WITH TEST AFTER
                       UNTIL F1-PRESSED OR F2-PRESSED
                           OR ESC-PRESSED
                       CALL GET-CHAR USING KEY-IN
                   END-PERFORM
               ELSE CONTINUE
               END-IF
           ELSE CONTINUE
           END-IF
       ELSE CONTINUE
       END-IF
    ELSE CONTINUE
    END-IF.
*
    IF F1-PRESSED
       MOVE SPACES TO LAST-NAME FIRST-NAME MIDDLE-NAME
                      AREA-CODE PHONE-1 PHONE-2
    ELSE IF F2-PRESSED
           PERFORM 400-WRITE-DATA
         ELSE IF ESC-PRESSED
                 SET BACK-TO-MENU TO TRUE.
*
400-WRITE-DATA.
    MOVE LAST-NAME TO L-NAME-OUT.
    MOVE FIRST-NAME TO F-NAME-OUT.
    MOVE MIDDLE-NAME TO M-NAME-OUT.
    MOVE AREA-CODE TO AREA-CODE-OUT.
    MOVE PHONE-1 TO PHONE-1-OUT.
    MOVE PHONE-2 TO PHONE-2-OUT.
    WRITE CUST-RECORD.
    MOVE SPACES TO LAST-NAME FIRST-NAME MIDDLE-NAME
                   AREA-CODE PHONE-1 PHONE-2.
```

FIGURE 14-5   SAMPLE INTERACTIVE COBOL PROGRAM.
(Continued)

```
     500-CHANGE-CUSTOMER.
*
*      This procedure not implemented.
*
     600-DELETE-CUSTOMER.
*
*      This procedure not implemented.
*
*
```

**FIGURE 14-5   SAMPLE INTERACTIVE COBOL PROGRAM.
(Continued)**

Reviewing the PROCEDURE DIVISION, the statement DISPLAY SPACE clears the screen. (Recall that statements such as DISPLAY SPACE are specific to each computer system and are shown here only as an example).

The CALL FUNCTION-KEY-ROUTINE calls out a special subprogram, defined by Micro Focus COBOL, that allows the user to define condition-names for selected keys. Referring to the early part of the DATA DIVISION, the reader will observe the 01 FUNCTION-KEYS definition, which, among other things, defines four condition-names:

88	ENTER-PRESSED	VALUE 1.
88	F1-PRESSED	VALUE 2.
88	F2-PRESSED	VALUE 3.
88	ESC-PRESSED	VALUE 4.

The four condition-names above can be checked during program execution to sense whether the following keys have been pressed, respectively: The Enter (return) key, the F1 function key, the F2, or the Esc (escape) key.

Note the strange VALUE designations in the DATA DIVISION, such as ... VALUE X"B0", or ... VALUE X"003B" in the FUNCTION-KEYS description. These are special (nonstandard) ways that Micro Focus has chosen to designate hexadecimal values needed to define parameters for special subroutines written for screen handling.

We now continue with our description of some of the highlights in the sample program.

In the 100-DISPLAY-MENU paragraph there are two CALL SCRN-IO commands. The first such CALL involves as its last argument the field MAIN-MENU-ATTR, which in the DATA DIVISION was defined with a ... FILLER PIC X(1920) VALUE ALL X"71". The X"71" is the Micro Focus way of specifying gray color background; thus, MAIN-MENU-ATTR was defined as 1,920 bytes with gray color attribute. The second CALL SCRN-IO involves MAIN-MENU as the last argument, which in the DATA DIVISION was defined as a group field describing the screen represented by Figure 14-3. Thus, the first CALL SCRN-IO defined the display attributes of the screen (all gray color), while the second CALL actually displayed the menu shown in Figure 14-3.

The last statement in the 100-DISPLAY-MENU paragraph is CALL CURSOR-POSITION, which puts the cursor in row 17, column 47.

The 200-GET-MENU-CHOICE paragraph receives a value from the keyboard by CALL GET-CHAR, another Micro Focus COBOL subroutine designed for character-by-character keyboard input. The subroutine is designed to wait until a key is pressed on the keyboard and then place the key-value in the argument field, which is called MENU-CHOICE in the sample program. The CALL PUT-CHAR USING MENU-CHOICE writes the contents of MENU-CHOICE at the position where the cursor is located (recall that the last statement in 100-DISPLAY-MENU placed the cursor at row 17, column 47).

If a VALID-CHOICE is not entered, the bell is sounded (CALL BEEPER), DISPLAY ERROR-MES AT 2124 is executed, and the cursor is positioned back at row 17, column 47 to await the next choice. The DISPLAY ERROR-MES AT 2124 demonstrates an alternate way for displaying messages on the screen with Micro Focus COBOL. The . . . AT 2124 signifies that the display is to begin at row 21, column 24.

When the user chooses menu choice "(1) ADD A NEW CUSTOMER", then the program executes 300-ADD-NEW-CUSTOMER. The first two CALL SCRN-IO statements are executed to prepare the screen for the display illustrated in Figure 14–4. The first CALL involves ADD-SCRN-ATTR, which defines blue (X"1F") and gray (X"71") areas on the screen. Although Figure 14–4 is not in color, the user should visualize that we have a completely blue screen except for the data, which are displayed in gray. The second CALL SCRN-IO involves NEW-CUST-SCREEN as the last argument. Examining NEW-CUST-SCREEN in the DATA DIVISION, we see a long, elaborate description of the screen format for the illustration in Figure 14–4. We have used mnemonic names in the form SCRN-xxxx to help us remember the implied position on the screen. Thus, SCRN-0228 is a mnemonic name for a field beginning in row 2, column 28.

Continuing with the 300-ADD-NEW-CUSTOMER routine, we ACCEPT the last, first, and middle name and the telephone number fields. In each case we test IF ENTER-PRESSED, which was defined as a condition-name for the condition of the Enter key having been depressed. If the respective ACCEPT operation was terminated by pressing the Enter key, then it is assumed that the user completed entering the respective field; and we are ready to proceed to ACCEPT the next field. Notice that we need not position the cursor prior to each ACCEPT because of the way the fields were defined. For instance, L-NAME-SCREEN contains a FILLER PIC X(495), which places the cursor at line 7, column 15 ($80 \times 6 = 480$; $495 - 480 = 15$).

The last part of 300-ADD-NEW-CUSTOMER checks as to whether or not one of the special keys, F1, F2, or Esc, was pressed. These keys are the three choices in Figure 14–4 for exiting from the ADD-NEW-CUSTOMER procedure.

When the user presses F1, either after typing in all four fields or in the course of typing any of the four fields, the program logic clears the contents of all fields and repeats the procedure of accepting data for a new customer. Thus, the user can in effect "cancel" and re-do an entry.

After entering all the data, it is assumed that the user will review it and, if satisfied, the F2 key will be pressed to tell the program to save the data. At that point the program executes 400-WRITE-DATA, which writes the customer name and telephone number in CUST-FILE.

The 500-CHANGE-CUSTOMER and 600-DELETE-CUSTOMER routines are not implemented in the program because their presence would not add to the purpose at hand. Still, their presence as "stub" paragraphs allow the sample program to contain a main menu that has more than one choice, thereby making that part of the program more realistic.

The sample program contains the majority of interactive features and operations that any interactive program contains; thus, the reader can use it as a basic framework for developing similar programs. Unfortunately, the detailed specifications are not in standard format since there is no standard format available. Still, the general approach used by the illustrated product, Micro Focus COBOL, is similar to the approach used by other vendors of COBOL compilers.

Exercises

14.1 Adapt the sample program to your computer system and execute it.

14.2 Take any previously written program that involved batch file input and change it so that input is entered via a keyboard.

15

DATA STRUCTURES

INTRODUCTION

COBOL provides convenient ways for structuring data to meet the needs for certain applications. In particular, the language provides convenient ways by which data can be grouped and referenced *within* a record, including reference to level numbers and associated elementary and group-item formations and the use of reference modification, the REDEFINES clause, and the RENAMES clause. In addition, data can be structured in the form of tables; and files can be organized in sequential, indexed, or relative form.

Even though COBOL provides considerable flexibility in structuring and referencing data, there are some occasions in which the data need to be structured differently from the ways provided for by the language. This chapter presents an overview of data structures that extends beyond the capability included in the COBOL language.

LOGICAL DATA STRUCTURES

An important characteristic of data structures is the ability to represent interrelationships among data items. There are two levels of data structure that can be considered: logical structure and physical structure. The *logical data structure* is concerned with the defined data relationships apart from their physical recording. *Physical data structure* is concerned with the actual storage representation of data and its relationships. In this section we consider four basic types of logical data structure: flat files, tree hierarchies, networks, and the relational model.

Flat Files

The sequential, indexed, and relative file structures that we have considered in this book are called *flat files*. We have viewed files as collections of records, each record consisting of a number of fields such as shown in Figure 15-1. Each row in Figure 15-1 constitutes a record. Each record is identified by a unique key, called the *entity identifier* or the *primary key*. In Figure 15-1 the EMPLOYEE-NUMBER is an example of an entity identifier. The term *attribute* is often used in lieu of the term field. Thus, a column in Figure 15-1, such as WAGE-RATE, constitutes an entity attribute. Flat files are often ordered on the basis of the entity identifier values, thereby establishing a logical relationship between records. However, no relationships are implied between the other attributes in the record.

Tree Hierarchies

A hierarchical data structure represents a relationship between a *parent* and a *child* data item. The relationship can be depicted in graphic form as a *tree*, as illustrated in Figure 15-2. At the head of the tree there is an element called

EMPLOYEE-NUMBER	DEPARTMENT	SKILL CODE	WAGE RATE	YEAR-TO-DATE GROSS
1234	10	A	3	10000
5678	20	B	1	7500
9101	10	L	2	8425

FIGURE 15-1   AN EXAMPLE OF A FLAT FILE.

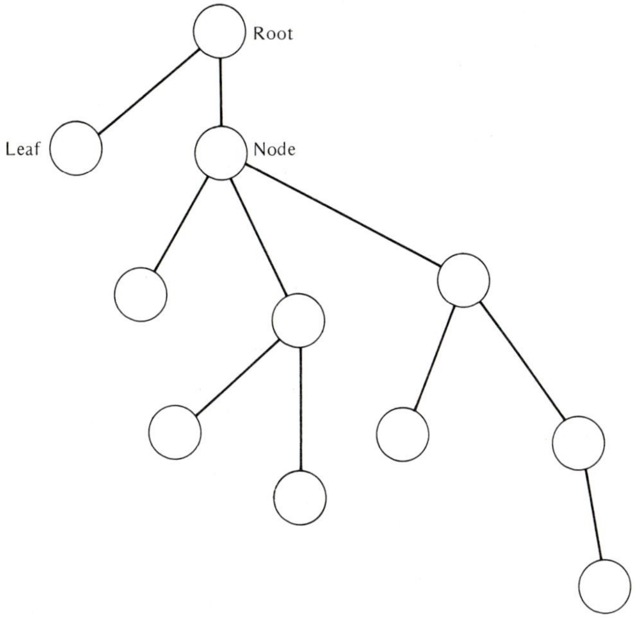

FIGURE 15-2   A TREE STRUCTURE.

the *root;* all other elements are hierarchically lower and are referred to as *nodes* in the tree. A node which has other dependent nodes is a parent element, while the dependent nodes are called the children. Children of the same parent are called (logical) *twins*. A node with no children is called a *leaf.*

Record descriptions in COBOL constitute hierarchies. The root element is the 01-level item, while subordinate group items constitute nodes and elementary items constitute leaves. Figure 15-3 serves to illustrate the concept.

The specific characteristic of a hierarchical structure is that each child has only one parent. (We will contrast this characteristic to network structures in the next section.)

Trees may be *balanced* (each parent has an equal number of children) or *unbalanced*. Balanced trees may be *binary* (each parent has two children).

An alternative to the parent-child terminology is *owner-member*. A hierarchy can be represented by a so-called *CODASYL set* as illustrated in Figure 15-4. The set terminology comes from the data base specifications of CODASYL.

Consider Figure 15-5, illustrating the hierarchical structure for a personnel file. The DEPT RECORD serves as the root of the tree hierarchy. EMPLOYEE RECORD and DEPT JOB RECORD are children of the root. Finally, EMPLOYEE RECORD is the parent to three logical children records: MAILING ADDRESS, JOB HISTORY, and DEPENDENTS.

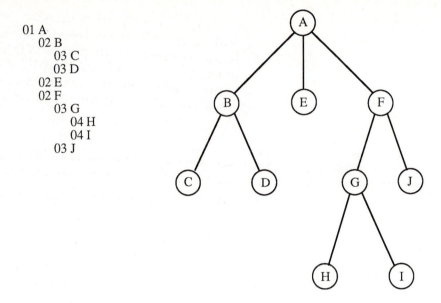

```
01 A
   02 B
       03 C
       03 D
   02 E
   02 F
       03 G
          04 H
          04 I
       03 J
```

FIGURE 15-3   HIERARCHICAL REPRESENTATION OF COBOL RECORD DESCRIPTION.

Networks

A *network* is a data structure such that a child in a hierarchy may have more than one parent. Consider a case where a company operates on the basis of projects. Employees are assigned to projects and machines are used by projects. The logical relationships are represented in Figure 15–6. A specific illustration is given in Figure 15–7, which is based on three employees, two projects, and three machines. The connecting lines indicate the relationships. For instance, Employee 1 has three parents, Project 1 and Machines 1

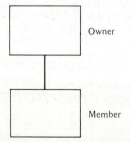

FIGURE 15-4   A CODASYL SET.

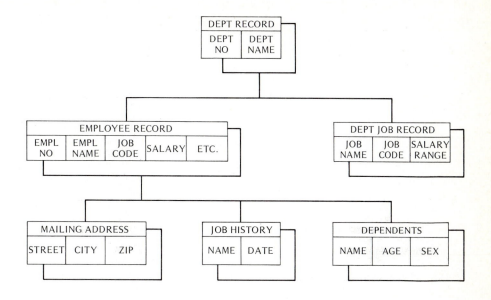

FIGURE 15-5   A HIERARCHICAL FILE STRUCTURE.

and 2. Similarly, Project 1 can be viewed to have as parents Machines 1 and 3 and Employees 1, 2, and 3.

Figure 15–8 illustrates the decomposition of the example network into six set hierarchies, while Figure 15–9 illustrates that the network could also be represented by six flat files (at the cost of great redundancy).

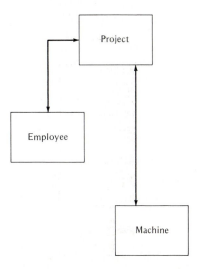

FIGURE 15-6   A NETWORK RELATIONSHIP.

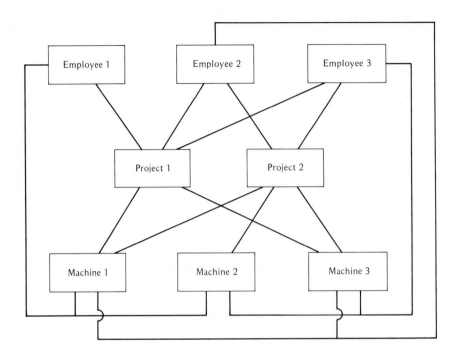

FIGURE 15-7   AN EXAMPLE OF A NETWORK STRUCTURE WITH THREE RECORD TYPES.

The Relational Model

The relational model is based on the fact that any data structure can be reduced to a set of flat files provided that some redundancy is allowed. A *relation* is a two-dimensional table. The table consists of rows called *tuples* and a fixed number of *attributes* (columns) such that the data in a column represents a homogeneous set—the data represents values for the same attribute. The data base user is equipped with language operators (relational algebra and/or relational calculus) which enable the formation of new tables (rela-

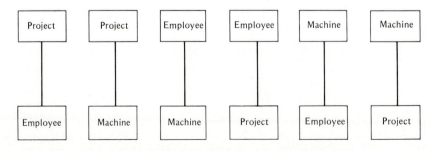

FIGURE 15-8   SUBSTITUTION OF SIX SET HIERARCHIES FOR A NETWORK.

P1	E1	P1	M1	E1	M1	E1	P1	M1	E1	M1	P1
P1	E2	P1	M3	E1	M2	E2	P1	M1	E2	M1	P2
P1	E3	P2	M1	E2	M1	E2	P2	M2	E1	M2	P2
P2	E2	P2	M2	E2	M3	E3	P1	M2	E3	M3	P1
P2	E3	P2	M3	E3	M2	E3	P2	M3	E2	M3	P2
				E3	M3			M3	E3		

FIGURE 15–9   REPRESENTATION OF THE NETWORK AS SIX FLAT FILES.

tions) by means of extracting a subset of columns, a subset of rows, or by combining columns and rows from two or more tables.

Consider Figure 15–10, which represents two relations, Project and Employee. The Project Table consists of two rows and two columns while the Employee Table consists of five rows and two columns. Relationships can be formed by reference to these tables. Suppose that we present the request: Identify the employees who worked on Project 2. This request could be satisfied by forming a new table that would consist of the second and fifth rows of the Employee Table, as follows:

E1	P2
E3	P2

As another example, consider the request: Find the customer names for the projects on which Employee 3 (E3) worked. This request would be satisfied by joining the fourth and fifth rows of the Employee Table and the two rows of the Project Table in Figure 15–10 to form a new table:

EMPLOYEE NO	PROJECT NO		PROJECT NO	CUSTOMER NAME		CUSTOMER NAME
E3	P1	+	P1	Jones	=	Jones
E3	P2		P2	Smith		Smith

PROJECT TABLE

PROJECT NO	CUSTOMER NAME
P1	Jones
P2	Smith

EMPLOYEE TABLE

EMPLOYEE NO	PROJECT NO
E1	P1
E1	P2
E2	P1
E3	P1
E3	P2

FIGURE 15–10   AN EXAMPLE OF A RELATIONAL MODEL DATA REPRESENTATION.

The appeal of the relational model is based on two factors. First, the concept of tabular structure seems easy to understand by users in general. In contrast, hierarchies and networks can become quite complex and difficult to comprehend. The second advantage of the relational model is that it is based on a formal, rational model whose logical manipulation can be described by means of the mathematical system of relational algebra or relational calculus.

Review

1   The data structure concepts which are concerned with defined data relationships, but not the physical recording of the data, are associated with _____ data structure.

logical

2   In the flat file structure, if each column represents a data field, or attribute, then each row represents a _____.

record

3   In the generalized terminology associated with data structure concepts, a record is called a _____ or a _____.

segment; tuple

4   In the flat file structure, each record is uniquely identified by one of the attributes which is used as the _____.

entity identifier (or primary key)

5   In hierarchical tree structures, the element at the head of the tree is called the _____, while all other elements, which are hierarchically lower, are called _____.

root; nodes

6   In hierarchical tree structures, a node which has other dependent

nodes is called a _____ element, while the dependent nodes are called _____.

parent; children

7   In hierarchical tree structures, a parent [can/cannot] have more than one child, and a child [can/cannot] have more than one parent.

can; cannot

8   In the network structure, a parent [can/cannot] have more than one child, and a child [can/cannot] have more than one parent.

can; can

9   If a file which has a network structure is represented by several flat files instead, the result is that there will be considerable _____ in data.

redundancy

10   When the relational model is used as the basis for logical data structure, the *relation* of interest can always be graphically portrayed as a two-dimensional _____.

table

11   In comparison with hierarchical tree structures and network structures logical data structures which follow the relational model are generally [easier/more difficult] to understand.

easier

POINTER STRUCTURES

The preceding section presented the basic concepts associated with logical data structures. Our ability to understand and communicate logical structure concepts is dependent on our use of graphic representations. But computers can store characters of data, not graphic figures, and thus we must use some other method of representation when it comes to considerations of *physical data structures. Pointers* provide us with an effective physical means of implementing logical data relationships in computer storage. A pointer is a data-item whose value is the storage address of some other data-item. Commonly, a pointer is a record field which contains the storage address of some other record.

In this section we present some of the common pointer structures. It should be recognized, however, that there are many other pointer structures that are also used.

Stacks

A *stack* is a one-dimensional table structure, also called a *linear list,* for which all additions and deletions take place at one end of the table. A simple example of a physical stack is the stack of trays in a cafeteria, given that new trays are added to the top of the stack and removals also are made from the top of the stack. In the terminology of the field of accounting, the term Last-In, First-Out (LIFO) describes the basic properties of a stack. In a data processing context, a stack can be used to represent the inventory of available rooms in a hotel given that the rooms are assigned according to which one was most recently cleaned. In a computer science context, a compiler can use a stack structure to store the return addresses of a series of nested PERFORM, or CALL, statements.

In order to implement a stack in COBOL, a table structure that includes a field to keep track of the head (or tail) of the stack can be used. Consider the following example:

```
01  STACK-STRUCTURE.
    02  STACK-HEAD        PIC 99.
    02  STACK-CAPACITY   PIC 99   VALUE 50.
    02  STACK-DATA.
        03  STACK-TABLE OCCURS 50 TIMES.
            04  HOTEL-ROOM   PIC X(4).
            04  ROOM-RATE      PIC 9(3)V99.
```

Initially, we could store a zero value in STACK-HEAD for the above example. When a new item is to be added to the stack, say the room-number in the field CLEAN-ROOM, we would execute the following procedure:

```
ADD-TO-STACK.
    IF   STACK-HEAD = STACK-CAPACITY
        THEN PERFORM STACK-IS-FULL
```

```
        ELSE ADD 1 TO STACK-HEAD
              MOVE CLEAN-ROOM-NO TO HOTEL-ROOM (STACK-HEAD)
              MOVE CLEAN-ROOM-RATE TO ROOM-RATE (STACK-HEAD)
    END-IF.
```

In order to assign (remove) the room that is at the head of the stack, the following procedure would be executed:

```
DELETE-FROM-STACK.
    IF STACK-HEAD < 1
        THEN PERFORM STACK-IS-EMPTY
        ELSE MOVE HOTEL-ROOM (STACK-HEAD) TO
              ROOM-ASSIGNMENT
              MOVE ROOM-RATE (STACK-HEAD) TO ASSIGNED-RATE
              SUBTRACT 1 FROM STACK-HEAD
    END-IF.
```

By the above examples we can observe that a stack can be maintained with relatively simple coding procedures. If a stack is stored in a relative file, a common approach is to store the stack head information on the first record of the file and to use the remainder of the file for stack storage. Assuming that REL-KEY was declared as the RELATIVE KEY, we would write:

```
MOVE 1 TO REL-KEY
READ STACK-FILE
        INVALID KEY . . .
etc.
MOVE STACK-FILE-REC TO STACK-HEAD.
```

Before terminating the program, the stack head would be saved by the following instructions:

```
MOVE STACK-HEAD TO STACK-FILE-REC
MOVE 1 TO REL-KEY
WRITE STACK-FILE-REC
        INVALID KEY . . .
```

In parallel with the table structure defined at the beginning of this subsection, the procedure to add a record to the stack might be written as follows:

```
ADD-TO-STACK.
    IF   STACK-HEAD = MAX-RECS-ALLOWED-IN-FILE
         THEN PERFORM STACK-IS-FULL
         ELSE ADD 1 TO STACK-HEAD
              MOVE STACK-HEAD TO REL-KEY
              MOVE appropriate data TO STACK-FILE-REC
              WRITE STACK-FILE-REC
                   INVALID KEY . . .
```

Again, we conclude that a stack is fairly easy to implement, either as a table structure or as a relative file.

Queues

A *queue* is a one-dimensional table representation with defined beginning and end locations that is operated on a First-In, First-Out (FIFO) basis. Records are added to the end of the list and are removed from the beginning of the list. An everyday example of a queue is a waiting line of customers at a post-office service counter. New customers are added to the end of the line (list) while servicing (removal) takes place at the beginning of the line (list). In a data processing context, a list of outstanding invoices (accounts payable) can be treated as a queue. A new invoice goes to the bottom of the list. When a payment is received it is applied against the oldest invoice first. If the payment is larger than that particular amount due, the remainder of the payment is applied to succeeding invoices. In computer science, a common use of a queue structure is in the scheduling algorithm for a multiprogramming operating system. Incoming jobs are stored as a queue, with the oldest job submitted being served first.

Referring to the hotel-room example in the previous subsection on stacks, a queue can be implemented with the following type of table structure, resulting in a FIFO basis for assigning rooms:

```
01  QUE-STRUCTURE.
    02   QUE-START        PIC 99    VALUE 1.
    02   QUE-END          PIC 99    VALUE 0.
    02   QUE-SIZE         PIC 99    VALUE 0.
    02   QUE-CAPACITY     PIC 99    VALUE 50.
    02   QUE-DATA.
         03   QUE-TABLE OCCURS 50 TIMES.
              04   HOTEL-ROOM     PIC X (4).
              04   ROOM-RATE      PIC 9(3)V99.
```

Initially, we set the values for QUE-START, QUE-END, and QUE-SIZE as shown in the above specifications. When an item is to be added to the queue, we write:

```
ADD-TO-QUE.
    IF    QUE-SIZE = QUE-CAPACITY
          THEN PERFORM QUE-IS-FULL
          ELSE ADD 1 TO QUE-END
               IF QUE-END > QUE-CAPACITY
                   THEN MOVE 1 TO QUE-END
               END-IF
               ADD 1 TO QUE-SIZE
               MOVE CLEAN-ROOM-NO TO HOTEL-ROOM (QUE-END)
               MOVE CLEAN-ROOM-RATE TO ROOM-RATE (QUE-END)
    END-IF.
```

In the above program segment, notice that QUE-START is not involved and therefore not affected by an ADD-TO-QUE operation. As items are added to the queue it may become full, hence the statement IF QUE-SIZE = QUE-CAPACITY THEN PERFORM QUE-IS-FULL. Another special case is that in which the QUE-START value is greater than 1 because of previous deletions. In such a case we wrap around the queue by the statement IF QUE-END > QUE-CAPACITY THEN MOVE 1 TO QUE-END. Figure 15–11 presents some example possibilities for queue contents in order to illustrate the circular implementation used. An alternative approach is to keep the queue contents "packed" at the top of the queue. By the latter approach, when an item is removed, then every item in the queue is moved up one place. The result is that the value of QUE-END would always be equal to QUE-SIZE, thereby making QUE-START and QUE-END unnecessary. However, this mode of operation is not the preferred one, because physically moving the contents of the queue is time consuming, especially for large queues.

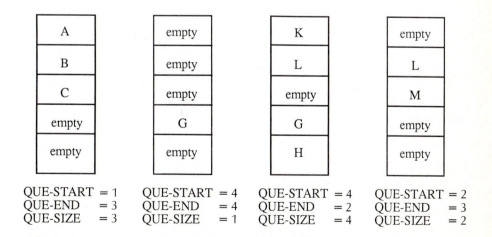

A	empty	K	empty
B	empty	L	L
C	empty	empty	M
empty	G	G	empty
empty	empty	H	empty

QUE-START = 1	QUE-START = 4	QUE-START = 4	QUE-START = 2
QUE-END = 3	QUE-END = 4	QUE-END = 2	QUE-END = 3
QUE-SIZE = 3	QUE-SIZE = 1	QUE-SIZE = 4	QUE-SIZE = 2

FIGURE 15–11   SAMPLE QUEUE CONTENTS AND STRUCTURE DESCRIPTORS.

Deletions from the queue can be handled by the following procedure:

```
DELETE-FROM-QUE.
    IF QUE-SIZE > 0
        THEN MOVE HOTEL-ROOM (QUE-START) TO ROOM-ASSIGNMENT
            MOVE ROOM-RATE (QUE-START) TO ASSIGNED-RATE
            ADD 1 TO QUE-START
            IF QUE-START > QUE-CAPACITY
                THEN MOVE 1 TO QUE-START
            END-IF
            SUBTRACT 1 FROM QUE-SIZE
            IF QUE-SIZE = 0
                THEN MOVE 1 TO QUE-START
                    MOVE 0 TO QUE-END
            END-IF
        ELSE
            PERFORM QUE-IS-EMPTY
    END-IF.
```

If the queue is not empty when the program segment above is executed (QUE-SIZE > 0), we advance the QUE-START by one position, wrapping around the queue if necessary. Notice that we do not bother to "erase" the deleted record in the sample procedure above. Deletion consists simply of advancing the value of QUE-START; thus, the "empty" cells in Figure 15–11 need not be empty. They may contain previously deleted but not yet overwritten items. Of course, an item being deleted can be erased by executing MOVE SPACES TO QUE-TABLE (QUE-START) *before* executing ADD 1 TO QUE-START.

Implementing a queue structure in a relative file can be done in a manner paralleling the method discussed in the previous subsection on implementing stack structures.

List Chains

A list is a data structure such that there is one starting (head) record, and each record (including the head) contains a pointer to the next record in sequence. The last record in the sequence has a special pointer value to indicate the end of the list chain. Figure 15–12 represents a simple list structure for five "Project Records." The spatial separation of the records is intended to represent the possible physical separations that may exist between records. The arrows in Figure 15–12 provide a pictorial view of the pointer structure. In computer storage the value stored in the pointer field gives the storage address of the record to which the arrow points in the figure.

The basic advantage of a simple list chain is that we may preserve log-

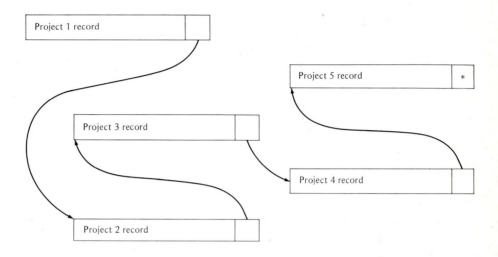

FIGURE 15-12   A SIMPLE LIST STRUCTURE.

ical order even though we may have "random" physical order. One disadvantage is that it is a forward-only system. If we have accessed a particular record through a chain of pointers and we wish to access its logical predecessor, there is no way to go backward. Figure 15–13 shows how we can have both forward and backward access capability by utilizing two pointers in each record. One pointer gives the storage address of the succeeding record

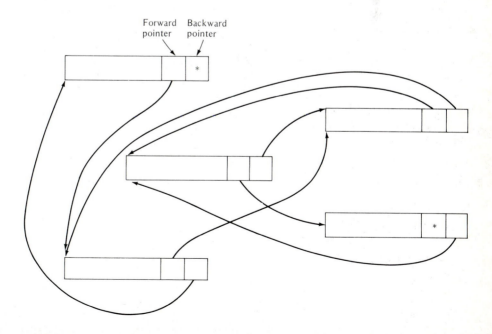

FIGURE 15-13   A LIST CHAIN WITH FORWARD AND BACKWARD POINTERS.

while the other pointer gives the storage address of the preceding record.

Figure 15–14 illustrates the applications of two-way pointers in the case of hierarchical structure involving two projects and the relationships of employees and machines assigned to projects. We form two list chains, one for each project. The Project records serve as heads of their respective chains. Each Employee record contains two pointers. One pointer points to the next employee record for Project 1 while the other pointer points to the next employee record for Project 2. The employee pointer (EP) in the Project 1 record points to Employee 1. The project 1 Pointer (P1P) in the Employee 1 record points to the Employee 2 record, which is the end of the chain. With respect

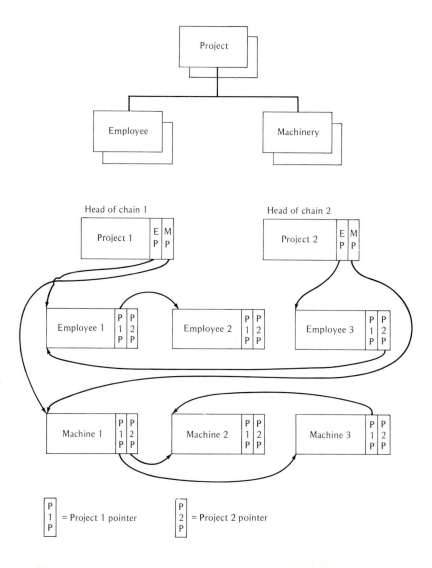

FIGURE 15–14 AN ILLUSTRATION OF A LIST CHAIN WITH TWO-WAY POINTERS.

to the Project 2 chain it should be noted that the first record in the employee chain is Employee 3, which is followed by Employee 1. This last example illustrates the ability of pointer structures to represent logical orders which are impossible as physical orders without redundancy. Specifically, the Employee 1 record is first in the Project 1 chain while it is last in the Project 2 chain.

The machine records also contain two pointers in a fashion analogous to that of the employee records.

Rings

A ring is a list chain such that the last record in the chain points to the head record. Figure 15–15 shows a simple ring structure. A ring provides an access path that is circular, and care must be taken to distinguish the head record. Suppose that in a ring of 500 records we are looking for a record which does not exist. We could have an infinite loop if we did not mark the header record as such.

Sometimes it is desirable to be able to return to the head of a chain from the record which we have just accessed without completing the entire path of the ring. Figure 15–16 illustrates the use of two pointers for quick return to the head record. One pointer points to the next record while the other points to the head record.

Reviewing Figure 15–16, it can be seen that the pointer structure allows return to the head of the chain, but is inefficient for returning to the predecessor record. Thus in such a ring of 500 records if we had accessed the 300th logical record and we wanted to access the 299th logical record, we would have to access all records from the first record (head) to the 299th record. We could consider the use of a third pointer to identify the predecessor record if we anticipate frequent need to backtrack. Obviously, pointer systems can proliferate as we strive for flexibility and efficiency. For instance, it is possible to have pointers that allow for "big jumps" instead of one record at a time. In general, as the number of pointers increases file updating

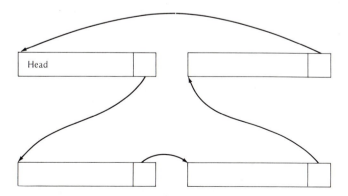

FIGURE 15–15   A SIMPLE RING STRUCTURE.

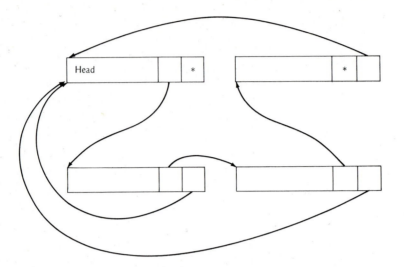

FIGURE 15–16   A TWO-POINTER RING STRUCTURE.

becomes more complex, since additions or deletions to the file require changes in many pointers.

Review

1   In terms of physical data structure, a data-item whose value indicates the storage location of some other record is called a _____.

                                                                                      pointer

2   The type of one-dimensional table structure that can be described as a Last-In, First-Out (LIFO) system is the _____ structure.

                                                                                      stack

3   The type of one-dimensional table structure that can be described as a First-In, First-Out (FIFO) system is the _____ structure.

                                                                                      queue

4   In a simple list structure, if there is only one pointer per record, that pointer usually identifies the [preceding/succeeding] record.

                                                                                      succeeding

5 When a simple list structure is used, it [is/is not] necessary that the records in the file physically be in a logical order.

is not

6 The type of list chain structure in which one or more records in the chain point to the head record is called a _____.

ring

SAMPLE COBOL PROGRAM

In this section the application of the pointer concepts discussed in the preceding section is illustrated by means of a complete COBOL program.

Pointer structures will be used to sort the data in a table in both ascending *and* descending order. We refer to this as the *chained records sort algorithm*. By the use of this method two additional fields are defined for each record of a given table of records. The first field, call it the predecessor field, contains a value that defines the location of the record that logically precedes the record in question. The other field, call it the successor field, contains a value that defines the location of the record that logically follows the given record. If such predecessor and successor fields are defined for each record, we say that we have a fully chained set of records. Such a set has both a forward and backward chain, since given any particular record we can determine all the records that precede it and all the records that follow it. In order to designate the first and last records of the table, the first can be assigned a predecessor value of zero while the last record can be assigned a successor value of zero.

In order to illustrate the procedure associated with the chained records sort algorithm, let us consider the table defined by the following DATA DIVISION statements:

```
01  DATA-TABLE.
      02  TABLE-ENTRIES OCCURS 50 TIMES.
            03  KEY-FIELD        PICTURE 9(4).
            03  DATA-FIELD       PICTURE X(76).
            03  PREDECESSOR      PICTURE 9(2).
            03  SUCCESSOR        PICTURE 9(2).
```

Conceptually, the table defined by the above statements has the following structure:

KEY-FIELD	DATA-FIELD	PREDECESSOR	SUCCESSOR

PREDECESSOR (1) and SUCCESSOR (1) refer to the predecessor and successor values of the first record in the table. Assume that the data to be stored consist of five records whose KEY-FIELDS are 3200, 3900, 2000, 4000, and 3500. For simplicity we ignore the DATA-FIELD values. In addition, it is useful to define the following data-names, whose values will be stored outside of the table as such:

NEW: new entry in the table

FIRST-PLACE: physical position of the record that is logically the first entry in the table

LAST-PLACE: physical position of the record that is logically the last entry in the table

For the five records whose keys as 3200, 3900, 2000, 4000, and 3500, we now consider the effects of entering each of these records to the table described above in a sequential fashion.

FIRST RECORD ENTERED

KEY-FIELD	DATA-FIELD	PREDECESSOR	SUCCESSOR
3200		00	00

NEW = 1, FIRST PLACE = 1, LAST-PLACE = 1

Since there is only one record in the table at this point, the PREDECESSOR and SUCCESSOR fields are both set equal to zero. Similarly, this one record is both the FIRST-PLACE and LAST-PLACE entry in the table. The value of NEW indicates the location of the new record.

SECOND RECORD ENTERED

KEY-FIELD	DATA-FIELD	PREDECESSOR	SUCCESSOR
3200		00	02
3900		01	00

NEW = 2, FIRST PLACE = 1, LAST-PLACE = 2

The KEY-FIELD of the second record is higher than the KEY-FIELD of the first record; therefore, the second record logically succeeds the first and SUCCESSOR (1) = 02. However, the first record is not logically preceded by any other record, and hence PREDECESSOR (1) = 00. Similarly, PREDECES-

SOR (2) = 01 and SUCCESSOR (2) = 00. The FIRST-PLACE in the table is at record 1 while the LAST-PLACE is at record 2.

THIRD RECORD ENTERED

KEY-FIELD	DATA-FIELD	PREDECESSOR	SUCCESSOR
3200		03	02
3900		01	00
2000		00	01

NEW = 3, FIRST PLACE = 3, LAST-PLACE = 2

The KEY-FIELD of the third record (2000) is compared with the KEY-FIELD of FIRST-PLACE (3900), and it is found to be smaller. Thus the search is completed and the predecessor and successor values are changed as indicated above.

The effects of processing the fourth and fifth records are illustrated in the following two tables. Note the logic of the changes in the predecessor and successor values in each table.

FOURTH RECORD ENTERED

KEY-FIELD	DATA-FIELD	PREDECESSOR	SUCCESSOR
3200		03	02
3900		01	04
2000		00	01
4000		02	00

NEW = 4, FIRST PLACE = 3, LAST-PLACE = 4

FIFTH RECORD ENTERED

KEY-FIELD	DATA-FIELD	PREDECESSOR	SUCCESSOR
3200		03	05
3900		05	04
2000		00	01
4000		02	00
3500		01	02

NEW = 5, FIRST PLACE = 3, LAST-PLACE = 4

Given the completed table above, suppose we wish to output the records in this table in ascending sequence. The contents of FIRST-PLACE indicates the location of the first record, that is, the record with the smallest key value. In the above example it is the third record, with the associated KEY-FIELD value of 2000. If the location of this record had not been stored in FIRST-PLACE, it could have been determined by checking the value of each PREDECESSOR field until the one with a value of zero was found. Of course, once the first record is identified, the location of each record which follows is determined by reference to the SUCCESSOR field.

Figure 15–17 presents a complete COBOL program that implements the general procedure just described in a specific context. The DATA-TABLE definition includes a REC-NO field designed to store the record-number of each record for ease of reference. The program is designed to output three tables. The first table is a listing of the original input data in the order presented in the INPUT-FILE. The second table is a listing of the DATA-TABLE records in physical order. The third table is a listing of the records in ascending order, along with the respective PREDECESSOR and SUCCESSOR values.

In the PROCEDURE DIVISION, PERFORM STORE-FIRST-RECORD is executed as a separate procedure in order to handle the very first record. One can reason that the same logic that adds any record to the table can be applied to the first such record as well. However, such an approach complicates the processing logic by requiring the program to differentiate first and nonfirst records. Reviewing the STORE-FIRST-RECORD paragraph, we observe that it consists of setting the appropriate values to define the one-record condition.

STORE-NEW-RECORD is the procedure that controls the logic of adding a new record. There are three possibilities represented by the three distinct procedures: PLACE-IN-FRONT, PLACE-AT-END, and PLACE-IN-MIDDLE. The last possibility represents the most complex case, since we need to travel through the chain until we find the position at which the new record "fits" (PERFORM TRY-NEXT UNTIL KEY-FIELD (NEW) NOT > KEY-FIELD (XTH)). It is interesting to note the content of the TRY-NEXT paragraph: MOVE SUCCESSOR (XTH) to XTH. That MOVE instruction provides the mechanism for accessing the next (XTH) record.

Figure 15–18 helps to illustrate the process of entering a new record "in the middle" of a file. In Figure 15–18, NEW represents the new record, X represents the current record with which NEW is being compared, and X − 1 and X + 1 represent the records preceding and following X, respectively. The dotted lines represent new pointer values that need to be set, while the remark "deleted pointers" identifies the pointers that need to be changed.

The program is substantially self-documenting, so the reader can follow the logic of the program by reading through it. However, the logic involving the pointers is rather difficult and terse; therefore, the best approach to understanding such logic is to use some sample data and to desk-check the program step by step.

```
 IDENTIFICATION DIVISION.
 PROGRAM-ID.  CHAINPR.
*
 ENVIRONMENT DIVISION.
 CONFIGURATION SECTION.
 SOURCE-COMPUTER. ABC-480.
 OBJECT-COMPUTER. ABC-480.
 INPUT-OUTPUT SECTION.
 FILE-CONTROL.
     SELECT INPUT-FILE  ASSIGN TO SOURCE.
     SELECT OUTPUT-FILE ASSIGN TO PRINTER.
*
 DATA DIVISION.
 FILE SECTION.
 FD  INPUT-FILE LABEL RECORD OMITTED
               DATA RECORD IN-RECORD.
 01  IN-RECORD.
     02 KEY-FIELD-IN       PIC 9(4).
     02 REC-DATA-IN     PIC X(76).
 FD  OUTPUT-FILE LABEL RECORD OMITTED
               DATA RECORD OUT-RECORD.
 01  OUT-RECORD        PIC X(133).
*
 WORKING-STORAGE SECTION.
*
 01  DATA-END          PIC XXX   VALUE "NO".
*
* POINTERS
*
 01  NEW         PIC 99.
 01  FIRST-PLACE  PIC 99.
 01  LAST-PLACE   PIC 99.
 01  XTH         PIC 99.
 01  I           PIC 99.
 01  NO-OF-RECS PIC 99 VALUE ZERO.
*
 01  DATA-TABLE.
     02 TABLE-ENTRIES OCCURS 50 TIMES.
         03 REC-NO      PIC 99.
         03 KEY-FIELD   PIC 9(4).
         03 DATA-FIELD  PIC X(76).
         03 PREDECESSOR PIC 9(2).
         03 SUCCESSOR   PIC 9(2).
*
 01  HEADER-1.
     02 FILLER     PIC X(13) VALUE "ORIGINAL DATA".
```

FIGURE 15-17   SAMPLE COBOL PROGRAM.

```
01   HEADER-2.
     02 FILLER    PIC X(4)   VALUE SPACES.
     02 FILLER    PIC X(6)   VALUE "REC-NO".
     02 FILLER    PIC X(2)   VALUE SPACES.
     02 FILLER    PIC X(10)  VALUE "IDENTIFIER".
     02 FILLER    PIC X(38)  VALUE SPACES.
     02 FILLER    PIC X(4)   VALUE "DATA".
     02 FILLER    PIC X(38)  VALUE SPACES.
     02 FILLER    PIC X(11)  VALUE "PREDECESSOR".
     02 FILLER    PIC X(2)   VALUE SPACES.
     02 FILLER    PIC X(9)   VALUE "SUCCESSOR".
*
01   REC-OUT.
     02 FILLER    PIC X(6) VALUE SPACES.
     02 REC-NO-OUT PIC Z9.
     02 FILLER    PIC X(5) VALUE SPACES.
     02 KEY-FIELD-OUT    PIC 9(4).
     02 FILLER         PIC X(5) VALUE SPACES.
     02 REC-DAT-OUT    PIC X(76).
     02 FILLER         PIC X(5) VALUE SPACES.
     02 PREDEC-OUT     PIC 9(2).
     02 FILLER         PIC X(11) VALUE SPACES.
     02 SUCCES-OUT     PIC 9(2).
*
PROCEDURE DIVISION.
PROGRAM-SUMMARY.
    OPEN INPUT INPUT-FILE
    OPEN OUTPUT OUTPUT-FILE
    WRITE OUT-RECORD FROM HEADER-1 AFTER PAGE.
    PERFORM READ-RECORD
*
    PERFORM STORE-FIRST-RECORD
*
    PERFORM STORE-NEW-RECORD
           UNTIL DATA-END = "YES" OR NEW = 50.
*
    PERFORM LIST-TABLE.
*
    PERFORM LIST-SORTED-TABLE.
    CLOSE INPUT-FILE OUTPUT-FILE
    STOP RUN.
*
READ-RECORD.
    READ INPUT-FILE
        AT END MOVE "YES" TO DATA-END.
    IF DATA-END NOT = "YES"
        MOVE SPACES TO REC-OUT
        MOVE KEY-FIELD-IN TO KEY-FIELD-OUT
        MOVE REC-DATA-IN TO REC-DAT-OUT
        WRITE OUT-RECORD FROM REC-OUT AFTER 2.
```

FIGURE 15-17   SAMPLE COBOL PROGRAM.   (Continued)

```
    STORE-FIRST-RECORD.
        MOVE 1 TO REC-NO (1)
        MOVE 1 TO NO-OF-RECS
        MOVE 1 TO NEW
        MOVE 1 TO FIRST-PLACE
        MOVE 1 TO LAST-PLACE
        MOVE ZEROS TO PREDECESSOR (1)
        MOVE ZEROS TO SUCCESSOR (1)
        MOVE KEY-FIELD-IN TO KEY-FIELD (1)
        MOVE REC-DATA-IN TO DATA-FIELD (1).
        PERFORM READ-RECORD.
*
   STORE-NEW-RECORD.
        ADD 1 TO NO-OF-RECS
        ADD 1 TO NEW
        MOVE NEW TO REC-NO (NEW)
        MOVE KEY-FIELD-IN TO KEY-FIELD (NEW)
        MOVE REC-DATA-IN TO DATA-FIELD (NEW)
*
        IF KEY-FIELD (NEW)  NOT >  KEY-FIELD (FIRST-PLACE)
           PERFORM PLACE-IN-FRONT
        ELSE
           IF KEY-FIELD (NEW)  NOT <  KEY-FIELD (LAST-PLACE)
              PERFORM PLACE-AT-END
           ELSE
              PERFORM PLACE-IN-MIDDLE.
*
        PERFORM READ-RECORD.
*
   PLACE-IN-FRONT.
        MOVE FIRST-PLACE TO SUCCESSOR (NEW)
        MOVE NEW TO PREDECESSOR (FIRST-PLACE)
        MOVE ZERO TO PREDECESSOR (NEW)
        MOVE NEW TO FIRST-PLACE.
*
   PLACE-AT-END.
        MOVE LAST-PLACE TO PREDECESSOR (NEW)
        MOVE NEW TO SUCCESSOR (LAST-PLACE)
        MOVE ZERO TO SUCCESSOR (NEW)
        MOVE NEW TO LAST-PLACE.
*
   PLACE-IN-MIDDLE.
        MOVE FIRST-PLACE TO XTH
*
        PERFORM TRY-NEXT UNTIL KEY-FIELD (NEW) NOT > KEY-FIELD (XTH)
*
        MOVE PREDECESSOR (XTH) TO I
        MOVE NEW TO SUCCESSOR (I)
                      PREDECESSOR (XTH)
        MOVE I TO PREDECESSOR (NEW)
        MOVE XTH TO SUCCESSOR (NEW).
```

FIGURE 15-17   SAMPLE COBOL PROGRAM.   (Continued)

```
    TRY-NEXT.
        MOVE SUCCESSOR (XTH) TO XTH.
*
  LIST-TABLE.
        WRITE OUT-RECORD FROM HEADER-2 AFTER PAGE
        PERFORM PRINT-DATA VARYING I FROM 1 BY 1
                UNTIL I > NO-OF-RECS.
*
  LIST-SORTED-TABLE.
        WRITE OUT-RECORD FROM HEADER-2 AFTER PAGE
        MOVE FIRST-PLACE TO I
        PERFORM GET-NEXT UNTIL I = ZERO.
*
  PRINT-DATA.
        MOVE REC-NO (I) TO REC-NO-OUT
        MOVE KEY-FIELD (I) TO KEY-FIELD-OUT
        MOVE DATA-FIELD (I) TO REC-DAT-OUT
        MOVE PREDECESSOR (I) TO PREDEC-OUT
        MOVE SUCCESSOR (I) TO SUCCES-OUT
        WRITE OUT-RECORD FROM REC-OUT.
*
  GET-NEXT.
        PERFORM PRINT-DATA
        MOVE SUCCESSOR (I) TO I.
```

FIGURE 15-17   SAMPLE COBOL PROGRAM.   **(Continued)**

INDEXING AND FILE INVERSION

It is often desirable to query a file or data base in the following fashion: retrieve all the employees who have a particular characteristic. If the file is ordered by that particular characteristic then the access to those records is
easy. If, however, the file is ordered on some other basis then the entire file
has to be read in order to retrieve all of the appropriate records. *File inver-*

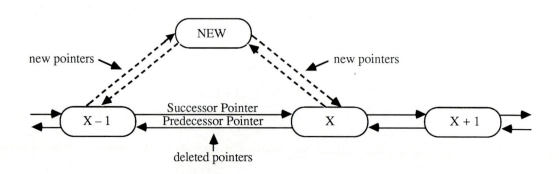

FIGURE 15-18   ILLUSTRATION OF ADDING A RECORD TO THE CHAIN.

EMPLOYEE-NO	DEPARTMENT	NAME	JOB	SALARY
100	30	Doe	Plumber	27,600
102	10	Johnson	Carpenter	24,400
105	30	Taylor	Welder	23,000
112	20	Prentice	Carpenter	25,000
113	10	Brown	Plumber	24,800
122	20	Smith	Carpenter	21,900
125	30	Burger	Carpenter	22,000

FIGURE 15-19   A FLAT EMPLOYEE FILE.

sion through appropriate indexing is a data structure which facilitates efficient data base interrogation. Let us consider an example, as presented in the following paragraphs.

Figure 15-19 presents an ordinary flat file. Records are identified by EMPLOYEE-NO, the primary key. The file is (partially) inverted in Figure 15-20, where we have created two indexes. The first index is ordered by the

EMPLOYEE FILE

EMPLOYEE-NO	NAME	SALARY
100	Doe	27,600
102	Johnson	24,400
105	Taylor	23,000
112	Prentice	25,000
113	Brown	24,800
122	Smith	21,900
125	Burger	22,000

DEPARTMENT INDEX

DEPT-NO	POINTER TO EMPLOYEE FILE		
10	102 ↑	113 ↑	
20	100 ↑	112 ↑	122 ↑
30	105 ↑	125 ↑	

JOB INDEX

JOB	POINTER TO EMPLOYEE FILE			
Carpenter	102	112	122 ↑	125 ↑
Plumber	100	113		
Welder	105			

FIGURE 15-20   AN ILLUSTRATION OF A PARTIALLY INVERTED FILE.

DEPT-NO values and for each department it contains a pointer to the storage address of the EMPLOYEE-NO indicated. The second index is ordered according to JOB, and also contains a pointer to the storage address of the employee. The little arrow is included to show that the value stored there would be the storage address for the record of the employee-number shown, and *not* the employee-number as such. The department index indicates, for instance, that the records of employee 102 and 113 contain the department-number value of 10. Now look back at the Employee file. It consists of only three data items per record. The DEPARTMENT and JOB attributes have been eliminated on the assumption that the indexes suffice to provide this information. (We will return to this point shortly.)

Figure 15–20 is an example of partial inversion. A fully inverted file is one with an index for each attribute. In our example, full inversion would also include an index for NAME and an index for SALARY. Indexes created for inversion are called *secondary* indexes. The primary index is, of course, based on the record identifier (primary key).

In general, only partial inversion is necessary. In our example in Figure 15–20 the file is not inverted on NAME or SALARY. On close observation it will be seen that an index for either of these two attributes would be as long as the original file, since the values of SALARY and NAME are unique. For that reason we might pause before deciding to invert fully, and consider whether queries about salary or name are going to be frequent. If it is expected that queries about names or salaries are going to be frequent, then it would be preferable to invert the file on those two fields, as well. In the absence of inversion, if we were looking for a name in the file there would be no knowledge available as to where in the file that name is located. With inversion, however, the name index would be sorted and quick reference to a particular name would be possible.

One more observation is in order. In Figure 15–20 the Employee file does not contain data for DEPT-NO and JOB, which are the basis for the two secondary indexes. Suppose we ask the question: In what department is Employee 112 located? The required access path would be to search the Department Index in a serial fashion until we have satisfied the question. If we did want to have the ability to retrieve efficiently all the attributes of a given employee's record, then we could retain all the data in the Employee file. But redundancy would thereby be introduced, since now the values for DEPARTMENT-NO and JOB would be stored both in the respective indexes and in the Employee file.

Review

1   When a file is inverted, this means that one or more _____ are created to facilitate efficient data base interrogation.

indexes

2   When indexes are created for some but not all of the attributes in the records, the file is said to be _____. When indexes are available for all attributes, the file is said to be _____.

partially inverted; fully inverted

3   An objective underlying file inversion is to facilitate data base interrogation by [including/not including] redundancy in the file system.

not including

4   Consider a file which is ordered on the basis of PART-NO and has an index for CUSTOMER-NO. If a report is prepared according to CUSTOMER-NO, then the efficiency of processing for this report is [greater than/equal to/less than] it would be if the file were ordered according to CUSTOMER-NO.

less than

DATA BASE MANAGEMENT SYSTEMS

We conclude this chapter by presenting some overview concepts with respect to data base management systems, since the various types of data structures discussed in this chapter find their most common use in such systems. Data base systems need to implement relationships among data without requiring that the data be physically moved or reorganized. Because of this requirement, pointers and other structures are the usual means of implementing data base constructs.

The conceptual design of a data base has to take into account the unique characteristics of each organization. However, the programming implementation need not be unique in the sense that file data definition and file processing as applied in different organizations are bound to include a great deal of common logic. Recognition of this fact has led to the development of a number of so-called data base management systems. These are software packages designed to minimize individual programming efforts in both the creation and use of data bases. Presently, they are mainly available from software firms for a rental or purchase fee. Based on their degree of sophistication, the purchase price for such systems varies from about a few hundred dollars for personal computers to over $100,000 for mainframes.

These generalized software packages represent extensive programming efforts. There are basically two types of data base management systems that have been developed: the host-language systems and the self-contained systems. The host-language systems are enhancements of procedure-oriented languages such as COBOL. Options within the language allow file management programming to be accomplished with a limited number of commands. The self-contained systems utilize their own language rules, and in this sense such a system can be thought of as a unique procedure-oriented language directed toward file management in data base systems. The Data Base Task Group (DBTG) appointed by the CODASYL Committee that oversees the development of COBOL has developed a set of specifications for incorporating data base management capabilities within the COBOL language. However, the CODASYL recommendations have not been widely adopted. Instead, there are many data base management systems, each with its own specific conceptual foundation and design.

As indicated above, from the user's standpoint the advantage of using a data base management system is that it minimizes the amount of individual program development on the part of the user. In more specific terms, the following advantages can be cited for using such a software package:

1   Allow the firm's programmer to work on complex tasks rather than on routine file maintenance and report generation.

2   Since the program statements in such systems are shorter than those in standard programming languages, reduce the amount of effort to create programs.

3   Eliminate duplicate file design efforts through the availability of easily restructured file definitions.

4   Allow the execution of multiple tasks concurrently and the production of reports in many different sequences given one set of specifications.

5   Give the user the advantage of a debugged common program logic, thereby making the user's own debugging task less complex and less time-consuming.

The term *schema* is used to denote the logical description of the data base. Typically, there is a Data Base Administrator (DBA) in an organization whose main responsibility is to define and maintain the data base schema. Applications programmers need not be bound by the schema. Each applications program defines a *subschema*, which is a description of data from the viewpoint of this particular program. It will be recalled that one of the reasons for a data base is to have the capability to look at data from different perspectives for individual uses (subschema), while at the same time the overall relationships of data are maintained in the background (schema). Figure 15–21 presents the main elements in the operation of a data base system. The Data Base Management System (DBMS) is the central element. The DBMS interacts with the operating system in controlling all aspects of data base operations. The schema describes the overall logical blueprint of the

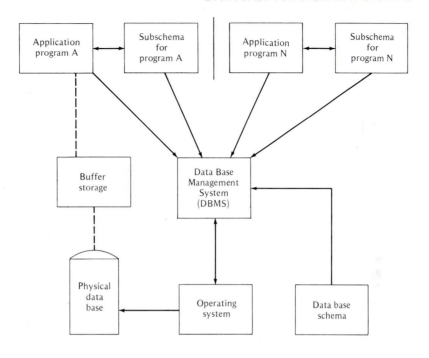

FIGURE 15–21 BASIC ELEMENTS OF A DATA MANAGEMENT SYSTEM IN OPERATION.

data base. The actual physical data base resides in direct access storage devices and it is stored and maintained there by the DBMS. Each subschema is used by the DBMS to access the physical data base and make it available through some buffer storage, which serves as the staging point for data access and manipulation.

In order to implement the functions required of a DBMS there are three types of languages needed. One is a language to enable the DBA to construct and maintain the schema. The CODASYL Data Base Task Group (DBTG) has proposed a Data Description Language (DDL) for such a purpose. A second language needed is one that can provide the interface between the applications programmer and the DBMS. The CODASYL proposed name is Data Manipulation Language (DML). In fact, the proposed CODASYL DML is an extension of COBOL and can be used by the COBOL programmer as part of the application program. For instance, the DML includes commands such as: CLOSE, DELETE, FIND, GET, INSERT, MODIFY, OPEN, ORDER, REMOVE, STORE.

The third type of language needed is one to describe data storage and retrieval at the physical level—a Device/Media Control Language (DMCL). This third type of language has to be oriented toward specific hardware, and therefore there is less of an agreement as to what such a language should be for general use. We might mention DL/I (Data Language I), an IBM product which can be used both for schema definition and for physical data description in that company's widely used IMS data base management system.

There are many data base software products available. These products vary in the conceptual basis for the data base and the features which are available, as well as the hardware for which they are programmed. Choosing among these many and varied software offerings is not an easy task. Lack of accepted standardization makes the choice rather critical, since portability from one system to another is nonexistent. CODASYL has proposed a standard, but there exists wide controversy about this standard.

Review

1   A data base management system is essentially a specialized type of _____ package.

software

2   Of the two types of data base management systems, the type for which the program statements used are similar to a procedure-oriented language such as COBOL is the [self-contained/host-language] system.

host-language

3   The main advantage associated with using a data base management system is that _____.

it minimizes the amount of programming and debugging that has to be done for a particular system (etc.)

4   The overall logical description of the data base is included in the _____ for the data base, while each applications program defines a _____ for specific uses of the data.

schema; subschema

5   In the context of data base management systems, DBA stands for _____ and DBMS stands for _____.

Data Base Administrator; Data Base Management System

6   A language which enables the DBA to construct and maintain a schema is the DDL, or _____.

Data Description Language

7   A language which serves to provide an interface between the applications programmer and the DBMS is the DML, or _____.

Data Manipulation Language

8   At the current stage of development, it can be said that the software to be used to implement the data base approach [has/has not] been standardized.

has not

Exercises

15.1   Differentiate the concepts of logical data structure and physical data structure in the design of a data base information system.

15.2   Give some examples of different logical data structures and describe some of the differences among these structures.

15.3   Various types of pointer structures provide the physical basis for implementing logical data relationships in computer storage. Describe some of the common pointer structures which are available.

15.4   What is the main objective associated with file inversion? Describe how this objective is achieved.

15.5   What are "data base management systems"? Describe the nature and availability of such systems at the present time, and the likely direction of future developments in this area.

15.6   Revise the sample program in Figure 15–7 to incorporate deletions as well as additions. Assume the source file records have the following format:

```
01  IN-RECORD.
    02  TRANS-CODE      PIC X.
        88  ADD-REC         VALUE 'A'.
```

```
       88   DELETE-REC    VALUE 'D'.
 02   KEY-FIELD-IN         PIC 9(4).
 02   REC-DATA-IN          PIC X(75).
```

In order to implement deletions, create a new chain whose head is in NEXT-PLACE. Initialize the table so that the SUCCESSOR values are 2, 3, 4, . . . , 50, 0, while NEXT-PLACE is equal to 1. Thus, starting with the value in NEXT-PLACE (which initially has a value of 1), the chain of empty records is at locations 1, 2, 3, . . . , 50. The successor of the 50th record is set to zero, indicating that there is no other empty record.

When you delete a record, place that record as the head of the empty-record chain. Thus, suppose that we have the following records:

Record Location	Key-Field	Predecessor	Successor
.			
10	MARY	13	08
.			
13	JOHN	33	10
.			
33	ANN	40	13

We are about to delete the record at 13. Assume NEXT-PLACE = 17. We would MOVE NEXT-PLACE TO SUCCESSOR (13) and we would MOVE 13 TO NEXT-PLACE. Of course, the PREDECESSOR and SUCCESSOR values of the records at 10 and 33 also need to be adjusted in order to effect the deletion.

V   Program design concepts and methods

16
PROGRAM COHESION

INTRODUCTION

The last part of this book presents concepts that relate to overall program design and testing. This chapter focuses on *program cohesion*. The application of this concept facilitates clear partitioning of a program into modules that have a central purpose, or theme, and that therefore can be understood, defined, designed, and modified more easily. Chapter 17 deals with the process of *program design*, which is concerned with how the individual (cohesive) modules are synthesized into a complete program. Finally, Chapter 18 describes *program testing*, or how to ascertain that (well-designed) programs are indeed coded to do the intended tasks.

THE BLACK BOX CONCEPT

In order to achieve good program design, a program module should have the property of being a black box. The *black box concept* means that a module should be capable of being described in terms of the *function* that it performs, rather than the *procedure* by which it performs the function. In other words, we should be able to describe *what* the module is designed to do rather than *how* it is done. The black box concept originated in engineering applications, and in that context it is conventional to speak of the input, the transform, and the output of a black box. Figure 16–1 illustrates this viewpoint schematically.

In the context of programming, the *input* to a black box consists of data supplied to the module and the *output* consists of data generated by the module. The *transform* consists of the combined effect of the series of statements that comprise the module. When the module is a single paragraph, a series of paragraphs, or even a section, the input and output data are not directly obvious in COBOL programs. The reason is that all of the data are defined in the one DATA DIVISION, and thus the input and output are specified indirectly. For instance, consider the following program segment:

```
⋮
    PERFORM READ-TRANS-REC
    MOVE 'NO' TO FILE-SEQ-FLAG
    PERFORM CHECK-FILE-SEQ
    IF FILE-SEQ-FLAG = 'YES' . . .
⋮
CHECK-FILE-SEQ.
    IF CUST-NO OF TRANS-REC < PREV-CUST-NO
        MOVE 'YES' TO FILE-SEQ-FLAG
    ELSE
        MOVE CUST-NO OF TRANS-REC TO PREV-CUST-NO.
```

The input to the CHECK-FILE-SEQ module consists of FILE-SEQ-FLAG, CUST-NO, and PREV-CUST-NO, while the output consists of the same three data items but with some changed values. Thus, even though the form of the program does not identify the input and output directly, a paragraph as a module does comply with the general black box concept.

FIGURE 16–1   THE BLACK BOX CONCEPT.

In the case where a module is a subprogram, the arguments of the CALL statement identify explicitly the input and output of the module. For example, if CHECK-FILE-SEQ was a subprogram, the CALL statement would be:

CALL 'CHECK-FILE-SEQ' USING CUST-NO
                        FILE-SEQ-FLAG
                        PREV-CUST-NO.

Therefore, regardless of the way that a module is represented in a program, from the design standpoint every module is a black box that can be described in terms of the input, the function performed (transformation), and the output.

Review

1   The fact that one should be able to describe a module in terms of the *function* performed, rather than the *procedure* followed, is reflective of the _____ concept.

black box

2   The three principal elements, or ingredients, associated with the black box concept are the _____, _____, and _____ associated with the black box.

input; transform; output

3   In the context of programming, the input and output associated with a black box are both forms of _____.

data

4   In COBOL programs, the input and output data are most obvious when the program module represents a [paragraph in the main program/subprogram].

subprogram

COHESION IN PROGRAMS

In addition to each module representing a black box, a well-designed program should consist of modules that have as much cohesion as possible. A module is *cohesive* if it performs only one function and all program statements in the module are directly related to that function only. Thus, a well-designed program ideally should be so partitioned that it consists of specific functions, each of which is represented by a cohesive module in the program.

From the practical standpoint, the question that arises is: What is a cohesive function? Unfortunately, there is no specific and comprehensive definition of a cohesive function. Nevertheless, a working knowledge of this concept can be developed by understanding some of its characteristics. Generally speaking, a cohesive function refers to a single task that can be described in just a few words of language. An example is: "Compute this week's F.I.C.A. tax for the employee." But what about the function: "Process the payroll for this week?" The latter function is too broad, and should be partitioned into several more specific tasks or functions. At the other extreme, however, the printing of a line of information or the addition of two numbers are tasks that are too specific to be represented as distinct program modules. Thus both experience and judgment serve as the basis for defining cohesive program modules. Still, the following two guidelines can be useful:

A cohesive module, when coded in COBOL, should not exceed a page of program statements (about 50 lines). However, the module may be represented by only 1 or 2 lines of program code if they constitute a distinct, cohesive function.

The module should be capable of being described in ordinary language *without* the use of multiple verbs, the conjunction "and," or use of a series of words such as "first," "then," and the like.

The above guidelines rely on indirect indicators that can alert the programmer to the existence of noncohesive functions. To further assist us in designing and recognizing cohesive modules, the remaining sections of this chapter describe several types of cohesion that can characterize a module.

Review

1   A module that performs only one function, and whose program statements are all directed toward that function, is described as being _____.

cohesive

2   Generally speaking, when a cohesive module is coded in COBOL the program statements should not exceed about _____ lines.

50

3   Generally speaking, the description of a cohesive module [may/should not] include a series of words such as "first," "then," and "next."

should not

FUNCTIONAL COHESION

Functional cohesion represents the highest form of cohesion and is the only type to which reference specifically was made in the preceding section of this chapter. Such a module is designed based on the definition of the function involved, and all the processing in the module is directly related to the defined function. For instance, a module described as Process-Transactions as contrasted to the module Process-Payment-Transactions illustrates the difference between a composite as contrasted to a cohesive function.

Consider now the following widely used type of paragraph in COBOL programs:

```
READ-RECORD.
      READ CUST-FILE RECORD
      AT END MOVE 'YES' TO FILE-END-FLAG.
```

It must be admitted that technically this is not a cohesive function. Its description would include two statements, such as "Read the next record, and if it is an end-of-file record, set a flag." The use of the conjunction "and" reveals the absence of functional cohesion. But the simplicity of the module plus the fact that the language syntax requires the AT END to be associated with a READ statement make it desirable to create such a module. Thus, functional cohesion is a programming objective that may not be strictly attainable in all situations because of practical considerations.

Review

1   In terms of general priority in program design, the highest form of cohesion for a module is _____ cohesion.

> functional

2   Modules that are not functionally cohesive [should never/may sometimes] be included in a well-designed COBOL program.

> may sometimes

COINCIDENTAL COHESION

Essentially, coincidental cohesion represents the other extreme from functional cohesion. A module has *coincidental cohesion* if it consists of a more-or-less random collection of statements or procedures. In reviewing programs, one can often find a "catchall" paragraph that includes a series of relatively unrelated statements, such as:

```
PAR-X.
    MOVE SPACES TO PRINTLINE
    MOVE CUST-NO TO SAVE-CUST-NO
    ADD TOT-1 TO TOT-ALL
    MOVE ZERO TO OLD-AMOUNT.
```

A practical way to recognize a module based on coincidental cohesion is to try to describe it with a simple statement. Module PAR-X above defies such description. Another practical test is to ask if it would make any difference if the single module were partitioned into two or more modules. For example, we could partition PAR-X above into PAR-X1 and PAR-X2 without impacting the cohesion of the new modules in any way:

```
PAR-X1.
    MOVE SPACES TO PRINT LINE
    MOVE CUST-NO TO SAVE-CUST-NO.
PAR-X2.
    ADD TOT-1 TO TOT-ALL
    MOVE ZERO TO OLD-AMOUNT.
```

As another kind of illustration, suppose that a program were arbitrarily subdivided into several modules of approximately equal size, as portrayed in Figure 16–2. We can observe that such a program would have several problems:

Functions that are inherently cohesive would become noncohesive because of program procedures being split across two or more modules.

Several small functions may come to be combined into one module.

Modules will need to reference each other extensively, because required information is located within other modules.

The black box concept would be difficult to apply.

The program would be difficult to understand and difficult to modify.

Of course, no one would set out to partition a program arbitrarily as implied in Figure 16–2. But some programs are so badly designed that they

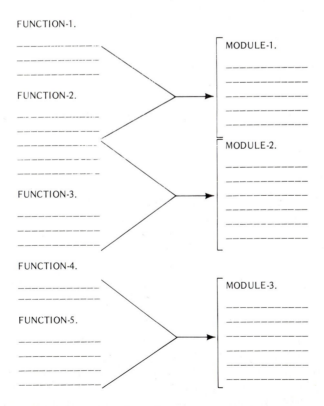

FIGURE 16–2   FORMING MODULES WITH COINCIDENTAL COHESION.

end up appearing as if the modules were formed by a random collection of statements or procedures.

Review

1   The type of cohesion that reflects a more-or-less random collection of the statements or procedures included in a module is _____ cohesion.

coincidental

2   In general, a well-designed program is one which [minimizes/maximizes] the use of coincidental cohesion in the formation of program modules.

minimizes

CLASS-ORIENTED COHESION

Modules characterized by *class-oriented cohesion* are formed by inclusion of elements that refer to the same broad class of logical processes or functions. For example, a module such as the one below is based on the general function of inputting files:

READ-FILES.
   READ TRANS-FILE RECORD
   ⋮
   READ MASTER-FILE RECORD
   ⋮

Although the module above seems to have a strong functional cohesion, the concept of function is misdirected. The purpose of having functional cohesion is to design modules based on *one* function relevant to the specific program. The READ-FILES module above is a broad class of functions that could be represented in many programs. The module preferably should be partitioned into two modules, one for inputting each file.

Another common example of class-oriented cohesion is the type of module that is often labeled Validate Data. Data validation is a general class of functions, and it would be better to construct a module for each specific type of data validation. For instance, we could have modules such as Validate Financial Data and Validate Customer Account Number.

Another common example of the use of class-oriented cohesion is a module that might be labeled Process-Transactions. Such a module often includes multiple functions, as indicated in the following program outline:

PROCESS-TRANSACTIONS.
   IF PAYMENT-TRANSACTION
      do . . .
      ⋮

   ELSE IF CHARGE-TRANSACTION
      do . . .
      ⋮

   ELSE IF NEW-RECORD-TRANSACTION
      do . . .
      ⋮

From the standpoint of good design logic, Process-Transactions is a composite-functions module that should be partitioned into several modules with strong functional cohesion, such as defining separate modules for processing payment transactions and for processing charge transactions.

The above example is so common in programming practice that it warrants further consideration. Is it really wrong to design a module such as Process-Transactions? The answer is: It depends. In general, modules characterized by class-oriented cohesion are not as good as modules based on functional cohesion. As a practical matter, however, if the Process-Transactions module is fairly simple it has to be admitted that such a composite-functions module does no real harm. But what do we mean by "simple"? If there are just a few types of transactions included in the module, perhaps not more than five, and their processing logic is not extensive or difficult, then we would be hard-pressed to argue against the composite module. Such a class-oriented module could be relatively easily comprehended, developed, and modified in the future. In particular, grouping several transaction-types in the same module does no harm if the processing logic of each transaction-type is distinct. The harm occurs if transaction-types share common procedures and the module is so designed that processing logic from several transaction-types is interwoven. In such a case an understanding of the processing of one transaction-type depends on an understanding of how it relates to the processing of one or more other transaction-types, thereby violating the concept of cohesiveness and resulting in poor partitioning of the program.

At this point it is appropriate to differentiate the appropriate orientation of a programmer during the design stage of a programming project as contrasted to the program-writing stage. At the design stage, we should not be concerned about the eventual implementation into program code. At the program-writing stage we may choose to implement a composite module because of the limited extent of code and the simplicity of logic in such cases as the use of a nested IF or EVALUATE statement. Nevertheless, in the long run we will write better programs if we design them apart from coding considerations. Such an approach would lead us to recognize, for instance, the processing of Payments, Charges, and New Records as distinct functions. As a likely result, we would probably end up with a coding structure that is improved in the long run. For example, instead of the program outline with one class-oriented module developed earlier in this section, we might have the following outline which includes one class-oriented module and then several modules with functional cohesion:

Using Nested If
Process-transactions.
    If payment-transaction
        Perform apply-payment
    Else
        If charge-transaction
            Perform apply-charge
        Else
            If new-record-transaction
                Perform add-new-record
    ⋮

Apply-payment.
    ⋮

Apply-charge.
    ⋮

Add-new-record.
    ⋮

Using EVALUATE
Process-transactions.
    Evaluate true
        When payment-transaction
            Perform apply-payment
        When charge-transaction
            Perform apply-charge
        When new-record-transaction
            Perform add-new-record.

Now, the modules Apply-Payment, Apply-Charge, and Add-New-Record have functional cohesion. If the credit department of the company should institute a new procedure for processing charges, for example, we need only focus on that module without being concerned about the other modules.

Review

1   Modules that are formed by inclusion of elements that belong in the same broad class of logical processes or functions are said to exhibit _____ cohesion.

class-oriented

2   For the programmer to anticipate program coding considerations during the program design stage, and to define modules accordingly, is [desirable/undesirable].

undesirable

TIME-RELATED COHESION

In time-related cohesion the only reason for combining the elements of a module into one unit is that they occur together in time. A common example of time-related cohesion is a module often named "Initialize," in which files are opened, counters and flags are set, headers are printed, and the like. Most programs contain such a module, even though such a module lacks functional cohesion.

Improved program design suggests that the use of time-related modules should be minimized. If an accumulator is to be set equal to zero, for example, it would be best to do so within a module for which this process is necessary in order to carry out a specific function. As we have acknowledged with respect to class-oriented cohesion, in many instances it is convenient to utilize time-oriented cohesion and to group steps that occur together in time. But it is better not to think in the time-oriented context of beginning, middle, and end when designing a program. Rather, the program designer should give principal attention to the functions to be carried out.

Review

1   The type of modular cohesion based on grouping items that occur together in time is _____ cohesion.

time-related

2   Although establishing a program module on the basis of time-oriented considerations is sometimes useful, the program designer should give principal attention to the _____ to be carried out by the module.

function

PROCEDURAL COHESION

Procedural cohesion involves a grouping of items that are associated with a particular type of procedure. The two most common procedures that serve as the basis for such a module are a program loop and a decision element. The program designer may identify the repeated performance of a series of steps and therefore choose to develop a module corresponding to the loop. For example, a program could include repeated analysis of company sales for each of the last 12 months. As much as possible, the repetition aspect of processing should not serve as the basis for module design. Instead, the focus should be on the functions to be performed.

As an example of a decision step serving as the basis for a program module, suppose that product prices are determined to be either "standard" or "exception." In such a case the program designer may choose to design a module that encompasses the processing for such prices. Again, the decision step is not the appropriate basis for module design, but rather the focus should be on function. Using function as the basis, we would disregard the decision aspect and proceed to design two (or more) modules to correspond to the functions involved in standard-price and exception-price processing.

Program designers who rely on flowcharts as the basis for design tend to develop modules that are heavily procedure-oriented. For example, refer to the flowchart in Figure 16–3. If a programmer based program design on this flowchart, it is highly likely that the modules labeled M1 and M2 would be defined solely on the basis of the loop and decision structures involved, respectively. Yet, when we consider the function involved, it may be that one module is appropriate.

Review

1   When items in a module are grouped because they are associated with a particular programming procedure, the basis for cohesion is described as _____ cohesion.

procedural

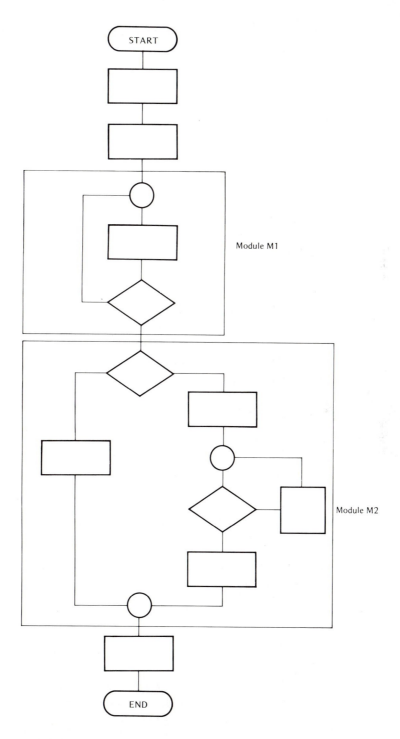

FIGURE 16–3   MODULES FORMED BY APPLICATION OF PROCEDURAL COHESION.

2   The two most common procedures that serve as a basis for procedural cohesion are the existence of a program _____ and a _____ element, or step.

loop; decision

3   The program designer who is likely to develop modules that are heavily procedure-oriented is one who relies on _____ as the basis for design.

flowcharts

DATA-RELATED COHESION

As the name implies, *data-related cohesion* is based on data categories. Such modules are most likely to be developed when a program is viewed in terms of data flow. For example, a module called Transactions Register might be developed based on transactions data being input and listed. The reason for the module is recognition of the data flow. Many program processes have the characteristic that data output with respect to one step is data input with respect to another step, and there is a tendency to combine the two steps into one module when data-related cohesion is applied. Again, this approach is less than ideal because the cohesion is not based on function and may result in multiple functions being combined into one module or one function being split into several modules.

Review

1   The type of module that is defined on the basis of the commonality of data exhibits _____ cohesion.

data-related

2   Data-related cohesion is most likely to be used by a program designer who views the program in terms of _____.

data-flow

SEQUENTIAL COHESION

Modules exemplifying *sequential cohesion* are designed on the basis of processing steps that occur in sequence. Therefore, the two or more steps that are combined may form a module with weak cohesion, because the module may include either a partial function or multiple functions. As an example, suppose that there are three steps, A, B, and C, as follows:

A   _____

       _____

       _____

B   _____

       _____

C   _____

       _____

       _____

Further, suppose that steps A and B in fact constitute one function, while C is another, distinct function. If sequence alone was the basis for modular design, any of the following four modular groupings is possible:

(A,B,C)	A and (B,C)
(A,B) and C	A and B and C

Of the possible groupings above, the only one that is functionally cohesive is the one consisting of the two modules, (A,B) and C.

Again, anticipation of program coding should not be considered in designing program modules. Suppose that there is a program segment consisting of 15 statements occurring in sequence. On a superficial basis (and before actual program coding) one might apply sequential cohesion and create a module (paragraph) containing all 15 lines. However, suppose the first 10 lines represent one function and the last 5 lines represent another function. Should a new module (paragraph) be defined beginning at line 11 even though the 15 lines will always be executed in the same sequential order in any event? We maintain that such partitioning of the module should be done. The separation leads to better documentation and makes future modification of the program easier.

Review

1   Modules that are based on including the processing steps that occur sequentially are said to exemplify _____ cohesion.

                                                                  sequential

2   Generally, a module that is based on sequential cohesion [would also/would not] incorporate functional cohesion.

would not

LEVELS OF COHESION

As indicated earlier, functional cohesion is the most desirable basis for modular design while coincidental cohesion is the least desirable basis. Where do the other forms of cohesion fall with respect to these two extremes? It has been suggested that the order from most desirable to least desirable forms of cohesion is as listed in Table 16–1.

Of course, the general rule is that functional cohesion should be achieved when possible. If functional cohesion is not attainable, the higher forms of cohesion in Table 16–1 should be preferred to the lower ones listed. But in actual programs it is difficult to justify any particular priority of types of cohesion other than the functional. That is, for a given program and particular circumstance a class-oriented basis for modular cohesion may be preferred to a data-related basis. Given the overall design of the program, there may be in fact little choice regarding the basis for a particular module of the program.

The most useful viewpoint to develop in studying the different forms of cohesion is to develop an awareness of the variety of approaches possible, but to follow a functional approach as the basic foundation for program design. As you design a program, you might for instance ask yourself: "Am I inadvertently relying on sequence to develop the program modules?" Such a questioning attitude leads to improved program design from the very start.

TABLE 16–1   PREFERRED ORDER OF COHESION

Functional
Sequential
Data-Related
Procedural
Time-Related
Class-Oriented
Coincidental

Once a program has been designed and found to be wanting, it is very difficult then to redesign the program. It is fundamentally easier to design it correctly in the first place. Still, it must be acknowledged that program design is an iterative process. We have to sketch a design, erase and resketch, and occasionally scrap the whole design and start all over.

Review

1   While the preferred order for the various forms of cohesion may vary to some extent from program to program, the most desirable is _____ cohesion while the least desirable is _____ cohesion.

functional; coincidental

2   If the concepts of good modular design are followed, iterative procedures involving revisions of early design attempts [are nevertheless/are not] required.

are nevertheless

Exercises

16.1   Explain the black box concept in COBOL programming.

16.2   Is cohesion an attribute of programs or of modules within programs?

16.3   Explain what is meant by "cohesion" in the context of program design.

16.4   Discuss several measures of cohesion and identify the highest and the lowest levels of cohesion.

16.5   Suppose that in a programming task sales transactions are processed. When a sales transaction is processed all of the following steps are required:

Check the credit of the customer.

Change the amount on hand in the inventory file.

Update the accounts receivable file.

Should these steps be included in one module or should they be partitioned into more than one module? Explain.

17

PROGRAM DESIGN

INTRODUCTION

As stated in Chapter 1, the ultimate objective of program design is to produce good programs. Chapter 16, "Program Cohesion," described the properties associated with good modules. In this chapter we describe several guidelines that can assist the programmer in attaining the objective of good program design. The emphasis in the preceding chapter was on the individual module, and it was concluded that good program design is enhanced when modules have as much cohesion as possible. In contrast, the emphasis in this chapter is on intermodule relationships and overall structure-chart considerations.

CONTENT COUPLING

Two program modules are *content-coupled* when one module references the contents of the other module. A general rule of good program design is that such coupling should be minimized. Content coupling is common in unstructured programs with abusive use of GO TO statements. For example, consider the program modules in Figure 17–1. Modules A, B, C, and D are highly content-coupled because in essence each module contains part of one or more other modules.

But the GO TO command is not the only culprit. Programs without this command can also include content coupling. Refer to Figure 17–2. If the A and B paragraphs happen to constitute a module because they constitute one function, then A would be content-coupled to C. For instance, suppose that PERFORM A THRU B is the control structure that uses this A-B function. Now, since module C PERFORMs B, part of the first module is also the content of C. To solve this problem, we could set up a separate function B which is PERFORMed by A and C. However, B must then be defined as a distinct module with functional strength. If B by itself is a series of statements that has little functional meaning, we should repeat the B program code within C rather than confusing the structure by avoiding the repetition of the code through the use of the PERFORM B statement.

Figure 17–3 illustrates another form of content coupling. In this case assume that we are using sections to represent functions. Paragraph PA references part of the X1 section, resulting in a situation similar to that described in Figure 17–2 except that content coupling occurs at a subsidiary level of the X1 and X2 modules.

A. _____
   _____
   GO TO C
   _____
   _____

B. _____
   GO TO A
   _____
   GO TO D
   _____

C. _____
   _____
   GO TO B
   _____
   _____
   _____

D. _____
   GO TO A

FIGURE 17-1   CONTENT-COUPLED MODULES USING GO TO.

PERFORM A THROUGH B

⋮

A. _____

  _____

  _____

  _____

B. _____

  _____

  _____

C. _____

  PERFORM B

  _____

FIGURE 17–2   ILLUSTRATION OF CONTENT COUPLING WITHOUT THE GO TO.

In general, content coupling should be avoided as much as possible in the design of programs. Such coupling results in having confusing and improper intermodule relationships that destroy the functional cohesiveness of the modules involved.

Review

1   When one program module references the contents of another module, the two modules are described as being _____.

content-coupled

2   Frequent use of the GO TO command leads to [many/few] modules being content-coupled.

many

SECTION X1.

P1. _____

  _____

P2. _____

  _____

  _____

SECTION X2.

PA. _____

  _____

  PERFORM P1.

PB. _____

  _____

  _____

FIGURE 17–3   ANOTHER FORM OF CONTENT COUPLING.

3   A principal problem associated with content coupling is that the functional _____ of modules is destroyed.

cohesiveness

MODULE SIZE

In the preceding chapter we indicated that the size of a module is governed
by the concept of functional cohesion. Thus, it might seem that module size
as such is not relevant as an indicator of good program design. However, in
practice well-designed programs tend to have modules that are not systematically too small or too large. At the limits, any given module cannot be
smaller than 1 line and should not be larger than about 50 lines. But within
these limits a program may become too complex because of a large number
of modules that are very small or a small number of modules that are very
large.

As illustrated in Figures 17–4 and 17–5, the basic solution for modules
that are too large is to partition them into smaller modules. In Figure 17–4(a)
the large module M consists of elements A, B, and C. We create a new hierarchical level in Figure 17–4(b) with AX as the superior module and modules B
and C as the subordinates. AX includes the original element A plus the coordinative elements to control B and C. In the case of Figure 17–5 the one
module subordinate to A is partitioned into three modules, but at the same
hierarchical level as before partitioning.

Similarly, modules that are too small can be combined to form larger
modules, as illustrated in Figures 17–6 and 17–7. In Figure 17–6 modules B
and C are combined into one module at the same hierarchical level. In the

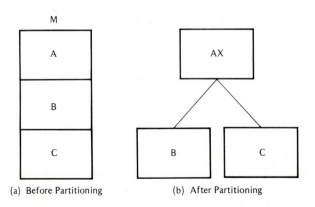

(a) Before Partitioning   (b) After Partitioning

FIGURE 17–4   REDUCING MODULE SIZE BY HIERARCHICAL PARTITIONING.

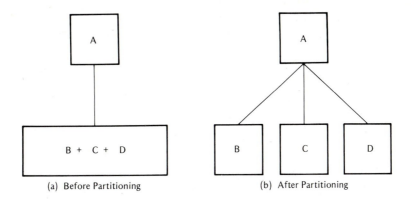

(a) Before Partitioning   (b) After Partitioning

FIGURE 17–5   REDUCING MODULE SIZE BY PARTITIONING AT THE SAME HIERARCHICAL LEVEL.

case of Figure 17–7 the two subordinates are incorporated into their superior to form a larger module. For instance, suppose the small module B is:

B.
      MOVE SPACES TO XYZ.

Instead of the statement PERFOM B in module A, that module could include the statement:

MOVE SPACES TO XYZ.

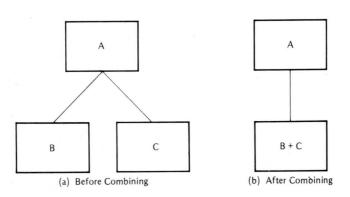

(a) Before Combining   (b) After Combining

FIGURE 17-6   INCREASING MODULE SIZE BY COMBINING AT THE SAME HIERARCHICAL LEVEL.

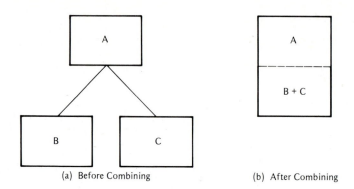

(a) Before Combining   (b) After Combining

FIGURE 17-7   INCREASING MODULE SIZE BY COMBINING SUBORDINATES INTO A SUPERIOR.

Sometimes it is desirable to have small modules because they provide programming flexibility and facilitate future modifications of the program. Refer to Figure 17-8. In Figure 17-8(a), before any combining of modules, X is a data item given to B as input from module A. On the basis of X, B invokes either module C or module D, and that is the extent of the function of module B in the program. For example, the program code on the following page could constitute B.

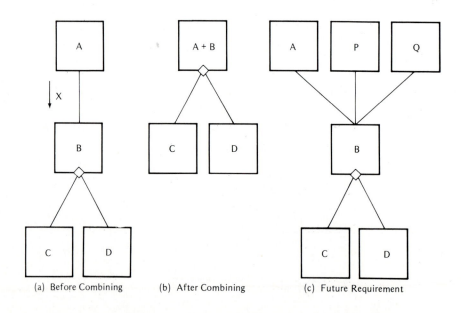

(a) Before Combining   (b) After Combining   (c) Future Requirement

FIGURE 17-8   SHOULD THE SMALL MODULE B BE ELIMINATED?

B.
```
IF X = 'DO-C'
    THEN PERFORM C
    ELSE
        IF X = 'DO-D'
            THEN PERFORM D.
```

The logical question arises: Why not incorporate module B into A as illustrated in Figure 17–8(b)? But suppose that a future modification would require that the C vs. D selection be invoked by the new modules P and Q, as shown in Figure 17–8(c). It is now clear that although module B is small and simple, it can play a useful role as a functional subordinate to several superior modules.

Of course, in all cases the primary consideration is the functional cohesion of each module. Our discussion above does not mean that we strive for "proper" module size as a main objective. Instead, module size is often an indirect indicator of functional cohesion, and we consider size changes only as an objective that is secondary to functional cohesion.

Review

1   The usual limits on module size are from _____ line(s) to approximately _____ lines of program code.

1; 50

2   When modules are too large, the basic solution is to _____ them into smaller (but cohesive) modules.

partition

3   Partitioning of modules [cannot/may] lead to more hierarchical levels in the structure chart.

may

4   Program modules that are too small often can be _____ to form larger modules without impacting the cohesion of each module.

combined

5   Combining small modules to form larger modules [cannot/may] lead to fewer hierarchical levels in the structure chart.

may

6   When a small program module is subordinate to several superior modules, it is generally [desirable/undesirable] to combine the module with one of the superior modules.

undesirable

SPAN OF CONTROL

The *span of control* is defined by the number of subordinates for a given superior module. In organization and management there is a counterpart concept that refers to the number of people that report directly to an organizational superior. In program design it is generally true that well-designed programs tend to have balanced spans of control in the range of 2 to about 7. A span of control of 1 suggests the possibility of composite functions which should be partitioned, while a span exceeding about 7 suggests that the modules may be too small and perhaps should be combined. Visual inspection of a structure chart often is sufficient to determine if the spans generally are too small or too large. For example, the unbalanced spans of control are readily observed in the two structure charts in Figure 17-9.

The term *fan-out* is also used to express the span of control. The fan-out of a given module is the number of its subordinates, and the term is derived from the structure-chart representation of the superior with respect to its subordinates. Another descriptive term is *pancaking*, which refers to a very wide span of control such as portrayed in Figure 17-9(a).

A span of control that is too narrow can be increased either by incorporating subordinates into their superiors or by partitioning and increasing the number of modules at a given level. Which approach is followed is of course reflective of the reason for the span being too narrow in the first place. Refer to Figure 17-10. The span of control has been increased for this structure by incorporating subordinates into their superiors and thereby also reducing the number of levels in the hierarchy. On the other hand, in Figure 17-11 the span of control has been increased by partitioning module B into B1, B2, and B3. Of course, in all cases span of control is an objective that is subordinate to the main objective of having functionally cohesive modules.

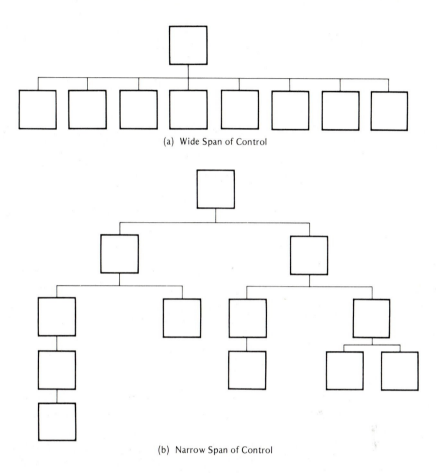

(a) Wide Span of Control

(b) Narrow Span of Control

FIGURE 17-9   UNBLANACED SPANS OF CONTROL.

Review

1   The number of subordinates for a given superior module defines the concept of _____.

span of control

2   Generally, the span of control should be within the range of _____ to about _____ subordinate modules.

2; 7

3   If a span of control that is too wide is reduced through combining

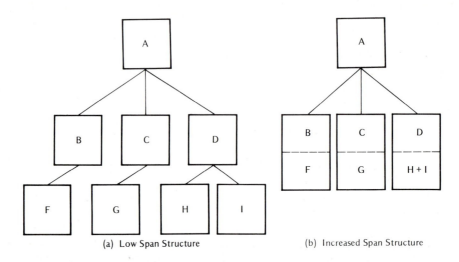

(a) Low Span Structure   (b) Increased Span Structure

FIGURE 17-10 **INCREASING SPAN OF CONTROL BY INCORPORATING SUBORDINATES INTO SUPERIORS.**

modules at the same level, then the number of levels in the structure chart is [reduced/unaffected].

unaffected

4 If a span of control that is too narrow is increased by combining modules at different levels (i.e., incorporating subordinates into their superiors), then the number of levels in the structure chart is [reduced/unaffected].

reduced

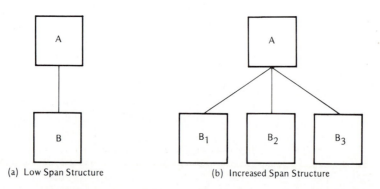

(a) Low Span Structure   (b) Increased Span Structure

FIGURE 17-11 **INCREASING SPAN OF CONTROL BY PARTITIONING MODULES.**

FAN-IN

The term *fan-in* refers to the number of superiors with respect to a given module. Refer to Figure 17–12. Figure 17–12(a) illustrates that module E has a fan-in of 4. Even though a strict hierarchy should not have modules with multiple superiors, in practice a high fan-in often is desirable because it reduces the amount of program code and provides the opportunity to develop well-tested common functions. From a program-coding standpoint we may well ask how high fan-in modules should be implemented. One approach is to set up such modules as independent subprograms that are CALLed by their superiors. Alternatively, they may be set up within the main program as paragraphs or sections to be PERFORMed. Occasionally, there may be objection to frequent use of the CALL and PERFORM commands because of the processing time required. If these commands are to be avoided, an alternative is to develop and test the high fan-in module separately and then incorporate it into each of its superiors, as illustrated in Figure 17–12(b). However, the avoidance of the CALL or PERFORM commands is generally not warranted except, perhaps, for a program with high data volume that is processed in a computer facility with minimum capacity.

A few words of caution are necessary regarding fan-in. Modules with multiple superiors (high fan-in) introduce a new form of relationship that may undermine the concept of hierarchical independence described in Chapter 1. In Figure 17–13, for example, modules B and C are hierarchical peers and therefore should be independent in their processing. Yet their sharing of module G as a subordinate introduces a form of relationship that may make them content-dependent on one another. For instance, suppose that a modification in C requires that G be modified. The modification in G may then lead to the requirement that B also be modified. Thus, the modules B and C have become dependent on one another because of the fan-in with respect to module G. Note that the fan-in need not be direct. In this

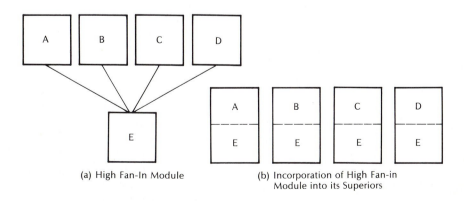

(a) High Fan-In Module

(b) Incorporation of High Fan-in Module into its Superiors

FIGURE 17–12   HIGH FAN-IN MODULES.

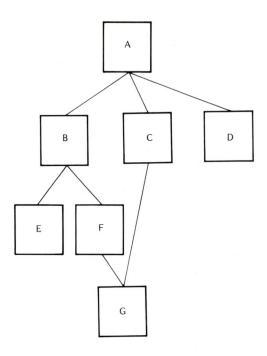

FIGURE 17-13   STRUCTURE CHART WITH FAN-IN AT MODULE G.

example, B is not the direct superior of G, but is one level removed in the hierarchy.

The possible adverse effects associated with sharing modules as subordinates makes it necessary that such sharing be clearly documented. In Figure 17-13 the sharing is documented by the multiple lines branching into module G. However, in structure charts with several high fan-in modules, the result may be many crossing lines, as illustrated in Figure 17-14(a). To avoid such a potentially confusing chart, the shared modules may be repeated in the chart with respect to each subordinate, and the repeated modules are then shaded in the upper right corner, as illustrated in Figure 17-14(b). But structure charts are only one form of documentation. Most compilers can produce a cross-reference listing that shows all of the PERFORM and CALL references to a given module, thereby providing a complete list of the superiors for that module. With such documentation being available, the programmer can maintain proper control over modification of shared modules. Whenever a change is required in such a module, one should review all instances of its use to ascertain whether the change applies in all cases. For example, suppose that a change in module H in Figure 17-14 results in module F having to be changed, but that F should not be changed with respect to its also being a subordinate to modules B and C. A new module, say F1, should be created as the subordinate of H, leaving the original module F unchanged as a subordinate of B and C.

Sometimes programmers change the procedure of a shared module so

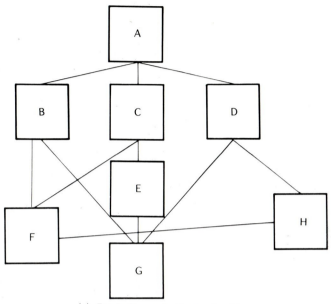

(a) Fan-In Shown by Connecting Lines

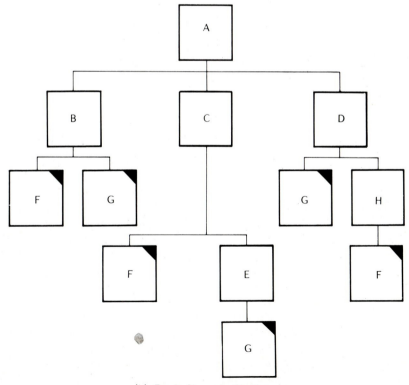

(b) Fan-In Shown by Shading

FIGURE 17-14   DOCUMENTATION OF HIGH FAN-IN STRUCTURE CHARTS.

that it "knows" whether it is being executed under the control of one or another of its superior modules, and does one function or another, accordingly. Such a practice is error-prone and leads to noncohesive modules. As stated in the preceding paragraph, it is preferable to create two separate modules instead, such as the F and F1 possibilities in the above example.

Review

1 The term that designates the number of superiors with respect to a given module is _____.

fan-in

2 In order to reduce the amount of program code, high fan-in generally is considered [desirable/undesirable].

desirable

3 The CALL verb is used to execute a high fan-in module when the module is coded [within the main program/as a subprogram].

as a subprogram

4 The PERFORM verb is used to execute a high fan-in module when the module is coded [within the main program/as a subprogram].

within the main program

5 An adverse effect associated with high fan-in modules is that the common superiors of such modules may become content-dependent on one another, thereby undermining the concept of hierarchical _____.

independence

6 When modules with multiple superiors are repeated in a structure chart, such shared modules are coded, or tagged, by _____ _____.

shading the upper right corner of
such modules

7   When a shared module has to be changed, it [is/is not] important to determine if the change is appropriate for its use with respect to all other superiors.

is

LEVELS OF DECISIONS

Good program design dictates that decisions be placed at the proper level in the hierarchy. Placement of decision steps at improper levels can lead to overly complex structures and to loss of hierarchical control in the program. Decision steps in a program often are not only local in their impact, but also may affect other parts of the program. The main objective from the standpoint of program design is to place a decision step at a level in the hierarchy such that the effect of a decision is limited to the module incorporating the decision and its subordinates.

As an example of improper design, refer to Figure 17–15. In this structure chart it is designated that the decision step in module F should also determine certain processing in module G. In order to implement such a design the programmer would probably create some special flag at F to codify the decision, and then this flag would have to be passed up the hierarchy

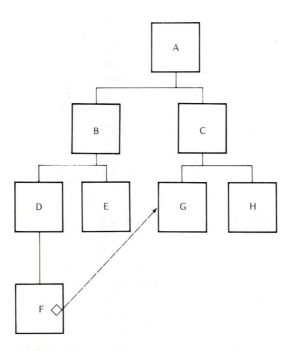

FIGURE 17–15   IMPROPER EFFECT OF DECISION STEP.

through D, B, and A, and then down the hierarchy through C until finally arriving at the destination, module G. Such implementation is error-prone. The fact is that even though modules F and G are under separate superordinates, they are control-coupled and therefore are dependent rather than independent modules. The proper way to handle the situation portrayed in Figure 17–15 is to remove the decision step from F and place it in module A, which is a superior with respect to both modules F and G.

Let us illustrate the placement of a decision step at the proper level by a specific example. Suppose that a program to merge two sequential files is being designed. The process involves comparing a record from each file, writing the smaller of the two records (say in terms of account/number), reading the next record from the file that contained the smaller record, and repeating the process. If two records are equal, both records should be written and a new pair of records should be read. An initial design for the program could be the one presented in Figure 17–16. The module called Write Smaller Record includes the logic of determining the record(s) to be written. That determination (decision) has an effect on the module at the same hierarchical level, Get Next Pair; the latter needs to know whether to read File-A, File-B, or both. We could try to force independence of these two modules by having both of them make the necessary determination regarding the file that contains the smaller record. Apart from the duplication of effort, the hidden dependence is dangerous. If we modify the module Write Smaller Record, we may not realize that we must also modify the module Get Next Pair.

Figure 17–17 presents an improved design for the program to merge two sequential files. In this design the four modules at the same hierarchical level are all independent of one another. In terms of program code, this design can be implemented as shown in Figure 17–18.

In the sample program in Figure 17–18, MERGING is the module

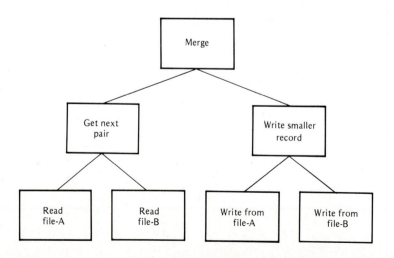

FIGURE 17–16   INITIAL DESIGN FOR THE MERGE PROGRAM.

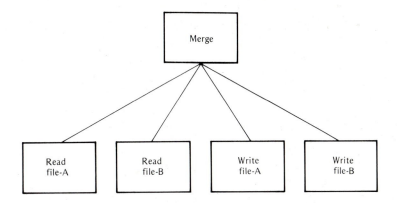

FIGURE 17-17   IMPROVED DESIGN FOR THE MERGE PROGRAM.

called Merge in the structure chart in Figure 17-17. Notice that this superior module contains the decision step that determines the processing in all of the subordinate modules.

Review

1   In terms of good program design, a decision step in a module [may/should not] affect processing in a module located in another section of the structure chart.

should not

2   In terms of good program design, a decision step in a module [may/should not] affect processing in another module with a common superior and at the same hierarchical level.

should not

3   In terms of good program design, a decision step in a module [may/should not] affect processing in the module in which it is located.

may

4   In terms of good program design, a decision step in a module [may/should not] affect processing in a subordinate module.

may

```
MERGING.
    PERFORM READ-A
    PERFORM READ-B
    PERFORM UNTIL A-ENDED = ' YES'
            AND B-ENDED = ' YES'
        IF A-REC <  B-REC
          THEN
                PERFORM WRITE-A
                PERFORM READ-A
          ELSE
                IF A-REC > B-REC
                  THEN
                        PERFORM WRITE-B
                        PERFORM READ-B
                  ELSE
                        PERFORM WRITE-A
                        PERFORM READ-A
                        PERFORM WRITE-B
                        PERFORM READ-B
                END-IF
        END-IF
    END-PERFORM.
READ-A.
    READ A-FILE
        AT END MOVE HIGH-VALUES TO A-REC
                MOVE 'YES' TO A-ENDED.
READ-B.
    READ B-FILE
        AT END MOVE HIGH-VALUES TO B-REC
                MOVE 'YES' TO B-ENDED.
WRITE-A.
    .
    .
    .
WRITE-B.
    .
    .
    .
```

FIGURE 17–18   SAMPLE MERGE PROGRAM OUTLINE.

INVERSION OF AUTHORITY

In a program hierarchy the flow of control is from a superior module to its subordinates. A subordinate module is activated by, and its processing may be affected by, a superior module. The superior module is written predicated on an understanding of the functions of all its subordinates. The concept of *inversion of authority* describes the circumstance in which a subordinate module seemingly controls or activates its superior by the result of its function. In the most typical case a flag is set equal to a value by the subordinate, and that flag value invokes certain action in the superior. However, note that the subordinate is not really controlling the superior in the usual sense of determining when or whether the module should be executed, and no knowledge of the superior's function is required in writing the subordinate module.

As a specific example of limited inversion of authority, suppose that the PERFORM statement below is in a superior module. While the READ-FILE module sets a flag to 'YES', writing the program statement requires no knowledge regarding use of the flag in the superior:

```
        PERFORM READ-FILE UNTIL E-O-F-FLAG = 'YES'.
          ⋮
READ-FILE.
        READ DATA-FILE RECORD
          AT END MOVE 'YES' TO E-O-F-FLAG.
```

In general, limiting the direction of control only downward in the hierarchy minimizes the number of relationships among program modules. If modules were systematically related to their peers and upward to their superiors, the number of intermodule relationships would be multiplied and the resulting complexity could be overwhelming. Therefore, even though limited inversions of authority may be unavoidable, they should be minimized.

Review

1   The concept which describes apparent control of a superior module by a subordinate module is _____.

inversion of authority

2   In the example of inversion of authority presented in this section, the

control by the subordinate module of its superior was relatively [extensive/limited].

limited

3   In a well-designed program, inversion of authority should occur [frequently/infrequently].

infrequently

CONTROL BASED ON PHYSICAL CONTIGUITY

In a strict program hierarchy, a program should be so designed as to have one single superior for the entire structure. The superior controls the execution of its subordinates which, in turn, do the same with respect to their subordinates. Subordinate control should be explicit, and as indicated earlier in this chapter, should be exercised by use of PERFORM or CALL statements. However, many programs include a third form of control structure that is implicit and tends to be error-prone. This kind of control is based on physical contiguity of modules in the program.

Figure 17–19(a) illustrates an example of a program outline with control based on physical contiguity. Module A is assumed to contain no end-of-program or GO TO statements. Thus, when module A finishes executing, then B starts to execute. B is in effect a subordinate of A by virtue of its physical position in the program. If a programmer later inserts a new module between A and B, the implied control structure between these two modules may be overlooked, resulting in programming errors. Similarly, modules D and E have the same control relationship because of their physical contiguity.

A related point is illustrated in Figure 17–19(b). Notice that PERFORM I THRU L in module A establishes the sequence of paragraphs as one module. One would therefore expect that I THRU L constitutes a cohesive function. But then notice that later in the program module N contains PERFORM J THRU K, which is part of the I THRU L sequence. One of two reasons most likely led to this program structure. One possible reason is that I THRU L is really a composite function which includes the J THRU K function. If such is the case, then the design may be appropriate. The other possibility is that I THRU L is in fact one cohesive function and the J THRU K sequence is a module with coincidental cohesion; the programmer noticed a sequence of code that was also needed in module N, and so made reference to J THRU K instead of writing the code again at N.

The two illustrations of programs that include control by physical

A. _____   A. _____
   _____   PERFORM I THRU L
B. _____   PERFORM M
   _____
   GO TO D   PERFORM N
C. _____
   End Program   I. _____
D. _____   _____
   _____   J. _____
E. _____   _____
   GO TO C   K. _____
      (a)   _____
                  L. _____
                     _____
                  M. _____
                     _____
                  N. _____
                     PERFORM J THRU K
                        (b)

FIGURE 17–19   ILLUSTRATIONS OF IMPROPER STRUCTURES INVOLVING CONTROL BY PHYSICAL CONTIGUITY.

contiguity in Figure 17–19 represent weak structures from the standpoint of program design. They are particularly likely to lead to errors when programs are altered or revised, and therefore control based on physical contiguity should be minimized.

Review

1   In a well-designed program, program control of a given module always originates from its _____.

superior

2   Explicit execution of a subordinate module is achieved by use of the verbs _____ or _____ in the superior module.

PERFORM; CALL

3   When a particular module H is executed because it happens to follow

module G in the program, module H in effect is a [superior/subordinate] of module G.

subordinate

4   The type of control of the execution of module H which is described in the preceding review item illustrates control based on _____ _____.

physical contiguity

5   A general rule in program design is that control based on physical contiguity should be [maximized/avoided].

avoided

TOP-DOWN DESIGN

In the preceding sections of this chapter we have described operational guidelines and characteristics of well-designed programs. We now describe the process by which well-partitioned modular programs can be structured into hierarchies. The process is known as *top-down design*.

In top-down design, we begin by identifying one module that describes the overall function of the program. Then we proceed to partition this overall function into its main components. For example, suppose that the overall function is Process Payroll. We ask ourselves: What has to be done to process the payroll? In response to this question we might initially identify four main functions, as shown in Figure 17–20: Edit Input Data, Process Transactions Against Master, Produce Paychecks, and Produce Reports. We then review these functions and determine whether the breakdown is complete and whether it contains redundancies. For instance, we might question whether or not the two modules Produce Paychecks and Produce Reports are really different functions, and if not, whether they could be replaced by a single module that could be called Produce Output. Or we might come up with a new module such as Sort Transactions.

When we are satisfied with the modules comprising the second level in the structure chart, we repeat the process, considering each of these modules in turn as if it were the top module. That is, for each main subfunction of the overall task we identify specific subfunctions which comprise that function. For example, we first ask: What are the main subfunctions that can be developed for Edit Input Data? As presented in Figure 17–21, two sub-

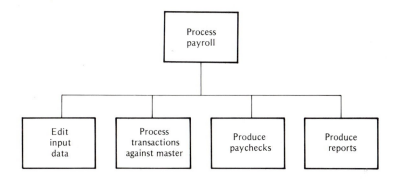

FIGURE 17–20   INITIAL DESIGN STRUCTURE FOR THE PAYROLL PROGRAM.

functions are identified: Check For Valid Employee and Check Time Cards Against Job Tickets. Although we do not continue with the analysis in Figure 17–21, the next step would be to determine subfunctions for the remaining second-level functions of Process Transactions Against Master and Produce Output.

The general process of identifying subfunctions continues with each lower level in turn. We stop when no function at any level can be partitioned any further, given that each function is a cohesive task that ultimately can be expressed in one cohesive module.

The top-down design by which modules are developed within a hierarchical structure permits the designer to concentrate on a single module at a time and to consider the relationship of that module to its subordinates only. By this approach, a large, complex programming task in essence can be reduced to a set of subtasks, each of which is substantially smaller and easier

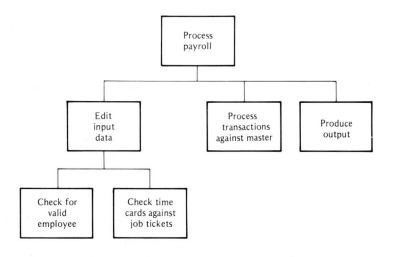

FIGURE 17–21   FIRST REVISION AND EXPANSION OF THE STRUCTURE CHART IN FIGURE 17–20.

than the total task. The property of independence in a structure chart is the one that allows us to proceed in this simplifying manner. Recall that each module should be independent in function from its peers. Thus, when we consider the Edit Input Data module in Figure 17–20 we need not focus on any of the other three modules that are its peers.

Top-down design is a well-tested and effective method for developing good program designs. Although the programmer should aspire to follow this approach closely, there are often reasons why top-down design cannot be followed strictly. For instance, one rule associated with top-down design is that all modules at a given level be reviewed and partitioned before proceeding to the next level. In practice, it may be necessary to violate this rule, as for example in a case in which there is a pressing need to implement a main function quickly. A function such as Edit Input Data may represent a priority function for operating reasons.

Further, try as we may to achieve perfect partitioning of modules, continued work at lower levels of the structure chart almost invariably brings to light the need for additional functions at a higher level or the desirability of consolidating certain higher-level functions. Thus, some bottom-up design is inevitable in most cases. Nevertheless, top-down design is the best general approach, and it is clearly superior to the bottom-up approach that was prevalent among programmers for many years. Attempts to structure a hierarchy by defining bottom-level functions and then assembling them into hierarchies leads to higher-level modules with low cohesion and to improper hierarchical dependencies.

Review

1 The approach to program design that begins by describing the one module for the overall function of the program and then proceeds to partition this function into its main components is called _____ design.

top-down

2 In terms of the top-down design, the programmer directs primary attention at partitioning [a single module/all modules at a single hierarchical level] at any one time.

a single module

3 A general rule associated with the top-down design is that all modules at a given rule [should/need not] be partitioned before proceeding to the next level.

should

4   An approach to program design that begins by defining bottom-level functions first and which leads to modules with low cohesion and to improper hierarchical dependencies is the _____ approach.

bottom-up

EXAMPLE OF TOP-DOWN DESIGN

We conclude the description of the top-down approach by illustrating the application of this approach for a specific programming task. Although the program is very simple, it serves to highlight the process involved.

Suppose that we have an employee file and we want to develop a program to tabulate salaries in a report such as illustrated in Figure 17-22. Asterisks are printed whenever an employee record is not encoded as being for a man or woman. We begin by defining the single top-level module, Produce Salary Report. We then ask the question: What are the main program functions? Our study of the report helps us to identify three main functions: Print Headings, Process Records, and Print Summary. This partitioning is illustrated in Figure 17-23. We might pause and ask whether these modules have sequential cohesion rather than functional cohesion, since they relate to the order in which they are processed. The answer is no; the functions were not so defined simply because of the order in which they occur, but because each represents a cohesive task. Incidentally, note that we show them on the chart from left to right, corresponding to their sequence. This is a recommended practice. As much as possible, the time sequence of the overall program functions should be presented from left to right.

The Print Headings is an elementary function and no partitioning is

	ANNUAL SALARY	
EMPLOYEE NAME	MEN	WOMEN
JONES, A.	18200.00	
ANDERSON, P.	12000.00	
ROBERTS, M.		15000.00
PROUST, K.*****		
NICHOLSON, J.	19600.00	
PHILLIPS, P.		18500.00
WORK, A.		20000.00
TOTAL	49800.00	53500.00
A V E R A G E	16600.00	17833.33

FIGURE 17-22   SAMPLE SALARY REPORT.

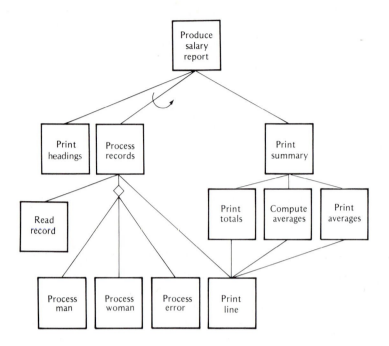

FIGURE 17-23   STRUCTURE CHART FOR THE SALARY REPORT PROGRAM.

necessary. It could also be considered so trivial that it does not deserve a module. Apart from the fact that this is an illustration to help us think in a particular way, we would also maintain that Print Headings should be left as a separate module in case future modifications require extended processing related to the headings of the report, such as a routine that centers the headings based on variable data or a routine that determines the day of the week.

Process Record is an iterative process (loop), and is so indicated by the curved arrow in Figure 17–23. It is partitioned into five modules. Notice that three of them are conditionally selected, as indicated by the diamond symbol.

The Print Summary module is partitioned into three modules. The reader might question the need for partitioning Print Summary. We agree that the simplicity of this specific program supports such questioning. However, Print Summary generally is a composite function. Suppose that in the future a more elaborate analysis is required in printing totals; our design would offer the independence among modules that could make such a change easy to implement.

The structure chart in Figure 17–23 is appropriate for a one-page report, but not necessarily for multiple-page output. Specifically, suppose we want the capability of printing a heading at the top of each page for a multi-page report. Under these circumstances the Print Headings module cannot be a direct subordinate of the top module. Figure 17–24 is a revised structure

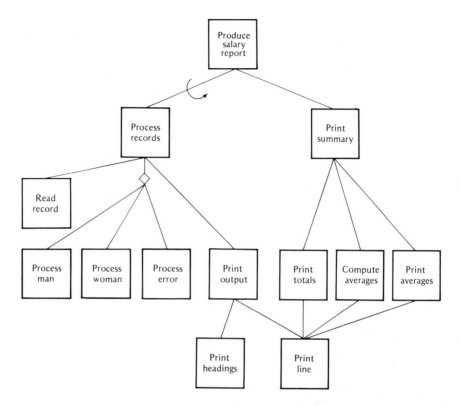

FIGURE 17–24   REVISED STRUCTURE CHART FOR THE SALARY REPORT PROGRAM.

chart that is appropriate for multiple- or single-page reports. The new module Print Output is subordinate to Process Records, and consists of the two functions Print Headings and Print Line. We assume that no heading is required for the Print Summary function.

Exercises

17.1   Why is content coupling via GO TO statements undesirable?

17.2   Suppose that a module has a size of 120 program lines. Is this necessarily a poorly designed module? Explain.

17.3   Consider the diagrams shown at the top of page 632. If a represents an original design and b and c two alternative modifications, what reasons would lead to choosing b or c?

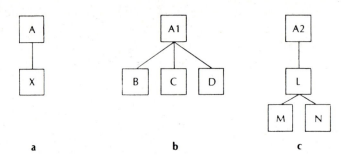

In other words, should we increase span by partitioning at the same level or by hierarchical partitioning?

17.4   Consider the diagrams below. If a represents an original design and b and c two alternative modifications, what reasons would lead to choosing b or c?

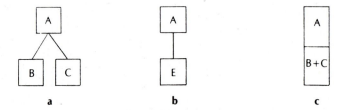

In other words, should we combine at the same hierarchical level, or should we combine subordinates into a superior?

17.5   Explain the term "fan-in" of a module and discuss both why it is desirable to have a high fan-in as well as the need to be cautious about high fan-ins.

17.6   What is the appropriate design for decision steps in a program? Suppose in the diagram below a decision is made in B which affects processing in C. How would you consider revising the program design?

17.7   Why is control based on physical contiguity undesirable?

17.8   Demonstrate the top-down design approach for a program that reads a file of student transcripts and prints a report as outlined below. There are three types of records on the file and they are so designated by a field called REC-TYPE. These records are: Name Records, Semester Records, and Course Records. The program lists each student name once and for as many semesters as are available it prints the semester identification and all the courses taken, and then computes the grade point average (GPA) for each semester. At the end, the total semester hours and the overall GPA are also given for each student. Finally, a summary report for all students is produced showing total credits and average GPA.

```
JOHN A. JOHNSON
     FALL 1987                      CREDITS        GRADE
     HISTORY                           3             B
     COBOL                             3             A
     ACCOUNTING                        3             C
        GPA   3.00
     SPRING 1988                    CREDITS        GRADE
           .                           .             .
           .                           .             .
           .                           .             .

     TOTAL CREDITS   126
     GPA   3.25

MARY M. MURPHY
           .
           .
           .

        TOTAL CREDITS FOR ALL STUDENTS   XXXX
        AVERAGE GPA FOR ALL STUDENTS   X.XX

                                                    .
                                                    .
                                                    .
```

18

PROGRAM TESTING

INTRODUCTION

Program testing refers to the steps and procedures undertaken in order to ascertain that the program is correct—i.e., that the program does what it was intended to do. The programmer goes through a number of steps in completing a programming project. These steps are summarized in Figure 18–1. As indicated in this outline, the actual program coding is just one of a large number of steps, and it constitutes only a relatively small part in the overall process. Program testing is involved in a multitude of single attempts, each

- Define the function of the program
- Design the program structure.
- Define required data and record layouts.
- Define test data and expected test results.
- Transform the program structure into a pseudocode program outline.
- Write the program in COBOL.
- Review and correct obvious syntactical or logical errors in this original version.
- If initial version was handwritten, key-in the program in machine-readable form; obtain a listing of the keyed-in version, correct typing errors and obtain revised listing.
- Compile the program and review syntactical and logical errors diagnosed by the compiler.
- Recompile the program until all compiler-detectable errors have been corrected.
- Execute the program using test data.
- Compare program results to established test results and revise the program. Repeat this step until satisfied that the program is correct.
- Execute the program with selected "real" data and verify correctness of processing. If errors are discovered, further revise the program until correct processing is achieved.
- Store program on library and release it for operation.

FIGURE 18–1   STEPS INCLUDED IN A PROGRAMMING PROJECT.

not as time-consuming as initial coding, but in total usually summing up to a large multiple of the coding time requirement.

Casual, sketchy, or haphazard approaches to program development results in a heavy penalty in error-correcting efforts. Well-managed installations have long recognized the importance of thoughtful, organized approaches to program development and demand that special emphasis and extensive effort be devoted to good program design. It is a fact that the greater the effort devoted to the first five steps in Figure 18–1, the less effort needed for the steps after coding. Good design is actually a high-yielding investment. A person who spends 5 days in design efforts may spend 3 days in program testing. In contrast, a person of comparable skills who spends 2 days in design efforts for the same task may spend 15 days in testing. Further, the second person will be working in the frustrating effort of endless error-correcting attempts, and will develop a program that is much more likely to be found in error in the future when untested conditions are encountered.

Ideally, we would like to produce programs with zero defects. In reality, we have no practical way to ascertain that a program is indeed correct. Well-designed and properly tested programs have a high probability of being error-free, but we have no logical way of ascertaining their absolute correctness. Inexperienced programmers and "laymen" often believe that exhaustive testing can remove all errors. They think that test data can be created to test the program under all possible conditions. Unfortunately, this is far from the truth. It has been shown that even for relatively small programs, testing of all possible paths under all possible data combinations would require hundreds or even thousands of years of continuous computer running!

There have been some efforts to develop a theoretical foundation for constructing unambiguous proofs of program correctness, comparable to the mathematical logic that guarantees the correctness of mathematical theorems. However, these developments are presently at an embryonic stage. Program development will remain an art for the forseeable future. Like any art, it can be practiced well or it can be practiced poorly. The current professional consensus is that programs can be developed so that errors are minimized and occasionally totally absent. Further, programs should be so constructed that errors, when discovered, can easily be traced to their causes and can be easily corrected. Thus, as a philosophy we can say that we should strive for minimal errors and easily correctable programs.

Review

1   With respect to an overall programming project, program design generally requires [less/more] time than program coding.

more

2   The more time devoted to establishing the functions of a program, designing the program structure, and defining test data, the [less/more] time generally is required for program testing.

less

3   As a general philosophy, the objective in programming projects is to develop programs that have [zero/minimal] errors.

minimal

TOP-DOWN PROGRAM DEVELOPMENT AND TESTING

One approach to program development and testing places emphasis on the system, where the system is the total program that consists of a collection of interrelated modules. This *top-down* testing approach requires that testing be implemented in stages, each stage corresponding to one hierarchical level in the program structure.

In a typical program structure, such as is illustrated in Figure 18–2, top-down testing would proceed as follows. First we test module 1 to see that it performs its function correctly. Next, we test module 1 together with modules 2, 3, and 10 to ascertain their correctness. The third test incorpo-

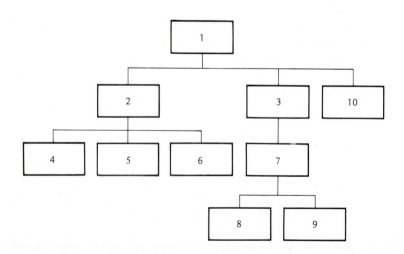

FIGURE 18–2   SAMPLE HIERARCHICAL PROGRAM STRUCTURE.

rates modules 4, 5, 6, and 7 along with 1, 2, 3, and 10, while the final test would also involve modules 8 and 9 in addition to the other modules.

In general, the top-down testing approach is associated with a top-down approach to program development. The advantage of following a top-down approach is that we make sure that the total program works properly before we refine any of its parts. It may be useful to relate this approach to the construction of a new building, where the total outside structure is created and tested before individual rooms are built inside. The top-down approach avoids "surprises" at the end of a programming project, such as incompatibility among the parts of the program. It is especially useful in large projects involving several programmers, where the need for integration of the parts is very important. But it is also useful in smaller, single-person programs. In either case the approach can be implemented through the development of *module stubs*, as explained in the following paragraph.

In order to implement the top-down testing approach we design the entire program module structure first, and then we code in detail at progressively lower-level modules. For example, for the program structure in Figure 18–2 we would first code only module 1 in detail, simply identifying all other modules by module names and by some identification-producing statements. In the next step we would code modules 1, 2, 3, and 10 in detail, while all other modules would be stubs, as illustrated in Figure 18–3. In our example we chose to DISPLAY a message in each stub module, identifying its execution. When we test this partial program all modules would be executed, albeit the lower-level ones perform a trivial function.

In this progressive testing approach, when modules 1, 2, 3, and 10 are tested and found to function correctly we then develop the full detail of modules 4, 5, 6, and 7 and test this expanded program. Finally, modules 8 and 9 are developed, and the whole system of modules is tested to ascertain its correctness.

A variant of the top-down approach is to subdivide the progressive module development and testing into stages that represent vertical rather than horizontal module order. For the example in Figure 18–2 we would first develop and test modules 1, 2, 4, 5, and 6, keeping 3, 7, 8, 9, and 10 as stub modules. In the next step we would expand the module development and testing to include module 3 and its subordinates, and finally we would add module 10.

The top-down approach has great merit in providing a systematic approach to program development and testing. However, it is often difficult to implement in pure form. Consider, for instance, module 2 in Figure 18–2. It is likely that some of its processing is conditional on the outcome of functions performed in its subordinate modules. The stub approach cannot simulate the required results in a satisfactory way. As a practical matter, then, we may consider two options. One option is to "fake" the results of a given module's assumed function. For instance, if module 2 is to receive an edited record from module 5 we might "hand-code" data in module 5, such as MOVE '123ABCD35982XYZ' TO RECORD-A, where RECORD-A is the one used by

```
        MODULE-1.
          :
          :

            PERFORM MODULE-2
              :
              :

            PERFORM MODULE-3
              :
              :

            PERFORM MODULE-10
              :
              :
              :

        MODULE-2.
            PERFORM MODULE-4
            PERFORM MODULE-5
            PERFORM MODULE-6
              :
              :

        MODULE-3.
            PERFORM MODULE-7
              :
              :

        MODULE-10.
          :
          :

        MODULE-4.
            DISPLAY 'THIS IS MODULE 4 EXECUTING' UPON DEVICE.
        MODULE-5.
            DISPLAY 'THIS IS MODULE 5 EXECUTING' UPON DEVICE.
        MODULE-6.
            DISPLAY 'THIS IS MODULE 6 EXECUTING' UPON DEVICE.
        MODULE-7.
            DISPLAY 'THIS IS MODULE 7 EXECUTING' UPON DEVICE.
        MODULE-8.
            DISPLAY 'THIS IS MODULE 8 EXECUTING' UPON DEVICE.
        MODULE-9.
            DISPLAY 'THIS IS MODULE 9 EXECUTING' UPON DEVICE.
```

FIGURE 18-3   PROGRAM WITH MODULE STUBS.

module 2 in its further processing. Or, if there is need for multiple records, we might include a READ instruction in module 5 to input manually tested correct records, but without doing the editing functions that will eventually be incorporated in module 5.

A second option is to temper the strict top-down method by fully developing the subordinate modules whose output is required by the superior module to be tested. For example, with respect to Figure 18–2, we might fully code modules 1, 2, 3, 10 and 5 in one stage, rather than keeping module 5 a stub.

Review

1   The approach to program testing that places primary emphasis on the total program, and by which program testing begins at the highest hierarchical level of the program structure is the _____ approach.

top-down

2   When a module is represented only by an identification statement during program testing, and is not in fact involved in data execution, such a module is often referred to as being a module _____.

stub

3   Whereas the basic top-down approach described in this section gives attention to modules according to hierarchical level, an alternative is to subdivide the progressive development and testing of modules according to [horizontal/vertical] order.

vertical

4   When the output of a subordinate module is required in order to test its superior, two options are available. One option is to enter the required output manually. The other is to _____.

fully develop the subordinate
module

BOTTOM-UP PROGRAM DEVELOPMENT AND TESTING

The bottom-up approach emphasized complete development and testing of the individual component modules before proceeding to their integration. It is the opposite of the top-down approach in that it proceeds from the lowest-level modules to the higher modules. The bottom-up approach is analogous to the approach taken in manufacturing, where parts are made and tested individually before they are assembled into units that are then tested as subassemblies or final products.

Refer back to Figure 18–2. Application of the bottom-up approach would begin by developing and testing modules 8 and 9 individually before developing module 7 and testing all three modules together. In the next phase modules 4, 5, and 6 would be completed, followed by 2, 3, and 10. Finally module 1 would be added and tested in conjunction with all the other modules.

The bottom-up approach is characteristic of programmers driven by a need to "keep working." They prefer to start early into the project by actually coding the most detailed and specific functions. Common candidates for such coding are input- and output-oriented modules. The programmer thinks, "I am going to need a 'read' module for each input file, so I might as well start coding them now." Similarly, printed reports are natural targets for early development, since the report formats and data transfer functions are clear and can be tested independently of the rest of the program.

The preceding paragraph implies some degree of arbitrary selection as to which modules to develop first. This need not be the case. The approach can be organized and systematic, and may dictate a precise order of module development and testing. In the strictest case, we proceed from the lowest level in the hierarchy chart to the top, main module.

In order to implement bottom-up testing it must be possible to "drive" lower-level modules. If a module is going to be eventually executed under control of a PERFORM or a CALL, that control must be provided in some way so that the module can actually be executed for the purpose of testing. This is accomplished in one of two ways. One method is to write *test-driver modules* that invoke execution of the modules undergoing testing. The test-driver can be a program that contains a PERFORM for each module to be tested. If modules to be tested are subprograms, then a main program that issues the appropriate CALLs is written so that the subprograms can be tested as such.

A second method of arranging for the execution of a lower-level module is to write the module to be tested so that it is an executable program. Instead of being under the control of a PERFORM or CALL, the procedures comprising the module are written as a complete program. For example, in the case of a subprogram the LINKAGE SECTION header can be written, but with an asterisk placed in column 7 of the COBOL Coding Form. Thus, the header is treated as a comment. Similarly, the PROCEDURE DIVISION header would contain no USING clause, although it is recommended that such a clause be included in a comment statement. Finally, STOP RUN would be used rather than EXIT PROGRAM, and thus instead of a subprogram we have an executable (main) program that can be tested by itself. When testing is completed the module is revised so that it can be used as a subordinate module that is executed under the control of a PERFORM or CALL in the next stage of program development and testing.

As is the case with the top-down approach, availability of necessary data becomes an issue with the bottom-up approach as well. A superior module often provides data upon which a subordinate module performs its function. If the superior module has not been developed as yet, the data output of the superior module needs somehow to be made available. As with the top-down approach, we may hand-code data into the program or we may include a READ statement preceding the PERFORM or CALL. The READ statement is used to input the needed data from a special test file that is used to simulate the required data.

Review

1   Modules that are particular candidates for early development in the bottom-up approach are those whose functions are oriented toward either _____ or _____.

input; output

2   Modules with PERFORM or CALL statements that are written specifically to invoke execution of the modules undergoing testing are called _____ modules.

test-driver

3   Instead of using test-driver modules, the procedures comprising the module to be tested can be written [so that it is under the control of a PERFORM or CALL/as a complete program].

as a complete program

4   In testing a module, the required data that would normally be obtained from a superior module can be hand-coded into the program or can be obtained from a special test file of such simulated data by use of the _____ statement.

READ

TOP-DOWN VS. BOTTOM-UP APPROACHES TO TESTING

Having described each of the two basic approaches to program development and testing, we may now raise the question as to which approach is better. In practice, most organizations are not purists with respect to either method and tend to use a combination of both approaches in the same project. Of course, they are fundamentally opposite approaches, and one must choose one or the other as the main approach.

The trend today favors the top-down approach for most environments. It has been concluded that it provides a better opportunity for continuous coordination and integration of all parts of a program project. But the top-down approach cannot always be successfully applied. Its success is tied to the prior development of a complete and correct program design. Such design is often an aspiration more than a reality because, simply, we are not perfect and we tend to overlook program requirements or make incorrect judgments. Often, it is not until we get into the details that we see some parts that were left out of the design or some misunderstandings and misconceptions upon which the design was based.

As much as possible, we want to proceed on the basis of the top-down approach. On the other hand, we have to accept the reality that design and implementation are iterative processes. We design, we implement, we redesign, and so on. Thus, we often use a bottom-up approach to some extent by necessity. We may also incorporate the bottom-up approach by design. If we have difficulty understanding the impact of a module's detailed code on the total program structure, we may choose to develop that module first, even if it is at a lower level. In either case, some of the bottom-up approach will thereby be incorporated together with the top-down approach.

From a historical perspective the bottom-up approach has often been associated with "sloppy" programming practices. Very often a team of programmers would work separately on different parts of a system. Then when the time came to integrate the whole it would be an endless chain of errors and incompatibilities in the parts. Just when the users were told "the system is almost ready—it is all coded and we only need to test it all together," the integration test would require months of effort. Also, on an individual basis, programmers who were not disciplined in their profession would tend to do a lot of coding but little designing, and then would spend endless hours testing the "almost-finished" program.

The top-down approach forces the design phase more explicitly, and for that reason it is the preferred choice. However, either method can be made to work successfully. If we do have a good, complete design, and if we do define clearly the data interfaces between modules, the bottom-up approach can be very effective. Under such circumstances each module is developed and tested within a clearly defined design framework, and incompatibilities and integration problems can be minimized.

The important point to keep in mind is that strict adherence to either the top-down or bottom-up approach is often indicative of narrow-minded management. No approach is *the* best in all cases. The effective programmer is one who understands all available methods and tools and is wise in selecting the right one for the appropriate occasion.

Review

1   The approach to program development and testing that generally is favored for use as the main approach is the _____ approach.

> top-down

2   The approach to program development and testing that historically has been associated with a lack of attention given to program design is the _____ approach.

> bottom-up

3   With reference to program development and testing, it is good organizational policy to use [one or the other approach explicitly/a combination of approaches].

> a combination of approaches

TESTING PROCEDURES

In this section we describe a number of specific procedures used in program testing.

Creation of Test Data

In order to test a single module or a whole program, we need input test data. Using a sample of real data is not the best approach because the sample is not likely to include all the special conditions to be tested.

The creation of test data requires considerable effort and thought. Inclusion of insufficient cases will allow hidden program deficiencies or "bugs," which will surface gradually over time as the overlooked cases are encountered in actual use of the program. Attempts to include all possible cases are futile, since the combinations of cases are literally overwhelming. We want to choose important cases, such as data in the extremes of the range as well as in the middle of the range of possible values. For instance, if a field can contain signed numeric data, include one positive, one negative, one zero, and one nonnumeric error value, as a minimum. However, we cannot rely too much on test data to "prove" that the program is correct. If there are 10 numeric fields in the input data and we want to test for most possibilities, we should include the following for each field: a large negative value, a small negative value, a zero value, a small positive value, a large positive value, and a nonnumeric (error) value. Given these six types of input for each field and considering that there are 10 fields, we would need to provide $6^{10} = 60,466,176$ sets of test data to include all the possible input combinations! Worse yet, we need to check that many test results to see how the program processed each combination. Thus we cannot rely on test data alone. Our main weapon against errors is the logical construction of the program and then the additional strength provided by selected test data.

There are some proprietary commercial software packages that generate test data based on PICTURE descriptions of fields. These are extremely useful aids and can be a great advantage for most routine testing. Having such automatic test data generation allows the programmer to concentrate on constructing special test data combinations.

Walkthroughs-Individual Review

After a program is written it is important to review the procedure logic of the program by walking through it on an individual basis. We take the test data and we apply the program instructions to it manually, thereby *desk-checking* the program execution. If erroneous results have been obtained from actual processing of the program, such desk-checking can also be used to search for the source of the error.

In the desk-checking review, it is useful to maintain a map of storage in order to keep track of the values stored in the various fields. A useful approach is to write field names as column headings and to enter the values stored in a given field under that column heading. When a value changes as a result of a READ, a MOVE, or an arithmetic instruction, then cross out the old value and write a new value underneath. Do not erase old values, so that you can refer back to a previous step in the program execution.

Walkthroughs-Peer Review

Most programmers have experienced the following situation. The programmer encounters a program error. Many frustrating hours or even days are spent trying to resolve the error, to no avail. Then the program is shown to a colleague and the nature of the error is explained. The colleague glances at the program and diagnoses the error or makes a suggestion as to how to resolve it in just a few minutes. This kind of experience has been actually formalized into an organizational procedure at many computer sites.

The term "structured walkthrough" has been used widely and originated with IBM, which formalized the concept and developed a set of rules and guidelines for such walkthroughs.

In general terms, a *walkthrough* is a peer review of a program. The program (module) author gives a copy of the code along with some documentation to a group of peers who will undertake the review. The group size is normally two to four persons, and may include all members of the team working on the same project. Each person studies the program individually and then they all meet at an appointed time. During this meeting they "react" to the program by bringing out ambiguities, possible errors, and visible errors. No suggestions are made on how to correct them—that is left to the author. Such a walkthrough lasts one-half to one hour and serves a very beneficial function. The programmer learns to program in understandable ways, tends to design better programs, and avoids "tricky," obscure code, and the group as a whole adapts to common company standards.

Many organizations have ritualized the process and are religious in the little details associated with such a review. We cannot, of course, comment on such individual practices. The important point is that it is very helpful to have your program reviewed by a small group of peers. Other people see quickly things that our own myopic view may prevent us from seeing. The author of a program often is so tied to the present structure that he or she cannot look at the program with the fresh viewpoint necessary to idenfity errors.

Traces

Most computer sites have available a software package that can *trace* or *monitor* program execution at the paragraph or even the data-name level. A printed trace captures the actual sequence of program execution and can be an invaluable aid in program testing and program error correction. Desk-checking a program often suffers from incorrect assumptions about the sequence of instructions to be executed, but a trace provides a record of the actual sequence.

In its simplest form, a trace prints the names of each paragraph executed in the order of execution. The programmer can check this sequence against the test data and ascertain that the program does indeed follow the expected paths with the test data. We recommend routine use of such a trace feature during program testing, since it requires a minimum amount of additional printout (a page or two) and it provides an invaluable aid. However, one word of caution is necessary. If the program contains a logical error that results in an interminable loop, you may generate an inordinately long printed trace! To prevent this problem, put an appropriate page limit in your job control statements so that the printing is checked.

If a software package trace is not available, the programmer can develop one rather easily by following each paragraph-name by a DISPLAY or WRITE statement that prints a literal which is the paragraph-name. When program testing is completed, an asterisk can be placed in column 7 to convert these trace statements into comments. Then, should the program need to be retested in the future, all we need to do is convert these asterisks to spaces and the "home-made" trace is reinstated.

Printing a trace of paragraph-names is a minimum trace. Most trace packages will allow selective control over tracing of individual records or data-names. For instance, if we have specified the tracing of data-name ABC, then when MOVE XYZ TO ABC is executed the trace will show the name of the field, ABC, its content before the move, and its content after the move. It is also possible to trace "all," in which case every paragraph and every instruction is traced, resulting in voluminous trace printouts. Occasionally such indiscriminate tracing is necessary, but it is usually a waste of time. It is much better to first localize the portion of the program that is likely to contain the suspected error and then, through controls in the trace package, monitor that portion of the program only. There are some trace-type packages, mostly available on minicomputers, that can be used from a terminal, and they allow the programmer to step through the program online. Such testing aids are bound to increase in availability and in sophistication.

Although it will always be important to make effective use of any testing aid, good program design should be used to minimize errors and testing efforts. No testing aid should be allowed to provide implicit encouragement of "sloppy" programming because of the belief that the testing package will uncover the errors.

Core Dumps

A *core dump* is a printing of central memory contents at an instant in time. It is a snapshot of central memory. The programmer can use reference data provided during compilation to locate any desired field and view its contents as they were at the moment that the core dump was executed. Normally the programmer uses the required job control statements to specify that a core dump be performed when the program abends. In this way the contents of memory can be viewed as they were at the time of the fatal error, and the programmer can see which record had been read from a given file, what the values of accumulator fields were at that time, and the like.

In many installations core dumps are a routine procedure, and some experienced programmers cannot imagine that anybody can develop and test programs without core dumps being used in the process. The practice can be very beneficial to those who are accustomed to it and know how to use if efficiently and effectively. On the other hand, core dumping has its roots in an era when other diagnostic and testing aids, such as traces, were not available, when compilers were much more prone to erroneous compilation, and when COBOL programmers were, at heart, assembler programmers and wanted to see the "real thing." In today's environment core dumps should have a very small place.

Most core dumps are produced in hexadecimal or other non-human-oriented output, and they take considerable time to read and interpret, even for experienced users. Just like any puzzle, they do generate interest on the part of the user, and many such users actually thrive on the ritual of getting the multipage dump and going through the process of deciphering it. But the practice can be wasteful in programmer time.

A trace can be both more efficient *and* more effective than a core dump because it is a picture of the dynamics of the program, rather than a static snapshot, and because trace packages are easier to use. There are occasions, however, when core dumps are indispensable, and that is when there is an error caused by the system software. Compiler and operating system software *do* contain errors, and occasionally they cause a COBOL program to execute in a strange way. When normal procedures cannot resolve an error, then core dump diagnosis is perhaps the only way to proceed. Thus, we advocate highly selective use of core dumps and recommend strongly against routine use of this testing procedure for every little program error.

Review

1   One appropriate procedure associated with program testing is to apply the program to a set of [actual sample data/artificial test data].

artificial test data

2   Test data for a numeric field [should/should not] include nonnumeric data.

should

3   The procedure of applying program instructions manually to test data is called _____.

desk-checking

4   The general term that is used to designate peer review of a program is _____.

walkthrough

5   A printed output that captures the actual sequence of program execution by including such information as the paragraph-names in the order of their execution is called a _____.

trace

6   Testing aids, such as trace packages, are becoming increasingly avail-

able. Programmers [can therefore/nevertheless should not] be less concerned about program efforts oriented toward minimizing initial programming errors.

nevertheless should not

7 The printing of central memory contents at an instant in time is called a
_____.

core dump

8 In general, a core dump is most appropriate for the diagnosis of apparent errors in [applications programs/system software].

system software

COMMON ERRORS

The purpose of this section is to describe a few common programming errors. There also are certain errors that are common to each specific computer site rather than being a general source of errors. These errors can be related to the type of applications programmed at that site, the standards adapted, or the systems software in use. Programmers have an extensive and highly efficient "grapevine" for passing along the appropriate warnings to one another. This is so even in the rather fluid college environment, in which any given student may only be involved in the programming process for a few months. In any case, avoiding errors that others have previously encountered makes good sense, and should be supported by documentation as well as informal communication.

Forgetting to Initialize or Reset

Forgetting to initialize or reset is a common error, and it can only be avoided by systematic review of every flag-type field and every accumulator.

Fields may be initialized in the DATA DIVISION by using a VALUE clause or they can be initialized in the PROCEDURE DIVISION by using a MOVE-literal or a SET . . . TRUE instruction. A good practice to follow is to initialize fields in the DATA DIVISION only when the values are to remain constant throughout the program. Fields which are used as "flags" or "switches," and therefore are set and reset during program execution, are best initialized in the PROCEDURE DIVISION, since the latter approach is more self-documenting.

In addition to forgetting to initialize a field, a common error is to forget to reset a value. For instance, in a nested PERFORM structure with iterative processing we may use a flag to control execution. We enter the procedure with the flag set to one value and then we change that value as an indicator that a condition has developed. However, we may forget to reset the flag back to the original value before it is again used in conjunction with the procedure.

Nonnumeric Data in Numeric Fields

Numeric data must consist of the digits 0–9, an operational sign (PIC S), and an implied decimal point (PIC V). Presence of other characters in a numeric field is an error. Some compilers abend the job when attempting to perform arithmetic or comparison (IF) with a numeric field that contains nonnumeric data; worse yet, other compilers process the nonnumeric data, yielding incorrect results. Abending is a nuisance, but incorrect arithmetic is a serious problem. In the latter case the error is hidden and may go undetected for a long time unless proper check-totals are used to detect such errors.

In order to avoid this kind of error it is important to review the program to ascertain that all fields used as operands in arithmetic statements have proper data. Data are entered into a field by a MOVE, a VALUE, or an input statement. Most often, it is through input statement execution that nonnumeric data originate. To prevent the error, all such data should be checked by a class condition test, such as IF NOT NUMERIC. . . .

Improper Use of Period

In any IF or other conditional statement the presence of a period is very important, since it terminates the domain of that statement. A common error is to have a period too early in the statement, and as a result to get subtle errors. For instance, if we have

```
IF QUANT > LIMIT
    MOVE A TO B
    ADD 1 TO LARGE.
```

it makes an important difference as to whether the period is at the end of the second line or the third line. Such a programming error is difficult to detect because the consequences of the error might never be encountered with the test data (recall that it is impossible to test all possible combinations of values). The best way to prevent such errors is to review each conditional statement individually for the proper placement of the period.

Another error associated with a misplaced period is the situation in which the period is in column 73 of the COBOL Coding Form. As the program is scanned it looks normal, yet it produces incorrect results (if we are fortunate to detect the error during testing). Anything written in columns 73–80 appears as part of the program in the listing, but it is treated as a comment by the compiler.

A related but relatively rare error is the situation in which an operand is written past column 72, such as COMPUTE X = Y + 1 and the "+ 1" is in columns 73–75.

Subscript Out of Range

Tables are defined using OCCURS clauses, which specify their size. If a two-dimensional table consists of 10 × 20 entries, the subscripts should be in the ranges 1–10 and 1–20, respectively. Yet for a variety of causes a subscript may lie outside that range, causing unpredictable results. Almost every programmer has been bitten by this bug. It often results in hidden errors, which are the worst kind. If we are aware of the type of error being committed, then we can try to correct it; but if we do not know what is happening operationally, then we have a serious problem.

Compilers do not generally provide automatic checking for out-of-range subscripts. The programmer can prevent such errors by preceding subscript uses by IF statements to check for invalid subscript values, or by checking input data and program logic to ascertain that the problem cannot occur undetected.

Improper Nesting of Perform Statements

Improper nesting of PERFORMs is another common error that results in unpredictable or strange results. Consider these statements:

A.   PERFORM B
:
:
B.
     PERFORM C
       :
       :
     PERFORM B.
C.
     PERFORM A.

The B paragraph should not PERFORM itself, and the C paragraph should not PERFORM its hierarchical superior. Such errors may lead to strange complications. Desk-checking will not work because the compiled program is in fact different from the source program. As you try to follow the source program against a trace of some kind it makes no sense. Rather than blaming the compiler, we should first check our program logic. If no answer for the difficulty can be found, then have peers review the program. The chances are that there are improper PERFORM statements or subscripts out of range, rather than errors in the compiler.

Processing the Last Input Record Twice

A common error is associated with use of the following type of structure:

```
    PERFORM A UNTIL X = 'YES'.
        .
        .
        .
A.  READ IN-FILE AT END MOVE 'YES' TO X.
    Process input record. . .
```

The programmer is thinking that moving 'YES' to X in the READ statement provides proper control. Yet the PERFORM . . . UNTIL will not catch the end of file condition until *after* the processing of the input record has taken place. As a result, the last record is still in the buffer and it is processed twice.

Improper Data Format

Some of the most difficult errors are ones that result from interaction between data and logic. When the program logic appears correct but the program is not performing correctly, good candidates for review are the data definitions and the actual data used as input. Suppose that we have:

```
02  PART-NO   PIC 9(4).
02  T-CODE     PIC 9.
```

If part-numbers are in fact 5 digits long, the fifth digit of the part number will be treated as a value for T-CODE. By coincidence, in limited testing the fifth digit of part number may have valid values as a T-CODE and the error may go undetected.

Length of records and length of fields must be checked thoroughly. In addition, we must accept the premise that input data may be recorded in error and may therefore cause problems, even if the data definitions in the programs are correct. To avoid source-data-related errors, the program should include checks to test the input data. Regardless of verification and checking, input data may still be incorrect. We cannot possibly eliminate all errors. A more realistic objective is to minimize errors and to provide for easy correction when errors do slip through. By coincidence, there may even be offsetting errors in a dual-entry system, but the probability of such occurrence is extremely low.

Environment-Related Errors

Occasionally there are errors that can be attributed to the environment. That is, they have their causes outside the program itself. For example, the operating system may have undergone a revision that is not compatible with the assumptions of the program about file handling. The human operator may be the cause of error; there may be a hardware malfunction; or a system software error can occur. There are many cases of programmers spending days puzzling over a bug, only to find out its removal was not within their control.

Environment-related errors often are temporary. Now and then a program does not run correctly on a given execution and yet, if resubmitted without any change in program or data, it runs just fine. It could be operator action, system error, or a rare combination of factors that was the cause. Our curiosity may be unsatisfied, but occasionally we have to accept the fact that trying to identify the cause of a temporary error may be futile. Fortunately, such error situations are rare.

Review

1   The content of flag-type field can be initialized in the DATA DIVISION by using a(n) _____ clause or it can be initialized in the PROCEDURE DIVISION by using a(n) _____ instruction.

VALUE;MOVE-literal

2   Because by their very nature, flag-type fields are changed and then reset in value during program execution, it is best to initialize such fields in the [DATA DIVISION/PROCEDURE DIVISION].

PROCEDURE DIVISION

3   In order to avoid the inadvertent input of nonnumeric data into a numeric field, such a test procedure as IF NOT NUMERIC . . . , which is a(n) _____ test, should be employed.

class condition

4   A common programming error is that of misplacing the period with respect to the conditional _____ statement.

IF

5   Anything written in columns 73–80 of the COBOL Coding Form, including a period in column 73, is treated as a(n) _____ by the compiler.

comment

6   The possibility of a subscript being out of range of a defined table can be detected by checking for invalid subscript values through the use of conditional _____ statements.

IF

7   Improper nesting of PERFORM statements is associated with faulty program [coding/logic].

logic

8   The error of processing the last input record twice typically is associated with the use of the PERFORM . . . _____ command.

UNTIL

9   When the program logic has been thoroughly reviewed and appears correct and environment-related errors are not a factor, likely sources of errors are the format specifications for the _____ and the actual _____ itself.

data; input data

10   Examples of environment-related errors are those associated with the computer operator, _____ malfunction, or system _____ error.

hardware; software

COBOL DEBUGGING FEATURE

The "debugging" feature enables the programmer to access pertinent information that may be useful in debugging and program testing. This feature has been placed in the "obsolete" category in the 1985 standard. Obsolete features continue to be available but are planned to be deleted from the language in the next revision of the COBOL standard when such revision occurs. Because it is still available, an overview of the COBOL debugging feature is presented in this section. It includes the following parts: a DECLARATIVES portion in the PROCEDURE DIVISION, debug lines in the ENVIRONMENT, DATA, and PROCEDURE DIVISIONs, and compile-time and object-time switches for selective control over the debugging feature.

DECLARATIVES Procedures

In the PROCEDURE DIVISION we may have a DECLARATIVES portion which specifies executable procedures and the conditions under which these procedures are to be executed. The programmer can write debugging-oriented procedures and specify that they are such by the special statement USE FOR DEBUGGING ON. ... The procedures so specified are executed based on the condition designated by the ON conditional expression in the USE statement. The format of the USE FOR DEBUGGING statement is presented in Figure 18–4. As indicated in the figure, we can specify that monitoring be performed on one or more identifiers, files, or procedures, or that it be performed with respect to all of the procedures.

The debugging feature works as follows. Suppose we have written

```
TRACE-BAL SECTION.
    USE FOR DEBUGGING ON BAL-FIELD.
LIST-BALANCE.
    MOVE DEBUG-ITEM TO PRINT-REC
    WRITE PRINT-REC AFTER ADVANCING 2 LINES.
```

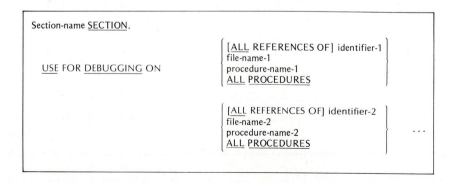

FIGURE 18–4   **FORMAT OF USE FOR DEBUGGING STATEMENT.**

In this example BAL-FIELD is an identifier. Every time that a program statement that makes explicit reference to BAL-FIELD is executed the system stores information about the statement and the contents of the identifier in DEBUG-ITEM. In the example above we chose to write this information on PRINT-REC, presumably for visual examination. During compilation the processor inserts instructions to store the information in the predefined record DEBUG-ITEM (explained below). If, for instance, there is a statement ADD X TO BAL-FIELD, DEBUG-ITEM will receive the contents of BAL-FIELD after this statement is executed and then control passes to the LIST-BALANCE paragraph. In concept, the compilation result is as follows:

ADD X TO BAL-FIELD.
Store the following information in DEBUG-ITEM:
    The line number identifying the (ADD) statement
    The name 'BAL-FIELD'
    The content of BAL-FIELD.
PERFORM LIST-BALANCE.

Essentially, the debugging feature makes information available in the DEBUG-ITEM and transfers control to a procedure in the DECLARATIVES portion of the program. What is done with that information is strictly dependent on what the DECLARATIVES procedures specify. Usually, however, it will be the printing of some data or some checking to determine if certain conditions have arisen.

The DEBUG-ITEM is defined by the compiler; therefore, it must not be defined by the programmer. Its definition is not listed as part of the program, but it is understood to be as presented in Figure 18–5. The meaning of each field is:

DEBUG-LINE: Contains source program line number identifying the line that resulted in execution of the debugging procedure.

DEBUG-NAME: Contains the identifier, file, or procedure-name involved.

DEBUG-SUB-1, DEBUG-SUB-2, DEBUG-SUB-3: If the item in DEBUG-NAME is a subscripted (or indexed) item, then the values of the subscripts (or indexes) are contained in these fields.

DEBUG-CONTENTS: In the case of an identifier, this field contains the value of the identifier. In the case of an input file, this field contains the record that was read. In the case of a procedure there may be spaces or a message in some special cases. These special cases are self-explanatory as part of the output but they are difficult to describe here briefly. As one example, if program control transfers implicitly

```
01 DEBUG-ITEM.
    02 DEBUG-LINE          PIC X(6).
    02 FILLER              PIC X      VALUE SPACE.
    02 DEBUG-NAME          PIC X(30).
    02 FILLER              PIC X      VALUE SPACE.
    02 DEBUG-SUB-1         PIC S9999 SIGN IS LEADING SEPARATE
                                     CHARACTER
    02 FILLER              PIC X      VALUE SPACE.
    02 DEBUG-SUB-2         PIC S9999 SIGN IS LEADING SEPARATE
                                     CHARACTER
    02 FILLER              PIC X      VALUE SPACE.
    02 DEBUG-SUB-3         PIC S9999 SIGN IS LEADING SEPARATE
                                     CHARACTER
    02 FILLER              PIC X      VALUE SPACE.
    02 DEBUG-CONTENTS      PIC X(n).
```

FIGURE 18-5   FORMAT OF DEBUG-ITEM.

from the end of one paragraph to the next paragraph, the message
FALL THROUGH is contained in DEBUG-CONTENTS to explain how
we got to the new procedure-name. The DEBUG-CONTENTS field is
as long as needed for the longest item being monitored.

Figure 18–6 presents some sample entries involving the debugging
feature. The first DECLARATIVES section, TRACE-PARAG SECTION, specifies
USE FOR DEBUGGING ON ALL PROCEDURES. Therefore, every time a pro-
cedure (paragraph or section) is entered in the program, the TRACE-PARAG
SECTION will be executed. For illustration, we defined in the DATA DIVI-
SION a DEB-REC record to which we transfer the procedure name (MOVE
DEBUG-NAME TO PROC-NAME) and then print that record in the PRINT-
PROC-NAME paragraph.

In the second section, TRACE-SUBSCRIPT SECTION, we specify monitoring of TABLE-A. In the case of TABLE-A we assume that I is a subscript
used to make references to TABLE-A. In CHECK-VALID-SUBS we check to
see if this subscript is within the valid range of subscripts (assumed to be
1–20), and if not, we print the content of DEBUG-ITEM as well as a message.

In the last sample section, we specify monitoring of AMOUNT-X and
SALES-FILE, and we simply choose to print the DEBUG-ITEM content in
either case.

Debugging Lines

As an alternative to using DECLARATIVES, the program can include so-
called debugging lines in the ENVIRONMENT, DATA, and PROCEDURE DI-
VISIONs. Such lines have a D in column 7 of the COBOL Coding Form and
thereby are recognized to be included for the purpose of debugging. What
the D does is to allow selective control over their execution. As we shall see,

```
          ⋮
01 DEB-REC.
    02 FILLER        PIC X(17) VALUE 'PROCEDURE = '.
    02 PROC-NAME PIC X(30).
          ⋮

PROCEDURE DIVISION.
DECLARATIVES.
TRACE-PARAG SECTION.
    USE FOR DEBUGGING ON ALL PROCEDURES.
PRINT-PROG-NAME.
    MOVE DEBUG-NAME TO PROC-NAME
    WRITE PRINT-REC FROM DEB-REC AFTER 2 LINES.
TRACE-SUBSCRIPT SECTION.
    USE FOR DEBUGGING ON ALL REFERENCES OF TABLE-A.
CHECK-VALID-SUBS.
    IF I < 1 OR I > 20
        MOVE 'SUBSCRIPT OUT OF RANGE' TO PRINT-REC
        WRITE PRINT-REC AFTER 2 LINES
        MOVE DEBUG-ITEM TO PRINT-REC
        WRITE PRINT-REC AFTER 1 LINE.
OTHER-EXAMPLES SECTION.
    USE FOR DEBUGGING ON ALL REFERENCES OF AMOUNT-X SALES-FILE.
PRINT-DATA.
    MOVE DEBUG-ITEM TO PRINT-REC
    WRITE PRINT-REC AFTER 1 LINE.
END DECLARATIVES.
FIRST-PROC-PARAG. etc. . . .
```

FIGURE 18–6   SAMPLE DEBUGGING FEATURE STATEMENTS.

such statements can be included or excluded from the compilation depending on the condition of the compile-time switch (to be explained below). Other than the fact that the D serves to so identify and control these statements, they are exactly like any other program statements.

As an example, suppose we have:

```
SAMPLE-PARAG.
        READ SALES-FILE AT END MOVE 'YES' TO END-OF-FILE.
D       IF END-OF-FILE NOT = 'YES'
D           AND SALES-AMT IS NEGATIVE
D           DISPLAY 'CONTENTS OF SALES RECORD ARE AS FOLLOWS'
D           DISPLAY SALES-REC.
```

The D characters in column 7 indicate that these lines will only be compiled if the compile-time debugging switch is on; otherwise they are treated as comments.

Thus, debugging lines are an alternate form of monitoring program execution. They serve a role similar to the statements in the DECLARATIVES, but there are differences. Some things are much easier to do via DECLARATIVES. For instance if we have 50 paragraphs in the program, the one clause ALL PROCEDURES can monitor all 50 paragraphs. On the other hand 50 D-type lines would be needed for monitoring the 50 paragraphs. Further, once D-type lines have been compiled they are part of the program during object-time execution. DECLARATIVES portions, however, can be selectively activated or inhibited before each execution of the program by using an object-time switch (explained below).

However, debug lines in the program also have some advantages. Such lines can be inserted in the ENVIRONMENT and DATA DIVISION, as well as the PROCEDURE DIVISION, thus providing a function that cannot be duplicated by DECLARATIVES. For instance, a debug-line data description in the DATA DIVISION can define data fields used for debugging only. As another advantage, by being written as part of the executable portion of the PROCEDURE DIVISION debug lines are more self-documenting. In reading such a program, it is easier to observe the role of debugging statements because they are part of the executable program. On the other hand, DECLARATIVES are only implicitly related to the executable procedures.

Compile-Time Switch

A compile switch provides control as to whether to compile debugging statements included in the program. Control is exercised by including/excluding the WITH DEBUGGING MODE clause in the SOURCE-COMPUTER paragraph:

SOURCE-COMPUTER.   ABC-480 WITH DEBUGGING MODE.

Inclusion of the clause results in compilation of debugging statements, while exclusion treats all such statements as comments. This applies both to debug lines and DECLARATIVES.

This compile-time control facilitates selective activation of debugging-oriented statements. In the course of testing a program if we wish to deactivate and then reactivate debugging statements, rather than "erase" such statements and then reinsert them every time, we simply change the SOURCE-COMPUTER statement. Further, once the program testing has been completed, the debugging statements may be left in the source program for possible future use with respect to program revision.

Object-Time Switch

The object-time switch feature enables dynamic control of debugging execution. This "switch" is set "on" or "off" by job control statements specific to each system. When the switch is on, then all debugging statements that have been compiled as a result of the WITH DEBUGGING MODE switch can execute. When the switch is off, then all DECLARATIVES-type debugging statements are suppressed. However, any debugging lines are executed, since they cannot be inhibited at object execution. If it is desired to exercise control over the execution of a debugging procedure, then the procedure should be included in the DECLARATIVES portion of the PROCEDURE DIVISION.

Review

1   The programmer can write debugging-oriented procedures and define the conditional execution of such statements in the _____ portion of the PROCEDURE DIVISION.

DECLARATIVES

2   Debugging-oriented procedures are identified in the DECLARATIVES portion of the PROCEDURE DIVISION by the special statement USE

_____.

FOR DEBUGGING

3   When the USE FOR DEBUGGING statement is used, monitoring can be performed with respect to [one/one or more] identifier(s), [one/one or more] file(s), and [one/one or more] procedure(s).

one or more; one or more; one or more

4   As an alternative to using DECLARATIVES, the programmer can include so-called _____ lines in the ENVIRONMENT, DATA, and PROCEDURE DIVISIONs.

debugging

5   Debugging lines are so identified by entry of the letter _____ in column 7 of the COBOL Coding Form.

D

6   Statements included in debugging lines are included or excluded

from compilation depending on the condition of the _____ switch.

compile-time

7 Brevity of required statements for debugging generally is achieved by use of [DECLARATIVES/debugging lines].

DECLARATIVES

8 Self-documentation of the debugging operations is enhanced by the use of [DECLARATIVES/debugging lines].

debugging lines

9 The clause in the SOURCE-COMPUTER paragraph that serves as the compile-time switch and thus provides control as to whether statements in debugging lines are compiled or are treated as comments is the _____ clause.

WITH DEBUGGING MODE

10 The switch that allows selective execution of the debugging procedures included in the DECLARATIVES portion of the PROCEDURE DIVISION is the _____ switch.

object-time

Exercises

18.1 Describe the top-down and bottom-up approaches to program testing.

18.2 In your own words, explain why extensive testing is not a sufficient substitute for good program design.

18.3 Apply the top-down testing approach using paragraph stubs with respect to a COBOL program that you have already written.

18.4 Incorporate the COBOL debugging feature into a program that you have already written.

A

Elements of COBOL: A Review

INTRODUCTION

The purpose of this appendix is to provide a brief review of the fundamentals of COBOL. It is intended for readers who have developed a basic command of the language in the past but need a refresher. Particular emphasis is placed upon reviewing the basic structure and rules of the language, rather than being concerned with numerous format specifications.

OVERALL STRUCTURE OF COBOL PROGRAMS

COBOL programs are written according to a special structure that is organized into a hierarchy of parts. In terms of an overall outline, the structure of this hierarchy is described as follows. Much of this text is concerned with developing the detail associated with this structure.

A *character* is the lowest form in the program structure.

A *word* is made up of one or more characters.

A *clause* consists of characters and words and is used to specify an attribute of an entry.

A *statement* is a syntactically valid combination of words and characters written in the PROCEDURE DIVISION of a COBOL program and beginning with a verb.

A *sentence* is a sequence of one or more statements, the last of which is terminated by a period followed by a space.

A *paragraph* consists of one or more sentences.

A *section* consists of one or more paragraphs.

A *division* consists of one or more paragraphs or sections. Every COBOL program consists of four divisions in the following order: IDENTIFICATION DIVISION, ENVIRONMENT DIVISION, DATA DIVISION, and PROCEDURE DIVISION.

COBOL CHARACTERS AND WORDS

The most basic and indivisible unit of the COBOL language is the *character*. The set of characters used to form COBOL source programs consists of the 51 characters identified in Figure A–1.

A sequence of characters can form a *word*. There are two types of COBOL words: *reserved words* and *user-defined words*. Reserved words are

Character	Meaning
0, 1, . . . , 9	digit
A, B, . . . , Z	uppercase letter
a, b, . . . , z	lowercase letter
	space
+	plus sign
−	minus sign (hyphen)
*	asterisk
/	slant (solidus)
=	equal sign
$	currency sign (represented as ¤ in the International Reference Version of International Standard ISO 646-1973)
,	comma (decimal point)
;	semicolon
.	period (decimal point, full stop)
"	quotation mark
(	left parenthesis
)	right parenthesis
>	greater than symbol
<	less than symbol
:	colon

FIGURE A–1   THE SET OF CHARACTERS IN COBOL PROGRAMMING.

defined by the COBOL language. (Appendix B presents a complete list of COBOL reserved words.) The programmer cannot use any of these words except in the form specified by the language. Much of this text is devoted to explaining the use of such reserved words.

User-defined words are supplied by the programmer (language user) in order to satisfy the format of a clause or statement in the language. A user-defined word may be 1 to 30 characters in length and may consist of letters, digits, and hyphens, except that a hyphen may not appear as the first or last character.

There are 17 types of user-defined words, examples of which are: condition-name, data-name, paragraph-name, record-name, and file-name. The reader will be exposed to different types of user-defined words as the text progresses. Special attention is given to data-names in the section that follows because data-names are used so frequently.

DATA-NAMES

Data-names are coined at the discretion of the programmer, except that there are certain rules that must be followed.

1   A data-name can be made up to 30 characters in length and can include alphabetic characters, numeric characters, and hyphens.

2   At least one character must be alphabetic.

3   The only special symbol permitted is the hyphen. A hyphen must always be embedded; that is, it cannot be the first or last character of the data-name.

4   Blanks cannot be included in the data-names.

5   Within the above rules the programmer may use any data-name, with the exception of the approximately 300 COBOL reserved words listed in Appendix B. (Language implementors often add some of their own words to the ANSI list.)

Some examples of legitimate data-names are:

HOURS	PREMIUM
ENDING-INVENTORY	A527157
SALES-TAX-TOTAL	31576X5

Of course, data-names do not have to be meaningful English words. A programmer can choose to use such data names as X, Y, Z, X1, X2, and the like. However, COBOL was designed specifically to allow self-documentation, which means that by reading the program one should be able to understand what the program does and what data it uses. The problem with using cryptic data-names is that their meanings are forgotten by the programmer and are never understood by others unless a list of definitions is supplied.

CONSTANTS

In addition to data-names, COBOL uses constants of three types: numeric literals, figurative constants, and nonnumeric literals.

Numeric literals without a decimal point are understood to be integers (whole numbers). If a decimal point is used, it must not be the last character. Thus, 35. is not correct, whereas 35.0 is acceptable. The reason for this rule is that in COBOL programming, the period is always used to signal the end of a sentence, just as in English, and it would be ambiguous whether a point following a number is a decimal point or a period.

The second type of constant used in COBOL is the *figurative constant*. The most common figurative constants are ZERO, ZEROS, ZEROES, SPACE, and SPACES, although a few others are available. These refer to zeros

IF LAST-NAME EQUAL 'BROWN' (etc.)

ZERO
ZEROS
ZEROES

All three forms are equivalent, and they reference the value of zero. In an instruction such as MOVE ZEROS TO AMOUNT, the storage field AMOUNT would be filled by as many zeroes as there are positions in that field. Thus the context determines the number of occurrences of the character 0.

SPACE
SPACES

Both forms are equivalent, and they reference one or more blanks, similar to the ZERO constant.

QUOTE
QUOTES

Both forms are equivalent, and they reference the quotation mark.

HIGH-VALUE
HIGH-VALUES

Both forms are equivalent, and they reference the highest value in the collating sequence for the particular computer system.

LOW-VALUE
LOW-VALUES

Both forms are equivalent, and they reference the lowest value in the collating sequence for the particular computer system.

ALL literal

References one or more occurrences of the single character nonnumeric literal, as in MOVE ALL "A" TO HEADER, which results in the storage field HEADER being filled with A's.

FIGURE A–2   FIGURATIVE CONSTANTS AND THEIR MEANINGS.

or blanks, respectively. Their general use can be illustrated by the following brief examples. Suppose we want to set AMOUNT equal to zero. We can write MOVE ZERO TO AMOUNT to accomplish this objective. Similarly, if we wish to ascertain that blanks are contained in the field called TITLE, we can write MOVE SPACES TO TITLE. Figure A–2 lists and defines the standard figurative constants used in COBOL programs.

In addition to numeric literals and figurative constants, the third class of constants is the *nonnumeric literal*. As contrasted to numeric literals and figurative constants, the nonnumeric literal is any alphanumeric value enclosed in quotation marks. For example, suppose we want to print the title INCOME STATEMENT. The words INCOME and STATEMENT are not intended to refer to data-names; rather, we simply want these exact words printed. This can be done by enclosing them in quotation marks.

As an example of how a nonnumeric literal might be used in a decision context, suppose we want to know if a customer's last name is BROWN. We could write something like this:

Any letter, number, or special symbol can be enclosed in quotation marks with the exception of a quotation mark itself. If we want to use quotation marks as part of the literal, we can accomplish this by use of the QUOTE figurative constant as follows:

QUOTE 'TOTAL AMOUNT' QUOTE

In this example the word QUOTE indicates a quotation mark. The use of the figurative constant QUOTE before and after the nonnumeric literal will result in quotation marks being printed. The quotation marks are printed as single or double marks, depending on the specific printer used.

Unlike a data-name, a nonnumeric literal can include blanks. The nonnumeric literal also can be composed entirely of numeric characters. This may seem like a contradiction, but it is not, since the term "nonnumeric" refers to how the characters are handled within the computer and not to their alphanumeric form as such.

STATEMENTS AND SENTENCES

Thus far we have given particular attention to types of COBOL characters and words and to the use of these words in designating variables and constants. We now turn our attention to the statements and sentences that constitute any series of program instructions. Similar to the English language, the general distinction between a statement and a sentence is that a statement may be part of a sentence, whereas a sentence is always signaled by a period and space. However, there are particular differences according to the types of statements and sentences.

The three types of statements and sentences are the imperative, conditional, and compiler-directing. An *imperative statement* indicates a specific unconditional action to be taken by the object program. Such a statement may also include a sequence of imperative statements. Examples of COBOL verbs used in imperative statements are READ, ADD, MOVE, GO, WRITE, and STOP. An *imperative sentence* is one or more imperative statements terminated by a period followed by a space.

A *conditional statement*, which is the second type of statement, specifies that the truth value of a condition is to be determined and that the subsequent action of the object program is dependent on this truth value. The COBOL verb frequently used in conditional statements is the IF. Incidentally, although IF is not a verb in English, it is a verb in the COBOL sense that determining a truth value is a form of action. A number of other verbs that by themselves are imperative become conditional verbs when used with particular options. For instance, the READ verb by itself is an imperative verb, but the READ ... AT END is a conditional verb. With the use of the option, subsequent action is dependent on the truth value of the AT END condition. A *conditional sentence* is a conditional statement that may be preceded by an imperative statement and which is terminated by a period followed by a space.

A *compiler-directing statement* consists of a compiler-directing verb and its operands, and execution of such a statement causes the compiler to take a specific action during compilation. The compiler-directing verbs are COPY, REPLACE, ENTER, and USE. A *compiler-directing sentence* is a single compiler-directing statement terminated by a period followed by a space. Thus, a compiler-directing sentence can include only one compiler-directing statement and no imperative or conditional statements.

COBOL FORMAT SPECIFICATIONS

The COBOL formats in Appendix C and referenced throughout this book serve to describe how each type of instruction should be structured and to identify the options available for each type of program instruction. The following set of conventions is followed in these format specifications for statements and sentences:

1   Words presented in uppercase are always *reserved words*.

2   Uppercase words which are underlined are the *key words* that are required in the type of program statement being described. Uppercase words that are not underlined are *optional words* and are used only to improve the readability of the program.

3   Lowercase words are used to indicate the points at which data-names or constants are to be supplied by the programmer. In addition to the words "data-name" and "literal," the term "identifier" is used to indicate a data-name, but it has a slightly broader meaning. It refers to either of the following cases: data-names that are unique in themselves, or data-names that are not unique in themselves but are made unique through qualification. Other lowercase words used to indicate items to be inserted by the programmer are:

file-name

record-name

integer

formula

condition

statement

any imperative statement

any sentence

4   Items enclosed in braces { } indicate that one of the enclosed items *must* be used.

5   Items enclosed in brackets [ ] indicate that the items are optional, and *may* be used at the option of the programmer.

6   An ellipsis (. . .) indicates that further information may be included in the program instruction, usually in the form of repeating the immediately preceding element any desired number of times.

   As an example, consider the format for a basic form of the ADD instruction:

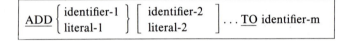

   If we apply the rules presented above, the word ADD is a reserved word because it is in uppercase, and it is required because it is underscored. The word TO is governed by the same rules. The braces following ADD indicate that one of the two alternatives enclosed *must* be used. Thus the required word ADD must be followed by either an identifier or a literal. The square brackets indicate that identifier-2 and literal-2 are both optional. In other words, the identifier or literal that immediately follows ADD may or may not be followed by a second identifier or literal. The ellipsis (. . .) indicates that the preceding element (in square brackets) may be repeated as many times as desired. Finally, the identifier-m indicates that there must be an identifier following the word TO. Note that the TO is not enclosed in braces, because it is the only option. Braces are used only when there is a choice between or among alternatives.
   Utilizing the general format above, we see that the following examples are legitimate ADD statements.

ADD AMOUNT TO TOTAL
ADD 100 TO TOTAL
ADD REGULAR OVERTIME TO GROSS
ADD 10 BONUS 100.25 TO GROSS

SOURCE TEXT MANIPULATION: THE COPY AND REPLACE VERBS

COBOL provides for the *insertion* and *replacement* of source code during the compilation process. The capability to do *source text manipulation* enables the programmer to do one or both of the following operations:

1   Copy prewritten portions of program code, such as record descriptions for files or report formats and "standard" paragraphs for tasks common to several programs, into the source program.

2   Replace existing source text with specified substitutes, such as replacing an abbreviation by a fully-spelled COBOL reserved word or renaming existing data-names to more meaningful new versions.

The capability to do source manipulation is provided in COBOL by the two specialized verbs, COPY and REPLACE. Figure A–3 presents the general format for the COPY statement. COPY is used in conjunction with a "library" facility, which is a file consisting of COBOL source program elements. Such a library contains COBOL elements that can be referenced by a *text-name*. It is also possible to have several such libraries, in which case the OF or IN library-name-1 qualifier in Figure A–3 is used. A well-planned and maintained library can reduce the time needed to write routines common to several programs, and it can serve to standardize such common routines.

For example, suppose that we have stored the following record description in a source library under the text-name CUST-REC:

```
02   CUST-NO       PIC 9(5).
02   CUST-NAME     PIC X(20).
```

Then in a program we could write as follows on the next page:

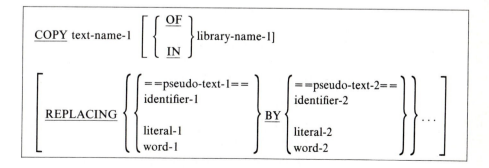

FIGURE A–3   GENERAL FORMAT FOR THE COPY VERB.

01   CUSTOMER-RECORD.   COPY CUST-REC.

As a result, the program would be compiled as if we had written:

```
01   CUSTOMER-RECORD.
     02   CUST-NO        PIC 9(5).
     02   CUST-NAME      PIC X(20).
```

The COPY facility not only saves time for the programmer, but even more importantly, it serves to reduce errors from inconsistent descriptions of the same file data. Commonly, the same file will be used by several programs. In such a case it is very productive to have the description of the file stored in a text library and then all the programs using that file would copy exactly the same descriptions.

The COPY can be used throughout the COBOL program. For instance, assuming that text-1 refers to specific stored program elements we could write:

```
SOURCE-COMPUTER. COPY text-1.
OBJECT-COMPUTER. COPY text-2.
     SELECT file-name COPY text-3.
FD file-name COPY text-4.
01      record-name. COPY text-5.
Section-name SECTION. COPY text-6.
Paragraph-name. COPY text-7.
```

In this fashion we need not rewrite corresponding portions of the programs that were prewritten.

Notice that it is also possible to COPY portions of the PROCEDURE DIVISION. This is not a common practice, but it can be very useful if we have one or more paragraphs or sections that can be used in more than one program.

It is also possible to use the REPLACING option with the copy verb, thereby modifying the copied items. For instance suppose that under the text-name F-REC we had stored the following:

```
02   A   PIC X.
02   B   PIC 99V99.
02   C   PIC X(10).
```

In a program we could write:

```
01      PROD-REC.
           COPY F-REC REPLACING A BY C-CODE
                                 B BY PRICE
                                 C BY NAME.
```

Then the compiler would generate:

```
01   PROD-REC.
       02   C-CODE      PIC X.
       02   PRICE       PIC 99V99.
       02   NAME        PIC X(10).
```

In a similar fashion, if we copy a PROCEDURE DIVISION paragraph which is identical in logic to one that is required in a program but which was written using different data-names, we could specify COPY ... REPLACING to change the data-names involved into the desired names.

The ==pseudo-text== designation provides the means for replacing a *series* of words, characters, and similar "pseudo-text" as contrasted to re-placing an individual identifier, literal, or word. The double equal sign is used as a *delimiter* to mark clearly the beginning and the end of the pseudo-text. Consider the following example of the use of the pseudo-text replacement feature:

```
COPY CUST-REC
     REPLACING ==02 FILLER PIC==
         BY ==02 PIC==.
```

The program segment above could be used to eliminate the word FILLER in CUST-REC by executing the indicated substitution. Two of the rules associated with this capability is that pseudo-text-1 must be in the range of 1 to 322 characters and that pseudo-text-2 may be empty. The latter designation makes it possible to eliminate specified text in the source code, as illustrated by the following:

```
COPY PROC-A
     REPLACING ==MOVE ZERO TO SUB-TOTAL==
            BY ====.
```

Setting up text-names and their content is specific to each computer site. Generally we set up a "library" containing "members" or "elements" that comprise the accessible text. Then, when a program is to be compiled, we submit job control statements to make the library available, so that copy operations can be carried out as parts of the compilation process.

The REPLACE statement provides the capability for text replacement independent of using the COPY verb. There are two formats available for the REPLACE statement, as presented in Figure A–4.

Format 1 works just like the REPLACING option of the COPY verb, as previously discussed, with the difference being that it applies to the entire source program, not just to the COPY text-name portion. For instance, suppose certain abbreviations that were used in writing a source program now need to be replaced throughout the program code. The following program segment serves as such an example:

```
REPLACE  ==#==  BY ==                    02  FILLER  PIC==
         ==/==  BY ==MOVE==
         ==CN== BY ==CUSTOMER-NAME==
```

Consideration of the above example illustrates that the REPLACE statement achieves the same result as any general-purpose text editor, and thus the first available format does not offer much that is new.

Format 2 of the REPLACE verb, which is REPLACE OFF, is used to deactivate a previously specified REPLACE operation. Thus, we can specify a REPLACE operation on, say, line 30 of the source code and then write RE-PLACE OFF on, say, line 100. The result is that the effect of the REPLACE is delimited to lines 31 through 99.

If both the COPY and the REPLACE verbs are used in the same program, all of the COPY verbs are executed first, before execution of the RE-PLACE verbs. Thus, the REPLACE verb could be applied to copied portions of a source program.

SUMMARY OF COMMON COBOL STATEMENTS

We now present a brief summary of some of the most common statements in the language. Figure A–5 is referenced throughout this presentation to exemplify the statements used.

Format 1

REPLACE [==pseudo-text-1== BY ==pseudo-text-2]...

Format 2

REPLACE OFF

FIGURE A-4   GENERAL FORMATS FOR THE REPLACE VERB.

```
 1.    IDENTIFICATION DIVISION.
 2.    PROGRAM-ID. SALESREPORT.
 3.    *
 4.    ENVIRONMENT DIVISION.
 5.    *
 6.    CONFIGURATION SECTION.
 7.    SOURCE-COMPUTER. ABC-480.
 8.    OBJECT-COMPUTER. ABC-480.
 9.    *
10.    INPUT-OUTPUT SECTION.
11.    *
12.    FILE-CONTROL.
13.       SELECT SALES-FILE ASSIGN TO CARD-READER.
14.       SELECT REPORT-FILE ASSIGN TO PRINTER.
15.    /
16.    DATA DIVISION.
17.    *
18.    FILE SECTION.
19.    *
20.    FD   SALES-FILE
21.         LABEL RECORDS ARE OMITTED
22.         DATA RECORD IS SALES-RECORD.
23.    01   SALES-RECORD.
24.         02 PRODUCT-NO                PIC 999.
25.         02 SALES-AMOUNT              PIC 9(4)V99.
26.         02 FILLER                    PIC X(71).
27.    *
28.    FD   REPORT-FILE
29.         LABEL RECORDS ARE OMITTED
30.         DATA RECORD IS REPORT-RECORD.
31.    01   REPORT-RECORD               PIC X(132).
32.    *
33.      WORKING-STORAGE SECTION.
34.    *
35.    01   END-OF-FILE-INDICATOR       PIC XXX VALUE 'NO'.
36.         88 END-OF-FILE VALUE 'YES'.
37.         88 NOT-END-OF-FILE VALUE 'NO'.
38.    *
39.    01   PREVIOUS-PRODUCT-NO         PIC 999.
40.    *
41.    01   PRODUCT-TOTAL               PIC 9(5)V99.
42.    *
43.    01   PAGE-SIZE                   PIC 99 VALUE 25.
44.    *
45.    01   PAGE-LINE-COUNTER           PIC 99 VALUE 25.
46.    *
```

FIGURE A–5   SAMPLE COBOL PROGRAM.

```
47.   *   BY INITIALIZING PAGE-LINE-COUNTER TO 25-PAGE-SIZE, WE
48.   *   WILL GET THE PAGE HEADING PRINTED PRIOR TO THE FIRST
49.   *   LINE OF OUTPUT.
50.   *
51.   *
52.   01   REPORT-HEADING.
53.        02 FILLER                    PIC X(10) VALUE SPACES.
54.        02 FILLER                    PIC X(11) VALUE 'PRODUCT NO.'.
55.        02 FILLER                    PIC X(3) VALUE SPACES.
56.        02 FILLER                    PIC X (12) VALUE 'SALES AMOUNT'.
57.        02 FILLER                    PIC X(4) VALUE SPACES.
58.        02 FILLER                    PIC X(11) VALUE 'TOTAL SALES'.
59.   *
60.   01   REPORT-LINE.
61.        02 FILLER                    PIC X(14) VALUE SPACES.
62.        02 PRODUCT-NO-OUT            PIC 999.
63.        02 FILLER                    PIC X(9) VALUE SPACES.
64.        02 SALES-AMOUNT-OUT          PIC Z,ZZ9.99.
65.        02 FILLER                    PIC X(7) VALUE SPACES.
66.        02 TOTAL-SALES-OUT           PIC $$$,$$9.99.
67.   /
68.     PROCEDURE DIVISION.
69.   *
70.     PROGRAM-SUMMARY.
71.   *
72.        OPEN INPUT SALES-FILE
73.            OUTPUT REPORT-FILE.
74.   *
75.        PERFORM PROCESS-FIRST-RECORD
76.   *
77.        PERFORM PROCESS-RECORD
78.            UNTIL END-OF-FILE
79.   *
80.        PERFORM PRINT-LAST-TOTAL
81.   *
82.        CLOSE SALES-FILE
83.            REPORT-FILE
84.   *
85.        STOP RUN.
86.   /
```

FIGURE A–5   SAMPLE COBOL PROGRAM.   **(Continued)**

```
 87.    PROCESS-FIRST-RECORD.
 88.       PERFORM READ-RECORD.
 89.       IF NOT-END-OF-FILE
 90.          MOVE PRODUCT-NO TO PREVIOUS-PRODUCT-NO
 91.          MOVE SALES-AMOUNT TO PRODUCT-TOTAL.
 92.       PERFORM PRINT-NEW-PRODUCT-LINE
 93.       PERFORM READ-RECORD.
 94.    *
 95.    READ-RECORD.
 96.       READ SALES-FILE
 97.          AT END MOVE 'YES' TO END-OF-FILE-INDICATOR.
 98.    *
 99.    PRINT-NEW-PRODUCT-LINE.
100.       MOVE SPACES TO REPORT-LINE
101.       MOVE PRODUCT-NO TO PRODUCT-NO-OUT
102.       MOVE SALES-AMOUNT TO SALES-AMOUNT-OUT
103.       PERFORM PRINT-LINE.
104.    *
105.    PRINT-LINE.
106.       IF PAGE-LINE-COUNTER = PAGE-SIZE
107.          WRITE REPORT-RECORD FROM REPORT-HEADING
108.             AFTER ADVANCING PAGE
109.          MOVE SPACES TO REPORT-RECORD
110.          WRITE REPORT-RECORD AFTER ADVANCING 1 LINE
111.          MOVE 2 TO PAGE-LINE-COUNTER.
112.       WRITE REPORT-RECORD FROM REPORT-LINE
113.          AFTER ADVANCING 1 LINE
114.       ADD 1 TO PAGE-LINE-COUNTER.
115.    /
116.    PROCESS-RECORD.
117.       IF PRODUCT-NO = PREVIOUS-PRODUCT-NO
118.       PERFORM PROCESS-REPORT-LINE
119.       ELSE
120.          PERFORM PROCESS-NEW-PRODUCT.
121.    *
122.       ADD SALES-AMOUNT TO PRODUCT-TOTAL.
123.    *
124.       PERFORM READ-RECORD.
125.    *
126.    PROCESS-REPORT-LINE.
```

FIGURE A–5   SAMPLE COBOL PROGRAM.   **(Continued)**

```
127.        MOVE SPACES TO REPORT-LINE
128.        MOVE SALES-AMOUNT TO SALES-AMOUNT-OUT
129.        PERFORM PRINT-LINE.
130.   *
131.     PROCESS-NEW-PRODUCT.
132.        MOVE SPACES TO REPORT-LINE
133.        MOVE PRODUCT-TOTAL TO TOTAL-SALES-OUT
134.        PERFORM PRINT-LINE
135.   *
136.        MOVE ZERO TO PRODUCT-TOTAL
137.   *
138.        PERFORM PRINT-NEW-PRODUCT-LINE
139.   *
140.        MOVE PRODUCT-NO TO PREVIOUS-PRODUCT-NO.
141.   *
142.     PRINT-LAST-TOTAL.
143.        MOVE SPACES TO REPORT-LINE
144.        MOVE PRODUCT-TOTAL TO TOTAL-SALES-OUT
145.        PERFORM PRINT-LINE.
```

FIGURE A–5   SAMPLE COBOL PROGRAM.   (Continued)

The SELECT Statement

SELECT file-name ASSIGN TO implementor-name

The SELECT statement is used to associate a file-name with a specific INPUT-OUTPUT unit (implementor-name). In Figure A–5, line 14 illustrates that a file named REPORT-FILE has been associated with a device called PRINTER. *Implementor* refers to the author(s) of the COBOL compiler.

Level Numbers

Data can be so described that reference can be made to either elementary or group items. Group items consist of one or more elementary or other group items. A level number precedes each data-name in the DATA DIVISION. The 01-level number is reserved for use with the all-inclusive items. A higher-level number denotes that the associated data-name is part of the preceding group item designated by a lower-level number. For instance, in Figure A–5, line 24, 02 PRODUCT-NO is an elementary item that is part of the 01 SALES-RECORD group item.

PICTURE Clause

Each elementary data item is described by a PICTURE (abbreviated PIC) clause that specifies the size of the item and the data characteristics. For instance, on line 24 of Figure A–5 PRODUCT-NO has PIC 999, denoting a numeric (9) field of 3 digits (three 9s). On the other hand, on line 31, 01 REPORT-RECORD is an elementary field of 132 alphanumeric positions, as denoted by PIC X (132). In the latter example the type of data is X (alphanumeric), where the field size is the number in parentheses.

VALUE Clause

Data items may be initialized to a specific content by means of the VALUE clause as illustrated on line 35, where END-OF-FILE-INDICATOR is initialized to the content 'NO' (VALUE 'NO'). Similarly, on line 43 PAGE-SIZE is initialized to the value 25. Such initialization results in the designated contents for the associated data items at the beginning of program execution.

Condition-Names

A special level number, 88, designates condition-names. On line 36, for example, END-OF-FILE is not a data-name; it is a condition-name of the preceding END-OF-FILE-INDICATOR data item. The VALUE clause in a condition-name does *not* serve to initialize data. Instead, it specifies the value that makes the condition specified by the condition-name to be true. Thus, for the example, on line 36 END-OF-FILE is true when END-OF-FILE-INDICATOR has a value of 'YES.'

The OPEN Verb

$$\underline{OPEN} \left\{ \begin{array}{l} \underline{INPUT} \\ \underline{OUTPUT} \end{array} \right\} \text{file-name-1 [file-name-2]} \ldots$$

In order to use a file, an OPEN statement must be executed. The file is designated as either INPUT (we are going to read data from this file) or as OUTPUT (we are going to write data into the file). Lines 72 and 73 illustrate use of the OPEN verb.

The READ Verb

$$\underline{READ} \text{ file-name RECORD AT } \underline{END} \text{ imperative-statement}$$

Contents of data records can be transferred from an input file into central storage with the READ verb, as illustrated on line 96. The AT END conditional statement specifies the action to be taken when a READ operation results in reading an end-of-file indicator record. Such a record contains a special code that signifies the end of the file.

The WRITE Verb

$$\text{WRITE record-name [\underline{FROM} identifier]} \begin{Bmatrix} \underline{BEFORE} \\ \underline{AFTER} \end{Bmatrix} \text{ADVANCING} \begin{Bmatrix} \text{integer LINES} \\ \underline{PAGE} \end{Bmatrix}$$

Contents of data records can be transferred from central storage to an output file using the WRITE verb. If the output file is associated with the printer, then we can also specify vertical spacing, as on line 110 (AFTER ADVANCING 1 LINE). Data can also be transferred (FROM) into the file record prior to writing. Lines 107–108 illustrate use of the FROM option as well as vertical spacing in the same WRITE statement.

The CLOSE Verb

$$\underline{CLOSE} \text{ file-name-1 [file-name-2] . . .}$$

Files should be CLOSEd when their processing has been completed, as illustrated on lines 82–83.

The MOVE Verb

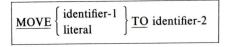

Data can be copied from one data item into another by use of the MOVE verb. Line 90, for example, specifies that the content of PRODUCT-NO be copied into PREVIOUS-PRODUCT-NO. The contents of the "sending" field remain unaffected by execution of the MOVE instruction. The "receiving" field contents depend on its size relative to the sending field. Depending on size and data characteristics, there may be truncation of leading or trailing characters and zero or space filling in the receiving field. As the verb format above indicates, it is possible to MOVE the value of a literal. The literal may be enclosed in quotation marks as on line 97, or it may be a figurative constant, as on lines 109 and 136.

The ADD Verb

> ADD identifier-1 TO identifier-2

Addition can be performed using the ADD verb, as on line 122. In this example, PRODUCT-TOTAL is incremented by the value in SALES-AMOUNT.

The PERFORM Verb

> PERFORM procedure-name [UNTIL condition]

Program execution proceeds line by line except when interrupted by *program control verbs,* such as PERFORM. This verb has the meaning "go to the specified paragraph, execute it, and return after completing the execution." Thus, on line 75 the paragraph named PROCESS-FIRST-RECORD is executed and then the program continues with the next line, 77, which also happens to be a PERFORM statement. The statement on line 77 illustrates conditional execution under PERFORM control. The "UNTIL condition" in the general format specifies that the program will first check to see if the specified condition is true. If it is *not* true, then the designated procedure is PERFORMed. If the condition is true, program execution continues with the next statement following the PERFORM. Thus, lines 77–78 specify the repeated execution (loop) of the PROCESS-RECORD paragraph.

The IF Statement

> IF condition statement-1 [ELSE statement-2]

The specialized conditionals associated with the READ, (AT END . . .) and the PERFORM, (UNTIL . . .) are specific to these verbs. IF is the general conditional statement. On lines 89–93 we specify that if the condition NOT-END-OF-FILE is true, then execute the four statements that follow (until the next period is encountered). Thus, "statement-1" in the format may stand for several individual statements. We may also specify the desired course of action if the condition is not true using the ELSE along with the IF. For example, on lines 117–120 we specify PERFORM PROCESS-REPORT-LINE if the condition PRODUCT-NO = PREVIOUS-PRODUCT-NO is true; ELSE PERFORM PROCESS-NEW-PRODUCT.

The STOP RUN Statement

Program execution is terminated when STOP RUN is encountered, as on line 85. There is, however, no comparable "start run" counterpart. Instead, execution begins with the first (executable) instruction in the PROCEDURE DIVISION.

B

COBOL reserved words

ACCEPT
ACCESS
ADD
ADVANCING
AFTER
ALL
ALPHABET
ALPHABETIC
ALPHABETIC-LOWER
ALPHABETIC-UPPER
ALPHANUMERIC
ALPHANUMERIC-
   EDITED
ALSO
ALTER
ALTERNATE
AND
ANY
ARE
AREA
AREAS
ASCENDING
ASSIGN
AT
AUTHOR

BEFORE
BINARY
BLANK
BLOCK
BOTTOM
BY

CALL
CANCEL
CD
CF
CH
CHARACTER
CHARACTERS
CLASS
CLOCK-UNITS
CLOSE
COBOL
CODE
CODE-SET
COLLATING
COLUMN
COMMA
COMMON
COMMUNICATION

COMP
COMPUTATIONAL
COMPUTE
CONFIGURATION
CONTAINS
CONTENT
CONTINUE
CONTROL
CONTROLS
CONVERTING
COPY
CORR
CORRESPONDING
COUNT
CURRENCY

DATA
DATE
DATE-COMPILED
DATE-WRITTEN
DAY
DAY-OF-WEEK
DE
DEBUG-CONTENTS
DEBUG-ITEM

DEBUG-LINE
DEBUG-NAME
DEBUG-SUB-1
DEBUG-SUB-2
DEBUG-SUB-3
DEBUGGING
DECIMAL-POINT
DECLARATIVES
DELETE
DELIMITED
DELIMITER
DEPENDING
DESCENDING
DESTINATION
DETAIL
DISABLE
DISPLAY
DIVIDE
DIVISION
DOWN
DUPLICATES
DYNAMIC

EGI
ELSE
EMI
ENABLE
END
END-ADD
END-CALL
END-COMPLETE
END-DELETE
END-DIVIDE
END-EVALUATE
END-IF
END-MULTIPLY
END-OF-PAGE
END-PERFORM
END-READ
END-RECEIVE
END-RETURN
END-REWRITE
END-SEARCH
END-START
END-STRING
END-SUBTRACT
END-UNSTRING

END-WRITE
ENTER
ENVIRONMENT
EOP
EQUAL
ERROR
ESI
EVALUATE
EVERY
EXCEPTION
EXIT
EXTEND
EXTERNAL

FALSE
FD
FILE
FILE-CONTROL
FILLER
FINAL
FIRST
FOOTING
FOR
FROM

GENERATE
GIVING
GLOBAL
GO
GREATER
GROUP

HEADING
HIGH-VALUE
HIGH-VALUES

I-O
I-O-CONTROL
IDENTIFICATION
IF
IN
INDEX
INDEXED
INDICATE
INITIAL
INITIALIZE
INITIATE

INPUT
INPUT-OUTPUT
INSPECT
INSTALLATION
INTO
INVALID
IS

JUST
JUSTIFIED

KEY

LABEL
LAST
LEADING
LEFT
LENGTH
LESS
LIMIT
LIMITS
LINAGE
LINAGE-COUNTER
LINE
LINE-COUNTER
LINES
LINKAGE
LOCK
LOW-VALUE
LOW-VALUES

MEMORY
MERGE
MESSAGE
MODE
MODULES
MOVE
MULTIPLE
MULTIPLY

NATIVE
NEGATIVE
NEXT
NO
NOT
NUMBER
NUMERIC

NUMERIC-EDITED

OBJECT-COMPUTER
OCCURS
OMITTED
OPEN
OPTIONAL
ORDER
ORGANIZATION
OTHER
OVERFLOW

PACKED-DECIMAL
PADDING
PAGE
PAGE-COUNTER
PERFORM
PIC
PICTURE
PLUS
POINTER
POSITION
POSITIVE
PRINTING
PROCEDURE
PROCEDURES
PROCEED
PROGRAM
PROGRAM-ID
PURGE

QUEUE
QUOTE
QUOTES

RANDOM
READ
RECEIVE
RECORD

RECORDS
REDEFINES
REEL
REFERENCE
REFERENCES
RELATIVE
RELEASE
REMAINDER
REMOVAL
RENAMES
REPLACE
REPLACING
REPORT
REPORTING
REPORTS
RERUN
RESERVE
RESET
RETURN
REWIND
REWRITE
RIGHT
ROUNDED
RUN

SAME
SEARCH
SECTION
SECURITY
SELECT
SEND
SENTENCE
SEPARATE
SEQUENCE
SEQUENTIAL
SET
SIGN
SIZE
SORT
SORT-MERGE
SOURCE
SOURCE-COMPUTER

SPACE
SPACES
SPECIAL-NAMES
STANDARD
STANDARD-1
STANDARD-2
START
STATUS
STRING
SUB-QUEUE-1
SUB-QUEUE-2
SUB-QUEUE-3
SUBTRACT
SUM
SUPPRESS
SYMBOLIC
SYNC
SYNCHRONIZED

TABLE
TALLYING
TAPE
TERMINAL
TERMINATE
TEST
TEXT
THAN
THEN
THROUGH
THRU
TIME
TIMES
TO
TOP
TRAILING
TRUE
TYPE

UNIT
UNSTRING
UNTIL
UP
UPON
USAGE
USE
USING

VALUE	WRITE	*
VALUES		/
VARYING	ZERO	**
	ZEROES	>
WHEN	ZEROS	<
WITH		=
WORDS	+	> =
WORKING-STORAGE	–	< =

C

Complete COBOL language formats

This appendix contains the composite language skeleton of the revised version of the American National Standard COBOL. It is intended to display complete and syntactically correct formats.

The leftmost margin on pages 688 to 689 and pages 690 to 696 is equivalent to margin A in a COBOL source program. The first indentation after the leftmost margin is equivalent to margin B in a COBOL source program.

On pages 696 to 704 the leftmost margin indicates the beginning of the format for a new COBOL verb. The first indentation after the leftmost margin indicates continuation of the format of the COBOL verb. The appearance of the italic letter *S, R, I,* or *W* to the left of the format for the verbs CLOSE, OPEN, READ, and WRITE indicates the Sequential I-O module, Relative I-O module, Indexed I-O module, or Report Writer module in which that general format is used.

The following are the formats presented on pages 688 through 707:

GENERAL FORMAT FOR IDENTIFICATION DIVISION

IDENTIFICATION DIVISION.
PROGRAM-ID.   program-name $\left[\text{IS} \quad \left\{ \left| \begin{array}{c} \underline{\text{COMMON}} \\ \underline{\text{INITIAL}} \end{array} \right| \right\} \quad \text{PROGRAM} \right]$.

[AUTHOR.   [comment-entry . . .]
[INSTALLATION.   [comment-entry . . .]
[DATE-WRITTEN.   [comment-entry . . .]
[DATE-COMPILED.   [comment-entry . . .]
[SECURITY.   [comment-entry . . .]

GENERAL FORMAT FOR ENVIRONMENT DIVISION

[ENVIRONMENT DIVISION.
[CONFIGURATION SECTION.
[SOURCE-COMPUTER.   [computer name   [WITH DEBUGGING MODE].]]
[OBJECT-COMPUTER.   [computer-name

$\left[\underline{\text{MEMORY}} \text{ SIZE integer-1} \left\{ \begin{array}{c} \underline{\text{WORDS}} \\ \underline{\text{CHARACTERS}} \\ \underline{\text{MODULES}} \end{array} \right\} \right]$

[PROGRAM COLLATING SEQUENCE IS alphabet-name-1]
[SEGMENT-LIMIT IS segment-number].]]
[SPECIAL-NAMES.   [[implementor-name-1

$\left\{ \begin{array}{l} \text{IS mnemonic-name-1} \\ \quad [\underline{\text{ON}} \text{ STATUS IS condition-name-1} \quad [\underline{\text{OFF}} \text{ STATUS IS condition-name-2}]] \\ \text{IS mnemonic-name-2} \\ \quad [\underline{\text{OFF}} \text{ STATUS IS condition-name-2} \quad [\underline{\text{ON}} \text{ STATUS IS condition-name-1}]] \\ \underline{\text{ON}} \text{ STATUS IS condition-name-1} \quad [\underline{\text{OFF}} \text{ STATUS IS condition-name-2}] \\ \underline{\text{OFF}} \text{ STATUS IS condition-name-2]} \quad [\underline{\text{ON}} \text{ STATUS is condition-name-1}] \end{array} \right\}$ . . .

[ALPHABET alphabet-name-1 IS

$\left\{ \begin{array}{l} \underline{\text{STANDARD-1}} \\ \underline{\text{STANDARD-2}} \\ \underline{\text{NATIVE}} \\ \text{implementor-name-2} \\ \left\{ \text{literal-1} \quad \left[\left\{ \begin{array}{c} \underline{\text{THROUGH}} \\ \underline{\text{THRU}} \end{array} \right\} \text{ literal-2} \right] \right\} \\ \quad \{\underline{\text{ALSO}} \text{ literal-3}\} \text{ . . .} \end{array} \right\}$ . . .

$$\left[\underline{\text{SYMBOLIC}} \text{ CHARACTERS } \left\{\left\{\{\text{symbolic-character-1}\} \ldots \begin{Bmatrix} \text{IS} \\ \text{ARE} \end{Bmatrix} \{\text{integer-1}\} \ldots \right\} \ldots \right.\right.$$

$$\left.\left. [\underline{\text{IN}} \text{ alphabet-name-2}]\right\}\right] \ldots$$

$$\left[\underline{\text{CLASS}} \text{ class-name IS } \left\{\text{literal-4} \left[\begin{Bmatrix} \underline{\text{THROUGH}} \\ \underline{\text{THRU}} \end{Bmatrix} \text{literal-5}\right]\right\} \ldots \right] \ldots$$

[\underline{CURRENCY} SIGN IS literal-6]
[\underline{DECIMAL-POINT} IS \underline{COMMA}].]]]
[\underline{INPUT-OUTPUT} \underline{SECTION}.
 \underline{FILE-CONTROL}.
     {file-control-entry} ...
[\underline{I-O-CONTROL}.

$$\left[\left[\left[\underline{\text{RERUN}} \left[\underline{\text{ON}} \begin{Bmatrix} \text{file-name-1} \\ \text{implementor-name-1} \end{Bmatrix}\right]\right] \underline{\text{EVERY}} \begin{Bmatrix} \begin{Bmatrix} [\underline{\text{END}} \text{ OF}]\begin{Bmatrix}\underline{\text{REEL}}\\\underline{\text{UNIT}}\end{Bmatrix} \\ \text{integer-1 } \underline{\text{RECORDS}} \end{Bmatrix} \text{ OF file-name-2} \\ \text{integer-2 } \underline{\text{CLOCK-UNITS}} \\ \text{condition-name-1} \end{Bmatrix}\right] \ldots \right.$$

$$\left[\left[\underline{\text{SAME}} \begin{bmatrix} \underline{\text{RECORD}} \\ \underline{\text{SORT}} \\ \underline{\text{SORT-MERGE}} \end{bmatrix} \text{AREA FOR file-name-1 } \{\text{file-name-2}\} \ldots \right] \ldots \right.$$

$$[\underline{\text{MULTIPLE}} \underline{\text{FILE}} \text{ TAPE CONTAINS}$$
$$\{\text{file-name-3} \quad [\underline{\text{POSITION}} \text{ IS integer-1]} \} \ldots] \ldots .]]]]$$

GENERAL FORMAT FOR FILE CONTROL ENTRY

<u>SEQUENTIAL FILE:</u>
<u>SELECT</u> [<u>OPTIONAL</u>] file-name-1

$$\underline{\text{ASSIGN}} \text{ TO } \begin{Bmatrix} \text{implementor-name-1} \\ \text{literal-1} \end{Bmatrix} \ldots$$

$$\left[\underline{\text{RESERVE}} \text{ integer-1 } \begin{bmatrix} \text{AREA} \\ \text{AREAS} \end{bmatrix}\right]$$

[[<u>ORGANIZATION</u> IS] <u>SEQUENTIAL</u>]

$$\left[\underline{\text{PADDING}} \text{ CHARACTER IS } \begin{Bmatrix} \text{data-name-1} \\ \text{literal-2} \end{Bmatrix}\right]$$

$$\left[\underline{\text{RECORD}} \underline{\text{DELIMITER}} \text{ IS } \begin{Bmatrix} \underline{\text{STANDARD-1}} \\ \text{implementor-name-2} \end{Bmatrix}\right]$$

[<u>ACCESS</u> MODE IS <u>SEQUENTIAL</u>]
[FILE <u>STATUS</u> IS data-name-2].

<u>RELATIVE FILE:</u>
<u>SELECT</u> [<u>OPTIONAL</u>] file-name-1

$$\underline{\text{ASSIGN}} \text{ TO } \begin{Bmatrix} \text{implementor-name-1} \\ \text{literal-1} \end{Bmatrix} \ldots$$

$$\left[\underline{\text{RESERVE}} \text{ integer-1 } \begin{bmatrix} \text{AREA} \\ \text{AREAS} \end{bmatrix}\right]$$

[ORGANIZATION IS] RELATIVE

$$\left[\underline{ACCESS} \text{ MODE IS } \left\{\begin{array}{l}\underline{SEQUENTIAL} \\ \underline{RANDOM} \\ \underline{DYNAMIC}\end{array}\right\} \begin{array}{l}[\underline{RELATIVE} \text{ KEY IS data-name-1}] \\ \underline{RELATIVE} \text{ KEY IS data-name-1}\end{array}\right]$$

[FILE STATUS IS data-name-2].

INDEXED FILE:
SELECT   [OPTIONAL]   file-name-1

$$\underline{ASSIGN} \text{ TO } \left\{\begin{array}{l}\text{implementor-name-1} \\ \text{literal-1}\end{array}\right\} \quad \dots$$

$$\left[\underline{RESERVE} \text{ integer-1 } \left[\begin{array}{l}AREA \\ AREAS\end{array}\right]\right]$$

[ORGANIZATION IS]   INDEXED

$$\left[\underline{ACCESS} \text{ MODE IS } \left\{\begin{array}{l}\underline{SEQUENTIAL} \\ \underline{RANDOM} \\ \underline{DYNAMIC}\end{array}\right\}\right]$$

RECORD KEY IS data-name-1
[ALTERNATE RECORD KEY IS data-name-2 [WITH DUPLICATES]]   ...
[FILE STATUS IS data-name-3].

SORT OR MERGE FILE:

SELECT file-name-1   ASSIGN TO $\left\{\begin{array}{l}\text{implementor-name-1} \\ \text{literal-1}\end{array}\right\}$ ...

REPORT FILE:
SELECT   [OPTIONAL]   file-name-1

$$\underline{ASSIGN} \text{ TO } \left\{\begin{array}{l}\text{implementor-name-1} \\ \text{literal-1}\end{array}\right\} \quad \dots$$

$$\left[\underline{RESERVE} \text{ integer-1 } \left[\begin{array}{l}AREA \\ AREAS\end{array}\right]\right]$$

[[ORGANIZATION IS]   SEQUENTIAL]

$$\left[\underline{PADDING} \text{ CHARACTER IS } \left\{\begin{array}{l}\text{data-name-1} \\ \text{literal-1}\end{array}\right\}\right]$$

$$\left[\underline{RECORD} \text{ } \underline{DELIMITER} \text{ IS } \left\{\begin{array}{l}\underline{STANDARD-1} \\ \text{implementor-name-2}\end{array}\right\}\right]$$

[ACCESS MODE IS SEQUENTIAL]
[FILE STATUS IS data-name-2].

GENERAL FORMAT FOR DATA DIVISION

[DATA DIVISION.
[FILE SECTION.
[file-description-entry
    {record-description-entry}   ...   ]   ...
[sort-merge-file-description-entry
    {record-description-entry}   ...   ]   ...
[report-file-description-entry]   ...   ]

[WORKING-STORAGE SECTION.
$$\begin{bmatrix} \text{77-level-description-entry} \\ \text{record-description-entry} \end{bmatrix} \quad \dots \quad \Big]$$
[LINKAGE SECTION.
$$\begin{bmatrix} \text{77-level-description-entry} \\ \text{record-description-entry} \end{bmatrix} \quad \dots \quad \Big]$$
[COMMUNICATION SECTION.
[communication-description-entry
[record-description-entry]   ...   ]   ...   ]
[REPORT SECTION.
[report-description-entry
    {report-group-description-entry}   ...   ]   ...   ]]

GENERAL FORMAT FOR FILE DESCRIPTION ENTRY

SEQUENTIAL FILE:
FD   file-name-1
     [IS EXTERNAL]
     [IS GLOBAL]
     $\Big[$ BLOCK CONTAINS   [integer-1 TO]   integer-2 $\begin{Bmatrix} \text{RECORDS} \\ \text{CHARACTERS} \end{Bmatrix}\Big]$
     $\Bigg[$ RECORD $\begin{cases} \text{CONTAINS integer-3 CHARACTERS} \\ \text{IS VARYING IN SIZE [[FROM integer-4] [TO integer-5] CHARACTERS]} \\ \quad \text{[DEPENDING ON data-name-1]} \\ \text{CONTAINS integer-6 TO integer-7 CHARACTERS} \end{cases}\Bigg]$
     $\Big[$ LABEL $\begin{Bmatrix} \text{RECORD IS} \\ \text{RECORDS ARE} \end{Bmatrix} \begin{Bmatrix} \text{STANDARD} \\ \text{OMITTED} \end{Bmatrix}\Big]$
     $\Big[$ VALUE OF $\Big\{$ implementor-name-1 IS $\begin{Bmatrix} \text{data-name-2} \\ \text{literal-1} \end{Bmatrix}\Big\}$ ... $\Big]$
     $\Big[$ DATA $\begin{Bmatrix} \text{RECORD IS} \\ \text{RECORDS ARE} \end{Bmatrix}$ {data-name-3}   ... $\Big]$
     $\Big[$ LINAGE IS $\begin{Bmatrix} \text{data-name-4} \\ \text{integer-8} \end{Bmatrix}$ LINES $\Big[$ WITH FOOTING AT $\begin{Bmatrix} \text{data-name-5} \\ \text{integer-9} \end{Bmatrix}\Big]$
         $\Big[$ LINES AT TOP $\begin{Bmatrix} \text{data-name-6} \\ \text{integer-10} \end{Bmatrix}\Big] \Big[$ LINES AT BOTTOM $\begin{Bmatrix} \text{data-name-7} \\ \text{integer-11} \end{Bmatrix}\Big]\Big]$
     [CODE-SET IS alphabet-name-1].
RELATIVE FILE:
FD   file-name-1
     [IS EXTERNAL]
     [IS GLOBAL]
     $\Big[$ BLOCK CONTAINS   [integer-1 TO]   integer-2 $\begin{Bmatrix} \text{RECORDS} \\ \text{CHARACTERS} \end{Bmatrix}\Big]$
     $\Bigg[$ RECORD $\begin{cases} \text{CONTAINS integer-3 CHARACTERS} \\ \text{IS VARYING IN SIZE [[FROM integer-4] [TO integer-5] CHARACTERS]} \\ \quad \text{[DEPENDING ON data-name-1]} \\ \text{CONTAINS integer-6 TO integer-7 CHARACTERS} \end{cases}\Bigg]$
     $\Big[$ LABEL $\begin{Bmatrix} \text{RECORD IS} \\ \text{RECORDS ARE} \end{Bmatrix} \begin{Bmatrix} \text{STANDARD} \\ \text{OMITTED} \end{Bmatrix}\Big]$

$$\left[\text{VALUE } \underline{\text{OF}} \quad \left\{ \text{implementor-name-1 IS} \quad \left\{ \begin{array}{l} \text{data-name-2} \\ \text{literal-1} \end{array} \right\} \right\} \quad \dots \right]$$

$$\left[\underline{\text{DATA}} \quad \left\{ \begin{array}{l} \underline{\text{RECORD}} \text{ IS} \\ \underline{\text{RECORDS}} \text{ ARE} \end{array} \right\} \quad \{\text{data-name-3}\} \quad \dots \right] \quad .$$

<u>INDEXED FILE:</u>
<u>FD</u>   file-name-1
    [IS <u>EXTERNAL</u>]
    [IS <u>GLOBAL</u>]

$$\left[\underline{\text{BLOCK}} \text{ CONTAINS } [\text{integer-1 } \underline{\text{TO}}] \quad \text{integer-2} \left\{ \begin{array}{l} \underline{\text{RECORDS}} \\ \text{CHARACTERS} \end{array} \right\} \right]$$

$$\left[\underline{\text{RECORD}} \quad \left\{ \begin{array}{l} \text{CONTAINS integer-3 CHARACTERS} \\ \text{IS } \underline{\text{VARYING}} \text{ IN SIZE [[FROM integer-4] [\underline{TO} integer-5] CHARACTERS]} \\ \quad\quad [\underline{\text{DEPENDING}} \text{ ON data-name-1}] \\ \text{CONTAINS integer-6 } \underline{\text{TO}} \text{ integer-7 CHARACTERS} \end{array} \right\} \right]$$

$$\left[\underline{\text{LABEL}} \quad \left\{ \begin{array}{l} \underline{\text{RECORD}} \text{ IS} \\ \underline{\text{RECORDS}} \text{ ARE} \end{array} \right\} \quad \left\{ \begin{array}{l} \underline{\text{STANDARD}} \\ \underline{\text{OMITTED}} \end{array} \right\} \right]$$

$$\left[\text{VALUE } \underline{\text{OF}} \quad \left\{ \text{implementor-name-1 IS} \quad \left\{ \begin{array}{l} \text{data-name-2} \\ \text{literal-1} \end{array} \right\} \right\} \quad \dots \right]$$

$$\left[\underline{\text{DATA}} \quad \left\{ \begin{array}{l} \underline{\text{RECORD}} \text{ IS} \\ \underline{\text{RECORDS}} \text{ ARE} \end{array} \right\} \quad \{\text{data-name-3}\} \quad \dots \right] \quad .$$

<u>SORT-MERGE FILE:</u>
<u>SD</u>   file-name-1

$$\left[\underline{\text{RECORD}} \quad \left\{ \begin{array}{l} \text{CONTAINS integer-1 CHARACTERS} \\ \text{IS } \underline{\text{VARYING}} \text{ IN SIZE [[FROM integer-2] [\underline{TO} integer-3] CHARACTERS]} \\ \quad\quad [\underline{\text{DEPENDING}} \text{ ON data-name-1}] \\ \text{CONTAINS integer-4 } \underline{\text{TO}} \text{ integer-5 CHARACTERS} \end{array} \right\} \right]$$

$$\left[\underline{\text{DATA}} \quad \left\{ \begin{array}{l} \underline{\text{RECORD}} \text{ IS} \\ \underline{\text{RECORDS}} \text{ ARE} \end{array} \right\} \quad \{\text{data-name-2}\} \quad \dots \right]$$

<u>REPORT FILE:</u>
<u>FD</u>   file-name-1
    [IS <u>EXTERNAL</u>]
    [IS <u>GLOBAL</u>]

$$\left[\underline{\text{BLOCK}} \text{ CONTAINS } [\text{integer-1 } \underline{\text{TO}}] \quad \text{integer-2} \left\{ \begin{array}{l} \underline{\text{RECORDS}} \\ \text{CHARACTERS} \end{array} \right\} \right]$$

$$\left[\underline{\text{RECORD}} \quad \left\{ \begin{array}{l} \text{CONTAINS integer-3 CHARACTERS} \\ \text{CONTAINS integer-4 } \underline{\text{TO}} \text{ integer-5 CHARACTERS} \end{array} \right\} \right]$$

$$\left[\underline{\text{LABEL}} \quad \left\{ \begin{array}{l} \underline{\text{RECORD}} \text{ IS} \\ \underline{\text{RECORDS}} \text{ ARE} \end{array} \right\} \quad \left\{ \begin{array}{l} \underline{\text{STANDARD}} \\ \underline{\text{OMITTED}} \end{array} \right\} \right]$$

$$\left[\text{VALUE } \underline{\text{OF}} \quad \left\{ \text{implementor-name-1 IS} \quad \left\{ \begin{array}{l} \text{data-name-2} \\ \text{literal-1} \end{array} \right\} \right\} \quad \dots \right]$$

[<u>CODE-SET</u> IS alphabet-name-1]

$$\left\{ \begin{array}{l} \underline{\text{REPORT}} \text{ IS} \\ \underline{\text{REPORTS}} \text{ ARE} \end{array} \right\} \quad \{\text{report-name-1}\} \quad \dots \quad .$$

GENERAL FORMAT FOR DATA DESCRIPTION ENTRY

FORMAT 1:

level-number $\begin{bmatrix} \text{data-name-1} \\ \text{FILLER} \end{bmatrix}$

[REDEFINES data-name-2]

[IS EXTERNAL]

[IS GLOBAL]

$\left[\begin{Bmatrix} \text{PICTURE} \\ \text{PIC} \end{Bmatrix} \text{IS character-string} \right]$

$\left[\text{[USAGE IS]} \begin{Bmatrix} \text{BINARY} \\ \text{COMPUTATIONAL} \\ \text{COMP} \\ \text{DISPLAY} \\ \text{INDEX} \\ \text{PACKED-DECIMAL} \end{Bmatrix} \right]$

$\left[\text{[SIGN IS]} \begin{Bmatrix} \text{LEADING} \\ \text{TRAILING} \end{Bmatrix} \text{[SEPARATE CHARACTER]} \right]$

$\left[\begin{array}{l} \text{OCCURS integer-2 TIMES} \\ \quad \left[\begin{Bmatrix} \text{ASCENDING} \\ \text{DESCENDING} \end{Bmatrix} \text{KEY IS} \quad \{\text{data-name-3}\} \quad \dots \right] \quad \dots \\ \quad \text{[INDEXED BY} \quad \{\text{index-name-1}\} \quad \dots \text{]} \\ \text{OCCURS integer-1 TO integer-2 TIMES DEPENDING ON data-name-4} \\ \quad \left[\begin{Bmatrix} \text{ASCENDING} \\ \text{DESCENDING} \end{Bmatrix} \text{KEY IS} \quad \{\text{data-name-3}\} \quad \dots \right] \quad \dots \\ \quad \text{[INDEXED BY} \quad \{\text{index-name-1}\} \quad \dots \text{]} \end{array} \right]$

$\left[\begin{Bmatrix} \text{SYNCHRONIZED} \\ \text{SYNC} \end{Bmatrix} \begin{bmatrix} \text{LEFT} \\ \text{RIGHT} \end{bmatrix} \right]$

$\left[\begin{Bmatrix} \text{JUSTIFIED} \\ \text{JUST} \end{Bmatrix} \text{RIGHT} \right]$

[BLANK WHEN ZERO]

[VALUE IS literal-1].

FORMAT 2:

66   data-name-1 RENAMES data-name-2 $\left[\begin{Bmatrix} \text{THROUGH} \\ \text{THRU} \end{Bmatrix} \text{data-name-3} \right]$.

FORMAT 3:

88   condition-name-1 $\begin{Bmatrix} \text{VALUE IS} \\ \text{VALUES ARE} \end{Bmatrix}$ $\begin{Bmatrix} \text{literal-1} \left[\begin{Bmatrix} \text{THROUGH} \\ \text{THRU} \end{Bmatrix} \text{literal-2} \right] \end{Bmatrix}$ $\dots$.

GENERAL FORMAT FOR COMMUNICATION DESCRIPTION ENTRY AND REPORT DESCRIPTION ENTRY

FORMAT 1:
CD   cd-name-1

FOR [INITIAL] INPUT

```
[[SYMBOLIC QUEUE IS data-name-1]
  [SYMBOLIC SUB-QUEUE-1 IS data-name-2]
  [SYMBOLIC SUB-QUEUE-2 IS data-name-3]
  [SYMBOLIC SUB-QUEUE-3 IS data-name-4]
  [MESSAGE DATE IS data-name-5]
  [MESSAGE TIME IS data-name-6]
  [SYMBOLIC SOURCE IS data-name-7]
  [TEXT LENGTH IS data-name-8]
  [END KEY IS data-name-9]
  [STATUS KEY IS data-name-10]
  [MESSAGE COUNT IS data-name-11]]
[data-name-1, data-name-2, data-name-3,
    data-name-4, data-name-5, data-name-6,
    data-name-7, data-name-8, data-name-9,
    data-name-10, data-name-11]
```

FORMAT 2:
CD   cd-name-1 FOR OUTPUT
      [DESTINATION COUNT IS data-name-1]
      [TEXT LENGTH IS data-name-2]
      [STATUS KEY IS data-name-3]
      [DESTINATION TABLE OCCURS integer-1 TIMES
          [INDEXED BY   {index-name-1}   . . .]]
      [ERROR KEY IS data-name-4]
      [SYMBOLIC DESTINATION IS data-name-5].

FORMAT 3:
CD   cd-name-1

FOR [INITIAL] I-O

```
[[MESSAGE DATE IS data-name-1]
  [MESSAGE TIME IS data-name-2]
  [SYMBOLIC TERMINAL IS data-name-3]
  [TEXT LENGTH IS data-name-4]
  [END KEY IS data-name-5]
  [STATUS KEY IS data-name-6]]
[data-name-1, data-name-2, data-name-3,
    data-name-4, data-name-5, data-name-6]
```

RD   report-name-1
      [IS GLOBAL]
      [CODE literal-1]
      $\begin{bmatrix} \begin{Bmatrix} \text{CONTROL IS} \\ \text{CONTROLS ARE} \end{Bmatrix} \quad \begin{Bmatrix} \text{\{data-name-1\}} \quad \ldots \\ \text{FINAL [data-name-1]} \quad \ldots \end{Bmatrix} \end{bmatrix}$
      $\begin{bmatrix} \text{PAGE} \quad \begin{bmatrix} \text{LIMIT IS} \\ \text{LIMITS ARE} \end{bmatrix} \quad \text{integer-1} \quad \begin{bmatrix} \text{LINE} \\ \text{LINES} \end{bmatrix} \quad \text{[HEADING integer-2]} \end{bmatrix}$
          [FIRST DETAIL integer-3]   [LAST DETAIL integer-4]

          [FOOTING integer-5]] .

GENERAL FORMAT FOR REPORT GROUP DESCRIPTION ENTRY

FORMAT 1:

```
01     [data-name-1]

       ┌                        ┌                          ┐ ┐
       │ LINE NUMBER IS         │ integer-1   [ON NEXT PAGE] │ │
       │                        │ PLUS integer-2            │ │
       └                        └                          ┘ ┘

       ┌                        ┌ integer-3        ┐ ┐
       │ NEXT GROUP IS          │ PLUS integer-4   │ │
       │                        │ NEXT PAGE        │ │
       └                        └                  ┘ ┘

                       ┌  ┌ REPORT HEADING   ┐                              ┐
                       │  │ RH               │                              │
                       │  ┌ PAGE HEADING     ┐                              │
                       │  │ PH               │                              │
                       │  ┌ CONTROL HEADING  ┐  ┌ data-name-2 ┐             │
                       │  │ CH               │  │ FINAL       │             │
       TYPE IS         ┤  ┌ DETAIL           ┐                              ├
                       │  │ DE               │                              │
                       │  ┌ CONTROL FOOTING  ┐  ┌ data-name-3 ┐             │
                       │  │ CF               │  │ FINAL       │             │
                       │  ┌ PAGE FOOTING     ┐                              │
                       │  │ PF               │                              │
                       │  ┌ REPORT FOOTING   ┐                              │
                       └  │ RF               │                              ┘

       [[USAGE IS] DISPLAY].
```

FORMAT 2:

```
level-number     [data-name-1]
       ┌                        ┌ integer-1   [ON NEXT PAGE] ┐ ┐
       │ LINE NUMBER IS         │ PLUS integer-2            │ │
       └                        └                          ┘ ┘
       [[USAGE IS]    DISPLAY].
```

FORMAT 3:

```
level-number     [data-name-1]
       ┌ PICTURE ┐
       │ PIC     │  IS character-string
       └         ┘
       [[USAGE  IS] DISPLAY]
       ┌                 ┌ LEADING  ┐                            ┐
       │ [SIGN IS        │ TRAILING │  SEPARATE CHARACTER        │
       └                 └          ┘                            ┘
       ┌ ┌ JUSTIFIED ┐          ┐
       │ │ JUST      │  RIGHT   │
       └ └           ┘          ┘
       [BLANK WHEN ZERO]
       ┌                    ┌ integer-1   [ON NEXT PAGE] ┐ ┐
       │ LINE NUMBER IS     │ PLUS integer-2            │ │
       └                    └                          ┘ ┘
       [COLUMN NUMBER IS integer-3]
       ┌ SOURCE is identifier-1                                          ┐
       │ VALUE IS literal-1                                              │
       │ { SUM   {identifier-2}  ...   [UPON {data-name-2}   ...  ]  }  ...│
       │         ┌                 ┌ data-name-3 ┐ ┐                     │
       │         │ RESET ON        │ FINAL       │ │                     │
       └         └                 └             ┘ ┘                     ┘
       [GROUP INDICATE].
```

GENERAL FORMAT FOR PROCEDURE DIVISION

FORMAT 1:
[PROCEDURE DIVISION   [USING   {data-name-1}   ...   ].
[DECLARATIVES.
{section-name SECTION [segment-number].
    USE statement.
[paragraph-name.
    [sentence]   ...   ]   ...   }   ...
END DECLARATIVES.]
{section-name SECTION [segment-number].
[paragraph-name.
    [sentence]   ...   ]   ...   }   ...   ]

FORMAT 2:
[PROCEDURE DIVISION   [USING   {data-name-1}   ...   ].
{paragraph-name.
    [sentence]   ...   }   ...   ]

GENERAL FORMAT FOR COBOL VERBS

ACCEPT identifier-1   [FROM mnemonic-name-1]

ACCEPT identifier-2 FROM
$\left\{ \begin{array}{l} \text{DATE} \\ \text{DAY} \\ \text{DAY-OF-WEEK} \\ \text{TIME} \end{array} \right\}$

ACCEPT cd-name-1 MESSAGE COUNT

ADD
$\left\{ \begin{array}{l} \text{identifier-1} \\ \text{literal-1} \end{array} \right\}$
   ...   TO {identifier-2 [ROUNDED]} ...
    [ON SIZE ERROR imperative-statement-1]
    [NOT ON SIZE ERROR imperative-statement-2]
    [END-ADD]

ADD
$\left\{ \begin{array}{l} \text{identifier-1} \\ \text{literal-1} \end{array} \right\}$
   ...   TO
$\left\{ \begin{array}{l} \text{identifier-2} \\ \text{literal-2} \end{array} \right\}$
    GIVING {identifier-3 [ROUNDED]}   ...
    [ON SIZE ERROR imperative-statement-1]
    [NOT ON SIZE ERROR imperative-statement-2]
    [END-ADD]

ADD
$\left\{ \begin{array}{l} \text{CORRESPONDING} \\ \text{CORR} \end{array} \right\}$
   identifier-1 TO identifier-2 [ROUNDED]
    [ON SIZE ERROR imperative-statement-1]
    [NOT ON SIZE ERROR imperative-statement-2]
    [END-ADD]

ALTER   {procedure-name-1 TO   [PROCEED TO]   procedure-name-2}   ...

CALL $\left\{\begin{array}{l}\text{identifier-1}\\\text{literal-1}\end{array}\right\}$ $\left[\underline{\text{USING}}\ \left\{\begin{array}{l}[\text{BY}\ \underline{\text{REFERENCE}}]\ \ \{\text{identifier-2}\}\ \ \dots\\\text{BY}\ \underline{\text{CONTENT}}\ \ \ \{\text{identifier-2}\}\ \ \dots\end{array}\right\}\ \ \dots\ \right]$
    [ON <u>OVERFLOW</u> imperative-statement-1]
    [END-CALL]

    CALL $\left\{\begin{array}{l}\text{identifier-1}\\\text{literal-1}\end{array}\right\}$ $\left[\ \underline{\text{USING}}\ \ \left\{\begin{array}{l}[\text{BY}\ \underline{\text{REFERENCE}}]\ \ \{\text{identifier-2}\}\ \ \dots\\\text{BY}\ \underline{\text{CONTENT}}\ \ \ \{\text{identifier-2}\}\ \ \dots\end{array}\right\}\ \ \dots\ \right]$
        [ON <u>EXCEPTION</u> imperative-statement-1]
        [<u>NOT</u> ON <u>EXCEPTION</u> imperative-statement-2]
        [END-CALL]

CANCEL $\left\{\begin{array}{l}\text{identifier-1}\\\text{literal-1}\end{array}\right\}$ $\ \dots$

SW CLOSE $\left\{\text{file-name-1}\ \ \left[\ \left\{\begin{array}{l}\underline{\text{REEL}}\\\underline{\text{UNIT}}\end{array}\right\}\ [\text{FOR}\ \underline{\text{REMOVAL}}]\\\text{WITH}\ \left\{\begin{array}{l}\underline{\text{NO}}\ \underline{\text{REWIND}}\\\underline{\text{LOCK}}\end{array}\right\}\ \ \right]\right\}\ \dots$

RI CLOSE $\{\text{file-name-1}\ \ [\text{WITH}\ \underline{\text{LOCK}}]\}\ \ \dots$

COMPUTE $\{\text{identifier-1}\ [\underline{\text{ROUNDED}}]\}\ \ \dots\ =\ $ arithmetic-expression-1
    [ON <u>SIZE</u> <u>ERROR</u> imperative-statement-1]
    [<u>NOT</u> ON <u>SIZE</u> <u>ERROR</u> imperative-statement-2]
    [END-COMPUTE]

CONTINUE

<u>DELETE</u> file-name-1 RECORD
    [<u>INVALID</u> KEY imperative-statement-1]
    [<u>NOT</u> <u>INVALID</u> KEY imperative-statement-2]
    [END-DELETE]

DISABLE $\left\{\begin{array}{l}\underline{\text{INPUT}}\ [\underline{\text{TERMINAL}}]\\\underline{\text{I-O}}\ \underline{\text{TERMINAL}}\\\underline{\text{OUTPUT}}\end{array}\right\}$ cd-name-1 $\left[\text{WITH}\ \underline{\text{KEY}}\ \left\{\begin{array}{l}\text{identifier-1}\\\text{literal-1}\end{array}\right\}\right]$

DISPLAY $\left\{\begin{array}{l}\text{identifier-1}\\\text{literal-1}\end{array}\right\}$ $\ \dots\ $ [<u>UPON</u> mnemonic-name-1]   [WITH <u>NO</u> <u>ADVANCING</u>]

DIVIDE $\left\{\begin{array}{l}\text{identifier-1}\\\text{literal-1}\end{array}\right\}$ <u>INTO</u> $\{\text{identifier-2}\ [\underline{\text{ROUNDED}}]\}\dots$
    [ON <u>SIZE</u> ERROR imperative-statement-1]
    [<u>NOT</u> ON <u>SIZE</u> <u>ERROR</u> imperative-statement-2]
    [END-DIVIDE]

DIVIDE $\left\{\begin{array}{l}\text{identifier-1}\\\text{literal-1}\end{array}\right\}$ <u>INTO</u> $\left\{\begin{array}{l}\text{identifier-2}\\\text{literal-2}\end{array}\right\}$
    <u>GIVING</u> $\{\text{identifier-3}\ [\underline{\text{ROUNDED}}]\}\dots$
    [ON <u>SIZE</u> <u>ERROR</u> imperative-statement-1]
    [<u>NOT</u> ON <u>SIZE</u> <u>ERROR</u> imperative-statement-2]
    [END-DIVIDE]

DIVIDE $\left\{ \begin{array}{l} \text{identifier-1} \\ \text{literal-1} \end{array} \right\}$ <u>BY</u> $\left\{ \begin{array}{l} \text{identifier-2} \\ \text{literal-2} \end{array} \right\}$
    <u>GIVING</u>   {identifier-3 [<u>ROUNDED</u>]} . . .
    [ON <u>SIZE ERROR</u> imperative-statement-1]
    [<u>NOT</u> ON <u>SIZE ERROR</u> imperative-statement-2]
    [<u>END-DIVIDE</u>]

DIVIDE $\left\{ \begin{array}{l} \text{identifier-1} \\ \text{literal-1} \end{array} \right\}$ <u>INTO</u> $\left\{ \begin{array}{l} \text{identifier-2} \\ \text{literal-2} \end{array} \right\}$ <u>GIVING</u> identifier-3 [<u>ROUNDED</u>]
    <u>REMAINDER</u> identifier-4
    [ON <u>SIZE ERROR</u> imperative-statement-1]
    [<u>NOT</u> ON <u>SIZE ERROR</u> imperative-statement-2]
    [<u>END-DIVIDE</u>]

DIVIDE $\left\{ \begin{array}{l} \text{identifier-1} \\ \text{literal-1} \end{array} \right\}$ <u>BY</u> $\left\{ \begin{array}{l} \text{identifier-2} \\ \text{literal-2} \end{array} \right\}$ <u>GIVING</u> identifier-3 [<u>ROUNDED</u>]
    <u>REMAINDER</u> identifier-4
    [ON <u>SIZE ERROR</u> imperative-statement-1]
    [<u>NOT</u> ON <u>SIZE ERROR</u> imperative-statement-2]
    [<u>END-DIVIDE</u>]

<u>ENABLE</u> $\left\{ \begin{array}{l} \underline{\text{INPUT}} \text{ [}\underline{\text{TERMINAL}}\text{]} \\ \underline{\text{I-O TERMINAL}} \\ \underline{\text{OUTPUT}} \end{array} \right\}$ cd-name-1 $\left[\underline{\text{WITH}}\ \underline{\text{KEY}}\ \left\{ \begin{array}{l} \text{identifier-1} \\ \text{literal-1} \end{array} \right\} \right]$

<u>ENTER</u> language-name-1   [routine-name-1].

<u>EVALUATE</u> $\left\{ \begin{array}{l} \text{identifier-1} \\ \text{literal-1} \\ \text{expression-1} \\ \underline{\text{TRUE}} \\ \underline{\text{FALSE}} \end{array} \right\}$ $\left[\underline{\text{ALSO}}\ \left\{ \begin{array}{l} \text{identifier-2} \\ \text{literal-2} \\ \text{expression-2} \\ \underline{\text{TRUE}} \\ \underline{\text{FALSE}} \end{array} \right\} \right]$ . . .

{{<u>WHEN</u>

$\left\{ \begin{array}{l} \underline{\text{ANY}} \\ \text{condition-1} \\ \underline{\text{TRUE}} \\ \underline{\text{FALSE}} \\ \text{[\underline{NOT}]} \left\{ \begin{array}{l} \text{identifier-3} \\ \text{literal-3} \\ \text{arithmetic-expression-1} \end{array} \right\} \left[\left\{ \begin{array}{l} \underline{\text{THROUGH}} \\ \underline{\text{THRU}} \end{array} \right\} \left\{ \begin{array}{l} \text{identifier-4} \\ \text{literal-4} \\ \text{arithmetic-expression-2} \end{array} \right\} \right] \end{array} \right\}$

[<u>ALSO</u>

$\left\{ \begin{array}{l} \underline{\text{ANY}} \\ \text{condition-2} \\ \underline{\text{TRUE}} \\ \underline{\text{FALSE}} \\ \text{[\underline{NOT}]} \left\{ \begin{array}{l} \text{identifier-5} \\ \text{literal-5} \\ \text{arithmetic-expression-3} \end{array} \right\} \left[\left\{ \begin{array}{l} \underline{\text{THROUGH}} \\ \underline{\text{THRU}} \end{array} \right\} \left\{ \begin{array}{l} \text{identifier-6} \\ \text{literal-6} \\ \text{arithmetic-expression-4} \end{array} \right\} \right] \end{array} \right\}$ . . . } . . .

imperative-statement-1} . . .
[<u>WHEN</u> <u>OTHER</u> imperative-statement-2]
[<u>END-EVALUATE</u>]

<u>EXIT</u>

<u>EXIT</u> <u>PROGRAM</u>

<u>GENERATE</u> $\begin{Bmatrix} \text{data-name-1} \\ \text{report-name-1} \end{Bmatrix}$

<u>GO</u> TO   [procedure-name-1]

<u>GO</u> TO   [procedure-name-1] . . .   <u>DEPENDING</u> ON identifier-1

<u>IF</u> condition-1 THEN $\begin{Bmatrix} \{\text{statement-1}\} \dots \\ \underline{\text{NEXT}} \ \underline{\text{SENTENCE}} \end{Bmatrix}$ $\begin{Bmatrix} \underline{\text{ELSE}} \ \{\text{statement-2}\} \dots \ [\underline{\text{END-IF}}] \\ \underline{\text{ELSE}} \ \underline{\text{NEXT}} \ \underline{\text{SENTENCE}} \\ \underline{\text{END-IF}} \end{Bmatrix}$

<u>INITIALIZE</u>   {identifier-1} . . .

$$\left[\underline{\text{REPLACING}} \ \left\{ \begin{Bmatrix} \underline{\text{ALPHABETIC}} \\ \underline{\text{ALPHANUMERIC}} \\ \underline{\text{NUMERIC}} \\ \underline{\text{ALPHANUMERIC-EDITED}} \\ \underline{\text{NUMERIC-EDITED}} \end{Bmatrix} \ \text{DATA} \ \underline{\text{BY}} \ \begin{Bmatrix} \text{identifier-2} \\ \text{literal-1} \end{Bmatrix} \right\} \dots \right]$$

<u>INITIATE</u>   {report-name-1} . . .

<u>INSPECT</u> identifier-1 <u>TALLYING</u>

$$\left\{ \text{identifier-2} \ \underline{\text{FOR}} \ \begin{Bmatrix} \underline{\text{CHARACTERS}} \left[\begin{Bmatrix} \underline{\text{BEFORE}} \\ \underline{\text{AFTER}} \end{Bmatrix} \text{INITIAL} \begin{Bmatrix} \text{identifier-4} \\ \text{literal-2} \end{Bmatrix} \right] \dots \\ \begin{Bmatrix} \underline{\text{ALL}} \\ \underline{\text{LEADING}} \end{Bmatrix} \begin{Bmatrix} \left\{ \begin{matrix} \text{identifier-3} \\ \text{literal-1} \end{matrix} \right\} \left[\begin{Bmatrix} \underline{\text{BEFORE}} \\ \underline{\text{AFTER}} \end{Bmatrix} \text{INITIAL} \begin{Bmatrix} \text{identifier-4} \\ \text{literal-2} \end{Bmatrix} \right] \dots \end{Bmatrix} \dots \end{Bmatrix} \right\} \dots \right\} \dots$$

<u>INSPECT</u> identifier-1 <u>REPLACING</u>

$$\left\{ \begin{matrix} \underline{\text{CHARACTERS}} \ \underline{\text{BY}} \begin{Bmatrix} \text{identifier-5} \\ \text{literal-3} \end{Bmatrix} \left[\begin{Bmatrix} \underline{\text{BEFORE}} \\ \underline{\text{AFTER}} \end{Bmatrix} \text{INITIAL} \begin{Bmatrix} \text{identifier-4} \\ \text{literal-2} \end{Bmatrix} \right] \dots \\ \begin{Bmatrix} \underline{\text{ALL}} \\ \underline{\text{LEADING}} \\ \underline{\text{FIRST}} \end{Bmatrix} \begin{Bmatrix} \begin{Bmatrix} \text{identifier-3} \\ \text{literal-1} \end{Bmatrix} \underline{\text{BY}} \begin{Bmatrix} \text{identifier-5} \\ \text{literal-3} \end{Bmatrix} \left[\begin{Bmatrix} \underline{\text{BEFORE}} \\ \underline{\text{AFTER}} \end{Bmatrix} \text{INITIAL} \begin{Bmatrix} \text{identifier-4} \\ \text{literal-2} \end{Bmatrix} \right] \dots \end{Bmatrix} \dots \end{matrix} \right\} \dots$$

<u>INSPECT</u> identifier-1 <u>TALLYING</u>

$$\left\{ \text{identifier-2} \ \underline{\text{FOR}} \ \begin{Bmatrix} \underline{\text{CHARACTERS}} \left[\begin{Bmatrix} \underline{\text{BEFORE}} \\ \underline{\text{AFTER}} \end{Bmatrix} \text{INITIAL} \begin{Bmatrix} \text{identifier-4} \\ \text{literal-2} \end{Bmatrix} \right] \dots \\ \begin{Bmatrix} \underline{\text{ALL}} \\ \underline{\text{LEADING}} \end{Bmatrix} \begin{Bmatrix} \begin{Bmatrix} \text{identifier-3} \\ \text{literal-1} \end{Bmatrix} \left[\begin{Bmatrix} \underline{\text{BEFORE}} \\ \underline{\text{AFTER}} \end{Bmatrix} \text{INITIAL} \begin{Bmatrix} \text{identifier-4} \\ \text{literal-2} \end{Bmatrix} \right] \dots \end{Bmatrix} \dots \end{Bmatrix} \right\} \dots \right\} \dots$$

<u>REPLACING</u>

$$\left\{ \begin{array}{l} \underline{\text{CHARACTERS}} \ \underline{\text{BY}} \ \left\{ \begin{array}{l} \text{identifier-5} \\ \text{literal-3} \end{array} \right\} \left[\left\{ \begin{array}{l} \underline{\text{BEFORE}} \\ \underline{\text{AFTER}} \end{array} \right\} \text{INITIAL} \left\{ \begin{array}{l} \text{identifier-4} \\ \text{literal-2} \end{array} \right\} \right] \cdots \\ \left\{ \begin{array}{l} \underline{\text{ALL}} \\ \underline{\text{LEADING}} \\ \underline{\text{FIRST}} \end{array} \right\} \ \left\{ \left\{ \begin{array}{l} \text{identifier-3} \\ \text{literal-1} \end{array} \right\} \underline{\text{BY}} \left\{ \begin{array}{l} \text{identifier-5} \\ \text{literal-3} \end{array} \right\} \left[\left\{ \begin{array}{l} \underline{\text{BEFORE}} \\ \underline{\text{AFTER}} \end{array} \right\} \text{INITIAL} \left\{ \begin{array}{l} \text{identifier-4} \\ \text{literal-2} \end{array} \right\} \right] \cdots \right\} \cdots \end{array} \right\} \cdots$$

<u>INSPECT</u> identifier-1 <u>CONVERTING</u> $\left\{ \begin{array}{l} \text{identifier-6} \\ \text{literal-4} \end{array} \right\}$ <u>TO</u> $\left\{ \begin{array}{l} \text{identifier-7} \\ \text{literal-5} \end{array} \right\}$

$\left[\left\{ \begin{array}{l} \underline{\text{BEFORE}} \\ \underline{\text{AFTER}} \end{array} \right\} \text{INITIAL} \left\{ \begin{array}{l} \text{identifier-4} \\ \text{literal-2} \end{array} \right\} \right] \cdots$

<u>MERGE</u> file-name-1 $\left\{ \text{ON} \left\{ \begin{array}{l} \underline{\text{ASCENDING}} \\ \underline{\text{DESCENDING}} \end{array} \right\} \text{KEY} \ \{\text{data-name-1}\} \cdots \right\} \cdots$

[COLLATING <u>SEQUENCE</u> IS alphabet-name-1]
<u>USING</u> file-name-2 {file-name-3} . . .

$\left\{ \begin{array}{l} \underline{\text{OUTPUT}} \ \underline{\text{PROCEDURE}} \ \text{IS procedure-name-1} \left[\left\{ \begin{array}{l} \underline{\text{THROUGH}} \\ \underline{\text{THRU}} \end{array} \right\} \text{procedure-name-2} \right] \\ \underline{\text{GIVING}} \ \{\text{file-name-4}\} \cdots \end{array} \right\}$

<u>MOVE</u> $\left\{ \begin{array}{l} \text{identifier-1} \\ \text{literal-1} \end{array} \right\}$ <u>TO</u> {identifier-2} . . .

<u>MOVE</u> $\left\{ \begin{array}{l} \underline{\text{CORRESPONDING}} \\ \underline{\text{CORR}} \end{array} \right\}$ identifier-1 <u>TO</u> identifier-2

<u>MULTIPLY</u> $\left\{ \begin{array}{l} \text{identifier-1} \\ \text{literal-1} \end{array} \right\}$ <u>BY</u> {identifier-2 [<u>ROUNDED</u>]} . . .

[ON <u>SIZE</u> <u>ERROR</u> imperative-statement-1]
[<u>NOT</u> ON <u>SIZE</u> <u>ERROR</u> imperative-statement-2]
[<u>END-MULTIPLY</u>]

<u>MULTIPLY</u> $\left\{ \begin{array}{l} \text{identifier-1} \\ \text{literal-1} \end{array} \right\}$ <u>BY</u> $\left\{ \begin{array}{l} \text{identifier-2} \\ \text{literal-2} \end{array} \right\}$

<u>GIVING</u> {identifier-3 [<u>ROUNDED</u>]} . . .
[ON <u>SIZE</u> <u>ERROR</u> imperative-statement-1]
[<u>NOT</u> ON <u>SIZE</u> <u>ERROR</u> imperative-statement-2]
[<u>END-MULTIPLY</u>]

S <u>OPEN</u> $\left\{ \begin{array}{l} \underline{\text{INPUT}} \ \left\{ \text{file-name-1} \left[\begin{array}{l} \underline{\text{REVERSED}} \\ \text{WITH} \ \underline{\text{NO}} \ \underline{\text{REWIND}} \end{array} \right] \right\} \cdots \\ \underline{\text{OUTPUT}} \ \{\text{file-name-2} \ [\text{WITH} \ \underline{\text{NO}} \ \underline{\text{REWIND}}]\} \cdots \\ \underline{\text{I-O}} \ \{\text{file-name-3}\} \cdots \\ \underline{\text{EXTEND}} \ \{\text{file-name-4}\} \cdots \end{array} \right\} \cdots$

RI <u>OPEN</u> $\left\{ \begin{array}{l} \underline{\text{INPUT}} \ \{\text{file-name-1}\} \cdots \\ \underline{\text{OUTPUT}} \ \{\text{file-name-2}\} \cdots \\ \underline{\text{I-O}} \ \{\text{file-name-3}\} \cdots \\ \underline{\text{EXTEND}} \ \{\text{file-name-4}\} \cdots \end{array} \right\} \cdots$

W   <u>OPEN</u> $\left\{ \begin{array}{l} \underline{OUTPUT}\ \{\text{file-name-1 [WITH }\underline{NO}\ \underline{REWIND}]\}\ldots \\ \underline{EXTEND}\ \{\text{file-name-2}\}\ldots \end{array} \right\}\ \ldots$

<u>PERFORM</u> $\left[\text{procedure-name-1}\ \left[\left\{ \begin{array}{l} \underline{THROUGH} \\ \underline{THRU} \end{array} \right\}\ \text{procedure-name-2} \right] \right]$

[imperative-statement-1 <u>END-PERFORM</u>]

<u>PERFORM</u> $\left[\text{procedure-name-1}\ \left[\left\{ \begin{array}{l} \underline{THROUGH} \\ \underline{THRU} \end{array} \right\}\ \text{procedure-name-2} \right] \right]$

$\left\{ \begin{array}{l} \text{identifier-1} \\ \text{integer-1} \end{array} \right\}$ <u>TIMES</u>   [imperative-statement-1 <u>END-PERFORM</u>]

<u>PERFORM</u> $\left[\text{procedure-name-1}\ \left[\left\{ \begin{array}{l} \underline{THROUGH} \\ \underline{THRU} \end{array} \right\}\ \text{procedure-name-2} \right] \right]$

$\left[\text{WITH }\underline{TEST}\ \left\{ \begin{array}{l} \underline{BEFORE} \\ \underline{AFTER} \end{array} \right\}\ \underline{UNTIL}\ \text{condition-1} \right]$

[imperative-statement-1 <u>END-PERFORM</u>]

<u>PERFORM</u> $\left[\text{procedure-name-1}\ \left[\left\{ \begin{array}{l} \underline{THROUGH} \\ \underline{THRU} \end{array} \right\}\ \text{procedure-name-2} \right] \right]$

$\left[\text{WITH }\underline{TEST}\ \left\{ \begin{array}{l} \underline{BEFORE} \\ \underline{AFTER} \end{array} \right\} \right]$

<u>VARYING</u> $\left\{ \begin{array}{l} \text{identifier-2} \\ \text{index-name-1} \end{array} \right\}$ <u>FROM</u> $\left\{ \begin{array}{l} \text{identifier-3} \\ \text{index-name-2} \\ \text{literal-1} \end{array} \right\}$

<u>BY</u> $\left\{ \begin{array}{l} \text{identifier-4} \\ \text{literal-2} \end{array} \right\}$ <u>UNTIL</u> condition-1

$\left[\underline{AFTER}\ \left\{ \begin{array}{l} \text{identifier-5} \\ \text{literal-3} \end{array} \right\}\ \underline{FROM}\ \left\{ \begin{array}{l} \text{identifier-6} \\ \text{index-name-4} \\ \text{literal-3} \end{array} \right\} \right.$

$\left. \underline{BY}\ \left\{ \begin{array}{l} \text{identifier-7} \\ \text{literal-4} \end{array} \right\}\ \underline{UNTIL}\ \text{condition-2} \right]\ \ldots$

[imperative-statement-1 <u>END-PERFORM</u>]

<u>PURGE</u> cd-name-1

SRI   <u>READ</u> file-name-1   [<u>NEXT</u>]   RECORD   [<u>INTO</u> identifier-1]
[AT <u>END</u> imperative-statement-1]
[<u>NOT</u> AT <u>END</u> imperative-statement-2]
[<u>END-READ</u>]

R   <u>READ</u> file-name-1 RECORD   [<u>INTO</u> identifier-1]
        [<u>INVALID</u> KEY imperative-statement-3]
        [<u>NOT</u> <u>INVALID</u> KEY imperative-statement-4]
        [END-READ]

I   <u>READ</u> file-name-1 RECORD   [<u>INTO</u> identifier-1]
        [<u>KEY</u> IS data-name-1]
        [<u>INVALID</u> KEY imperative-statement-3]
        [<u>NOT</u> <u>INVALID</u> KEY imperative-statement-4]
        [END-READ]

<u>RECEIVE</u> cd-name-1 $\begin{Bmatrix} \underline{MESSAGE} \\ \underline{SEGMENT} \end{Bmatrix}$ <u>INTO</u> identifier-1

    [<u>NO</u> <u>DATA</u> imperative-statement-1]
    [WITH <u>DATA</u> imperative-statement-2]
    [<u>END-RECEIVE</u>]

<u>RELEASE</u> record-name-1   [<u>FROM</u> identifier-1]

<u>RETURN</u> file-name-1 RECORD   [<u>INTO</u> identifier-1]
    AT <u>END</u> imperative-statement-1
    [<u>NOT</u> AT <u>END</u> imperative-statement-2]
    [<u>END-RETURN</u>]

S   <u>REWRITE</u> record-name-1   [<u>FROM</u> identifier-1]

RI   <u>REWRITE</u> record-name-1   [<u>FROM</u> identifier-1]
        [<u>INVALID</u> KEY imperative-statement-1]
        [<u>NOT</u> <u>INVALID</u> KEY imperative-statement-2]
        [<u>END-REWRITE</u>]

<u>SEARCH</u> identifier-1 $\left[\underline{VARYING} \begin{Bmatrix} \text{identifier-2} \\ \text{index-name-1} \end{Bmatrix} \right]$
    [AT <u>END</u> imperative-statement-1]
    $\begin{Bmatrix} \underline{WHEN} \text{ condition-1} \begin{Bmatrix} \text{imperative-statement-2} \\ \underline{NEXT} \ \underline{SENTENCE} \end{Bmatrix} \end{Bmatrix}$ . . .
    [END-SEARCH]

<u>SEARCH</u> <u>ALL</u> identifier-1   [AT <u>END</u> imperative-statement-1]
    $\underline{WHEN} \begin{Bmatrix} \text{data-name-1} \begin{Bmatrix} \text{IS } \underline{EQUAL} \text{ TO} \\ \text{IS } = \end{Bmatrix} \begin{Bmatrix} \text{identifier-3} \\ \text{literal-1} \\ \text{arithmetic-expression-1} \end{Bmatrix} \\ \text{condition-name-1} \end{Bmatrix}$
    $\left[\underline{AND} \begin{Bmatrix} \text{data-name-2} \begin{Bmatrix} \text{IS } \underline{EQUAL} \text{ TO} \\ \text{IS } = \end{Bmatrix} \begin{Bmatrix} \text{identifier-4} \\ \text{literal-2} \\ \text{arithmetic-expression-2} \end{Bmatrix} \\ \text{condition-name-2} \end{Bmatrix} \right]$ . . .
    $\begin{Bmatrix} \text{imperative-statement-2} \\ \underline{NEXT} \ \underline{SENTENCE} \end{Bmatrix}$
    [<u>END-SEARCH</u>]

SEND cd-name-1 FROM identifier-1

SEND cd-name-1 [FROM identifier-1] $\left\{ \begin{array}{l} \text{WITH identifier-2} \\ \text{WITH ESI} \\ \text{WITH EMI} \\ \text{WITH EGI} \end{array} \right\}$

$\left[\left\{ \begin{array}{l} \underline{\text{BEFORE}} \\ \underline{\text{AFTER}} \end{array} \right\} \text{ADVANCING} \left\{ \begin{array}{l} \left\{ \begin{array}{l} \text{identifier-3} \\ \text{integer-1} \end{array} \right\} \left[\begin{array}{l} \text{LINE} \\ \text{LINES} \end{array} \right] \\ \left\{ \begin{array}{l} \text{mnemonic-name-1} \\ \underline{\text{PAGE}} \end{array} \right\} \end{array} \right\} \right]$

[REPLACING LINE]

SET $\left\{ \begin{array}{l} \text{index-name-1} \\ \text{identifier-1} \end{array} \right\} \ldots$ TO $\left\{ \begin{array}{l} \text{index-name-2} \\ \text{identifier-2} \\ \text{integer-1} \end{array} \right\}$

SET {index-name-3} ... $\left\{ \begin{array}{l} \underline{\text{UP}}\ \underline{\text{BY}} \\ \underline{\text{DOWN}}\ \underline{\text{BY}} \end{array} \right\}$ $\left\{ \begin{array}{l} \text{identifier-3} \\ \text{integer-2} \end{array} \right\}$

SET $\left\{ \text{\{mnemonic-name-1\}} \ldots \text{ TO } \left\{ \begin{array}{l} \underline{\text{ON}} \\ \underline{\text{OFF}} \end{array} \right\} \right\} \ldots$

SET {condition-name-1} ... TO TRUE

SORT file-name-1 $\left\{ \text{ON } \left\{ \begin{array}{l} \underline{\text{ASCENDING}} \\ \underline{\text{DESCENDING}} \end{array} \right\} \text{ KEY \{data-name-1\}} \ldots \right\} \ldots$

[WITH DUPLICATES IN ORDER]
[COLLATING SEQUENCE IS alphabet-name-1]
$\left\{ \begin{array}{l} \underline{\text{INPUT}}\ \underline{\text{PROCEDURE}} \text{ IS procedure-name-1} \left[\left\{ \begin{array}{l} \underline{\text{THROUGH}} \\ \underline{\text{THRU}} \end{array} \right\} \text{ procedure-name-2} \right] \\ \underline{\text{USING}} \quad \text{\{file-name-2\}} \ldots \end{array} \right\}$

$\left\{ \begin{array}{l} \underline{\text{OUPUT}}\ \underline{\text{PROCEDURE}} \text{ IS procedure-name-3} \left[\left\{ \begin{array}{l} \underline{\text{THROUGH}} \\ \underline{\text{THRU}} \end{array} \right\} \text{ procedure-name-4} \right] \\ \underline{\text{GIVING}} \quad \text{\{file-name-3\}} .. \end{array} \right\}$

START file-name-1 $\left[\underline{\text{KEY}} \left\{ \begin{array}{l} \text{IS } \underline{\text{EQUAL}} \text{ TO} \\ \text{IS } = \\ \text{IS } \underline{\text{GREATER}} \text{ THAN} \\ \text{IS } > \\ \text{IS } \underline{\text{NOT}}\ \underline{\text{LESS}} \text{ THAN} \\ \text{IS } \underline{\text{NOT}} < \\ \text{IS } \underline{\text{GREATER}} \text{ THAN OR } \underline{\text{EQUAL}} \text{ TO} \\ \text{IS } >= \end{array} \right\} \text{data-name-1} \right]$

[INVALID KEY imperative-statement-1]
[NOT INVALID KEY imperative-statement-2]
[END-START]

STOP $\left\{ \begin{array}{l} \underline{\text{RUN}} \\ \text{literal-1} \end{array} \right\}$

STRING $\left\{ \left\{ \begin{array}{l} \text{identifier-1} \\ \text{literal-1} \end{array} \right\} \ldots \underline{\text{DELIMITED}} \text{ BY } \left\{ \begin{array}{l} \text{identifier-2} \\ \text{literal-2} \\ \underline{\text{SIZE}} \end{array} \right\} \right\} \ldots$

<u>INTO</u> identifier-3
[WITH <u>POINTER</u> identifier-4
[ON <u>OVERFLOW</u> imperative-statement-1]
[<u>NOT</u> ON <u>OVERFLOW</u> imperative-statement-2]
[<u>END-STRING</u>]

<u>SUBTRACT</u> $\left\{ \begin{array}{l} \text{identifier-1} \\ \text{literal-1} \end{array} \right\}$ . . . <u>FROM</u> {identifier-3 [<u>ROUNDED</u>]}. . .
    [ON <u>SIZE</u> <u>ERROR</u> imperative-statement-1]
    [<u>NOT</u> ON <u>SIZE</u> <u>ERROR</u> imperative-statement-2]
    [<u>END-SUBTRACT</u>]

<u>SUBTRACT</u> $\left\{ \begin{array}{l} \text{identifier-1} \\ \text{literal-1} \end{array} \right\}$ . . . <u>FROM</u> $\left\{ \begin{array}{l} \text{identifier-2} \\ \text{literal-2} \end{array} \right\}$
    <u>GIVING</u> {identifier-3 [<u>ROUNDED</u>]} . . .
    [ON <u>SIZE</u> <u>ERROR</u> imperative-statement-1]
    [<u>NOT</u> ON <u>SIZE</u> <u>ERROR</u> imperative-statement-2]
    [<u>END-SUBTRACT</u>]

<u>SUBTRACT</u> $\left\{ \begin{array}{l} \underline{\text{CORRESPONDING}} \\ \underline{\text{CORR}} \end{array} \right\}$ identifier-1 <u>FROM</u> identifier-2 [<u>ROUNDED</u>]
    [ON <u>SIZE</u> <u>ERROR</u> imperative-statement-1]

    [<u>NOT</u> ON <u>SIZE</u> <u>ERROR</u> imperative-statement-2]
    [<u>END-SUBTRACT</u>]

<u>SUPPRESS</u> PRINTING

<u>TERMINATE</u> {report-name-1} . . .

<u>UNSTRING</u> identifier-1
   $\left[\underline{\text{DELIMITED}} \text{ BY } [\underline{\text{ALL}}] \left\{ \begin{array}{l} \text{identifier-2} \\ \text{literal-1} \end{array} \right\} \left[\underline{\text{OR}} \ [\underline{\text{ALL}}] \left\{ \begin{array}{l} \text{identifier-3} \\ \text{literal-2} \end{array} \right\} \right] \ \cdots \right]$
   <u>INTO</u> {identifier-4 [<u>DELIMITER</u> IN identifier-5] [<u>COUNT</u> IN identifier-6]} . . .
   [with <u>POINTER</u> identifier-7]
   [<u>TALLYING</u> IN identifier-8]
   [ON <u>OVERFLOW</u> imperative-statement-1]
   [<u>NOT</u> ON <u>OVERFLOW</u> imperative-statement-2]
   [<u>END-UNSTRING</u>]

<u>USE</u> [<u>GLOBAL</u>] <u>AFTER</u> STANDARD $\left\{ \begin{array}{l} \underline{\text{EXCEPTION}} \\ \underline{\text{ERROR}} \end{array} \right\}$ <u>PROCEDURE</u> ON $\left\{ \begin{array}{l} \text{\{file-name-1\}} \ \cdots \\ \underline{\text{INPUT}} \\ \underline{\text{OUTPUT}} \\ \underline{\text{I-O}} \\ \underline{\text{EXTEND}} \end{array} \right\}$

W <u>USE</u> <u>AFTER</u> STANDARD $\left\{ \begin{array}{l} \underline{\text{EXCEPTION}} \\ \underline{\text{ERROR}} \end{array} \right\}$ <u>PROCEDURE</u> ON $\left\{ \begin{array}{l} \text{\{file-name-1\}} \ \ \cdots \\ \underline{\text{OUTPUT}} \\ \underline{\text{EXTEND}} \end{array} \right\}$

<u>USE</u> [<u>GLOBAL</u>] <u>BEFORE</u> REPORTING identifier-1

$$\text{\underline{USE} FOR \underline{DEBUGGING} ON} \left\{ \begin{array}{l} \text{cd-name-1} \\ \text{[\underline{ALL} REFERENCES OF] identifier-1} \\ \text{file-name-1} \\ \text{procedure-name-1} \\ \underline{\text{ALL}} \text{ \underline{PROCEDURES}} \end{array} \right\} \cdots$$

S \underline{WRITE} record-name-1   [\underline{FROM} identifier-1]

$$\left[\left\{ \begin{array}{l} \underline{\text{BEFORE}} \\ \underline{\text{AFTER}} \end{array} \right\} \text{ADVANCING} \left\{ \left\{ \begin{array}{l} \text{identifier-2} \\ \text{integer-1} \\ \text{mnemonic-name-1} \\ \underline{\text{PAGE}} \end{array} \right\} \left[\begin{array}{l} \text{LINE} \\ \text{LINES} \end{array} \right] \right\} \right]$$

$$\left[\text{AT} \left\{ \begin{array}{l} \underline{\text{END-OF-PAGE}} \\ \underline{\text{EOP}} \end{array} \right\} \text{imperative-statement-1} \right]$$

$$\left[\underline{\text{NOT}} \text{ AT} \left\{ \begin{array}{l} \underline{\text{END-OF-PAGE}} \\ \underline{\text{EOP}} \end{array} \right\} \text{imperative-statement-2} \right]$$

[\underline{END-WRITE}

RI \underline{WRITE} record-name-1   [\underline{FROM} identifier-1]
     [\underline{INVALID} KEY imperative-statement-1]
     [\underline{NOT} \underline{INVALID} KEY imperative-statement-2]
     [\underline{END-WRITE}]

GENERAL FORMAT FOR COPY AND REPLACE STATEMENTS

$$\underline{\text{COPY}} \text{ text-name-1} \left[\left\{ \begin{array}{l} \underline{\text{OF}} \\ \underline{\text{IN}} \end{array} \right\} \text{ library-name-1} \right]$$

$$\left[\underline{\text{REPLACING}} \left\{ \left\{ \begin{array}{l} \text{==pseudo-text-1==} \\ \text{identifier-1} \\ \text{literal-1} \\ \text{word-1} \end{array} \right\} \underline{\text{BY}} \left\{ \begin{array}{l} \text{==pseudo-text-2==} \\ \text{identifier-2} \\ \text{literal-2} \\ \text{word-2} \end{array} \right\} \right\} \cdots \right]$$

\underline{REPLACE}   {==pseudo-text-1==   BY   ==pseudo-text-2==} ...

\underline{REPLACE} \underline{OFF}

GENERAL FORMAT FOR CONDITIONS

\underline{RELATION CONDITION:}

$$\left\{ \begin{array}{l} \text{identifier-1} \\ \text{literal-1} \\ \text{arithmetic-expression-1} \\ \text{index-name-1} \end{array} \right\} \left\{ \begin{array}{l} \text{IS [\underline{NOT}] \underline{GREATER} THAN} \\ \text{IS [\underline{NOT}] >} \\ \text{IS [\underline{NOT}] \underline{LESS} THAN} \\ \text{IS [\underline{NOT}] <} \\ \text{IS [\underline{NOT}] \underline{EQUAL} TO} \\ \text{IS [\underline{NOT}] =} \\ \text{IS \underline{GREATER} THAN \underline{OR} \underline{EQUAL} TO} \\ \text{IS >=} \\ \text{IS \underline{LESS} THAN \underline{OR} \underline{EQUAL} TO} \\ \text{IS <=} \end{array} \right\} \left\{ \begin{array}{l} \text{identifier-2} \\ \text{literal-2} \\ \text{arithmetic-expression-2} \\ \text{index-name-2} \end{array} \right\}$$

\underline{CLASS CONDITION:}

$$\text{identifier-1 IS [\underline{NOT}]} \left\{ \begin{array}{l} \underline{\text{NUMERIC}} \\ \underline{\text{ALPHABETIC}} \\ \underline{\text{ALPHABETIC-LOWER}} \\ \underline{\text{ALPHABETIC-UPPER}} \\ \text{class-name-1} \end{array} \right\}$$

<u>CONDITION-NAME CONDITION:</u>
condition-name-1

<u>SWITCH-STATUS CONDITION:</u>
condition-name-1

<u>SIGN CONDITION:</u>

arithmetic-expression-1 is [<u>NOT</u>] $\left\{\begin{matrix}\underline{POSITIVE}\\ \underline{NEGATIVE}\\ \underline{ZERO}\end{matrix}\right\}$

<u>NEGATED CONDITION:</u>
<u>NOT</u> condition-1

<u>COMBINED CONDITION:</u>
condition-1 $\left\{\left\{\begin{matrix}\underline{AND}\\ \underline{OR}\end{matrix}\right\}\ \text{condition-2}\right\}$ · · ·

<u>ABBREVIATED COMBINED RELATION CONDITION:</u>

relation-condition $\left\{\left\{\begin{matrix}\underline{AND}\\ \underline{OR}\end{matrix}\right\}\ [\underline{NOT}]\ \text{[relational-operator]}\ \text{object}\right\}$ · · ·

GENERAL FORMAT FOR QUALIFICATION

<u>FORMAT 1:</u>

$\left\{\begin{matrix}\text{data-name-1}\\ \text{condition-name}\end{matrix}\right\}$ $\left\{\begin{matrix}\left\{\left\{\begin{matrix}\underline{IN}\\ \underline{OF}\end{matrix}\right\}\ \text{data-name-2}\right\}\ \cdots\ \left[\left\{\begin{matrix}\underline{IN}\\ \underline{OF}\end{matrix}\right\}\ \left\{\begin{matrix}\text{file-name-1}\\ \text{cd-name-1}\end{matrix}\right\}\right]\\ \left\{\begin{matrix}\underline{IN}\\ \underline{OF}\end{matrix}\right\}\ \left\{\begin{matrix}\text{file-name-1}\\ \text{cd-name-1}\end{matrix}\right\}\end{matrix}\right\}$

<u>FORMAT 2:</u>

paragraph-name-1 $\left\{\begin{matrix}\underline{IN}\\ \underline{OF}\end{matrix}\right\}$ section-name-1

<u>FORMAT 3:</u>

text-name-1 $\left\{\begin{matrix}\underline{IN}\\ \underline{OF}\end{matrix}\right\}$ library-name-1

<u>FORMAT 4:</u>

LINAGE-COUNTER $\left\{\begin{matrix}\underline{IN}\\ \underline{OF}\end{matrix}\right\}$ file-name-2

<u>FORMAT 5:</u>

$\left\{\begin{matrix}\text{PAGE-COUNTER}\\ \text{LINE-COUNTER}\end{matrix}\right\}$ $\left\{\begin{matrix}\underline{IN}\\ \underline{OF}\end{matrix}\right\}$ report-name-1

FORMAT 6:

$$\text{data-name-3} \quad \left\{ \begin{array}{l} \left\{ \begin{array}{l} \underline{IN} \\ \underline{OF} \end{array} \right\} \quad \text{data-name-4} \quad \left[\left\{ \begin{array}{l} \underline{IN} \\ \underline{OF} \end{array} \right\} \quad \text{report-name-2} \right] \\ \left\{ \begin{array}{l} \underline{IN} \\ \underline{OF} \end{array} \right\} \quad \text{report-name-3} \end{array} \right\}$$

MISCELLANEOUS FORMATS

SUBSCRIPTING:

$$\left\{ \begin{array}{l} \text{condition-name-1} \\ \text{data-name-1} \end{array} \right\} \quad \left(\quad \left\{ \begin{array}{l} \text{integer-1} \\ \text{data-name-2 } [\{\pm\} \text{ integer-2}] \\ \text{index-name-1 } [\{\pm\} \text{ integer-3}] \end{array} \right\} \quad \cdots \quad \right)$$

REFERENCE MODIFICATION:
data-name-1 (leftmost-character-position: [length])

IDENTIFIER:

$$\text{data-name-1} \quad \left[\left\{ \begin{array}{l} \underline{IN} \\ \underline{OF} \end{array} \right\} \quad \text{data-name-2} \right] \quad \cdots \quad \left[\left\{ \begin{array}{l} \underline{IN} \\ \underline{OF} \end{array} \right\} \quad \left\{ \begin{array}{l} \text{cd-name-1} \\ \text{file-name-1} \\ \text{report-name-1} \end{array} \right\} \right]$$

[({subscript} . . .)]   [(leftmost-character-position: [length])]

GENERAL FORMAT FOR NESTED SOURCE PROGRAMS

IDENTIFICATION DIVISION.
 PROGRAM-ID.   program-name-1   [IS INITIAL PROGRAM].
[ENVIRONMENT DIVISION.   environment-division-content]
[DATA DIVISION.   data-division-content]
[PROCEDURE DIVISION.   procedure-division-content]
[[nested-source-program]   . . .
 END PROGRAM program-name-1.]

General Format for NESTED-SOURCE-PROGRAM:

IDENTIFICATION DIVISION.

$$\text{PROGRAM-ID.} \quad \text{program-name-2} \quad \left[\text{IS} \quad \left\{ \left| \begin{array}{l} \underline{COMMON} \\ \underline{INITIAL} \end{array} \right| \right\} \quad \text{PROGRAM} \right] .$$

[ENVIRONMENT DIVISION.   environment-division-content]
[DATA DIVISION.   data-division-content]
[PROCEDURE DIVISION.   procedure-division-content]
[nested-source-program]   . . .
 END PROGRAM program-name-2.

GENERAL FORMAT FOR A SEQUENCE OF SOURCE PROGRAMS

{<u>IDENTIFICATION</u> <u>DIVISION.</u>
 <u>PROGRAM-ID</u>.   program-name-3   [IS <u>INITIAL</u> PROGRAM].
[<u>ENVIRONMENT</u> <u>DIVISION</u>.   environment-division-content]
[<u>DATA</u> <u>DIVISION</u>.   data-division-content]
[<u>PROCEDURE</u> <u>DIVISION</u>.   procedure-division-content]
[nested-source-program]   . . .
 <u>END</u> <u>PROGRAM</u> program-name-3.}   . . .
 <u>IDENTIFICATION</u> <u>DIVISION.</u>
 <u>PROGRAM-ID</u>.   program-name-4   [IS <u>INITIAL</u> PROGRAM].
[<u>ENVIRONMENT</u> <u>DIVISION</u>.   environment-division-content]
[<u>DATA</u> <u>DIVISION</u>.   data-division-content]
[<u>PROCEDURE</u> <u>DIVISION</u>.   procedure-division-content]
[[nested-source-program]   . . .
 <u>END</u> <u>PROGRAM</u> program-name-4.]

INDEX